LONGING FOR THE LOST CALIPHATE

FRONTISPIECE. The last Abbasid caliph of Baghdad al-Mustaʿṣim (bottom left) brought on his knees as a captive before the Mongol commander Hülegü (top right) sitting on a throne.

LONGING *for the* LOST CALIPHATE

A TRANSREGIONAL HISTORY

MONA HASSAN

PRINCETON UNIVERSITY PRESS
PRINCETON AND OXFORD

Published by Princeton University Press, 41 William Street, Princeton, New Jersey 08540

In the United Kingdom: Princeton University Press, 6 Oxford Street, Woodstock, Oxfordshire OX20 1TR

press.princeton.edu

First paperback printing, 2018
Paper ISBN: 978-0-691-18337-4

The Library of Congress has cataloged the cloth edition of this book as follows:

Names: Hassan, Mona, author.
Title: Longing for the lost caliphate : a transregional history / Mona Hassan.
Description: Princeton, N.J. : Princeton University Press, [2016] | Includes bibliographical references and index.
Identifiers: LCCN 2016016011 | ISBN 9780691166780 (hardcover : alk. paper)
Subjects: LCSH: Caliphate—History. | Islam and state.
Classification: LCC BP166.9 .H37 2017 | DDC 297.6/1— dc23

British Library Cataloging-in-Publication Data is available

This book has been composed in Adobe Text Pro and Poetica

For my mother with infinite gratitude
and my children with deepest love

CONTENTS

ILLUSTRATIONS AND MAPS

ILLUSTRATIONS

MAPS

ACKNOWLEDGMENTS

"WHOEVER DOES NOT thank people, does not thank God," is a statement attributed to the Prophet Muhammad in *Sunan al-Tirmidhī*. And the debts of appreciation I have accumulated over the many years of researching and writing this book are boundless. To all those who helped in ways, large and small, thank you.

The germination of this book began deep in the library stacks of Princeton University, where I was working toward my doctoral degree. In those early days, the word "caliphate" had not yet become a topic of contemporary American discussion and geopolitics, although an older generation of Americans and Europeans may have fondly recalled the stories of *One Thousand and One Nights* set in Baghdad, the capital of the Abbasid Caliphate, as a land of fabled luxury and romantic mystique. As I worked on my research paper on Islamic law for Hossein Modarressi, though, I noted with surprise the distraught exclamations of Jalāl al-Dīn al-Suyūṭī over the absence of a caliphate for three and a half years following the Mongol invasion of Baghdad in 1258, more than two hundred years before his time. Correlating that observation with a fortuitous Turkish assignment for Erika Gilson on the last Ottoman sultan-caliphs, I began to calculate the number of years since the Grand Nationalist Assembly abolished the Ottoman Caliphate in 1924 and wonder about its potential ramifications.

Michael Cook and Şükrü Hanioğlu, my dissertation co-advisers, who firmly anchored me in early Islamic as well as late Ottoman and early Republican Turkish history respectively, warmly encouraged this project and supported it in many ways over the years. I am grateful for all of their help and guidance. Michael Adas at Rutgers University fostered my love of and training in global history from early on. His encouragement to see Islamic history as global history permeates this book and inspired me to follow his path of scholarly and teaching excellence.

I would also like to thank Stephen Reinert, Peter Golden, Al Howard, Jackson Lears, Matt Matsuda, and Carolyn Brown for their early training and support at Rutgers, as well as Gyan Prakash, Bob Tignor, Bernard Haykel, Kerry Walk, Ann Jurecic, and Patricia Armstrong for offering teaching opportunities at Princeton. I am also grateful to Muhammad Qasim Zaman for serving on my doctoral dissertation committee at Princeton with insight and intellectual generosity. I am additionally indebted to Nadia Moustafa of Cairo University and Ali Gomaa of al-Azhar University for supervising and facilitating my research and scholarly development in Egypt. In Turkey, Nejdet Gök of Necmettin Erbakan University, İsmail Kara of Marmara University, Azmi Özcan of Sakarya University, and Recep Şentürk of Fatih Sultan Mehmet University offered invaluable assistance.

As an assistant professor of Religious Studies and History at Duke University, I greatly benefitted from the university's support as well as an American Council of Learned Societies Fellowship and a Social Science Research Council Postdoctoral Fellowship for Transregional Research that together granted me a full year for further reflection, research, and writing.

Duke's Franklin Humanities Institute awarded me the opportunity to convene a book manuscript workshop in 2013–14, and I am deeply grateful for the insightful participation of Elizabeth Castelli from Barnard College of Columbia University and José Casanova from Georgetown University, my outstanding editor Fred Appel from Princeton University Press, and my participating colleagues in the Triangle who carefully read my lengthy draft manuscript Anna Bigelow, Bruce Hall, Jehangir Malegam, and Sumathi Ramaswamy.

I also greatly appreciate the suggestions and feedback on various portions of the manuscript that I received from Rodrigo Adem, Kalman Bland, JH Brown, Carl Ernst, Kathy Ewing, Tom Ferraro, Robert Gibbs, Shalom Goldman, Malachi Hacohen, Engseng Ho, Amaney Jamal, Ira Lapidus, John Martin, Sucheta Mazumdar, Adam Mestyan, David Morgan, Maha Nassar, Michael Provence, Ann Marie Rasmussen, Francis Robinson, S. Sayyid, Mariam Sheibani, Carol Symes, Mustafa Tuna, Brett Whalen, Tim Winter, Joe Winters, Erik Zitzser, and Erik Jan Zürcher. I did not always follow their and others' sagacious advice, but I wholly value their discerning remarks, assistance, and provocations.

I am especially grateful to my colleagues in the Religious Studies Department, the History Department, and the International Comparative Studies Program for creating a vibrant community at Duke University as well as to my colleagues in the Triangle Medieval Studies Seminar, the Global Asia Working Group and Initiative, the Global History Seminar, and the Theory Reading Group. My colleagues in the Religion, Memory, History Group of the American Academy of Religion have always offered rich and thought-provoking discussions across our diverse areas of expertise.

Portions of this research were also presented at the meetings of the American Academy of Religion, the American Historical Association, and the Middle East Studies Association as well as in lectures and presentations at Duke University, King's College—London, the Norwegian University of Science and Technology, Oxford University, Rutgers University, Stanford University, the University of North Carolina—Chapel Hill, and Virginia Tech University.

I thank the librarians at Duke University, Princeton University, the University of Chicago, and the University of North Carolina—Chapel Hill, especially Bill Blair, Stephen Ferguson, Christof Galli, Glenda Lacoste, Heidi Madden, Denise Soufi, Larisa Walsh, Cheryl Wilkins, and Erik Zitzser, for cheerfully feeding my insatiable appetite for books and helping with my queries often above and beyond the call of duty.

I also appreciate the indispensable assistance of the staff at al-Azhar Library, al-Azhar University Faculty of Arabic Language Library, the American University in Cairo libraries, the ʿAyn Shams University Library, the Beyazıt State Library, the British Library, the British National Archives, the Center for Islamic Studies (İSAM) Library, the Egyptian National Archives, the Egyptian National Library, the Istanbul Metropolitan Municipality Taksim Atatürk Library, the Köprülü Library, the National Library of France, the Nuruosmaniye Library, the Ottoman Archives, the personal library of Ali Gomaa, the Turkish Presidential Archives, the Research Centre for Islamic History, Art, and Culture (İRCİCA) Library, and the Süleymaniye Library.

At Princeton University Press, Fred Appel has been a superb editor, and I have been deeply appreciative of his involvement and our many profound conversations. My production editor Sara Lerner and copyeditor Brittany Micka-Foos have also ensured a smooth and convivial production process in finally bringing this book to light. Rob McCaleb and Chris Ferrante skillfully arranged my maps and illustrations respectively. And I also appreciate Jan Williams's attentive work in developing the index.

The debts I owe to my family are the longest, deepest, and most difficult to encapsulate in a matter of words. My late grandmother, who called me Dr. Mona from the moment I began my doctoral program, and extended family always warmly embraced and encouraged me. And my Uncle Hani and his family put up with me and my growing archive for far longer than they could have anticipated. My father met my budding academic prospects with great enthusiasm. My husband kept me grounded and listened to endless ruminations on my research. My children reminded me to shut my computer to be more fully present with them and enjoy every precious moment. My mother patiently and impatiently waited for the fruits of all her labor and love to blossom. I dedicate this book to her for everything, and to my children with a heart full of love and hope. May they grow up to contribute to a more peaceful world for all people, premised on our shared humanity, enduring compassion, and selfless cooperation.

NOTE ON TRANSLITERATION AND DATES

I UTILIZE A modified form of the IJMES transliteration system for Arabic and Persian words that are not necessarily commonplace in English. Words commonly used in English, however, are noted as such, hence: Qur'an instead of Qur'ān, Mecca instead of Makkah, Sunni instead of Sunnī, Abbasid instead of ʿAbbāsī, Mamluk instead of Mamlūk, and so on.

For Ottoman Turkish works, I utilize modern Turkish orthography to maintain some measure of continuity with the post-1928 materials. Names of authors who were primarily trained in the Ottoman Empire before its dismemberment and wrote in Ottoman Turkish (even if they used other languages as well) are also transcribed into modern Turkish, hence: Mustafa Sabri instead of Muṣṭafā Ṣabrī. The newly acquired last names of Turkish authors who lived through the transition from the Ottoman Empire to the Turkish Republic (after the Surname Law of 1934) are given in parentheses the first time they are mentioned.

Dates are often given according to the Islamic calendar (*Anno Hegirae* or AH) preceding a slash, followed by their Common Era (CE) equivalent, such as 656/1258 for the year of the Mongol conquest of Baghdad. Dates given alone follow the Common Era calendar, such as 1924 for the year of the Turkish nationalist abolition of the Ottoman Caliphate.

LONGING FOR THE LOST CALIPHATE

INTRODUCTION

The cosmopolitan, scholarly language of Islamic religious discourse cuts across multiple frontiers, constructing a universe of reciprocal benefit to those who master it. This religious discourse is at once flexible and transferable across time and space. Not only did it span the known world of the fourteenth century, but it also persisted across the vicissitudes of political and economic change that separated the premodern from the modern world system.

—*MUSLIM NETWORKS FROM HAJJ TO HIP HOP*, ED. MIRIAM COOKE AND BRUCE LAWRENCE[1]

Overall, the best historians of memory are like the ogre who looks for human voices and emotions. They capture the haunted images of the past that hover in a given society, the obsession with certain events, periods, or beliefs, and they attempt to understand how and why they made sense to people in the past.

—"HISTORY AND MEMORY," ALON CONFINO[2]

WORKING AT THE Foreign Office in London, a British diplomat reviewed the stunning news emanating from Turkey on March 3, 1924. D. G. Osbourne had just learned of the legislative acts passed by the nascent Turkish Republic's Grand National Assembly and updated the confidential file before him:

> The Caliphate of the house of Osman is abolished and all members of the house are to follow the Caliph—and the late Sultan—into exile. Their property is to revert to the state. Justice and education are to be entirely purged of their religious associations. The policy of disestablishment or laicization is carried to its logical limit.[3]

For years, the Foreign Office had amassed thousands of files during the Great War out of fear of the Ottoman Caliphate's capacity to stir the effuse sympathies of Muslims in British India, Egypt, and around the globe. And perhaps pondering the demise of this centuries-old institution and potent symbol for Muslim unity, Osbourne carefully penned in between the lines of his typed update, "This is an historical event of the first importance."[4]

In France, a young doctoral student in law and political science sent by Egypt, at the wave of his country's modernization efforts in education, was connected through Rashīd Riḍā's Cairene Islamic modernist periodical *al-Manār* to a global readership of Muslims. Through its pages, he learned of the dramatic news, which would greatly shape the course of his doctoral thesis at the University of Lyon, published in 1926. For this young legal scholar, ʿAbd al-Razzāq al-Sanhūrī, the 1924 disappearance of the Ottoman Caliphate was intimately connected with its historical precedent: the Mongols' violent destruction of the Abbasid Caliphate in Baghdad in 1258. For the second time in the history of Islam, he wrote, Muslims, like himself, were left without a caliph to shepherd the temporal and spiritual interests of the community, even if only symbolically. And like his religious predecessors, al-Sanhūrī felt that resolving this dilemma of caliphal absence was among the most pressing issues of his age.[5]

Longing for the Lost Caliphate: A Transregional History explores these complex constellations of meanings and networks that shaped Muslim reactions to the remarkably unexpected disappearance of an Islamic caliphate in the thirteenth and twentieth centuries. It probes the collective memories encircling the caliphate, as an institution enmeshed with the early history of Islam, which circulated widely across Afro-Eurasia and created a shared sense of community among disparate peoples at the same time as it gave rise to differing and competing visions of the community's past, present, and future. *Longing for the Lost Caliphate* asks two essential questions: What did Muslims imagine to be lost with the disappearance of the Abbasid and Ottoman Caliphates in 1258 and 1924 respectively? And how did they attempt to recapture that perceived loss, and in doing so redefine the caliphate for their times, under shifting circumstances?

As a contribution of global Islamic history to the study of cultural memory, *Longing for the Lost Caliphate* pursues a challenging investigation of Islamic interconnectivities across Afro-Eurasia in both the thirteenth and the twentieth centuries. The traumatic disappearance of the Abbasid and Ottoman caliphates in 1258 and 1924 generated an outpouring of emotion far beyond the territorial boundaries of imperial domains and illustrates the limitations of conventional political and historiographical boundaries in investigating such phenomena. In the case of the Abbasids, this emotive response emanated from as far away as Spain in the west to India in the east, along with Egypt, western North Africa, geographical Syria, Mesopotamia, Yemen, and Persia—regions that had long been independent of Abbasid rule or even boasted of rival states and institutions. And in the case of the Ottomans, Muslims from Southeastern Europe, North Africa, the Middle East, South Asia, and Southeast Asia expressed profound consternation—again beyond the political and territorial reach of the Ottoman Empire at the time of its demise. In analyzing these vivid materials, I explore the poignant sense of symbolic loss among Muslims across Afro-Eurasia to the disappearance of an Islamic caliphate in the thirteenth and twentieth centuries as well their various, and sometimes conflicting, attempts to reconstruct the lost institution and the religious communal bonds it represented. This fascinating circulation of ideas and debates in response to the dilemma of caliphal absence highlights exceptionally well the vivacity of transregional social and intellectual networks among Muslims in the premodern and modern eras.

This revisionist enterprise also shifts the prevailing historiographic lens from focusing on the political developments associated with the caliphate at disparate junctures to bringing its deep-seated cultural associations to the fore. An earlier generation of scholars presumed a dearth of Muslim sentiment regarding the Islamic caliphate as a corollary to the institution's political deterioration and imperial decline. Continuously in print since 1950, Bernard Lewis's *The Arabs in History* downplays the shock of the Abbasid Caliphate's violent demise in 1258: "The Caliphs had long since lost almost all their real power, and miltary Sulṭāns, both in the capital and in the provinces, had begun to arrogate to themselves not only the powers, but even some of the prerogatives, of the Caliphs. The Mongols did little more than lay the ghost of an institution that was already dead."[6] And in 2004, Patricia Crone acknowledged the scholarly lacuna in assessing Muslim reactions to the Mongol invasion of Baghdad but expected little expression of emotion to surface from the primary source material. As Crone writes, "In 656/1258 the Mongols sacked Baghdad and killed the last Abbasid caliph, al-Mustaʿsim. The reaction awaits a study, but the sources are not exactly brimming over with grief."[7] Yet, as my first chapter illustrates, the poetry, music, historical chronicles, and other works that contemporaries and near contemporaries left behind tell another story, one of deep and abiding anguish.

Poets, in particular, utilized inherited literary forms to shape new and powerful expressions of loss and mourning. The first usage of elegies in Arabic poetry for entire cities, as opposed to individuals, had been inspired by devastation inflicted on Baghdad long before the Mongol invasions, during the civil war between al-Amīn and al-Maʾmūn, the two sons of Hārūn al-Rashīd, as they vied for the caliphate following their father's death. Inhabitants of the city, and travelers as well, sought to evoke the golden age of the Abbasid Caliphate's luminous capital and to preserve its living memory.[8] But in the aftermath of 1258, the elegiac form and its tropes gained new meaning. The level of destruction wrought by the Mongols was unparalleled in the city's long and sinuous history.[9] And faced with the death of hundreds of thousands in the once-bustling metropolis, the classical poetic form of searching for the ruined dwelling of a beloved and mourning days past became chillingly appropriate.

The resulting articulations of grief over the catastrophe of 1258 were so potent and pregnant with meaning that they continued to be evoked by Muslims over the centuries as a cultural touchstone, especially during moments of distress. The British invasion of Egypt in 1882 found Muslim masses called upon to recite a "soul-stirring poem" written as a prayer to God when the Mongols took Baghdad in the thirteenth century; the Khedive's imam urged Muslims to recite the poem in public gatherings following their recitation of the blessed accounts of Prophet Muḥammad recorded in *Saḥīḥ al-Bukhārī*. The famed Muḥammad ʿAbduh also published the moving poem in Egypt's *Official Gazette* so that the troops could read and benefit from it as well.[10] Another powerful anecdote replete with stanzas reflecting on divine justice following the 1258 Mongol conquest that had been preserved in fourteenth- and fifteenth-century histories was widely disseminated via an early nineteenth-century text of theology and reproduced during the twentieth and twenty-first centuries.[11] The collapse of the Ottoman Caliphate in 1924 elicited its own neoclassical poems mourning the institution's premature passing, and this latter form of elegiac loss contributes to my fourth chapter tracing these cultural continuities into the new forms and contexts of the early twentieth century. More recently, the American invasion of Iraq in 2003 also provoked journalists to deride marauding Americans as modern-day Mongols (including the satiric depiction of George W. Bush in Mongol attire) as an evocative illustration of their insensitivity and barbarism.[12] And in the throes of the Arab Spring and its ensuing counterrevolutions, the aforementioned stanzas composed in the thirteenth century and cited in works of history and theology even reached the Twittersphere when they were tweeted out on May 23, 2013 to over five thousand followers.[13]

Moreover, in another revision of prevalent scholarly assumptions, the first fall of Baghdad in 1258 did not signal an end to Islamic jurisprudential engagement with the concept of an Islamic caliphate and the active desire to reconcile contemporary circumstances with the ideals of Islamic political theory. This classical intellectual pursuit took shape during the abating of caliphal power in the tenth and eleventh centuries, and it continued as the idealized conception of the caliphate less and less mirrored reality. Even though histories of Islamic political thought typically end with the fall of the Abbasids in Baghdad in 1258, Mamluk-era scholars in Egypt and Syria continued to embrace and engage this vibrant intellectual heritage, as I demonstrate in my second and third chapters. The wide resonance of these interpretations, rooted in powerful communal memories, enhanced the religious authority as well as the social and political relevance of the Abbasid caliphs in Cairo. This analysis overturns the suppositions of academics like Sir Hamilton Gibb that "the setting up of a nominal 'shadow-caliphate' at Cairo made no difference, since few if any jurists of the period recognized it."[14] Instead, I explore how Muslim jurists along with other religious scholars and social actors actively supported the reinauguration of the Abbasid Caliphate in Cairo and contemplated what it meant for Mamluk state and society over nearly three centuries. In the sixteenth century, Ottoman scholars, like the Grand Vizier Lütfi Paşa, also marshaled this rich corpus of Islamic political thought and jurisprudence to legitimize the ruling dynasty's caliphate. And the quest for legitimate Islamic leadership did not end with the demise of the Ottoman Caliphate in 1924—far from it. In the aftermath of World War I, many Muslim intellectuals, activists, and politicians grappled with how to reconfigure a modern caliphate for their age, as I address in my fifth and sixth chapters.

The Abbasid and Ottoman Caliphates were not the only caliphates of Islamic history, nor were their dynasties the only ones to fall with dramatic consequences. One could point to the Ismaʿīlī caliphate of the Fatimids in North Africa or the Umayyad Caliphate of Spain, among others. Indeed, the loss of Muslim Spain has remained a key cultural signifier similarly evoking pained nostalgia for its cosmopolitanism and brilliance.[15] Yet among the Sunni majority, the Abbasids and Ottomans laid claim to a more broadly universal caliphate that was interwoven into a seamless narrative of Islamic leadership that traveled in general terms from the great centers of Medina to Damascus to Baghdad to Cairo to Istanbul. This storyline, as al-Sanhūrī indicated in the opening above, was only punctured by the worrisome absence of a caliphate following the calamities of 1258 and 1924. These two periods of disruption form the basis of my study because they surface and accentuate what was at stake for Muslim contemporaries and near contemporaries invested in the myriad meanings and extensive religious discourse of a universal Sunni caliphate. As a prelude to analyzing the successive waves of communal loss and aspirations for collective regeneration, the following pages present a contextualizing overview of the caliphate's development.

EARLY HISTORY OF THE CALIPHATE

The institution of the caliphate itself emerged upon the Prophet Muḥammad's death in 11/632 when his close companions assumed leadership of the early Muslim community. Precisely what this new form of leadership and authority would entail was initially unclear, but the vision of a caliphate as temporal succession to the Prophet Muḥammad over the entire Muslim community's affairs, and not merely those of one faction, tribe, or region, was quickly articulated and implemented by the Prophet's close friend and father-in-law, Abū Bakr (r. 11–13/632–34). His election, as an upright leading Muslim figure descended from Quraysh, to follow the book of God and the example of God's messenger in his stewardship established a number of important legal precedents and ideals for Islamic leadership and politics among the majority of the community. And Abū Bakr's brief reign as caliph, or temporal successor to the Prophet Muḥammad, was critical in laying the foundations for a cohesive and expansive Islamic polity after the Prophet's passing away.[16]

Abū Bakr and the first few righteous caliphs who followed him, for a period of thirty years until 41/661, are known collectively as the Rightly Guided Caliphs (*al-khulafāʾ al-rāshidūn*) in the Sunni tradition. Despite the array of problems and turmoil that surfaced during this period, particularly following the assassinations of the second, third, and fourth caliphs ʿUmar (r. 13–23/634–44), ʿUthmān (r. 23–35/644–56), and ʿAlī (r. 35–40/656–61), Sunni Muslims view this era as a golden age with righteous individuals, closely affiliated with the Prophet Muḥammad and steeped in his teachings, at the helm of communal leadership. For affirmation of this view, Muslims have pointed to related *ḥadīths* on the topic, such as the Prophet Muḥammad's instruction to follow the righteous and rightly guided caliphs (*al-khulafāʾ al-rāshidīn al-mahdiyyīn*) who would come after him,[17] along with other traditions that relate the sequential actions of Abū Bakr, ʿUmar, ʿUthmān, and ʿAlī in the lifetime of the Prophet in highly symbolic succession.[18] Other important references in the ḥadīth literature indicate that a period of righteous successors emulating the prophetic model (*khilāfat al-nubuwwah*) would last for only thirty years.[19] And others yet convey the Prophet's prediction that his grandson al-Ḥasan (through his daughter Fāṭimah and son-in-law ʿAlī) would ultimately reconcile two great warring Muslim factions.[20]

Bringing an end to the first civil war among Muslims that had plagued his father's reign, this grandson of the Prophet, al-Ḥasan b. ʿAlī, ceded his right to the caliphate in 41/661 to his father's rival, Muʿāwiyah b. Abī Sufyān (r. 41–60/661–80), who had been a latecomer to Islam towards the end of the Prophet's life. According to the primary sources cited by Wilferd Madelung in his *Succession to Muhammad*, al-Ḥasan had stipulated, among other terms, "that Muʿāwiya should not be entitled to appoint his successor but that there should be an electoral council (*shūrā*)" to determine the next caliph.[21] Such a return to earlier models of caliphal election was not, however, adopted by Muʿāwiyah, to the chagrin of many piously minded individuals.[22] And instead, Muʿāwiyah sought to impose his son Yazīd (r. 60–64/680–83) upon the Muslim community as his heir through a mixture, typically attributed to Muʿāwiyah's political finesse, of enticement and potent threats of violence. In this instance, however, Yazīd's ascension to the throne provoked a second outbreak of civil war that was finally put to rest a long eleven years later by the Umayyad caliph ʿAbd al-Malik (r. 65–86/685–705), who furthered the bureaucratization and Arabization of a specifically Umayyad imperial regime rooted in dynastic succession.[23]

THE ABBASID CALIPHATE

Resentment over the despotic and dissolute ways of the Umayyads, not to mention their descent from the ʿAbd Shams branch of Quraysh, boiled over into a series of revolts and rebellions during their reign seeking to establish alternative, and presumably more suitable, candidates as caliph. Ultimately one movement coalescing around an unnamed member of the Prophet Muḥammad's family was successful in overthrowing the last Umayyad caliph, Marwān b. Muḥammad b. Marwān b. al-Ḥakam (r. 127–32/744–50), in the second/eighth century. After the untimely death of the original candidate in the midst of these revolutionary preparations, his brother Abū'l-ʿAbbās, who was also a descendent of the Prophet's uncle al-ʿAbbās, was openly proclaimed caliph in 132/749 in Kufah, over other possible candidates descended from the line of the Prophet's son-in-law ʿAlī. A confluence of factors had brought the Abbasids to power: their noble lineage, promise of pious and just rule, and careful and protracted political and military preparations, as well as ancestral, ethnic, factional, and regional rivalries.[24] The successful assumption by Abū'l-ʿAbbās, inducted as al-Saffāḥ (r. 132–36/749–54), of the Islamic caliphate inaugurated a reign of Abbasids based in Mesopotamia that would last for over five hundred years until the fateful Mongol invasion of 656/1258.

The Abbasids had grown progressively weaker as rulers over the duration of their lengthy reign as caliphs, which itself was not immune from rebellions and riveting contests over power. Disputes over succession surfaced early and often, and the empire's expansive domains became increasingly autonomous. Hereditary governorships encouraged the decentralization of power within the empire's core provinces, while tributary rulers of peripheral regions assumed even greater independence. Within the capital, rivalries among the military regiments and among factions of the bureaucracy crippled the central government's efficacy and limited its reach. And with the establishment of the post of *amīr al-ʿumarāʾ* in 324/936, the Caliph al-Rāḍī (r. 322–29/934–40) conferred his power to govern upon a supreme military commander—an arrangement that would last throughout the sway of the Buyids and the Saljuqs down to the end of the sixth/twelfth century.[25] The Abbasid caliph al-Nāṣir (r. 575–622/1180–1225) sought to reassert meticulous control over governance during his lengthy reign, and his vigorous example is reputed to have been followed by his son and grandson who ascended to the caliphate in succession.[26] What happened next, during the reign of Baghdad's last Abbasid caliph, al-Mustaʿṣim (r. 640–56/1242–58), lays the stage for the Mongol conquest of the Abbasid capital.

Muslim contemporaries and near contemporaries in the seventh/thirteenth and eighth/fourteenth centuries seek to lay the blame for the fall of Baghdad to the Mongols, in a number of quarters. Notably, the personal characteristics of the last caliph al-Mustaʿṣim come in for heavy criticism. He was reputed to have been pious, gentle, and easygoing but also, to his detriment and that of the Abbasid Caliphate in Baghdad, lacking vigilance, decisiveness, and high aspirations, and he was known for his weakness of opinion, inability to manage affairs, and inexperience.[27] Yet these individual flaws also point to some of the systemic problems that had developed over the course of the late Abbasid Empire. Was it not leading figures of the Abbasid state, including the *Duwaydār*[28] and the *Sharābī*,[29] who chose al-Mustaʿṣim over stronger and more suitable candidates because they thought he would be more susceptible to their control and influence? One contemporary historian, Ibn Wāṣil (604–97/1208–98), recounts how al-Mustaʿṣim's highly determined and courageous uncle known as al-Khafājī[30] used to declare, with great boldness and independent spirit, that if God placed him in power, he would eradicate the Mongols and wrest the lands away from them.[31] And another early historian, ʿAbd al-Raḥmān b. Ibrāhīm Sunbuṭ Qanītū al-Irbilī (650–97 / ca. 1252–97 / 1317), relates how all of the Abbasid princes, except for one,[32] initially refused to pledge their allegiance to al-Mustaʿṣim as caliph in 640/1242. Only after orders were issued and enforced to prevent food and other provisions from reaching them in their homes did the Abbasids ultimately relent.[33] The elaborate secrecy in which the preliminary transfer of the caliphate from al-Mustanṣir to al-Mustaʿṣim was conducted appears as another measure designed to ward off anticipated resistance to his selection[34] and further reveals the imbalance of powers in the late Abbasid regime.

Similarly, festering sectarian tensions among bureaucrats of the Abbasid Empire as well as among the general populace of Baghdad and its environs significantly exacerbated the system's weaknesses. Contemporaries point to the recurring outbreaks of violence among Sunni and Shi'i Muslims in Baghdad as a major catalyst for the Mongol conquest of the capital. In response to a Shi'i attack on Sunnis, the Shi'i neighborhood of al-Karkh was plundered in retribution. Egyptian historical sources indicate that this raid was undertaken at the direct command of the caliph,[35] while Syrian historians explain that the aggrieved Sunnis of Bāb al-Baṣrah had complained directly the *Duwaydār* Rukn al-Dīn and one of the caliph's sons[36] who independently ordered the army to raid al-Karkh.[37] The retribution exacted, however, was egregiously excessive, as houses were looted, people were killed, and women were raped.[38] The caliph's Shi'i vizier, Muʾayyad al-Dīn Muḥammad Ibn al-ʿAlqamī,[39] is widely reported to have identified with his coreligionists in al-Karkh and, unable to stop the mortifying plunder, to have resolved secretly to exact his own revenge upon the caliph and his Sunni clique.[40]

The details of Ibn al-ʿAlqamī's treachery vary slightly from one source to another, growing most colorful in later sources, but the basic plot remains essentially the same: that he wrote to the Mongol Hülegü and invited him to capture Baghdad.[41] Some seventh/thirteenth- and eighth/fourteenth-century historians explain that Ibn al-ʿAlqamī (d. 656/1258) was behind the reduction in the stipends and numbers of al-Mustaʿṣim's troops, from the initial one hundred thousand or so he inherited from his father al-Mustanṣir to less than twenty thousand,[42] so that when the two armies finally met in Muḥarram 656 / January 1258, the caliph's army was ultimately defeated.[43] When the Mongols then laid siege to the city of Baghdad, Ibn al-ʿAlqamī is reputed to have gone out to assure his own position with the Mongols, under the ruse that he was seeking an amicable truce for all.[44] At this time, the inhabitants of Baghdad were instructed not to fire arrows back at the Mongols as that could potentially derail the crucial negotiations.[45] When the caliph was later asked to go outside the city to meet with the Mongols, some historians explain that Ibn al-ʿAlqamī had deceived the caliph into believing that Hülegü wanted his daughter to marry the caliph's son in order to seal their supposed arrangements.[46] And in seeking to absolve Ibn al-ʿAlqamī from such accusations, the Shi'i historian Ibn al-Ṭiqṭaqā (660–709 / ca. 1262–1309) argues that Hülegü would not have reappointed the vizier over Baghdad once it fell to the Mongols, if had he indeed betrayed the caliph—an argument which places primacy on loyalty in governance and assumes that Hülegü would not reward treachery undertaken on his behalf.[47] But a contemporary resident of Baghdad, Jamāl al-Dīn Sulaymān b. Fakhr al-Dīn ʿAbdillāh Ibn Raṭlayn, who was reputed to be a trustworthy witness, reported from his father, who was also deemed a trustworthy witness and was one of only seventeen people kept with the caliph inside the Mongol camp during the siege of Baghdad, that Ibn al-ʿAlqamī had personally advised Hülegü to kill al-Mustaʿṣim rather than finalize an armistice or else Mongol rule of Mesopotamia would never be secure.[48] In the end, the Mongols killed the caliph, the other members of the Abbasid dynasty, and the leading figures of Baghdad, then indiscriminately plundered, raped, and murdered the city's inhabitants,[49] and the former Abbasid capital became a provincial backwater in the newly rising Mongol Empire.[50]

THE OTTOMAN CALIPHATE

Another Abbasid Caliphate was reestablished in Cairo (as I examine in chapter 2) only a few years after the destruction of Baghdad, and it was from this Cairene institution that the rights to the caliphate were allegedly transferred in the sixteenth century to the Ottomans in Anatolia.[51] The first awareness Europeans gained of this tradition about the Ottomans inheriting the caliphate from the Abbasids of Cairo was through Georgius Fabricius (1516–71 CE) and Johannes Rosinus (c. 1550–1626 CE) in the sixteenth and seventeenth centuries and later from Muradcan Tosunian (also known as Ignatius Mouradgea d'Ohsson, 1740–1807 CE) in the eighteenth century.[52] In the late nineteenth and early twentieth centuries, certain Russian, British, and Italian orientalists,[53] whose ideas have gained great traction, sought in collaboration with imperial administrations to frame the notion of a formal transfer of the caliphate to the Ottomans as a fabrication of the late eighteenth century designed to beguile European governments. The inconsistency of this dating aside, other more recent scholars like Naimur Rahman Farooqi and Azmi Özcan have convincingly demonstrated critical weaknesses in the earlier arguments aimed at undermining Ottoman claims to the caliphate, including the acknowledgment that holding an official ceremony had never been a prerequisite to transfer the caliphate from one dynasty to another and that the Ottomans relied primarily on other approaches to bolster their caliphal legitimacy.[54] In the sixteenth century, the Ottomans commissioned legal works explicating their claims to the caliphate despite their non-Qurashī lineage, such as the *Khalāṣ al-Ummah fī Maʿrifat al-Aʾimmah* of the Grand Vizier Lütfi Paşa (d. 970/1562), and utilized the titles caliph (*khalīfah*), commander of the faithful (*amīr al-muʾminīn*), and the preferred juristic term *imām* in official documents, along with a panoply of other titles legitimizing and glorifying their reign. As early as 923/1517, the same year that the Ottomans conquered Mamluk Egypt and took custody of its Abbasid caliph, the Ottoman sultan Selim I officially proclaimed that he alone possessed the right to be called caliph.[55] J. W. Redhouse, another British scholar of the late nineteenth century, sought at length to dispel his contemporaries' assertions that the Ottoman sultan's status as "the Caliph of the world of Islam" was a new and baseless pretension as being "erroneous, futile, and impolitic."[56] And indeed, Muslims of the early twentieth century were far from dissuaded from rendering material and moral support to the Ottoman caliphs on the grounds of politicized foreign scholarship.

For millions of them, both within and without Ottoman imperial domains, the Ottomans were perceived as the rightful guardians of this venerable Islamic tradition of the universal Islamic caliphate before its eventual obliteration in 1924. The Ottoman sultan-caliph who ascended the throne in 1876 and reigned for over thirty years, Abdülhamid II, actively cultivated these Islamic loyalties as a means to consolidate his increasingly Muslim-populated and Asiatic, yet ethnically diverse, empire and stave off the threat of alternative ideologies like separatist nationalism.[57] By highlighting his caliphal role as the spiritual guardian and temporal protector of all Muslims, Abdülhamid II also succeeded in developing a powerful counterweight in his relations with other European empires, whose sovereigns and administrators were mindful of his abilitity to persuade, or even incite, the millions of Muslims under their imperial rule. More than once did they call upon Abdülhamid II's help in quelling potential Muslim resistance, and the possibility that he could alternatively ignite it also figured into their calculations.[58] For as Israel Gershoni and James Jankowski have articulated:

> In much of the Islamic world by the beginning of the twentieth century, identity as a Muslim had come to mean political solidarity with the Ottoman Empire and manifested itself in declarations of allegiance to its Sultan/Caliph, acceptance of its theoretical authority as an alternative to final subjection by Europe, and support for it in the international crises in which it was involved.[59]

Even after Abdülhamid II's deposition in 1909 by the Young Turks, Muslims in places such as Egypt and India, although initially concerned, continued to display their religious loyalty to the Ottoman state, often translating adoring rhetoric into concrete action. Coming to a fever-pitch in the 1911–12 Italian-Ottoman conflict over Tripolitania (modern-day Libya) and the 1912–13 Balkan wars, Muslims in a number of countries raised immense sums of money to assist the Ottomans through public fundraising drives, actively espoused the Ottoman cause in the press and literature, organized hundreds of meetings as well as boycotts, sent medical missions, and even arranged for the dispatch of military volunteers.[60]

Yet the termination of the Ottoman Caliphate ultimately came from within its own domains, acutely ravaged by World War I,[61] as the unpredictable culmination of several significant intellectual and socio-political trends. The push to modernize the Ottoman Empire emerged in the eighteenth century in order to save the empire from military defeat at the hands of its European counterparts. Yet the attempt to establish new military schools and Europeanize the army led to the deposition of one sultan in 1807 by the traditional Janissary corps, who were later eliminated by his successor, the Sultan-Caliph Mahmud II, [62] in 1826. The imbalance in political powers that this created, with the removal of a main check upon the central government and the concurrent weakening of other traditional elites, like the *ʿulamāʾ* (religious scholars or learned class), paved the way for more reforms throughout society. On the one hand, during the remainder of Mahmud II's reign and the subsequent era of Tanzimat (1839–76), schools like the Royal Medical Academy (*Tıbbiye*), where an early version of the influential Committee of Union and Progress (CUP) would emerge in 1889, were established and exposed new generations of young Ottomans to European instructors, texts, and philosophies.[63] Yet on the other hand, the growing concentration and centralization of power in the palace and, increasingly, the imperial bureaucracy, over the next several decades, also fostered the desire for a constitutional and representative rule of law, among emerging secular as well as disempowered traditional elites. Ottoman constitutionalism, highly conservative and Islamic, was created by the amalgam of diverse groups and interests that broadly sought to establish parliamentary and constitutional government in the Ottoman Empire.[64]

Yet ironically, the subsequent Hamidian, Unionist, and Kemalist eras of late Ottoman and early Turkish Republican history were all dominated by authoritarian reformers, who, after brief experimentations with constitutional and parliamentary democracy, sought to consolidate power into a single-party or single-person rule, in order to implement a particular vision of Europeanized modernity. The Unionists, or the CUP forming the major umbrella organization of the Young Turks, were able to wrest control of the empire from Abdülhamid II in 1908, restore the constitution of 1876 and the parliament he had prorogued in 1878, and ultimately facilitate what Şükrü Hanioğlu notes is the most significant sociopolitical legacy of the Second Constitutional period, "the emergence of an intellectual nationalist vanguard at the expense of the traditional religious and propertied elites."[65] In the waning days of World War I, the Unionists also laid down the foundations for a nationalist resistance movement in Anatolia against the Allied Powers to preserve Ottoman territory and sovereignty, by storing, sending, and later smuggling officers, arms, ammunition, money, and supplies, establishing key organizations to continue the armed and public defense of Turkish Muslim rights, and mobilizing Muslim public opinion for the nationalist cause.[66] Not surprisingly, this Anatolian-based nationalist struggle was markedly religious in tenor.[67] Although the Unionist deputy in these plans for nationalist resistance, Mustafa Kemal Paşa (1880 or 1881–1938), grew increasingly independent and irksome, he was able to maintain his position through the continued loyalty of the armed forces, including Kazım

(Karabekir) Paşa (1882–1948), the deportation of prominent Unionist leaders to Malta by the British in March 1920, the Bolsheviks' deluding and delaying another eminent Unionist Enver Paşa (1881–1922) from action, and Mustafa Kemal's ultimate military victory over the invading Greek army in September 1922.[68] Over the next few years, Mustafa Kemal Paşa, later known as Atatürk or the Father of the Turks, skillfully and ruthlessly outmaneuvered his fellow nationalists and war heroes in accumulating the reigns of power and political influence in the fluid post-war environment.[69]

The ultimate push to abolish the Ottoman Caliphate as a rival source of power in March 1924 came from Mustafa Kemal, who had already secured his appointment as president of a Turkish Republic a few months earlier, in October 1923. Yet this was by no means the only or the most logical outcome of the Turkish War of Independence, which had been waged to preserve the integrity of the Ottoman Sultanate and Caliphate.[70] The Grand National Assembly was established in Ankara on April 23, 1920 to continue the work of the Ottoman Parliament that had been impeded by the British occupation of Istanbul on March 16, 1920.[71] And approximately two years of nationalist struggle later, the assembly's representatives were annoyed that the Grand Vizier Ahmet Tevfik (Okday) Paşa (1845–1936) in Istanbul seemed to insist pretentiously on sending a joint delegation to the peace negotiations at Lausanne, despite the negative reply sent from Ankara, which, unbeknownst to the assembly delegates at large, he had never received. Sinop Deputy, Rıza Nur (1879–1942), introduced a motion that the assembly separate the sultanate and caliphate from one another, in order to isolate and eradicate the temporal power of the imperial bureaucracy associated with the former (and thereby get rid of presumptuous grand viziers once and for all), while still preserving the high spiritual office of the caliphate. The modified resolution finally adopted in the early hours of November 2, 1922, declared that the sovereignty of the sultanate was formally incorporated and executed by the government of Turkish Grand National Assembly alone, and it also preserved the caliphate for the Ottoman Royal House.[72]

Yet, as Michael Finefrock has argued, by not simultaneously delineating the precise form of the state that was to replace the Ottoman Sultanate, these moderate and conservative nationalists placed themselves at a distinct political disadvantage. Although liberals and conservatives alike in the assembly increasingly argued "in favor of the Caliph playing an important role in whatever political system ultimately was established,"[73] they were undermined by political intimidation (for example, the brutal murder of a vocal pro-caliphate assembly member[74] in 1923 by Mustafa Kemal's lead bodyguard), Mustafa Kemal's modification of the 1920 High Treason Law on April 15, 1923, (making it a crime to campaign for the return of the sultanate broadly defined, i.e., any form of temporal power for the caliph),[75] and his adroit arrangements for a more loyal second assembly.[76] Following the isolation of the army politically[77] and during an absence of highly regarded opposition figures from Ankara,[78] the rest of the personally vetted assembly moved on March 4, 1924, to abolish the Ottoman Caliphate along with the religious foundations of law and education. The centuries-old institution was struck down by a legislative act of the Grand National Assembly, and all members of the Ottoman dynasty were expelled from the newly formed Turkish Republic.[79]

DIACHRONIC REFLECTIONS ON SYMBOLIC LOSS, DESTRUCTION, AND RENEGOTIATION

Juxtaposing this disappearance of the caliphate in the twentieth century with its brief absence in the thirteenth century also raises certain questions about the commonalities between such seemingly different scenarios. The two events are separated by nearly seven centuries, their capitals in Baghdad and Istanbul are lands apart, their territories do not fully converge, and one institution was obliterated by a foreign army whereas the other was swept away through the internal act of an assembly. Yet what binds these two scenarios together is the abiding significance of the caliphate within the Islamic context and the elusive desire for a righteous locus of central authority and leadership grounded in the Islamic tradition. Even so, certain contextual similarities facilitated Muslim contemporaries' heightened emotions at the point of the caliphate's demise in the premodern and modern eras. The territories of both the Abbasid and the Ottoman Empires had greatly dwindled and the political power of the nominally supreme ruler in both instances had ebbed, fomenting a greater sense of loss and nostalgia for their glorious pasts. And in both cases, individual caliphs, the Abbasid al-Nāṣir li-Dīnillāh (who ruled 1180–1225 CE) and the Ottoman Abdülhamid II (who ruled 1876–1909 CE), sought to rejuvenate the institution of the caliphate as a means of augmenting their dynasty's political position and power at a time of weakness and intentionally enhanced the spiritual claims of the caliphate upon Muslims across Afro-Eurasia. Transregional networks of literary and cultural elites in both eras facilitated the circulation of such caliphal claims to spiritual and moral, if not functional political, authority, which strongly resonated with deeply ingrained religious traditions as well as the particularities of various local contexts.

The symbolism of the caliphate, augmented by the often romanticized memory of what the institution represented and what it could still represent in the lives of contemporaries and their progeny, was potent. For many Muslims, the caliphate even constituted a symbol of Islam itself, one deeply embedded in a rich intellectual and cultural discourse that could readily evoke a sense of the wider community's glory, righteousness, and esteem. For some, harkening back to the earliest caliphal models, it signified the potential of the Muslim community to live up to the best interpretations of the Prophet Muḥammad's teachings, to constitute a model and mercy for the rest of humanity, and to assume a position of virtuous leadership and benevolent guidance. Mandated by Islamic law as necessary to safeguard the Muslim community's temporal and spiritual affairs, the caliphate was enmeshed with numerous jurisprudential rulings that had developed over centuries of vibrant discussion and debate. As an institution with its genesis in the early days of Islam, the caliphate offered a potent mode of connectivity with the Muslim community's cultural, religious, legal, and historical heritage as well as with its ideals of solidarity. Therefore, its absence seemed inconceivable and created an aching void for many.

In probing this complex constellation of meanings and sensations, I have necessarily had to establish what I hope are some meaningful and feasible, if not exhaustive, parameters for analysis. The premodern portion is roughly demarcated by the first geographical zone identified by Marshall Hodgson for what he calls the High and Late Middle Ages where "Arabic continued to predominate as [a] literary tongue even where it was not the spoken language," with Cairo functioning as "the intellectual capital of this zone." Encompassing Arabia, Syria, Mesopotamia, Egypt, western North Africa, and Spain, these territories loosely correspond to the former western territories of the Abbasid Caliphate, and hence this delineation allows us to assess the reactions to its disappearance in lands where its cultural imprint was both deep and lasting, bearing religious meaning and significance long past its gradual political disintegration and ultimate destruction. Yet we should also acknowledge that this delineation does not fully encompass Hodgson's second geographical zone from "the Balkans east to Turkestan and China and south to southern India and into Malaysia" where Persian matured and flourished as another significant "language of culture." Nor does it address all of the many regions to which Islam was rapidly and remarkably expanding after the fourth/tenth century, including Sub-Saharan Africa, Southeast Asia, Central Eurasia, South Asia, and China.[80] Although it would make for another intriguing study to analyze in full the reactions in Persian literature to the demise of the Abbasid Caliphate (especially recognizing that many of these territories came to be ruled by Turkic-Mongolic sovereigns who continued to derive prestige from their lineage even after their Islamization) as well as perceptions of it among newly Islamized populations across the world (and specifically what, if anything, was culturally transmitted to them about the Abbasid Caliphate at various points in time and how), both sets of these dynamics lie beyond the scope of this current manuscript.

Similarly faced with the sheer unfeasibility of studying the reactions of all Muslim nations in the modern era to the demise of the Ottoman Caliphate, I have selected a few particular sites for investigation, with an eye to their varying relationships with the Ottoman Empire and experiences of European colonialism. The histories of Anatolia, geographical Syria, Egypt, and India present different forms of interaction with the Late Ottoman Empire. While Anatolia represented the birthplace of the Ottomans and remained a central province for the duration of their rule, geographical Syria was conquered in the course of the sixteenth century and remained a provincial part of the empire until its dismemberment in the early twentieth century. Although Egypt had been acquired during the sixteenth-century campaigns of the Ottoman sultan Selim I (r. 918–26/1512–20), by the nineteenth century it had become a semi-autonomous state under its Ottoman Albanian governor Mehmed Ali Paşa, never to be fully reintegrated into the empire. India, on the other hand, was never was an official part of the Ottoman Empire, to begin with. Yet there, the British established a strong commercial then imperial presence, ultimately overcoming the remnants of the Mughal Empire. And in Egypt too, first Napoleon Bonaparte (1769–1821) led a French expedition in 1798, followed nearly a century later by British military occupation and administration. Meanwhile, geographical Syria and Anatolia faced the prospect of European colonization much later, during the course of the First World War. These different variables help contextualize and elucidate the various reactions of Muslims in the early twentieth century to the unforeseen abolition of the Ottoman Caliphate by the Turkish Grand National Assembly.

Longing for the Lost Caliphate examines the profuse reflections of Muslims in the premodern and modern eras upon these dramatically unexpected disappearances of an Islamic caliphate. The premodern materials include predominantly Arabic as well as some Persian poetry, historical chronicles, legal treatises, commentaries on prophetic narrations, works of Qur'anic exegesis, topographical surveys, musicological compositions, and eschatological works, in both manuscript and published formats. The modern source materials expand to include Arabic, English, French, Ottoman Turkish, and Turkish archival documents, memoirs, poetry, periodical literature, and specialized treatises. This wide range of materials helps provide insight into the world of Muslim literary and cultural elites (jurists, exegetes, traditionists, theologians, historians, musicians, poets, intellectuals, bureaucrats, activists, and journalists) at the same time as it provides a tantalizing, if elusive, glimpse of their interactions with broader Muslim populations. Poetry regularly recited in public in the premodern world or disseminated through newspapers in the twentieth century, folk musical performances seeking to preserve forms inherited from the thirteenth century, premodern processions and ceremonies, and modern mass rallies and petitions, all illustrate the vibrant and myriad means of transmitting collective memories of the Islamic caliphate.

Yet, in *Longing for the Lost Caliphate,* I would also like to suggest that this fascinating intertwining of faith, community, and politics is not exceptional to the Muslim religious imaginary. In many ways, it parallels the experiences of other religious communities amid poignant moments of symbolic loss and reconstruction, such as the destruction of the Second Temple, the fall of Rome, and the capture of Constantinople, as well as the renegotiation of transregional religious identities and institutions amid the modern world system of nation-states, such as the rearticulation of the papacy and the global rise of politicized religious movements and parties. These allusions to the comparative religious experiences of other communities are integrated into the body of book, where I hope they will most effectively illuminate Muslim engagement and entanglement with the notion of a vanished caliphate, irrevocably lost in its past forms, and passionately desired in potential new configurations (whether political, spatial, spiritual, or communal).

In exploring how premodern and modern Muslims conceptualized the past and reimagined a collective future, I begin with the Mongol destruction of Baghdad in 1258 and its ramifications before delving into the later aftermath of the Ottoman Caliphate's abolition in 1924. I analyze the cultural, political, and intellectual dimensions of Muslims' multiple engagements with the idea of an Islamic caliphate at these historic junctures through chapters that are thematically, rather than chronologically, structured around analytical arguments. In painting these broad strokes, I also pay attention to the importance of local context as well as personal and professional formations in the shaping of regional and individual perspectives. And by focusing on different angles through each of my chapters, I strive to illustrate the multifarious refractions of Muslim cultural memories of the caliphate: in poetic and prosaic descriptions as well as musical resonances, but also in the realms of social, political, and intellectual engagement, activism, and debate. These cultural memories pervade both discursive language and the social sphere; they inform the movements of peoples' tongues and pens as well as their hands and feet. As such, I hope that this book elucidates some of the ineffable ways that Muslims have vividly imagined their past in relation to the caliphate and striven to reconfigure their political and intellectual constructs as part of a living and dynamic cultural memory.

Beginning with a striking dream and travel narrative, the opening anecdote of chapter 1, "Visions of a Lost Caliphal Capital: Baghdad, 1258 CE" establishes the intense desire and nostalgia for Baghdad as the Abbasid Caliphate's cosmopolitan capital and its centrality in the Muslim imaginary, among the near and the far. Poetry, historical chronicles, and scholarly literature from Muslim Spain in the west, Yemen in the south, and Egypt, western North Africa, geographical Syria, Mesopotamia, Persia, and India further east richly illustrate a shared perception among interconnected literary elites about the Abbasids' temporal and spiritual preeminence, despite all of their political reversals. Poetic elegies and moralizing tendencies over the destruction of the Second Temple and the fall of Rome suggest similarities. Yet the world without a caliph was so unimaginable for many premodern Muslims that it boded the imminent end of time itself—an eschatological interpretation that reverses contemporaneous Christian views of empire.

Chapter 2, "Recapturing Lost Glory and Legitimacy," opens with a prominent Islamic scholar refusing to pledge allegiance to the Mamluk ruler, intimating his slave status, in order to highlight the intensely problematic questions of political and legal legitimacy for premodern Muslim states in the wake of the Abbasid Caliphate's demise. Similar to the self-image of Byzantium as a Second Rome or the way that medieval rulers in western Europe appropriated Roman symbols, the Mamluk State reinvented the Abbasid Caliphate of Cairo through elaborate rituals and ceremonies reminiscent of a glorious past, and legal scholars articulated creative jurisprudential solutions. Within Mamluk domains, the dilemma of caliphal absence was thus resolved by resurrecting the Abbasid Caliphate in Cairo as a doubly political and spiritual institution, where the caliph delegated his authority to govern to the sultan and radiated metaphysical blessings through his continued physical presence. This fraught relationship between caliphal authority and the wielding of power notably continued to surface as a magnet for political activity and debate, including the ever-potent threat of rebellion, over the centuries of Mamluk rule. Other premodern polities, however, adopted different solutions, and in South Asia, the Delhi Sultanate clung to the remaining legitimizing vestiges of the last Abbasid caliph of Baghdad, by propagating his name on its coinage and during Friday sermons, for decades. It was only much later that ambitious military leaders began to seek official delegation of rule in South Asia from the Abbasid caliph in Cairo and interject his legitimizing authority into local politics.

Chapter 3, "Conceptualizing the Caliphate, 632–1517 CE," begins with a discussion of how the embodied practice of the earliest generations of Muslims was essential in consolidating a nearly universal Islamic consensus upon the obligation of appointing a leader for the Muslim community. As such, the caliphate was incorporated into Sunni Islamic law as a legal necessity and a communal obligation, and Muslim scholars attempted to address the institution's increasing divergence from ideals over time. Following the destruction of the Abbasid Caliphate in Baghdad in 656/1258, Muslim scholars of Mamluk Egypt and Syria drew from this rich tradition of Islamic political thought and jurisprudence to articulate creative solutions that bolstered the socio-legal foundations of the reconstituted caliphate in Cairo. As intellectual predecessors, teachers, disciples, colleagues, rivals, and adversaries, these premodern scholars were connected to each other through intricate social webs that traversed the centuries of Mamluk rule from the thirteenth to the sixteenth centuries. In the works of these authors, the issue of the caliphate builds upon the legal scaffolding of past scholarship while reflecting contemporary social contexts and the relevant issues of their day.

In chapter 4, "Manifold Meanings of Loss: Ottoman Defeat, Early 1920s," a protracted poetic debate between one of the last Ottoman *şeyhülislams* Mustafa Sabri and the Egyptian Prince of Poets Aḥmad Shawqī, conducted through the Egyptian press in the 1920s, aptly illustrates how modern regional contexts and professional affiliations created divergent interpretations of the Ottoman Caliphate's significance, even among those Muslim elites who shared an intense devotion to defending its legacy. For Mustafa Sabri, who hailed from the

Ottoman religious hierarchy, the abolition of the caliphate meant a loss of the primacy of Islamic law, whereas for Aḥmad Shawqī, who assailed the British with his poetic pen, it meant the loss of the last great Muslim power in an age of colonialism. More broadly, Anatolia was home to the Turkish War of Independence waged to save the Ottoman Caliphate from foreign occupation yet overtaken by a gradual and strategic Kemalist revolution. Egypt and India, chafing under British colonialism, idealized the Ottoman Caliphate as the last great Muslim empire and a rallying symbol for local nationalist movements. And geographical Syria, agitated by the centralization policies, often castigated as Turkification, of the CUP while an Ottoman province, leaned towards a more vocally independent Arab nationalism and the competing caliphal claims of the Hashemite Sharīf Ḥusayn. Wary of the political implications of these contending claims and religious debates for their overseas holdings, the British and French imperial bureaucracies closely watched and documented any developments through their global network of officials and informants.

Chapter 5, "In International Pursuit of a Caliphate," analyzes the vibrant discussions of the early twentieth century over how to revive a caliphate best suited to the post-war era. While some advocated preservation of a traditional caliphal figurehead, many Muslim intellectuals were greatly persuaded by new models of internationalism embracing the nation-state and proposed international caliphal councils and organizations, similar to the League of Nations, or other purportedly spiritual institutions, similar to the refashioned papacy, to preserve the bonds of a transregional religious community. To varying degrees, all the participants in the debate over reviving a twentieth-century caliphate were influenced by an intriguing confluence of both the historic tranregionalism of the Muslim community as well as the modern thrust of the new age of global internationalism.

Chapter 6, "Debating a Modern Caliphate," explores the contentious debates among modernist and traditional Muslim scholars in the Turkish Republic and Egypt over the future of the caliphate. Scholars and intellectuals on both sides of the divide faced serious consequences for their positions: İsmail Şükrü's publisher was brutally murdered by Mustafa Kemal's lead bodyguard, Seyyid Bey was sidelined from power after justifying the new Turkish regime, the Head of the Istanbul Bar Association Lütfi Fikri was put on trial for treason, ʿAlī ʿAbd al-Rāziq was expelled from the ranks of Egypt's illustrious Azharite scholars, and Mustafa Sabri lived for a while in double exile in Egypt. And although not directly instigated by his intriguing views on the caliphate, Said Nursi survived multiple poisonings, imprisonment, and exile within Republican Turkey for his charismatic potential and activism. The separation of the caliphate from the Ottoman Sultanate followed by the Ottoman Caliphate's abolition had opened up the possibilities for new and passionately contested configurations of power.

The book's epilogue, "The Swirl of Religious Hopes and Aspirations," presents the later birth and development of Islamist movements of widely divergent strains, contrasts their stances with those held by the majority of Muslims, and further contemplates some of the book's central themes. It emphasizes broader patterns regarding the dynamic intersection of faith, community, and politics across time and space and also highlights differences among the premodern and modern contexts of religious communities and their imaginaries.

As *Longing for the Lost Caliphate* reveals, the caliphate signifies a pivotal cultural symbol that Muslims have imbued with different meanings according to their particular social contexts, bound by distinct parameters of time and space. It constitutes a cultural grammar that people readily identify and utilize to create new meanings. Building on the insights of Émile Durkheim, Maurice Halbwach's notion of collective memory, shorn of his positivist understanding of history, is particularly useful in understanding this phenomenon. His emphasis on the power of social frames in shaping memories reveals their immense fluidity and malleability on the one hand and their woven threads of connectivity with the past on the other. Elizabeth Castelli observes:

> Religion, in Halbwach's account of it, is in essence a form of cultural memory work. What makes it different from the cultural memory work of other collectivities or modes of social life is the heightened importance attached to religion's complex and potentially paradoxical relationship with the past. This is particularly amplified at moments of ideological and institutional stress or change.

This interpretative framework underscores that people's memories, including those of religious communities, are shaped by their social affiliations and interactions and that the strength of their identification with particular groups may change, wane, or present different reflections on past events and emotions. It further recognizes the idealization and distortion of specific recollections, as their particularities dissolve over the passage of time, into tradition and collective imaginaries. Or to utilize another metaphor, it slowly irons out the wrinkles of the past. As Patrick Hutton elucidates in his *History as an Art of Memory*, "Only an historian scanning particular representations of a tradition at intervals over a long time is in a position to observe the change."[81] The clearly different conceptual spaces of 1258 and 1924 help illuminate this gradual process of transformation among Muslims while simultaneously revealing lasting and recognizable cultural resonances associated with the notion of an Islamic caliphate. In short, *Longing for the Lost Caliphate* probes Muslim understandings of the caliphate, dramatically accentuated by its absence in the thirteenth and twentieth centuries, and reflects upon the broader implications of symbolic loss in the cultural memories of religious communities across the *longue durée*.

CHAPTER 1

VISIONS OF A LOST CALIPHAL CAPITAL: BAGHDAD, 1258 CE

Memory is an index of loss.

—NATALIE ZEMON DAVIS AND RANDOLPH STARN[1]

Listen to the story told by the reed,
of being separated.
"Since I was cut from the reedbed,
I have made this crying sound.
Anyone apart from someone he loves
understands what I say."

—MAWLĀNĀ JALĀL AL-DĪN AL-RŪMĪ[2]

THE STRIKING TRANSFORMATIONS that befell the cosmopolitan City of Peace (*Dār al-Salām*), as Baghdad was known, following the Mongol conquest in 656/1258 were painful to all those, near and far, who had witnessed or imagined its grandeur. One contemporary who survived the Mongol onslaught, Ẓahīr al-Dīn Ibn al-Kāzarūnī (611–97/1214–98), exemplified this cosmopolitan culture and learning of the devastated city: an historian, litterateur, mathematician, traditionist, jurist, agriculturalist, and public official,[3] whose two surviving works, one historical, the other literary, each memorialize the loss of the Abbasid caliphs and their capital. In a piece of prose (*maqāmah*) that he dedicated to Baghdad, Ibn al-Kāzarūnī lucidly conveys the intense desire and nostalgia people could hold for the destroyed capital of the Abbasid Caliphate. In the evocative narrative he constructs, a man, who once served as the Judge of Tabriz, dreamt literally and figuratively of the majestic city of Baghdad, when one night a voice called out in a vision and resoundingly affirmed his intentions to set off for the Abbasid capital. Accordingly, he prepared his provisions for the long journey and said farewell to his children in pursuit of Baghdad, which he called:

> the Kaʿbah [i.e., mecca or religious focal point] of Islam, the sanctuary of the Muslim community's leader (*al-imām*), the trove of the generous and noble (*maʿdin al-kirām*), the Abode of the Caliphate, and the safe asylum from all fear (*maḥall al-amn min al-makhāfah*). In it are the center and throne of kingship

> and the current leader and commander of the Muslims (*imām al-ʿaṣr wa-amīrihi*), the Caliph of God, the descendant of the uncle [al-ʿAbbās] of the tender-hearted (*awwāh*) Prophet [Muḥammad]. Kings submit in obedience to [Baghdad's] power and crowd at its doors to kiss its foundations.

The description continues on to mention the widespread justice, knowledge, and religiosity of the city, where Islam itself is protected by the venerable Abbasid caliphs. But by the time the yearning traveler reached his destination, the Mongols had besieged and destroyed the illustrious seat of the caliphate, leaving it a shambles, a hollow and broken shell of its former self. And the poor man recited mournful poetry to express the depth of his disappointment, "I bewail its ruins at times, / and I cry over those who have departed; so if eyes were to vanish from crying / out of excessive desire, we would have gone blind." After such an arduous journey, the Baghdad that had so preoccupied his imagination and inspired intense desire had vanished.[4]

Yet nearby stood another man weeping inconsolably due to another sense of loss and bereavement; his tears were those of one who had lived in the Abbasid capital before its devastation and had therefore experienced its majesty firsthand. This resident of Baghdad initially shunned the traveler's inquires about the cause of his tears, protesting that if he had only seen the city's former condition, he too would have succumbed to the same psychological state. The long-distance visitor was intrigued by these words and pleaded to be shown around the ruins of the city in the company of this knowledgeable guide, who, after some persuasion, assented. Their tour began with the sanctified caliphal complex, which they noted to be neglected and abased after having served as a symbolic focal point for Muslims. The resident showed his guest around some of its former palaces and the throne of the caliphs' lost dominion. Here, as in all of the subsequent sites of the devastated city, the guide revealed to his curious companion how affairs used to be conducted in the capital of the Abbasid Caliphate. The architectural ruins elicited lengthy conversations about the Abbasids' days of glory along with meticulous details about their bureaucracy and noteworthy seasons, like the times of pilgrimage, fasting, major holidays, commemorating the deceased, and celebrating spring. In the end, the recollection of the more joyous occasions also prompted the resident of Baghdad to remember that moral deviance had seeped into society and evoked the wrath of God, as manifested by the Mongols' invasion. He had decided for himself that the temporal world was simply not worth the effort and therefore sought to turn back to God and follow the model of the righteous. The pious traveler encouraged his host along these lines of sincere repentance, and, solidifying their noble intentions with a solemn pact, the two finally parted.[5]

Ibn al-Kāzarūnī's narrative deftly weaves together many of the prominent themes expressed by contemporaries and near contemporaries writing in the seventh/thirteenth and eighth/fourteenth centuries about the fall of Baghdad.

On the one hand, Ibn al-Kāzarūnī evokes the centrality of Baghdad in the Muslim imaginary. It is depicted as the focal point of Islam both spiritually and temporally for it is from there that the Abbasid caliphs reigned. Drawing from a shared constellation of potent signifiers, he conveys the Abbasids' worldly and religious preeminence as celebrated rulers, protectors of Islam, guardians of the Muslim community, political inheritors of the blessed Prophet, and his blood relatives. And on the other hand, he highlights the moral dangers that laced the Abbasids' power and wealth, leading to extravagance, decrepitude, and ultimately divine retribution. Its remedy, particularly for the broader community following the Abbasids' demise, lay in sincere repentance and embodied acts of piety. Such propositions were not limited to Ibn al-Kāzarūnī's poetic prose. As I demonstrate in this chapter, despite the weakened state of the Abbasid Caliphate by the time of the Mongol invasions, such poignant and layered expressions of anguish over what had been lost and shattered enjoyed wide resonance and circulation across diverse literary forms and lands in the world of the seventh/thirteenth and eighth/fourteenth centuries.

MAPPING AN ISLAMIC CULTURAL DISCOURSE

Poetic elegies composed to the memory of the fallen city of Baghdad were once so numerous and deeply rooted in the cultural discourse of the Muslim humanities that many premodern historians felt it sufficed merely to allude to the plethora of poems on the subject.[6] But in 1923, when Muḥammad al-Hāshimī recovered the famed Persian poet Saʿdī's Arabic elegy from manuscript form and published it in his Baghdad periodical *al-Yaqīn*, he lamented the poem's neglected state. "We must wonder," he wrote, "how historians have forgotten this poem and litterateurs have neglected narrating and compiling it, for this is a sin that cannot be forgiven."[7] And ten years later, in 1933, the Orientalist scholar Joseph De Somogyi referred to a *qaṣīdah* written by the Syrian Taqiyy al-Dīn Ibn Abī Yusr with the words, "It is to our knowledge the only poem lamenting the fall of Baghdad, and it is an excellent poetical expression of the contemporary sentiment felt at the fall of the Abbasids and at the tragedy of their capital."[8] However, with the advantage of the accelerated publication of works from the Islamic literary heritage over the course of the twentieth century and facilitated access to Islamic manuscript libraries, I was fortunate to locate and translate over twenty more such poems expressing the eloquent grief of contemporaries and near contemporaries regarding this historic event as well as scores of historical chronicles, biographical dictionaries, eschatological treatises, topographical surveys, exegetical works, and commentaries on prophetic traditions that address the cultural trauma of 656/1258. Pinpointing some of the locales associated with these authors on a map reveals just how widely these ideas were expressed and circulated, from Muslim Spain and North

Africa in the west to India in the east, and from Anatolia in the north to Yemen in the south, with the heaviest concentration in the central lands of Egypt, Syria, and Mesopotamia. It also raises questions about the networks that facilitated the interactions of these literary elites and helped them maintain shared sensibilities, along with a sense of greater community, across such vast swaths of territory in the premodern world.

Despite the obvious realities of political fragmentation and dynastic competition, the social and cultural networks that crisscrossed Afro-Eurasia and tied people together across geographical and political boundaries helped perpetuate Islamic ideals of communal unity. Long gone was the unified empire of early Islamic history. Over the course of centuries, far-flung and even central provinces had slipped out of the imperial control of the Abbasid caliphs, becoming autonomous and independent political units under local elites and nomadic peoples. Andalusia and the Maghreb were lost to the Umayyads and subsequent dynasties. Egypt, Khurasan, and Transoxania first succumbed to the increasingly autonomous rule of military governors and were later conquered by invading armies. And Syria, Mesopotamia, and the Hijaz too came to be ruled by others. From the middle of the tenth to the middle of the twelfth centuries, even the caliphs themselves fell subservient to a series of powerful military commanders, the Buyids from northwestern Iran then the Turkish Seljuqs.[9] Yet despite having lost effective political and military control, the Abbasid caliphs retained their symbolic socio-cultural and religious prestige as nominal leaders of a universally conceived Sunni Muslim community.

Significantly, the Islamic culture that had emerged during the age of the imperial caliphate, with Arabic as its lingua franca, did not disintegrate with the collapse of centralized political power. John Voll has argued for the existence of a special discourse-based Islamic world system that offered a "sense of cohesion and shared identity" following the onset of political disintegration in the fourth/tenth century:

> The Islamic discourse was able to cross the boundaries between urban-based and pastoral agrarian societies and those between the different major traditions of civilization in the Afro-Eurasian landmass. Networks of personal and organizational interaction created at least a minimal sense of corporate, communal identity in the vast emerging world-system.[10]

The widely noted mobility of Muslim pilgrims, scholars, mystics, artisans, litterateurs, and merchants helped integrate disparate domains, as did the institutions that gradually developed in order to serve this high circulation of people across premodern Afro-Eurasia, offering lodging, hospitality, opportunities for exoteric and esoteric study, and fellowship. So too did the emergence of multiple political centers assist in fostering the fluorescence of this cultural expression, as rulers sought to attract and patronize these streams of peripatetic

MAP 1. Distribution of premodern authors and poets.

Black Sea
Caspian Sea
Tabriz
Antep
Aleppo
Sinjar
Mosul
Qazwin
Hamadan
Baalbek
Damascus
Baghdad
Mada'in
Kufa
Basra
Cairo
Shiraz
Delhi
Red Sea
Arabian Sea
Taiz
INDIAN OCEAN

scholarly, literary, and artistic production at their courts to help bolster their claims, as Ira Lapidus notes, of regnal status on par with their rivals and peers.[11] Still, it would be a mistake to conflate this far-reaching socio-cultural cohesion with blanket uniformity. This " 'commonwealth' of regional Muslim states, united by their participation in an emerging Islamic culture" after the fourth/tenth century, could be characterized by what Fred Donner has called "distinctive variants of a recognizably common Islamic culture."[12] The celebrated eighth/fourteenth-century travels of Ibn Baṭṭūṭah from his home in Tangiers across Afro-Eurasia have frequently and justifiably been called upon to epitomize this ability of premodern Muslim individuals to traverse distant and unfamiliar lands while remaining socio-culturally conversant actors and participants.

Particularly in the expansive former western territories of the Abbasid Empire on which this study is based, the idea of an Islamic caliphate retained deep cultural resonance among Arabic literary and scholarly elites. There are hints in the extant literature of mass popular participation and consumption of this discourse, but such references remain deeply tantalizing. Religious scholars speak of the intense trepidation engulfing "everyone" at the destruction of the Abbasid Caliphate in Baghdad.[13] And one composer of multiple poetic elegies for the Abbasid capital and its caliphs was known by the epithet "al-Wāʿiẓ" or the Admonisher, indicating that his poems were likely intended for even wider audiences than the historians who transcribed them. He may have utilized these elegies in order to preach popular sermons, or the etymologically related *waʿẓ*, and touch the emotions of large gatherings of people of all ranks.[14] A prominent scholar of the era, Tāj al-Dīn ʿAbd al-Wahhāb al-Subkī, commented on the proper execution of an inspirational preacher's duties and closely associated it with the preaching of the more formal Friday sermons at congregational prayers, and indeed the same person could sometimes perform both functions. He urged both types of preachers to project their voices clearly in the mosques to be heard and understood by the masses, and the inspirational preacher or *wāʿiẓ* received particular advice to remind people of God and their duties toward Him, to evoke fear of God in their hearts, and to convey the stories of pious predecessors as exemplary models and lessons.[15] The story of the Abbasids and their demise in Baghdad offered rich material for such evocative poetic exhortation. Chroniclers also described people's joy at the ultimate restoration of the Abbasid Caliphate in Cairo and how they turned out to watch the fantastic spectacles of the associated processions and ceremonies.[16]

Although we cannot read the inner thought processes of these popular audiences in the mosques and on the streets, we do have some measure of access to their authors and performers, who exerted disproportionate influence in establishing broader cultural norms and understandings. Or as Peter Brown has eloquently urged in the context of Late Antique intellectual elites and the study of their extant work, authors often articulate broader religious currents in society:

> The word "elite" can be misleading. It invites us to assume an absence of contact between leading minds and the wider body of opinion and practice that surrounds them. This is a false assumption. I prefer the judgment of Louis Gernet, writing on Greek religion in the classical period: "An elite does not invent. It renders explicit what many others think."[17]

The Arabic poems, histories, and scholarly works that have traversed the centuries into our hands are the shared records of premodern literary scholars, documenting and revealing their hopes, fears, insights, and understandings of the calamitous events of 656/1258 afflicting the wider, interconnected Muslim community with which they identified, belonged, and participated.

AL-SUBKĪ'S LIVING HISTORY: AN ENDURING SENSE OF LOSS

One such scholar was the aforementioned Tāj al-Dīn al-Subkī (728–71/1328–70), who was born in Cairo roughly seventy years after the fall of Baghdad to the Mongols. Born into an eminent scholarly lineage, al-Subkī began his studies at an early age with his own father, who also took every care to expose his son to the leading male and female scholars of his time.[18] When his father was appointed to the Mamluk State's highest Damascene legal position of chief justice or *Qāḍī'l-Quḍāt,* a position to which he too would eventually ascend by the remarkably young age of 28, al-Subkī relocated around the age of eleven to Damascus. There, he continued to frequent the city's wide range of offerings, displaying remarkable acumen and application, and al-Subkī grew close to and was dearly beloved by the historian and traditionist al-Dhahabī (673–748/1274–1348), maintained a lifelong poetic correspondence with the biographer and litterateur al-Ṣafadī (696–764/1297–1363), and was highly honored in his youth by the stern and renowned traditionist and jurist al-Mizzī (654–742/1256–1341). By the age of eighteen, al-Subkī had demonstrated such a dexterous proficiency in the Shāfiʿī school of law that he was already licensed to teach and issue legal opinions in its domain. Over the course of his illustrious and prolific career, al-Subkī developed a reputation for his flowing eloquence, courage, clemency, compassion, and sheer brilliance.[19]

Throughout his interactions with the scholars of his day, al-Subkī maintained a deep interest in history from a young age and set about poring over and gathering biographies of past scholars and avidly observing his contemporaries. As a youth, he made a point to attend al-Dhahabī's lessons twice a day and even engaged in copying for him for a spell. Early on, al-Subkī also began compiling and arranging his own materials,[20] which he would eventually integrate into three major and interrelated intellectual histories of individuals affiliated with the Shāfiʿī school of law. The histories or *Ṭabaqāt al-Shāfiʿiyyah,* referred to in modern terms as biographical dictionaries, bore deceptively similar titles corresponding to their length, the Major (*al-Kubrā*), Minor (*al-Sughrā*), and Medial (*al-Wusṭā*), two of which he composed in tandem. Despite their overt similarities, in titles and in the structural utilization of biographical entries, al-Subkī conceptualized each of these works for a different purpose. As he was preparing his most ambitious history, *Ṭabaqāt al-Shāfiʿiyyah al-Kubrā*, the prolonged duration necessary to complete this encyclopedic work inspired him to compose a second shorter one that scholars could consult for a comprehensive list of Shāfiʿī jurists' biographies, *al-Wusṭā*, which he completed in 754/1353 at the age of twenty-six. The larger work took him twelve more years to complete, in 766/1365, after roughly ten years of serving as Damascene chief justice, since al-Subkī sought to integrate his vast learning and expound on multiple fields of knowledge via this biographical rubric. As al-Subkī clarified in his introduction, "This book is [a work of] prophetic narrations, jurisprudence, history, literature, and collected [topics of] benefit, in which we mention complete biographies in the manner of traditionists and litterateurs."[21] al-Ṣafadī extolled these efforts with poetry and prose, referring to al-Subkī's work as not mere biographies but rather luminous constellations of stars. And al-Subkī's writings enjoyed wide circulation both during his life and after his death.[22]

In discussing the Mongol invasion of Baghdad in his *Ṭabaqāt al-Shāfiʿiyyah al-Kubrā*, al-Subkī reveals that the critical aim of his narrative is to perpetuate the collective significance of this disaster for an enduring affective community of believers. The entry on al-Ḥāfiẓ Abū Muḥammad ʿAbd al-ʿAẓīm al-Mundhirī begins benignly with a description of the deceased as a friend of God, a foremost narrator of the traditions of the Prophet, and a jurist of the legal school whose eponymous founder, al-Shāfiʿī, emerged from among the Prophet's extended relations. The occasion of his death in 656/1258, however, presents an opening for al-Subkī to elaborate on the broader historical significance of this catastrophic year. Mere mention of the fateful year elicits a string of eloquent phrases bemoaning it as inflicting the worst of calamities and encompassing the ugliest of horrific crimes, which were perpetrated by the Mongols against the Muslims. Writing around one hundred years or so after the traumatic events, they were no less vivid to al-Subkī's mind, and he sought to ensure that their memory was preserved, transmitted, and continued to generate intense depths of emotions. He sought to elicit moral reflection and dread, to evoke the heated tears of "Muslims across the passage of time" (*al-muslimūn ʿalā mamarr al-zamān*), and to inspire historians' realization that they had never heard the likes of this invasion that rendered sky earth and earth sky, violently rupturing the recognizable order of life and destroying its calm. In doing so, al-Subkī actively reaches and projects across time the cultural symbolism of the Abbasid caliphal capital's demise.

Both of the two audiences that al-Subkī specifies at the beginning of his narration are associated with this unique temporality: Muslims who may live at any future point of time and historians who engage in sifting through and evaluating traces of the past. Illustrating the "the relativity of time from the perspective of memory" across generations, al-Subkī's work indicates new social dimensions of the major contribution of Henri Bergson, with whose ideas Maurice Halbwachs later wrestled, that the time of memory "does not exist in discrete, measurable units. Rather, it endures, and it may be telescoped or expanded in our recollections by the intensity of the emotions it inspires or the vividness of the imagery it evokes."[23] At the close of his account, al-Subkī layers on another dimension of transregionality, passionately articulating a vision of these historical events' import beyond those immediately afflicted in Baghdad. Returning to his initial point, addressed to historians, of the unprecedented carnage and horrors of the Mongol invasion, al-Subkī reflects that even if the world had experienced worse than it, the events of 656/1258 and the killing of the Abbasid caliph, in the heart of Muslim domains, were associated with the "humiliation of the religion" of Islam (*hawān al-dīn*) and therefore constituted "a tribulation that was not limited but rather afflicted all other Muslims" (*balāʾ alladhī lam yakhtaṣṣ bal ʿamma sāʾir al-muslimīn*).[24] This vision of the past conceives of an integral Muslim community, interconnected across time and space that is carefully attuned to the cultural symbolism of the assault on Baghdad and its caliph. And writing in Mamluk Syria roughly one hundred years later, it is a vision that al-Subkī assiduously seeks to cultivate.

His doing so reveals the continuing social frameworks that shaped Arabic literary and scholarly elites' understanding of the past. Through their scholarship and writing, through their travels and tutelage, Muslim scholars and litterateurs not only transmitted discrete bodies of knowledge but also the sensibilities that were integral to their comportment. al-Subkī's evocative narration, a century after the Mongol onslaught, points to the cumulative impact of accounts by eyewitnesses, contemporaries, and the intervening generations that sustained this vivid imagery and its symbolism within Mamluk domains. As the seminal contributions of Maurice Halbwachs toward understanding the dynamics of collective memory suggest, these shared conceptions, passed continually back and forth, allow for the reconstruction and reinvigoration of past events. The interconnected body of scholars, with whom al-Subkī identified and to which he eminently belonged, sustained such conceptions and viewpoints. This living history, differentiated in Halbwachs's mind from the positivist written history of his age, "perpetuates and renews itself through time," shifting, changing, and reflecting present concerns, while maintaining its connection to a bygone era.[25]

Yet the form of al-Subkī's narrative, historical writing under a biographical rubric, along with his chosen audience, Muslims in general and historians more particularly, are also especially significant. Here dissolves the distinction Halbwachs draws between lived and written history, one revealing past thoughts and sensibilities and the other registering an official record of the nation. Formed in the late nineteenth and early twentieth centuries, Halbwachs's understanding of written history reflects the modern European historicist enterprise. Yet for al-Subkī, written history was lived history. And even more crucially, contrasting with the lucid work of Yosef Hayim Yerushalmi contemplating Jewish history and memory, it also represented a major channel of Muslim memory. As Yerushalmi persuasively argues, "Historiography, an actual recording of historical events, is by no means the principal medium through which collective memory of the Jewish people has been addressed or aroused" although medieval Jews did write historical works. Rather, "memory flowed, above all, through two channels: ritual and recital." Yet for Muslims of the premodern era, who as Yerushalmi notes excelled in forging an important historiographic tradition,[26] the inscription of historical events was central in preserving communal memories.

CHANNELING MUSLIM MEMORY THROUGH HISTORY

Building on these insights, I would like to probe further and suggest that the main vehicle of Muslim collective memory was historical. This analysis both includes and moves us beyond the textual inscription of the past, proposing four intertwined strands of history that preserve and convey a living Muslim memory: what I refer to as narrative history, embodied history, discursive history, and the artistic. By narrative history, I mostly mean the formal historiographic tradition, encompassing chronicles, biographies, and other written records of the past, such as al-Subkī's *Ṭabaqāt* elaborated above. By discursive history, I incorporate the ḥadīth tradition,[27] in its oral and written forms, that developed elaborate and carefully scrutinized chains of narration for anecdotes of varying accuracy conveying what the Prophet Muḥammad may have said, done, or approved of during his lifetime—a critical tradition that greatly influenced other fields of intellectual inquiry. By embodied history, I refer to the important tradition of communal precedent, or *ʿamal*,[28] which considers the cumulative heritage of the Prophet Muḥammad's community, especially in Medina, to identify historical acts and practices signifying the prophetic way. Both these discursive and embodied practices of history notably form the substance of much discussion and debate among proponents of multiple Islamic legal methodologies, articulating supple and distinctive visions of ritual and transactional law. Yet legalized Islamic rites, such as the daily ritual prayer or the once-in-a-lifetime pilgrimage to Mecca, do not only preserve an overall meaning of history for the Muslim community—as divine intervention in human affairs through the sending of merciful messengers to call people back to God—a process Paul Connerton refers to as "commemorative ceremonies."[29] They also further seek to reflect and reenact historical realities, by emulating a prophetic model: to pray the way the Prophet Muḥammad prayed, to perform pilgrimage the way he modeled it. Or in the words of his reported instructions, "Pray the way you saw me pray" and "Take from me your rituals of pilgrimage, for perhaps I may not perform pilgrimage after this year."[30] Thus, even ritual forms of Muslim memory, according to communal understanding, are grounded in historical acts witnessed by the earliest believers. As for artistic forms of history, I mean those poetic and musical endeavors that sought to narrate and preserve past events along with their emotive import for future generations.

Most importantly, the cultural history of the Islamic caliphate interwove all of these strands together, the narrative, embodied, discursive, and artistic aspects of Muslim collective memory, hence elucidating the institution's immense symbolic weight. The caliphate, as a vehicle or *lieu* of Muslim collective memory, combined the profane (or the mundane narrative history of the community) with the prophetic (or the religious injunctions derived from the community's discourses and embodied practices). The worldly, or secular, and the sacred, or metaphysical, conjoined in particularly powerful ways to imbue the caliphate with utterly deep cultural resonance that traversed vast lands and even centuries.

As a result, Muslim authors who lived during the fateful events of 656/1258 as well as those of subsequent generations who remained within the western Arabic literary orbit interpreted the fall of Baghdad as a tragedy not only for those murdered in the Mongol onslaught but more abstractly as a tragedy for Islam itself. Abū ʿAbdillāh Muḥammad b. al-Ḥusayn b. Abī Bakr b. Aḥmad al-Mawṣilī Ibn al-Sharawī of Mosul captures in his poetry how dreams died away, amidst profuse tears, with the loss of the City of Peace and how "the star of guidance has fallen and Islam has weakened and perished (*taḍaʿḍaʿa*)."[31] And the Kufan preacher and poet Shams al-Dīn Muḥammad b. ʿUbaydallāh al-Kūfī al-Wāʿiẓ bewails, "Because of their being far away, ruination has come closer, and because of losing them, / guidance was lost and Islam was shaken."[32] The well-traveled historian Ibn Wāṣil reflects on the Mongol capture of Baghdad and killing of its caliph that "Islam has not been afflicted with a more tremendous or piercing calamity (*dāhiyah*)," and, writing in Baalbek, Quṭb al-Dīn Mūsā b. Muḥammad al-Yūnīnī (640–726/1242–1348), affirms that Islam has not met with a more tremendous or horrendous catastrophe,"[33] as did Ibn Shākir al-Kutubī (686–764/1287–1363) years later.[34] For Ibn al-Dawādārī, who began work on his voluminous chronicle in Egypt in 709/1309 and completed it in 736/1335, these same events constituted the perishing of Islam (*halāk al-Islām*).[35] And expressing his personal sense of bereavement, the esteemed historian and teacher of Tāj al-Dīn al-Subkī, Shams al-Dīn al-Dhahabī, in Syria, even adapts a supplication traditionally invoked by the immediate relatives of the deceased for this historical occasion, "Oh God! Recompense us in our misfortune (*muṣībah*)—the likes of which has never [before] befallen Islam and its people."[36] The dreadful calamity of initially hearing that the Mongols were besieging Baghdad was so dire that the influential scholar ʿIzz al-Dīn Ibn ʿAbd al-Salām (577–660/1181–1262) ordered all the preachers and imams in Cairo's

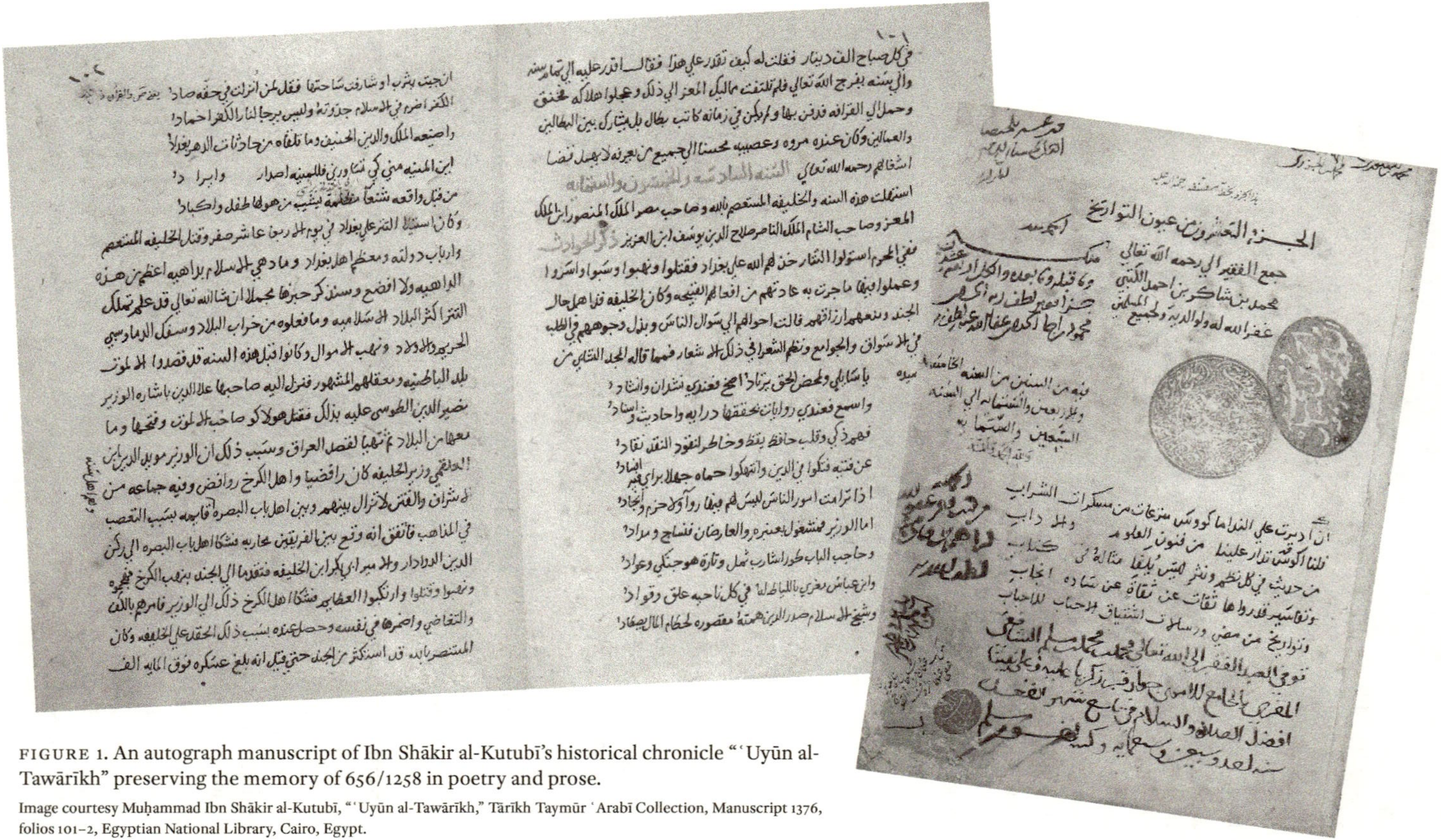

FIGURE 1. An autograph manuscript of Ibn Shākir al-Kutubī's historical chronicle "ʿUyūn al-Tawārīkh" preserving the memory of 656/1258 in poetry and prose.

Image courtesy Muḥammad Ibn Shākir al-Kutubī, "ʿUyūn al-Tawārīkh," Tārīkh Taymūr ʿArabī Collection, Manuscript 1376, folios 101–2, Egyptian National Library, Cairo, Egypt.

mosques to take the extraordinary measure of performing *qunūt,* or standing supplications, in the five daily prayers, beseeching God for the caliphal capital's safe and victorious deliverance. When news reached them instead that Baghdad had fallen, as Ibn Wāṣil reports, the Muslims' grief and mournful sorrow intensified (*ishtadda asaf al-muslimīn ʿalā dhālika wa-ḥuznuhum*).[37]

For these Muslims living across geographical and temporal distances, the Mongol conquest of Baghdad and the killing of the Abbasid caliph represented the most catastrophic calamity. With the loss of Baghdad, the inviolable was violated, the sacred was desecrated, and the worldly was abased. The obliteration of the caliph and his dynasty ruptured one of the community's most significant and symbolic modes of connectivity to the Prophet Muḥammad and their shared history. The caliph's death, along with that of his potential successors, signified an inconceivable loss, and the transgressions against the caliph and all associated with him and his rule—the city, his throne and palace, his household, his subjects, and the sanctuaries he was supposed to safeguard—painfully underscored the great tragedy of what had transpired.

LOSS OF THE ABBASIDS

This inability of the caliph to protect the sacrosanct bodies, rites, and spaces of his own capital was deeply traumatic for contemporaries and near contemporaries as etched in the works of Muslim Arabic literary and scholarly elites. The annihilation of the Abbasid caliph himself, as the titular Commander of the Faithful and temporal successor to the Prophet Muḥammad, was the first such critical loss to this community. Early accounts by the contemporaries Ibn Raṭlayn in Baghdad and al-Juzjānī in Delhi stress the role that Muslim loyalties to the Abbasid caliph played in Hülegü's deliberations about his execution. According to Ibn Raṭlayn's father, who had accompanied the caliph inside the Mongol camp, negotiations had been all but settled between al-Mustaʿṣim and the invaders that the Mongols would receive half of the income of Mesopotamia as tribute, when Ibn al-ʿAlqamī is said to have intervened with the advice that it was preferable to kill the caliph, or else Mongol rule over Mesopotamia would never be secure.[38] Based in Delhi, al-Juzjānī widens the scope of Muslims in his narrative willing to rise in support of the caliph. In his reconstruction of those fatal events, treacherous Muslims advised Hülegü that if the caliph remained alive, all Muslim troops and Muslim peoples in other countries would rise in order to liberate him and punish Hülegü instead by death.[39] But Hülegü was also reported to have been frightened by other Muslims of the cosmological consequences that would ensue should the caliph's blood be shed: drought and fiery brimstone according to the Syriac historian Ibn al-ʿIbrī, a destructive earthquake according to al-Juzjānī, and the darkening of the world and destruction of Hülegü's house according to al-Subkī.[40] The Ilkhanid vizier Rashīd al-Dīn attributes the most elaborate rendition of these

FIGURE 2. The last Abbasid caliph of Baghdad al-Mustaʿṣim brought before the Mongol commander Hülegü. In contrast to the image of this scene on the frontispiece, al-Mustaʿṣim is depicted standing in captivity in the black robes associated with Abbasids on the bottom right.
Image courtesy Rashīd al-Dīn Faḍl Allāh al-Hamadhānī, "Jāmiʿ al-Tawārīkh," Supplément Persan Collection, Manuscript 1113, folio 186, Bibliothèque nationale de France, Paris, France.

prophesies specifically to the Mongols' Muslim court astrologer Ḥusām al-Dīn, albeit before Hülegü's march on the Abbasid capital:

> Neither to attack the house of the caliphate nor to lead an army to Baghdad is auspicious, for until now no ruler who has attacked Baghdad and the Abbasids has enjoyed either freedom or life. If the padishah does not heed my words and goes there, six catastrophes will befall—first, all the horses will die and the soldiers will fall ill; second, the sun will not rise; third, rain will not fall; fourth, a cold destructive wind will arise, and the world will be destroyed by earthquake; fifth, the plants will not grow from the ground; sixth a great ruler will die within the year.

Whether Ḥusām al-Dīn believed in the validity of his astrological predictions or merely sought to protect the Abbasid Caliphate and its capital, he would later pay for these claims of dire consequences with his life.[41] And although

Naṣīr al-Dīn al-Ṭusī does not discuss it in his personal account of Baghdad's conquest, Rashīd al-Dīn ascribes to him the initial, flat refutation of any such harm to ensue. Hülegü reportedly took well to al-Ṭusī's views, and "from the wise man's speech, the prince's heart lit up like a tulip in spring."[42] In all likelihood, al-Mustaʿṣim was given an honorable death by Mongol standards by not spilling royal or noble blood on the ground,[43] but for Muslim contemporaries and near contemporaries, whether the caliph was trampled in a sack, suffocated, strangled, or drowned to death, it was catastrophic.[44]

The emotive element of poetry brought to life the pain of this loss, in agreement with the contemporaneous evaluation of historians, discussed earlier, that the destruction of Baghdad represented a signal tragedy for Muslims and their religion. In his elegy mourning the loss of the Abbasids, ʿAlī b. Mamdūd b. Masʿūd al-Sinjārī poignantly informs their forsaken capital that its noble inhabitants were what had given meaning to the people of the world and the city itself (*kānū maʿānī banī'l-dunyā wa-maʿnākī*). This meaning-making associated with the Abbasids as fervently desired luminaries inspires al-Sinjārī to refer to Baghdad longingly as "the City of the Beloved Ones" (*Dār al-Aḥibbah*). Love, pain, and loss of orientation in the world are all intertwined. For al-Sinjārī, adapting Qur'anic and prophetic descriptions of the celestial, the Abbasids are like stars upon which people rely for guidance and direction. Their absence then, leaves him adrift, pondering, "Where are they who illuminated the days / with their light and to whom all complaints were directed? // Where are those radiant stars of ours?"[45] Like the sun and stars, the Abbasids are depicted as focal points of the world that have gone into a mysterious eclipse, sinking people who long for their symbolic presence into darkness and bewilderment.

al-Kūfī al-Wāʿiẓ also weaves together these themes of the agonizing loss and love of the once-paramount Abbasids in his poetry. In one elegy, he elaborates on the spiritual solace that the Abbasids had formerly brought to a far-reaching community of Muslims, "You were a breath of life (*rūḥan*) for hearts and nations and a comfort for souls; then you were overtaken by what everyone (*kullu shakhṣ*) would have ransomed you from, with his life and valuables, were it only possible."[46] And elsewhere, he depicts the preeminence and dominance of the Abbasids, those luminous guiding stars and awe-inspiring monarchs, on the spiritual as well as the political plane. As he petitions the fallen city:

> I called out to it: "O Abode! What happened to those who were
> the desired ones (*al-awṭār*) among all the lands?
>
> Where are they whom you knew (so) well when, before whose might,
> crowned heads bowed out of abjection?
>
> They were the stars people followed (*nujūm man iqtadā*), so over them
> cry (spiritual) guidance (*al-hudā*) and the rites of faith."[47]

Along with those Muslims who regarded the caliphs as an aspirational focus, Islamic rites and guidance are personified in their grief over the Abbasids' absence. And in yet another poem, where he addresses the Abbasids and the ruins of Baghdad in turn, al-Kūfī al-Wāʿiẓ creates a chilling image of this devastation and his own distraught state:

> The quarters of guidance became desolate after you went far away
> while the blood of Islam was shed;
>
> Where are they who ruled all peoples? Where are they who acquired
> [treasures]?
> Where are they who dominated?
>
> I stood in the dwelling after they [left], asking it about them,
> and about what they stored in it, and what they possessed.
>
> The deteriorating ruins and desolate quarters answered me,
> "Yes, they were indeed here, and they have perished."
>
> Do not deem (my) tears to be merely water flowing over cheeks,
> For verily they are the essence of ardent love pouring forth.[48]

In Arabic poetic works, such as these, Muslim contemporaries and near contemporaries continued to evoke a wrenching image of the Abbasids as beloved stewards of a far-reaching Muslim community, possessing power and prestige on a global scale, despite the greatly weakened fortunes of the dynasty by the time it was finally eliminated by the Mongols in 656/1258. The poetry does not speak so much to the political efficacy of the Abbasid caliphs as it does to their complex religious and cultural symbolism, which was reconfigured into an idealized form through the frequent recollection of their past glories. The Abbasids were intertwined with Islamic ideals as caliphs of the Sunni Muslim community, but when attention concentrated on the worldliness of the Abbasid dynasty, contemporaries' mournful reminiscences were also laced with a subtle critique of their transitory power.

This debasement of the once-glorious Abbasids inspired many to affirm the ephemerality of worldly pursuits and to focus instead on God's everlasting grace. Saʿdī in his poem even asks God to look after the person who awakens to this reality and the certainty that wealth disappears.[49] The wealth, power, and standing of the Abbasids had evanesced—and their worldly indulgences exposed them to ethical critiques in the aftermath of the Mongol invasions as well as created a moral parable of their fleeting opulence and rank. When al-Kūfī al-Wāʿiẓ witnessed that the ancient Abbasids had been disinterred from their resting place in the cemetery of al-Ruṣāfah and that their skulls and bones lay strewn about the burnt quarters, he wrote a couple of lines of reflective poetry on one of its remaining walls: "If you want a moral lesson (*ʿibrah*), then these are the Abbasids, / upon whom perdition (*āfāt*) has descended; Their women have been taken as booty, / after the ones who were alive were killed and the dead were burned."[50] And ʿAlī b. Mamdūd al-Sinjārī ponders, "The adversities of time have destroyed (*akhnat*) and divided them, / so they have become an admonition (*ʿibrah*) that is spoken of."[51] For the Yemeni ruler al-Malik al-Ashraf (761–803/1359–1400), the disappearance of the Abbasid dynasty in Iraq, despite all of its awesome majesty and the lengthy duration of its power, exemplified the Prophet Muḥammad's teaching that God would never elevate something except that it would ultimately be abased.[52] The Caliph al-Mustaʿṣim is said to have acknowledged the moral irony of his own condition shortly before his death while at the Mongol encampment outside his besieged capital, "We began the morning with an abode like the heavens and paradise, / and we entered the evening without any abode as if it had not even existed yesterday."[53] This swift dissipation of wealth and worldly preeminence inspired numerous historians of the Abbasids' demise to evoke God's excellence and eternal permanence by way of contrast. In the words of the Andalusian bureaucrat Lisān al-Dīn Ibn al-Khaṭīb (713–76/1313–74), for instance, "The Abbasid dynasty was eradicated from Baghdad, [and remains so] up until now, and Baghdad was settled by the Mongols; so glory be to the One whose dominion and power are never extinguished nor are His benevolence and excellence."[54] Such recollections of God's benevolent omnipotence were a significant source of consolation for countless others as well. One contemporary in Cairo, however, was so disturbed by the horrific abasement of the Abbasids that he wondered how God could have permitted such a calamity to occur, only to have subsequently heard in his dream a voice instructing him not to complain about God and His infinite wisdom. This solemn rebuke stirred him to awaken in remorseful penitence.[55] Similarly, the ascetic ʿAfīf al-Dīn Yūsuf b. al-Baqqāl (d. 666/1298) recounted that when he was residing in Cairo, he was so shaken by news of the massacre in the Abbasid capital and the ensuing desecration of its bodies, texts, and sites of worship that he pleaded with God over how He could have allowed it. The response came via a poem delivered to ʿAfīf al-Dīn in a dream asking him to cease complaining about God's decisions and to trust in His absolute justice and divine decree.[56]

BODILY DESECRATION

In addition to the assassination of the caliph and his heirs, the atrocious murder and rape of his subjects as well as the extensive pillage and arson of his capital painfully pierced the socio-cultural depiction of the Abbasid Caliphate's symbolic centrality, power, and benign protection. After the Mongols defeated the Abbasids' army and then successfully besieged the capital, they unleashed their swords on Baghdad's inhabitants for roughly forty days.[57] Men, women, the elderly, and children were all slaughtered by the Mongols.[58] Ibn Kathīr (ca. 700–774 / ca. 1301–73) describes how some people tried to lock themselves in the urban warehouses and hostelries (*khānāt)*, mosques, and Sufi hospices (*ribāṭ*) for protection, but the Mongols would either break or burn their way inside and then kill those who had fled to the roofs, with the result that the drainage pipes poured out blood instead of water.[59] al-Kūfī al-Wāʿiẓ bewails this indiscriminate slaughter that befell the people of Baghdad with the words:

Oh! what a catastrophe from which no one was saved,
so the slave and the king were the same.

After [the days of] might of our beloved ones, the hands of the enemies seized them,
so they did not spare [anyone] or leave [anything] behind.

If only they could have been ransomed from what befell them (*nālahum*),
Oh, how I would have, with my soul (*muhjatī*) and all that I own.[60]

And in his poetic elegy, Muḥammad b. al-Ḥusayn b. Abī Bakr al-Mawṣilī draws an analogy with the heinous massacre of Karbalā'.[61] In total, hundreds of thousands of people lost their lives in Baghdad at the hands of the Mongols, at least eight hundred thousand according to the Muslim sources and over two hundred thousand according to Hülegü himself.[62] The anonymous primary source erroneously attributed to Ibn al-Fuwaṭī (642–723/1244–1323) further describes how the dead lay in piles in the streets and markets of the city, where they had met their fate, while rain fell and horses trampled upon their corpses, all together disfiguring and leaving them to putrefy.[63] Traumatized by the enormity of these atrocities, Ibn al-Ṭiqtaqā, author of *al-Fakhrī*, explains, "So much widespread killing, tremendous plunder, and grave mutilation [of the dead] took place that it is difficult to listen to in general terms, so imagine [listening to] the details!"[64]

Poets recalling the fall of the Abbasid Caliphate also link its debasement with the horrific affronts that the Mongols perpetrated against the women of Baghdad. Countless women were raped and murdered or taken captive, including members of the Abbasid dynasty,[65] and all three of the last caliph al-Mustaʿṣim's living daughters, Fāṭimah, Khadījah, and Maryam, entered Mongol captivity.[66] In the words of the famed Saʿdī from Shirāz (ca. 580–700 / ca. 1184–1300):

Can I adequately express what happened to the Caliphate?
Come see how the matter all ended;

Oh that my ears (*ṣamākhī*) had gone deaf before hearing
of the ripping apart of the women's veils (*hatk asātīr al-maḥārim*) in captivity;

They pass barefoot through rugged desert after rugged desert—
delicate ladies (*rakhāʾim*), unable to walk over a bridge.

. . . .

They rise and stumble in fields and rugged terrain;
can the walking of those used to luxurious comfort (*nawāʿim*) be concealed?

They are driven like goats in the middle of a waterless desert—
Considered precious by their people, they were not even startled by reproaches;

They were taken captive with their faces exposed (*sāfirāt wujūhuhā*)—
fine-figured young women (*kawāʿib*) who had never emerged from the shade (*ḥalak*) of their chambers;

The Mongols (*ʿItrat Qanṭūrāʾ*), in every house,
cry out concerning the children of the Barmakids, "Who will buy?"[67]

Here, Saʿdī depicts a striking contrast between all the privileges the women of Baghdad had known under the Abbasid caliph and their harsh treatment at the hands of the Mongols. The image he illustrates is one of delicate and lovely women, accustomed to luxurious ease, ensconced in the comfort of their homes, now found stumbling amidst rugged and waterless deserts. After having been honored and held dear by their people, to the rhetorical extent of their not ever experiencing the alarm of being reproached, the women of Saʿdī's poem are treated like mere animals by the Mongols. The ripping apart of their protective clothing encapsulates the degradation of these women's ennobled status. Their veils are rent asunder as they enter Mongol captivity, and they are dragged off in torment and full exposure. The children of notable and cultured aristocrats, like the Barmakids, who were once close to the Abbasid caliph and at the center of power, have become slaves to be sold off by the vile Mongols. Such, he deems, is the sorrowful fate of the caliphate and its people.

In an elegy that the renowned Syrian Taqiyy al-Dīn Abū Muḥammad Ismāʿīl b. Ibrāhīm Ibn Abī Yusr (589–672/1193–1273),[68] penned for the fallen Abbasid capital, he frames the section concentrating on the people afflicted by the Mongol scourge by opening and closing with an emotive description of its female victims.

How many inviolate women (*ḥarīm*) have the Mongols captured by force!
and before that veil (*sitr*) there were [so many] layers of protection (*astār*);

And how many full moons (*budūr*) eclipsed at al-Badriyyah!
and no more will full moons rise from there;

And how many treasures have become scattered
among the plunder and were seized by unbelievers!

And how many punishments did they inflict with their swords
on [people's] necks, by which [people's] sins were erased.

I called out while the exposed captives (*sabiyy mahtūk*) were dragged
to ravishment by licentious enemies,

FIGURE 3. Siege of Baghdad by the Mongol army.

Image courtesy Rashīd al-Dīn Faḍl Allāh al-Hamadhānī, "Jāmiʿ al-Tawārīkh," Supplément Persan Collection, Manuscript 1113, folio 180v and 181r, Bibliothèque nationale de France, Paris, France.

while they were being driven to [their] death[s], which they beheld,
"The Fire, O my Lord, rather than this, and not this shame!"[69]

Like Saʿdī, Ibn Abī Yusr emphasizes the irreproachable status of Baghdad's women, describing them as *ḥarīm*, inviolate members of respectable households, and *budūr*, or full moons, in an allusion to their radiant beauty. This aura of respectability and attractiveness only serves to magnify the extent of the poignant tragedy. His play on words simultaneously associated with various stages of dress and undress further emphasizes the unexpected ignominy inflicted by the Mongols; *sitr* and its plural *astār* doubly point to the veil(s) and the layers of protection that these women had once enjoyed in their households. It was inconceivable that they be enslaved by a foreign army, when they had been so well protected from far lesser degrees of effrontery. And his description of these honorable women as *mahtūk*, once they pass into the possession of the Mongols, linguistically implies their violent exposure, degradation, and rape, all at once, thereby evoking multiple connotations for their denudement and even greater sexual humiliation. Employing rhetoric to move and disturb the feelings of his listeners and readers, Ibn Abī Yusr further emphasizes the horror of this tragedy, both in his repetition of the opening phrase "How many," "How many," "How many," to build up emotive tension and in his crying out to God that even the torment of fire would be preferable to witnessing this suffering and disgrace.

The symbolism of rape also enters Tāj al-Dīn al-Subkī's narrative of Baghdad's fall, and he draws attention to the danger posed to the metaphorical marital bed of the Prophet's familial relation, the Abbasid caliph, dramatizing the immediacy of this threat by referring to him as the Prophet's "nephew." Thus, al-Subkī recounts how Hülegü himself lusted after the wife of the caliph, and she continually sought to distract him with one precious object after another in the caliphal palace. When she realized the firmness of his intent to ravish her, the caliph's wife was said to have contrived a plot with her servant to protect her honor. In short, the noble woman pulled out a sword that she said belonged to the caliph and would only inflict harm if it were used by him. She offered to demonstrate its harmlessness upon her servant, who screamed out according to her instructions. Feigning disbelief, the caliph's wife then asked her servant what was wrong and offered that the worried servant demonstrate the sword's absolute harmlessness on her instead. Then, according to her mistress's final wishes, the servant struck the wife of the caliph with all her force, splitting her into two. And thus, the caliph's wife arranged to meet her own death rather than suffer the ignominy of rape. The anecdote concludes with Hülegü's remorse over having lost such a shrewd woman and al-Subkī's appreciation for how she protected her own purity and did not permit Hülegü to enjoy what had been reserved for her husband. Thus, in al-Subkī's narrative, the wicked Mongol assailant is triumphantly, although tragically, thwarted in his attempts to disgrace the noble relative of the Prophet Muḥammad and last Abbasid caliph of Baghdad, al-Mustaʿṣim billāh.[70]

The sister of the caliph, and hence a direct descendent of the Prophet Muḥammad's family herself, was also said to have avoided humiliation at the hands of the Mongols, although through markedly dissimilar tactics. According to the history composed by Yemen's Rasūlid ruler, al-Malik al-Ashraf, when Sitt al-Sharaf heard that the Mongols had set out for Baghdad in 655/1257 she began fasting and pleading with God that He take her so that she would not witness their terror, and the Almighty accepted her supplications so that she died of an illness after only a matter of days. Her funeral was well attended by state officials and leaders of the Abbasid army, in keeping with her status, and she was buried in the cemetery of al-Ruṣāfah.[71] Religiosity is given primacy in this anecdote, and it is through her personal piety and acts of devotion, rather than her cunning, that Sitt al-Sharaf is saved from experiencing the affliction that the Mongols wreaked upon Baghdad. Her very name means Lady of Honor, and she is taken to manifest this concept through her pious acts and noble lineage.

Within seven years of the Mongol conquest of Baghdad, Ẓahīr al-Dīn Ibn al-Kāzarūnī completed a history, recording and preserving the caliphal past, entitled *Mukhtaṣar al-Tārīkh.*[72] Eighteen years later, in 681/1283, he appended an update to the last entry on al-Mustaʿṣim to address what had happened to the last Abbasid caliph's daughters since they were captured and removed from Baghdad twenty-five years ago. Fāṭimah had died in Mongol captivity, Khadījah had married the pious ascetic Muḥyīʾl-Dīn Abūʾl-Maḥāmid Yaḥyā al-Makhzūmī al-Shabadhī and returned to Baghdad for the last four years of her life, and Maryam continued to live in the captivity of the Mongols. In light of the infamy of the Mongols' atrocities, Ibn al-Kāzarūnī takes care to emphasize that all three women were honorable—a point he does not feel the need to stress in connection with the two other daughters of al-Mustaʿṣim, ʿĀʾishah and Karīmah, who predeceased him during his caliphate. In the case of Maryam, who remained among the Mongols until his day, Ibn al-Kāzarūnī also describes her as respected there, perhaps to assuage the reader, and even to gradually rehabilitate the Islamisizing Mongols. But the more satisfying story of restoration for contemporaries clearly belongs to Khadījah.[73]

Both Ibn al-Kāzarūnī and his student Ibn al-Fuwaṭī (642–723/1244–1323), another eminent historian from Baghdad who survived the Mongol invasions, detail her story. Ibn al-Fuwaṭī elucidates in his biographical dictionary arranged by honorifics, *Majmaʿ al-Ādāb fī Muʿjam al-Alqāb*, that Hülegü had sent Khadījah back to Möngke upon the conquest of Baghdad and how Ibn al-Fuwaṭī's other teacher, Shams al-Dīn Abūʾl-Majd Ibrāhīm al-Makhzūmī al-Shabadhī, had avidly sought her release and then married her off to his son Muḥyīʾl-Dīn. After they had departed Transoxania together, Hülegü's eldest son Abaqa, who had succeeded his father to the Ilkhanate in 663/1265, commissioned Muḥyī'l-Dīn with the directorship of the Mustanṣiriyyah Library in Baghdad. (And remarkably, on some occasion, Abaqa gave him another granddaughter of the Caliph al-Mustanṣir, al-Ḥājjah Zaynab bint al-Amīr Abī'l-Qāsim ʿAbd al-Azīz, as a gift.)[74] Muḥyī'l-Dīn and Khadījah took up their residence in the Palace of Sūsiyān[75] in Baghdad in 672/1273; this palace had been long associated with her family and preserved, along with its gardens, as a charitable endowment by her father al-Mustaʿṣim, the last Abbasid caliph of Baghdad, in 652/1254 only a few years before the Mongol invasion.[76] Over the course of her marriage, Khadījah bore three children, two sons and a daughter: ʿAbd al-ʿAzīz Abū'l-Qāsim, who bore the honorific ʿIzz al-Dīn or ʿAzīz al-Dīn, ʿAbd al-Ḥaqq Abū'l-Faḍl Muẓaffar al-Dīn, and Karīmah, who went by Sitt al-ʿArab Mubārakah. Khadījah, however, would not live very long in the former capital of her father, and she passed away in Baghdad on Monday, Muḥarram 18, 676 / June 21, 1277; her husband followed only a few years later on the eve of Friday, Rajab 7, 682 AH, corresponding to the evening of September 30, 1283 CE. Nevertheless, Ibn al-Kāzarūnī's and Ibn al-Fuwaṭī's emphases in recounting Khadījah's life denote a restorative paradigm and a vital restitution of the past. Her legally sound contraction of marriage to a pious transmitter of prophetic ḥadīth, her return to the former Abbasid capital, and her bearing of children of good character and learning who merged the lineage of the Prophet's companion Khālid b. al-Walīd with that of the Prophet's uncle and progenitor of the Abbasid dynasty, al-ʿAbbās, symbolically reorder and set aright the grievous wrongs inflicted by the Mongols during their conquest.[77]

LITERARY DIMENSIONS OF RELIGIOUS RITES

The poetry and historical anecdotes of Baghdad's fall formed an important cultural repertoire of agony and loss transmitted through wide readership, cross-generational instruction, and public performance, whereas Jewish mourning of the Temple's destruction in 586 BCE and again in 70 CE was commemorated primarily through ritual and liturgical means. The Ninth of Av, when the Talmud indicates the Second Temple was destroyed, became a day to observe mourning rites memorializing both catastrophes as well as other calamities to befall the Jewish people, symbolizing their relentless persecution and suffering. The rites are to take on a weight similar to observing the death of one's immediate kin, and fasting on the Ninth of Av entails abstaining from food, drink, sexual intercourse, bathing, fragrances, leather footwear, elevated seating, working, and studying Torah, with the exception of certain passages, including the day's liturgical centerpiece: The Book of Lamentations. While the first and fifth chapters of Lamentations reference captive maidens and ravished women, who form a key element of Muslim poems and narratives about Baghdad, the whole of the first chapter is strikingly framed by the gendered personification of Jerusalem as a shamed and forsaken woman. In *Ḥurban*, Alan Mintz argues that this personification, ascribing individual experiences to an integral whole, aims to express "the maximum register of pain" for a collective entity. The once-glorious Jerusalem has become like an abandoned widow, bereaved by her loss, and a dishonored woman, reduced to the pitiful state of calling out to those who pass her by in the road. Her thoughtless transgressions, and promiscuousness, have lead to even further violation of her sanctity, signified by rape. As Adele Berlin and Marc Zvi Brettler comment, the poetic language plays with allusions of uncleanliness and impurity, disgrace and nakedness, and sexual immorality as a metaphor for idolatry, in Judah's pursuit of " 'friends' other than her 'husband,' God." Critically, it is Daughter Zion's disobedience to the Lord that has incurred His wrath, and her sinfulness that is the ultimate cause of her immense distress. In search of the ancient history that may have inspired such liturgical poetry, Judah Mosconi reflects in the thirteenth century on the repercussions of "the deeds of our ancestors because of whose sins the city [of Jerusalem] was destroyed" with the words: "They ate the sour grapes, but our teeth are set on edge."[78]

While the loss of the Abbasid caliph in Baghdad was not ritually memorialized, the impact of his death upon the sanctity of Islamic rites was a major concern for Muslim poets and authors in the seventh/thirteenth and eighth/fourteenth centuries. Although poetry of the era did not attempt to resolve the very real juristic questions of how to legitimate congregational daily and Friday prayers or other key functions of state in the absence of a caliph, which we will discuss in the next two chapters, they do reflect on the cultural void and anguish created by this dilemma. Saʿdī questions in his Arabic elegy how it could be possible for Muslims not to acknowledge the Abbasids as their spiritual and temporal leaders in the course of their Friday prayers. He asks, "Can a sermon be made from the top of pulpits, / while al-Mustaʿṣim billāh is not in existence?" This line powerfully speaks to multiple registers of whether it was conceivably possible to issue sermons after al-Mustaʿṣim's death, juristically and emotionally. How could people be gathering for congregational prayers delegitimized by the lack of a caliph? How could people bring themselves to go on in his absence? It is further agonizing for Saʿdī to consider how they, "Banū'l-ʿAbbās," who were "the pride of all of humankind" (*muftakhar al-warā*) have been relegated to mere pastime conversations.[79] In another poem, Ibn Abī Yusr conjoins the loss of the Abbasids in the context of the Friday congregational prayers with the disappearance of their rule: "The pulpits and thrones are devoid of them, / so peace upon them until [our] death."[80] While the Abbasid caliphs of Baghdad may no longer receive Damascene supplications for a ruling sovereign at the end of Friday sermons, Ibn Abī Yusr poetically invokes God's peace upon them for the remainder of his life.

Later authors also dwell on the disruption and desecration of Islamic rites in Baghdad following the Mongol conquest. Ibn Kathīr reflects on the religious void caused by the sheer number of those killed in the Mongol invasion. "The preachers, prayer leaders, and memorizers of the Qur'an were killed, and the mosques, daily congregational prayers, and Friday prayers were obstructed and discontinued (*ta ʿaṭṭalat*) for months in Baghdad."[81] And al-Subkī comments on the public denigration of Muslims, who, he writes, were forced to break their fast during the sacred month of Ramaḍān and ordered to drink wine and consume the flesh of swine, both prohibited substances, instead of maintaining their religious observances. He bemoans that wine was spilled in mosques and that Muslims were prevented from issuing the call to prayer as they had always done; Baghdad, he complains, had always been a Muslim city and never before subjected to such disgrace.[82] Whether through massive carnage or through imposition of non-Muslim rule, it was inconceivable that such elementary religious obligations would be abandoned in the once-illustrious metropolis of the Abbasid Caliphate. And the incorporation of these elements in Ibn Kathīr's and al-Subkī's narratives highlights the extent of the cultural trauma envisioned and felt by these later authors.

AN ALTERED LANDSCAPE

Furthermore, the Mongol invasion of Baghdad was perceived as a disconcerting affront to the city's sacred topography. As the Ayyūbid courtier Taqiyy al-Dīn Ibn Abī Yusr ruminates in his elegy for Baghdad, "The crown of the Caliphate and the quarters that were honored / by the distinguishing characteristics [of Islam] have been obliterated by devastation."[83] The Mongols tied their horses at the city's mosques,[84] reducing the noble houses of worship to the status of common stables, and Hülegü even rode his horse directly into the caliphal palace. Rather than dismounting, Hülegü continued astride his beast past the vestibule where people had humbly sought an audience with the caliph and often been denied access and the privilege of entry. To al-Subkī, it was as if Hülegü was mocking this great tradition and the Abbasid legacy, while the symbolic locus of Abbasid power was defiled by the strident manner of its Mongol conqueror and the hooves of his mount.[85] Even the privacy of people's homes was not treated as sacrosanct, and blood was shed in these Islamically inviolable spheres of personal safety and comfort. In such torment, Baybars al-Manṣūrī and others saw parallels with the punishment visited upon the Children of Israel by their powerful enemies who had fought into the depths of their homes.[86] Nor was the blood of Baghdad's innumerable scholars spared, and the extensive killing of these exemplary figures was deeply troubling. As Saʿdī laments, "The misfortunes of time (*nawāʾib dahr*), Oh that I had died before them, / and not witnessed the aggression of the insolent fool (*al-safīh*) against the savant (*al-ḥibr*)."[87] Ibn Khaldūn (732–84/1332–82) mourns the loss of their scholarly production, emblematized by the treasure of books, torn from the repositories of learning, that the Mongols threw and drowned in the waters of the Tigris.[88] Most of the city's dwellings were burnt to the ground, as were Baghdad's most symbolic sites, including the august caliph's mosque, a saint's shrine, and the graves of the past Abbasid caliphs.[89] And even Rashīd al-Dīn, in the service of the Ilkhanids, acknowledged the sanctity of these sites burnt and destroyed by the Mongols (*al-amākin al-muqaddasah fī'l-madīnah*).[90] For Muslim authors, these vigorous assaults were only further evidence of the Muslim community's devastating humiliation at the hands of the Mongols and a horrible reversal of fortune.

For survivors, beyond the symbolic defilement of sacred sites, it was the lost lives that had once breathed life and memories into the spaces of Baghdad as well as their own traumatic experiences that irrevocably altered the city's landscape and quarters. As one survivor wrote in a personal letter to Abū Shāmah (599–665/1203–67) in Damascus, what had happened was even worse than anything Abū Shāmah could have possibly heard.[91] Those who were saved from the massacre had hid themselves in wells, canals, tunnels, and the subterranean vaults of the dead for roughly forty days during the Mongol rampage. Exposed to hunger, thirst, and cold during this lengthy duration, many of these refugees died from the poor conditions of their temporary asylum.[92] Those who weathered the harrowing ordeal faced a most gruesome return to the heart of the city. In the words attributed to Ibn al-Fuwaṭī, "Then [after forty days] general amnesty (*al-amān*) was proclaimed; so those who remained came out [of hiding] and their skin had become discolored [from lack of exposure to the sun] and their minds had vanished from the horrors they had witnessed which cannot be described in words. They were like the dead emerging from their graves on the Day of Resurrection."[93] Emerging from their subterranean places of hiding, these few survivors would have been confronted with the sight of Baghdad lying in complete ruin and its streets filled with the decaying and disfigured corpses of hundreds of thousands of the city's former residents. The stench was reported to be overwhelming, and combined with the contamination of the city's water by the dead and the descent of flies upon Baghdad, which also contaminated the food supply, these drastic changes were considered to be the cause of the last source of death, the plague, which claimed the lives of almost everyone who had escaped the sword.[94]

The eyewitness accounts of the trustworthy (*al-ʿadl*) Jamāl al-Dīn Abū'l-Manṣūr Sulaymān b. Fakhr al-Dīn Abī'l-Qāsim ʿAbdillāh Ibn Raṭlayn al-Ḥanbalī al-Baghdādī,[95] who was a young boy during the Mongol siege of Baghdad, exceptionally elucidates the palpable trauma of these events. Transmitted through the historical works of Ibn Wāṣil (604–97/1208–98), al-Jazarī (658–739/1260–1338), al-Dhahabī, and Ibn al-Dawadārī, Jamāl al-Dīn seems to have recounted his story on at least a couple different occasions, highlighting various aspects of his experience, as he did in one session at the beginning of the year 698 AH, which corresponds to October 1298 CE, roughly forty years after their occurrence. According to him, after the Abbasid army was defeated, the Mongols requested that the caliph go out to meet them, which al-Mustaʿṣim did, in

FIGURE 4. Siege of Baghdad by the Mongol army.

Image courtesy Staatsbibliothek zu Berlin-Preussischer Kulturbesitz, Orientabteilung, Diez A fol. 70, S. 4 + S. 7. Photo credit: bpk/Berlin.

the company of the city's judges, jurists, college teachers (*al-mudarrisūn*), leaders of the hospices (*mashāyikh al-ribāṭ*), mystics, and approximately seven hundred cavalry. After the city's luminaries had reached their destination, the Mongols then requested that only seventeen people continue on to accompany the caliph, and Jamāl al-Dīn explains that one of the Mongols took his father's hand, almost as if at random, saying that this one completes the number. As for the rest of Baghdad's elite, they were made to dismount and disrobe (*ʿarrawhum qumāshahum*) and were then all massacred by the sword. With the elimination of the Abbasid notables, the Mongols then entered the city and unleashed their swords upon the rest of its inhabitants for forty days, so that blood flowed profusely and congealed in the alleys of Baghdad like immense livers of camels. The seventeen survivors who were chosen to accompany the caliph also witnessed his momentous execution by the Mongols, who proceeded to finish off this small group, starting off with one of them at a time, until after only two persons were killed, the lives of the rest were almost miraculously spared. So the fifteen who were left alive after this lengthy ordeal reentered Baghdad in order to return home to their families and found only absolute devastation with no one left behind to console or even inform them of what had happened.[96] The bereaved group then headed for the Mughīthiyyah legal college, which must have still been standing, while Jamāl al-Dīn, who had survived the massacre, was also searching for his father. None of the fifteen initially recognized Jamāl al-Dīn, not even his own father; perhaps hunger, thirst, lack of exposure to the sun from hiding, general disarray, or even injury may have dramatically altered his appearance. Or perhaps they themselves had been altered by the combined stress of all the traumatic events they had endured. When the boy explained that he wanted Fakhr al-Dīn Ibn Raṭlayn because he was his son, the man looked at him carefully and then wept upon recognition. The young boy also happened to have some sesame seeds with him that he distributed among his father's companions.[97] The horrific trauma of the Mongol destruction of Baghdad vividly emerges from this unique narrative, where a small group of survivors witness immense death and bloodshed, barely escaping the horror with their own lives, and experience a heart-wrenching separation from their own families and all that they knew.

The poignancy of such traumatizing experiences was also expressed musically. Among the folk musical repertoire of Iraq, one *maqām*, or melodic mode, is said to have originated in the aftermath of the Mongol onslaught on Baghdad in 656/1258. Known as *maqām mukhālif*, this melancholic modal structure continues to be taught by musical masters as the epitomization of the searing agony inflicted by these tragic events.[98] Although little is known about how *maqām mukhālif* was historically composed, it had spread and gathered enough renown within seventy-two years of the Mongol conquest of Baghdad that Badr al-Dīn Muḥammad b. al-Khaṭīb al-Irbilī ennumerated it as one of six melodic modes in his didactic poem of musicology composed in 729/1328.[99] In his

FIGURE 5. Various musical definitions of *Maqām Mukhālif.*

Image from Rob Simms, *The Repertoire of Iraqi Maqam* (Oxford: Scarecrow Press, 2004), 181.

earlier musicological treatise, Ṣafiyy al-Dīn ʿAbd al-Muʾmin al-Urmawī (613–93/1216–94) had already elucidated how melodic modes were imbued with particular expressive properties, and, as Amnon Shiloah elaborates, "until the nineteenth century almost all available sources dealing with modal theory were concerned with specifying the manifold affiliations of the *maqāmāt* and *awāzāt* to ethical, therapeutical and cosmological values."[100] Orally transmitted across generations from master to apprentice as part of the folk musical tradition particular to Iraq, *maqām mukhālif* has retained a deep connotation with sorrow. Reflecting a rich vein of collective memory in the emotive soundscape, one contemporary musician Rahim Alhaj clarifies how he uses his oud in playing *maqām mukhālif* to "capture the sadness that this maqām portrays, and uses the space between the notes to express edginess, stress and tension."[101] Or as another contemporary musician Amir Elsaffar explains, "Mukhalif is one of the saddest maqam melodies in the Iraqi repertoire, and the legend is that the opening phrase of this Maqam is the long, gasping sigh of the survivors of the 1258 massacre as they picked through dead bodies, looking for family and loved ones."[102]

The intense, personal grief that those who had lived in Baghdad felt upon the loss of their relatives, friends, and the city as they once knew it also found an expressive outlet through poetry. The court scribe Jamāl al-Dīn Yāqūt al-Mustaʿṣimī (d. 698/1298), who had been born in Anatolia in the early seventh/thirteenth century, was brought to Baghdad as a young boy to serve the last Abbasid caliph al-Mustaʿṣim, from whom he gained his sobriquet. Raised and educated in the caliphal palace, Yāqūt al-Mustaʿṣimī grew to be widely renowned for his literature and calligraphic script, leaving an indelible impact upon the development of Arabic calligraphy.[103] His poetry was also noted for its elegance, some of which he mournfully dedicated to the loss of his former masters, the Abbasid caliphs:

> Oh that gathering whose splendor I have lost—
> [oh how] events have conjoined against me;
>
> Since I lost sight of those faces,
> my eyes have not seen beauty;
>
> I miss all those who used to keep me company,
> I am a wandering stranger in my own country;
>
> May my soul never reach its aspirations (*maʾāribahā*),
> if it should find solace after you in [any other] dwelling;
>
> The one who loves you, Oh people of Baghdad,
> taught the pigeon on a branch how to wail.[104]

Yāqūt al-Mustaʿṣimī vividly brings out the emotional sense of bereavement that he and others felt in this short but eloquent piece, raising themes that other

FIGURE 6. The calligrapher Yāqūt al-Mustaʿṣimī writing while hiding in a minaret during the Mongol siege.

(Left) Image courtesy © The State Museum of Oriental Art (Moscow). Qāḍī Aḥmad al-Ḥusaynī, "Gulistān-i Hunar (Traktat o kalligrafakh i khudozhnikakh)," folio 19a, The State Museum of Oriental Art, State Federal Budget Institution of Culture, Moscow, Russian Federation. (Right) Image courtesy © The Institute of Oriental Manuscripts, Russian Academy of Sciences. Qāḍī Aḥmad al-Ḥusaynī, "Gulistān-i Hunar (Traktat o kalligrafakh i khudozhnikakh)," Manuscript B 4722, folio 19b, the Institute of Oriental Manuscripts, Russian Academy of Sciences, Moscow, Russian Federation.

poets would also explore. The absence of those faces familiar and dear leaves him exceptionally disoriented in his own land, a sudden stranger, unable to find inner comfort or even appreciate the sight of beauty because of the extent of his grief. Immersed in this painful state of alienation and deep mourning, Yāqūt al-Mustaʿṣimī supposes that it must be one who has loved these vanished dwellers of Baghdad who has inspired the Arabic poetic emblem of sorrow, the cooing of a lone pigeon.

Yāqūt al-Mustaʿṣimī's poem also raises the question of whether survivors of the Mongol onslaught could find solace following the irrevocable alteration of their city and the death of their companions and friends. Yāqūt al-Mustaʿṣimī issues a poetic rebuke to himself should he ever forget the personal attachments that had adorned his life in Baghdad. And indeed he never left the city. But how did survivors who remained in Baghdad, or in other areas subsumed under Mongol influence and control, cope with the trauma of their losses and the enduring sites of their past? Halbwachs stresses the importance of continuing identification and interactions with social groups in order to maintain the vivacity of shared memories. "What we remember," as Patrick Hutton encapsulates Halbwachs's contribution, "depends on the contexts in which we find ourselves and the groups to which we happen to relate. The depth and shape of our collective memory reflect this configuration of social forces that vie for our attention." Did Yāqūt al-Mustaʿṣimī's expressions of alienation fade as he went on to gain employment, renown, and patronage among the Ilkhanids? Or did the altered landscape continue to provoke painful memories of alienation? Or like Saʿdī's Persian poem dedicated to his Salghurid patron in Shiraz, Abū Bakr-i Saʿd, a vassal to the Mongols who even assisted in their conquest, did he continue to artfully weave the poetic obligations of patronage with lingering remorse and longing for al-Mustaʿṣim and a vibrant recollection of the traumatic past? In this Persian elegy on the fall of the Abbasid Caliphate, Saʿdī praises Abū Bakr-i Saʿd as "the just king, the leader of power and faith, emperor of happy fate, savior of the day" who extends his protection in the aftermath of the caliphate's destruction. And yet, "Heaven would be right if it wept blood upon the earth—[because] Commander of the Faithful Mustaʿsim's kingdom has fallen." Through a powerful marshalling of words, Saʿdī also invokes the lasting bitterness of this loss and emphasizes the deep impression of sadness that cannot be washed away because it is emblazoned, like a brand, upon the heart.[105]

Other elegies composed for Baghdad similarly articulate a deep-seated grief over the loss of cherished relationships that had defined the city's spaces and enriched the poets' lives. ʿAlī b. Mamdūd al-Sinjārī in his elegy, for instance, reminisces over the fond days he used to spend in Baghdad and all of the close relations he had cultivated and enjoyed in the once-flourishing metropolis. He speaks of the depth of his longing for those lost times, wondering how people could have preferred to be anywhere else in the world.[106] The poet Muwaffaq al-Dīn Ibn Abī'l-Ḥadīd is gripped by the devastating end meted out to his compatriots among the once-illustrious people of Baghdad:

> I miss the Exalted Abode (*Dār 'Ilwah,* i.e., Baghdad) and cannot see
> its people either in my days or nights;
>
> The crow has cawed at its inhabitants so they were dispersed
> by plunder between the sword blades and spears;
>
> They left their homes and became neighbors to
> wild beasts among deserts and outskirts.[107]

Pining for the city's illustrious days and the sight of its inhabitants once more, he artistically contrasts their former unity and strength with the disastrous events of 656/1258. Baghdad's residents have become scattered victims of war, refugees who have lost the comfort of their homes and past lives. The survivors of this debacle have been reduced to living among the wild beasts on the periphery of their former seat of power and dominance. And al-Kūfī al-Wāʿiẓ grieves over the sorrowful absence of his friends and neighbors:

> I wish that I had died before you departed,
> and never lived to witness the moment of farewell;
>
> Oh why has the mutability of time deranged
> my condition, and left me without my friends?
>
> Oh why are the houses divested
> of my people and my neighbors?
>
> I swear by your lives, nothing has occupied them after you,
> except for deterioration, destruction, and fire;
>
> ....
>
> Oh why do I look around and not see
> my beloved ones among people;
>
> Oh my grief, Oh my loneliness, Oh my bewilderment,
> Oh my desolation, Oh my distressful anguish.[108]

For al-Kūfī al-Wāʿiẓ, the drastic changes wrought by the Mongol siege and destruction of Baghdad have disrupted his very sense of well being. His friends and neighbors have vanished, their dwellings are left in ruin, and the poet is left to his own mental distraction and torment.

This immense loss of life and ruination of the city combined to destroy all that Baghdad had represented as the glorious capital of the Abbasids and a celebrated cosmopolitan center of learning, wealth, comfort, and prestige. In his topographical study, Ṣafī al-Dīn ʿAbd al-Muʾmin b. al-Khaṭīb ʿAbd al-Ḥaqq al-Baghdādī al-Ḥanbalī (658–739/1260–1338) remarks of the city's lost glory:

> The Mongols came and destroyed most of it and killed all of its inhabitants, so none of them were left except for a few individuals, who served as good examples. People from other places have [since] come and settled there, and its [own] people were annihilated. And now it is not what it used to be, nor are its people the same ones with whom we [people of Baghdad] were acquainted. The pronouncement rests with God the Exalted.[109]

And Ibn Kathīr laments, "Baghdad, after it had been the most gregarious (*ānas*) of all cities, was reduced to ruins, with very few people left, [living] in fear, hunger, humiliation, and insignificance."[110] As the Egyptian historian Baybars al-Manṣūrī, who died in 725/1325 in his eighties, elaborates:

> The city of Baghdad was the City of Peace and the sanctuary of Islam, the location of the Commander of the Faithful and the destination of Muslims' travels, the center of towns and the expected location of merchants; in it was the multitude of Islam and those of knowledge and eminence, and artisans and traders; gathered in it were all classes and groups who filled its localities and quarters. So this event was the most bitter of events, and this disaster was among the most distressing of calamities.[111]

In clarifying the palpable pain of contemporaries like himself, Baybars al-Manṣūrī's description of Baghdad evokes the imagery of an earthly paradise (through its honorific title "the Abode of Peace" and its bustling cosmopolitanism) and points to the city's sanctity and centrality among Muslims. Highly prominent among its ennobling traits was the presence of the Abbasid caliph, whom Baybars al-Manṣūrī chose to describe as the Commander of the Faithful and thereby stress the religious bonds between him and an interconnected community of Muslims. Given these powerful associations, the traditionist Abū Jaʿfar Aḥmad b. Ibrāhīm Ibn al-Zubayr al-Thaqafī (627–708/1230–1308) in Spain commiserates over the loss of Baghdad as the greatest of all Muslim cities,[112] while Zakariyyā b. Muḥammad b. Maḥmūd al-Qazwīnī (ca. 600–682 / ca. 1203–83) similarly begins his topographical and anecdotal description of Baghdad by assessing it as "the mother of the world, the mistress of all lands, paradise on earth, the City of Peace, and the dome of Islam."[113] In doing so, al-Qazwīnī draws upon this theme of the city as Islam's majestic and sacred metropolis, which rendered its brutal capture and devastation so utterly shocking. Along these lines, the Egyptian chronicler ʿAlāʾ al-Dīn Mughulṭāy b. Qilīj b. ʿAbdillāh (ca. 689–762/1290–1361) exclaims in passionate rhymed prose, "Hülegü (forcefully) occupied the lands and caused iniquity to spread therein. And he destroyed the City of Peace—rather, the sanctuary of Islam—Baghdad!"[114] Indeed, as the Aleppan historian Ibn Ḥabīb al-Ḥalabī (710–79/1310–77) reflected on these catastrophic events, the Mongol destruction of

Baghdad was "a tribulation whose convulsions were immense and an ordeal that passed but the layers of grief over it remain" (*wa-laqad kānat fitnatan zalzalatuhā ʿaẓīmah, wa-miḥnatan raḥalat wa-lākin ḥasarātuhā muqīmah*). Drawing a specific analogy to an earthquake, Ibn Ḥabīb al-Ḥalabī rhetorically describes the tremendous aftershocks of the loss of Baghdad and its caliphate as producing lasting waves of sorrow, pain, and distress over the passage of time.[115]

ESCHATOLOGICAL ENDINGS

The world without a caliph was so unimaginable for many premodern Muslims that the destruction of Baghdad boded the imminent end of time itself—an eschatological interpretation that reverses some contemporaneous Christian views of world order and the ultimate end. The eleventh through fourteenth centuries saw the articulation of an expanding ecclesiastical vision of Christendom, united under the papal leadership of Rome and predicated on the subsuming and subduing of non-Christian infidels and Christian heretics into a triumphant world order that would hasten the apocalyptic realization of God's kingdom. As Brett Whalen explains, "The papacy and its clerical supporters, in large part to assert their claims of primacy within Europe, redefined their place in God's plan for salvation, arguing that the Roman Church would assume a role of worldly leadership and pastoral dominion over rulers, churches, and communities everywhere as a prelude to the end of history." And for Pope Innocent III, who epitomized papal claims of spiritual and temporal primacy, "The universality of Peter's commission was reinforced by the location of his ecclesiastical dominion in Rome, the seat of imperial monarchy and the ruler of nations."[116] The crusades that Pope Innocent III and other popes before and after him authorized to wrest control of the holy land away from Muslims were an important part of that global vision and reach.

In the thirteenth century, Latin Christian ideas about crusading and conversion converged in unprecedented and powerful ways in pursuit of papal dominion, and the dramatic expansion of the Mongols was integrated into these "papal hopes for the worldwide spread of Christendom" toward the end of time. As John Tolan elaborates in his study of Islam in the medieval European imagination:

> Throughout the thirteenth century, indeed, the advances of the Mongols fueled Christian hopes that a universal victory of Christendom was imminent: missionaries were sent to the Mongols, letters exchanged proposing alliances. The Muslim world could be outflanked through the aid of this powerful new ally; Christianity would emerge victorious. These apocalyptic scenarios also led to hopes that missions to Muslims could lead to widescale conversions.

As apocalyptic prophecies developed in new directions, the Mongol conquest of Baghdad was incorporated into Latin Christian expectations of the impending collapse of Islam. Writing approximately twelve years after the Mongol sack of Baghdad in his *Opus Majus*, the English Franciscan Roger Bacon derived great consolation from his reading of the concurrence of astrological and scriptural predictions about "the destruction of the law of Mahomet" in relation to the Apocalypse. He rejoiced, "It may happen that the Saracens will be destroyed by the Tartars or Christians. Already the greater part of the Saracens have been destroyed by the Tartars, as well as the capital of their kingdom, which was Baldac, and their caliph, who was like a pope over them." Baghdad, or "Baldac," the "royal city, in which the caliph lord of the sect of the Saracens has established the seat of his dignity" had been destroyed. The anonymous author of *De statu Saracenorum*, compiled in 1273 only a few years after Bacon's *Opus Majus*, was similarly comforted by the annihilation of the Abbasid caliph as assuring the path toward a triumphant Christendom. In reiterating the prophesies of William of Tripoli, *De statu Saracenorum* predicted the imminent demise of Islam in the aftermath of the Mongols' invasion of Baghdad and their murder of its caliph. "The Tartars, under the rule of their prince Hulaon, captured Baghdad and its Caliph (who was the forty-third) and murdered him with all his servants and relatives of the lineage of Machometus, so that no one of his lineage remained, who could succeed Machometus and be called Caliph." Reassured by these extraordinary events, the anonymous author hoped for the subsequent peaceful conversion of Muslims to the Christian faith, noting that they were already very close in their essential beliefs and convictions. The anticipated passing of Islam as a dynamic faith and power on the global stage was considered crucial to realizing Latin Christian aspirations of divine dominion under the Roman Church in a perceived fulfillment of the messiah's promise about the last days.[117]

For premodern Muslims, however, the loss of a universal Islamic caliphate, represented by the Abbasids, was unfathomable because all of the community's historic channels of memory and meaning, from law, prophetic narrations, praxis, and culture, undergirded the very necessity of the institution. The world without a caliph—this disruption of the natural order of things—therefore boded the imminent end of time. And a series of dramatic natural disasters were woven into this explanation of the approaching Day of Judgment. Already two years before the Mongol destruction of Baghdad, a number of cataclysmic events in 654/1256 had created an aura of dreadful expectation about the impending dramatic end. In the sacred city of the Prophet Muḥammad, Medina, a terrifying earthquake beset its inhabitants over a period of four days, followed by an immense volcanic eruption nearby in Ḥarrat Rāḥat.[118] The people of Medina sought refuge in the Prophet's mosque for days and months on end, imploring God's forgiveness and salvation,[119] while the awesome fire rapidly burst forth from the six or seven scoria cones in massive quantities,[120] reminding those who witnessed it of the flaming rage of hellfire, as described in some Qur'anic passages.[121] Even the city's governor was prevailed upon to redress the

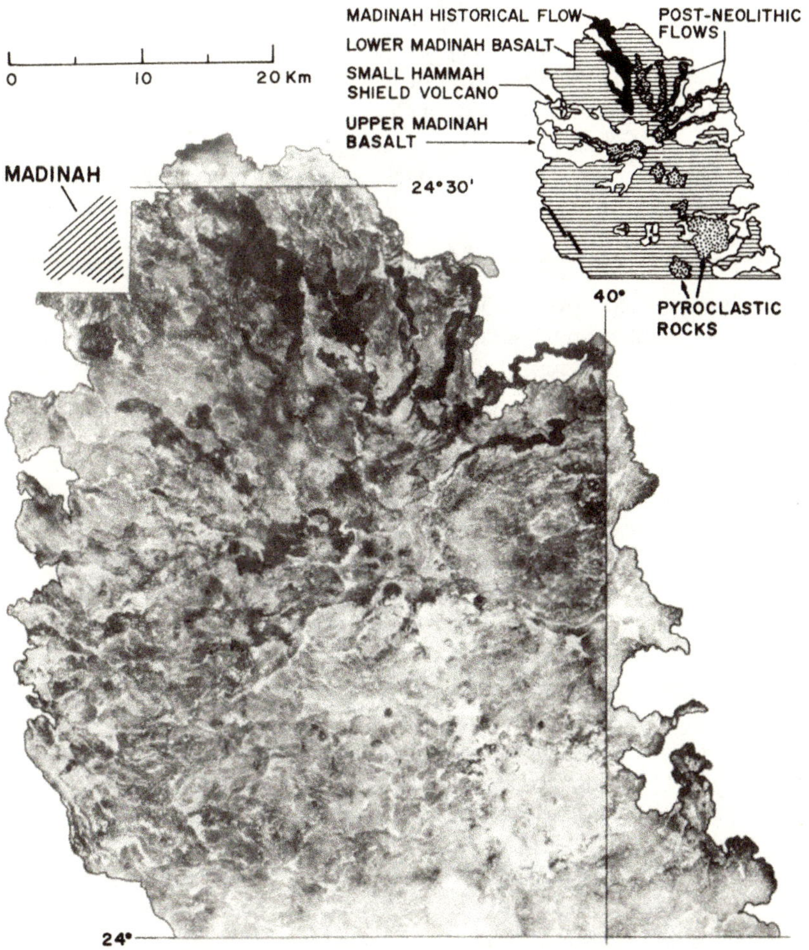

FIGURE 7. Aerial photograph of the historic lava flows in Ḥarrat Rāḥat. The lava flows of the 654 AH / 1256 CE volcanic eruption are designated by the label "Madinah Historical Flow."

Image courtesy Victor E. Camp and M. John Roobol, "The Arabian Continental Alkali Basalt Province: Part I. Evolution of Harrat Rahat, Kingdom of Saudi Arabia," *Geological Society of America Bulletin* 101, Issue 1 (January 1989), 75.

numerous wrongs he had committed against Medina's populace as well as to manumit all of his slaves.[122]

Yet even more astounding for contemporary and later Muslims was the Prophet Muḥammad's accurate prediction that such a fire, this spurting of volatile magma through the earth's surface, would emerge from the land of Hijaz sometime before the Day of Judgment would commence.[123] As a signpost along the way, it was a poignant reminder that the end of time was approaching.[124]

And contemporaries verified the Prophet's description of this volcanic eruption's magnitude, which he had specified would illuminate as far as Bosra in Syria.[125] This visible manifestation of the Prophet's prediction was deemed nothing short of a marvelous sign of God and a revelatory miracle bestowed upon His mortal messenger.[126] Like other poets of his era, inspired by the Prophet Muḥammad's miraculous foretelling of these events, Sayf al-Dīn ʿUmar b. Qizil composed a poem in which he personally addressed the Prophet and celebrated his veracity,[127] and another unnamed poet declared the matter to be a manifest miracle for those endowed with profound understanding.[128] In this fashion, the recorded text made its way from the earlier canonical collections of the Prophet Muḥammad's sayings and deeds into newer compositions on the Prophet's many miracles as well as eschatological works discussing the end of time. This cultural imprint was deep, and centuries later, the late Mamluk scholar Jalāl al-Dīn al-Suyūṭī (849–911/1445–1505) continued to point to Prophet Muḥammad's prediction of this specific volcanic eruption before the end of time as one of the miracles with which he was uniquely blessed as God's beloved messenger to humanity.[129] During the eruption itself, however, the Shaykh of the Prophet's Sanctuary in Medina, the trustworthy (*al-ʿadl*) Maḥmūd b. Yūsuf al-Amʿānī, sent a letter that was copied down from the original by Ibn al-Sāʿī (593–674/1197–1275) and ultimately preserved in the history of Ibn Kathīr, admonishing the people of Baghdad. It read: "[This volcanic eruption] is an awesome sign and a sound indicator that the Hour is nearing; so the felicitous one is he who avails himself of the opportunity before death and sets his affairs aright by improving his standing, before dying, with God the Almighty."[130] Thus, the volatile eruption near Medina ominously inspired al-Amʿānī to warn the people of Baghdad of death and the approaching Day of Judgment.

Muslim scholars and historians later integrated this volcanic eruption, as well as an unprecedented flooding of Baghdad and burning of the Prophet's Mosque, which all occurred in the year 654/1256,[131] into a comprehensive narrative of Baghdad's subsequent demise. While discussing these three major occurrences in his chronicle, Abū Shāmah notes that his contemporaries considered all of them to be signs warning of what was to come in the very near future with the Mongol conquest of Baghdad. Abū Shāmah himself composed a few lines of poetry delineating a connection among these inauspicious events:

> In 654 A.H. occurred [all] in the same year,
>
> A volcanic eruption in Hijaz and the burning
> of the [Prophet's] Mosque, along with the flooding of the City of Peace;
>
> Then the Mongols took Baghdad at
> the beginning of the following year after that;

Its people did not escape while the forces of disbelief
gathered against them; oh the loss of Islam![132]

The Caliphate was extinguished from there,
And al-Mustaʿṣim became without refuge (*iʿtiṣām*);

O Lord, preserve, safeguard, and protect the rest of the cities,
O Majestic and Generous One!

And show compassion toward Hijaz and Egypt,
And send peace upon the lands of Syria-Palestine.[133]

Years later, al-Subkī likewise asserted that the volcanic eruption, fire, and flooding were causal preludes leading up to the Mongol conquest of Baghdad (*umūr kānat muqaddimāt li-hādhihiʾl-wāqiʿah*).[134] And in his well-regarded eschatological work, *al-Tadhkirah*, composed in Andalusia, the contemporaneous scholar al-Qurṭubī (d. 671/1272) closes his discussion of the miraculously prophesized eruption in Ḥarrat Rāḥat with the striking occurrence of the more commonplace fire that burned the Prophet's mosque, ominously followed by the Mongol destruction of Baghdad. On the latter occurrence, he comments:

> Then occurred the taking of Baghdad through conquest by the Mongols, so its inhabitants were killed and taken captive. And that had been the pillar of Islam and its throne, so fear spread widely, people's distress became immense, fright prevailed everywhere, and there was great sadness over the spreading of the Mongols throughout the land. People became distraught, like drunkards, without a caliph or imam. So the affliction has increased and the tribulation has become great [and can only persist]—unless God the Glorious encompasses us with His forgiveness, benevolence, and grace![135]

And his contemporary, the Syrian historian Ibn Wāṣil, shares the sentiment, noting how the volcanic eruption and accidental fire in the Prophet's mosque greatly pained people and overwhelmed them with fear—all of which were merely preludes to the loss of the caliphate (*buṭlān amr al-khilāfah*) and the disappearance (*zawāl*) of the Abbasid dynasty.[136]

In addition to the unique combination of cataclysmic natural disasters, the Mongol conquest of Baghdad itself was perceived as an ominous portent of the appointed hour of resurrection and judgment. According to the widely reported ḥadīth of the Prophet Muḥammad, recorded in most of the canonical collections, the Day of Judgment would not occur until after the Muslims had fought with a people possessing small eyes, flat noses, white reddish faces that were broad, round, rough, and shiny like hammered shields (*al-majānn al-muṭraqah*), and shoes made of hair.[137] Contemporary and subsequent Muslim scholars of ḥadīth and eschatology concurred that this prediction was fulfilled by the appearance of the Mongols and their invasions of Muslim lands.[138] The miraculousness of the Prophet's Muḥammad's foretelling these events was

FIGURE 8. The City of Baghdad in flood. The accompanying Persian couplets from the *Dīvān* of the fourteenth-century poet Nāṣir of Bukhārā (d. 772/1370) translate as:

This year the Tigris had a strangely drunken gait,
With feet in chains and foaming at the mouth—rather, it's a madman!

Heaven poured water and filled it up around the citadel,
As if Baghdad were a candle and the Tigris was a moth.

considered a manifest affirmation of the truth of his mission and of the nearing of humanity's final reckoning before their Creator. As the eminent scholar Muḥyī'l-Dīn Abū Zakariyyā Yaḥyā b. Sharaf al-Nawawī (631–76/1233–77) observes:

> All of these [words] are miracles of the Messenger of God, May God's peace and blessings be upon him, for the fighting has taken place with those [Mongols] possessing all of the attributes that he, May God's peace and blessings be upon him, mentioned... they were found to have all of these attributes during our time and have fought the Muslims a number of times including now. We ask God the Generous [to grant] a good ending for the Muslims in this and all other affairs and for the continuation of his grace and protection. And may God send his blessings upon His messenger who does not speak based on his own whims but only through revelation revealed to him [by God].[139]

Or as al-Qurṭubī affirms the realization of the Prophet's prediction regarding the Mongols in his discussion of the known signs of the Day of Judgment, "This has indeed happened in the way that he, may God's peace and blessings be upon him, informed."[140]

Furthermore, the horrific manner in which the Mongols conquered Baghdad only accentuated this perception of the nearing of the end of time. As al-Qurṭubī goes on to describe their dreadful manifestation in his times, "No one can turn them away from the Muslims except for God; it was as if they were Gog and Magog or [at least] their predecessors."[141] So atrocious was the violence and humiliation that the Mongols inflicted upon the Muslim community that their eruption from the east was commonly associated with the traumatic appearance of Gog and Magog expected towards the end of time. Scholarly descriptions of the Mongols' lineage even include the explanation that they were the cousins of these dreadful peoples.[142] And the distressful trauma of their appearance was often depicted as analogous to the Day of Judgment itself, as in Ibn Abī Yusr's closing lament in his longer poetic elegy:

> Truly the Day of Judgment took place in Baghdad,
> When prosperity turned into adversity;
>
> The family of the Prophet and the people of knowledge were taken captive;
> So whom do you think cities will contain after them?
>
> I never hoped that I should remain while they had departed,
> But destiny intervened against what I would choose.[143]

By highlighting the Abbasids' familial connection with the Prophet Muḥammad, Ibn Abī Yusr accentuates the symbolic tragedy of their loss for the Muslim community along with the loss of the religious scholars who convey the prophetic message, thereby elevating the catastrophe to its highest level. In his elegy, Saʿdī mourns the moment when Baghdad's women, including those of the caliphal household, were taken into captivity as distressing and harrowing as the Day of Judgment.[144] And the overall calamity of these events similarly inspired Ibn Khaldūn to remark, "The Mongols and their ruler Hülegü advanced towards Baghdad and seized the seat of the Caliphate. They killed al-Mustaʿṣim and obliterated the distinguishing characteristics of the religion [of Islam]. It was as if it were one of the signs of the Hour."[145]

THE CONSOLATION OF PROPHETIC TRANSMISSIONS

In the face of such excruciating death and destruction, praise of the Prophet Muḥammad, who had foretold the fighting with the Mongols and reminded people of their mortality and coming judgment, became an increasingly important source of solace. Literary critics Thomas Emil Homerin, ʿUmar Mūsā Bāshā, and Muḥammad Zaghlūl Sallām even indicate that a poetic genre of panegyrics dedicated to the Prophet Muḥammad continued to grow and flourish precisely against the backdrop of this menacing threat from the Mongols, which allowed people, in the words of Homerin, to indulge in "a deep nostalgia for an idyllic time of peace, religious purity, and moral order" and also "fostered a conscious sense of Muslim identity."[146] Perhaps we can even trace elements of this trend in the sorrowful elegies dedicated to the lost seat of the caliphate in Baghdad and the consolation that at least one poet sought in commemorating the Messenger of God and his mission. As Ibn Abī Yusr expresses his misery:

> After the enslavement of all of the Abbasids,
> may no aurora illuminate the face of the dawn;
>
> Nothing has given me pleasure since their departure,
> except prophetic accounts (*aḥādīth*) and post-prophetic reports (*āthār*)
> that I narrate;
>
> There does not remain, now that they have vanished,
> any desire (*shawq*)[147] for glory in religious and worldly affairs,
> for they have parted and perished.[148]

The one source of comfort that Ibn Abī Yusr identifies in the disheartening aftermath of the Abbasids' death and enslavement, his transmitting the sayings and deeds of the Prophet Muḥammad and his righteous followers (as *aḥādīth* and *āthār*), is a fitting consolation for the magnitude of the calamity. For over five hundred years, the Abbasids had represented a tradition of guardianship over the Muslim community's affairs—the caliphate (*khilāfah*)—with its roots in the early origins of Islam following the death of the Prophet Muḥammad. With the living links of this venerable institution broken and destroyed, it is as if Taqiyy al-Dīn Ibn Abī Yusr seeks to hold on to the textual chains (*isnāds*) that preserve all else remaining of the Islamic tradition.[149] Like the Abbasid

Caliphate that had symbolically bonded Muslims from far-off regions to one another and to their distinctly Islamic heritage, despite the undeniable realities of political fragmentation, the discursive preservation of the faith through the textual transmission of narratives, to which Ibn Abī Yusr refers, suggests yet another, ultimately more resilient, mode of maintaining devotional unity and solidarity among the diverse members of a universally conceived Sunni Muslim community.

CHAPTER 2

RECAPTURING LOST GLORY AND LEGITIMACY

Islam is par excellence the social, even the political religion. Since the time of the Madina Caliphate it has been unable to fulfill its goal of a social order in which the religious and the political aspects shall be one. But the aspiration could not be laid aside by seriously pious Muslims. It might, however, be transformed.

—MARSHALL HODGSON (D. 1968)[1]

The one to whom the possessor of power pledges allegiance is the Caliph. And the one who monopolizes power and obeys the Caliph in the matter of the Friday prayer and coinage is the Sultan who implements law and justice with full validity.

—IMAM ABŪ ḤĀMID AL-GHAZĀLĪ (D. 505/1111)[2]

IN THE YEAR 658/1260, Rukn al-Dīn Baybars al-Bunduqdārī (d. 676/1277) sought to ascend the throne of Egypt as head of the military slave elite, the Mamluks, who had wrested control away from their Ayyubid masters only two years prior. The Ayyubid dynasty founded nearly a century before by Ṣalāḥ al-Dīn al-Ayyūbī (532–89/1138–93), known in Europe as Saladin, had restored the country's allegiance to the Abbasid caliph of Baghdad,[3] and so too had the last Ayyubid prince, al-Malik al-Nāṣir Yūsuf (627–58/1230–60), based in Syria, visibly supported the Abbasid Caliphate.[4] Yet as the Mongols invaded northwest Mesopotamia and geographical Syria, al-Malik al-Nāṣir was induced to flee from the city of Damascus, which was soon captured by the Mongols.[5] When the Mongols turned to press onwards toward Egypt, their advance was halted by the Mamluk ruler al-Malik al-Muẓaffar Quṭuz, who secured a resounding victory at ʿAyn Jālūt on Ramaḍān 25, 658 / September 3, 1260.[6] Yet while Quṭuz was returning to his citadel in Cairo and the throne of the Mamluk domains, he was assassinated at al-Quṣayr by some disgruntled Mamluks.[7]

One of these assassins was Rukn al-Dīn Baybars al-Bunduqdārī, who is said to have wielded the sword that fatally struck Quṭuz. Gathering in the camp at al-Quṣayr, the Mamluks present deliberated over who would next assume leadership and ultimately settled upon Baybars. Rushing back to Cairo with his Mamluk supporters to take advantage of the element of surprise, Baybars rapidly ascended the throne in the fortified citadel and began accepting people's pledges of allegiance to him as the newly designated ruler. Yet it is reported that Baybars faced an unexpected challenge to his legitimacy to reign at this juncture. The religious scholar, ʿIzz al-Dīn ʿAbd al-ʿAzīz Ibn ʿAbd al-Salām (577–660/1181–1262), known as *Sulṭān al-ʿUlamāʾ* or the Leading Power among Scholars, openly refused to pledge his allegiance. Instead, Ibn ʿAbd al-Salām assuredly called out, " O Rukn al-Dīn, I only know you as the mamluk of Bunduqdār," intimating that Baybars's slave status disqualified him from serving as head of state. This challenge from a formidable scholar whose political stances could lead vast numbers of the city's populace to follow him in droves could not be easily dismissed. And it was not until a reliable witness was procured who testified that ownership of Baybars had been transferred from his original owner ʿAlāʾ al-Dīn Aydekin Bunduqdār (d. 684/1285) to the Ayyubid prince al-Malik al-Ṣāliḥ Najm al-Dīn Ayyūb (d. 647/1249) who had manumitted him that Ibn ʿAbd al-Salām was satisfied enough to pledge his allegiance.[8]

Although the immediate crisis was averted, this account of Ibn ʿAbd al-Salām's conscientious refusal points to a wider problem of legitimacy facing the mostly Turkic Muslim rulers of post-Abbasid polities, in what Richard Bulliet has called the Muslim North,[9] and their increasing dependence upon religious scholars to sanctify and authenticate their rule. The disappearance of the Abbasid Caliphate of Baghdad had deprived rulers of the sheen of legitimacy that caliphal affirmation of their regional power as his deputies or sultans could offer, and military prowess alone was not enough to establish political authority. In this post-Abbasid era, Muslim rulers and scholars developed a symbiotic relationship of scholarly patronage and religious legitimation that burnished the reputation of ruling elites as the demonstrably righteous endowers of the institutional infrastructure necessary to support flourishing scholarly production and transmission. Amid these vexing questions over legal and political legitimacy for premodern Muslim polities in the wake of the Abbasid Caliphate's demise, the luster of the Abbasid caliphal heritage continued to hold evocative promise and appeal in multiple contexts. Its memory was continually invoked in the ways that Mamluk-era social and political actors, in particular, sought to reinvent the Abbasid Caliphate for their times. The past was not dead and forgotten, but a fecund source of inspiration to be creatively reconfigured and imagined, with tangible consequences and implications for Mamluk state and society.

REMEMBERING AND RECREATING A GLORIOUS PAST

This enduring significance of the Abbasid legacy mirrors the way that Roman traditions contributed to the cultural formations of early medieval Europe, long after Rome, as an ancient imperial capital, had been rendered obsolete. As Julia Smith masterfully demonstrates in her book *Europe after Rome: A New Cultural History 500–1000*, the idea of Rome was a powerful imaginative device.

In 381 CE, Constantinople was officially designated a new Rome at an ecumenical council and promoted in hierarchy over the apostolic sees of Alexandria, Antioch, and Jerusalem. The bishop of the new eastern imperial capital accrued this "prerogative of honor" second only to the bishop of the old Roman capital itself. By the sixth century, "warlords who established kingdoms within the provinces of the crumbling western Roman Empire had legitimized their position by eagerly appropriating symbols of Roman rule—portraits on coins, seals, dress, insignia of office, flattering epithets." And Irish and British origin legends from that era also reveal "the significance of Roman history and Christian Latin texts as the cultural rubble out of which fundamentally different edifices could be built, even in places at or beyond the outermost margins of former imperial rule." Rome's imperial past continued to be appropriated at the beginning of the ninth century, and the coronation of Charlemagne as emperor in 800 gave new rise to the imitation of Roman ceremonial. The following year, Charlemagne invested in the "rhetorical mantle of historical authentication" by including the motto "the renewal of the Roman empire" on his seal—even though he did not aspire to rule from Rome, and Carolignian writers embellished their accounts of his palace complex in Paderborn with various poetic allusions to how "Golden Rome is reborn and restored anew to the world." Rome was also replicated in the British archipelago and Germany in the ninth and tenth centuries, "through name transference, building forms, liturgy, dedications, and imported martyrial relics," when Christian communitites sought to create local links, which were otherwise lacking, to Roman apostolic authenticity. Remembering Rome connected medieval European rulers and their subjects to a glamorous and secure past.[10]

Likewise, in the fluid post-Ayyubid context of geographical Syria and Egypt, the glorious heritage of Abbasid Baghdad loomed large. And the aura of legitimacy that could be won through the act of recognizing and being recognized by a new Abbasid caliph inspired several political contenders to perpetuate this prestigious caliphal legacy and visibily associate themselves with its living memory. Scions of the Abbasid dynasty were in short supply. Aside from the caliph's youngest son, al-Mubārak, who had been captured by the Mongols, all of the well-known Abbasid candidates for the caliphate and their families had been systematically murdered. These included the reigning caliph al-Mustaʿṣim, his two eldest sons,[11] his uncles who were the sons of the Caliph al-Ẓāhir,[12] and two of his cousins who were the grandsons of the Caliph al-Nāṣir.[13] The latter two groups had been considered even more imposing candidates for the caliphate than their younger nephew or cousin al-Mustaʿṣim back in 640/1242 when he first ascended the throne amid great secrecy and exertion of pressure.[14] Yet despite these drastic limitations following the Mongol invasion, the institution of the caliphate remained firmly associated with the Abbasid dynasty. So strong was this cultural imprint that all of the multiple attempts to restore an Islamic caliphate centered on an Abbasid claimant.

GOING BEYOND BAGHDAD

In the aftermath of the Mongol conquest of Baghdad, at least five individuals identifying themselves as Abbasid survivors of the debacle or at least descendants of the august dynasty sought recognition for themselves as caliphs, often in competition with one another and in collaboration with the rival military factions of geographical Syria and Egypt. The most colorful of these candidates for a resurrected caliphate was Abū'l-ʿAbbās Aḥmad (d. 701/1302). Reputedly a lineal descendent of the twenty-ninth Abbasid caliph al-Mustarshid (r. 512–29/1118–35), Abū'l-ʿAbbās Aḥmad had escaped Baghdad early in 657/1259 in the company of Zayn al-Dīn Ṣāliḥ b. Muḥammad b. Abī'l-Rushd al-Asadī al-Ḥākimī (known as Ibn al-Bannāʾ), the latter's brother Shams al-Dīn Muḥammad b. Muḥammad, and Najm al-Dīn Muḥammad b. al-Mashshāʾ.[15] After becoming honored guests of the Khafājah Bedouin of Iraq and their leader Ḥusayn b. Fallāḥ, the small retinue was directed towards geographical Syria on the advice of Jamāl al-Dīn Mukhtār al-Sharābī, who had recently departed Baghdad himself. As the contemporary sources report, this decision was motivated by the greater public good that could be achieved by transferring the surviving Abbasid to those domains rather than his remaining among the nomadic Khafājah.[16] Making the journey in the company of a certain Nuʿaym, a leader of the Iraqi Bedouins of ʿUbādah to the west,[17] Abū'l-ʿAbbās and his retinue were well-received and honored by a number of Bedouin leaders. They stayed with the Amīr Nūr al-Dīn Zāmil (d. 670/1272),[18] son of the Amīr Sayf al-Dīn ʿAlī b. Ḥudhayfah the leader of the Āl Faḍl[19] at the time, then with al-Shaykh Birrī, then ʿĀmir b. Ṣaqr, until they came to reside with the Amīr ʿĪsā b. Muhannā (d. 683/1284)[20] of the Āl Faḍl.

It was this Amīr ʿĪsā b. Muhannā of the Āl Faḍl Bedouins who first brought Abū'l-ʿAbbās Aḥmad to the attention of the contemporary rulers of Syria and Egypt. When the Ayyubid prince of Syria al-Malik al-Nāṣir Yūsuf learned about the survival of the Abbasid caliph al-Mustarshid's grandson Abū'l-ʿAbbās and that he was residing as a guest among the Āl Faḍl Bedouins,[21] he ordered that the royal Abbasid be brought to him in Damascus. Yet despite al-Malik al-Nāṣir's former display of reverence to the Abbasid Caliphate of Baghdad, the historical possibilities of his intentions vis-à-vis Abū'l-ʿAbbās were lost in the subsequent Mongol invasions of northwest Mesopotamia and geographical Syria.[22] Only a couple of months following al-Malik al-Nāṣir's death, the Mamluk ruler of Egypt al-Malik al-Muẓaffar Quṭuz and his subordinates recognized the caliphal rights of Abū'l-ʿAbbās, after having defeated the Mongols at ʿAyn Jālūt in 658/1260.[23] The contemporary account of al-Yūnīnī notes that Quṭuz assigned a commander, the Amīr Sayf al-Dīn Qilij al-Baghdādī, to accompany the caliphal figure of Abū'l-ʿAbbās in reclaiming his patrimony in Baghdad.[24] And other slightly later figures who were likely influenced by subsequent historical developments, Ibn al-Dawādārī, who completed his chronicle *Kanz al-Durar* in 736/1335, and Ibn Abī'l-Faḍā'il, who completed his chronicle *al-Nahj al-Sadīd* in 759/1358, add that Quṭuz had intended to reestablish Abū'l-ʿAbbās as caliph in Cairo. In their accounts, he instructed ʿĪsā b. Muhannā of Āl Faḍl to send the royal Abbasid on to Cairo with the words: "When we return to Cairo, dispatch him to me so that, God willing, we may reinstate him."[25] In any event, Quṭuz's commander swore allegiance to Abū'l-ʿAbbās as caliph, and the two managed to reconquer a number of Mesopotamian towns along the way to Baghdad,[26] which also suggests a limited Mongol presence in the region following the Mamluk victory at ʿAyn Jālūt. Yet like al-Malik al-Nāṣir before him, Quṭuz was prematurely murdered, and any further plans he had for Abū'l-ʿAbbās were aborted.[27] Nevertheless, Quṭuz and his commander's recognition of Abū'l-ʿAbbās as caliph spread widely among the Bedouins of geographical Syria, where Abū'l-ʿAbbās would reside for many months.[28] By the time Abū'l-ʿAbbās had received an invitation to Cairo from the next Mamluk ruler al-Malik al-Ẓāhir Baybars al-Bunduqdārī[29] and physically managed to arrive, another Abbasid descendant had already been installed as caliph. Fearing for his life and liberty, Abū'l-ʿAbbās promptly turned back and fled from Baybars's capital.[30]

During the invasion of Baghdad, the Mongols had reportedly released this other Abbasid descendant, Abū'l-Qāsim Aḥmad (d. 660/1261), the son of the thirty-fifth caliph al-Ẓāhir (r. 622–23/1225–26), from prison. He had been kept there by his nephew al-Mustaʿṣim during his own ill-fated caliphate. After his serendipitous release, Abū'l-Qāsim Aḥmad left Baghdad to seek refuge among the Khafājah Bedouins of Iraq.[31] And he later arrived in the vicinity of Damascus, among a group of nearly fifty horsemen of these Khafājah Bedouin, including the Amīrs Naṣir al-Dīn Muhannā b. Shahrī, Washshāḥ b. Shahrī, Muhammad b. Qibyān al-ʿUbbādī, and seven other military commanders.[32] Word of his arrival reached the ears of the newly appointed Mamluk ruler Baybars who issued an invitation to Abū'l-Qāsim Aḥmad to come to Cairo,[33] as he also did with Abū'l-ʿAbbās Aḥmad. Abū'l-Qāsim arrived first on Thursday, Rajab 9, 659 / June 9, 1261, and he was received with great ceremony and paraded throughout the city in the presence of al-Malik al-Ẓāhir Baybars, the most eminent members of the Mamluk State, other representatives of the military, judiciary, bureaucracy, and different religious communities. Even the populace of Cairo and Fustat are reported to have turned out in great numbers for the memorable event. To this all-inclusive reception, Abū'l-Qāsim entered Cairo through the Gate of Victory (*Bāb al-Naṣr*) wearing the symbolic attire of the Abbassids, transversed the city in ceremonious procession, and exited through the Zuwaylah Gate (*Bāb al-Zuwaylah*) on his way to the citadel, where he took up residence in the Tower of Well-Being (*Burj al-ʿĀfiyah*).[34]

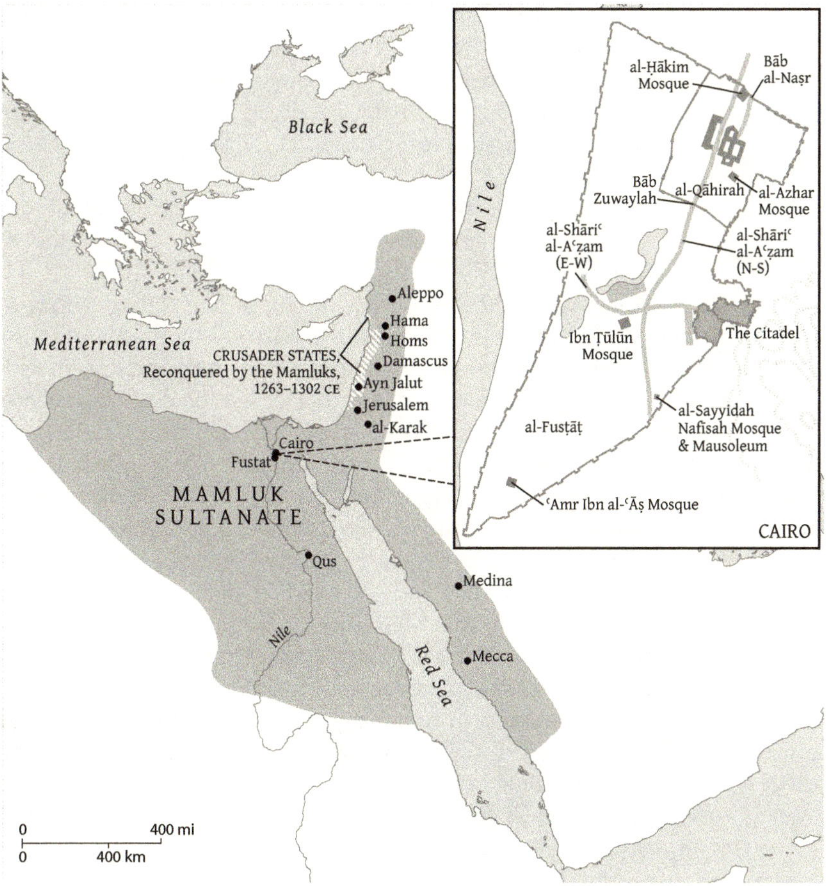

MAP 2. Mamluk Sultanate and ceremonial processional route.

COMMEMORATING THE CALIPHATE

Having recently assumed the throne, al-Malik al-Ẓāhir Baybars was acutely aware of the myriad challenges to his rule. The Abbasid Caliphate had been eradicated from Baghdad and its populace massacred. The Ayyubid dynasty had been eliminated from geographical Syria, leaving no clearly defined successor. Crusader states occupied territories in the north. Mongol armies had invaded and occupied much of the east. He had assassinated Quṭuz and assumed his place as Mamluk ruler of Egypt, but he still had to contend with the military factions loyal to the former head of state. And it was possible for religious elites to challenge his authority and legitimacy, as Ibn ʿAbd al-Salām had once done. Internally and externally it was a tumultuous era. And as Peter Holt and Stefan Heidemann have argued, Baybars astutely recognized the symbolic utility of the Abbasid refugee's presence for his own conduct of foreign and domestic affairs.[35] The new Mamluk ruler effectively utilized the arrival of Abū'l-Qāsim Aḥmad (inaugurated as the Caliph al-Mustanṣir) and later of Abū'l-ʿAbbās Aḥmad (inaugurated as the Caliph al-Ḥākim) to consolidate his reputation and his rule.

Critical to this endeavor was the image Baybars helped cultivate of himself as the restorer of the Abbasid Caliphate after its eradication from Baghdad, through the inauguration of acknowledged scions of that noble dynasty. [36] The links in Abū'l-Qāsim's and Abū'l-ʿAbbās's genealogies to Abbasid caliphs as their forefathers signified the continuity of this illustrious heritage, and they were prominently presented and proclaimed. Shortly after Abū'l-Qāsim's arrival, his genealogy was publicly confirmed before a large and diverse audience in the Grand Reception Hall of al-ʿAmad in the Citadel. On Monday, Rajab 13, 659 / June 13, 1261, al-Malik al-Ẓāhir Baybars assembled the judges and jurists, congregational prayer leaders, scholars, military commanders, Sufis, merchants, and all shades of people to recognize Abū'l-Qāsim's Abbasid lineage and to therefore honor him as their rightful caliph. A caliphal eunuch (or *ṭawāshī*)[37] from Baghdad by the name of Mukhtār as well as the Khafājah Bedouins who had accompanied Abū'l-Qāsim from Mesopotamia were asked to confirm his identity, and they testified that he was indeed Aḥmad the son of the Abbasid caliph al-Imām al-Ẓāhir and the grandson of the Abbasid caliph al-Imām al-Nāṣir. Upon this declaration, a prominent group of religious scholars and functionaries[38] bore witness to the Chief Justice Tāj al-Dīn Ibn Bint al-Aʿazz (604–65/1208–67)[39] regarding the veracity of his descent. After recording his legal affirmation of the evidence, Ibn Bint al-Aʿazz stood up and proclaimed his own confirmation and judgment in favor of Abū'l-Qāsim's Abbasid lineage before the entire assembly. With the refugee's genealogy thus legally affirmed, the eminent scholar Ibn ʿAbd al-Salām, followed by al-Malik al-Ẓāhir Baybars and the Chief Justice Ibn Bint al-Aʿazz, then all the rest of the attendees, according to their station, proceeded to pledge their allegiance to Abū'l-Qāsim as the newly proclaimed Abbasid caliph al-Mustanṣir.

This public ceremony and the rituals of the following Friday openly celebrated the restoration of the caliphate as an integral part of Islamic law and culture. The pledges of allegiance to al-Mustanṣir acknowledged the necessity of his position as head of state, as delineated by Islamic jurisprudence, in order to facilitate good public governance. The legitimacy of state affairs, public finances, court judgments, marital contracts, and even congregational prayers all hinged on his existence. Thus, al-Mustanṣir was called upon to uphold the word of God and the model of His messenger, to enjoin good and forbid wrongdoing, to fight in God's way, and to acquire and distribute wealth properly.[40] As it was customary to pray for the caliph and his success in the course of Friday congregational prayers, the very presence of al-Mustanṣir at the first such occasion following his inauguration was similarly resplendent. On Friday, Rajab 17, 659 / June 17, 1261, the Caliph al-Mustanṣir personally led the Friday congregational prayer in the Grand Mosque of the Citadel. He preached on the merits of the Abbasids and the tremendous honor of their dynasty, reinscribing the religious and cultural connotations of their virtues in a public space of worship. al-Mustanṣir also recited passages from the Qur'an, and the citadel mosque was bedecked with gold and silver coins copiously strewn about to mark the auspicious return of an Abbasid to the pulpit and the caliphate.[41]

By prominently demonstrating his support and reverence for the new Abbasid caliph as the embodiment of the community's revitalizing memories, Baybars was also able to assert his own political and even spiritual primacy within Mamluk society. The official correspondence that he dispatched for wide dissemination on the occasion of al-Mustanṣir's inauguration takes care to stress how Baybars had honored and received the Abbasid scion with the great respect befitting his lofty station.[42] And at the inaugural ceremony itself, this marked elevation of status was physically exemplified by their sitting arrangements. In a display of manners, Baybars did not sit on a cushion in the caliph's presence and reserved that mark of distinction for al-Mustanṣir alone.[43] But it was not enough for Baybars as a military leader to exhibit his respect for the newly designated caliph; hence, the official dispatch carefully emphasizes the widespread scholarly and popular approbation of al-Mustanṣir as the legitimate caliph of his age. In addition to al-Malik al-Ẓāhir Baybars and the military elite (*al-umarāʾ wa'l-ḥalqah*[44]), "all the people have pledged their allegiance to him and are in accord with his caliphate."[45] As a result, Baybars ordered that al-Mustanṣir's caliphate be officially recognized on the coinage and during Friday congregational prayers,[46] and recognition of al-Mustanṣir's caliphate was intimately bound with recognition of Baybars's pivotal role in facilitating the institution's restoration. As such, the letter sent to the Damascene chief justice Najm al-Dīn b. Sanī al-Dawlah (d. 680/1281)[47] and read aloud in the ʿĀdiliyyah legal college of Damascus[48] boldly proclaimed that al-Malik al-Ẓāhir Baybars had rectified the lamentable state of public affairs through the official recognition of a caliph of sound lineage.[49] And the reception of this news in Damascus, as depicted by Abū Shāmah (599–665/1203–67), was ecstatic:

> The people were immensely happy with this (*surra al-nāsu bi-dhālika surūran ʿaẓīman*) and thanked God for the return of the Abbasid Caliphate after the disbelieving Mongols had cut it off by killing the Caliph al-Mustaʿṣim ibn al-Ẓāhir, who was the nephew of this one given allegiance (*bayʿah*) in Egypt, and by destroying Baghdad and killing its inhabitants; and that was in the year [6]55 [AH], so the people remained without a caliph for about four and a half years.[50]

As Baybars's biographer Ibn Shaddād (613–84/1217–85) would later write, this appointment of a caliph on whom "the religious foundations" of Islam and "the legal obligations" of Muslims depend was one of Baybars's greatest merits and epitomized his observance of Islamic law and justice as a ruler.[51]

Baybars marshaled a panoply of visual, textual, performative, and legal means to envelop himself in the prestige of the Abbasid Caliphate that drew deeply from the wells of communal meaning and strategically positioned himself as the caliph's political and spiritual deputy. Approximately two weeks after al-Mustanṣir's inauguration, the new caliph officially designated Baybars as his legitimate sultan and delegated him to take care of all the military and administrative affairs that were his legal responsibility as leader of the Muslim community. As the head of the Egyptian chancery at the time, Fakhr al-Dīn Ibrāhīm Ibn Luqmān (612–93/1215–94), who prepared the ornate document of investiture with his own hand, declared there was no one more deserving of this trust than the one who had resurrected the Abbasid Caliphate after its abysmal disappearance. Thus, al-Mustanṣir entrusted al-Malik al-Ẓāhir Baybars with the military and civil affairs of the lands of Egypt, Diyarbakr, Hijaz, Yemen, and Mesopotamia, as well as any other domains to be conquered in the future—lands beyond Baybars's immediate control, but for which he was granted suzerainty. In the words of Fakhr al-Dīn, the Muslim community, or *ummah*, had found someone to bear the weight of its governance. According to this investiture, it was therefore Baybars's responsibility to locate suitable delegates to administer these regions on his behalf, and he would answer to God for their actions. The expectations of a just ruler were laid squarely on Baybars's shoulders.[52]

On Monday, Shaʿbān 4, 659 / July 4, 1261, in an elaborate ceremony to commemorate this designation of Baybars as sultan, he was literally and figuratively cloaked in the mantle of Abbasid authority and power. Dressed lavishly in what was described as Abbasid attire, Baybars wore black and purple garments embellished with gold to project his newfound authority. He in turn bestowed robes as the caliph's legitimate delegate upon the religious elite to honor them and likewise enrobed leading Mamluk military commanders, who could have constituted potential opposition to his rule, as his clear subordinates. During the procession back to the Citadel, through the festively decorated and cloth carpeted streets of Cairo, this subordinate group remained on foot while al-Malik al-Ẓāhir Baybars rode astride a grey stallion. The only other designation of elevated prominence was assigned to the caliphal document of Baybar's investiture as sultan, raised up high above people's heads.[53]

Yet al-Mustanṣir's designation of Baybars as rightful sultan was not the sole mark of privilege that he bestowed. On the completion of the three sacred months of Rajab, Shaʿbān, and Ramaḍān that had coincided with al-Mustanṣir's arrival in Cairo, the new caliph initiated Baybars into the *futuwwah* order that had been reorganized by his grandfather in Baghdad, the Abbasid caliph al-Nāṣir. Originally men's lodges infused with spiritual teachings that celebrated "feasting, hospitality, and good fellowship," al-Nāṣir transformed the important social institution of *futuwwah* into a vehicle of asserting caliphal supremacy. al-Nāṣir designated himself as the official head of all *futuwwah* branches in 604/1207 and developed a courtly version where he initiated and presided over other Muslim rulers and members of the military elite. Supposedly initiated into the *futuwwah* by his father, the Caliph al-Ẓāhir, who had been initiated by his grandfather, the Caliph al-Nāṣir, the newly inaugurated al-Mustanṣir embodied the continuation of this poignant Abbasid inheritance. In 659/1261, al-Malik al-Ẓāhir Baybars was integrated into this spectacular initiatic chain of chivalry traversing through the Abbasid caliphs al-Ẓāhir and al-Nāṣir, back to the Prophet Muḥammad's companion Salmān the Persian, and ultimately to the Prophet Muḥammad's son-in-law and spiritual successor Alī b. Abī Ṭālib. Invested with the trousers of *futuwwah*, al-Malik al-Ẓāhir Baybars was elevated and consecrated by his incorporation into this potent lineage and empowered to initiate other rulers and members of the elite beneath his own authority.[54]

CONTESTING CALIPHS

All of the pomp and circumstance surrounding Baybars's delegation as the political and spiritual representative of the new Abbasid caliph helped to entrench his authority and position as ruler above all the other military commanders who could vie for power with him in Egypt, geographical Syria, and Mesopotamia. In this regard, Baybars met with great success. When he traveled to Syria to assert his power in the company of the widely acknowledged Abbasid caliph al-Mustanṣir, the populace of Damascus rejoiced to receive them both. And Baybars received delegations from the Ayyubid princes al-Malik al-Ashraf Mūsā b. al-Manṣūr (r. 644–58/1246–60) and al-Malik al-Manṣūr Muḥammad b. al-Muẓaffar (r. 642–83/1244–84) ruling Homs and Hama respectively in order to submit their acquiescence.[55] Baybars graciously accepted their submission and delegated them as his vassals responsible for governing lands that had previously been under their sole control and discretion. Likewise, the Ayyubid prince al-Malik al-Mughīth ʿUmar of al-Karak (d. 661/1263) sent a letter to Baybars to acknowledge Baybars's suzereinty as Mamluk sultan and to express remorse for his past actions treacherously depleting Baybars's forces upon his ascension to the throne and allying himself with the Mongols.[56] And when the Abbasid Abū'l-ʿAbbās who had turned back and fled from Cairo, fearing his own imprisonment as an extraneous caliphal rival to al-Mustanṣir,[57] attempted to take over the Mesopotamian town of ʿĀnah, its people refused. News had reached them that al-Malik al-Ẓāhir Baybars had pledged allegiance to a caliph in Cairo and that he was on the way to retrieve his patrimony; they would not submit ʿĀnah to anyone else but that rightful caliph al-Mustanṣir.[58]

Yet Baybars's early efforts upon seizing power from Quṭuz to arrest potential Mamluk rivals in order to neutralize them had inadvertently created an alternative locus of regional power. Fearing his imminent arrest, one commander, the Amīr Shams al-Dīn Āqqūsh al-Barlī al-ʿAzīzī, along with his followers among the ʿAzīziyyah and Nāṣiriyyah, managed to escape Damascus by night.[59] These roaming Mamluk forces wreaked havoc in Baybars's plans for regional stability and ultimately entrenched themselves in the important city of Aleppo, outwitting Baybars's own men on multiple occasions and attracting the loyalty and services of the Turkomans as well as the disaffectioned Bedouin leader Zāmil and his group of supporters.[60] When the wandering Abbasid survivor Abū'l-ʿAbbās narrowly escaped death and detention in a skirmish that was actually intended to neutralize the forces of Āqqūsh al-Barlī, he was ironically pushed, in order to maintain his own security, into the arms of al-Barlī,[61] who showed the Abbasid great deference. Thus, during al-Barlī's second occupation of Aleppo, which began in August 1261,[62] Abū'l-ʿAbbās was instated as a rival Abbasid caliph under the regnal name, al-Ḥākim bi-Amrillāh, or the one who rules by God's command. al-Barlī and all of the inhabitants of Aleppo pledged their allegiance to him as caliph, and as the contemporary Abū Shāmah observes, the name of al-Ḥākim was both inscribed on the coinage of Aleppo and proclaimed from its minbars during Friday congregational prayers. Thus, the significant military force and political domain of al-Barlī was united with the legitimizing presence of an Abbasid caliph, who garnered oaths of loyalty and allegiance from other towns and groups in the region, including for example the Banū Taymiyyah in Ḥarrān.[63]

As contemporaries clearly recognized, Baybars had a significant problem on his hands with the installation of a rival Abbasid caliph, by a Mamluk commander with a significant military coalition, in one of the region's most influential provinces. Therefore, he assiduously sought to demonstrate the superiority of both his military force *and* the claims of his Abbasid caliph in a symbolically charged tour aimed at subduing the contested domains of geographical Syria and Mesopotamia. On Friday, Dhū'l-Qaʿdah 10, 659 / October 7, 1261, al-Malik al-Ẓāhir Baybars and his acknowledged Abbasid caliph al-Mustanṣir made separate grand entrances at the Damascene congregational mosque and attended the Friday sermon and prayers together. Afterwards, Baybars publicly displayed his servitude and respect for al-Mustanṣir as caliph, while people prayed for the success of them both.[64] From Damascus, Baybars dispatched a military expedition to crush the Aleppan resistance to his rule, which was ultimately successful,[65] and another expedition led by the Cairene Abbasid caliph al-Mustanṣir to regain the original seat of the Abbasid Caliphate in Baghdad, which ended in the death of al-Mustanṣir and many of his troops.[66] However, al-Barlī's Caliph al-Ḥākim, who had briefly joined forces with al-Mustanṣir in attempting to retake Mesopotamia and Baghdad,[67] sought refuge with Baybars in Cairo after the death of his relative at the hands of the Mongols.[68]

In the meanwhile, a third simultaneous movement to establish an autonomous caliphal regime had also been underfoot. In the aftermath of the Mongol destruction of Baghdad, a man presented himself to the Kurdish military faction, the Shahrazūriyyah, as the son of al-Amīr al-Gharīb (d. 614/1217), who had arrived in Irbil much earlier claiming to be the son of the Abbasid caliph al-Nāṣir. The approximately three thousand military members of the Shahrazūriyyah, who had been put to flight by Hülegü's troops and arrived in geographical Syria in 656/1258, sought to install this supposed grandson of al-Imām al-Nāṣir as caliph. However, when they were dispersed, presumably by the Ayyubid al-Malik al-Nāṣir or possibly by Baybars before his assumption of the sultanate,[69] the Abbasid claimant was imprisoned. There, he encountered the Judge Kamāl al-Dīn al-Khiḍr b. Abī Bakr b. Aḥmad al-Kurdī, who was known to contemporaries for his shameless love of power, and indeed had been imprisoned on account of it.[70] The two agreed to strive for the establishment of another political regime, with one man as an Abbasid caliph and the other as his vizier. Although the supposed grandson of al-Imām al-Nāṣir died before al-Khiḍr's release from prison, the ambitious judge continued to strive for the realization of their plans, with the former's son as caliph in his stead. al-Khiḍr contacted other notables, colluded with the Shahrazūriyyah and other Kurds, and even promulgated official announcements on behalf of the new regime. With news reaching al-Malik al-Ẓāhir Baybars of these affairs, the Mamluk sultan had al-Khiḍr arrested and hung on Jumādā al-Ākhirah 18, 660 / May 10, 1262, with the state documents he had issued symbolically dangling from his neck.[71]

The ultimately successful bid to reinstate an Abbasid Caliphate after the destruction of Baghdad by the Mongols emerged against the backdrop of this internal competition for regional supremacy, but even more significantly it also represented a move to claim even broader, transregional supremacy for the Mamluks ruling in Egypt. In contrast to Baybars's speedy recognition of al-Mustanṣir, the more formidable Abbasid figure of al-Ḥākim had to wait several months before he was officially installed as caliph. Therefore, it was not until the beginning of Muḥarram 661 / mid-November 1262 that al-Malik al-Ẓāhir formally pledged allegiance to al-Ḥākim bi-Amrillāh as the Abbasid caliph of his times. Speculating on the cause of this delay, Holt remarks:

> Personally, al-Ḥākim was clearly a more considerable candidate than al-Mustanṣir. He had already twice been recognized as caliph—but by two of Baybars' defeated rivals, Quṭuz and al-Barlī, and was thus to some extent a potential focus of opposition. Baybars' haste to install al-Mustanṣir may indeed have been due partly to a desire to anticipate the arrival of this second and less attractive claimant. Al-Ḥākim had gained military experience and some success in his earlier adventures, and he had a powerful friend who could provide him with a fighting force in ʿĪsā b. Muhannā.[72]

It is important to extend these salient observations with some modification. al-Malik al-Ẓāhir Baybars must undoubtedly have been concerned about al-Ḥākim's active political and military past, yet ʿĪsā b. Muhannā's previous association with

FIGURE 9. Silver and gold coins from the Mamluk Sultanate. (Top) Damascus silver dirham of Baybars invoking the first Abbasid caliph of Cairo al-Mustanṣir as "Amīr al-Mu ʾminīn al-Imām al-Mustanṣir Abū'l-Qāsim Aḥmad b. al-Imām al-Ẓāhir," circa 659–60 AH / 1260–61 CE. (Bottom) Cairo gold dinar of Baybars invoking the second Abbasid caliph of Cairo al-Ḥākim as "al-Imām al-Ḥākim bi-Amrillāh Abū'l-ʿAbbās Aḥmad Amīr al-Mu ʾminīn," 661 AH / 1262 CE.

Top image courtesy American Numismatic Society, New York, NY, ANS 1971.286.1. Bottom image courtesy A H Baldwin and Sons, London (www.baldwins.co.uk), #4777.

al-Ḥākim during the days of al-Malik al-Nāṣir Yūsuf and al-Malik al-Muẓaffar Quṭuz could hardly have been a cause of distress in 660 / 1262. Far from there being grounds for an antagonistic relationship between Baybars and ʿĪsā b. Muhannā, the two had forged strong bonds of loyalty back when the former had fled Cairo during the reign of al-Malik al-Muʿizz Aybek al-Turkumānī (r. 640–55/1250–57). When Baybars was elevated to the position of sultan, he repaid ʿĪsā b. Muhannā's generous acts of kindness by designating him to be the leader of the Āl Faḍl, investing him with the towns of Sirmīn and Salamiyyah, and allotting him the region between Aleppo and Homs (*ammarahu ʿalā nuqrat Ḥalab ilā Ḥimṣ*).[73] Thus, the line of ʿAlī b. Ḥudhayfah, who had declined to assist Baybars in his former state of destitution, was deprived of its traditional position of Āl Faḍl leadership. Zāmil, the son of this ʿAlī b. Ḥudhayfah, sought to reclaim his hereditary role from Baybars, but the sultan was averse to risking the loss of the devotion and assistance of ʿĪsā b. Muhannā. Therefore, Zāmil had turned to the truly potent locus of internal resistance to Baybars's rule, that of Āqqūsh al-Barlī.[74]

Far from being an obsolete concern, the insurrection of Āqqūsh al-Barlī remained a troublesome menace well through the end of 660 AH. Even though al-Barlī was defeated and wounded by the Mongols near Sinjār on Sunday, Jumādā al-Ākhirah 14, 660 / May 6, 1262 while coming to the assistance of the besieged al-Malik al-Ṣāliḥ, he continued to remain outside of Baybars's orbit of influence for some time.[75] In order to resolve the matter, al-Malik al-Ẓāhir attempted to both cajole and threaten al-Barlī, stationed in al-Bīrah, in turn. Baybars al-Manṣūrī even asserts that al-Barlī defeated an army belonging to al-Malik al-Ẓāhir that was led by Jamāl al-Dīn al-Muḥammadī at this time, however al-Yūnīnī indicates that most of al-Barlī's troops defected to Egypt following their defeat by the Mongols. This latter point appears to be corroborated by Ibn ʿAbd al-Ẓāhir (620–92/1223–92), who notes the arrival of such troops at the court of the Mamluk sultan al-Malik al-Ẓāhir in the month of Shaʿbān (corresponding to June or July). Yet on the other side of the struggle for regional dominance, Hülegü dispatched al-Barlī's cousin Qūnū and Zayn al-Dīn Qarāghā al-Jamadār al-Nāṣirī, who had been captured from Aleppo, as messengers to persuade al-Barlī to enter the service of the Mongol ruler—an offer that he resolutely declined. Perhaps confronted by his inability to resist further Mongol encroachment beyond the lands of Mosul, al-Barlī determined to present himself to al-Malik al-Ẓāhir in Cairo and demonstrate his loyalty, whereupon al-Barlī insisted on deferring possession of al-Bīrah to his seemingly gracious and generous host. Upon al-Barlī's arrival and submission, al-Malik al-Ẓāhir at long last was able to consolidate his rule over geographical Syria.[76]

It was only after al-Barlī had submissively surrendered himself to Baybars's authority and power in Dhū'l-Ḥijjah 660 / October 1262, which also coincided with the arrival of Mongol delegation seeking the Mamluk sultan's protection, that Baybars recognized al-Ḥākim as caliph the following month. With the main locus of internal Mamluk resistance finally neutralized, the sudden dissension within the Mongol army between Berke and Hülegü, which resulted in the arrival of these roughly two hundred or so Mongol refugees, provided additional incentive for the inauguration of a caliph in their midst.[77] The Mongols were integrated into the Mamluk military system with the distribution of robes, horses, wealth, housing, and positions of leadership, converted to Islam, and witnessed yet another elaborated ceremony instating al-Ḥākim as the second

Abbasid caliph of Cairo. Similar to the earlier inauguration of al-Mustanṣir, al-Ḥākim's Abbasid pedigree was recited aloud and confirmed before an assorted congregation, and the military commanders, bureaucrats, judges, soldiers, and jurists of all ranks gave their allegiance to al-Ḥākim as caliph. And like al-Mustanṣir before him, al-Ḥākim was called upon to uphold the word of God and the model of His messenger, to enjoin good and forbid wrongdoing, to fight in God's way, and to acquire and distribute wealth properly. But perhaps in light of the wider audience for al-Ḥākim's pledge of allegiance, it also includes specific mention of the fulfillment of covenants, the establishment of criminal law and justice, and all else that imams are obliged to execute in matters of religion and protection of the Muslim community. Without delay, al-Ḥākim immediately delegated his caliphal duties to Baybars, and the Mamluk sultan was assigned to administer all territories and govern with justice. The following day, al-Ḥākim eloquently led the Friday congregational prayer with a speech prepared by Judge Muḥyī'l-Dīn Ibn ʿAbd al-Ẓāhir and then took up residence in the Cairene Citadel as the thirty-ninth Abbasid caliph.[78]

This elevation of an Abbasid caliph under Mamluk sovereignty presented a unique opportunity to establish a critical geo-political alliance between the Mamluk Sultanate and the Golden Horde and solidify the bonds of Islam, across conventional boundaries. In addition to matters of state, messengers were dispatched with vital news of al-Ḥākim's inauguration to the disaffected Mongol Khan Berke, a convert to Islam who had recently fallen out with Hülegü. In order to impress him with the new caliph's sacred lineage, the Egyptian chancery prepared a gold illuminated genealogy of al-Ḥākim linking him to the immediate family of the Prophet Muḥammad, who had been the nephew of the Abbasid dynasty's progenitor al-ʿAbbās. This document of the caliph's illustrious pedigree was ceremoniously utilized during his inauguration in front of the Mongol delegation and Mamluk elites before being sent to Berke, along with Chief Justice Tāj al-Dīn Ibn Bint al-Aʿazz's affirmation of its veracity. And since al-Ḥākim had not been invested with the sacramental trousers of *futuwwah* of his ancestors, al-Malik al-Ẓāhir Baybars delegated Atabeg Fāris al-Dīn Aqṭāy to initiate him on the sultan's behalf into the order's hallowed chain passing through the deceased al-Mustanṣir back to the Prophet's son-in-law ʿAlī. The following day, al-Ḥākim in turn delegated the atabeg to incorporate the Mongol emissaries to Berke into the *futuwwah* order associated with Abbasid caliphal supremacy.[79]

Illustrating the continued potency of the Abbasid dynasty in the aftermath of the Mongol conquest of Baghdad, yet another man asserting to be an Abbasid prince and potential claimant of the caliphate emerged during the reign of al-Malik al-Ẓāhir Baybars. In Ramaḍān 664 / June 1266, a man declaring himself to be al-Mubārak, the youngest son of the last Abbasid caliph al-Mustaʿṣim of Baghdad arrived in geographical Syria accompanied by a number of Bedouin leaders.[80] The story was plausible since it was well known that al-Mubārak was the only son of al-Mustaʿṣim to have been spared in the massacre. al-Mustaʿṣim's eldest son Abū'l-ʿAbbās Aḥmad (born in 631 / ca. 1233) and his middle son Abū'l-Faḍāʾil ʿAbd al-Raḥmān (born in 633/1235) had been killed shortly after their father in the Mongol encampment outside of Baghdad in 656/1258. Abū'l-Manāqib al-Mubārak (born in 640/1242), however, had been spared death and was taken as a captive of the Mongols.[81] As a result of his arrival in Muslim territory, the Mamluk sultan's deputy in Syria, the Amīr Jamāl al-Dīn al-Nujaymī (d. 677/1278),[82] ordered that he be hosted in the most dignified place and fashion. When Sultan Baybars arrived himself to Damascus, he dispatched the Baghdadian servant, a *ṭawāshī* named Mukhtār, who had recognized the now-deceased al-Mustanṣir Abū'l-Qāsim Aḥmad[83] and Jamāl al-Dīn b. al-Dawādār to see the Caliph al-Mustaʿṣim's youngest and only surviving son. However, neither one of them recognized him, and it was discovered that the man was not whom he claimed to be. As a result, the imposter was sent off to Cairo and held there for safe keeping,[84] presumably so that he could not foment any further trouble in Syria or attract a following eager to elevate a son of al-Mustaʿṣim to prominence. The claim of such a noble lineage, to be the son of the last Abbasid caliph of Baghdad, was clearly an invitation to restore the Islamic caliphate to the more immediate and symbolically charged line of the family, since al-Ḥākim was approximately four or five generations removed from his forefather, the twenty-ninth Abbasid caliph, al-Mustarshid, who had ruled so long ago in the early sixth/twelfth century.

The real al-Mubārak, however, lived out the rest of his days among the Mongols, where Ibn al-Kazarūnī says he was treated with respect (*kāna muḥtaraman ʿindahum*). There, he married and had children, before his death roughly twenty years later on Thursday, Jumādā al-Ūlā 2, 677 / September 21, 1278. al-Mubārak was then buried near the grave of the Abbasid caliph al-Mustarshid, who had been murdered in his camp outside of Marāghah and buried inside the town in 529/1135. It was an ironic place for the displaced son of the last Abbasid caliph of Baghdad to be buried, considering that al-Mustarshid was the Abbasid caliph from whom al-Ḥākim reigning in Cairo claimed his descent. Yet perhaps the decision to bury al-Mubārak there was a statement about the transfer of temporal power and legitimacy to the Mongols as much as it may have been a sign of respect for his dynastic heritage. Nevertheless, al-Mubārak was disinterred two years later and transferred from Marāghah to the former capital of his father. His coffin arrived in Baghdad on Thursday, Rajab 11, 679 / November 6, 1280 in the company of his eldest son, Abū Naṣr Muḥammad, and was taken to the Palace of Sūsiyān, where al-Mubārak's sister Khadījah and her husband Muḥyī'l-Dīn had resided after their own return. There on family grounds, next to the grave of his sister Khadījah, the youngest son of the last Abbasid caliph of Baghdad was finally laid to rest.[85]

FIGURE 10. Mausoleum of the Abbasid caliphs in Cairo next to the mosque of Sayyidah Nafīsah.

"Kairo: Kalifengräber" (1894), photographed by Charles Scolik (1853–1928), *Reise der Orietalischen Gesellschaft zu Leipzig: Sommer 1894* (Meiningen: Verlag von Junghanss & Koritzer, 1894–95). Princeton University Library, General Manuscripts Collection (Bound 2nd Series), C0938, no. 461, vol. 1.

Nonetheless, two months after the supposed appearance of al-Mubārak, a fifth man surfaced in Mamluk domains in Dhū'l-Qaʿdah 664 / August 1266 claiming to be a descendent of the Abbasid caliphs. The man was dark in coloring,[86] like al-Mustanṣir had been, and, in seeking out Baybars's dominion, perhaps he hoped to imitate the successful ascendance of al-Mustanṣir Abū'l-Qāsim Aḥmad to the caliphate in Cairo. This first Abbasid caliph of Cairo, al-Mustanṣir, even owed the popular nickname al-Zarabīnī to his coloring.[87] And al-Dhahabī indicates, by way of explanation, that al-Mustanṣir's mother was of Ethopian descent.[88] The attempt of this most recent Abbasid claimant to gain recognition as a member of that august family and hence access to ceremonial power and prestige was not, however, met with the same success. And the claimant was duly shipped off to Egypt as the man claiming to be al-Mubarak had been sent off before him.[89] Instead of being dislodged by such rival claimants, al-Ḥākim continued to reign as caliph under Mamluk suzereignty until his death many decades years later on Jumādā al-Ūlā 18, 701 / January 19, 1302. He was buried near the tomb of the Prophet Muḥammad's saintly great-great-great-granddaughter al-Sayyidah Nafīsah (145–208/762–824) in Cairo,[90] solidifying his connection with the prophetic household and their spiritual role in sheparding the Muslim community. And al-Ḥākim was the progenitor of a new line of Abbasid caliphs in Cairo that would last until the Ottoman conquest of Egypt in the tenth/sixteenth century.

EMBRACING COMMUNAL CONTINUITY

Thus, within Mamluk domains, the dilemma of caliphal absence was resolved by resurrecting the Abbasid Caliphate in Cairo as a doubly political and spiritual institution, where the caliph delegated his authority to govern to the sultan and radiated metaphysical blessings through his mere presence. Emblematic of this resolution was the momentous approbation of Ibn ʿAbd al-Salām, who was reputed to never swerve in his pursuit of truth and justice. Baybars is even reported to have said that he never felt fully secure in his rule until the death of this formidable scholar, who inspired intense popular loyalty and adherence. So immense was the wide regard in which he was held that Muslim congregations across Egypt, geographical Syria, Mesopotamia, Mecca, Medina, and Yemen gathered to perform funeral prayers for Ibn ʿAbd al-Salām in absentia upon receiving news of his death, and the streets of Cairo themselves were thronged with people following his funeral procession.[91] Given his standing, Ibn ʿAbd al-Salām's attendance at the ceremony elevating al-Mustanṣir to the caliphate was widely noted. As a link in the community's transmission of knowledge and practice, or the substance of communal memory, Ibn ʿAbd al-Salām's participation conveyed an importance sense of scholarly approval of the renewed institution, its integrity, and the legal soundness of its reestablishment.[92] al-Dhahabī additionally mentions a first-hand account from Ibn ʿAbd al-Salām to Jamāl al-Dīn Muḥammad al-Mālikī of how this leading figure among the scholars, *Sulṭān al-ʿUlamāʾ*, commanded and even preceded the Mamluk sultan Baybars in pledging allegiance to the new caliph:

> When we began to pledge our allegiance to al-Mustanṣir, I said to al-Malik al-Ẓāhir, "Give your pledge to him (*bāyiʿhu*)." So he replied, "I cannot do it well, but you give your pledge first, and I will [pledge] after you."

Discussing the events of the next day following al-Mustanṣir's inauguration as caliph, Ibn ʿAbd al-Salām further communicated:

> So after we contracted the pledge, we came the next day to the Sultan who praised the Caliph and said, "Among his blessings is that I entered the house yesterday and intended to find a place to pray, and I saw an obtrusive bench (*maṣṭabah nāfirah*). So I said to a servant, 'Destroy this.' And when they razed it, an underground passage opened up beneath it (*infataḥa taḥtahā sarab*). So they descended into it, and lo and behold, there were numerous boxes filled with gold and silver from the treasure of al-Malik al-Kāmil, May God have mercy on him."[93]

Through this narration, Ibn ʿAbd al-Salām conveys the sultan's appropriate deference to the position of the learned in society as well as his humble recognition of the caliph's metaphysical blessings upon his military patron and host. The dramatic contrast between this warm approval and Ibn ʿAbd al-Salām's earlier resistance to legitimize Baybars's assumption of the sultanate, because of his questionable origins, indicates just how powerfully the reconstituted Abbasid Caliphate of Cairo continued to resonate politically, legally, and culturally within Mamluk society.

Within Mamluk domains, Muslim literary and cultural elites energetically embraced this new caliphate as a continuation of the Islamic caliphate lost to them in Baghdad. By recalling the pain of disruption, the sermon that the Egyptian judge Muḥyī'l-Dīn Ibn ʿAbd al-Ẓāhir composed in 661/1262 for al-Ḥākim to read from the pulpit, for the Friday congregational prayers following his assumption of the caliphate, eloquently makes this case. It centers on the poignant theme of the caliphate's traumatic eradication that is followed by jubilant restoration. Beginning with the words, "O people, know that the imamate is an obligation among the obligations of Islam," the sermon continues to dwell on the heinous atrocities committed by the Mongols in the Abode of Peace, Baghdad. The indiscriminate slaughter, the illicit usurpation of wealth, the mortifying rape of its women, and the atrocious assault on the sanctity of the caliphate are coupled with emotive evocations of the screaming, weeping, and terror experienced by the city's Muslim inhabitants. Remembering these painful circumstances helps to augment the sensations of gratitude that the sermon ultimately seeks to inspire. al-Malik al-Ẓāhir Baybars has aided and revived the august Abbasid Caliphate, and the restoration of such an integral Islamic institution is a blessing from God Himself. And when the congregation is reminded of their religious obligations to obey the community's leaders (the caliph, the sultan, and the scholars of the community), it is through invocation of a Qur'anic verse (4:59) that reinscribes the continued discursive relevance and necessity of the restored caliphate in Cairo.[94]

Such active participation of the day's most prominent judges, jurists, and scholars of all ranks at the inaugural and subsequent ceremonies for al-Mustanṣir and al-Ḥākim affirmed the legality of the resuscitated caliphate and underscored its broad socio-cultural acceptance.[95] And in their written works, contemporary and near contemporary historians of the era paralleled Ibn ʿAbd al-Ẓāhir's concerns over the riveting cultural trauma of the caliphate's absence, which served to enhance their expressions of joy over its reconstitution. Thus, the disquieting notions of caliphal absence and disruption figure prominently in historical records of the interim period, with frequent reference to the caliphate's disturbing vacancy.[96] In his *Siyar Aʿlām al-Nubalāʾ*, for instance, al-Dhahabī remarks, "The Abbasid imamate was disrupted for three years and some months with the death of al-Mustaʿṣim." By selecting the jurisprudential word *imāmah* to refer to the caliphate, as many authors of this era frequently did, al-Dhahabī both indicates and incorporates the dominant juristic discourse about the institution's legal necessity into his biographical dictionary of Muslim luminaries.[97]

Chroniclers also frequently draw attention to the dilemma of caliphal absence at the beginning of each annual assessment following the Mongol destruction of Baghdad. al-Yūnīnī, Ibn Shākir al-Kutubī, and Ibn al-Dawādārī, for example, often state that such-and-such a year commenced while the Muslims were without a caliph. And al-Yūnīnī particularly emphasizes this fact for the years in which al-Mustanṣir and al-Ḥākim are installed as caliphs, as if seeking to provide a contextual backdrop to highlight the significance of what would later transpire—and be recorded amid the events of those years.[98] For those specific years, 659 and 661 AH, al-Yūnīnī additionally acknowledges the presence of the Hafsids in western North Africa among various other local rulers, without in fact bestowing universal legitimacy and authority upon their claims to a regional caliphate.[99] For Ibn Shākir al-Kutubī and Ibn al-Dawādārī, however, the calamity appears to be so overwhelming that it dominates the opening lines of each and every year of caliphal vacancy.[100] Nor does Ibn al-Dawādārī seem willing to acknowledge the yawning gap between al-Mustanṣir's death and al-Ḥākim's reinstatement, which effectively constituted another transitory moment of official caliphal absence. Rather, he asserts that the caliphate was filled by al-Ḥākim's mere arrival on Egyptian soil in 660 AH, well before official recognition of his position.[101] Strikingly mirroring Ibn al-Dawādārī's arrangement, the Coptic historian Ibn Abī'l-Faḍāʾil likewise notes the absence of a caliph for the year 659 AH in a reflection of broader historiographical norms.[102] Ibn Shākir al-Kutubī, on the other hand, makes subtle reference to the advent of al-Ḥākim while later acknowledging the vacancy of the caliphate until his reappointment in 661 AH.[103] Even generations later, Jalāl al-Dīn al-Suyūṭī (d. 911/1505) continues to emphasize the calamity of this period of caliphal absence by dramatically repeating the following annual notations:

> Then entered the year 657, and the world was without a caliph.... Then entered the year 658, and the period (*al-waqt*) was still without a caliph.... Then entered the year 659, and the period (*al-waqt*) was still without a caliph, until Rajab when the caliphate was established in Egypt and the *bay'ah* was given to al-Mustanṣir as we will relate. And the period of the caliphate's absence was three and a half years.[104]

Or as Ibn Duqmāq (d. 809/1407) had earlier exclaimed, "The caliphate was cut off from Baghdad, and the world remained without a caliph until the year 659 during the time of al-Malik al-Ẓāhir Rukn al-Dīn Baybars al-Bunduqdārī."[105]

This devastating absence of a caliphate, mandated by Islamic law and culturally associated with poignant communal memories of Muslim glory and prestige, therefore prefigures and contextualizes contemporaries and near contemporaries' expressions of joy over its continuation. One contemporary from Basra, Alī b. Abī'l-Faraj b. al-Ḥusayn al-Baṣrī, was relieved to see how the symbolic absences of a caliph that had caused great anxiety and despondency were redressed; gold and silver coins were minted in the name of al-Mustanṣir, and the pulpits of congregational mosques rung out with prayers for the new caliph by name on Fridays after a disruption of three long years. In al-Baṣrī's estimation, the whole world rejoiced over al-Mustanṣir's caliphate, and his leadership (imamate) steadied the foundations of Islam (*tabāsharat al-dunyā bi-khilāfatih wa'staqarrat da'ā'im al-islām bi-imāmatih*).[106] On the later inauguration of al-Ḥākim, Baybars al-Manṣūrī similarly exulted in seeing the legal and ritual vacuum of the caliphate filled. Indeed, he perceived it as a duty, commenting, "It would not have been befitting to neglect pledging allegiance to the leader of humankind from whom the legality of the Friday congregational prayer and the daily congregational prayers of Islam would be derived."[107] This affective element continued to draw the attention of future generations of historians, like Ibn Ḥabīb al-Ḥalabī, who discussed the restoration of the Abbasid Caliphate in Cairo as the foundation of the nascent Mamluk Sultanate. In the succinct picture he paints, political legitimacy was restored, the affairs of state were stabilized, people's inner thoughts were made happy (*surrat al-khawāṭir*), their chests expanded in relief (*insharaḥat al-ṣudūr*), and they could now pluck the fruits of emotive elation (*quṭifat min jinān al-hanā' thimāruhā al-janiyyah*). The palpable emotions that caused physical constriction and political instability gave way to readily abundant joy with the elevation of al-Mustanṣir, followed by al-Ḥākim, as caliph.[108]

In this vein, Muslim authors in the seventh/thirteenth and eighth/fourteenth centuries clearly emphasize the continuity of the Abbasid Caliphate at the helm of Islamic leadership between Baghdad and Cairo. In addition to the public celebrations of al-Mustanṣir's and al-Ḥākim's genealogies, literary sources of the era express a remarkably near universal recognition of the familial bond of al-Mustanṣir and al-Ḥākim with previous Abbasid caliphs and embrace the authenticity of their noble descent from the Abbasid dynasty. Even though the primary accounts contain divergent genealogies in the case of al-Hākim, the veracity of both caliphal candidates' lineage is acknowledged by the overwhelming majority of those who transmit it.[109] Among Mamluk-era historians, statistical analyses as well as descriptive phrases and personal markers were essential tools in asserting the continuity between the new Abbasid caliphs in Cairo with the earlier Abbasids of Baghdad. Baybars al-Manṣūrī, for instance, extols al-Mustanṣir as "the first to arrive from the caliphs of the Abbasid dynasty (who have reigned) since the beginnings of the Islamic community (*al-millah al-Islāmiyyah*)."[110] And other contemporaries observe that the first caliph inaugurated in Cairo was even granted "the honorific title of his brother," al-Mustanṣir Abū Jaʿfar, who ruled in Baghdad from 623/1226 to 640/1242. With the familial relationship perceived as a matter of fact, this unprecedented duplication of regnal titles among Abbasid caliphs evoked al-Mustanṣir Abū'l-Qāsim's personal and political connection with the dynastic past as well as the blessings (*tabarruk*) contemporaries saw in those living links. al-Baṣrī also conveys the auspicious sign that both brothers were inaugurated as caliph on the same date of Rajab 13th, though some thirty-seven years apart.[111] Even such seemingly trivial information as al-Mustanṣir's being one of the five pairs of brothers ever appointed to the Abbasid Caliphate or the rarity of al-Ḥākim's not having inherited his position in the footsteps of his father or grandfather offer the chance for these historians to incorporate the Cairo-based caliphs fully into the Abbasid dynasty by prompting citations of all parallel examples among the previous Abbasid caliphs.[112] An even more concise mechanism of integration is the simple references to al-Mustanṣir and al-Ḥākim as the thirty-eighth and thirty-ninth Abbasid caliphs respectively, continuing the numeration from Baghdad.[113] The new caliphs are also referred to as *Amīr al-Muʾminīn* (Commander of the Faithful), *Khalīfat al-Muslimīn* (Caliph of the Muslims), *al-Imām* (the Leader), *Mawlānā al-Khalīfah* (Our Master the Caliph), and *al-Sayyid* (The Master). Mention of their names could also elicit the invocation *alayhi al-salām* ("Peace be upon him") typically reserved for prophets, thereby establishing a mental association between the caliphs and the most honorable of men appointed by God. Even upon their deaths, authors invoked the superior posthumous supplication *raḍiya Allāhu ʿanhu* ("May God be pleased with him") rather than the more conventional invocation of God's mercy, *raḥimahu Allāhu* ("May God have mercy on him").[114] Or as Baybars al-Manṣūrī skillfully encapsulates the history of the institution's reestablishment, "The caliphate had been vacant since the time of al-Mustaʿṣim's killing, so the sultan rejoiced to bring about the means of restoring it (*ittiṣāl asbābihā*), to renew its robes (*athwāb*), to establish its light (*manār*), and to manifest its distinguishing features (*shiʿār*) so that it would rest on a firm foundation and be connected to the Abbasids."[115]

ENDURING SALIENCE

Given the deep religious and socio-cultural resonances of the reconstituted caliphate in Cairo, the relationship of caliphs' authority to the wielding of power continued to crop up as a magnet for political discussion, activity, and debate over the centuries of Mamluk rule. In particular, the caliphs repeatedly found themselves at the center of intrigues to wrest control away from ruling sultans, to whom they, after all, had theoretically delegated their powers. And it was precisely fear of this potent threat embodied by the Cairene Abbasid caliphs that induced multiple Mamluk sultans to limit the extent of the caliphs' mobility and social interactions. In response, Mamluk sultans often encountered active resistance and resentment over their treatment of Abbasid caliphs from among the populace, religious scholars, and other members of the military elite, who upheld the memorialized claims of the institution to religious sanctity and socio-political esteem.

One early contestation (and subsequent precedent) over the caliph's primacy and legal prerogatives within the Mamluk State involved a thorny case of leadership and succession. When the Sultan al-Malik al-Nāṣir Muḥammad b. Qalāwūn (d. 741/1341) retreated to al-Karak, closing the second of his three reigns, Mamluk military commanders requested that the Cairene Abbasid caliph al-Mustafkī II Sulaymān (683–740/1285–1340) officially designate his replacement. With the symbolic and legal weight of the caliphate behind him, al-Mustafkī delegated Baybars al-Jāshankīr (d. 709/1310) as sultan. Yet this alternate sultanate was shortlived. Within a year, al-Malik al-Nāṣir resumed control of the Mamluk State. Nevertheless, some chroniclers take the view that the sultan never forgot the caliph's supposed preference for Baybars al-Jāshankīr. Years later, the sultan made al-Mustafkī and his family virtual prisoners in the citadel. For several months, al-Mustafkī neither came nor went nor received visitors, who might prove to be seditious in the eyes of the sultan. After a fleeting reprieve, a renewed aggravation prompted the sultan to banish the caliph and reportedly almost one hundred of his relatives to Qūṣ in Upper Egypt, once and for all, far from the locus of power. His contemporary, the historian Ibn al-Wardī (689–749/1290–1349), composed a poem, invoking the literary heritage of al-Maʿarrī (d. 449/1057), to lament the Abbasids' forcible departure: "They have exiled you to Upper Egypt, with an excuse that bears no glory in my religion and belief. Upper Egypt will not alter you, rather you will be like swords in their scabbards." Although the Abbasid caliph was hidden away in Qūṣ like a sword tucked into its scabbard, his inherent worth and potency—and that of his heirs—would not be diminished. Even in his early twenties, the Caliph al-Mustafkī's aura of gravitas had inspired such awe and reverence that the eminent historian al-Dhahabī admiringly recalled the details of his personage, bearing, and dress decades later. In exile, in his venerable fifties, the longstanding caliph designated his successor to the Abbasid Caliphate, his son Aḥmad, in front of a grand assembly of forty well-respected witnesses.

Upon the caliph's death in 740/1340, however, the sultan refused to acknowledge this selection of a successor. The judge presiding over the region of Qūṣ, where al-Mustafkī had lived, had legally certified the validity of Aḥmad's designation as the new caliph. Initially, he was referred to as al-Mustanṣir III, adopting the same regnal title as the very first recognized Abbasid caliph of Cairo, thereby signaling his legitimacy and caliphal continuity. Yet the sultan was adamant. In seeking to deprive al-Mustafkī's son of the prestige and power of the caliphate, the Sultan al-Malik al-Nāṣir identified another member of the Abbasid family for the position, Abū Isḥāq Ibrāhīm, who was the deceased caliph's dissolute nephew. Leading scholars informed the sultan that Ibrāhīm was not personally qualified for the honor and attempted to dissuade him. Nevertheless, the sultan brought Ibrāhīm to Cairo and had him publicly display his repentence of past immoralities. When the scholars still did not assent to endorse Ibrāhīm's suitability for caliphal office, the sultan unilaterally declared him caliph as al-Wāthiq II. However, registering their disapproval, preachers conspicuously abstained from mentioning his name in prayer from the pulpits on Fridays. And people generally referred to him insultingly as al-Mustaʿṭā rather than as al-Wāthiq. Chroniclers commonly refused to consider him to be a caliph at all. Within four months, the Sultan al-Malik al-Nāṣir died, and Chief Justice Ibn Jamāʿah along with other Mamluk judges reaffirmed the Islamic legal rights of al-Mustafkī's son Aḥmad, who was restored amid wide acclaim to his position as Abbasid caliph. Henceforth, he would be known as al-Ḥākim II (r. 741–53/1341–52), which evoked the glorious memory of his grandfather as the first long-lived Abbasid caliph of Cairo. On the other hand, in the more colorful interpretation of what the later polymath Jalāl al-Dīn al-Suyūṭī would describe as divine retribution for mistreating the Abbasids; the son whom al-Malik al-Nāṣir had chosen to succeed him was speedily dislodged from the sultanate and sent into exile in Qūṣ.[116] Reciprocal recompenses aside, in the fine balancing act between the prerogatives of the caliph and the sultan, there were limits. And all of the parties involved wielded some measure of power within Mamluk society. Even when the sultan unilaterally imposed his position, scholars and religious functionaries could withhold their approbation and consent. And popular dissent could also translate into rebellion.

The memorable reign of al-Mutawakkil II ʿAbdullāh (who lived ca. 745–808 / ca. 1344–1406) as Abbasid caliph highlights the potential perils for the foremost

Mamluk to lose his grip on power if he exceeded these bounds. During al-Mutawakkil's sixteenth year as caliph, in the year 779/1377, the military leader Aynbek b. ʿAbdallāh al-Badrī (d. 780/1378) assumed control of the Mamluk State as the atabeg domineering over a seven-year-old sultan installed following the rebellion that had deposed his father. Initially, al-Mutawakkil, who was described by the contemporaneous al-Qalqashandī (756–821/1355–1418) as a handsome and unassuming man of intellect and stature, had been asked to assume the sultanate instead, but he had declined. Aynbek was reportedly envious of the caliph and presumably wary of him as a rival for power, and in their histories of the era, Ibn Qāḍī Shuhbah (779–851/1377–1448) and Ibn Ḥajar al-ʿAsqalānī (773–852/1372–1449) mention that al-Mutawakkil had adamantly refused to sign off on Aynbek's plans to depose the young sultan. Aynbek therefore sent al-Mutawakkil into exile to Qūṣ, to which al-Mustafkī had been banished before him. Yet people interceded on the caliph's behalf, and Aynbek relented. The next day, however, he attempted to install another Abbasid, Najm al-Dīn Zakariyyā, who was the son of the discredited al-Wāthiq II, as caliph instead—without a proper pledge of allegiance. Yet this illicit attempt to elevate a rival caliph lasted only a matter of weeks. This time, it was other Mamluk military leaders who pointedly persuaded Aynbek that his actions to depose al-Mutawakkil as caliph were not justifiable. Aynbek's deputies rebelled, and the once-powerful atabeg soon lost his life. In al-Qalqashandī's estimation and attention to affect, Aynbek's overreach and transgression against the Abbasid caliph alienated the army and caused their hearts to turn against him (*taghayyarat ʿalayhi al-mamālik [al-mamālīk] wa-nafarat minhu qulūb al-ʿaskar*). Indeed, the Turkish Ibn Duqmāq (750–809/1349–1406), another contemporary who was the grandson of a Mamluk military leader and closely connected with the military sphere, lauded al-Mutawakkil as a guiding beacon who embodied the luminous and affective cultural memories of his Abbasid forefathers and the Islamic caliphate. One of the supplications that Ibn Duqmāq made for al-Mutawakkil also beseeches God to nurture the Abbasid in the way of the first Rightly Guided Caliphs who abided by truth and justice. Such prayers intimate how musings about the contemporary Cairene Abbasid caliph were anchored in the seminal memories of the Islamic community's formation.[117]

When a later and more tenacious Mamluk sultan al-Malik al-Ẓāhir Barqūq (d. 801/1399) escalated his efforts to dislodge al-Mutawakkil as caliph, he ended up losing his own throne. Prompted by the rumor of a rebellion brewing with caliphal support, Barqūq took the precaution of imprisoning the Abbasid caliph al-Mutawakkil in the citadel in 785/1383. Reportedly informing the sultan's decision were the admissions of two badgered and somewhat improbably accused men, who were all too ready upon interrogation to cast the blame at al-Mutawakkil's feet. But the Abbasid caliph assiduously denied any knowledge or involvement. Only recently installed as sultan, and the first of the Circassian Mamluk rulers, Barqūq must have felt insecure in his control of affairs, and the general plausibility of a plot against him and in favor of the Abbasid caliph of many years must have stoked his ire. Barqūq is said to have flown toward al-Mutawakkil in a rage, sword unsheathed, and one of the sultan's deputies had to intervene and shield the caliph (as well as his patron's reputation). And when the sultan expressed a desire for his presumed adversary's public execution, the sultan's deputy and all those present invoked their explicit fear that attempting to kill the caliph would incite the masses to attack them instead (in one rendition, *matā samarnā al-khalīfah rajamatnā al-ʿāmmah*). Thus, Sultan Barqūq had to content himself with imprisoning al-Mutawakkil and deposing him as caliph.[118]

In his stead, the sultan elevated ʿUmar, yet another son of the disreputable al-Wāthiq II, to the Abbasid Caliphate. The bold selection of al-Wāthiq III as ʿUmar's regnal name clearly asserted the sultan's primacy in such matters of leadership and authority, harkening back as it did to an earlier sultan's intrepid choice of caliph. Like al-Malik al-Nāṣir before him, Barqūq would not relent from this course of action, despite the avid efforts of people to persuade him that al-Mutawakkil should be restored to the caliphate. Upon al-Wāthiq III's death in 788/1386, Barqūq even turned to Aynbek's short-lived candidate for the position (from nearly a decade before) and installed him too as caliph, rather than revert to the venerable al-Mutawakkil. In fact, it was precisely the deposed Abbasid caliph's popularity that rendered him so potentially perilous from the sultan's perspective. Throughout the long six years of al-Mutawakkil's imprisonment, as his contemporary al-Qalqashandī reports, people considered him alone to be the legitimate caliph. And the same year that Barqūq inaugurated his second substitute caliph in 788/1386, he also successfully squelched a small popular rebellion that listed the sultan's mistreatment of al-Mutawakkil among its chief grievances. Known as the Ẓāhirī revolt, this obscure idealistic clique aspired to resuscitate an Islamic caliphate with a strong Qurashī leader at the helm rather than a corrupt and oppressive Mamluk sultan. But without broader social and military support, they were doomed to fail.[119]

Just three years later, however, Barqūq was not so successful in preserving his sultanate. In 791/1389, a large military coalition of Mamluks from Syria, led by the governor of Aleppo, Yalbughā al-Nāṣirī (d. 793/1391), underscored the imprisonment of the Abbasid caliph al-Mutawakkil as one of their main arguments for overthrowing Barqūq. Certainly, other factors were involved, not the least of which was the soured personal histories of al-Nāṣirī and the others with Sultan Barqūq—as detailed by Ibn Khaldūn (732–808/1332–1406), who by then had been a resident of Cairo for some seven years and was a careful observer. But as Ibn Khaldūn additionally notes, al-Nāṣirī got on his soapbox, as it were, and railed long and hard about how the sultan had imprisoned the caliph (*taʿālā ʿalā al-Sulṭān bi-ḥabsihi al-khalīfah wa-aṭāla al-nakīr fī dhālik*). Therefore, as the hostile armed forces closed in and captured the major city of Damascus, Barqūq apologized to the long-suffering Abbasid in Cairo, freed him, and officially reappointed him to the caliphate. Moreover, the increasingly beleaguered sultan now sought to demonstrate his reverence for the Abbasid in public. After undertaking necessary preparations, he ostentatiously celebrated al-Mutawakkil's resumption of the caliphate with a magnificent ceremony followed by a major procession through the streets of his capital, rippling with the black banners of the Abbasids. The glorious event projected an image of harmonious unison among Mamluk commanders, judges, and the jubilant masses in support of the Abbasid Caliphate. Yet it was too late for Barqūq: the Mamluk sultan soon found himself dethroned and imprisoned in al-Karak. In the meantime, his victorious opponent al-Nāṣirī went out of his way to honor al-Mutawakkil and proudly declared in at least one gathering of Mamluk military leaders that he had only raised his sword against Barqūq in order to aid the Commander of the Faithful (*Yā Amīr al-Mu'minīn, mā ḍarabtu bi-sayfī hādhā illā fī nuṣratik!*).[120]

Barqūq's intriguing efforts to control the caliphate illustrate the various arts of persuasion and compulsion that could be brought to bear upon a Mamluk sultan to honor the rights of an Abbasid caliph. Barqūq likely interpreted his predecessors' lack of success to al-Malik al-Nāṣir's rapid demise and Aynbek's inherent weakness. Yet the more Barqūq exerted his will to deny the caliphate to the distinguished al-Mutawakkil, the more dissent spread and took increasingly dangerous forms. This broad social undercurrent shifted from persuasive advice, to wider discontent, to popular rebellion, to successful military revolt. Moreover, this last dramatic turn of events met with some measure of official religious sanction. After the completion of al-Nāṣirī's coup, the state council of high-ranking jurists in Damascus issued a legal decision against the defeated Barqūq (which intriguingly the visiting Ibn Khaldūn also signed) on the grounds that the former sultan had transgressed egregiously. Central among these offenses was Barqūq's unlawful deposition of the caliph. Thus, for scholars and soldiers alike, the claims of the Cairene Abbasid Caliphate on communal memories and emotions remained a potent force to be duly respected. Accordingly, after Barqūq successfully managed to regain the Mamluk Sultanate, following many months in exile plotting his return, the chastened ruler wisely honored al-Mutawakkil as caliph and demonstrated a more symbolically symbiotic relationship with the Abbasid for the duration of his reign.

Yet in his magisterial work, Ibn Khaldūn further clarifies what was at the heart of it all, what exactly the Abbasid Caliphate meant for the Mamluk society of his day. Having been appointed to the formal institution of the caliphate, it was al-Mutawakkil who was necessary to legitimate religious offices according to the Sacred Law, as will be elaborated in the next chapter. Moreover, it was invocation of his name from all the region's pulpits as caliph that invited divine blessings, through a combination of people's reverence for his Abbasid ancestors, their act of continuing righteous customs in seeking such blessings, the perfection of people's faith by loving them, and the Cairene Abbasids' realization of all the legal prerequisites for the imamate.[121] This powerful blend of memorial practices—the imitation of the community's righteous predecessors, the following of prophetic guidance by implementing Sacred Law, the perpetuation of august historical institutions—coalesced around the figure of the Cairene Abbasid caliph. By imprisoning him, Barqūq had affronted the community's deeper sense of meaning. And by honoring him, such Muslims communally sought to attain God's grace and individually strove to perfect their faith through love.

Even so, the evocative memory of a ruling caliph was such that al-Mutawakkil's son, the Cairene Abbasid al-Mustaʿīn II al-ʿAbbās (r. 808–16/1406–14), was briefly declared to be the sultan in 815/1412. al-Mustaʿīn had assumed the caliphate upon his father's death in 808/1406 as his designated heir and had cooperated with the Mamlūk sultan al-Malik al-Nāṣir Faraj (791–815/1389–1412), joining him on some of his expeditions. But several years later, al-Mustaʿīn unexpectedly found himself in Damascus in the middle of a contest for power. As a group of officers and officials waged a protracted uprising against al-Nāṣir, they had a brilliant inspiration: it would dramatically improve their chances of success if they could draw on the Abbasid caliph's authority and influence by declaring *him* to be the new sultan. The rebels chose one of their own, the chief secretary of the Mamluk chancery, to approach al-Mustaʿīn with the idea, but the caliph adamantly declined. So they devised a ruse. Lured by lucrative promises, the caliph's half-brother rode through the streets reciting a proclamation in al-Mustaʿīn's name, disparaging and deposing al-Nāṣir Faraj as sultan and forbidding anyone from assisting him. If he had feared for his life in opposing al-Nāṣir Faraj before, al-Mustaʿīn was now faced with no other option, and he threw himself into his new role, declaring a sultanate while fully expecting dismal failure.

Yet if the rebels had repeatedly failed in their previous attempts to dislodge al-Malik al-Nāṣir Faraj, the intense appeal of the Abbasid Caliphate would alter their destiny. As Ibn Taghribirdī shrewdly observed, they would not have been able to assume control of the state without the caliph (*lawlā al-khalīfah mā 'ntaẓama lahum amrun li-ʿiẓam mayl al-turkumān wa'l-ʿāmmah li'l-Malik al-Nāṣir*). However, the claims of the caliph upon people's hearts and minds would outweigh the popularity of al-Nāṣir Faraj. And al-Mustaʿīn's contingent was sure to exploit the powerful attraction of an Abbasid caliph once again resuming absolute sovereignty—long a nostalgic memory—by assuming the Mamluk Sultanate for himself. Utilizing his expertise in crafting persuasive rhetoric, the chief secretary effectively argued al-Mustaʿīn's case in public declarations. And they placed a throne for al-Mustaʿīn at an open-air site of high visibility across from the large congregational mosque Jāmiʿ Karīm al-Dīn al-Khilāṭī. Rather comically, al-Mustaʿīn's formal Abbasid attire as sultan-caliph was the black outfit that the mosque's preacher used for his regular sermons. More poignantly, the clothes that the preacher wore on Friday to signal his legitimacy—

that he was appointed in a state symbolically consecrated by an Abbasid caliph (with black being considered as the Abbasids' color)—had become the very clothes to signify the sultan-caliph's supreme dominion. On Saturday afternoon, Muḥarram 25, 815 / May 7, 1412, as al-Mustaʿīn sat regally on his throne, the crier rode back and forth so all could hear him and loudly proclaimed that al-Nāṣir Faraj had been deposed as sultan and replaced by the caliph, the Commander of the Faithful, al-Mustaʿīn. It was therefore unlawful for anyone to aid or abet the deposed al-Nāṣir Faraj, and whoever came over to the caliph's side would be safe with respect to his wealth and his life. And the caliph had declared a grace period until Thursday for people to declare their allegiance and assistance to him. These strident proclamations were repeated at various locations for maximum effect among al-Nāṣir Faraj's troops and the population of Damascus.

Faced with these unexpected developments after over one hundred and fifty years of more-or-less anticipated arrangements, the city was divided. One camp of people declared it utter disbelief to disregard the caliph's command—that it was, in essence, disobedience to God and his messenger. And another camp declared it was obligatory to support the Sultan al-Nāṣir—that it flouted Islamic law to rebel against the ruling sovereign. Ironically, both sides had their arguments rooted in the same Islamic legal and religious discourses. But as the expedient pact between Abbasid caliph and Mamluk sultan ruptured, who should be considered as the head of state? Subsequently, al-Nāṣir Faraj's fortunes began to decline. And, in the end, the question was settled by the military victory of al-Mustaʿīn's allies, which received the sanction of a consortium of Egyptian and Syrian scholars. Thus, the Mamluk State came to be presided over by a sultan-caliph, unified in the person of al-Mustaʿīn. In his official documents and correspondence, al-Mustaʿīn's magnificence was proclaimed through a multitude of honorifics. He was the Commander of the Faithful, Leader of Muslims, Caliph of the Lord of the Worlds, Nephew of the Master of Messengers, the Slave of God and His Protected Friend, and the Imam. Such succinct phrases telegraphed that his authority derived from the weighty precedents of Islamic law and history and that the sanctity of his rule was bound to God, His prophet, the righteous successors, and a glorious dynasty thereafter. In keeping with this singular status, the official coinage was reputedly reissued in al-Mustaʿīn's name alone.

Nevertheless, the established patterns of Mamluk politics quickly derailed the experiment. Initially, the two rebel leaders, Shaykh (d. 824/1421) and Nawrūz (d. 817/1414), had established themselves quite literally by the sultan-caliph's side. Still at the palace in Damascus, they both sat in official gatherings of the sultan-caliph with Shaykh on al-Mustaʿīn's right and Nawrūz on al-Mustaʿīn's left. But after Shaykh reportedly deployed some tactics of reverse psychology, Nawrūz resolved to assume the governorship of Damascus along with a free hand in the lands of Syria, leaving the affairs of Egypt to Shaykh as the atabeg.

Yet back in the Mamluk capital in Cairo, Shaykh gradually encroached upon the caliph's powers as sultan until he had supplanted him entirely in that role. The by-now old and familiar patterns of retaining a capable sultan from the military elite alongside a blessed caliph to preside over ceremonial occasions had reasserted themselves. Yet in Damascus, Nawrūz, clinging to the ideal of absolute caliphal supremacy, procured a legal opinion that Shaykh's actions were illegitimate and resolved to fight the new usurper. In turn, Shaykh consulted with the chief justice (who had incidentally lost this post for a spell under al-Mustaʿīn's sultanate) and deposed al-Mustaʿīn as caliph.[122] Even as al-Mustaʿīn's unique sultanate and then caliphate unraveled, the intricacies of the situation continued to reveal how deeply the Abbasid caliphs were enmeshed in the travails of Mamluk society and politics. And as the Mamluk Sultanate entered a period of relative stability, the Abbasid Caliphate remained an integral component of social thought and identity. As for the panegyric that Ibn Ḥajar had composed during the Caliph al-Mustaīn's seventh-month reign as sultan, it remained a famous piece of cultural lore for over a century,[123] down through the last years of the Mamluk Sultanate and through the Ottoman conquest.

Although the Abbasid Caliphate was resurrected in the Mamluk State as a significant religio-political institution, other premodern polities adopted different solutions to the dilemma of caliphal absence. In South Asia, for example, the Delhi Sultanate clung to the remaining legitimizing vestiges of the last Abbasid caliph of Baghdad, propagating his name on its coinage long after his death—as did the independent Muslim rulers of Bengal. The silver tanka of the Delhi sultan Kayūmarth included in figure 11, for example, still mentioned the last Abbasid caliph of Baghdad al-Mustaʿṣim in 689/1290, more than three decades after his death. Similar numismatic patterns, discussed by Heidemann, appeared in Yemen and Anatolia. Yemeni coins continued to invoke the last Abbasid caliph of Baghdad into the ninth/fifteenth century, and Anatolian coins variously included posthumous references to al-Mustaʿṣim, the testimony of faith, and fictive caliphs whose names may have provided opportunities for local political maneuverings.[124]

It was only many decades after al-Mustaʿṣim's death in the Mongol onslaught on Baghdad that ambitious military leaders in South Asia began to seek official deputization of their rule from the Abbasid caliph in Cairo thus interjecting his authority into local politics. Delegations from India came during the reigns of al-Mustakfī II, al-Ḥākim II, al-Mutawakkil II, and al-Mustaʿīn II, all of whom have been discussed in this section in the context of Mamluk politics, as well as during the reign of al-Muʿtaḍid III (r. 817–45/1414–41), who figures in the next chapter. In this new landscape, various leading figures sought to harken back to the days when the caliph could legitimize local rulers through the act of investiture. In 731/1331, for example, the Sultan of Delhi Muḥammad ibn Tughluq (r. 725–52/1325–51) sent messengers to Cairo requesting that the Caliph al-

FIGURE 11. Silver and gold coins from the Delhi Sultanate. (Top) Delhi silver tanka of Kayūmarth dated 689 AH [1290 CE] still invoking legitimacy through the last Abbasid caliph of Baghdad al-Mustaʿṣim as "al-Imām Amīr al-Muʾminīn al-Mustaʿṣim." (Bottom) Delhi gold tanka of Fīrūz Shāh invoking the Abbasid caliph of Cairo al-Muʿtaḍid as "al-Imām Amīr al-Muʾminīn Abū'l-Fatḥ al-Muʿtaḍid billāh," circa 753–63 AH / 1352–62 CE

Top image courtesy American Numismatic Society, New York, NY, ANS 1973.56.313. Bottom image courtesy The David Collection, Copenhagen, inventory no. C 338. Photo by Pernille Klemp.

Mustakfī designate him as his deputy. And extant coins from his reign in Delhi from 742, 743, and 744 AH invoke the name of al-Mustakfī as caliph, even though this Abbasid caliph had passed away in 740/1340. A few years after the internal Mamluk controversy over al-Mustakfī's successor as caliph had been settled, Muḥammad ibn Tughluq additionally received and celebrated an investiture from al-Ḥākim II in 744/1343 with great ceremony. And his court poet, Badr-i Chāch (d. 815/1412), memorialized the auspicious occasion with a triumphant ode. Moreover, faced with a series of splintering movements, both Muḥammad ibn Tughluq and his cousin and successor Fīrūz Shāh Tughluq (r. 752–90/1351–88) began to seek out yearly confirmation of their caliphal investiture as sultans of Delhi. And after the middle of the eighth/fourteenth century, even the rebels further south in the Deccan began to cloak themselves in the mantle of Cairene Abbasid caliphal legitimation and formal investiture to dissuade the Delhi sultans from reconquering their breakaway Mābār and Bahmanī sultanates.

Ibn Khaldūn also discusses how Indian and other rulers sought out investiture from al-Mutawakkil during his caliphate. And the Aleppan historian Ibn al-Shiḥnah (804–90/1402–85) further specifies that the early Ottoman sultan Bayezid I (r. 791–804/1389–1402), also known as Abū Yazīd ibn ʿUthmān in Arabic chronicles, sent precious gifts to the Abbasid caliph al-Mutawakkil along with the request to be honored as his deputized ruler of Anatolia or *Sulṭān al-Rūm* in 797/1394, a request which was granted. During the caliphate of al-Mustaʿīn, the third Bengal sultan of the Ilyās dynasty, Ghiyāth al-Dīn Aʿẓam Shāh ibn Iskandar (r. 792–814/1389–1411), also inquired about a caliphal investiture towards the end of his reign, sending money to the Abbasid caliph as well as a gift to the Mamluk sultan, and then boasted of his allegiance to the caliph on his coinage. And leading a new Raja Ganesh dynasty in Bengal in 833/1429, Jalāl al-Dīn Muḥammad (r. 818–36/1415–32) requested the honor of a caliphal investiture as the deputized ruler of India or *Sulṭān al-Hind*, in the manner of the Delhi sultans before him, to which the Cairene caliph al-Muʿtaḍid assented. Overjoyed at receiving his official designation, Jalāl al-Dīn Muḥammad Shāh sent back large gifts to the Abbasid caliph and the Mamluk sultan in 834/1430.[125] Just as the rejuvenated caliphate had long figured in Mamluks politics, renewed recognition by a current Abbasid caliph had come to be perceived as a valuable asset in the struggle for political preeminence elsewhere.

Yet perhaps we can begin to contemplate an even more profound global series of transformations following the destruction of Baghdad and the massacre of the Prophet's presumed successors in 656/1258. It may be that we can detect an increasing cultural shift in emphasis upon educational, mystical, and narrative chains of transmissions that rapidly gained ascendance in part because they signified Islamic scholarly and spiritual bonds as alternative modes of community and connection to the prophetic heritage. At least within the Mamluk domains, however, and to an extent outside of them, those burgeoning communal constellations continued to draw meaning from a living heir to the Prophet.

CHAPTER 3

CONCEPTUALIZING THE CALIPHATE, 632–1517 CE

THE PROPHET MUḤAMMAD had been ill with a fever for days, much to the concern of his companions. But the curtain separating his wife's compartment from the mosque was pulled aside and suddenly revealed the Messenger of God standing there. He broke into a radiant smile at the sight of his followers praying together to God, and they were so overjoyed at his apparent recovery that they nearly lost all their concentration in prayer. Yet that same day, the Prophet Muḥammad passed away in the lap of his beloved wife ʿĀʾishah, requesting with his last words not the companionship of his family, friends, or followers but that of God the Exalted. His community was devastated. His close companion ʿUmar vehemently denied that the Prophet had passed away. He volubly asserted that the Prophet Muḥammad had only gone to meet his Lord as Moses had done and that he would return shortly. Yet Abū Bakr, after having entered his daughter ʿĀʾishah's house and kissed the forehead of the deceased Prophet farewell, called for the people's attention and proclaimed, "Whoever among you [mistakenly] used to worship Muḥammad, know that Muḥammad has died, but whoever among you worships God, verily God is alive and will not perish!" He then reminded them of the Qur'anic verse, "Muḥammad is only a messenger before whom many messengers have been and gone. If he died or was killed, would you revert to your old ways?" (3:144) ʿUmar's legs gave way, and he fell down in shock at the realization that the Prophet Muḥammad had died.[1] For the early Muslim community, the Prophet Muḥammad's death signaled an end to an immediate flow of divine revelation and the loss of God's messsenger's comforting and illuminating presence. His passing also opened a void in the temporal leadership of the community, and the speed with which his companions sought to appoint a pious political successor at its helm established a key precedent.

This ideal of leadership formed a cornerstone of Islamic political thought and jurisprudence with which Muslim scholars continually engaged, even as—or especially as—contemporary realities increasingly degenerated. In the aftermath of the Abbasid Caliphate's demise in Baghdad in 656/1258, Muslim scholars of Mamluk Syria and Egypt continued to grapple with this notion of an Islamic caliphate—or succession to the Prophet Muḥammad—as an integral aspect of their state and society. Indeed, their ongoing engagement with the concept of the caliphate in these new circumstances was a testament to the powerfully affective memories of the Prophet Muḥammad's merciful legacy and the shattering agony of his loss. Even if God's Messenger had returned back to his Lord, leading Mamluk-era intellectuals urgently sought to maintain a communal connection with his prophetic leadership and the institutionalized forms of his succession that had coalesced in Islamic law and history over the course of centuries.

CLASSICAL ARTICULATION OF THE ISLAMIC CALIPHATE AS A LEGAL NECESSITY AND COMMUNAL OBLIGATION

It was above all the embodied practice of the earliest generations of Muslims, following the example set by the Prophet's closest companions, that was critical in consolidating a nearly universal Islamic consensus upon the obligation of appointing an individual to lead the community. Immediately following confirmation of the Prophet Muḥammad's death, his companions rushed to appoint a temporal successor. So concerned were they with the matter of securing subsequent leadership that they gave it precedence over preparation of the beloved Prophet's body for burial. The first two Rightly-Guided Caliphs, Abū Bakr then ʿUmar, who assumed these duties following the Prophet's death, made a point of designating their own successor or outlining the procedures for choosing him.[2] As Ibn Khaldūn explains in the celebrated introduction to his universal history:

> Appointing a leader is obligatory. Its mandatory nature is known through revelatory law (*sharʿ*) by the consensus of the Companions and the next generation of Followers, because the Companions of the Prophet (God's peace and blessings be upon him) hastened upon his death to pledge allegiance and submit consideration of their affairs to Abū Bakr (May God be pleased with him). And it was thus in every age thereafter, and the matter was established as consensus indicating the obligation of appointing a leader.[3]

For Sunni scholars, the continued presence of such a leader, whether he was referred to as caliph (*khalīfah*) in his capacity of succeeding the Prophet's guardianship over the community's affairs, *imām* in reference to his leadership position, or *amīr al-muʾminīn* for his role in commanding the faithful, was meant to ensure stability and harmony within the domains of Islam.[4]

Sunni scholarly interpretations of Qur'anic verses and prophetic directives affirmed this legal necessity of a communal leader rooted in the exemplary model set by the earliest generations of Muslims. In his seminal exegesis of the Qur'anic verse 4: 59 of Sūrat al-Nisāʾ, al-Ṭabarī (d. 310/923) asserted the religious roots of the communal obligation to elect and maintain a caliph through documenting and interpreting the opinions of the Prophet's companions. In this matter, al-Ṭabarī solidly favored the opinion of Abū Hurayrah, Ibn ʿAbbās, and others that "those vested with authority" (*ulū'l-amr*), to whom qualified obedience was due, were the community's political and military commanders (*al-umarā'*).[5] And by the seventh/thirteenth century, al-Qurṭubī could readily point to this position as the majority opinion of all Muslim scholars, while simultaneously expressing his appreciation for a secondary interpretation that advocated deference towards Islamic religious authorities (*al-fuqahā' wa'l-'ulamā' fī'l-dīn*).[6] Toward the end of the Umayyad era, as Wadad Kadi has demonstrated, exegetical discussions about God's creation of Adam also drew connections between the Qur'anic term *khalīfah* and the caliphate's historical manifestation—in addition to recognizing general human responsibility for the cultivation and custodianship of the earth.[7] And in medieval Spain, Ibn Ḥazm (d. 456/1064) further pointed to the Qur'anic treatment of legislative imperatives and judicial rulings designed to guide and regulate human society as logical evidence for the caliphate's obligatory status.[8] Among the collected corpus of the Prophet Muḥammad's statements and deeds, topics like the necessity of pledging one's allegiance to a ruler and the prophetic command to appoint a leader for groups consisting of even three persons garnered further elaboration and discussion through centuries of ḥadīth commentary.[9]

The universality of the general obligation to designate a leader for the Muslim community was so widely recognized that only a few third/ninth-century Mu'tazilite figures, chiefly al-Aṣamm (d. 200/816)[10] and Hishām al-Fuwaṭī (d. 215/830),[11] are mentioned as adopting a position contrary to this overwhelming consensus, as are the Najadāt sect[12] of the Kharijites.[13] In observing the extent of this agreement among Muslims, Ibn Ḥazm remarks in his comparative study of religious communities:

> All the Sunnis, all the Murji'ites, all the Mu'tazilites, all the Shi'is, and all the Kharijites have agreed upon the obligatory nature of imamate and that it is mandatory upon the community to submit to a just leader who establishes the laws of God among them and governs according to the rules of the Sacred Law with which the Prophet (God's peace be upon him) came—except for the Najadāt among the Kharijites, for they have said that people need not adhere to the obligation of imāmate and that they only need observe their rights among one another, though no one remains of this group.[14]

It was not the necessity of recognizing a leader for the Muslim community that engendered disagreement among these different groups, but rather the interpretative specificities surrounding that leader's designation and essential attributes. As such, the absurdity of the notion that having a leader could be merely permissible, and not actually obligatory, could elicit scathingly disparaging remarks. In this vein, al-Qurṭubī pointedly invokes the definition of the word *aṣamm*, meaning deaf, in his masterly work of Qur'anic exegesis:

> There is no disagreement among the community or among the leading scholars about the obligation of that [i.e., appointing a caliph]—except what has been nar-

> rated about al-Aṣamm since he was deaf (*aṣamm*) towards matters of Sacred Law, as are all those who adopt his statement and follow his opinion and way.[15]

And in his political treatise, Imām al-Ḥaramayn Abū'l-Maʿālī ʿAbd al-Malik al-Juwaynī (419–78/1028–85) similarly remarks:

> ʿAbd al-Raḥmān b. Kaysān [al-Aṣamm] took the view that it [i.e., appointing a leader] is not obligatory and that it is permissible for people to be left in disagreement, clashing with one another under all sorts of circumstances, without a means of governance to gather them nor a means of coalescence to bind their diverse opinions. This man is an assailant, based on the chasm of disobedience and the equation of rights with recalcitrance, who does not respect the boundary of justice nor find difficult the path of deviation. He is never mentioned except for slipping away from the grip of consensus and diverging from the paths of observance. [On this issue of the imamate,] he is preceded by the consensus of all those upon whom the sun has shone in the East and the West and by the agreement of the views of all scholars collectively.[16]

Aside from the divergent opinions of individuals widely considered to be few in number and held in general disregard, the requirement of appointing a leader for the Muslim community was a well-established facet of Sacred Law.

Yet not only was establishing a caliphate mandatory in its own right, it was also the necessary means to fulfill other obligatory aspects of Islamic law as elaborated by Sunni jurists. Therefore, in addition to securing the community's spiritual well-being, the caliph was expected to participate actively in the military, administrative, financial, and judicial aspects of government. Along with supervising official military expeditions, the caliph's responsibilities in this domain entailed that he garrison and fortify Muslim frontiers and protect the populace from all external threats to their safety. Internally, armed bandits, criminals, and highway robbers were to be sought out and criminal activities to be eliminated from their roots so that peace, stability, and economic prosperity could be allowed to prevail. On the judicial plane, the caliph was held ultimately accountable for the administration of justice, the implementation of criminal punishment, the resolution of disputes, and the redress of the grievances of the wronged. His duties included overseeing the proper collection and distribution of public revenues and financial resources in accordance with Islamic law, while addressing the plight of the poor and needy was to rank among his greatest concerns. As legal guardian for all those who lacked close relatives to serve in that capacity, the caliph was also obliged to protect any material wealth that they might possess before they came of age as well as assure that their personal interests were secured upon marriage. Although the caliph was expected to devote personal attention to these diverse details of government, he was also obliged to appoint the most competent and trustworthy officials whenever delegating limited, or even unrestricted, authority to others.

Congregational prayer leaders, pilgrimage guides, judges, distributors of charity, marketplace regulators, guild supervisors, bureaucrats, and military officers all derived legitimacy from their appointment by the caliph.[17] The implications of these rulings were wide-ranging for ordinary Muslims in the public sphere.

Furthermore, the caliph's existence was deemed essential in enabling ordinary Muslims to fulfill their own religious obligations in the political sphere, by obeying the caliph's just command, refraining from political divisiveness, aiding and assisting the caliph's rightful stance, and advising him with sincerity.[18] In elaborating on the meaning of *naṣīḥah* as sincere advice, Muḥyī'l-Dīn al-Nawawī encapsulates all of these duties within a prophetic framework:

> As for the *naṣīḥah* towards the leaders of the Muslims, that means cooperating with them towards Truth, obeying them in it, commanding them with it, exhorting and reminding them (of God-consciousness) with gentleness and kindness, and informing them of what they have unknowingly neglected of the rights of Muslims, abandoning rebellion against them, and warming people's hearts towards obeying them.[19]

The disintegration and potential disappearance of the caliphate over time, which would hinder the fulfillment of a caliph's multiple roles as agent, object, and facilitator of Sacred Law as it had developed through centuries of scaffolding discussions and debates, was deeply unsettling for Muslim jurists and presented a veritable legal predicament.

It was with the gravity of such a situation in mind that Abū Ḥāmid al-Ghazālī (450–505/1058–1111) declined to strip the waning Abbasid Caliphate of his day of its legitimacy. As he explained in his theological work *al-Iqtiṣād fī'l-Iʿtiqād*:

> Good grief, who would not agree with this [argument] and would decree the invalidity of the imamate in our times because of the absence of its conditions, while he is incapable of replacing the person filling the position—rather he even lacks someone characterized by its necessary conditions (to begin with). So which situation is better, to say that the judges are discharged and public functions are invalid and marriages cannot be contracted and all the transactions of the holders of public office across the world cannot be implemented and that all creation is engaged in what is forbidden, or to say that the imamate is contracted and that transactions and public functions can be implemented based on contemporary circumstances and necessity?![20]

Clearly, denial of the Abbasid caliph's legitimate rule would have created a legal void in the workings of society according to Islamic political theory. Yet as Wael Hallaq and Patricia Crone have alluded,[21] despite the great attention paid to al-Ghazālī's articulation of these concerns, it was one of al-Ghazālī's teachers, the renowned Imām al-Ḥaramayn al-Juwaynī, who most thoroughly examined the jurisprudential questions surrounding the caliphate's historical deficiencies and attempted to find solutions to its increasing divergence from absolute ideals, even to the extent of contemplating its possible extinction. al-Juwaynī's seminal insights on this vexing dilemma informed the work of Muslim jurists across the centuries of Mamluk rule and continued to be referenced amid the discussions and debates of the twentieth and twenty-first centuries.

AL-JUWAYNĪ'S SEMINAL FIFTH/ELEVENTH-CENTURY RESOLUTION

Confronted with the intellectual turmoil surrounding the plight of the Abbasid Caliphate in the fifth/eleventh century, Imām al-Ḥaramayn Abū'l-Maʿālī ʿAbd al-Malik al-Juwaynī (419–78/1028–85) composed a treatise addressing the laws of leadership and government, which he dedicated to the ruling Seljuq vizier Niẓām al-Mulk (d. 408–85/1018–92).[22] Playing on one of Niẓām al-Mulk's eponyms as "Ghiyāth al-Dawlah," al-Juwaynī titled his work *Ghiyāth al-Umam fī Iltiyāth al-Ẓulam*, or *The Succor of Nations amidst the Confusion of Darkness*.[23] In establishing the groundwork of his treatise, al-Juwaynī brilliantly lays out the main juridical questions associated with the imamate and its representatives through a lucid distinction and evaluation of the definitive matters at hand. Inspired by the analytical approach of Islamic legal theory (*uṣūl al-fiqh*), al-Juwaynī methodically examines the obligatory nature of the imamate, the qualifications of the imam and his electors, the procedures for the installation and deposition of an imam, and the dimensions of law entrusted to the imam and his deputies.[24] It is only after having fully clarified these essential matters that al-Juwaynī moves on to examine the supposition of the absence of the caliph and his representatives.

In addressing this perplexing question, al-Juwaynī adopts a three-part approach that reflects the progressive stages by which the legal expectations of the Muslim community's leader might gradually erode. The first stage entails the difficulty of locating a candidate who combines all the ideal prerequisites. The next level of deterioration supposes the appearance of a militarily and socially powerful figure who thrusts himself upon public office, whether he be fully qualified for the position of imam or not. And the last set of developments presents an imagined scenario of complete political vacuum created by the absence of all officially appointed and militarily entrenched Muslim leaders, that is to say, a complete state of anarchy. al-Juwaynī considers this last scenario to be a highly unusual and unlikely exception to the normal course of events, since military leaders, whether juristically qualified or not, are ever-present within society.[25]

In the first level of caliphal absence that al-Juwaynī discusses, he supposes the impossibility of satisfying the required characteristics of an imam, one trait after another, beginning with those aspects that are the most easily dispensable until he reaches those that are of pivotal consequence. Thus, al-Juwaynī enumerates the Qurashī lineage of a caliph as the least consequential attribute of all, stipulated merely out of honor and respect for the family of the Prophet Muḥammad. The overall purpose of establishing a leader for the Muslim community, al-Juwaynī argues, is not affected by the question of genealogy, whereas to insist upon a leader of Qurashī blood may in fact be detrimental. Preference, al-Juwaynī explains, should be assigned at all times to a scholarly, capable, and pious candidate for caliph over one who is merely Qurashī. Should a candidate who possesses these former three traits in addition to being of Qurashī descent suddenly emerge, however, those extenuating circumstances would constitute grounds for the deposition of the non-Qurashī already in office. Yet were it somehow unfeasible or undesirable to adopt that course of action, the partially qualified leader's position could be legally confirmed.[26]

The level of scholastic competence that would enable someone to engage in independent legal reasoning, or *ijtihād*, was also required of the imam. In contrast to the stipulation of lineage, the absence of *ijtihād* could significantly impair the leader of the Muslim community's ability to perform his duties. al-Juwaynī resolves this dilemma by suggesting that the otherwise capable Muslim leader refer matters requiring juridical investigation to the scholars of the community. These religious scholars would be in a position to guide the caliph's policy by clarifying Islamic rulings on any perplexing issues that should emerge. According to Islamic principles, such a resolution would be far more preferable than allowing the community to flounder in a political and administrative void.[27]

Next, al-Juwaynī judiciously addresses the deficiencies of piety among the available candidates for caliph by drawing a careful distinction of degree. A person thoroughly immersed in the ways of insolence and depravity, who flagrantly indulges in all that is Islamically forbidden and discouraged, could never be appointed leader of the Muslim community. Even if elected to office, his appointment would be baseless and invalid. To entrust such an individual with the reigns of power and authority would only exacerbate matters and cause extensive harm to the community's interests. As al-Juwaynī asserts, encouraging the proliferation of moral deviance and political instability in this manner would be utterly incomprehensible.[28]

However, al-Juwaynī argues that a candidate who drinks wine or commits other similar acts of perdition, yet still exhibits an earnest desire to establish the foundations of righteousness and overall well-being in the community, merits further consideration. As long as this individual possesses the political, social, and military abilities necessary to sustain the office, and as long as there is no one else better qualified, he may be appointed as imam while every effort is made to rectify his moral deficiencies. This appointment is motivated solely by the necessity of maintaining a dedicated leader to manage and direct the affairs of the Muslim community and assure their collective safety and prosperity. The caliph's ability to actually do so, termed *kifāyah,* is all that remains after al-Juwaynī's process of intellectual distillation as the most essential qualifying attribute for an imam.[29]

al-Juwaynī concludes his discussion on the imam's required traits by subjecting these imperiled characteristics to oppositional combinations. Thus, while a pious, capable, and scholarly candidate is given preference over a Qurashī who possesses none of those elements, al-Juwaynī proceeds to ask how to weigh the merits of a scholarly Qurashī who is not independently capable of holding office in contrast with a thoroughly independent and capable non-Qurashī candidate.[30] For al-Juwaynī, the answer hinges upon the Qurashī's intellectual perceptiveness and ability to learn. Therefore, should the Qurashī be astute and easily absorb sensible means of governance when explained to him, then al-Juwaynī considers his appointment to be the most preferable of the two options. Once established as imam, this individual could, and by all means should, rely upon the wise counsel of intelligent and experienced advisors in making his decisions. Were the Qurashī candidate intellectually dull, sluggish, and obtuse, however, little hope could be sustained for training him to rule well, and the other pious and capable non-Qurashī candidate would therefore take precedence. Thus, religious knowledge alone was not sufficient to outweigh the communal benefits of a leader's strength and political abilities.[31]

The second segment of al-Juwaynī's analysis regarding the various degrees of caliphal absence supposes the emergence of a powerful individual who forcibly assumes office without election. al-Juwaynī begins this discussion of the forceful assumption of leadership without regular procedures of election after having clarified the complete set of characteristics desired in an imam as well as having evaluated the possible scenarios induced by their gradual disappearance. Therefore, in organizing this section, al-Juwaynī distinguishes between the powerful individual who possesses all the attributes required of an imam and one who lacks most of these traits but retains the quality of dedicated political capability (*kifāyah*). In the case of the fully qualified individual, al-Juwaynī first analyzes the supposition that he is also the only qualified candidate of his time. If no one remains who possesses the necessary traits of electors (*ahl al-ḥall wa'l-ʿaqd*), then this fully qualified candidate who calls people to follow him and assumes the role of imam on his own is indeed the leader of the community, by virtue of being both the elector and the elected at once.[32]

However, should there exist qualified electors at the time, there is the possibility that they may or may not choose to elect him. If they refuse, then the uniquely qualified candidate should still call people to his support, whereupon they would be obliged to acquiesce.[33] As al-Juwaynī states, it is not permissible to delay a matter of such widespread importance in preserving the domains of Islam. Should the electors readily respond, though, the question remains whether the imamate is contracted by the election process or by the presentation of the matter to the electors in the first place. Noting that previous scholars have differed on the matter, al-Juwaynī records his own conclusion that a formal election is not necessary under these particular circumstances. Since there was no plurality of candidates, which would normally necessitate an election to ward off disagreements among them, the election of a sole candidate who must be established in office, in any case, is shorn of any actual effect.[34]

In conclusion, al-Juwaynī observes that the sole qualified candidate for imam is obliged to rely upon his strength and power to call others to his obedience. By doing so, he becomes the rightful leader of all. Even if he should lack the necessary material support, people would still be obliged to follow and appoint him to office out of the great temporal and spiritual need for such a leader. However, al-Juwaynī notes that a number of speculative juridical arguments could be made both in favor and against the establishment of his imamate if no one were to respond to his call or if he were only supported by a weak following. al-Juwaynī himself favors recognition of this uniquely qualified candidate as the rightful leader to whom obedience is due. Yet were the qualified candidate to turn away from calling others to his aid, it would be a grievous wrongdoing on his part, and his insistence would actually preclude him from office.[35]

Having exhausted the possible scenarios associated with a single qualified candidate for leadership, al-Juwaynī proceeds to imagine a plethora of similarly qualified candidates, one of whom has forcibly assumed the position. Were this course of action a result of the electors' neglecting their duties to select a Muslim leader to the extent of causing political instability, then a qualified individual who assumed power to preserve political integrity could and should be confirmed in office. al-Juwaynī again questions whether this imamate is legally established by the demonstration of force itself, yet here he argues that the election process is fundamentally necessary since the person who took matters into his own hands (because of the electors' inaction) was not the sole possible candidate. An imamate, al-Juwaynī contends, can only be confirmed through the appointment of a successor by the previous leader, the pledge of allegiance by qualified electors, or the deserving of office by virtue of being the sole qualified candidate, as previously discussed. Although al-Juwaynī notes that some scholars consider the assumption of office by power in combination with the difficulty of opposing that person as sufficient reason to establish the imamate, he considers the election process mandatory under these circumstances to calm the political waters.[36]

For al-Juwaynī, the difficulty in even imagining this scenario lies in the implication of willful iniquity against the person who boldly assumes the reigns of power without first undergoing a proper election. As al-Juwaynī has previously discussed, the imamate cannot be conferred upon a degenerate person, and this course of action seems to indicate a large degree of unscrupulousness. Therefore, if after rising up for valid reasons, such a person in fact tried to force his own election as caliph, his immoral insistence on dominating would disqualify him from office. It is only that qualified individual who seeks to step aside to no avail once his noble aims are accomplished who should definitively be established as imam, preferably by means of election.[37]

In addressing contemporary circumstances, al-Juwaynī's main concern turns to reaching a juridical understanding of the assumption of leadership by a primarily powerful and competent candidate who lacks the other desired traits. In the absence of completely qualified and independent candidates, this individual who bears the sole qualification of political, social, and military competence can be elected to office, and if he assumes power on his own, then he is treated in the same fashion as a fully qualified candidate would be. If he is the only person capable of fulfilling the necessary duties of an imam, then his appointment likewise becomes mandatory. With no fully qualified candidates for the position, this capable leader serves in the role of one enjoining what is beneficial and dissuading others from what is harmful (*al-āmir bi'l-maʿrūf wa'l-nāhī ʿan al-munkar*). And by undertaking direction of the affairs of the Muslims, he saves the entire community from the perils of political vacuum, military weakness, and spiritual chaos. In this particular set of passages, al-Juwaynī implicitly and openly encourages the Seljuq vizier Niẓām al-Mulk to continue managing the affairs of the Muslim community, as there is no one else capable of assuming the responsibility.[38]

This person who addresses the Muslim community's greatest concerns is not allowed to abandon his heavy burdens and resign. Even the individual obligation to perform the pilgrimage to Mecca should be deferred in the interest of fulfilling the broader obligations of his position. Indeed, all of the duties associated with the imam in Islamic law are entrusted to him. He is also obliged to pay attention to the transmission of information and communications, to consult Islamic scholars, and to remain alert to any possible turmoil in religious affairs. All of these remarks are again subtly directed to Niẓām al-Mulk.[39]

What al-Juwaynī is advocating by urging Niẓām al-Mulk to maintain the integrity of the Muslim community may be legally classified as an instance of replacing the absent locus of an Islamic ruling with another.[40] Even in the physical presence of an Abbasid caliph, al-Juwaynī recognized his inability, as defined in realistic legal terms, to fulfill the expectations of a Muslim leader. The person who actually undertakes the affairs of the Muslim community, i.e., the true *qāʾim bi-hādhā al-amr*,[41] is the one who merits al-Juwaynī's attention and juridical concern. Thus, the responsibilities and obligations of an imam are transferred and entrusted to Niẓām al-Mulk as the person who is best able to discharge them. While remedying the predicaments of his age, al-Juwaynī consciously crafted his legal treatise in anticipation of increasingly dire circumstances yet to come. With the devastation of the remnants of the Abbasid Caliphate in Baghdad in 656/1258, his discerning methodology acquired new relevance.

POST-656/1258 THEORISTS OF THE CALIPHATE

Following the destruction of Baghdad, Muslim scholars of Mamluk Egypt and Syria articulated creative solutions to solidify the legal foundations of the reconstituted Abbasid Caliphate in Cairo based upon this rich tradition of Islamic political thought and jurisprudence. Far from boxing themselves into illogical absurdities that lent themselves to extinction, premodern jurists continued to build upon and develop the scholarly contributions of their predecessors with an eye towards changing circumstances. Unfortunately, however, the dramatic events surrounding the Mongol conquest of Baghdad in 656/1258 persuaded Sir Hamilton Gibb and his student Ann Lambton in their influential writings on Islamic political thought to read a definitive end for the Islamic caliphate into the works of Muslim jurists from the seventh/thirteenth and eighth/fourteenth centuries. The contributions of scholars such as the Shāfiʿī judge Badr al-Dīn Muḥammad Ibn Jamāʿah (639–733/1241–1333) and the notorious Ḥanbalī Taqiyy al-Dīn Aḥmad Ibn Taymiyyah (661–728/1262–1328) have been designated as the last segment of a downward spiraling trajectory of Islamic political jurisprudence on the caliphate. In this narrative, Ibn Jamāʿah and Ibn Taymiyyah represent polar opposites, as might be historically fitting given their roles across each other in real life as judge and accused respectively.[42] For Gibb and Lambton, Ibn Jamāʿah represents the absurdity of the classical tradition pushed to its extremes, by introducing the bankrupt concept of *ghalabah*, and hence constitutes its final disintegration,[43] and Ibn Taymiyyah represents the rabid puritan reformer who sought to cleanse Islam from the fiction of a caliphate once and for all.[44] Yet a closer look at the works of both Ibn Jamāʿah and Ibn Taymiyyah negates this presentation and reveals that both authors' views of the caliphate were far more mundane. By analyzing their writings within the historical context of their times and the broader juristic discourse on the caliphate, we discover that both Ibn Jamāʿah and Ibn Taymiyyah sought to uphold the Islamic caliphate of their times, the Abbasid Caliphate in Cairo, by rooting their work within the Islamic discursive tradition.

GHALABAH, THE SULTANATE, AND THE CALIPHATE IN IBN JAMĀʿAH'S *TAḤRĪR AL-AḤKĀM*

This role consigned to Ibn Jamāʿah in the narrative of Islamic political thought first articulated by Gibb, and widely reiterated in various forms thereafter, rests on two essential premises: one, that Ibn Jamāʿah, who lived in the seventh/thirteenth and eighth/fourteenth centuries, introduced the concept of justifying caliphal rule by sheer military force, or *ghalabah*,[45] following the destruction of the Abbasid Caliphate in Baghdad, and two, that these historical circumstances compelled him to collapse the caliphate and sultanate into one another, as the final travesty of Islamic jurisprudence on the Muslim community's leadership. As such, Ibn Jamāʿah is said to have initiated the idea that "the seizure of power itself gave authority"[46] or "the notion that might makes right, the final absurdity in any constitutional system."[47] Or in Gibb's words, Ibn Jamāʿah obscured the principle that "the sole authority was that of the sharīʿa and temporal power could be validated only by association with the sharīʿa" and developed a doctrine that "amounted in effect to a complete divorce of the imamate from the sharīʿa and the abandonment of the Law in favor of secular absolutism."[48] As a result, Gibb observed that Ibn Jamāʿah's ideas were a "patent contradiction, which could not be accepted by the general Community of Muslims . . . but at least it served to show that the whole theoretical structure from which it derived had to be rejected."[49]

However, this historical trajectory of Islamic political thought developed by Gibb and further elaborated upon by Lambton in her book *State and Government in Medieval Islam* overlooks the early strains of Ḥanbalism that considered *ghalabah* to be a legitimate means of procuring the caliphate as well as similar discussions among both Ḥanafī and Shāfiʿī jurists. Basing their analysis on the Prophet Muḥammad's statements that righteous succession to him (*khilāfat al-nubuwwah*) would last for only thirty years before being transformed into a rule characteristic of kingship (*mulk*), early Ḥanbalīs and Ḥanafīs had limited expectations of post-*Rāshidūn* (post-Rightly Guided) caliphs after the year 41/661. The minimal legal conditions established by Aḥmad ibn Ḥanbal for these caliphs who behaved as though they were worldly emperors included recognition that their rule could become binding without the desired act of recognition by the community.[50] Nor was Ibn Jamāʿah's discussion of *ghalabah* in *Taḥrīr al-Aḥkām fī Tadbīr Ahl al-Islām*[51] a novelty even within the school of Shāfiʿī legal thought. Although the earlier Shāfiʿī jurist Imām al-Ḥaramayn al-Juwaynī disagreed with the notion that one's candidacy for the caliphate could be legally established by the demonstration of force itself,[52] he also clearly stated that "some of our scholars" held the position that if one could not repulse a person who had assumed the caliphate by sheer force, and if the duties of the institution could be fulfilled by his assumption of it, then he should be legally established in the position he had forcibly assumed as caliph.[53]

Blending the problematics of *ghalabah* into the question of the sultanate, Lambton also states:

> Ibn Jamāʿa, forced by the circumstances of the time, goes further [than al-Ghazālī] and accepts the possibility of the absorption of the caliphate itself into the sultanate. He states that if at any time there was no *imām* and someone not properly qualified assumed charge of the office and exercised dominion over the people by his power and military force without having received a *bayʿa* or being appointed by the previous holder of office, the *bayʿa* must be concluded for him and obedience to him was incumbent so that he could order the affairs of the Muslims and unite them. [54]

Whereas Malcom Kerr observes, "[Ibn Jamāʿah's] remarks on 'the imamate of conquest' on the one hand, read like Ghazālī's view of the sultan, extended one step further by being applied to the imam himself."[55] Yet the irony of such statements is that much of Ibn Jamāʿah's work draws upon the writings of al-Juwaynī, who was the teacher of the very person, al-Ghazālī, whom Ibn Jamāʿah is assumed to have superseded. As Ibn Jamāʿah himself indicates in his preface, *Taḥrīr al-Aḥkām* was an abbreviated summary of Islamic laws on governance and leadership that relied upon the positions of earlier scholars and was rooted in Islamic traditions.[56] And one can clearly see the echoes of al-Juwaynī's *Ghiyāth al-Umam* even in Lambton's cursory summation cited above, minus the two jurists' differences within the domains of earlier legal discourse over the validity of *ghalabah* in other passages.

By restoring the earlier Shāfiʿī jurist al-Juwaynī's *Ghiyāth al-Umam* to its proper place in the scaffolding of Islamic political thought and jurisprudence, we can better appreciate the continuity of Islamic legal discourse and its application to new and evolving circumstances after 656/1258, not its premature extinction. In his *Taḥrīr al-Aḥkām*, Ibn Jamāʿah upholds the jurisprudential edifice constructed by al-Juwaynī over two centuries earlier. It is a legal construction that maintains the image of the caliphate, although the caliph may in fact be inept, while ensuring that another competent individual, whether he be the Seljuq vizier or the Mamluk sultan, executes the necessary duties of an imam. Thus, when Ibn Jamāʿah discusses the imam's delegation of authority to others, he remarks how comprehensive delegation of one's duties (*tafwīḍ ʿāmm*) was customary in his times, which legitimately included the transfer of responsibility for appointing judges and other public officials, organizing military forces, and ensuring internal and external security, as well as administering the collection and distribution of state finances. Immediately thereafter, Ibn Jamāʿah notes that the (Mamluk) sultan who is appointed by the (Cairene Abbasid) caliph should meet all of the juristic qualifications of the caliph, except for that of Qurashī lineage, since the sultan is filling in for the caliph in the execution of his responsibilities (*wa-yuʿtabar fīʾl-Sulṭān al-mutawallī min jihat al-Khalīfah mā yuʿtabar fīhī illā al-nasab li-annahu qāʾim maqāmah*).[57] Clearly, the sultan and caliph in question are the Mamluk sultan who was ceremoniously delegated by the Abbasid caliph repeatedly during the lifetime of Ibn Jamāʿah.[58] As chief justice in Cairo, Ibn Jamāʿah personally participated in and legitimated this dual system on multiple occasions, such as when he ceremoniously led the gathered congregation in prayers following al-Ḥākim's second public Friday sermon in 661/1262 at the beginning of al-Malik al-Ashraf Khalīl b. Qalāwūn's sultanate.[59] The text manifestly both parallels Ibn Jamāʿah's historical context and is aligned with Ibn Jamāʿah's stated purpose in offering his composition as sincere advice (*naṣīḥah*) to a contemporaneous political leader entrusted with the affairs of the Muslim community by God.[60] Furthermore, while continuing in the next passage to articulate his approval of *ghalabah* in this context, Ibn Jamāʿah holds that if such a worldly figure or king were to take over the lands by force and power (implying someone aspiring to be sultan over the totality of Muslim lands as the Mamluks claimed rather than a local commander interested in controlling only one particular territory), the caliph should then delegate the affairs of state to him in order to preserve a state of communal unity and obedience, even if this worldly ruler or "king" did not meet the full qualifications of the imamate (without regard for lineage, which as mentioned above, was reserved for the caliph alone). In what appears to be a reference to the Mamluk position of *Nāʾib al-Sulṭān*, however, the deputy (*nāʾib*) of this newly instated ruler should ideally compensate for his superior's missing traits that are essential to Islamic leadership of the community.[61]

As a result of the Mamluk sultan's filling in for the Abbasid caliph in the execution of his legal responsibilities as head of state or imam, though, the language in Ibn Jamāʿah's discussion of his rights and those of the populace remains necessarily rather ambiguous. Although Ibn Jamāʿah notes that both the caliph and the sultan have ten rights vis-à-vis the populace, his language morphs into a singular masculine pronoun while discussing those rights as well as the ten rights that the populace can expect in return. On the first right of these rights, that the caliph and sultan deserve obedience, Ibn Jamāʿah cites (for the second time in his treatise) the Qur'anic verse from Sūrat al-Nisāʾ discussed at the beginning of this chapter, and he states in no uncertain terms that the *ulūʾl-amr* consist of the chief political leader of the community (*al-imām*) and his deputies, according to the majority of scholars.[62] Thus, the caliph maintains his symbolic place in the overall state structure because of his Qurashī lineage (which Ibn Jamāʿah has already noted is legally necessary)[63] and his Abbasid heritage (to which he owes his elevation to the post-1258 caliphate), but by handing over his duties to the sultan, the caliph recedes into the background of these legal and moral discussions. Like the Seljuq vizier Niẓām al-Mulk in al-Juwaynī's treatise before him, the Mamluk sultan in Ibn Jamāʿah's *Taḥrīr al-Aḥkām* is the real locus of the Islamic legal discussions of leadership and governance, known juristically as the imamate, and its practical implementation. Commencing with al-Juwaynī in the fifth/eleventh century and reiterated by Ibn Jamāʿah following the Mongol conquest of Baghdad in the seventh/thirteenth century, the person who actually rules, and not the caliph whose role is one of symbolic legitimation, comes to be acknowledged as the "imam" of juristic discourse.

IBN TAYMIYYAH'S VIEWS ON THE CALIPHATE

Rather than seizing the Mongol destruction of Baghdad as an opportune moment to declare the end of the caliphate as it had been previously known, a position that has been erroneously ascribed to Ibn Taymiyyah ever since the publication of Henri Laoust's influential work on his social and political views in 1939,[64] Ibn Taymiyyah also engages in a process similar to the one that had preoccupied Sunni jurists for centuries—namely, how to comprehend the historical position of the caliphate from a sound Islamic legal perspective. Ibn Taymiyyah develops his ideas on the caliphate in a lengthy non-binding legal opinion or *fatwa*, in which he addresses the well-known statement of the Prophet that there would be a thirty-year period of *khilāfat al-nubuwwah* (righteous vice-regency of the Prophet after his passing away) that would be ultimately superseded by *mulk* (kingship). Historically, this *ḥadīth* provides affirmation of the righteous leadership of the first few caliphs. In terms of a juristic evaluation, however, the key question arises: What then are the appropriate legal classifications of *khilāfat al-nubuwwah* and of *mulk*? Ibn Taymiyyah delineates four main responses among Muslims to this question; two of them he identifies as unacceptable extremes, and two as representing centrist positions. The first of the two potentially acceptable middle paths is to proclaim *khilāfat al-nubuwwah*—or the highest representation and standard of the caliphate—obligatory (*wājibah*), which means that deviations from this model are only permissible by necessity of circumstance (*an yuqāl al-khilāfatu wājibah wa-innamā yajūzu al-khurūju ʿanhā bi-qadr al-ḥājah*). According to this classification, *mulk*—or political rule associated with the worldly detractions of kingship—is a case of dire need (*ḥājah*) and not inherent permissibility (*jawāz aṣlī*). The other centrist position, which Ibn Taymiyyah associates at one point with Abū Yaʿlā Ibn al-Farrāʾ (d. 458/1066), is to consider *khilāfat al-nubuwwah* meritorious (*mustaḥabbah*). This position leaves slightly more conceptual room for the permissibility of *mulk* (which Ibn Taymiyyah specifies as caliphal rule besmirched by elements of kingship (*shawb al-khilāfah bi'l-mulk*), so long as it facilitates the actual intent behind this Islamic public office of the caliphate (*an yuqāl yajūzu qabūluhā min al-mulk bi-mā yuyassiru fīʿl al-maqṣūdi bi'l-wilāyah wa-lā yuʿassiruhu*).[65]

In contradistinction to both these middle positions are the two extremes. The first is the position adopted by religious innovators like the Kharijites, Mu'tazilites, and some pious ascetics who deem *khilāfat al-nubuwwah* to be obligatory under all conditions, regardless of any extenuating circumstances, and accordingly condemn anyone who falls short of it (*yūjibu dhālika fī kulli ḥālin wa-zamānin wa-ʿalā kulli aḥadin wa-yadhummu man kharaja ʿan dhālika muṭlaqan aw li-ḥājatin*). The other extreme, which Ibn Taymiyyah identifies as the purview of oppressors, libertines, and some Murji'ites, is to declare the absolute permissibility of *mulk*, or worldly rule, without holding it to the standards of the righteous caliphs (*yubīḥu al-mulk muṭlaqan min ghayr taqayyudin bi-sunnat al-khulafāʾ*). A fully modern interpretation of these last two categories would identify religious extremism as the first excess and excessive secularism at the other opposing extreme. As for Ibn Taymiyyah's middle path, achieving an exemplary caliphate, one that realistically embraces the guidance of the Prophet and his righteous successors, is the ideal form of Islamic governance.[66]

In drawing this normative distinction between *khilāfat al-nubuwwah* and *mulk*, Ibn Taymiyyah does not seek to negate the historical development of the caliphate. Rather he recognizes the validity of referring to rulers subsequent to the Rightly Guided Caliphs as caliphs themselves—even if the substantive character distinguishing their rule was that of kingship (*mulk*). He locates religious grounds for this position in the saying of the Prophet Muḥammad, as reported by Abū Hurayrah and recorded in the two most authoritative ḥadīth collections of al-Bukhārī and Muslim:

> The Israelites were led by prophets; each time a prophet passed away, he was succeeded by another prophet. Yet there will be no prophet after me; there will be vice-regents (*khulafā'* or caliphs), and they will be many. [The Companions] asked, "What do you order us to do?" He said, "Be loyal to your pledge of allegiance (*bay'ah*), to one after the other, and give them their rights, for God will ask them about how they shepherded you."[67]

According to Ibn Taymiyyah's analysis, the acknowledgment of a future multitude of caliphs indicates that there would be more caliphs than just the first few righteous ones (since they alone could not be considered "many"). The Prophet's instruction to be loyal to one's pledge of allegiance to whoever had assumed the caliphate first also suggested to Ibn Taymiyyah that, unlike the time of the Rightly Guided Caliphs, succession would later become a matter of dispute. Ibn Taymiyyah further regards the Prophet's injunction to respect the rights of those later caliphs, who would eventually be taken to task by God for their shepherding of the Muslim community, as evidence supporting the Sunni position of recognizing temporal political authority.[68] Thus, while acknowledging the oppressive character of Yazīd b. Mu'āwiyah's rule in *Minhāj al-Sunnah* (*kāna fīhi min al-ẓulm mā kāna fīhi*),[69] Ibn Taymiyyah does not hesitate to refer simultaneously to that period of rule as "the caliphate of Yazīd" (*khilāfat Yazīd*).[70] And Ibn Taymiyya more generally refers to the Umayyad and Abbasid caliphs (*khulafā' banī Umayyah wa-banī 'Abbās*), while acknowledging that the word "caliph" is a common term for those entrusted with political authority among Muslims.[71]

In his legal exposition, though, Ibn Taymiyyah also remains unequivocally clear that all such rulers should be held to the standards of the Righteous Caliphs in their governance. He condemns the notion that worldly rulers should not be bound to the exemplary model of the caliphs (*min ghayr taqayyud bi-sunnat al-khulafā'*) while concomitantly recognizing the likelihood that such rulers might occasionally have to diverge from this standard of governance due to circumstances rendering it impossible (*ta'adhdhur*) or even simply difficult (*ta'assur*) to adhere to it. Wanton disregard for the noble path of caliphs, however, would be inadmissible (*ammā mā lā ta'adhdhur fīhi wa-lā ta'assur, fa-inna al-khurūj fīhi 'an sunnat al-khulafā' ittibā'un li'l-hawā*).[72] Elsewhere, Ibn Taymiyyah also recalls the injunction of the Prophet Muḥammad that Muslims should follow his example and the example set by the Righteous and Rightly Guided Caliphs (*al-khulafāʾ al-rāshidīn al-mahdiyyīn*) who would follow him.[73] Yet Ibn Taymiyyah does not lay the blame for the degeneration of political rule into worldly kingship solely at the feet of the leaders of state; for him, the metaphorical flock also shares its portion of the blame, as in the aphorism: "People will be appointed over you according to how you are" (*kamā takūnūna yuwallā ʿalaykum*).[74] Therefore, in addition to people improving their own condition and maintaining political order through general yet qualified obedience, the Muslim community's duty to offer sincere advice (*naṣīḥah*) to those placed in authority over them acquires immense significance within the sphere of Ibn Taymiyyah's political thought.[75]

In light of his assessment of *naṣīḥah,* Ibn Taymiyyah's well-known treatise *al-Siyāsah al-Sharʿiyyah fī Iṣlāḥ al-Rāʿī wa'l-Raʿiyyah* can be understood as a composition designed to advise the ruling elite and elevate their moral standards of governance in a creative scholar's iteration of the genre of advice literature, as I have elaborated at greater length elsewhere.[76] Ibn Taymiyya explains in his opening remarks how the treatise was solicited by a member of the ruling class whom God had made it obligatory to advise (*iqtaḍāhā man awjaba Allāh nuṣḥahu min wulāt al-umūr*). He then expounds upon this obligation by quoting the prophetic ḥadīth, which praises the offering of sincere advice to such officials (*an tanāṣiḥū man wallāhu Allāh amrakum*) as an act pleasing to God. Though one would not necessarily expect theoretical legal explications in a work of this genre aimed at rectifying contemporary malaise, Ibn Taymiyyah nevertheless firmly roots his arguments in *al-Siyāsah al-Sharʿiyyah* within an Islamic discursive tradition that revolved around the caliphate. As Ibn Taymiyyah explains in the introduction, the conceptual framework of *al-Siyāsah al-Sharʿiyyah* springs from those two Qur'anic verses in Sūrat al-Nisāʾ (4:58–59) that demonstrate, in the majority opinion among Muslim scholars by the seventh/thirteenth century, the Muslim community's obligation to elect and maintain a caliph, with those vested with authority (*ulū'l-amr*) signifying the community's political and military leaders (*al-umarāʾ*).[77] Ibn Taymiyyah embraced this explanation of the Qur'an's conceptual terminology, readily interchanging the expression derived from these verses "those in authority" (*wulāt al-umūr*) with those for the political and military authorities (*al-umarāʾ*), the caliphs (*al-khulafāʾ*), and the imams (*al-aʾimmah*) as though they were synonymous.[78] In this fashion, he embraces the lengthy trajectory of Muslim scholars' highly practical considerations regarding the caliphate.

In *al-Siyāsah al-Sharʿiyyah,* Ibn Taymiyyah also acknowledges the caliph's place at the head of the state's political and military hierarchy. While explaining the weighty responsibility of judging truthfully among people, and hence ruling over them, he addresses all key officials of the state, "whether he is caliph (*khalīfah*), sultan (*sulṭān*), vice-regent (*nāʾib*), governor (*wālī*), a Sharʿī judge, or his deputy."[79] Rather than directing specific bureaucratic advice to each of these government officials within the Mamluk system, Ibn Taymiyyah begins *al-Siyāsah al-Shar'iyyah* by offering general advice regarding how such responsible members of state could best discharge the public duties entrusted to them.[80] And notably, Ibn Taymiyyah specifically places the caliph at the head of this state bureaucracy above and before the actual sultan. Written in the context of the Mamluk State, Ibn Taymiyyah's choice of words in this descending order of rank is an unmistakable reference simultaneously paralleling and legitimizing the contemporaneous bureaucratic structure. Specifically, it acknowledges the Abbasid caliph as the symbolic figurehead who transferred all of his essential functions and duties over to the Mamluk sultan for execution. Accepting the legitimacy of the Mamluk State structure for what it was, with an Abbasid caliph nominally at its pinnacle, Ibn Taymiyyah thus directs most of his attention in *al-Siyāsah al-Shar'iyyah* towards ameliorating the actual performance and execution of Islamic governance, by addressing the administration of finances and criminal punishment,[81] as well as offering essential reminders regarding the need for wise exercise of the government's resources and power.[46] All of this advice is directed towards improving the actual daily functioning of the state under which Ibn Taymiyyah lived—comprised of a ceremonial Abbasid caliph, a governing Mamluk sultan, and numerous other administrative officials.

SHAMS AL-DĪN AL-DHAHABĪ'S POLEMICAL TREATISE ON THE GRAND IMAMATE

In Mamluk Syria, Shi'ism, as Stefan Winter has argued, "still represented a moral and historical alter-ego to dominant Sunni society, not an ideological threat," and it was not until the sixteenth century, with the adversarial ideologies and hostilities between the Safavid and Ottoman Empires, that the political and personal boundaries more fully ossified. In the Mamluk centuries, however, Shi'is occupied an "ambivalent position" in Syrian society and participated in Sunni scholarly circles and networks.[82] Some Shi'i scholars, like al-'Allāmah Ḥasan Ibn al-Muṭahhar al-Ḥillī, enjoyed the patronage of the Ilkhanids in the recently conquered lands of Mesopotamia. Shortly after he was appointed an advisor to the Ilkhanid ruler Öljeitü in 710/1311, al-Ḥillī composed his *Minhāj al-Karāmah fī Ma'rifat al-Imāmah*, which "challenged the Sunni concept of legitimate leadership." It was in response to it that Ibn Taymiyyah composed his *Minhāj al-Sunnah fī Naqḍ Kalām al-Shī'ah wa'l-Qadariyyah*, criticizing Shi'i ideology and articulating a Sunni defense of the caliphate as exemplifying the prophetic way.[83] Yet a lesser-known treatise written by the prominent historian and traditionist Shams al-Dīn Muḥammad al-Dhahabī (673–748/1274–1348) around 744/1344, close to the end of his life, also expounds the Sunni understanding of the imamate. Unlike *Minhāj al-Sunnah*, al-Dhahabī's manuscript "al-Muqaddimah al-Zahrā fī Īḍāḥ al-Imāmah al-Kubrā"[84] does not refute a particular author or text, but it exemplifies a broader pattern of scholarly engagement and debate with the social expression of Shi'i sympathies. Adopting a personal and impassioned tone, al-Dhahabī deploys rational arguments to plead against the logic of particular Shi'i positions, given the countervailing weight of scriptural and sociological evidence.

After praising God and praying for peace on His prophets, the manuscript opens with a reminder of the obligation to appoint a leader for the Muslim community. al-Dhahabī notes:

> Sunnis ("The people of the prophetic way"), Mu'tazilites, Murji'ites, Kharijites, and Shi'is [all] agree upon the necessity (*wujūb*) of the imamate and that it is obligatory (*farḍ*) upon the Muslim community (*ummah*) to follow a just leader (*inqiyād ilā imām ʿadl*). The only exception is the Najadāt among the Kharijites who say that the imamate is not necessary and that people only need to give each other their rights, and this statement is null and void (*sāqiṭ*).

From this overall point of agreement, al-Dhahabī launches into his disputations with divergent Shi'i interpretations of that Islamic leadership. One of al-Dhahabī's preliminary points concerns the dominant legal opinion that there should be only one leader at any particular point in time. This assertion appears to serve multiple purposes. On the one hand, it highlights his sympathies for ʿAlī and al-Ḥusayn as the rightful caliphs in their disputes with the Umayyad contester for the caliphate, Muʿāwiyah, which may have appealed to his intended audience. And on the other hand, it underscores the validity of Abū Bakr's caliphate in immediate succession to the Prophet Muḥammad, as it would not have been valid for both ʿAlī and Abū Bakr to have been recognized leaders of the same community. Yet the point bears even upon his contemporary social context; al-Dhahabī's stress on the singularity of Islamic leadership also bolsters the legitimacy of the contemporaneous Abbasid caliph of Cairo vis-à-vis the Twelver Shi'i imam in occultation. They cannot both be rightful guardians of the community in his view, and al-Dhahabī vehemently disparages the notion of the twelfth imam's continued leadership over Muslims roughly 470 years after his disappearance.[85]

As for the Shi'i assumption that the Prophet Muḥammad's companions willfully disregarded his command to appoint ʿAlī as his first caliph and successor, al-Dhahabī insists on the rational implausibility of their having done so. These were the Prophet's close companions, he notes among several other arguments, and they eagerly followed his instructions and defended his sacred mission with their lives. These were the foremost Companions who fought with him when they were outnumbered at the Battle of Badr and who pledged their unswerving allegiance to him at the *Bayʿat al-Riḍwān* where they earned God's pleasure and grace. Even God Himself, al-Dhahabī points out, describes them in the Qur'an as being truthful (*ulāʾika hum al-ṣādiqūn*, 49:15). al-Dhahabī, therefore, asks his interlocutors to reflect on the enormity of their accusation.

He colorfully asserts that what his Shi'i contemporaries accuse the faithful supporters of the Prophet of having done is so abominable that it is worse than anything ever done by the Mongols who had become Muslim, indeed worse than even what the disbelieving Mongols had ever done! (*Fa-ramaytahum bi-khazyah la takādu taqa ʿu min awbāsh al-ajnād wa-lā min muslimat al-Tatār bal wa-lā min kafaratihim wa-lā min ḥarāmiyyat al-Khuwārazmiyyah wa-lā min adhillat al-munāfiqīn!*)[86] The contemporary reference to Mongol misconduct in the context of this religio-political treatise is intriguing.

al-Dhahabī's reverence for the Mamluk State as the Islamic polity and imamate of his age (a position that Ibn Taymiyyah, whom he admired, also held[87]) surely colored his interpretation of the ongoing hostilities between the Mamluks and the Ilkhanids. Could this reference to misdeeds in the context of Islamic leadership therefore imply that the recently Islamized Ilkhanid Mongols had wrongfully assaulted the rightful caliphate of their age? It is certainly an argument that has been deployed in the reverse direction to explain the repeated military assaults of the Ilkhanids against the Mamluks over the course of the eighth/fourteenth century. As Reuven Amitai–Preiss speculates regarding Ilkhanid strategy:

> The Mongols surely understood that the Mamluk sultans had become the *de facto* leaders of the Muslim world and had resurrected the ʿAbbāsid Caliphate. The leadership of the Ilkhanid state may have feared the impact on their own Muslim subjects of a strong Muslim state which was outside their control and offered resistance.[88]

As for the non-Muslim Mongols, al-Dhahabī indicates that had the Prophet's companions concealed his instructions about caliphal succession, it would have been worse than those despicable actions for which the Mongols were notorious: the destruction of Baghdad and the murder of its caliph. And it would have been worse than the audacity of the "Khawārazmian bandits" who expressed open hostility to the Abbasid caliphs of Baghdad and briefly propped up an alternative ʿAlid caliph in the early seventh/thirteenth century. The exalted Companions' supposed disobedience to the Prophet's command to appoint ʿAlī as his immediate political successor would have been worse than the misdeeds of the basest of hypocrites.

To the contrary, al-Dhahabī affirms the virtue of the Prophet's companions and the soundness of their judgment in appointing Abū Bakr and then ʿUmar as leaders of the Muslim community after the Prophet Muḥammad's death. Elsewhere, in his historical expositions of the continued tradition of Sunni leadership, al-Dhahabī enthusiastically embraces the Abbasid caliphs in Cairo during his lifetime as the rightful bearers of that prophetic trust. Continuing the numbering of Abbasid caliphs from Baghdad, al-Dhahabī celebrates the advent and inauguration of al-Mustanṣir as the thirty-eighth Abbasid caliph as well as "the establishment of the imamate" (*ʿuqidat lahu al-imāmah*) of al-Ḥākim,

"The Present-Day Caliph" (*khalīfat al-waqt*). During al-Ḥākim's forty-year tenure as caliph, one of al-Dhahabī's own teachers, Sharaf al-Dīn al-Maqdisī (622–94/1225–95), himself a disciple of Ibn ʿAbd al-Salām,[89] was called to Cairo and spent roughly one year instructing the caliph in the religious sciences and writing for him as a caliphal secretary. Furthermore, al-Dhahabī carefully notes the ascension of al-Ḥākim's son and grandson to the caliphate in succession, al-Mustakfī II Sulaymān in 701/1302 and al-Ḥākim II Aḥmad nearly four decades later in 740/1340. They are the last of the Abbasid caliphs whom al-Dhahabī included in the addendum or *dhayl* of his highly regarded and widely disseminated corpus of historical writings before al-Dhahabī's own death in Damascus on Dhū'l-Qaʿdah 3, 748 / February 4, 1348.[90]

TĀJ AL-DĪN AL-SUBKĪ AND THE RESTORATION OF BLESSINGS

Doubtless Tāj al-Dīn ʿAbd al-Wahhāb al-Subkī (ca. 727–71 / ca. 1327–70) absorbed historical lessons such as these, regarding the enduring significance of the Abbasid Caliphate in Cairo, from the close-knit scholarly networks of his times and from his close tutelage with al-Dhahabī, some fifty-four years his senior. When al-Subkī would return from his twice-daily lessons with al-Dhahabī, al-Subkī's father the Damascene chief justice Taqiyy al-Dīn ʿAlī b. ʿAbd al-Kāfī al-Subkī (683–756/1284–1335) would announce, "You've come from your shaykh," as an indication of their mutual endearment. Other scholars were referred to by the location of their instruction or the texts that they taught the younger al-Subkī: "You've come from the Tinkuz Congregational Mosque (*jāmiʿ*)[91]" or "You've come from *al-Shāmiyyah*," and so on. The eminent al-Mizzī garnered special mention, however, and the father wanted to inculcate deep reverence for him in his son, so al-Mizzī was referred to as "*the* Shaykh," with particular enunciation and strength. Yet al-Subkī in his youth shied from the stern nature of al-Mizzī with whom he studied intentionally only twice a week and preferred the affection showered on him by al-Dhahabī. The amiable scholar favored al-Subkī among his students, and once al-Dhahabī even defended the merits of the young al-Subkī's knowledge in prophetic traditions to his father. Indicative of this trust in al-Subkī's potential, al-Dhahabī penned an entry for him in his biographical collection of noteworthy traditionists: "I hope he will distinguish himself as a scholar" (*arjū an yatamayyaza fī'l-ʿilm*). Indeed, as his studiousness and wit as a youth had indicated, Tāj al-Dīn al-Subkī did grow into scholarly eminence, becoming Damascene chief justice and a prolific author of great erudition. Or as al-Dhahabī later added, "then he taught and issued legal opinions" (*thumma darrasa wa-aftā*).[92]

In one of his works focused on moral edification, *Muʿīd al-Niʿam wa-Mubīd al-Niqam*, al-Subkī neatly weaves together the contemporary social context of the Abbasid Caliphate of Cairo and the influential juristic precedent of al-Juwaynī and his *Ghiyāth al-Umam*, which he had read and admired. In response to a personal inquiry on how to restore God's worldly favors after they have been lost, al-Subkī designed the treatise to be concise and accessible to the broadest of audiences. al-Subkī clarifies that divine blessings are only removed when due gratitude is not manifested in one's heart, in one's words, and in one's actions. One must spiritually acknowledge that the source of all blessings is God alone, praise Him, speak openly of His grace, and adhere to what He, the Bestower, commands. Furthermore, each blessing has a form of gratitude that is particular to it, and one must therefore use God's blessing in obedience to Him and in the way that such a divine favor especially merits and necessitates. al-Subkī then presents specific examples, which constitute the body of his treatise, of how gratitude should be expressed properly in over one hundred cases. The first deals with the gift of one's two eyes, the second with the gift of one's two ears, and the third addresses the caliph.[93]

In his discussion of how those endowed with authority should properly demonstrate their gratitude to preserve God's blessings, al-Subkī begins with the caliph himself. As al-Subkī explains, "The third example encompasses the Caliph and then those beneath him (*fa-man dūnahu*), the Sultan, his deputies, the judges, and all other public officials." By using the participle (*fa*) and the preposition (*dūna*) in this construction, al-Subkī clearly indicates a hierarchical sequence with the caliph at the pinnacle of government. He is both above and before all other temporal as well as religious representatives of the state, whether that be the sultan, his deputies, the judges, or others. The advice al-Subkī has in mind, however, is applicable to them all. In this third example, al-Subkī advises the caliph and other lesser officials to look out for the interests of the populace, to implement justice among them, and to treat them equally and fairly without any hint of favoritism. To show gratitude for the blessing of public office, these state officials should realize that they are not necessarily better than the populace over which they rule by God's grace alone. They should remain mindful of God, who raised them to power and is fully capable of demoting them, and they should fulfill their obligations to Him as well as fulfill the rights of the proverbial flock of His servants.[94]

After acknowledging the primacy of the caliph and the importance of advising *waliyy al-amr*, referring to the political leader in the terminology of Qur'anic exegesis, al-Subkī turns to the sultan in his fifth example of where gratitude is due. In a fascinating phrase, al-Subkī states, "The Sultan—I mean the Grand Imam" (*al-Sulṭān aʿnī al-imām al-aʿẓam*). He then clarifies that jurists have written much under the section of the imamate in their legal works as well as devoted special works to laws of Islamic governance (*al-aḥkām al-sulṭāniyyah*), and he intends to point out only the most important of these matters neglected by kings (*al-mulūk*). al-Subkī then discusses details of the sultan's duties regarding the military, the system of *iqṭāʿāt*, respect and material support for scholars and mystics, the Public Treasury, and matters of religion and prayer.[95]

It is utterly fascinating that al-Subkī has transferred the legal discourse of the imam's responsibilities to the sultan with a quick stroke of the pen. The caliph remains a ceremonial figurehead—he is not disregarded in the overall conception of the state or the ranking of its officials, but the sultan functions as the actual chief executive—the locus of Islamic rulings regarding the imamate, which were once synonymous with the caliphate and not the sultanate. Similar to al-Juwaynī before him, who was concerned about the actual exercise of power in the state, or the true *qā ʾim bi-hādhā al-amr* in al-Juwaynī's poignant words, al-Subkī recognizes that the sultan is the one who has assumed the onus of the imām's actual responsibilities despite the physical presence of a presiding caliph. Indeed, al-Subkī records his admiration for al-Juwaynī's contributions in *Ghiyāth al-Umam* in another context.[96] Yet by the eighth/fourteenth century, al-Subkī no longer needed to adduce jurisprudential proofs of the soundness of this approach as al-Juwaynī had done in the fifth/eleventh century nor even to clarify the process of comprehensive delegation in this context as Ibn Jamāʿah had done in the seventh/thirteenth century. Over the passage of four centuries, the profound legal reasoning first introduced by al-Juwaynī had become so entrenched and widely embraced that al-Subkī could afford to make merely a passing reference. In composing a moral work intended for a broad audience spanning the social spectrum, al-Subkī could reasonably expect that his non-specialist readership would comprehend his allusions to the proper roles of the Abbasid caliph and Mamluk sultan in the Islamic legal and cultural discourse of his times.

THE INTER-SCHOOL POLEMICS OF NAJM AL-DĪN AL-ṬARSŪSĪ

Over a decade after having served as Damascene chief justice, al-Subkī could also reflect on the lessons of his youth and evaluate his own teachers with the retrospective distance of a matured scholar. As much as he had adored al-Dhahabī and still appreciated his scholarly patronage, al-Subkī also felt compelled to be honest in his criticism of his teacher. Despite belonging to the Shāfiʿī school of law, al-Dhahabī leaned heavily toward the minority theological opinions of the Ḥanbalīs and belittled the majority of Sunni scholars who identified as Ashʿarites.[97] In al-Subkī's mind, the natural association between Shāfiʿī law and Ashʿarī theology was clear; the vast majority of Shāfiʿīs in his age were Ashʿarī, as were many Ḥanafī and Mālikī jurists. al-Dhahabī had adopted a marginal stance. Reading against the grain of such assertions inspired George Makdisi to argue that the Ḥanbalī school "spearheaded a traditional revival between the eleventh and thirteenth centuries" to become the main religious current among Muslims. Yet as Wilfred Madelung and Khaled El-Rouayheb have demonstrated, Ashʿarism, along with Maturidism, had conclusively reached social and intellectual predominance and the two theological schools were regarded as Sunni orthodoxy by the fifth/eleventh century. The charismatic Ḥanbalī anthropomorphist Ibn Taymiyyah and his partisans were relegated to social marginality and faced discretionary punishments and imprisonment when they clashed with the power of the Mamluk State and its scholarly elites.[98]

With access to power, resources, and reputations at stake, academic rivalries, especially across legal schools of thought, continued to roil throughout the Mamluk era. These tensions remained even after—or perhaps particularly because of—the Mamluk sultan al-Malik al-Ẓāhir Baybars's alteration of the judicial system to appoint four chief justices in Cairo in 663/1265 and in Damascus in 664/1266, selected from each of the main legal schools of thought. Although the Shāfiʿī chief justice would retain jurisdiction over questions exclusively associated with the state, namely the public treasury, the property of orphans, and the supervision of charitable endowments, as well as some administrative oversight of the judiciary, his authority and power were circumscribed. No longer could the Cairene chief justice Ibn Bint al-Aʿazz decline to implement the contravening rulings of his Mālikī, Ḥanafī, and Ḥanbalī judicial subordinates. As Yossef Rapoport has argued, the Mamluk sultan's reform was not "merely a matter of political expediency" but institutionally helped foster a more flexible yet stable legal system by multiplying the number of judicial recourses available. This legal plurality was especially significant given that Mamluk-era judges were expected to rule according to the established positions of their particular school rather than follow individual judicial discretion.[99]

Despite a high degree of cooperation among the judges who referred cases to one another to facilitate greater leniency and realization of public interest in recognition of their institutional limitations, friction between adherents of the different legal schools remained. Both Tāj al-Dīn al-Subkī, as well as his father before him, and Najm al-Dīn Ibrāhīm b. ʿAlī al-Ṭarsūsī (710–58/1310–57) served as chief justices in this new quadruple system, representing the Shāfiʿī and Ḥanafī schools of law respectively. Framing his work as a gift of advice on matters of governance, al-Ṭarsūsī wrote a treatise for the Mamluk sultan of his day, al-Malik al-Nāṣir Ḥasan b. Muḥammad b. Qalāwūn (735–62/1334–61), which he titled *Tuḥfat al-Turk fī mā Yajibu an Yuʿmala fīʾl-Mulk*. As Riḍwān al-Sayyid has argued though, the composition more closely resembles the genre of juristic disagreement (*ikhtilāf fiqhī*) than any other. And through this juristic disputation, al-Ṭarsūsī hoped to persuade al-Malik al-Nāṣir of the superior merits of the Ḥanafī school for the Mamluk Sultanate. "He tries to convince the Mamluk Sultan to transform the Ḥanafī school into state law and to neglect the other schools of law," al-Sayyid writes, "by virtue of the Mamluks being Ḥanafīs and the Ḥanafī school being best suited for the Sultanate and the Sultan."[100]

First and foremost, al-Ṭarsūsī seeks to discredit his Shāfiʿī counterparts through his polemical representation of their position on the imamate. Citing authoritative figures of the Shāfiʿī school of law, including its eponymous founder

Imam al-Shāfiʿī from the second/eighth century, a compiler of political rulings al-Mawardī from the fifth/eleventh century, and the school's "modern" pillars al-Rāfiʿī and al-Nawawī from the seventh/thirteenth century, al-Ṭarsūsī stresses the Shāfiʿī stipulation that an imām must be a *mujtahid* and a *qurashī*. In other words, the imām must be a scholar of the highest caliber able to exert independent judgment, and he should be descended from the Prophet's kinsfolk of Quraysh, among several other credentials. Yet it is these two criteria in particular that interest al-Ṭarsūsī, for he utilizes them to argue that the Shāfiʿī school mandates that the Mamluk *sultan* must possess them. And, as al-Ṭarsūsī takes care to stress, al-Malik al-Nāṣir as a member of the ruling non-Arab Turkic military elite clearly did not meet these standards. As a result, al-Ṭarsūsī asserts that the Shāfiʿīs regard the Mamluk sultan as an illegitimate ruler and that his legal rivals are therefore unsuited for, and should be debarred from, public office. Given the Shāfiʿī position on the imamate, al-Ṭarsūsī argues, "The Sultan should not appoint any one from the Shāfiʿīs to public office or judgeship at all because they claim that the Sultanate belongs to Quraysh and that the Turks should not have any Sultanate." Instead, the overall position of legal supremacy and lower-level judgeships should go to Ḥanafīs, who having no such foul preconditions in al-Ṭarsūsī's mind, are more suited to serve the sultan.[101]

Editing this manuscript, Riḍwān al-Sayyid is horrified by these vehement allegations and even inserts parenthetical exclamation marks where al-Ṭarsūsī equates the words *sulṭān* and *imām* in his anti-Shāfiʿī polemics. Yet the situation appears to be even more complex. By the eighth/fifteenth century, it seems that all Mamluk legal schools were referring to the *sulṭān* as the *imām*. The younger al-Subkī certainly did so in his *Muʿīd al-Niʿam* discussed above, and al-Ṭarsūsī himself repeatedly interchanges the two terms throughout his *Tuḥfat al-Turk* while advocating Ḥanafī positions on governance. In order to ensure the continuity and stability of the Islamic legal system in the Mamluk era, it appears that Muslim jurists by the eighth/fifteenth century had transferred the jurisprudential discourse of the *imām*, or leader of the community, from the caliph to the sultan with the transfer of his executive powers by comprehensive delegation, or *tafwīd ʿāmm*. As such, the sultan, as executive head of state, remained obliged to follow the guidelines of Islamic political jurisprudence. Orphans still needed to be taken care of, the public treasury still needed to be administered, appointments to public office still needed to made, and so on. These responsibilities of the "imām" to administer public affairs did not disappear with the realignment of political positions. Yet the Shāfiʿīs did *not* in fact transfer stipulation of Qurashī descent from the caliph, who remained a ceremonial head of state, to the Mamluk sultan. Ibn Jamāʿah had made this point expressly clear in his *Taḥrīr al-Aḥkām*. And as for the question of *ijtihād*, Shāfiʿīs had long argued that it was possible for the head of state to rely on others for the necessary knowledge he individually lacked. Yet al-Ṭarsūsī certainly did not cite these nuances in the Shāfiʿī school's position as it had evolved over time. Instead, he attempted to terrify the sultan by warning him of the potential consequences of lacking full legitimacy according to the Shāfiʿīs: He could lose the respect and obedience of the populace and even worse lose the loyalty of his army. All the more reason, al-Ṭarsūsī argues, for the sultan to entrench the Ḥanafīs in power.[102]

al-Ṭarsūsī even cites a conversation he had with the elder al-Subkī to disparage the suitability of "*his* madhhab" as a Shāfiʿī for the Mamluk State. As the Shāfiʿī chief justice, the elder al-Subkī was entrusted with overseeing the overall working of the quadruple legal system in Damascus, including the three other schools' affairs, as well as adjudicating certain matters of state according to his own school. Clearly irritated by this arrangement, al-Ṭarsūsī argues that the Shāfiʿīs are not particularly suited to a position of legal primacy in the Mamluk system, by Taqiyy al-Dīn al-Subkī's own admission. In particular, al-Ṭarsūsī seeks to undermine the Shāfiʿī position on the public treasury, broadly considered to be favorable to the state. The Shāfiʿī school held that the treasury would inherit from a deceased person in the absence of legal heirs, which typically excluded some extended family members (*dhawī'l-arḥām*) if they lacked a designated bequest. Yet when asked about this matter by al-Ṭarsūsī, Taqiyy al-Dīn al-Subkī indicated that the corruption of the public treasury had led to the suspension of the practice. Although this point of perceived Shāfiʿī advantage was rendered moot, al-Ṭarsūsī highlights eleven other matters of state where he considers the Ḥanafī school to be more favorable to the sultan than the Shāfiʿī school. In all of these issues, the Shāfiʿīs appear to encroach upon and delimit the power of the sultan, in comparison to the freer hand permitted by the Ḥanafī position.[103] With the discussion over the imamate as a lynchpin, al-Ṭarsūsī vigorously argues for the greater elegibility of his own school of thought over that of his judicial counterparts among the Shāfiʿīs and aspires to Ḥanafī supremacy within the Mamluk legal system.

IBN KHALDŪN'S POLITICAL ENTANGLEMENTS AND IDEALS

Called "the greatest theoretician of history" and a "father of sociology," Ibn Khaldūn (732–84/1332–1406) also served as chief justice in the Mamluk capital, representing the Mālikī school of law. Escaping a life of public prominence in North Africa and Spain, Ibn Khaldūn moved in 784/1383 to the cosmopolitan city of Cairo where he would spend the last twenty-three years of his life. There, however, he quickly became enmeshed in Mamluk politics, developing close relations with the first Circassian Mamluk sultan Barqūq and eventually serving as Mālikī chief justice a total of six tumultuous times. On the first occasion in 786/1384, the appointment of a recently arrived "foreigner" reportedly caused great resentment in Egyptian scholarly circles, perhaps all the more so since Ibn Khaldūn refused to don the customary judicial attire of Mamluk Egypt and continued to identify himself in person and in dress as a western

North African. Within roughly nine months, however, Ibn Khaldūn had resigned this position, to which he would return several times over the years. Yet his sojourn in the Mamluk domains also offered Ibn Khaldūn the time and wider horizons with which to revise his celebrated universal history and its prolegomena.[104]

Evaluating the fluctuating circumstances of civilizations, Ibn Khaldūn carefully observed the contemporary polities of his times and reflected on those of the past. In his estimation, an Islamic caliphate that fulfilled its purpose constituted the ideal form of governance. Ibn Khaldūn considered political rule to be a social necessity for human beings, in order to organize their affairs, and recognized it could take multiple forms. Visceral power (*al-mulk al-ṭabīʿī*) derived from anger and people's animal nature, compelling others to comply with otherwise narrow and selfish interests, typically resulting in wide injustices. The policies of rational politics (*siyāsah ʿaqliyyah* and *al-mulk al-siyāsī*), however, were crafted by society's intelligentsia and statesmen to achieve broader, public interests. The Sacred Law, Ibn Khaldūn asserts, does not condemn such rational politics or even the human drive for leadership, but it censures the attendant oppression, use of force, and unnecessary indulgences in luxury and instead directs and elevates these human instincts to a higher plane. Rational politics could be sufficient to govern a society in Ibn Khaldūn's view, but it was also limited. It only considers the temporal dimension of life on earth, and it does not additionally discern matters with the light bestowed by God. Thus, religious politics, also known as the caliphate (*siyāsah dīniyyah* and *khilāfah*), as Ibn Khaldūn clarifies, looks out for people's temporal as well as their eternal interests. And the Sacred Law revealed by God to his prophets leads people back to Him through rectifying their worship, social transactions, and political affairs. This form of leadership was undertaken by the prophets and then the caliphs as their successors.[105]

Islamic history, Ibn Khaldūn observes, had begun with a pure caliphate when the Rightly Guided Caliphs assumed leadership of the Muslim community one after another for thirty years following the death of the Prophet Muḥammad; yet the situation soon changed. After this initial period, the aims of royal and caliphal authority blended and intertwined. And ultimately, the Muslim community was left with pure kingship (*mulk*), and the forces of socio-political cohesion or *ʿaṣabiyyah* for kingship and the caliphate went their separate ways. As Ibn Khaldūn argued in theory, *ʿaṣabiyyah* was the solidarity necessary among people to propel their government to political heights; it could be used for good, like securing people's general welfare, or for evil, like succumbing to false pride and imagining shared superiority over others. People would be wiser, Ibn Khaldūn argued, to think of their fate in the hereafter and humble standing before God.[106]

Perhaps it may have been a desire to restore this socio-political cohesion or *ʿaṣabiyyah* of the caliphate that helped persuade Ibn Khaldūn to sign the fatwā against his patron sultan Barqaq during the 791/1389 rebellion. As detailed in the previous chapter, the fatwā produced and signed by a state council of scholars in Damascus, where Ibn Khaldūn was visiting, had complained of Barqūq's poor treatment and removal of al-Mutawakkil II as caliph—even after Barqūq had preemptively reinstated al-Mutawakkil II to stem the swelling tide of popular and military discontent. As Ibn Khaldūn had elucidated, the indispensible presence of al-Mutawakkil II as Abbasid caliph enabled the legitimate functioning of religious offices, such as those of prayer-leaders, preachers, pilgrimage guides, collectors of charity, as well as other offices, and garnered God's blessings upon the whole of society.[107]

Yet the heated dispute with Barqūq was not Ibn Khaldūn's only encounter and adjudication in the contemporary contestation over caliphal legitimacy during the early Circassian period. Over a decade later, in 803/1401, within the first couple of years of the reign of Barqūq's son al-Nāṣir Faraj as Mamluk sultan, another Abbasid staked his claim before none other than the ferocious Timur (728–807/1328–1405),[108] known in Europe as Tamerlane. During Timur's siege of Damascus, one of the descendants[109] of al-Ḥākim I, the long-lived progenitor of the Abbasid dynasty in Cairo, sought Timur's intervention in the affairs of the caliphate. In the words of Ibn Khaldūn, translated by Walter Fischer:

> He presented himself before Sultan Timur and asked of him justice in his cause, claiming from him the position of Caliph as it had belonged to his ancestors. Sultan Timur replied to him, "I will summon the jurists and the judges for you, and if they decide anything in your favor I will render justice to you accordingly."

Yet the Abbasid claimant inadvertently squandered his opportunity to have Timur instate him as caliph. In presenting his case, the Abbasid explained that a sound tradition, or *ḥadīth* of the Prophet, declared that the caliphate belonged to the Abbasids for as long as the world endured (*inna al-amr li-Banī ʿAbbās mā baqiyat al-dunyā yaʿnī amr al-khilāfah*). And he argued that he had more of a right to the caliphate than its current holder in Cairo, al-Mutawakkil II, who had assumed it without a solid legal foundation, whereas the claimant's own Abbasid forefathers had rightfully deserved the office (*innī aḥaqq min ṣāḥib al-manṣib al-ān bi-miṣr li-anna ābāʾī alladhī* [*sic*] *warathtuhum kānū qad istaḥaqqūhu wa-ṣāra ilā hādhā bi-ghayr mustanad*). The scholars were silent. Perhaps they were reluctant to interfere and hesitant to create havoc. What would it have meant for the invading Timur to have elevated a rival Abbasid caliph in Damascus against the intensely popular al-Mutawakkil II based in Cairo? And from all appearances, the individual claims of this particular Abbasid were weak.

Conveniently, the Timurid advisor ʿAbd al-Jabbār b. Nuʿmān (ca. 770–805 /ca. 1368–1403)[110] provided an opening and a way out of the uncomfortable situation. He asked what his fellow scholars thought about the reputed prophetic tradition itself—and not about the supplicant's rights within the Abbasid family vis-à-vis al-Mutawwakil. This statement they readily disavowed as not being sound (*laysa bi-ṣaḥīḥ*). And upon hearing this, Timur inquired, perhaps with some measure of surprise, how then the caliphate had devolved upon the Abbasids until the present, and Ibn Khaldūn recounted the vital history of the caliphate from the death of the Prophet Muḥammad down to the Abbasids of Cairo. He concluded with the flourish, "Authority has been transmitted from members of his [i.e., al-Ḥākim's] family down to the present one who is in Cairo. Nothing is known contrary to that," whereupon Timur turned to his Abbasid supplicant with the chastisement, "You have heard the words of the judges and jurists, and it appears that you have no justification for claiming it [the caliphate] before me; so depart—may God guide you aright!"[111] Far from remaining an abstract theoretical concern, Ibn Khaldūn's interpretations of the caliphate once again intermingled with the vicissitudes of contemporary politics.

THE MAMLUK CHANCERY CONTRIBUTIONS OF AL-QALQASHANDĪ

Like his elder contemporary Ibn Khaldūn, the Egyptian scholar Shihāb al-Dīn Aḥmad al-Qalqashandī (756–821/1355–1418) was another Muslim jurist affiliated with the Mamluk State apparatus. A descendant of the Arabian tribe Banū Badr that had settled in the Egyptian delta, al-Qalqashandī was born in a rural town north of Cairo and later began his Islamic studies in Alexandria. In his early twenties, al-Qalqashandī received his license to teach and issue legal opinions according to the Shāfiʿī school from Sirāj al-Dīn ʿUmar b. ʿAlī Ibn al-Mulaqqin (726–804/1323–1401), and he also composed a couple of legal commentaries on Shāfiʿī texts. But rather than pursue the professional path of the judiciary, al-Qalqashandī entered government service through the chancery. He first served the Mamluk governor of Alexandria Salāḥ al-Dīn Ibn ʿArrām for a spell, before transferring to Cairo in 791/1389 to work under the chief secretary (*Kātib al-Sirr*) of the Mamluk sultan Barqūq, Badr al-Dīn Muḥammad Ibn Faḍl Allāh al-ʿUmarī (d. 796/1394). In his prestigious position as secretary in the royal administration, al-Qalqashandī sat in the company of the Mamluk sultan during the public dispensation of justice, affixed the sultan's signature to executive decisions, and wrote out the most important of official documents. al-Qalqashandī eventually assumed even higher judicial office in the Mamluk State (*nabā fī'l-ḥukm*) for a number of years.[112]

In addition to the renowned encyclopedic tome he wrote on the secretarial profession, *Ṣubḥ al-Aʿshā fī Ṣināʿat al-Inshā*, al-Qalqashandī authored a comprehensive work on the caliphate, *Maʾāthir al-Ināfah fī Maʿālim al-Khilāfah*, during the last few years of his life. This composition he dedicated to the one person he recognized as the Muslim leader of his age (*al-imām al-aʿẓam* and *khalīfat al-ʿaṣr*), the Abbasid caliph in Cairo, al-Muʿtaḍid billāh III Dāwūd (r. Muḥarram 4, 817–Rabīʿ al-Awwal 4, 845 / March 26, 1414–July 23, 1441). Subtly linking the caliph's personal name Dāwūd (or David) with the accumulated scholarly tradition regarding the caliphate (including the exegetical discussion of God's designation of Prophet David as a vicegerent on earth in Qur'an 38:26), al-Qalqashandī allows that "no one can deny the virtues of the caliphate of Dāwūd." And in elaborating on the merits of al-Muʿtaḍid, al-Qalqashandī states, "He is, in reality, the leader of the religion and the caliph of Islam, and [he is] the religious leader whose lineage connects him to the other religious leaders [of Islam], for he is the *imām* son of the *imām* son of the *imām* son of the *imām*." In this vision, the transregional Muslim community (*al-ummah*) surrenders its affairs to his care, its members hasten from everywhere to him, and they find that his "generous qualities" and "glorious deeds" (*maʾāthir*) cannot be delimited nor his wonders enumerated. With great rhetorical skill, al-Qalqashandī evokes the emotive pith of a deep-rooted religious discourse surrounding the caliphate; he conjures the Abbasid caliph of Cairo as the religious pinnacle of an interconnected Muslim community and its shepherd. As such, the latest transfer of the Islamic caliphate from Baghdad to Cairo, upheld by continuously linked generations of Abbasid caliphs, elicits his praise and gratitude to the Almighty.[113]

In broadly conceptualizing the Islamic caliphate in his *Maʾāthir al-Ināfah*, al-Qalqashandī presents multiple context-specific definitions, including a flowery and impassioned description, a technical linguistic and professional assessment, and a hagiographic distinction of the institution from baser forms of political power. In seeking to stress the importance of his subject matter in his prefatory remarks, al-Qalqashandī emphasizes the vital necessity of the caliphate for Muslims. It is "the enclosure of Islam, the protection of its domain, the meadow of its flock, and the pasture of its weary (*ḥaẓīrat al-islām, wa muḥīṭ dāʾiratih, wa marbaʿ raʿāyāh, wa martaʿ sāʾimatih*). By it the religion is preserved and protected, the territory of Islam is safeguarded, and the populace dwell in peace." And by incorporating material from his chancery manual *Ṣubḥ al-Aʿshā*, al-Qalqashandī professionally dissects and analyzes the key terms of *Maʾāthir al-Ināfah*: caliphate (*khilāfah*), caliph (*khalīfah*), and other associated expressions. In explicating the meaning of the word "caliphate," al-Qalqashandī discusses its morphology and common usage before noting that it constitutes "public office over the entire community, the undertaking of its affairs, and the bearing of its burdens." And while acknowledging the customary application of the term "caliph" to all holders of this public office, even beyond the initial thirty-year period of righteous caliphate that the Prophet predicted would be followed by kingship, al-Qalqashandī also points to the term's higher moral connotations of true justice. As the Prophet's Persian companion Salmān once reportedly clarified the distinction between a caliph and a king in response to the second caliph ʿUmar's inquiry, "[The caliph] is the one who deals with his flock justly and apportions [resources] among them fairly, who shows compassion and concern for them the way a man has compassion for his wife or a parent for his child, and who judges among them by the Book of God the Exalted."[114]

As the subsequent portions of *Ma'āthir al-Ināfah* illuminate, al-Qalqashandī's legal exposition of the caliphate—both in his first full chapter and in his *Ṣubḥ al-A'shā*—were composed to bolster the theoretical foundations of the Cairene institution. He deftly crafts a legal argument for the enduring necessity of the caliphate, the validity of the Abbasid Caliphate of Cairo (as meeting individual and procedural conditions), and the fallaciousness of competing claimants past and present. In this context, the first point al-Qalqashandī addresses is the Islamic legal obligation of contracting the imamate with someone who can fulfill the position. He notes the broad scholarly consensus on this point and comments that the rare exception, in the form of al-Aṣamm, only confirms the rule. Whether scholars affirmed this legal obligation on the basis of rational thought (that every people need a leader to avert injustice, oppression, and social chaos) or revelation (because that leader also needed to uphold religion and the prophetic way), there was no difference of opinion over its obligatory nature for the Muslim community (*farḍ kifāyah*). Citing the work of al-Māwardī and al-Nawawī in particular, al-Qalqashandī observes that were the institution not to be established, the sin of omission would fall upon the potential electors and those qualified to serve as caliph.[115]

Furthermore, al-Qalqashandī invokes the legal stipulations concerning the necessary qualifications for caliphal office and electoral procedure to uphold the sanctity of the Abbasid Caliphate of Cairo and to undermine the claims of the past Umayyads of Spain as well as the bygone Fatimids and contemporaneous Hafsids of North Africa. In the first instance, al-Qalqashandī discusses the legal necessity of a caliphal candidate's possessing the right lineage to legitimize his imamate. After presenting textual support for stipulating descent from Quraysh, he also cites the analyses of his Shāfi'ī predecessors al-Rāfi'ī (555–623/1160–1226), al-Baghawī (d. ca. 510/1117), and al-Mutawallī (426–78/1035–86) regarding the proper course of action in the potential absence of a fully qualified Qurashī candidate. al-Rāfi'ī sequentially enlarged the pool of qualified candidates from members of Quraysh, to those of Kinānah, to the descendants of Ishmael, to any other qualified individual, whereas al-Baghawī and al-Mutawallī immediately reassign the role to a non-Arab or Arab candidate respectively. But by according initial preference to Quraysh, al-Qalqashandī paves the way to affirming the legitimacy of the Abbasid caliphs of Cairo because of the unquestioned veracity of their genealogical claims. By contrast, he castigates those of the Fatimids and the Hafsids as spurious, which only confirms the invalidity of their caliphal assertions—a position, as Nasser Rabbat notes, of wide scholarly consensus in Mamluk Egypt.[116] In terms of electoral procedure, al-Qalqashandī also discusses the scholastic difference of opinion within the Shāfiʿī legal school over validating more than one caliphate at a given time. Yet he affirms the majority opinion that it is impermissibile. In doing so, al-Qalqashandī marshals his strongest scriptural and legal arguments against the caliphal claims of the Andalusian Umayyads, the Fatimids, and the Hafsids despite their great distance from the Abbasids of Baghdad and Cairo. The true caliphs, he remarks, form a continuous line (*jārūna ʿalā nasq wāḥid*) from the Rightly Guided Caliphs, to the Umayyads in Syria, to the Abbasids in Iraq, to the Abbasids in Egypt up until his day, one after the other.[117]

Even in the event that a caliph is imprisoned or his movement restricted by his deputies, which occurred frequently in Mamluk Egypt as readily shown by al-Qalqashandī's own historical narrative, he stresses the continuing legal foundation of such a caliphate. Utilizing the work of al-Māwardī as a precedent in constitutional law, al-Qalqashandī embraces this theoretical extension of the legally valid assumption of the imamate by force. The argument as a whole hinges on the powerful deputy's sustained declaration of obedience to the Abbasid caliph; his legally deputized Seljuq or Mamluk sultan has not openly rebelled. As a result, the valid execution of Islamic laws and Muslim communal unity are not imperiled under such a sultanate, in the same way that they would be preserved under a forcefully assumed imamate. Whether the rule of law is administered by a powerful imam or a domineering yet deputized sultan is materially irrelevant. In fact, al-Qalqashandī naturalizes this subtle transformation as part and parcel of the institution's historical development: whereas in the past a caliph used to appoint all public officials as demonstrated by his signature on their papers, following the caliphate's transfer from Baghdad to Cairo, a caliph directly deputized only the sultan, giving him all-encompassing powers (*tafwīḍ al-umūr al-ʿāmmah*) in order for the sultan to designate all other official appointees.[118]

Through his discussion of such official documents, correspondence, and customs, al-Qalqashandī further integrates the Abbasid caliphs of Cairo into an illustrious caliphal heritage extending all the way back to Abū Bakr as the first successor to the Prophet Muḥammad. He does so by detailing how the traditions of the Islamic caliphate and its chancery have evolved over the centuries and noting the specific ways in which Cairene practices either follow or diverge from earlier precedents. The pledge of allegiance to al-Ḥākim II as caliph in the year 661/1262, for instance, exemplifies the third of four patterns that al-Qalqashandī identifies for the preparation of these caliphal documents since the first Islamic century. Yet the pledges of allegiance that al-Qalqashandī personally composed for Cairene Abbasid caliphs as well as the one drawn up for al-Muʿtaḍid III in 817/1414 follow the fourth and final pattern by opening with the praise of God as had become customary in the Egyptian chancery of his day. Steeped in this accretionary chancery tradition, al-Qalqashandī additionally describes how he had utilized an earlier eighth/fourteenth-century document to prepare al-Mutawakkil II's official designation of al-Mustaʿīn as his successor to the Abbasid Caliphate in Cairo.[119]

al-Qalqashandī's presentation of these various approaches also offers intriguing insights into the ongoing development and discussion of these secretarial practices in Mamluk Egypt even as he intentionally honors the Abbasid caliph as part of a living and lasting heritage. For a caliph's deputation of other Muslim leaders and rulers, al-Qalqashandī records four different documentary approaches, the first of which was initiated in imitation of the Prophet Muḥammad's own example and utilized over the centuries. From his own participation in the bureaucracy, al-Qalqashandī attests that this particular chancery tradition signified the prevailing mode in Mamluk Egypt and adduces three examples written by al-Shaykh Shihāb al-Dīn Maḥmūd al-Ḥalabī and al-Mawlā Shams al-Din Ibrāhīm b. al-Qaysarī from the caliphal reigns of al-Ḥākim I and al-Ḥākim II. However, the Egyptian chief secretary Fakhr al-Din Ibn Luqmān contravened this dominant practice in his preparation of al-Ḥākim I's documents, discussed in the previous chapter, deputizing and legitimizing Baybars as his sultan in 659/1261. Even though this fourth distinct pattern was later adopted by the Judge Muḥyī'l-Dīn Ibn ʿAbd al-Ẓāhir as a model for the caliphal investiture of the Mamluk sultan Qalāwūn in 678/1279, the divergence from standard secretarial practice earned the later censure of the eminent Shihāb al-Dīn Aḥmad Ibn Faḍl Allāh al-ʿUmarī (700–749/1301–49), the author of *al-Taʿrīf bi'l-Muṣṭalaḥ al-Sharīf* who headed the Mamluk chancery in Cairo and Damascus and was also known as al-Maqarr al-Shihābī. Yet al-Qalqashandī demurs at this critical assessment by recording an earlier chancery precedent from Baghdad dating from Rajūb 630 / April 1233. This crucial Abbasid antecedent, written by the Vizier Abu'l-Azhar Aḥmad b. Nāqid on behalf of the Caliph al-Mustanṣir for the Ayyubid sultan al-Malik al-Kāmil, maintains a legitimizing link between the two Abbasid bureaucracies.[120]

Moreover, al-Qalqashandī's assessment of the state bureaucracy through its evidentiary materials and customs reveals his personal and professional attachment to acknowledging the Abbasid caliph as its acclaimed leader. On the one hand, al-Qalqashandī details the various regalia associated with caliphs past and present, taking care to note the marks of honor still accorded to the Abbasid caliphs of Cairo. And he documents in great detail the manner in which caliphs have deputized other rulers in their presence and absence, including the Buyids, Seljuqs, Ayyubids, and Mamluks. But even more significantly, he interprets the arguably diminished role of the caliph in Mamluk Egypt as evidence of his lofty stature. For al-Qalqashandī, the change in official correspondence from addressing the person of the caliph to addressing his administration (the Mamluk bureaucracy) denotes a deep and enduring respect for the caliphal office and its representative in his age. In this matter, he documents the opinion of al-Maqarr al-Shihābī that this transformation in correspondence was motivated by humility towards the exalted caliph; one should address him by praying for the success of the administration that was both intimately associated with the caliphal personage and drew its entire legitimacy from his sanction. Yet al-Qalqashandī also registered his disagreement with this approach as not being sufficiently reverential. It was more appropriate, he argued, for such letters to begin addressing the caliph by rhetorically kissing the ground before him in an even greater display of humility and subservience "because kings are [the caliph's] representatives and his followers and not above him in station" (*idh al-mulūk nuwwābuh wa-atbāʿuh wa lā aʿlā minhu rutbatan*).[121] Through his legal and secretarial work within the Mamluk bureaucracy, al-Qalqashandī vigorously affirmed the significance and stature of the Abbasid Caliphate of Cairo.

AL-SHĪRĀZĪ'S METAPHYSICAL EXALTATION OF THE ABBASID CALIPH IN CAIRO

Another Shāfiʿī jurist who expressed his adoration for the Abbasid caliph al-Muʿtaḍid III was ʿAlāʾ al-Dīn ʿAlī b. Aḥmad al-Shīrāzī (788–861/1386–1457). al-Muʿtaḍid had assumed the caliphate following the deposition of his brother al-Mustaʿīn, the short-lived sultan-caliph discussed in chapter 2. Yet far from denigrating the institution and displaying cynicism over al-Muʿtaḍid's comparative lack of executive powers, al-Shīrāzī continued to uphold and venerate the Abbasid Caliphate of Cairo as the bedrock of all society and politics. Born in Baghdad, al-Shīrāzī was descended from the Prophet Muḥammad's Companions, among the *Anṣār*, and began his religious studies later in life. He became especially distinguished in the fields of positive law, legal methodology, grammar, logic, and spirituality, among others, to the extent that the readily acerbic biographer al-Sakhāwī (830–902/1427–97) noted with admiration how his knowledge was unsurpassed in some specialties. al-Shīrāzī eventually moved from Mesopotamia to the sacred environs of Mecca under Mamluk suzerainty. There, as an honored inhabitant of the noble sanctuary, he taught many people and grew in fame and stature. al-Sakhāwī himself came to listen to portions of al-Shīrāzī's books read out loud by the author, including a Qur'anic exegesis and a legal commentary, and commended al-Shīrāzī's mastery of theology, his eloquence, his luminosity, and his character. al-Sakhāwī may have also heard portions of a special composition that al-Shīrāzī had prepared some thirteen years prior. After a new sultan had come to power in Cairo on Rabīʿ al-Awwal 19, 842 / September 10, 1438, al-Shīrāzī benefited from his munificence and patronage, especially in facilitating al-Shīrāzī's efforts to rebuild and revive al-Sayyidah Khadījah's birthplace in Mecca as a spiritual center for teaching and fellowship. As a gift of appreciation, al-Shīrāzī composed a lengthy manuscript called "Tuḥfat al-Mulūk wa'l-Salāṭīn fīmā Yaqūmu bihi Usus al-Dīn," advising the new sovereign al-Malik al-Ẓāhir Abū Saʿīd Jaqmaq (ca. 777–857 /

FIGURE 12. A copy of al-Shīrāzī's ninth/fifteenth-century manuscript "Tuḥfat al-Mulūk" portraying the Mamluk sultan's obedience to the Abbasid caliph as the key to every success.

Image courtesy Alī b. Ahmad b. Muḥammad b. Abī Bakr b. Muḥammad al Shīrāzī, "Tuḥfat al-Mulūk wa-ʾl-Salāṭīn," Ijitmāʿ Taymūr Collection, Manuscript 72, folios 82–83, Egyptian National Library, Cairo, Egypt.

ca. 1375–1453) on how to conduct his affairs.[122] The foundation for the sultan's success, al-Shīrāzī argued, depended upon his demonstration of respect and obedience to the Abbasid caliph.

Writing nearly two centuries after the Mongol conquest of Baghdad, al-Shīrāzī's insistence on the centrality of the Cairene Abbasid caliph for contemporary affairs, in both legal and metaphysical terms, is simply stunning. In his explanation, the honor of the caliphate originates with the first of men and prophets: Adam. al-Shīrāzī invokes God's words to the angels, "I am putting a trustee (*khalīfah*) on earth" (Qur'an 2:30) to convey the honor of God's designating Adam as the first of caliphs responsible for tending to God's creation. In addition to selecting Adam for this high and noble station, God further distinguished him by placing this successive leadership in his progeny (*khalāʾif* in Qur'an 6:165). Accordingly, al-Shīrāzī describes the word caliph or *khalīfah* as the noblest of all titles. The best of creation in each era inherit this paternal role (*maqām al-ubuwwah*) from the father of humankind. No king or sultan can compare with the glory of a caliph, al-Shīrāzī asserts. Indeed, al-Shīrāzī explains that on a metaphysical plane, the caliph commands what God commands, and therefore opposition to him in reality means disobedience of God. As he elaborates, the caliphate traveled from prophet to prophet until it reached the Prophet Muḥammad, the final seal of prophets—and then from saint to saint after him and from him, until it reached "Our Master, the Commander of the Believers" al-Muʿtaḍid III Dāwūd. The caliph has been granted all the lands of Islam, al-Shīrāzī explains, as well as executive authority over them as the metaphorical shadow of God on earth in whom all the weak and powerless can seek refuge. His very presence provides stability and order in the world and yields immense blessings and benefit to all. In al- Shīrāzī's eyes, supporting religion and the welfare of Muslims are synonymous with taking care of the caliphate and appreciating its worth and the cause of success, salvation, and every good.[123]

Moreover, al-Shīrāzī explains that the success of the Mamluks in Egypt and Syria derives from and depends upon their sincere demonstrations of subordination to, love of, and respect to the Abbasid caliph in their midst. In strengthening their position through delegation and investiture on the part of the caliph, the sultans of Egypt managed to attain heights that no other sultans had achieved—although the sultans of India rank a close second for maintaining their connection with the Abbasid Caliphate in Cairo. Because the Mamluks are the caliph's own military forces, his blessings envelop them (*shamalahum barakatuh*) and elevate the Mamluk sultan of Egypt, as the Commander of the Believers's deputy, above the rest of kings and sultans. And al-Shīrāzī emphatically notes that no public office on the face of the earth, East or West, is valid without the caliph's delegation and authorization. Through his words, al-Shīrāzī offers a stirring reminder of the proper ordering and rank as well as the deep meanings and foundational value of the caliph in Mamluk State affairs.[124]

He also seeks to counter potential doubts over the caliphate's centrality, which appear to have been in common circulation. First, al-Shīrāzī rejects the notion that the caliphate had become obsolete after its destruction in Baghdad by restating the communal obligation to maintain a caliphate according to the Sacred Law. He also argues that the caliphate is not bound to a particular place, noting how it had transitioned from Medina to Mecca to Kufah to Damascus to Baghdad to Cairo. Next, al-Shīrāzī critiques the idea that the caliphate had ever gone into abeyance following the Mongol conquest of Baghdad. Rather, he argues that it was merely hidden while the Mongols and other oppressors afflicted Islam, Muslims, and the followers of the prophetic way—until God gave victory to the religion and supported the Sunni Muslims of Egypt. Under these favorable conditions, the caliphate once again became manifest. Third, al-Shīrāzī addresses the question of the caliph's actual power (*shawkah*) as a stipulation of office. His rejoinder is that the sultans of Egypt and their soldiers are the current caliphate's source of power (*hum shawkat al-khilāfah al-ān*)—even though al-Shīrāzī does not consider clout to be a necessary condition for the caliphate, following the much earlier opinion of al-Māwardī in the fifth/eleventh century. Nevertheless, he deems that the military leaders and electors in Mamluk Egypt have fulfilled their duties by lending their support to the caliphate and hence to truth itself. Since the Mamluk sultan and his predecessors have been continuously appointed by the Abbasid caliph to rule on his behalf, al-Shīrāzī remarks, the might of the sultan is in fact that of the caliph. Likewise, the rule of a Mamluk sultan after his delegation and appointment by the Abbasid caliph is actually the rule of caliph himself. [125]

In recognition of the caliph's legal, moral, and spiritual supremacy, al-Shīrāzī also explains how the Abbasid caliph al-Muʿtaḍid Dāwūd is the true leader (*al-imām al-ḥaqq*) of his times and that all Sunni Muslim rulers should obey and submit to him and request their deputation and delegation from him. As an exemplary model in this regard, the Mamluk sultan can be assured of his legitimacy and glory. And even the rulers of India, despite their great distance from the caliph, military might, and immense wealth, are honored by the caliph's deputization and cloaked in his authority, thereby assuring their legality and success. As for al-Muʿtaḍid himself, his august lineage, noble birth, religiosity, piety, good character, and fulfillment of all the conditions for a caliph, only augment the dignity and honor he bestows upon the Muslim community as its leader. Egyptians, in particular, are distinguished by the blessed caliph's presence in their midst (*innahu manqabah ʿaẓīmah li-ahl Miṣr ajmaʿihim*) and their longstanding support of him. And as the seat of the caliphate, Egypt is the most illustrious and glorious of lands (e.g., *innahā ashraf al-bilād* and *lahā al-fakhr ʿalā ghayrihā bi-qiyām al-khilāfah al-ṣaḥīḥah al-ʿAbbāsiyyah bihā khāṣṣatan duna ghayrihā*), and the many merits and diverse members of Mamluk State and society elicit al-Shīrāzī's extensive praise. al-Shīrāzī is distinctly grateful for their rising to fulfill the religious obligation of appointing and supporting the Islamic caliphate and considers it to be a clear proof of their rectitude and certitude.[126]

Throughout his discussion of the caliphate, al-Shīrāzī takes care to bolster and repeat at frequent intervals his central argument that obedience and submission to the Cairene Abbasid caliph is the foundation of every success, and conversely that disobedience to him is the root cause of perdition. Whether in the detailed intricacies of defining and explaining the caliphate or clarifying Muslims' responsibilities toward it, al-Shīrāzī felt the point must be made. By way of conclusion, he even devotes an entire section to the matter. Less frequently, yet certainly critically in political terms, al-Shīrāzī folds the Mamluk sultan into this schema of obedience as the caliph's deputy. In his framing, religio-political obedience is due to the caliph as the ultimate leader (*al-imām al-aʿẓam*), to the Mamluk sultan who had been designated and delegated by the caliph to execute his affairs, and to his designated public officials (*ulū'l-amr*) in turn. Obedience to them was obedience to God, following the verse (Qur'an 4:59) that has coursed through the history of Islamic political thought. And accordingly, evinced by love, it was a means to achieve divine pleasure.[127]

By contrast, though, al-Shīrāzī cautioned that rulers who had not yet submitted to the authority of Abbasid caliph and his deputy sultan without a valid cause were in a state of immoral defiance. And he feared that without the caliphal substantiation stipulated by the Sacred Law they could be encumbered with religious deficiencies and the invalidity of legal contracts. Echoing the worries of al-Ghazālī centuries before, al-Shīrāzī cautions that marriages could not be legally contracted under such circumstances and depicts the ensuing mayhem in families, vitiating the dignity of their progeny, their wealth, and all legal transactions, throwing society into complete disarray. Yet ultimately, al-Shīrāzī hopes that all Muslim states and their rulers would unite under the leadership of the Caliph al-Muʿtaḍid Dāwūd, putting an end to infighting among them, and securing their worldly and eternal benefit in obedience to God the Exalted. A couple of succinct phrases encapsulate these sentiments that al-Shīrāzī dwells upon at great length, namely, that the presence of the caliph brings legal order and stability to the world (*intaẓama bi-wujūdihi aḥkām al-ʿālam*) and that the caliph's manifestation sets the world aright, while his light rectifies affairs in the hereafter (*istaqāma bi-ẓuhūrihi al-dunyā wa-bi-nūrihi al-ukhrā*).[128]

al-Shīrāzī's aspirational vision of a pax Islamica is explicitly rooted in his loving memories of the time when the Prophet Muḥammad led the Muslim community in righteousness, followed by the Rightly Guided Caliphs who succeeded him at the community's helm. al-Shīrāzī held that it was from these previous generations that the caliph of his age had inherited his august position in an unbroken chain of sanctity. Not only did al-Muʿtaḍid Dāwūd ably meet all the legal requirements that jurists like al-Māwardī had required for a caliph, in al-Shīrāzī's view, but he was also fulfilling a cosmic role. Additionally, al-Shīrāzī saw the Abbasid caliph's presence in his day as a healing salve after the great catastrophe of 656/1258, which he reviewed and relived in his manuscript. The Mongol invasion of the caliphal capital of Baghdad nearly two hundred years before underscored the deep pain of past events and the necessity of the caliphate's transfer to Cairo. All of these strong threads of communal memory, emotion, divine designation, Sacred Law, and tragedy are adroitly woven together in al-Shīrāzī's narrative.[129]

As for al-Malik al-Ẓāhir Jaqmaq, his reign as Mamluk sultan would last for a little over thirteen years after al-Shīrāzī completed his manuscript as a gift on Jumādā al-Ākhirah 12, 843 / November 20, 1439. It extended beyond the remaining nearly two years of Muʿtaḍid III's caliphate into those of his caliphal successors al-Mustakfī III Sulaymān (r. 845–55/1441–51) and then al-Qāʾim II Ḥamza (r. 855–59/1451–55). And whether he took al-Shīrāzī's words to heart or not, historical sources of his era acknowledge Jaqmaq's visible respect for the Abbasid caliphs as well as his evident concern for the poor and orphans and securing their welfare. Considered blessed as a result, Jaqmaq's own reign as Mamluk sultan ended with his illness and death in 857/1453. Further north that same year, the young Ottoman sultan Mehmed II Fatih (835–86/1432–81) conquered the former capital of the Byzantine Empire, Constantinople, unleashing waves of celebration and mourning among the parties concerned. Another Rome had fallen, and yet another imperial version of it was in the making under the Ottomans.[130]

JALĀL AL-DĪN AL-SUYŪṬĪ'S DEVOTIONAL LOVE OF THE PROPHET'S FAMILY

It is often noted that Jalāl al-Dīn ʿAbd al-Raḥmān al-Suyūṭī (849–911/1445–1505) auspiciously began his scholarly career when he was born in his father's library, where his mother was retrieving a book and succumbed to the pangs of labor. Their child earned the sobriquet "the son of books" (*ibn al-kutub*)[131] and grew up to author hundreds of his own compositions as one of the most prolific and prominent scholars of the late Mamluk era. When the boy Jalāl al-Dīn was only three, his father, Kamāl al-Dīn Abū Bakr al-Suyūṭī, had taken care to have him attend, at least once, the lessons of the venerable traditionist Ibn Ḥajar al-ʿAsqalānī, who was by that time in his late seventies. Yet the scholastic inheritance of al-Suyūṭī's father extended beyond his appreciation of books and academic gatherings. The elder al-Suyūṭī was personally engaged in the service of the Abbasid caliph of Cairo al-Mustakfī III Sulaymān as his imām and was deeply attached to him. The father had composed the official documents designating al-Mustakfī III Sulaymān as the caliphal successor of his brother al-Muʿtaḍid III Dāwūd (whom al-Qalqashandī and al-Shīrāzī had so admired), "the leader of the believers, the son of the master of [all] messengers' uncle, and the inheritor of the rightly guided caliphs." Relating his father's high regard for al-Mustakfī III Sulaymān to his own, Jalāl al-Dīn al-Suyūṭī remarks that he grew up in the caliph's household witnessing the family's generosity and virtue. "His family is the best of families in religiosity, worship, and good," al-Suyūṭī reflects, "and I do not think there has been another caliph on the face of the earth after the family of ʿUmar b. ʿAbd al-ʿAzīz more devoted to worship than the family of this caliph." So close was his father to al-Mustakfī II that Jalāl al-Dīn al-Suyūṭī even connects their deaths: Kamāl al-Dīn al-Suyūṭī only lived for forty days or so after the passing of his beloved caliph in 855/1451 while young Jalāl al-Dīn was still a child.[132] Yet beyond material effects, Jalāl al-Dīn al-Suyūṭī inherited a deep and abiding love for the Abbasid Caliphate of Cairo, born of intimate personal experience and connections, which he cherished and elaborated through his scholarship.

Within the intricate social web of patronage and academic rivalry of late Mamluk Cairo, al-Suyūṭī utilized his close ties to the Abbasid caliphs to his distinct advantage. In matters of scholarship, al-Suyūṭī's proximity to the Abbasid family allowed him to consult even its female members as oral sources of historical information. Whereas Ibn Ḥajar had recorded in his earlier history that al-Muʿtaḍid III Dāwūd had passed away close to the age of seventy in 845/1441, al-Muʿtaḍid III's own niece—possibly the daughter of al-Mustakfī III Sulaymān herself—had informed al-Suyūṭī that her uncle was sixty-three upon his death.[133] Moreover, al-Suyūṭī's father Abū Bakr had taught the young ʿAbd al-ʿAzīz who married the daughter of al-Mustakfī III and would later become the Cairene ʿAbbasid caliph al-Mutawakkil III.[134] These connections also helped further al-Suyūṭī's professional career. In 891/1486, al-Mutawakkil III Abd al-ʿAzīz arranged for al-Suyūṭī's illustrious appointment as supervisor of the Foundation of Baybars al-Jāshankīr responsible for administering and allocating its endowment.[135] And roughly ten years later in 902/1496, al-Suyūṭī persuaded al-Mutawakkil III to create a new supreme judicial post for him that gave al-Suyūṭī discretionary powers over the entire Mamluk judiciary—although this arrangement was quickly rescinded upon the judges' collective protest. Certainly, al-Suyūṭī had felt entitled to such a position in the intellectual maturity of his fifties since he deemed himself to be the only living scholar who could claim the highest level of independent reasoning (*ijtihād*) within an existing legal framework, which in al-Suyūṭī's case was the Shāfiʿī school of law.[136]

Yet al-Suyūṭī's view of *ijtihād*, or independent legal reasoning, was also connected to the continued relevance of the Abbasid Caliphate. In his treatise *al-Radd ʿalā Man Akhlada ilā al-Arḍ,* justifying the attainability and contemporary existence of *ijtihād*—particularly his own—al-Suyūṭī points to its well-established recognition as a caliphal prerequisite. As he argues:

> Among the matters of collective obligation for which jurists stipulate *ijtihād,* from which one understands that *ijtihād* is a collective duty, is the grand imamate (*al-imāmah al-ʿuẓmā*). The scholars of the Shāfiʿī, Mālikī, and Ḥanbalī schools

> of law have agreed that the overall leader of Muslims (*al-imām al-aʿẓam*) should be capable of exercising independent legal reasoning (*mujtahid*).

al-Suyūṭī's logic was that because *ijtihād* was a requirement for the caliph, whose continued existence was a collective obligation upon the Muslim community, *ijtihād* by corollary was a collective obligation (*farḍ kifāyah*). After enveloping his argument in the general mantle of authority associated with the majority of Islamic legal schools, al-Suyūṭī cites the specific articulations of earlier Shāfiʿī jurists stipulating *ijtihād* in a caliph: al-Baghawī in his *Tahdhīb*, al-Mutawallī in his *Tatimmah*, and al-Juwaynī in his *Irshād*. That the Abbasid caliph, whether in Baghdad or Cairo, was no longer an independent *mujtahid* was another question of practicality that jurists like al-Juwaynī had previously addressed, as we have seen, by suggesting that the caliph could rely instead upon the scholars of his community. Given al-Suyūṭī's familiarity with al-Juwaynī's *Ghiyāth al-Umam*, which he used as a precedent for other compositions, a caliph's reliance upon such scholars in theory and practice must have been a foregone conclusion on his part. Indeed, al-Suyūṭī's suggestions to al-Mutawakkil III over administrative and judicial affairs may be seen in this light as his intending to fulfill this necessary advisory capacity to the caliph. Considering that al-Suyūṭī viewed himself as satisfying the collective obligation of *ijtihād* on behalf of the wider community and hoped to be the Muslim renewer (*mujaddid*) of his age, it is also plausible that he regarded his exercise of independent legal reasoning as bolstering the legal foundations of the caliphate. al-Suyūṭī may very well have envisaged himself as helping to actualize the community's aspirations for a caliphate informed by scholarship of the highest caliber, and in any case he argued that both the caliphate and *ijtihād* remained solid legal obligations.[137]

In fact, al-Suyūṭī expressed his astonishment that anyone could imagine otherwise. He was incredulous to discover through a discussion with a reputable non-Arab (*baʿḍ fuḍalāʾ al-ʿajam*) that someone of his standing could be so ignorant of such an essential matter. In response to this man's inquiry about whether the caliphate had a sound legal foundation, was transmitted through prophetic narrations, or was merely a matter of custom, al-Suyūṭī composed "Kitāb al-Ināfah fī Rutbat al-Khilāfah."[138] In this manuscript, al-Suyūṭī strenuously asserts that the caliphate is among the very foundations of Islam. And for the benefit of his interlocutor, al-Suyūṭī explains that he has gathered a number of prophetic traditions designating the caliphate as for Quraysh and promising it eventually to the progeny of the Prophet's uncle al-ʿAbbās. Both of these two sections are replete with multiple transmissions, linguistic variations, and scholarly commentaries, establishing the legality of the caliphate belonging to members of Quraysh in general and to the Abbasids in particular.

Beyond the legalism of these arguments, however, for Jalāl al-Dīn al-Suyūṭī, granting the Abbasid Caliphate of Cairo its full due was above all a matter of love and devotion to the Prophet Muḥammad. In the manuscript that al-Suyūṭī composed for al-Mutawakkil III Abd al-ʿAzīz on the virtues of the Abbasids, "al-Asās fī Manāqib Banī'l-ʿAbbās,"[139] he predictably lavishes high praise upon its commissioner. His panegyrics reflect al-Mutawakkil III's status as the pillar and nexus of Islamic leadership. He is "our master, the commander of the faithful, the refuge (*ʿiṣmah*) of Muslims, the nephew of the Master of Messengers, the leader (*imām*) of the people of the world and religion, the successor (*khalīfah*) of the Messenger of God," and so on. In al-Suyūṭī's lavish imagery, the pulpits and thrones are ennobled by the elevated rank of the Abbasids, who have inherited the caliphate one after the other in accordance with the promise of the truthful prophet. And al-Suyūṭī invokes God's peace and blessings upon His messenger for as long as the pulpits resonate with the honorifics of the fortunate caliphate of the Abbasids and its black emblems soothe the eyes of its lovers.

Yet it is remarkable how al-Suyūṭī conjoins love of the Abbasids with the reverence and love due to God's messenger, which is the central premise of his manuscript. For al-Suyūṭī, love of the Abbasids is a branch stemming from the love of the Prophet, which itself develops out of bearing witness to the absolute oneness of the Divine. God Himself obligated love of the family of al-Mutawakkil III's ancestor, al-ʿAbbās, and made it among the best acts of virtue by which sincere souls could prepare for the Day of Judgment. al-Suyūṭī clarifies that he hastened to comply with al-Mutawakkil III's request for a composition on the virtues of the prophetic family because he believed that doing so would bring him closer to God and His messenger and be a means of his own salvation and protection.

al-Suyūṭī establishes these principles of his treatise based on sound narrations from the authenticated collections of al-Bukhārī and Muslim as his essential framework, which open and close his selection of forty ḥadīths on the virtues of the Abbasids. In the first narration from Muslim, the Prophet Muḥammad reminds people of his mortality and indicates that he is leaving behind two weighty matters for their benefit. In this speech given at a place called Khumm between Mecca and Medina, he urges people to hold on to the Book of God, which is full of guidance and light, and to be mindful of his family (*udhakkirukum Allāh fī Ahl Baytī*), which he repeats thrice for emphasis and clarity. Upon questioning, the original narrator explains that this category does not refer to the Prophet's wives in the most intimate sense of family but rather to those family members who were forbidden from accepting charity, namely the families of his paternal cousins ʿAlī, ʿAqīl, and Jaʿfar (the sons of Abū Ṭālib) and the family of his paternal uncle al-ʿAbbās (*Āl al-ʿAbbās*).[140] Thus, the Prophet's uncle al-ʿAbbās and his family the Abbasids are specifically recognized as exemplary members of the Prophet's family about whom he exhorted the Muslim community.

And in the two narrations from al-Bukhārī, the model words and actions of the Prophet's close companions and first two successors as caliphs, Abū Bakr and ʿUmar, reveal their own reverence for the Prophet's family. Abū Bakr exhorts the community to be mindful of the Prophet Muḥammad by treating his family well (*urqubū Muḥammadan fī Ahl Baytih*). And indicating the lofty station of al-ʿAbbās, ʿUmar would implore God by the uncle of the Prophet for rain the way they used to implore Him by the Prophet during his lifetime and receive rain (*Allahumma innā kunnā natawassalu ilayka bi-Nabiyyinā fa-tasqīnā, wa innā natawassalu ilayka bi-ʿamm Nabiyyinā fa'sqinā*). This narration communicates God's acceptance, approval, and love since the community would be rewarded with the mercy of rain (*fa-yusqawna*), through the blessings of the Prophet's uncle and progenitor of the Abbasids, al-ʿAbbās. As such, al-Suyūṭī hopes that his own compilation sharing their merits will water the quarters of Muslims with their succoring rain. [141]

To convey the affective force of the love due to the Cairene Abbasids as members of the Prophet Muḥammad's family, al-Suyūṭī presses the argument through a wide assortment of traditions (*ḥadīths*) of varying quality. [142] Weak material, as Jonathan Brown has detailed, was often employed in non-legal discussions like the virtues of actions, especially if they were corroborated by other narrations with stronger chains of transmission or "buttressed by communal practice."[143] Substantiated by the principles expressed in the soundest of his narrations, al-Suyūṭī's essential argument was clear: love of the Cairene Abbasids was inextricably intertwined with love of the Prophet Muḥammad through their status as extended members of his blessed family. This love of the Prophet's family received divine sanction through the interpretative circumstances surrounding the revelation of particular verses (*ḥadīths* 16, 17, and 24). It was a barometer of a person's faith (*ḥadīths* 4 and 7). It offered a means of safety and salvation (*ḥadīths* 10 and 18). It was personally recompensed by the Prophet (*ḥadīth* 27). It offered an opportunity to align oneself with those exalted in heaven (*ḥadīths* 8 and 13). And by contrast, hatred of them could land one in hell (*ḥadīths* 9 and 15). Recognizing and bestowing their rights was key (*ḥadīths* 23, 25, and 38). And in essence, the Prophet reportedly urged, "Love God for all His blessings with which He nurtures you, love me for the love of God, and love the people of my family (*ahl baytī*) for my love" (*ḥadīth* 11).[144] Several of these and other traditions specify the virtues of the Prophet's uncle al-ʿAbbās and his son ʿAbdullāh (*ḥadīths* 5, 6, 8, 12, 20–22, 24, 40c), and others seem to foretell the rise of the Abbasid caliphs from their progeny (*ḥadīths* 28–37). Perhaps ironically, a number of the narrations legitimizing Abbasid rule that had circulated in the early years of their dynasty in Mesopotamia[145] were utilized to legitimize the reign of Abbasid caliphs toward the end of their dynasty in Cairo.

Based on his reading of some of these prophetic traditions of dubious authenticity, al-Suyūṭī expected the Abbasids to remain the rightful leaders of the Muslim community until the second coming of Jesus, son of Mary. Even though al-Suyūṭī asserted that the narrations included in al-Daylamī's (d. 509/1115) collection *Firdaws al-Akhbār* were unreliable on the whole, he selects one particular tradition from there and from al-Ṭabarānī's (d. 360/971) similarly uncritical compilation *al-Muʿjam al-Kabīr* to convey his expectations on the matter. In this narration, the Prophet Muḥammad's wise wife Umm Salamah is said to have reported his prediction that "the caliphate will be in the hands of the progeny of my uncle—the brother of my father—until they surrender it to the Messiah" (*al-khilāfah fī walad ʿammī ṣinwa abī ḥattā yusallimūhā ilā al-masīḥ*).[146] al-Suyūṭī further adduces this point about the Abbasid Caliphate enduring until the end of time as evidence in his history of Muslim caliphs against the spurious claims of the long-gone Fatimids. In addition to the arguments deployed by other jurists—including the Fatimids's false genealogy, heretical beliefs, and procedurally invalid election—al-Suyūṭī cites these eschatological expectations as a final flourish confirming their illegitimacy. He elaborates:

> Prophetic transmissions indicate that once leadership of the Muslim community reaches the offspring of al-ʿAbbās it will not leave their hands until they surrender it to Jesus son of Mary or the Mahdī. Therefore, it is understood that whoever claims to assume the caliphate while they uphold it is an illegitimate and misguided rebel (*khārij bāgh*).[147]

An urge to discredit the Ismāʿīlī eschatology once held by the Fatimids or that of other more contemporary ʿAlid groups may have also influenced al-Suyūṭī's views on the longevity of the Abbasid Caliphate.

Consequently, al-Suyūṭī did not anticipate the demise of the Abbasid dynasty a mere twelve years after his death, when the Ottomans invaded Mamluk Egypt in 923/1517 and took custody of its Abbasid caliph. Clearly, the Ottomans, who hailed from the Turkish tribes of Central Asia, were not descendants of the Prophet's immediate family or even members of his Arabian tribe of Quraysh. Nevertheless, able scholars affiliated with the Ottoman court in mid-tenth/mid-sixteenth century tapped other veins of the caliphate's rich intellectual legacy and Islamic constitutional law to uphold the Ottoman dynasty as the legitimate bearers of the Islamic caliphate, as vicegerency of the Prophet Muḥammad, into a new era. And the articulations of devotion and esteem expressed by late Mamluk-era scholars, such as the widely read Jalāl al-Dīn al-Suyūṭī, helped shape ongoing Muslim sentiments of attachment to the memory of an Islamic caliphate far and wide. These voices from "the tradition"—the Islamic literary heritage—continued to speak across immense gulfs of time to new and dramatically different audiences who brought with them a multitude of interpretative tools and concerns of their own.

CHAPTER 4

MANIFOLD MEANINGS OF LOSS: OTTOMAN DEFEAT, EARLY 1920S

> An institution hallowed with traditions of thirteen centuries, an embodiment of might and grandeur of the Orient in the eyes of European nations and a shield of defence for Islam during the last four hundred years, passed away as if in the twinkling of an eye. This edifice which looked as firm as a rock and promised to last as long as the world would last, was swept away by the flood of phenomena. Is the earth of faith shaken by a terrible shock, and are the mountains of beliefs crumbled to pieces and diffused in the air like dust?
>
> —MOHAMMAD BARAKATULLAH OF BHOPAL, INDIA, 1924[1]

IN THE AFTERMATH of World War I, Turkish nationalists gradually reconfigured a truncated Ottoman Empire. They resisted the physical colonization of Anatolia, established a Grand National Assembly, and stripped the Ottoman Caliphate of political power (*saltanat*) in 1922. Amid these rapid developments, the former şeyhülislam of the Ottoman Empire Mustafa Sabri (1869–1954) vigorously defended a Sunni traditionalist position of the caliphate's juridical and socio-cultural necessity. His spirited adherence to these traditionalist positions ultimately led Sabri to flee the Ottoman Empire in its final years during the upheavals caused by the Kemalist seizure of power. He continued to respond in writing to the threats of radical secularist and Islamic modernist interpretations at home and in his initial and final abode of exile, Egypt.

On the other hand, after having composed many pan-Islamic and pro-Ottoman poems dedicated to sultans like Abdülhamid II, the Egyptian Prince of Poets Aḥmad Shawqī (1868–1932) was inspired by the Turkish War of Independence (1919–23) to bestow his poetic laurels upon a new hero: Mustafa Kemal. One such piece was published in the Egyptian newspaper *al-Ahrām* in 1923 to commemorate the return of the former Khedive ʿAbbās II's mother from abroad. The poet asks her to describe Istanbul and the "ally of oppressors" (*waliyyan li'l- ṭawāghīt*) there whom people undeservedly call *amīr al-mu'minīn* or Commander of the Believers: in other words, the Ottoman sultan-caliph Vahideddin. Shawqī hurls a number of poetic insults at Sultan Vahideddin for having cloaked Islam in disgrace with his arbitrary, unjust, and incompetent caliphal rule that dared to repudiate Mustafa Kemal. By contrast, Mustafa Kemal in Shawqī's poem is the valiant hero who strove to liberate Turkish lands and abolished the sultan's rule for "the rule of the individual [or perhaps one could say autocratic rule] is debased, accursed."[2] Emblematic of its social context, the poem conveys Egyptian admiration for Mustafa Kemal as the perceived initiator of the successful Anatolian War for Independence, a regard inspired in part by longing for Egypt's own liberation from British colonial domination. And it also articulates a broader political criticism of authoritarian rule and extols the merits of popular democracy.

Yet, shortly thereafter, Mustafa Sabri responded in print with his "Qaṣīdah Nūniyyah" of the same meter and rhyme as Shawqī's poem. He forcefully retorted that the man Shawqī had made a hero of was more akin to the oppressors of old (and a debased monkey) and invoked God's curse upon Shawqī for his poetic lies. It was not autocratic rule that Mustafa Kemal had eliminated—he was particularly adept on that front—rather it was the Sacred Law of the Lord of the Worlds that he had clearly abolished, Sabri argued, despite the negligence and blindness of Muslims like Shawqī to this truth. Accompanying this vehement poem published in the Egyptian newspaper *al-Muqaṭṭam*, Sabri wrote an open letter to Shawqī declaring that the poet neither knew Mustafa Kemal in order to praise him nor Sultan Vahideddin in order to censure him in these terms. In Shawqī, Sabri found a poet who did not just say what he did not do (in reference to the Qur'anic chapter regarding poets, Sūrat al-Shuʿarāʾ (26: 224–27) but who also spoke about what he did not even know![3] More intimately acquainted with the intense hostility towards religion that positivist Unionists like Mustafa Kemal harbored, Sabri acutely perceived the gradual dismantling of the state's Islamic character and argued that stripping political sovereignty from the Ottoman Caliphate and transferring it to the Turkish Grand National Assembly was a frontal attack upon Islamic law. As he pointed out elsewhere, the caliphate was composed of two parts: government and representation of the Prophet, and neither one without the other could be called a caliphate.[4]

Upon the declaration of the Turkish Republic later that same year, Shawqī composed yet another congratulatory poem and countered Mustafa Sabri's accusations by continuing to draw auspicious, and as he argued informed, comparisons between the Kemalists and early Islamic forces at Khaybar and Tābūk, complete with a condescending gesture towards Sabri (*al-lāḥī*) as being completely oblivious.[5] For Sabri, then, the final abolition of the Ottoman Caliphate less than one year later on March 3, 1924, was a bitter confirmation of his predictions. And it took Shawqī entirely by surprise. Shawqī's astonishment is captured in his eloquent and moving elegy of the caliphate, where he utilizes the painful imagery of a bride who unexpectedly passes away on her wedding night. He describes how the joyous anticipation of Muslims across the world had turned into despondent mourning. Tears began to flow heavily from all the faces that had been smiling at her good fortunes, since the victories of the Turkish resistance movement in Anatolia following World War I had been interpreted as a source of regained strength for the Islamic caliphate. Egypt and

India are left to wallow in these pools of sadness, and lands such as geographical Syria, Iraq, and Persia ask out of an astonished disbelief whether someone could have possibly eradicated the Islamic caliphate:

> Minarets and pulpits have clamored over you [oh, Caliphate],
> And over you, kingdoms and [far-off] regions have wept;
>
> India is appalled, and Egypt is despondent,
> Crying over you with overflowing tears;
>
> And Syria-Palestine, Iraq, and Persia all ask:
> Has someone obliterated the Caliphate from [the face of] the earth?![6]

The deposed Ottoman caliph Abdülmecid II (1868–1944) admired Shawqī's poem when it finally reached him in exile, and he had his personal secretary write a note of appreciation praying for the poet's success in serving the Islamic cause.[7] But Mustafa Sabri's printed response to Shawqī was sharp, "Yes, it has been obliterated, despite the ignorance of those who do not heed warnings when it is time!" Shawqī's belated mourning was of little comfort or use in Sabri's eyes, and the former shaykh of Islam thought that the least that such previously staunch supporters of Mustafa Kemal could do was to raise their expressions of censure so high as to dislodge their former idol from power and restore the caliphate and Islamic practices to Turkey.[8]

Yet in his elegy of the abolished caliphate, Shawqī struggles with the heroic image of Mustafa Kemal that he had created in his earlier poetry, passionately celebrating the Anatolian resistance movement. The depth of Shawqī's turmoil caused by the caliphate's abolition led the poet to disparage and condemn the Turkish nationalists, and Mustafa Kemal in particular, harshly as the perpetrators of this atrocity:

> Prayer has cried [over you, oh, deceased Caliphate], and this is a tribulation
> [caused by] one who plays with Islamic Law, evil and drunken in his judgment, shameless;
>
> A fool has pronounced his opinion, offering misguidance,
> and openly bringing disbelief to the lands;
>
> Those who have followed his "jurisprudence"
> Were [only] created for understanding battalions and weapons;
>
> If they discuss, they only speak with the muteness of regiments,
> Or if they are spoken to, they only hear with the deafness of arrows.

But after reproaching the Kemalists as ignorant soldiers who are senselessly and shamelessly immersed in depravity, Shawqī attempts to reconcile this biting reproach with his own earlier praise, and in fact he apologizes in the elegy for this seeming contradiction. Mentioning the past laurels he has cast at Mustafa

Kemal even leads Shawqī to reflect momentarily on the leader's remarkable merits, as if to say that it was not for naught that he had garnered the poet's initial admiration. This predicament makes the current situation all the more perplexing for Shawqī. To restate the conundrum posed by his poem: Should he "declare the reviver of a people to be an atheist or say that the restorer of rights is a libertine?"[9] For Sabri, however, the matter was entirely clear: whether or not Shawqī chose to say it, Mustafa Kemal was indeed an atheist and a libertine.[10]

As this protracted poetic debate conducted through the Egyptian press in the 1920s aptly illustrates, modern regional contexts and professional affiliations created divergent interpretations over the significance of the Ottoman Caliphate's demise, even among those Muslim elites who shared an intense devotion to defending its legacy. For Mustafa Sabri, who hailed from the Ottoman religious hierarchy, the abolition of the caliphate meant a loss of the primacy of Islamic law. Hailing from the Ottoman imperial center of power, his familiarity with the internal political machinations and intellectual currents that had endangered its existence also shaped his perspective. According to the vivid imagery drawn by Mustafa Sabri, the two swords of atheism and nationalism had slaughtered the Ottoman Caliphate. And in fleeing abroad, he mistakenly assumed that Egypt would be a refuge from similar intellectual battles. Instead, Mustafa Sabri expressed his disappointment that he had found strong advocates of secularism and European rationalist, materialist thought in Egypt, along with multiple divisions between religious scholars that critically hampered their ability to defend Islam.[11] Yet for Aḥmad Shawqī, who assailed the British with his poetic pen, the lines of battle were drawn very differently. For him, the struggle to defend the Ottoman Caliphate and the independence of its former territories following World War I were associated with his own nationalist aspirations for Egypt. And for him, like many other far-flung Muslim intellectuals in the early twentieth century who echoed the themes of his poignant elegy, the abolition of the Ottoman Caliphate signified the disturbing loss of the last great global Muslim power in an age of encroaching colonialism.

NOTIONS FROM AFAR

Although Ottoman claims to the Islamic caliphate date from the sixteenth century, the Ottoman sultan's title of caliph gained new saliency in the increasingly globalized political context of the eighteenth through twentieth centuries. As early as 1517, Ottoman sultans asserted for themselves in official documents and treatises the sole right to be caliph (*khalīfah*), commander of the faithful (*amīr al-mu'minīn*), and leader (*imām*) of the Islamic jurisprudential discourse.[12] Yet by the late eighteenth century, a combination of internal reforms and external developments prompted a modern-day rearticulation of the Ottoman caliphal institution. Seen as a watershed moment, the 1774 treaty of Küçük Kaynarca is

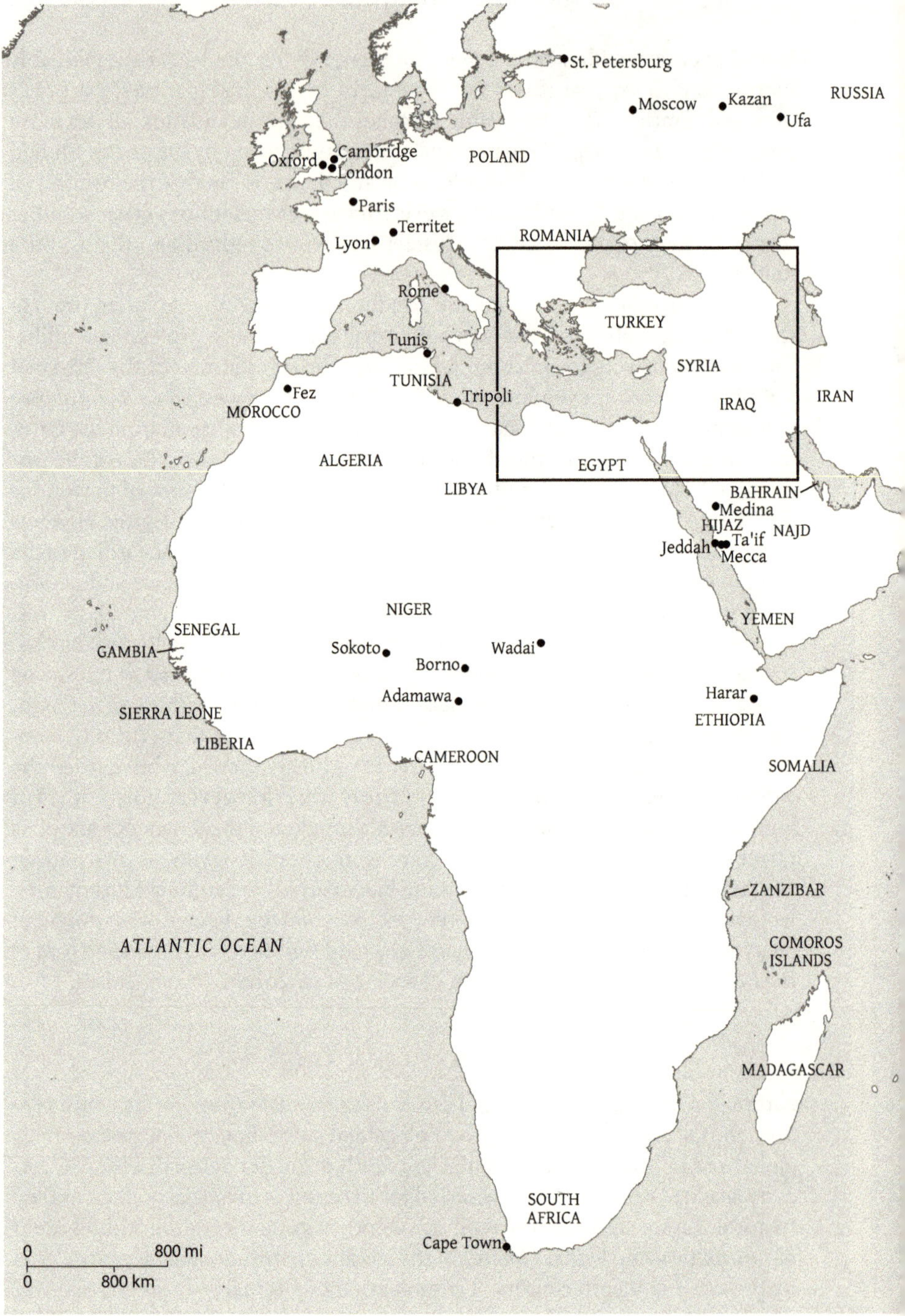

MAP 3. Afro-Eurasia, 1920s.

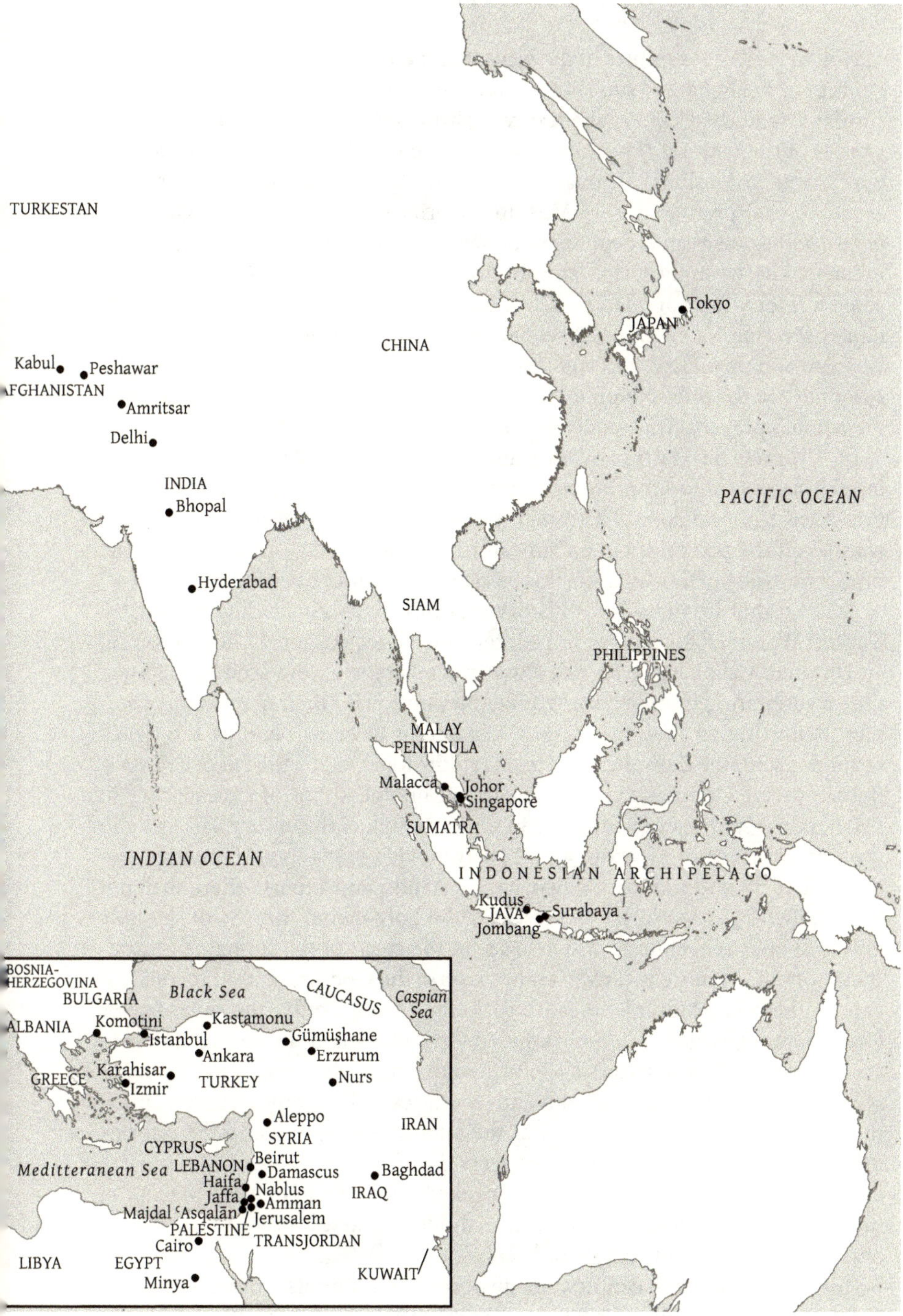

TURKESTAN
CHINA
Tokyo
JAPAN
Kabul
Peshawar
AFGHANISTAN
Amritsar
Delhi
INDIA
Bhopal
PACIFIC OCEAN
Hyderabad
SIAM
PHILIPPINES
MALAY
PENINSULA
Malacca
Johor
Singapore
SUMATRA
INDIAN OCEAN
INDONESIAN ARCHIPELAGO
Kudus
JAVA
Surabaya
Jombang
BOSNIA-
HERZEGOVINA
BULGARIA
Black Sea
CAUCASUS
Caspian
Sea
ALBANIA
Komotini
Kastamonu
Istanbul
Gümüşhane
Ankara
Erzurum
GREECE
Karahisar
Izmir
TURKEY
Nurs
Aleppo
SYRIA
IRAN
CYPRUS
Beirut
Meditteranean Sea
LEBANON
Damascus
Baghdad
Haifa
Nablus
Jaffa
Amman
IRAQ
Majdal
ʿAsqalān
Jerusalem
PALESTINE
TRANSJORDAN
Cairo
LIBYA
EGYPT
KUWAIT
Minya

one of the earliest examples of the ways that the Ottoman Empire adapted the concept of a caliphate to such novel circumstances. Despite the Ottomans' territorial loss of the Crimea, the treaty enshrined the Ottoman sultan's role as Leader of the Faithful (*imamü'l-müminin*) and caliph (*halifetü'l-muvahhidin*) over Crimean Muslims. Through these diplomatic means, the Ottoman state retained legal prerogatives in Muslim-majority Crimea, even though it had been established as an independent buffer state (albeit under Russian political influence) between the Ottoman and Russian Empires. While Russia occupied some former Ottoman fortresses in and around the Crimea, the Ottomans retained the caliph's ceremonial recognition of appointments to the Crimean Khanate and its judiciary as well as acknowledgment of the Ottoman caliph's suzerainty in the public supplications associated with Friday and holiday congregational prayers. This emphasis, as Tufan Buzpinar has argued, helped assuage Ottoman devastation over the unprecedented loss of the Crimea and offered justification for continuing Ottoman interest in Crimean affairs. It also preserved the principle of Ottoman preeminence over Crimean Tatars and warded off the possibility of a Crimean Khan's elevation as a rival caliph. The primary novelty of this situation was its articulation in an inter-imperial treaty.[13]

It is a rather ironic twist of history that this treaty concluding the Russo-Turkish War of 1768–74 came to be interpreted as the original "fabrication" of an Ottoman Caliphate given that Russian intellectuals were around the same time resuscitating another sixteenth-century notion for their new vision of empire. Reflecting on how the "tragic" Council of Florence, uniting the Greek Orthodox with the Catholics, had been rapidly followed by the fall of Constantinople to the Ottomans in 1453, the monk Filofei, abbot of a monastery in Pskov, composed a series of letters in the early sixteenth century. His letter to the Grand Prince of Moscow Vasilii III Ivanovich (1479–1533) famously predicted that "two Romes have fallen, a third stands, and a fourth there shall not be." Filofei urged Vasilii III to preserve "the holy divine thrones of the holy universal apostolic church, which arose in the stead of the Roman and Constantinopolitan [churches] which now exists in the God-protected city of Moscow." Otherwise, Moscow, the "Third Rome," would suffer the same fate as Constantinople when it had abandoned Orthodoxy and, moreover, usher in the apocalypse. These letters by Filofei were copied and circulated as manuscripts in the sixteenth and seventeenth centuries. When some Orthodox practitioners, later known collectively as the Old Believers, opposed the reforms introduced by Patriarch Nikon in the second half of the seventeenth century to emulate Greek rites and liturgy, they invoked Filofei's admonitory concept of the Third Rome, in defense of Russian Orthodoxy, and would continue to do so over the next couple of centuries.[14]

Yet in the eighteenth century, the invocation of Rome also found innovative political expression. In the analysis of Stephen Baehr, rhetorical connections with Rome in eighteenth-century Russian culture represented new articulations of a theory of the transference of empire, or *translatio imperii*. He arrestingly notes:

> In a 1759 article "On the Use of Mythology" Grigorii Kozitskii, a Latin teacher and future secretary to Catherine the Great, wrote that "there is no history that is closer to our age than that of ancient Rome." During the eighteenth century statements of this sort, identifying eighteenth-century Russia with the glories and powers of ancient Rome—the archetype of empire in the Western mind—echoed in Russian history and literature and formed the basis for a cultural myth, resurrecting, at least tacitly, the earlier idea of Moscow (the Russian Empire) as Third Rome.

During the 1770s and 1780s, when the treaty of Küçük Kaynarca was contracted, this Russian "dream of Empire" frequently surfaced as a reflection of the expansionist foreign policy of Catherine the Great (1729–96). In commemoration of what Catherine had accomplished at Küçük Kaynarca, the well-known Russian poet Vasili Ivanovich Maikov (1728–78) even crowed how "the Russian state [*derzhava*] has spread out like ancient Rome." Indeed, Baehr observes, "The political situation of the reign of Catherine, with its long wars with Turkey, was perhaps the factor most responsible for the continuation and expansion of the Roman myth" and the aspirational vision of a Holy Russian Empire.[15] It was with the 1861 publication of one of Filofei's sixteenth-century letters, however, that the advantageous interpretation of "the Third Rome" as a foundational imperial Russian ideology—shorn of its ecclesiastical implications—took deep hold in the late nineteenth and early twentieth centuries. Not only was this the way that educated Russians had come to understand their own history, but it also resonated with the aspirations of late imperial intellectuals, including the Pan-Slavists, as well as interwar Communists.[16]

In this same time period, a confluence of domestic and foreign concerns elevated the Ottoman Caliphate to growing prominence. The Ottoman sultan Abdülhamid II, who ruled over the tumultuous era from 1876 to 1908, emphasized the caliphal aspect of his rule to stave off the deleterious effects of separatist nationalism in his increasingly Muslim-populated yet ethnically diverse empire. He also recognized its effectiveness and weight as a tool in dealing with his European imperial counterparts.[17] And following the Young Turk Revolution in 1908, the materialist positivists of the CUP continued to marshal and manipulate religious arguments to their political advantage. During World War I, the CUP, as cynical as they were of religion, even asked Muslims to side with the holy cause of the Ottoman sultan-caliph and his allies.

In the aftermath of the Great War, the Turkish War of Independence was similarly waged in the name of saving the Ottoman Caliphate and elicited broad popular support among Muslims residing within and beyond the empire's boundaries, especially those negotiating colonial contexts. Muslims occupied by the French and Italians in North Africa, subdued by the British in Egypt and

India, and dominated by the Dutch in the Indonesian Archipelago aspired toward the preservation of the Ottoman Empire as the rightful Islamic caliphate of their age. Having been shocked by the Ottomans' defeat in the First World War, Indonesian Muslims disparaged the unduly harsh terms of the Allied occupation of Istanbul and felt that "in acting against the caliph [the victors] were interfering with the entire Muslim world."[18] The Khilafat Movement in South Asia famously and fervently advocated for the rights of the Ottoman Empire and its caliphate.[19] And in his poignant elegy for the abolished institution, Shawqī records how he had faithfully devoted his pen to the cause of the Ottoman Caliphate and only glorified the victories of prominent military figures such as Enver, Ethem (1883–1949), and Mustafa Kemal for its sake.[20] Galvanized by their struggles to sustain the Ottoman Caliphate both during and immediately following World War I, such Muslim supporters of the institution, residing far from the imperial center, were ill-prepared to embrace or even anticipate its internal collapse.

In India and Egypt, in particular, aiding the cause of the Ottoman Caliphate had contributed to the Islamic foundations of local nationalist agitation against British rule, while in the Dutch East Indies, the crisis over the caliphate in the 1920s increased Muslims' awareness of their colonial subjugation and helped foster an Islamic-based nationalism.[21] The plight of the Ottoman Caliphate emerged as a focal point for localized action in response to a wider global crisis, allowing space for the articulation of multiple identities and loyalties that could simultaneously coexist. As Gail Minault has documented in her study of the Indian Khilafat Movement, the rallying symbolism of a besieged Ottoman Caliphate enabled diverse populations of Indians to overcome religious, ethnic, and political differences in support of the Indian nationalist movement. Through their local and internationalized activism, Indian Muslims negotiated a space where they could be fully sympathetic with their Arab and Turkish brethren as fellow believers and equally loyal to India as sincere nationalists.[22] In similar terms, Shawqī's poetry during World War I characterizes Egyptian pan-Islamic activity on behalf of the Ottoman Caliphate as one of harmoniously coexisting loyalties born of a mutual bond. In one composition he declares:

> O House of Othman! Our cousins! How could you complain of a wound,
> and we not complain of its pain?
>
> We sympathize with you and do not forget
> our homeland (*waṭan*), throne, crown, or (national) flag.[23]

In this constellation of meanings, it was possible to be both Ottoman and Egyptian as well as loyal to the Ottoman caliph and the Egyptian homeland alike, and, as Gershoni and Jankowski have observed, it was only with the Turkish nationalist abolition of the Ottoman Caliphate following World War I that this option vanished.[24]

These modern political contexts and configurations of caliphal support drew upon a deep cultural reservoir of the caliphate's significance for a globally conceived Muslim community. Therefore, authors writing in the wake of the Ottoman Caliphate's demise utilized rich literary inheritances to express the profound spiritual bonds that the institution had engendered and signified in order to express their remorse. Reflecting on the meanings that the Ottoman Caliphate held for Muslims across the world, Shawqī's moving elegy emphasizes both the spiritual attachments it had generated among them as well as how the caliphate had enabled the fulfillment of their religious duties and rites, such as legitimizing the Friday congregational prayer:

> [It was] an honor (*ḥasab*) that that lasted throughout all of the nights,
> And then disappeared between a single evening and morning;
>
> A relationship whose supports were destroyed (*ʿalāqatun fuṣimat ʿurā asbābihā*),
> It was the most virtuous of spiritual bonds;
>
> It gathered upon righteousness those who were near,
> And many a time it brought together thrones of the distant;
>
> It organized the lines of the Muslims and their steps,
> In the coming and passing of every Friday.[25]

Symbolic of personal engagement in communal piety, the caliphate, in Shawqī's eyes, had sustained spiritual and social formations. Drawing an association between the startling events of March 1924 and a deep sense of bereavement felt among religiously minded individuals, one Afghani author wrote in the pages of *Amān-i Afghān*: "This news has affected and grieved the hearts of all sincere Moslems, especially those who cling most closely to their religion and to the maintenance of Islamic law, obligations and institutions."[26] And on March 19, 1924, the Albanian newspaper *Shpresa Kombëtare* also lamented these disquieting developments:

> At the time of the Young Turk Revolution in Constantinople Sultan [Abdül-] Hamid was dethroned, but no one suspected that bold commencement would end by wiping out, not only the Imperial House and the ancient might of the House of Osman, but would also drive out of Turkey that which for three hundred million Moslems is the religious centre of their lives.[27]

Indeed, the Turkish abolition of the caliphate, coming rapidly on the heels of glorious military victory against foreign occupation, left a bitter sense of betrayal among those Muslims across Afro-Eurasia who had lent their material and moral support to the defense and regained strength of the Ottoman Empire. The neoclassical Egyptian poet Muḥammad ʿAbd al-Muṭṭalib (1871–1932), for instance, had been composing a piece lauding the victories of the Turks over the Greeks at the battle of Sakarya a few years ago and had only been able to complete six lines before news of the caliphate's abolition reached him. As ʿAbd al-Muṭṭalib acknowledges in his collected volume of poetry, he was so surprised and hurt by the news of this deviation (*inḥirāf*) of the Turks from Islam that the "freezing of his faculties" (*jumūd al-qarīḥah*) forced him to leave his poetic composition in praise of them incomplete.[28] Likewise, the British Consulate in Sarajevo, Bosnia, reported profound bewilderment and indignation among religious scholars and educated Muslims there, whose hopes of the revival of the empire had been dashed by the eradication of the Ottoman Caliphate.[29] And on the pulpit of the most prestigious congregational mosque in Damascus, the Umayyad Mosque, Shaykh ʿAbd al-Qādir al-Khaṭīb gave a rousing speech, on March 7, 1924, as part of the first Friday prayer following the caliphate's abolition. In his speech, Shaykh ʿAbd al-Qādir recounted how the Ottoman Caliphate had guarded the honor of Muslims globally and declared that when the empire had been occupied by outside forces, those Muslims had fervently prayed for the Ottoman Turks until they achieved victory through the efficacy of such unified and sincere supplication and assistance. Yet those very Turks who had led the defense efforts, bemoaned Shaykh ʿAbd al-Qādir, repaid the good will of their brethren through the ignoble acts of abolishing the caliphate and expelling the caliph and his family from their land, "and this has left a bitter impression on every Muslim believer."[30] Even in the city of Fez in Morocco, described as "the theological centre of the Moslems in North Africa," a similar reproach of the Turks' ingratitude was raised. As one British official encapsulated these sentiments circulating in Fez:

> Whilst the old order prevailed, Turkey was looked up to by all the Moslems; funds were readily subscribed (so it is said) to support the "Defenders of the Faith"—the Turkish soldiers—and Turkey owed her recent gains, not so much to the force of her armies, as to the moral power of the Moslems abroad. Had it not been for that influence Constantinople would now be in Christian hands.[31]

These words of hurt, sadness, and indignation emanating from Egypt, Bosnia, Syria, and Morocco give expression to the sense of betrayal that Muslims felt on a broad scale toward the unexpected course of action adopted by the Turks. The abolition of the Ottoman Caliphate was perceived as a flouting of the trust that other Muslims had placed in the Turks as custodians of this Islamic institution, a breach of the reciprocity due to their faithful support in times of need, and the breaking of the bonds of a global brotherhood.

This dismay caused by the severing of the ties created by the caliphate was noticeable even in the Hijaz, which could not claim to have rendered material or moral assistance to the Ottoman Empire during World War I. To the contrary, the Hashemite king Sharīf Ḥusayn had rebelled against the Ottomans in 1916 and then quickly proclaimed his own caliphate in the wake of the Turkish abolition in 1924. Yet even there, news of the Ottoman Caliphate's disappearance reportedly extinguished the glimmer of hope among Sharīf Ḥusayn's constituents that their region would ultimately remain within the empire's dominion. As the British Consul Reader William Bullard (1885–1976) reported nearly a year into his foreign service there, "The Jeddah people are greatly depressed. The assumption of the caliphate by King Hussein they regard as a farce, but the abolition of the Turkish Caliphate has given check to the hope that had hitherto sustained them: that sooner or later the Turks would recover the Hedjaz and the nightmare reign of Hussein I would come to an end."[32] Here, the recurring theme of formerly allied and subjugated Muslim regions' hopes for the revival of the Ottoman Empire and for receiving salvation at its hands reemerges with a slightly different twist. In this case, the despised sovereign represents a rival Muslim figure of power whose personal ambitions are rejected out of longing for the comparative stability and prestigious stature of Ottoman caliphal rule, as observed through the eyes of a British official.

Such mourning at the passing of the Ottoman Caliphate quickly turned into its corollary of harsh censure and repudiation of the Kemalists' irreligious and irresponsible act. In Libya, the ʿUlamāʾ of Tripoli addressed an open letter of protest to Mustafa Kemal Paşa as the president of the Turkish Republic on April 5, 1924, citing how the abolition of the Ottoman Caliphate had "deeply offended the Ulema and Moslem[s] of Tripoli." In arguing that the caliphal institution was founded by the Prophet Muḥammad to maintain the social welfare of Muslims, these Libyan religious scholars drew an analogy of the caliphate as the life-giving essence of Islam, namely that the caliphate was to the religion of Islam as the soul was to the human body. The language utilized by the Judge of Tripoli and other leading scholars of this region speaks of their profound anguish and indignation; they were "much pained," and they felt it necessary to "strongly protest" the heinous act that had "wounded the religious sentiments of all true believers."[33] Earlier on March 15, 1924, the Grand Shaykh of al-Azhar in Cairo had also resolutely declared to the Egyptian press and the wider Muslim community, "I repudiate the action of the Kemalists in its entirety."[34] "In Palestine as well," British archival documents reveal, "the news of the expulsion of the Caliph and his family caused a revulsion of feeling against the Angora Government."[35] And in Albania, words were spoken of the "Young Turks'" astounding arrogance.[36] Through the field reports gathered by British officials regarding the situation in each of the Indian provinces after the Ottoman Caliphate's abolition, a picture of overall shock, resentment, and condemnation vividly emerges. So integral was the caliphal institution to their perceived sense of welfare that many Indian Muslims expressed a collective sense of ownership in the Ottoman Caliphate as an Islamic institution. It did not "belong" to the Turks alone in order for them to have abolished it without consulting their Muslim brethren around the world.[37]

Criticism often focused on the very person of Mustafa Kemal as the leader who had heroically defended the Ottoman Caliphate from the external assaults upon its land and sovereignty.[38] In a moment of poignant rhetorical irony, Shawqī himself paused to observe in his elegy how they who had protected the caliphate in war had now killed it in peace.[39] The esteemed leader of these valiant efforts had now turned into an "Unbeliever" and a "Salonica Renegrade" in the eyes of many Bosnian Muslims,[40] and the sense of ardent censure likewise emerges from the British High Commissioner Lord Edmund Allenby's (1861–1936) assessment of Egyptian sentiments in March of 1924:

> There is no doubt that the action taken by the Turkish Government against the Caliph's position and person has profoundly affected the country and is greatly deprecated. Attempts to justify the action of Mustapha Kemal and his government are not tolerated and the present Turkish policy is characterized as religious bolshevism, which if pursued will rob Turkey of her claim to a place among Islamic nations of the world.[41]

In the Dutch East Indies, the startling paradox of the deeds of the Turkish Nationalists seemed only to add to the "hesitation and bewilderment" gripping Muslims of the region, who appeared to be "divided between allegiance to the historic institution of the Caliphate and the admiration which [they had] been taught to feel for that institution's chief destroyer, Kemal Pasha."[42]

Indeed, it was difficult for many to accept the new role that such a venerated hero as Mustafa Kemal had adopted for himself as the destroyer of the Islamic caliphate. Muslims farthest removed from the Ottoman imperial city of Istanbul and the new Turkish Nationalist capital of Ankara, such as those in the Dutch East Indies and India, seemed to wait keenly for further information in order to fathom the most recent developments in Turkey.[43] Members of the Central Khilafat Committee of India hastened to obtain further clarification from Ankara via telegram, as if the alarming news itself was suspect,[44] and then to send an eight-person delegation "to persuade the Turkish Government to continue [its] association with [the] Caliphate and retain [its] central position in [the] Islamic world."[45] The Central Khilafat Committee and the Jamiat ul-Ulama also sent communications to the Shaykh of al-Azhar and Saʿd Zaghlūl Pasha (1859–1927) in Egypt requesting that they exercise restraint until the results of their own discussions with Ankara became clear. In the words of vigilant British officials, "They greatly prefer that the Khilafat should remain associated with the Turkish nation, and will spare no efforts in trying to convince their Turkish brethren that in the interests of their own nation and its Republic as well as of Islam, they should continue to appoint the Khalifa from among themselves."[46] They were so eager to preserve the prestige of the caliphal office among the Turkish nation and simultaneously preserve the efficacy of the institution that, according to British Air Staff Intelligence headquartered in Iraq, the Indian Muslim delegation even intended to propose that Mustafa Kemal himself should assume the position of caliph. When their repeatedly sincere efforts met with ultimate and persistent rebuff, the Indian Caliphate Committee lapsed into a state of despair and dismay.[47]

Elsewhere, the stern condemnation of Mustafa Kemal's actions was mingled with the memory of his courage and bravery as well as the hope of his once again utilizing his potential in service of the Muslim community and the emblem of its unity, the caliphate. After bemoaning the passing of the Ottoman Caliphate and its caliphs from Istanbul, along with the symbols of Ottoman rule, the Egyptian "Poet of Islam," as Aḥmad Muḥarram (1877–1945) was known, displays momentary ambivalence towards the problematic figure of Mustafa Kemal and urges clemency towards the former protagonist of much pan-Islamic Egyptian poetry. He demurs:

> The *Ghāzī* [Mustafa Kemal] has decreed the matter, so do not decry
> the affairs of government [literally, kingship] until they become clear.[48]

In keeping with the honored position reserved for the Gazi Mustafa Kemal, regarded as the leader of the Anatolian resistance movement on behalf of the caliphate, Muḥarram's poem lapses into this temporary lull as if to await an explanation. Yet by the conclusion of the poem, the travesty of the caliphate's abolition and the expulsion of the Ottoman family from Turkey overwhelm Muḥarram's own sense of justice and propriety, and he concludes his composition with an anguished sense of irony:

> We prevented transgression from overwhelming them,
> so they betrayed us, and they were the transgressors.
>
> We are afflicted for their sake, and we are afflicted by them,
> And if you are surprised, well, that is what has happened to us.[49]

For Muḥarram, the intense loyalty of Egyptians and countless other Muslims towards the Islamic caliphate was met with betrayal by its own Turkish custodians, who had inflicted utterly agonizing wounds with their act of abolition.

THE TURKISH REPUBLIC

In fact, this external censure of the caliphate's abolition was a major source of discomfort and concern to members of the new nationalist government in Ankara. Despite the Turkish nationalist projection of other Muslim countries' indifference towards the caliphate and its fate, a position deeply embedded in the official historiographic reconstruction of events, contemporary observers such as Ronald Charles Lindsay (1877–1945) at the British Consultate reported on the anxiety circulating among government circles in Ankara in 1924.[50] Prime

FIGURE 13. Mustafa Kemal greeting Shaykh Aḥmad al-Sanūsī during the War of Independence in Anatolia.

Image courtesy Osmanlı Arşivi Daire Başkanlığı, YEE.KP 86/41-4110.

Minister İsmet (İnönü)'s (1884–1973) own telegram sent via secret code to a Turkish representative abroad, which was intercepted and deciphered by another branch of His Majesty's Government, confirms these intimations:

> We understand that certain publications (? press news) are appearing among Mussulman peoples whose... are unfavourable to their proper appreciation of the position as regards the abolition of the Caliphate. That Europeans (? interpret) these publications against us is (? probable). I would request you to forward any information from EGYPT, INDIA and other countries and give me your views as to the (? activities) and schemes of European Governments, while also reporting any (? countervailing) measures that may occur to you. I would further ask you to keep an eye on any changes in the position as regards the Caliphate and keep me posted.[51]

As evident from İsmet's instructions, concern over the possible manipulation of Muslims' adverse reactions ran so high that the Turkish government actually sought out other measures through which to preserve its international standing. Probing into the domestic dimensions of the dilemma faced by the nascent Turkish Republic, Lindsay relates:

> The Angora Government [i.e., Ankara Government] are in a somewhat difficult position. I happen to know that they are very anxious to reduce to a minimum the amount of news from outside on the subject of the Caliphate. On the other hand, they wish to avoid any appearance of curtailing the liberty of a very sensitive press. The result is that direct reports from abroad are apt not to appear in the papers when they arrive here by telegraph, but are published a few days later in a medley of European comment, when the foreign newspapers reach Constantinople by post. [52]

As a result of these government measures, even as newsworthy a telegram as the one reporting the deposed caliph Abdülmecid's manifesto decrying the validity of the Kemalists' actions and his appeal for a global Muslim congress was kept from the domestic press, and overall, in Lindsay's words, "Little or no news of how the change has been received in other Muslim countries has yet become public property here." Clarifying why the developments among Muslims abroad elicited such anxiety among Kemalists, Lindsay elaborates:

> Turkish extremists would be happy enough if all they had to fear were a contest of several rival Caliphs, each enjoying recognition only in a limited area. What would really worry the responsible leaders would be to see a candidate like King Hossein accepted by Moslems outside Arab countries, or to see Abdul Mejid Effendi receive any wide measure of sympathy or support. Any such development would, apart from its placing Turkey in an awkward position vis-à-vis of the world of Islam generally, tend to stimulate criticism at home. [53]

Even with the news of foreign reactions eventually filtering into the country through European newspapers, albeit to a far more limited audience, the words and actions of the Istanbul press and all those who would otherwise openly express their disapproval of the caliphate's abolition had already been severely limited by the preemptory passage and execution of the 1923 High Treason Law as a precautionary measure to contain domestic opposition.[54] In his reports back to England, Lindsay notes that the amended Law on Treason and its exemplary implementation through the Independence Tribunals earlier on had predictably squelched any outbreaks of popular discontent upon the departure of the caliph and his relatives, particularly while the threat of the courts' possible reconstitution was volubly aired as an unremitting deterrent.[55] Lindsay's impression of the impact these tactics made led him to remark, "The general attitude in Constantinople, and, so far as I know elsewhere is one of outward indifference or subdued resignation, bred of lassitude and fear of a triumphant minority."[56] His partiality toward perceiving Oriental lassitude notwithstanding, the British Consul nevertheless depicts a general atmosphere of trepidation. And while attempting to analyze the factors contributing to this predicament in slightly more depth, one Afghani author explains to the reading public of the newspaper *Amān-i Afghān*:

> Among the Turkish liberators are many persons of conservative and moderate views who have no desire for a republic and do not accept either the separation of administration from religion or the abolition of the Caliphate. This class has the support of the general public; but since the Army is controlled by the extremists, the moderate, conservative, and orthodox parties are in an inferior position.[57]

Writing only two days after the caliphate's abolition, Nevile Henderson (1882–1942) alternatively strives to capture the simmering of internal dissent in one of his reports back to the British Foreign Office with a flair for cautious poetics:

> It is too soon to judge the effects of this bold stroke of the Angora Government. There is undoubtedly much disquiet in men's minds. There must be many who think in their hearts with a poor madman who on the 3rd March snatched a green coverlet from a shrine in Stamboul and ran through the streets, crying "O Caliph, whither art thou going?" There are, however, no signs of overt opposition to the decrees of Angora. Should saner people think to follow the madman's example, they have had their warning in unofficial intimations from the capital that an addition is to be made to the Law of Treason making it an offence against the law to criticize the reforms, and that independence courts, with power to inflict the death penalty without reference to the Assembly, are to be set up in various places, including Constantinople. It is a proof of the despair of the Conservatives that on the 2nd March Velid Bey, the editor of the one strongly Islamic daily paper in Constantinople, left unexpectedly abroad.[58]

Henderson's poignant imagery of the lunatic's open anguish accentuates the denial of such vocal and visible expressions of grief and dismay to those of sound mind. Only the "madman" could be free from the strictures of political restraint and intimidation.

Nevertheless, moderate and conservative nationalist leaders and members of the intelligentsia did seek less discernible ways to express their discontent, open up further discussion, and bring about the possibility of change. Noting the cautious reserve of the Istanbul press leaning in this direction, Lindsay observes, "Certain opposition newspapers here, which do not venture themselves to attack the Government, have been saying of late that it should answer foreign critics of what it has done."[59] And in the months to come, a former Unionist like Cavid Bey (1875–1926) would continue to "persecute the Government with a mordant pen" in the papers.[60] Rauf (Orbay) Bey (1881–1961), Refet (Bele) Paşa (1881–1963), Kazım (Karabekir) Paşa (1882–1948), Ali Fuat (Cebesoy) Paşa (1882–1968), Cafer Tayyar (Eğilmez) Paşa (1877–1958), and Cevad (Çobanlı) Paşa (1870–1938) were among those nationalist leaders who reportedly demonstrated negative reactions towards the caliphate's abolition.[61] And yet, with a less than generous assessment of his former colleagues who had struggled in Turkey's war for independence, Ali Fuat Cebesoy recollects in his memoirs, "When it became impossible to express their opinions or discuss the form of the administration openly after the modification of the treason law, they secretly began negative propaganda against Gazi [Mustafa Kemal] Pasha's ideas for the future."[62] Assessing the motives of this increasingly alienated and marginalized nationalist elite in his observation of the political opposition that had begun to crystallize against Mustafa Kemal's policies, Lindsay acknowledges both a "natural desire felt for the fruits of office by those who have been kept from them for too long" combined with "conservative opinion which is shocked at the irreligion of Mustapha Kemal and at his policy of secularization."[63] In Erik-Jan Zürcher's estimation, the people in Rauf's circle are best characterized as constitutional monarchists, and he astutely observes:

> For them, the office of the Ottoman Caliphate held prestige and value and also figured as a possible counterweight to the growing personal power of President Mustafa Kemal. Its abolition increased their fear that a dictatorship was in the making. It was . . . frustration with Mustafa Kemal's increasing power monopoly that drove them into the opposition.[64]

In the second half of 1924, rumors circulated about the plots and strategies variously ascribed to religious scholars, Unionists, and nationalists, who were by no means mutually exclusive groups, to restore a caliphate. Oddly enough, in July 1924, one *hoca* reputedly confided to British consular officials that he and other religious figures were making plans to reinstate a caliph and saw the disillusioned politicians as potential allies. He reportedly disclosed that they had contacted and made arrangements with the CUP, "as represented by the notorious Kara Kemal Bey" (d. 1926), and that "they would like to work with Reouf, but considered that he should throw over Mustafa Kemal more completely than he has done."[65] As Rauf grew more distant from Mustafa Kemal and eventually split from the People's Party in November 1924, speculation was rife over his contemplated course of action. In the conjecture of consular reports, "It is even suggested by those in touch with Rauf Bey that if he cannot moderate Mustapha Kemal Pasha's policy by constitutional means he will endeavor to bring back the late Vahid-ed Din, perhaps not as Sultan, but at any rate, as Caliph."[66] And in its surveillance of the opposition, secret British intelligence even gave credence to such elaborate schemes as the following:

> At a recent secret meeting of the Union and Progress Committee it was resolved in principle to invite all Moslem countries to send delegates to a congress to examine the proposal that some city—such as Adrianople—should be chosen to be the seat of the Khalif. The city would be considered a holy city and would form a neutral state under the Khalifah flag. Each Moslem country would have its own representative there and would undertake to send and maintain a number

> of soldiers in the Khalif's bodyguard. A yearly or half-yearly congress would be held for the consideration of Islamic affairs, or, in case of emergency such as the threat of war, could be summoned immediately in extraordinary session.[67]

These plans seem almost reminiscent of a sovereign Muslim version of what would officially become, in only a few short years with the signing of the Lateran agreements in 1929, the Vatican City.

Although it is difficult to discern what grains of truth, if any, contributed to these rumors of prominent nationalists' deliberations regarding the caliphate, Mustafa Kemal and his new entourage were apprehensive of the palpable threat that they posed. Mustafa Kemal and the loyal leaders of his People's Party coordinated a series of key arrests, mounted an investigation into the matter, and placed eminent nationalists, such as Refet, Rauf, Cavid, Kara Kemal, and another person by the name Hossaret Han, under the strict surveillance of the secret police, alongside that of Mustafa Kemal's private police, to ward off such an eventuality. As British intelligence services divulge, "The definite emergence of a Khilafat Party is thought to be merely a matter of time and strenuous efforts are being made to hamper its development."[68] Certainly, prominent Turkish nationalist leaders were increasingly discontented with their exclusion from positions of power and political influence in the new Turkish Republic and acutely distressed at the growing radical and despotic tendencies of the state which they had helped bring to life,[69] yet, as Zürcher has demonstrated, they also attempted to work and remain within Mustafa Kemal's People's Party for as long as conceivably possible.[70]

Indeed, the only person among the cadre of Turkish nationalists who belonged to the People's Party and openly expressed his dissatisfaction with the deposition of the caliph in the event's immediate aftermath was Halit (Akmansu) Bey (1884–1953). A veteran of the Turkish War of Independence and founding member of the Association for the Defense of the National Rights of Anatolia and Rumelia, Halit had argued his case against the caliphate's abolition inside the Turkish assembly as the deputy of Kastamonu. He did not find fault with the minister of justice's Islamic legal justifications for abolishing the caliphate and acknowledged that the institution no longer retained actual power. Yet he urged the assembly to consider the political dimensions. To eradicate an institution that had lasted for over 1,300 years required further deliberation, especially since they had waged the national resistance movement by promising the people that they were going to save the caliph (*Arkadaşlar hepimiz biliyoruz ki İstiklal Mücadelatı ilan edildiği zaman halkımızın halife makamına olan merbutiyetini nazar-ı itibara alarak hepimiz "Halifeyi kurtaracağız. Şöyle yapacağız böyle yapacağız." diye telkinatta bulunduk*). Halit also recalled how they had included many religious scholars in the Grand National Assembly out of respect for the people's feelings and how he and all his other nationalist colleagues had urged the soldiers on during the war saying that they were going to save the caliphate along with the entire homeland (*"Makam-ı hilafeti, bütün vatanla beraber kurtaracağız"*). And now, as Halit conveyed it, the people did not believe that their Friday congregational prayers would be valid without the caliphate, and he was certain that the love and regard that the Islamic world showed them as Turks, despite all the mistakes of their rule, was rooted in more than mere religious sentiments of brotherhood—it stemmed from their country's preservation of the caliphate. If the caliphate lacked any substantive influence and esteemed status among Muslims, then why, Halit asked, had they enshrined it as part of their party's electoral principles only six months ago as well as in the laws of November 1922? Why had they told the people it was necessary? He argued that declaring the abolition of the caliphate would be a source of great political harm and suggested instead that they should absorb it into the corporative person of the Grand National Assembly.[71] Ironically, this idea that Halit articulated was later adopted by the famous South Asian poet Mohammad Iqbal (1877–1938) "that the Turkish assembly should be seen as a legitimate stand-in for the defunct imam"[72]—however, that notion was resoundingly rejected by the assembly itself. [73]

When the proposed bill to abolish the caliphate passed despite his earnest interjections, Halit promptly resigned from the People's Party of Mustafa Kemal the same day, March 3, 1924, as a matter of principle. In his succinct note of resignation, Halit explained to the party's leadership that although he remained a loyal populist, committed to the principles he and the other party members had espoused in the 1923 elections, he could no longer in good conscience remain part of the People's Party after witnessing it diverge from these electoral principles. As Halit had conveyed to his colleagues in assembly, the nine-point platform upon which all members of the People's Party had been instructed to base their electoral campaigns in 1923 included the key principle that "The Turkish Grand National Assembly is the support of the office of the Caliphate which is an exalted office among Muslims" (*İstinadgahı Türkiye Büyük Millet Meclisi olan makam-ı hilafet, beynel'islam bir makam-ı mualladır*). [74] For Halit, the principles of this electoral platform, including the one pledging support for the caliphal institution, were a sacrosanct contract with the people who had brought him to office that he was, therefore, not at liberty to break. At first, Mustafa Kemal as chairman of the party and president of the Turkish Republic attempted to persuade Halit to withdraw his resignation through the intercession of four other assembly deputies,[75] but Halit responded by declaring his firm resolution to preserve the commitment he had made towards the Turkish people and fulfill the heavy responsibility placed on his shoulders by them and history alike, through remaining loyal to his electoral campaign promises. He saw no other alternative but to resign from the People's Party.[76]

The rejoinder to this unwavering articulation of principles was swift. Within two days, a telegram from the Governor of Kastamonu, Halit's electoral district, was published in large-sized font in the newspapers of Ankara. The Governor,

توحید افكار

مقام خلافتك الغاسی، شرعیه و كالتنك، اركان حربیه ریاستنك قابینه‌دن اخراجی، توحید تدریسات لایحه‌لری مجلسجه قبول ایدلدی

بیوك ملت مجلسنك دونكی جلسه‌سی ایی كورولتولی اولدی

قرار عبدالمجید حضرتلرینه تبلیغ ایدلدی

طولمه باغچه سراینده صوك وضعیت

قابینه‌نك بو كون استعفاسی بكله‌نیور

FIGURE 14. Newspaper Announcement of the Ottoman Caliphate's abolition in *Tevhid-i Efkar* (Istanbul), March 1924, including portraits of Zeki Bey (top right) and Halit Bey (top left).

Image courtesy *Tevhid-i Efkar*, 3, no. 969–3997 (March 4, 1924), Beyazit Devlet Kütüphanesi, Hakkı Tarık Us Bölümü, No. 3052, Cilt 19.

Fatin Bey, along with six other signatories, comprising the mayor, the jurisconsultant (*müftü*), the judge (*kadi*), and three *tekke* shaykhs, explained at length how there was no need to retain the caliphate and concluded with a pointed quip doubting the insight and mental capacities of anyone who hesitated over this matter. Regardless of such foolish individuals, the telegram claimed, the Turkish people would continue on their path to progress and development. Not stopping at that, the following orders were also sent in secret code from Ankara to Kastamonu: "Tell the municipality's mayor to start working on having the people of Kastamonu remove Halit from his deputyship in parliament." When the mayor declined on the basis of how much the people of Kastamonu loved Halit, the instructions from Ankara then changed to have the mayor himself removed from office so that an incoming mayor could do the job. When Necip Bey, Kastamonu's mayor who had thus fallen out of official favor, related these events back to Halit, the latter exclaimed in ironic allusion to the principles of the nationalist movement, upon which the Republic was founded, something along the lines of: "So much for the sovereignty of the people!"[77]

The only other assembly member to speak out against the abolition of the caliphate during the actual proceedings was the sole independent deputy of the second session, Zeki (Kadirbeyoğlu) Bey (1884–1952), who represented the Gümüşhane province in the Black Sea region. Hailing from a prominent Gümüşhane family, Zeki was a popular merchant and moderate liberal nationalist figure who served as vice-chair for the Trabzon Association for the Defense of National Rights's first and second congresses in 1919. Representing Gümüşhane at the subsequent Erzurum Congress, Zeki reportedly insisted that Mustafa Kemal could not enter the premises without first removing his uniform and insignia that paraded his status as the Ottoman sultan's aide-de-camp, adding hostility to their divergent visions for the nationalist movement's future. The longstanding tensions between these two men significantly increased during the Grand National Assembly's second electoral cycle some four years later, when Mustafa Kemal pulled out all the stops to exclude Zeki from joining the personally vetted assembly. According to Zeki's memoirs, the denizens of Gümüşhane repeatedly urged him to announce his candidacy as well as to select two other candidates for the remaining assembly seats that would represent their region. Zeki recalled warning the other notables to expect opposition from the Ankara government, which only wanted to elect its own representative from the People's Party, but assured of local support, Zeki and his two colleagues ran for office. After it became clear in the first round of elections that Zeki would win, members of the People's Party asked the central government to intervene in the second stage when local electors would winnow down and select three assembly members from among the remaining candidates. Accordingly, Ankara sent orders to the local gendarmerie to pressure and intimidate the electors into voting for the People's Party candidates. Armed conflict broke out in one district resisting the gendarmes and only fifteen out of sixty of its electors were able to cast their votes, and in another district the electors were arrested and released on the condition that they solemnly swore to vote for the People's Party slate; the election commissioners followed up by insisting on writing out their ballots by hand even for literate electors until Zeki intervened. In yet another district where the gendarmes entered the polling station to ensure voting for the People's Party, the electors and, in this case, the mayor Hacı Alaeddin Bey, who was presiding over this district's election, walked out. Baffled by what to do, the gendarmerie telegraphed Mustafa Kemal who then summoned the mayor. He conveyed that the population was adamant in electing Zeki who had helped them during World War I and warded off starvation afterwards by providing food and seeds; otherwise, they would rather load up their ox carts and tools and leave. Faced with such intransigence, Mustafa Kemal relented for the time being. Notwithstanding the combined pressures, Zeki was elected to the assembly, though his running mates were not as successful, and the other two seats went to the People's Party candidates. Yet when Zeki traveled to Ankara, to receive his official designation as an assembly member, he was told that there were some insurmountable difficulties with his paperwork. The People's Party accused him of pressuring voters in the district where armed conflict had broken out in resistance to the gendarmes. And when Zeki told them to simply subtract that district's votes since he would still have enough to be seated as an assembly member, he was told they could not because the orders came personally from Mustafa Kemal. Only after Zeki threatened them to reject his membership in the assembly so that he could go back and inform his constituents about what had transpired, did Mustafa Kemal reconsider and reportedly contemplate that having a few independents in an assembly full of his political party members might have offered some semblance of fair and independent elections.[78]

On March 3, 1924, after several months in the assembly, Zeki ascended the podium to express his disagreement with the proposed motion to abolish the caliphate. In a climate of political intimidation, he courageously expressed that he represented the people—therefore he had a right to talk—and that he was neither beholden to the ruling party nor afraid of them. Using nationalist language, Zeki recalled asserting that the Ottoman dynasty had not usurped power over a people it did not represent and invoking the glorious memories of the past Ottoman sultans Yildirim Bayezid, Fatih Mehmed, and Yavuz Selim that contradicted the negative sentiments of his fellow assembly members toward the dynasty as a whole. He reminded the assembly of their electoral platform under the People's Party as well as the text of the previous November 1922 law immutably (*layetegayyerdir*) preserving the Ottoman Caliphate after its separation from the sultanate. To eliminate the caliphate would contravene the people's express wishes to maintain it as well as the current constitutional framework, and Zeki held that such actions could only legitimately take place after a popular referendum or a new set of elections. Yet Zeki also contended that the Ottoman dynasty was not an obstacle to the Republic, and instead of abolishing the caliphate and expelling its members, he proposed settling them in three mansions out in Etlik, then a suburb of Ankara. Nationalists' enmity was not toward the sultanate per se, Zeki argued, but rather toward personal autocracy—and Zeki openly declared that he saw the Republic moving in the direction of becoming an autocratic sultanate itself (under Mustafa Kemal).[79] Zeki boldly carried on in the assembly despite being repeatedly interrupted, harangued, and insulted, as Mustafa Kemal quietly signaled various assembly members to rise and object. Accused of spying for the palace or trying to curry favor with the caliph, Zeki was infuriated and reminded Mustafa Kemal of *his* intimate ties to the palace; Mustafa Kemal had once wanted to become the caliph's son-in-law by marrying Vahideddin's daughter Sabiha Sultan (1894–1971) and was rebuffed. Zeki's objections were motivated by his conviction that it was foolish to abandon Turkey's global leadership of the Muslim community. In his view, the only beneficiaries of the caliphate's abolition would be other governments with large Muslim populations, like the British Empire. Why would Turks destroy such a valuable institution with their own hands, when their enemies had not been able to accomplish that for centuries, he wondered.[80] Yet the vote to dismantle the caliphate and expel the Ottoman dynasty proceeded despite Zeki's protests, and he later bore the consequences for speaking out.

For the remainder of Mustafa Kemal's life, Zeki was ominously followed wherever he went. Soon after the voting, as Zeki narrates in his memoirs, he heard that Mustafa Kemal had ordered his assassination. And others warned him that the pro-caliphate politician, Ali Şükrü, who was murdered by Mustafa Kemal's bodyguard nearly one year prior, had not said nearly as much as Zeki. When Zeki was called to Prime Minister İsmet Paşa's office immediately after the vote and locked in with three other hostile representatives from the People's Party, the outnumbered politician attempted to defend himself from an ambush by brandishing his two guns, until the Turkish general Rüştü Paşa (1872–1926) heard the quarreling and demanded that the door be opened and Zeki set free. Returning home, Zeki learned that three suspicious men had been observing his house all day. And after receiving a warning one day that a car waiting outside the assembly would try to kill him, Zeki attempted to avoid the car following him from work. Despite his caution in walking back with Rüştü Paşa and another assembly member for company, the car rushed forward to hit him crossing an intersection and, after missing, returned the next day to follow Zeki again. That day, Zeki managed to outsmart the driver and forced him to drive to the nearest police station at gunpoint—only to find that the would-be hit-and-run driver was himself a plainclothes police officer. These disturbing events in the immediate aftermath of the caliphate's abolition were but the beginning of nearly two decades of persecution and intimidation, endangering Zeki's personal safety, political participation, and commercial transactions.[81]

Resigning from his deputyship in the Turkish assembly in 1924 and leaving the country altogether two years later, another disaffected nationalist of prominence, Dr. Rıza Nur, availed himself of the freedom to express his personal opinions abroad. After lengthy sojourns in France, Egypt, and England, Rıza Nur bequeathed a handwritten copy of his copious memoirs, *Hayat ve Hatıratım*, to the British Museum on June 4, 1935.[82] Strikingly, Rıza Nur was not personally religious and had been deeply influenced by the vulgar materialism popular at the Royal Medical Academy at the turn of the century. Furthermore, even though he had been one of Turkey's signatories at Lausanne and was the assembly deputy who initiated the separation of the sultanate from the caliphate back in 1922 to assert national sovereignty, the abolition of the caliphate was for him an altogether different matter—it was an outright crime (*cinayet*) and an act of insanity (*çılgınlıktır*). It was madness for Turkey to throw away the material and spiritual strength that the caliphate had represented to the country, and immoral to leave the Muslims of the world "powerless, without a center, hopeless, and as forlorn as strangers" (*Müslümanlar kuvvetsiz, merkezsiz, ümitsiz, garip bırakıldı*). He also comments that while Mustafa Kemal had left the poor Muslim world "without a head" (*Zevallı Alem-i İslam başsız kaldı*), even Mussolini (1883–1945) had not abolished the papacy. Rıza Nur recognized that Muslims of the world had loved the Turks as custodians of the caliphate and that this had signified immense spiritual power, which translated into material strength. Angry at Mustafa Kemal's selfish and politically motivated denial of any foreign benefit that the Turks had derived from upholding the caliphate, Rıza Nur recounts how the Red Crescent had successfully gathered funds for Turkey in India, how the Indians had also interceded politically on Turkey's behalf to secure more equitable terms for the country, and how even an Egyptian Coptic Christian had intervened militarily to minimize the harm inflicted upon the Ottoman army during its assault on the Suez. All this assistance, Rıza Nur exclaims, was coming from occupied and oppressed peoples; how much more could be forthcoming, he speculates, when they were free and liberated? While imagining the possible advantages of retaining the caliphal institution, Rıza Nur further contemplates the economic advantages and how love for the caliphate's upholders could have translated into a widespread desire for their commercial products, the budding of which was already evident. In light of all of these considerations, Rıza Nur was deeply affected upon learning the news of the caliphate's abolition, which came to him as a shock. The institution that he had deemed worth strengthening and modernizing was now gone.[83]

Others also took the opportunity to register their opposition to the caliphate's abolition and the direction in which the government's political party was heading. A certain *hoca* of Erzurum officially resigned from the People's Party, and "in his letter of resignation stated quite frankly that his religious principles would not allow him to remain any longer in the party." In Lindsay's assessment of the matter on November 24, 1924, "This is open Khalifism, and is the most outspoken declaration of it that I have yet seen. The Hoja does not stand alone, but he has not many adherents in the Assembly, and I do not think that they amount to much at present, but there seems to be geographical character in this movement—they all hail from the eastern provinces."[84] Despite Lindsay's commentary on this group's insignificant numbers, their presence at all in the second session of the Turkish assembly is significant, for it indicates the strain that was steadily building among the assembly deputies whose candidacies for office had been personally vetted by Mustafa Kemal in 1923 for potential loyalty.[85]

And in spite of our general conceptions of the war-strained and intimidated Anatolians' general quiescence, popular demonstrations protesting the removal of the Ottoman Caliphate also broke out in the Northwest, South, and Southeast. In Silifke, along the Mediterranean, an imam named Askeri Hoca preached spiritedly against the government's policies in the Alaaddin Mosque during the Islamic month of Ramaḍān. When this imam did not come to the mosque for the noonday prayer on April 28, 1924 (Ramaḍān 23, 1342 AH), the disappointed populace of the town set out to look for him and discovered that he had been arrested for his intrepid words. Angered, the large crowd of men and women determined to rescue the *hoca* and headed towards the government building in town, drawing increasingly more people along the way. Frightened by this large and indomitable gathering, the government officials inside the building where the *hoca* was being kept for interrogation either hid or fled, and the province's head commissioner (*Vilayet Serkomiseri*) had to face the crowd alone. The people of Silifke then proceeded to beat up the head commissioner, and, in the absence of the police and gendarmerie, they set the *hoca* free and brought him back to the mosque where he openly condemned those who had led the nationalist movement and now ran the government as sinners who had deceived the people. In the midst of this passionate sermon, reinforcements arrived from nearby Mersin and arrested the *hoca*, who was ultimately tried and hung for supporting the caliphate, as an act of high treason, by the reconstituted Independence Tribunals.[86]

Similar demonstrations erupted in Bursa, Reşadiye, and Adapazarı, not far from Istanbul.[87] And the Egyptian newspaper *al-Akhbār* even reported of a demonstration occurring in the heart of Istanbul, where a large crowd marching towards the Dolmabahçe Palace in protest against the caliphate's abolition was only dispersed through brute force.[88] In Southeastern Anatolia, the resentment over the Turkish government's abolition of the caliphate resulted in an armed brawl in late March 1924 in the town of Gaziantep, where people responded to the insulting taunts by supporters of Mustafa Kemal against the caliphate, with knives and rifles, ultimately leaving four or five people dead. Similar tensions likewise emerged in Urfa and Birecik amidst general "disgust and anger against the Turkish Government," while the Alevi partisans of Mustafa Kemal, alongside the Turkish government itself, were also said to be

MAP 4. Public protests and tensions over the caliphate's abolition in the Turkish Republic (1924) and the Shaykh Said Rebellion (1925).

pressuring the religious and/or conservative supporters of the caliphate, including some of the region's most prominent families, to leave the country, perhaps for Syria, on the basis of their partisanship. While some families reportedly began to leave, "opposition to this form of persecution is stiffening daily... So far from complying, it is stated that a movement of opposition is growing and that the Government is being defied."[89]

The widespread resentment in Southeast Anatolia towards the caliphate's abolition even fed into the momentous rebellion among Kurds led by Shaykh Said in early 1925.[90] Initial preparations for the revolt were made by Kurdish nationalists who had coalesced into a clandestine organization, *Ciwata Azadi Kurd* (Society for Kurdish Freedom), which then turned to traditional community figures, namely religious and tribal leaders, to assume initiative, out of a recognition for their greater ability to influence and mobilize the ethnically Kurdish population.[91] One of the few grievances that this sociologically and ideologically diverse group of individuals held in common was the abolition of the caliphate by the Turks. In the time of Abdülhamid II, the Kurdish population had immense regard for the caliph and viewed him as a fatherly figure. And as van Bruneissen describes their continued attachment to the caliphate:

> Especially among the Kurds, the caliphate had been held in high esteem. When, at the outset of the First World War, the Sultan in his capacity of Caliph or supreme leader of all orthodox Muslims proclaimed a *cihad* (holy war), most Kurds rallied to the call. The large sums that had been spent by Russians in an attempt to buy some Kurdish chiefs' loyalties were of no avail, nor could emotional appeals by Kurdish nationalists compete against the Caliph's word. To many, the

> caliphate was the very embodiment of Islam, and its abolition seemed a blow dealt at Islam itself.[92]

The peasants, in van Bruneissen's view, perceived the caliphate's abolition as a symbolic attack upon their own beliefs and resented the disappearance of the institution that had served as a rallying point for "uniting the Kurdish tribes in a common struggle."[93] Even though their voices had been obscured by those calling for loyalty to the Ottoman sultan-caliph, Kurdish nationalists also deeply felt the loss of the caliphal institution. When members of *Ciwata Azadi Kurd* who were officers in the Turkish army prematurely mutinied and then fled to Iraq for safety in September 1924, second on their list of eleven grievances, which predominantly consisted of complaints about various forms of ethnic discrimination, was that "the caliphate, one of the last ties binding Kurds and Turks together, had been abolished."[94] As van Bruneissen observes, it was not until this supra-ethnic bond was severed with the elimination of the caliphate that "more or less nationalist-inspired revolts" began to emerge among the Kurds.[95] And in this particular instance, according to Robert Olson and William Tucker, the objective most referred to by the broad spectrum of those participating in the rebellion of 1925 was the restoration of the caliphate.[96] In the words of Shaykh Said, the Naqshbandi shaykh who assumed a leading role in planning and coordinating the revolt, "the [Turkish] Nationalists had reduced the Caliph to the state of a parasite."[97]

The consequences of this Kurdish revolt were wide-ranging. The military launched a series of assaults to quell the rebellion,[98] while on February 25, 1925, the Turkish assembly unanimously approved the implementation of martial law in the Eastern provinces along with that of Malatya and, with some debate, also modified the Law of High Treason to include the political abuse of religion and religious objects as a treasonous undertaking.[99] Up to fifty-two thousand troops were dispatched to the area of the rebellion by the middle of April, captured towns were taken back from the rebels, the Kurdish military forces were destroyed, and the leaders of the rebellion who were not killed in battle were ultimately tried and hung for their sedition.[100] Yet, writing primarily about vindictive tactics implemented after the capture of Shaykh Said in mid-April 1925, Olson comments, "The greatest suffering of the Kurds was not from the numbers killed or the casualties they sustained, but rather from the lands destroyed, villages burned, people deported, and persecution and harassment by Turkish officers, soldiers, and gendarmes."[101]

Around this time, an internal shift within the ruling Republican People's Party over the severity of the tactics necessary to handle the situation had resulted in a change of prime ministers and an increasingly hardline approach to domestic politics both within the Eastern provinces and in the country at large. The very next day, March 4, 1925, following İsmet's re-appointment as prime minister, proposals to institute an emergency law on the Maintenance of Order

(*Takrir-i Sükun Kanunu*) granting the government virtually unlimited powers for two years and to reconstitute Independence Tribunals in the capital itself, Ankara, along with the eastern city of Diyar-ı bekir, were successfully passed in the assembly despite the new Progressive Republican Party's strenuous opposition.[102] These latest assembly developments would have acutely far-reaching consequences. All of the major newspapers, except for the two official and semi-official government organs *Cumhuriyet* and *Hakimiyet-i Milliye*, were shut down, thereby silencing those who would criticize the ruling party.[103] Key socialists and communists were arrested and tried by the Independence Tribunal newly established in Ankara.[104] And ultimately, the tribunal moved to close down the offices of the Progressive Republican Party on June 3, 1925, insinuating that its very existence as an opposition party and declared respect for religious customs and beliefs had contributed to the Kurdish uprising in the Southeast.[105] In the words of Lindsay:

> Now that the revolt has broken out the Turks have exploited it promptly to crush the opposition that was growing throughout the country against the radical and secular tendencies of the present régime and to strengthen the *de facto* autocracy of Mustafa Kemal; this is the incidental advantage arising out of an otherwise bad situation.[106]

The outbreak of the Shaykh Said rebellion would not be the last time Mustafa Kemal found an excuse to silence other politicians who could potentially utilize poor economic conditions and the unpopularity of his reforms to their advantage.

Although the progressive party members had continued to communicate and coordinate assembly tactics informally with one another, an Izmir plot to assassinate Mustafa Kemal discovered almost exactly one year later, in June 1926, served as an opportunity, as Zürcher has elucidated, to "eliminate all potential competitors for leadership of the national movement through a series of two political show trials." Over one hundred people were arrested on charges of treason, including nearly all of the remaining leaders of CUP and prominent members of the Progressive Republican Party. Declared the "mastermind" of the plot, Rauf who was abroad at the time was not arrested, but sentenced in absentia to ten years imprisonment. A relatively minor though nettlesome figure, Zeki was tried and eventually acquitted. Although put on trial, the Turkish independence heroes Refet, Kazım Karabekir, Ali Fuat, and Cafer Tayyar were eventually "released under the pressure of public opinion and signs of discontent from the army." Cavid Bey was executed, and so was Rüştü Paşa, who had been active in leading the War of Independence on the Eastern front and later tried to save Zeki from danger in the aftermath of the caliphate's abolition. Kara Kemal, who had initially gone into hiding, was also among the nineteen people sentenced to death. Many others received prison sentences of varying lengths.

The political influence of the surviving nationalists with the experience, skills, and popularity to raise a vigorous challenge was thoroughly crushed, ending any effective opposition to Kemalist policies for decades to come.[107]

THE LEVANT

Chafed by the centralization policies of the CUP following the Young Turk Revolution of 1908,[108] popular opinion in the former Ottoman provinces of the Levant leaned more heavily in support of a vocally independent Arab nationalism and the competing caliphal claims of Sharīf Ḥusayn (1854–1931). Only days after the Turkish nationalist assembly's decision to abolish the Ottoman Caliphate in 1924, Ḥusayn ibn ʿAlī, the Sharīf of Mecca and a longtime client of the British, arranged for his recognition as caliph while visiting his son, the Amīr ʿAbdullāh (1882–1951), in Transjordan. As early as March 5, news of Ḥusayn's assumption of the office was transmitted back to his kingdom in the Hijaz, replete with 101 gun salutes to accompany the official announcements made in Mecca, Medina, Jeddah, and Ṭāʾif.[109] Many saw Sharīf Ḥusayn's move as the fulfillment of his longstanding ambitions to be instated as caliph, but it could also be seen as a desperate play for continued relevance. British support for him was waning in the aftermath of the Great War with the successful defeat of the Ottoman Empire in hand, and hostilities with the Sultan of Najd and later founder of the Kingdom of Saudi Arabia ʿAbd al-ʿAzīz Ibn Saʿūd (1875–1953) were still simmering.[110] Nevertheless, according to an interview that Sharīf Ḥusayn gave to the *Manchester Guardian*'s correspondent in Shūnah in March 1924, the position of caliph had been forced upon him:

> I have not sought or desired the Khilafate; it has been thrust upon me. From everywhere they come to me and say: "Islam must have a Khalif to protect it, and the Khilafate must not be allowed to die out. You are the only Prince competent to fill it. You are the independent ruler of a great Moslem and Arab State. In your charge are the Holy Cities. You are of the tribe of Koreish. Your orthodoxy and zeal for the true faith are beyond all question. You are an Arab of the Arabs." If I had not accepted I should have failed in my duty, and my people would have turned against me.[111]

Sharīf Ḥusayn's official gazette, *al-Qiblah*, likewise takes pains to emphasize that he had not asked to be caliph, but rather that he was obliged by Islamic law to accept and confirm Muslims' pledges of allegiance, by virtue of his fulfilling all caliphal criteria, to preserve the institution. In flowery language, "the Caliphate had come to him submissively and cast its reins between his hands."[112] Given the skepticism of contemporaries and subsequent historians alike over the way in which these urgent summonses to embrace the caliphate were in fact engineered by Sharīf Ḥusayn and his sons, Sharīf Ḥusayn's assessment of his

FIGURE 15. Newsreel stills of Sharīf Ḥusayn's proclamation as caliph in Transjordan, March 1924.

Image courtesy "Ruler of 60,000,000 Moslems: King Hussein proclaimed Caliph in place of deposed Abdul Mejid," British Pathé, issue date: March 24, 1924, Stills #5, #22, #32.

qualifications most amply reflects his own perception of reality that he desired others to embrace as well. Certainly, the fact that the Amīr Fayṣal (1885–1933) had openly recognized his father as caliph in the name of his government in ʿIrāq and then prevented the Reuters report to the effect that Sharīf Ḥusayn had "accepted the Caliphate from the Moslems of Mesopotamia" from circulating locally because his ʿIrāqī subjects were actually still discussing among themselves whether or not to recognize Sharīf Ḥusayn as caliph gives one pause.[113] So also does the promotion in *al-Qiblah* of a small cohort of Penang schoolboys studying in Mecca to the status of an official delegation offering their pledge of allegiance on behalf of "5,000,000 Moslems of the Malay peninsula."[114] Yet despite the dubiousness of such concerted efforts to aggrandize the recognition of Sharīf Ḥusayn's caliphate into a universal acclaim, it was, in fact, heartily embraced in some diverse quarters, as in the Levant, among his distant relatives the Haḍramī sayyids in Southeast Asia,[115] and among a portion of Indian Khilafatists who aspired to locate the caliphate within the Meccan sanctuary.[116]

In the Levant, where the Hashemites had become associated with the Arab nationalist demand for complete independence, Sharīf Ḥusayn's caliphate met with popular acclaim. In his negotiations with the British government, Sharīf Ḥusayn remained steadfastly committed to securing the implementation of the wartime promises he argued were made to him for an independent Arab kingdom encompassing all of what was to be divided into Syria, Lebanon, Palestine, Transjordan, and Iraq, in addition to the Hijaz.[117] His son Fayṣal, meanwhile, had worked closely with the region's local nationalists during the war to sustain the Arab revolt against the Ottoman Empire and subsequently established the first Arab Kingdom, based in Damascus, until he was overcome and expelled by the French in July 1920.[118] In their bid to "give the Arab nationalist movement an appearance of unity while stressing the continuity of nationalist demands with the unfulfilled promises made by Britain to Sharīf Husayn during the war," in the words of Mary Wilson, Fayṣal's supporters also made the symbolic move of inviting his brother ʿAbdullāh (1882–1951) to come from the Hijaz and assume the lead of their regrouped movement in Amman.[119] These connections that the Hashemites had astutely cultivated with Arab nationalists over the years also fed into a measure of recognition for Sharīf Ḥusayn as caliph in March 1924 as an emblem of nationalist aspirations to full independence. Support for the caliphate of Sharīf Ḥusayn was a pragmatic and seemingly viable path to independence among a wide array of politically conscious Arabs in the spring of 1924. It also appears to have resonated with wider perceptions of a need to return the Islamic caliphate to the Prophet's tribe of Quraysh.

Such arrangements were swiftly made in Damascus. On Friday, March 7, "the Chief Preacher" Shaykh ʿAbd al-Qādir al-Khaṭīb climbed the pulpit of the Umayyad Mosque[120] to bewail the termination of the caliphate by the Turkish nationalists, explaining that it was a legal obligation upon the Muslim community to maintain a spiritual and temporal leader. "Oh Muslims!" he exclaimed,

"You have to choose a Caliph who could preserve both religious and civil order and protect the honor of the Muslims," and he proceeded to clarify the necessary attributes of such a leader. If Shaykh ʿAbd al-Qādir was indeed nervous before ascending the pulpit with the encouragement of younger Arab activists, as others observed, the end of his sermon clearly reveals why. His conclusion consisted of the following declaration, "O gathering of Muslims, all the conditions of the caliphate exist in the King of the Arabs al-Huṣayn b. ʿAlī, so I pledge allegiance to him by virtue of the Book of God and the way of His messenger. So will you too pledge allegiance to him by that?" At this point, the political activists scattered throughout the crowd reportedly replied in fervent affirmation, evoking general acclamation of Sharīf Ḥusayn ibn ʿAlī as the rightful caliph among an estimated thirty to forty thousand congregants in attendance. Afterwards, Shaykh ʿAbd al-Qādir al-Khaṭīb telegraphed the news to Sharīf Ḥusayn.[121] As reported by the Damascene periodical *Fatā al-ʿArab*, a formal declaration of Sharīf Ḥusayn's caliphate was also signed on March 11, 1924, by the chief of the ʿUlamāʾ, the Qāḍī, and the Naqīb al-Ashrāf along with other religious scholars and notables of Damascus.[122] And the Palestinian periodical *Filasṭīn* further reported that the Muslims of Homs and Hama pledged their allegiance to Sharīf Ḥusayn as caliph after the congregational Friday prayers on March 7, 1924.[123]

A large proportion of Muslims in Aleppo were likewise said to have accepted Sharīf Ḥusayn as the caliph succeeding Abdülmecid, and preachers, including the one at the town's most important mosque, prayed for the new caliph by name on Friday, March 7. The Shaykh of Aleppo's Great Mosque[124] additionally commended acceptance of Sharīf Ḥusayn as caliph on March 10, 1924, to the worshippers who had gathered there for the afternoon prayers. And in an attempt to rally further popular support, pamphlets arguing the importance of acknowledging Sharīf Ḥusayn as caliph were distributed towards evening.[125] On March 7, preachers in two of Beirut's mosques included the name of Sharīf Ḥusayn as caliph, simply as a matter of fact, during the Friday prayers, and a third earnestly urged the people adopt this course. By the following Friday, several meetings had been held in Beirut to discuss the matter, which culminated in the recognition of Sharīf Ḥusayn's caliphate by the Muslims of Beirut and its environs. This confirmation took place over the objections of Prince Saʿīd al-Jazāʾirī (1883–1966), who was the grandson of the exiled Amīr ʿAbd al-Qādir of Algeria (1808–83) and had urged the Muslims of Beirut to wait until an Islamic conference could look into the matter. In general, as elsewhere in geographical Syria, popular sentiment seemed favorably disposed to recognizing Sharīf Ḥusayn as the new symbolic leader of their community.[126]

In Palestine, the bid to recognize Sharīf Ḥusayn as caliph took significant shape. Under the leadership of al-Ḥājj al-Amīn al-Ḥusaynī (1897–1974), the Supreme Islamic Council (*al-Majlis al-Islāmī al-Aʿlā*) convened a meeting in Jerusalem on March 10, 1924, to evaluate the question democratically. Muslim scholars, notables, judges, electors (*ahl al-ḥall wa'l-'aqd*), and a swath of representatives from across Palestine attended. While the majority of the elected delegates representing Palestinian towns and villages were in favor of acknowledging Sharīf Ḥusayn's caliphate, the deputies from Nablus were firmly opposed to hastening into such a recognition without first learning the opinions of the rest of Muslims around the world and consulting them. Accordingly, the morning's proceedings focused on three possible options: offering an unconditional pledge of allegiance to Sharīf Ḥusayn as caliph, making a conditional pledge of allegiance to him, and waiting to hold a conference in the Aqṣā Mosque in two-months' time with the participation of Muslims from Egypt, India, Syria, and all other lands. After a midday break, the Palestinian representatives reconvened, listened to a presentation by Muslim scholars about the election of a caliph according to Islamic legal texts, and ultimately voted to support a conditional pledge of allegiance to Sharīf Ḥusayn as caliph. Their four main conditions were that the new caliph rely upon consultation (*shūrā*), as was commanded by God, that he not contravene the general public interests of Muslims, that he not undertake any decisions regarding Palestine or its government without first consulting its own Palestinian inhabitants, and that he not recognize any foreign occupation of Arab lands in general or of Palestine in particular. These lofty expectations of a caliph were written out twice and signed with pen and ink by all in attendance, followed by a fervent prayer offered by the Mufti of Gaza. The resulting documents along with the two pens used to write each one were sent on to separate destinations. One set was conveyed to Sharīf Ḥusayn who was receiving pledges of allegiance in Shūnah, and the other was hung symbolically in the Aqṣā Mosque in Jerusalem, revealing a potent blend of their aspirations for independence and faithful representation as Palestinians, Arabs, and Muslims.[127]

Yet Palestinian Christians who were active in the public domain also vocally supported the caliphate of Sharīf Ḥusayn. The prominent Melkite Christian writer Jamīl al-Baḥrī (d. 1930) who, in the words of his brother, struggled for the homeland and nationalism (*al-waṭan wa'l-waṭaniyyah*) above all else,[128] opened the March 1924 issue of his literary magazine produced in Haifa, *al-Zahrah*, with the embellished words of Sharīf Ḥusayn's note of commendation. Sharīf Ḥusayn flowerily reported that he had received his copy as a mark of Arab progress with great delight and esteem and prayed for its owner's success and happiness, both worldly and eternal. Similarly effusive, al-Baḥrī waxed eloquent over Sharīf Ḥusayn's refined sentiments and appreciation of literature, asking God to prolong his days and preserve His Majesty, "the Pride of the Arabs, their Reliance, and the one who raises the banner of their dignity, by God's grace and generosity" (*fakhr al-'Arab wa-sanadahum wa-rāfi' liwā' 'izzihim bi-mannihi ta'ālā wa-karamih*). He then devoted the next nine pages of *al-Zahrah* to preserving for posterity the historic events of the selection of Sharīf Ḥusayn as caliph, especially in Palestine. And in closing his account,

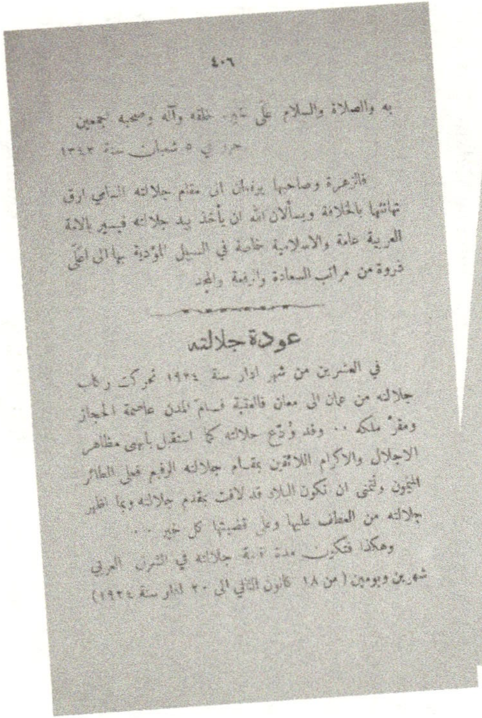
٤٠٦

به والصلاة والسلام على خير خلقه وآله وصحبه اجمعين

حرر في ٥ شعبان سنة ١٣٤٢

فالزهرة وصاحبها يرفعان الى مقام جلالته السامي ارق تهانيها بالخلافة ويسألان الله ان يأخذ بيد جلالته فيسير بالامة العربية عامة والاسلامية خاصة في السبل المؤدية بها الى اعلى ذروة من مراتب السعادة والرفعة والمجد

عودة جلالته

في العشرين من شهر اذار سنة ١٩٢٤ تحركت ركاب جلالته من عمان الى معان فالعقبة فسائر المدن عاصمة الحجاز ومقر ملكه .. وقد ودع جلالته كما استقبل بأبهى مظاهر الاجلال والاكرام اللائقين بمقام جلالته الرفيع

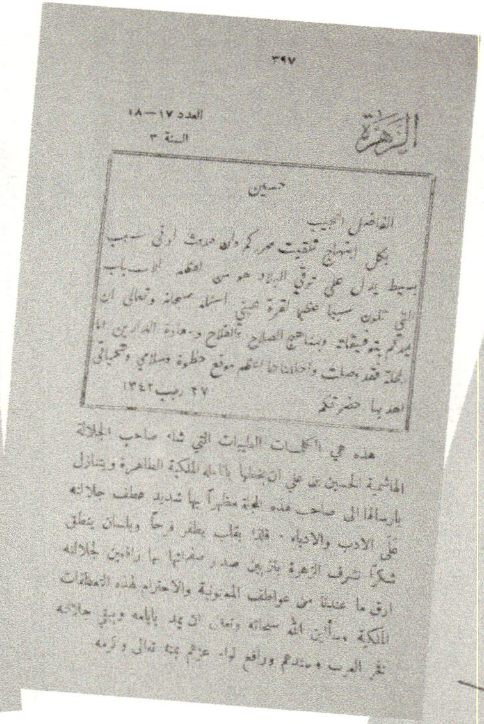
٣٩٧

الزهرة

العدد ١٧—١٨

السنة ٣

حسين

الفاضل الحبيب

٢٧ رجب ١٣٤٢

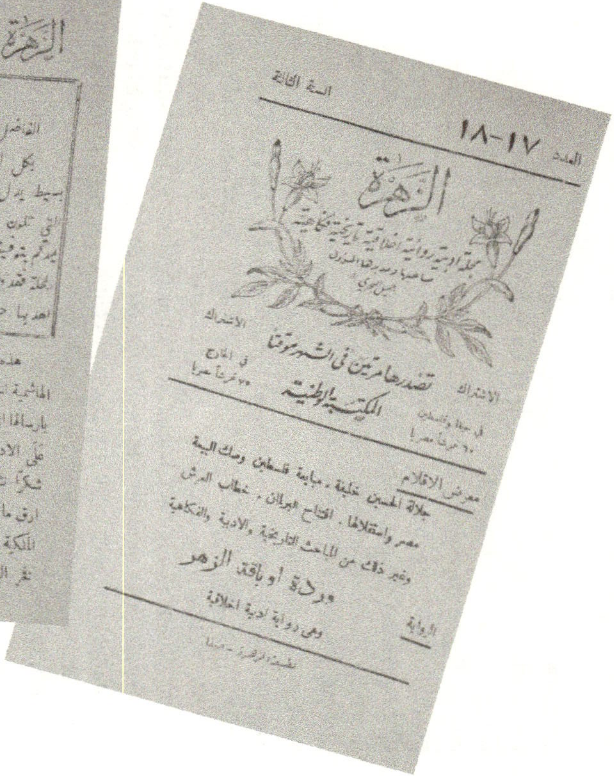
العدد ١٧-١٨

السنة الثالثة

الزهرة

الاشتراك

الكتبة الوطنية

معرض الاقلام

وردة او باقة الزهر

الرواية

FIGURE 16. Endorsement of Sharīf Ḥusayn's caliphate in Jamīl al-Baḥrī's literary magazine *al-Zahrah* (Haifa), March 1924.

Image courtesy *al-Zahrah* 3, no. 17–18 (March 1924), The British Library, Endangered Archives Programme, Periodical Collection of the al-Aqsa Mosque Library, EAP119/1/9.

al-Baḥrī offered his own sublime congratulations and prayers for the new caliph. He asked God to "take His Majesty by the hand so that he leads the Arab nation (*ummah*) in general and the Islamic one in particular to the pinnacle of happiness, prominence, and glory." From al-Baḥrī's perspective, Arab identity was the overarching marker of an inclusive community that stood to benefit from Sharīf Ḥusayn's caliphate, and Islam was denoted as a specific subset. [129]

In Jaffa, the respected Arab nationalist and Greek Orthodox journalist ʿĪsā al-ʿĪsā (1878–1950) offered support through what Rashid Khalidi has described as "the most influential Palestinian newspaper during the first half of the twentieth century," *Filasṭīn*.[130] Published three times a week during this epoch, their widely circulated newspaper proudly noted that the denizens of Jaffa had first pledged allegiance to Sharīf Ḥusayn as caliph in 1919 following the death of the Ottoman sultan Mehmed V Reşad (r. 1909–18). At the time, ʿĪsā al-ʿĪsā himself was serving in King Fayṣal's Royal Chancery in Damascus, capital of the short-lived independent Arab Kingdom. However, Fayṣal's father Sharīf Ḥusayn had not accepted Jaffa's allegiance back then, saying that its time had not yet come. In March 1924, however, al-ʿĪsā noted how circumstances had changed in the intervening years and expressed his explicit joy that his Muslim brethren in Palestine had unified around the caliphate of His Majesty. Even before the official gathering in Jerusalem, Muslim scholars in Jaffa had convened and decided to arrange for recognition of Sharīf Ḥusayn's caliphate after the Friday congregational prayers in the Great Mosque[131] on March 7. Accordingly, Shaykh ʿĪsā Efendi Abū'l-Jabīn made a speech to the congregation about what the Turks had done, how they had mistreated the caliph and held Muslim feelings in contempt, and he expounded on the qualifications of Sharīf Ḥusayn to be caliph. On Abū'l-Jabīn's request that the congregation pledge its allegiance to Sharīf Ḥusayn, they affirmed it all together. A group of Muslim scholars then announced the news to the Muslim and Christian Association's Center (*Markaz al-Jamʿiyyah al-Islāmiyyah al-Masīḥiyyah*) and its vice president Saʿīd Abū Khaḍrah and then conveyed their pledge to "His Majesty, Our Master, Commander of the Faithful, Ḥusayn b. ʿAlī the Magnificent" in Shūnah by telegram.[132]

Aside from conveying news of these developments in Jaffa and across Palestine, al-ʿĪsā took an active stance in urging and commending them. In the early days, he advised that it would be expedient for Palestinians to accept Sharīf Ḥusayn's caliphate to ward off the possibility of other rival candidates—although he hoped the Muslim community in Palestine would first ascertain Sharīf Ḥusayn's positions and stipulate his support for Palestinian independence (*istiqlāl Filisṭīn*) and his rejection of the devastating Balfour Declaration that endangered it by denying national rights to the "existing non-Jewish communities in Palestine" who formed the great majority of the population. al-ʿĪsā praised the speed with which "our brothers" in the Hijaz and Transjordan had pledged their allegiance by presenting the Muslim community with a *fait accompli* that it seemed could prevent disunity and foreign interference. Pleased with the ensuing Palestinian recognition of Sharīf Ḥusayn's caliphate, al-ʿĪsā hoped that the new Arab caliphate marked the beginning of a resplendent era and that Muslims everywhere would gather around his Hashemite Majesty and lend him their affective and material support in realizing the aspirations of Arab lands for independence, especially those of Palestine, home to the third-most sacred Islamic sanctuary and afflicted by the Balfour Declaration that arrogated exclusive national rights to a small minority. Indeed, al-ʿĪsā identified the appeal of Sharīf Ḥusayn's caliphate firstly in his resolve and determination for securing the future of Arab lands (*taqrīr maṣīr al-bilād*) as a king to whom England had promised their independence through treaties, secondly in his ardor to serve the Aqṣā Mosque as caliph, and thirdly, in the Islamic legal stipulation that the caliphate should be led by the Prophet's family of Quraysh.[133]

Even when Palestinian villagers from Majdal ʿAsqalān (now Ashkelon) telegraphed *Filasṭīn* to complain first of the unsavory words then of the house arrest (*imtiḥāninā fī dārinā*) that they had received at the hands of Sharīf Ḥusayn's delegation that had been sent to seek out their allegiance, which they withheld, al-ʿĪsā deflected the blame. It appeared to him that such deficiencies lay at the feet of Sharīf Ḥusayn's deputies, not His Majesty or his sons. While finding fault in the reprehensible reaction of the Hashemite delegation's leader, al-ʿĪsā also did not think the villagers were justified in retaining their pledge of allegiance to the deposed Ottoman caliph Abdülmecid after Egyptian religious scholars had recently invalidated it—though he remained silent on their expressed desire to await the decision of an Islamic conference to be held in Cairo regarding the caliphate. Rather, al-ʿĪsā advised, it would be better for the people of Majdal ʿAsqalān to follow the example set by the people of Palestine more broadly when they rushed to pledge their allegiance to Sharīf Ḥusayn as caliph, since it symbolically strengthened his hand in advocating for their cause (*li-mā yarawna fī bayʿatihi al-quwwah al-maʿnawiyyah lahu fī nuṣrat qaḍiyyatihim*).[134]

Given these associations of Sharīf Ḥusayn with Arab demands for political independence combined with French mistrust of his ties to the British as a rival imperial force, the French were vociferously opposed to his candidacy for the caliphate and actively sought to squelch local recognition of him in their newly acquired territories. Periodicals advocating Sharīf Ḥusayn's caliphate, such as the Beirut newspaper *al-Ḥaqīqah*, were suppressed and their offices raided.[135] Mosque leaders were repeatedly instructed not to pray for Sharīf Ḥusayn as the new caliph on Fridays, with the threat of dire consequences looming over them.[136] The police confiscated petitions circulating the streets of Aleppo on behalf of Sharīf Ḥusayn's caliphate.[137] And a number of individuals considered to be acting in the Sharifian ruler's interests were officially deported from Lebanon to Palestine as other activists were arrested and expelled from the towns of Homs and Hama.[138] The telegraph administration halted all messages from Damascus to Amman pledging allegiance to Sharīf Ḥusayn.[139] And the gendarmes pointedly walked through the streets of Damascus to impress the force of their presence upon the city's inhabitants.[140]

The results of these measures, however, were not always to the liking of the French authorities. When the Mufti of Damascus Muḥammad ʿAṭṭā al-Kasīm issued a circular, which he made clear was "by virtue of an order received from His Excellency the Governor of Damascus," on Thursday, March 13, 1924, to the mosque preachers that "the prayer tomorrow should be only in the name of the caliph of Muslims without any particular name, as has been ordained in Beyrut and Aleppo," the city's bazaars shut down in silent protest. Nor did the preachers of Damascus's principal mosques comply. Reportedly angered at the government's interference, tens of thousands of people turned up at the Umayyad Mosque on March 14 to see what the preacher would do and finally regained their composure upon hearing supplications made for Sharīf Ḥusayn's success as caliph. At the governor's insistence, the mufti issued yet another circular repeating the official directives on the following Thursday. And Shaykh ʿAbd al-Qadīr of the Umayyad Mosque was brought before the governor himself to be admonished into compliance. The next day, Friday, March 21, 1924, Shaykh ʿAbd al-Qadīr followed the letter of his instructions, if not the spirit, by notifying his congregation:

> Oh! Men, you know that Homage to the Caliph has been paid, and this cannot be denied. The KORAN says: "[Anyone who breaks his pledge does so to his own detriment (48:10)]", and the Prophet said: "He who dies without having done homage to an Imam, will die [in a state of ignorance]." Notwithstanding all of this, the Government have seen fit that the name of the Caliph should not be mentioned in the Friday Prayer, but this will not affect the homage we did, because the prayer will only be directed to the Caliph to whom homage has been done. Then he added:—"Oh Lord! Grant Victory to the Caliph of the Muslims—the Guardian of the Two Sacred Cities." [141]

In addition to Shaykh ʿAbd al-Qadīr's affirming the inviolability of the congregation's earlier pledge of allegiance to the new caliph, the reference in his prayers to Sharīf Ḥusayn, as the official protector of the religious sanctuaries in the Hijaz, remained obvious and omitted only his proper name. This model of purported compliance was followed in some of the other mosques, while other preachers simply continued to disregard openly the orders emanating from the French colonial authorities.[142] The official head of Damascus's religious scholars, the *raʾīs al-ʿulamāʾ*, was also summoned before the city's governor to retract his written and signed declaration of allegiance to Sharīf Ḥusayn as caliph. When the *raʾīs al-ʿulamāʾ* refused to do any such thing, the governor insisted that he resign his position, which the recalcitrant scholar also refused. Thereupon, the governor consulted the French high commissioner's delegate about how to resolve the dilemma and then implemented a seemingly satisfactory resolution; the governor informed the disobedient religious leader that his very post as *ra'īs al-'ulamā'* had been abolished.[143] Throughout geographical Syria, people's feelings were aroused by the heavy-handed interference of the French colonial authorities in their selection of a new caliph.[144]

While the French were deeply implicating themselves in the tumult of the caliphate, the British were anxious to distance themselves from any semblance of involvement in the affair. In the course of their early negotiations in 1914 and 1915, British officials had tempted Sharīf Ḥusayn and his sons with support for the idea of an Arab caliphate to counter and supplant that of the Ottomans. On October 31, 1914, Lord Herbert Kitchener (1850–1916) brazenly wrote to 'Abdullāh, the son of Sharīf Ḥusayn, "It may be that an Arab of true race will assume the Caliphate at Mecca or Medina, and so good may come, by the help of God, out of all the evil that is now occurring." And Sir Henry McMahon (1862–1949) reiterated these tidings nearly one year later, on August, 30, 1915, "We declare once more that His Majesty's Government would welcome the resumption of the Caliphate by an Arab of true race." Approximately ten years later, however, after the defeat and dissolution of the Ottoman Empire following the First World War and Sharīf Ḥusayn's open declaration of his alternative caliphate, the British waffled. A lengthy internal memorandum on British commitments to Sharīf Ḥusayn was rapidly prepared and widely circulated, on March 12, 1924, to absolve His Majesty's Government of any obligation to acknowledge and support these caliphal claims. In the Foreign Office's vindicating assessment of their policy:

> His Majesty's Government have succeeded so far in making it clear that they regard the question of the Caliphate as a purely Moslem affair, without causing Shereef Hussein to doubt their goodwill towards his aspirations in the matter. We have two purely negative desiderata—avoidance of offence, on the one hand, to Moslem opinion, and, on the other hand to the Shereef —which have to be reconciled with one another, and hitherto we have avoided committing ourselves in either direction in a way that would compromise us in the other.[145]

Their overriding concern, therefore, was to maintain this appearance of impartiality. And then there was the disquieting question of His Majesty's Indian subjects. On March 8, 1924, the British viceroy telegrammed the secretary of state for India his riveting apprehension that Sharīf Ḥusayn's assumption of the caliphate would provide ample opportunity for Khilafat activists to blame the policy of His Majesty's Government for promoting this "attack on the unity of Islam, already imperiled by British hostility and precipitate action of the Turks."[146] The solution to this dilemma was almost simultaneously devised by the India Office and the Foreign Office alike: clarification of governmental policy by means of a parliamentary question.

Before such a parliamentary question could be contrived, Brigadier-General Ernest Makins (1869–1959) in the House of Commons submitted his own inquiry to ward off, in his words, "any misconceptions which may react on public tranquility in the different parts of the Empire" regarding the Turkish abolition of the caliphate. This opportunity was readily taken up by the Foreign Office staff to propagate their newly adopted position through the prime minister's official response, "His Majesty's Government are not entitled, either on political or religious grounds, to comment on, or interfere in any way in a matter in which their policy has consistently been, and will remain, one of complete disinterestedness."[147] When, days later, Lord Colum Chrichton-Stuart (1886–1957) and Captain Anthony Eden (1897–1977) additionally contemplated offering the expelled Ottoman caliph Abdülmecid asylum within the border of the British Empire to appease His Majesty's Muslim subjects, as "a most effective reply to previous anti-British agitation," the prime minister returned what was intended to be "as brief and elastic a reply as possible," so as not to offend either the Indians or the Turks, and reaffirmed his earlier response.[148] The text of the prime minister's initial statement was then distributed among the British high commissioners in predominantly Muslim territories across the world so that the consular officials could publicize this policy in accordance with local circumstances and remain cautiously guarded on all matters related to the caliphate.[149] On this basis, the telegram informing government offices of the formal ceremony proclaiming Sharīf Ḥusayn as caliph was not given the slightest reply of acknowledgment.[150] And the parliamentary exchange provided an effective foundation for the prime minister to decline a visit from Sharīf Ḥusayn's representative in London, Dr. Nājī al-Aṣīl (1897–1963), while retaining his good graces.[151] At home and abroad, His Majesty's Government endeavored to maintain this position of "complete disinterestedness."

Nevertheless, allegations began surfacing in Syria that British agents had been surreptitiously distributing money to secure people's allegiance to Sharīf Ḥusayn as caliph. Ten thousand pounds sterling were said to have been distributed in Aleppo for this purpose.[152] Ostensibly, the ultimate aim of these clandestine activities was to ensure Great Britain's domination of Muslim lands through Sharīf Ḥusayn as their agent and protégé. According to the Aleppan newspaper, *al-Taqaddum*, recognition of Sharīf Ḥusayn therefore meant that "Great Britain would become the official Protector of all the Moslems."[153] An alternative thesis broached in the Syrian press was that the British merely wanted to sow discord among Muslims by advocating Sharīf Ḥusayn's caliphate, and through dividing Muslims from one another in this way, the malevolent British would "succeed in setting their feet on their lands and having a preponderating influence over them."[154] Per the advice proffered by one author seeking to assess and redress the situation:

> The British have been accustomed in the past to use their well-known astuteness to profit by events, and at the present time they are again doing their utmost to

> influence the trend of events in the East, to suit their policy. Consequently, we see them trying to make out of this purely religious question a political one. We must not permit them to do so.[155]

Given that the logical consequence of these allegations would be to decrease support for Sharīf Ḥusayn's caliphate by stripping away any possible claims to Arab nationalist ambitions, it is not at all surprising that these rumors in fact originated among French intelligence officers, who sought to accomplish the same ulterior motives they had attributed to the British, though through their own press subsidies. The Damascene newspaper that started the controversy was receiving monetary support from the French intelligence service.[156]

While aiming to undermine support for Sharīf Ḥusayn's caliphate in greater Syria, the French colonial authorities also attempted to promote the candidacy of other prominent figures in his stead. Far more palatable, for instance, was the Sultan of Morocco, Yūsuf bin Ḥasan (1882–1927), also a *sharīf*, but whose country was already a French protectorate since the signing of the Treaty of Fez in 1912.[157] Several members of the Ottoman dynasty who were expelled from Turkey took up residence in Beirut, and Prince Selim (1870–1937), son of the pan-Islamist caliph Abdülhamid II, was rumored to be singled out for his illustruous parentage and political ambitions as potentially the next caliph, under French tutelage, in greater Syria.[158] It was even reported in the press that the French authorities were considering offering the last Ottoman caliph Abdülmecid himself residence in Damascus to counter the claims of Sharīf Ḥusayn there.[159] And when plans were afoot in Damascus to secure caliphal recognition of ʿAbd al-ʿAzīz Ibn Saʿūd, the Sultan of Najd and Sharīf Ḥusayn's main rival in the Arabian Peninsula, it was natural for many to assume a role for the French somewhere in the midst of these intrigues.[160] By contrast, in Paris, Monsieur Jules Gasser (1865–1958) of the Gauche Démocratique, advised his colleagues on the Senate's Foreign Affairs Committee that "France should be very reserved regarding the Caliphate and should do nothing to assist the establishment of a general Caliphate, which [he] feared would lead to Pan-Islamism... [adding that] it was in French interests that the Caliphate should be divided, each Moslem country having its own Caliph."[161]

Without intentionally seeking to comply with French colonial interests, a plethora of candidates for the position of caliph emerged for consideration by Muslims across Afro-Eurasia. Nearly every Muslim ruler aspired to augment his prestige with the supreme title of caliph, were it only possible, and the leaders of national resistance movements warding off colonial incursions into Muslim territories appeared to many as natural contenders because of their undeniable valor. Thus, in addition to the claims of the deposed Ottoman caliph Abdülmecid and the apparent ambitions of Sharīf Ḥusayn of Mecca, the names of King Fuʾād (1868–1936) of Egypt,[162] Amīr Amānullāh Khan (1892–1960) of Afghanistan,[163] Imam Yaḥyā (1869–1948) of Yemen,[164] the Sultan Ibn Saʿūd of Najd,[165] the Sultan Yūsuf bin Ḥasan of Morocco,[166] the Nizam of Hyderabad Mir Osman Ali Khan (1886–1967),[167] the Shaykh Aḥmad al-Sanūsī (1873–1933) of Libya,[168] the Amīr Muḥammad bin ʿAbd al-Karīm al-Khaṭṭābī (1882–1963) of the Moroccan Rīf,[169] and even that of Mustafa Kemal[170] were all aired about. Reporting from Delhi, one British diplomat assessed local reactions to this situation following the collapse of the Ottoman Caliphate with the words, "The number of candidates for the vacant caliphate is rather bewildering to the ordinary Muhammadan public."[171] Cognizant of the challenges that such a multitude of candidates would present, the Qāḍī's deputy in Fez, Sīdī Ḥāmid Jilālī, expressed his disquietude as early as mid-March 1924, saying that he feared "the presence of rival candidates for the position of Caliph will put off, indefinitely, Moslem unity."[172]

CHAPTER 5

IN INTERNATIONAL PURSUIT OF A CALIPHATE

> We moslems of the world should thank God that Khilafate is released from the bloody hands of the Turks, and we have now God given opportunity to revive and reconstruct the True Khalifate. By the revival of the Khilafate Islam will be regenerated and will again lead the world from the present chaos to highest security. The greatest force which is latent in Islam will be liberated to save and reconstruct the world on the safest and soundest lines of eternal peace and progress.
>
> —THE REPRESENTATIVE COUNCIL OF THE INCORPORATED MOSLIM [*SIC*] COMMUNITY OF BERLIN, APRIL 1924[1]

ON MARCH 11, 1924, the deposed Ottoman caliph Abdülmecid welcomed representatives of major news agencies, including Reuters, Havas, Wolf, and Stephanie, to his new abode in exile, the Grand Hôtel des Alpes in Territet, Switzerland, overlooking Lake Geneva. The day before, Muslims from Egypt, India, and Indonesia had telegraphed messages to the deposed caliph conveying their deep sorrow and concern over the latest turn of events, while journalists had gathered in the hotel lobby in search of news following the arrival of such an eminent personage. Feeling the need to address both sets of concerns, Abdülmecid decided to organize a press conference where he could simultaneously clarify his position and convey his response to Muslims across the world. Decrying what he termed the irreligious Turkish Republic's claim to have abolished the Islamic caliphate, Abdülmecid declared the heinous act to be "fundamentally sacrilegious, null, and void" (*şeriat-ı garray-i Ahmediyye'yi münkir böyle bir karar-ı batılı keenlemyekun*) and called for the leaders and representatives of the Muslim community to cooperate with one another, in communication with him, on the planning of a grand international conference to discuss and ultimately rectify this lamentable state of affairs.[2] However, Abdülmecid's own position as caliph was in actuality crippled by the unfolding of events precipitated by the Turkish Republican assembly. As Abdülmecid himself acknowledged, the only resource he could still claim as his own was that of Muslim solidarity and loyalty,[3] yet a plethora of other contending candidates for the position of caliph quickly emerged in the aftermath of Abdülmecid's sudden loss of stature and morally persuasive power. The suggestion for an Islamic conference where Muslims from across the world could assess the situation as a

FIGURE 17. The last Ottoman caliph Abdülmecid II, 1922–24.
Image courtesy TBMM Milli Saraylar Daire Başkanlığı, Dolmabahçe Sarayı Fotoğraf Koleksiyonu, Sebah & Joaillier, Env. No. 100/4779.

collective body was widely embraced and promoted. However, a complex array of intersecting as well as conflicting personal, national, and colonial interests worked to undermine the fundamental quest for the caliphate's resurrection, following its abolition by the Turkish assembly in March 1924, at the same time that the very possibility of regeneration allowed for a fecund overflowing of ideas among Muslims globally on how to best conceptualize and reconstitute a caliphate in the post-war era. These vibrant discussions of the early twentieth century over how to revive a caliphate best suited to the modern world merged a sensibility of Islamic tranregionalism with the infectious spirit of a new age of global internationalism.

AN INTERNATIONALIST ERA

In the aftermath of the Great War, the massive and prolonged loss of life and ensuing economic depression ruptured the legitimacy and superior moral claims of the old imperial order on a global scale. At the same time, rapid technological transformations, induced by trains, steamships, telegraphs, telephones, radio transmission, and airplanes, seemed to shrink the world and made it possible to conceptualize a politically integrated globe. Rushing to fill the vacuum, the articulation of Wilsonian principles and the Bolshevik revolution inspired new models of international order rooted in liberalism and socialism that intellectually challenged the European imperial legacy and contributed to the creation of the League of Nations and the Communist International. Yet religious networks of various hues also aspired to shape an emerging world order in pursuit of peace and prosperity, as a spate of scholarly investigations have recently revealed. Reaching back to nineteenth-century France, Lisa Moses Leff describes how "Jewish identity itself became tied to the process of global integration, and the divinely ordained mission of the Jews was defined to facilitate the construction of the liberal world system." And Malachi Hacohen discusses a rich spectrum of Jewish internationalist networks in the interwar years, including active Jewish involvement in Marxist and liberal internationalism, seeking Jewish emancipation through proletarian redemption or national integration, as well as the internationalizing effects of extensive "anti-internationalist" networks of Zionists and Orthodox Jews. American Protestant organizations, like the Young Men's Christian Association, aligned themselves with a liberal internationalist vision, and Protestant leaders affiliated with the YMCA established the Institute of Pacific Relations in 1925 to stimulate international cooperation on issues of race relations and regional security. The Vatican sought to propagate a new Catholic vision of international affairs, as Guiliana Chamedes has shown, and "in the years following 1918, it sought to instantiate an alternative mode of 'governing the world'; one that was opposed to the new forms of secularism it saw built into the League of Nations's minority protection schemes and in the expansion of a left-wing radicalism across much of the European continent." And Cemil Aydin examines how Ottoman and Japanese elites reshaped pan-Islamic and pan-Asian ideas in relation to the rising tides of liberal internationalism, socialist internationalism, and nationalism.[4] Like their contemporaries, a wide spectrum of Muslim intellectuals and activists creatively engaged the challenges posed by the post-war era and strove to formulate an Islamic internationalism that represented notably modern articulations of deeply rooted religious sentiments.

In particular, the notion of a grand international conference had broad appeal among many Muslims of the early twentieth century who regarded the controversies besetting the caliphate as issues of direct and pressing concern to the entire community of the faithful. Many viewed such an international forum as an effective means to stave off precipitate action by any one segment of the global brotherhood to claim the illustrious caliphate for its own national, ethnic, or ideological leaders. For example, the Indian Central Khilafat Committee and Jamiat al-Ulama feared that the Egyptians would rush into such an arrangement with King Fuʾād, as Reuters had already reported of the religious scholars at al-Azhar, so they telegraphed the Shaykh al-Azhar and Saʿd Zaghlūl Pasha to urge that they refrain from behaving as regrettably as King Ḥusayn had done and to leave the question of a successor caliph to be settled by an international Muslim conference.[5] Also, the Afghani newspaper *Amān-i Afghān* pointedly edified its readers:

> It is obvious that a great Islamic question, which affects the whole people of Islam, cannot be solved and settled according to the views of any one section or the decision of the people of a single country. The Caliphate is a matter common to all Islam, and the proper way for Moslems to settle the question is by holding a general Islamic conference of the general representatives of Islam in a purely Islamic country which is free both from external intrigues and from foreign influences. The members of this conference should first settle by agreement among themselves the form which the Caliphate is to take and then elect to the Caliphate one of the famous leaders of Islam. This is our opinion and the view commonly held by the Moslems of Afghanistan. In this view all enlightened Moslems who adopt the religious standpoint and desire the maintenance of Islamic institutions will certainly concur. It is essential to avoid haste in this matter; the question must be decided with patience and full consideration.[6]

Mixed in with these words of brotherly parity are veiled allusions to the local advantages of Afghanistan, noted for its political independence, both as a potential site for the much-discussed conference and as a viable domain for the proposed caliphate of Amīr Amānullāh Khan. Ultimately, however, it was in Egypt that the efforts to organize an international conference of Muslims to discuss and resolve the pressing dilemma of the caliphate coalesced.

CHAPTER 5

PROMOTING AN INTERNATIONAL CONFERENCE

On March 9, 1924, a spiritual association, *al-Jamʿiyyah al-ʿAzāʾimiyyah li-Iḥyāʾ al-Akhlāq*, under the leadership of Muḥammad Māḍī Abū'l-ʿAzāʾim, met to discuss the recent crisis over the caliphate and proclaimed its denunciation of the Turkish parliamentary decision as well as affirmed the members' continuing loyalty to Abdülmecid as caliph, at least until a qualified body of Islamic scholars could satisfactorily resolve the dilemma.[7] Shortly thereafter, Abū'l-ʿAzāʾim issued an open invitation to Muslim scholars, journalists, and laymen to gather in his home on March 20, 1924, to lay down plans for a possible solution. The outcome of the evening's deliberations was the established goal of a general conference that would represent all Muslim peoples and the formation of an administrative committee and its subsidiaries to carry out this arduous task. Notably, Abū'l-ʿAzāʾim himself, a representative of the nationalist political party *al-Ḥizb al-Waṭanī* and its founder's brother ʿAlī Fahmī Kāmil (d. 1927), the exiled Tunisian nationalist ʿAbd al-ʿAzīz al-Thaʿālabī (1874–1944) who had led the Tunisian Liberal Constitutional Party, and the Algerian Khālid al-Ḥasanī al-Jazāʾirī were among those at the helm of this new organization, which also garnered support from the Egyptian prince ʿUmar Ṭūṣūn (Ömer Tosun in Turkish, 1872–1944).[8] One of the guiding principles of this new Society of the Islamic Caliphate in the Nile Valley, or *Jamāʿat al-Khilāfah al-Islāmiyyah bi-Wādī al-Nīl*, was that the pledge of allegiance to Abdülmecid remained binding until another caliph could be elected via an international Muslim conference. Another included that Egypt was an unfit location for this Islamic conference, much less the caliphate itself, because of the degree of foreign influence upon the country. Branches espousing these two positions quickly proliferated throughout Egypt.[9]

In addition to the work undertaken by Abū'l-ʿAzāʾim and his cohorts, simultaneous efforts were underway at the renowned Islamic university of al-Azhar to push for an international caliphate conference. Beginning at al-Azhar's institute in the provincial town of Ṭanṭa, Muslim scholars and students urged that all of al-Azhar's religious institutes form delegations to investigate the contemporary problems surrounding the caliphate that they could collectively discuss in a preliminary conference that they hoped would be organized by al-Azhar's most prominent individuals.[10] Another scholarly committee headed by Shaykh Muḥammad Farrāj al-Minyāwī called upon Prince ʿUmar Ṭūṣūn on March 16, 1924, to lay the foundations for an international conference of Muslims to be held in Egypt regarding the caliphate as well as to rally Egypt's leading figures to form an international delegation in conjunction with other Muslim world leaders that could be sent to the Kemalists in support of Abdülmecid and his caliphate.[11] And three days later, on March 19, 1924, yet another group of Azharī scholars and students called upon the *Hayʾat Kibār al-ʿUlamāʾ* and other Egyptian leaders to examine the issue of the caliphate in their times as well as formed a fourteen-person caliphate committee to pursue the matter.[12] In response to these various appeals, *al-Hay'ah al-'Ilmiyyah al-Dīniyyah al-Islāmiyyah al-Kubrā bi'l-Diyār al-Miṣriyyah* or the "Supreme Islamic Body of Egypt," which included the Shaykh al-Azhar, the grand muftī, the Sharī'ah Supreme Court's chief justice, the Shaykh al-Mashāyikh of the Sufi orders, and the director of al-Azhar's religious institutes, among others, convened an historic and well-attended meeting on March 25, 1924, in the administrative building of al-Azhar's religious institutes.[13]

The decision that the committee of high-ranking dignitaries announced as the result of its deliberations broke with the majority position that had been held in Egypt up until that time by declaring the caliphate of Abdülmecid to have been null and void from its very inception. The committee rebuked the Turkish Parliament for its decision of 1922 to separate the powers of the sultanate and caliphate from one another and invest Abdülmecid with a solely spiritual position, which, as the committee members clarified, defied the Islamic legal definition of the caliph as possessing combined temporal and spiritual authority. Given these conditions, the committee members explained, Muslims' very pledge of allegiance to Abdülmecid as caliph in 1922 was legally inadmissible, and, because he was shorn of the power to rule, his caliphate was categorically invalid. Even if one were to overlook these serious problems, they argued, Abdülmecid would have definitively lost his position as caliph through his inability to handle the affairs of Muslims or even protect himself and his family from expulsion from their own dominion by the Turks in 1924. As such, the committee resolved that there was no outstanding debt of allegiance due to the expelled Ottoman "prince" Abdülmecid upon the Muslims of the world. And instead, they issued a call for an international Islamic conference to be held in Cairo in March 1925 under the leadership of Egypt's Shaykh al-Islām to resolve who should assume the mantle of the caliphate.[14]

This delegitimization of Abdülmecid's caliphate was a striking departure from Egyptian popular support for the expelled Ottoman, and secret Egyptian government documents point to the ulterior political motives—long suspected by contemporaries and subsequent analysts—to proclaim King Fu'ād as caliph, as likely being behind this move. On March 2, 1924, for instance, only one day before the abolition of the caliphate, Abdülmecid's younger brother Prince Seyfeddin expressed an interest in relocating to Egypt, the original domicile of his wife, "owing to [the] impending banishment of [the Ottoman] family." Since Prince Seyfeddin had applied for a visa through the British Consulate in Istanbul, High Commissioner Lindsay telegraphed the British Residency in Cairo to check how he should deal with such requests, especially since other members of the Ottoman royal dynasty, including perhaps the caliph himself, were likely to follow suit. At the residency, approval was sought two days later from the Egyptian government, whose Foreign Ministry returned the reply on March 6, "Mr. Landsay's [*sic*] telegrams has [*sic*] been duly considered by H. E.

the Minister who asked me to inform you that the views of the Egyptian Government are that, to avoid complication of religious and political nature, it is inadvisable to allow the Caliph or members of his family to proceed to Egypt." Despite, or perhaps more accurately because of, the numerous ties of the Ottoman dynasty to Egypt, as in the case of Prince Seyfeddin through marriage to its royal family, the Egyptian government deemed it politically expedient to exclude such potentially volatile additions to the country's political and religious scene. Given the immense attachment and devotion shown to the Ottoman Caliphate and those who upheld the sacred institution during the travails of World War I, the prospective arrival of the Ottoman caliph and his family made King Fu'ād and his ministers wary of losing their grip on all claims of domestic supremacy. Perhaps it also made them wary of losing the even greater chance to claim the caliphate for Egypt anew.[15]

Another letter sent by King Fu'ād's representative in London on March 7, 1924, only four days after the caliphate's abolition, further substantiates this notion. Declaring his loyalty and sincerity towards His Royal Majesty of Egypt, 'Azīz 'Izzat Pasha felt compelled to summarize what news about the caliphate had come his way through the print media and numerous personal conversations as well as to convey his own stirring ideas on the matter. In short, while acknowledging the many burdens accompanying the position of caliph, 'Izzat Pasha strongly believed that were King Fu'ād to assume the caliphate it would be to the monarch's distinct advantage and also to that of the Muslim world at large. From 'Izzat Pasha's perspective, attaining the caliphate would strengthen the Egyptian state, ward off foreign interference in its affairs, and prevent colonizing European powers from expropriating its land, including the Sudan. As evidence, he cites how Istanbul remained in the hands of the Turks after the Treaty of Sevrès[16] due to its sanctified position in the hearts of Muslims, who had made numerous entreaties on its behalf. In the hands of King Fu'ād, 'Izzat Pasha envisions the caliphate becoming a wellspring of civilization that would spread throughout the other Muslim lands, whose inhabitants would gather round the caliph in love and admiration. Thus, despite the distances and ethnic differences that would otherwise separate those devotees, the caliphate of King Fu'ād would foster bonds of Islamic unity between Muslim nations, even in the political domain.[17]

Procedurally, however, how would King Fu'ād actually come to be recognized as caliph? 'Izzat Pasha acknowledged that it was important for King Fu'ād to obtain the support of the Muslim masses and conveyed his conviction regarding the relative ease of this task given the monarch's outstanding qualifications: his incomparable intelligence, majesty, and illustrious lineage; the preeminent position of his kingdom, Egypt, among Muslims as well as its Arabo-Islamic heritage; Egypt's progressive intellectual activity and national renaissance; and finally its central geographic position. Critical in this equation was the role of Egypt's venerable Islamic institution, al-Azhar. And 'Izzat Pasha suggested an Islamic conference, convened by conservative Egyptian scholars and attended by representatives of all Islamic lands, as the ideal means for King Fu'ād to procure the caliphate. Rather naively, or perhaps by means of flattery, he imagined that it was inevitable for King Fu'ād to receive the majority of votes under these circumstances and thus be elected to the caliphate by unanimous international consent. Crucially, from 'Izzat Pasha's perspective, official recognition from an international Islamic conference would silence King Fu'ād's potential critics, among both Muslims and non-Muslim Europeans, since this conference would represent the authoritatively unanimous voice or *ijmā'* of the Muslim community.[18] The striking resemblances between these policy recommendations of 'Izzat Pasha that Egyptian scholars should convene an international Islamic conference to secure the caliphate for King Fu'ād and the arresting decisions promulgated by Egypt's supreme Islamic body, almost three weeks later, in preparation for an international caliphate conference in Cairo are simply too great to be ignored.[19]

Supported by the venerable reputation of al-Azhar, preparations for the conference proposed by Egypt's Supreme Islamic Body quickly assumed an aura of officiality that enabled it to surpass the parallel activities of Abū'l-'Azā'im's group of nationalist religious scholars. From the beginning, the caliphate committee of Abū'l-'Azā'im reacted with tenacity to the Supreme Islamic Body's decision of March 25, 1924, reiterating their own support for Abdülmecid, at the very least as an interim caliph, and that Egypt was an unsuitable location for the future conference due to the undesirable presence and influence of the British.[20] These emphases earned Abū'l-'Azā'im's committee the ire of two powerful groups. On the one hand, Egyptian nationalists belonging to the Wafd Party were suspicious of their avowed loyalty to non-Egyptian figures as well as their leaders' alliance with the rival nationalist party *al-Ḥizb al-Waṭanī*. And, on the other hand, royalists, who expressly sought a future Egyptian caliphate by means of a Cairene conference, were also provoked by their declaration of Egypt's unsuitability for such a venue. As an unreliable or contradictory thorn in the side of these two formidable forces in Egyptian politics, the forlorn caliphate committee's ability to continue coordinating their preparatory activities for an international conference would greatly suffer. For their part, the Wafd government issued decrees prohibiting meetings of the Abū'l-'Azā'im caliphate committee in Cairo and Alexandria, which Abū'l-'Azā'im and his cohorts would unsuccessfully protest to Egyptian parliamentarians as constituting unconstitutional measures.[21] And when the royalist Unionist party came to power in November 1924, the situation deteriorated even further, with the arrest of some of Abū'l-'Azā'im's committee members in the provinces, a raid upon Abū'l-'Azā'im's residence, the confiscation of the minutes of their meetings and the journal *al-Madīnah al-Munawwarah*, and the prohibition of Abū'l-'Azā'im's traveling to the annual pilgrimage in Mecca, where he could possibly spread his ideas and organization among Muslims from around the world.[22] As

British High Commissioner Lord Lloyd observed in Cairo, "It soon became apparent that the Committee of Al Azhar alone enjoyed official approval and the benefit of recognition by the authorities."[23] Yet even foreign delegations of Muslims tended to regard the caliphate committee springing from the prestigious and internationally renowned university of al-Azhar as the more official of the two parties, sometimes acknowledging the views and efforts of Abū'l-ʿAzāʾim's group, but according fuller deference to the former.[24] Consequentially, Abū'l-ʿAzāʾim's *Jamāʿat al-Khilāfah al-Islāmiyyah* was rendered both ineffectual and inconsequential by this adverse combination of factors, leaving the Azhar caliphate committee to conclude its mission.

IMAGINING THE GLOBAL COMMUNITY AND ITS LEADERSHIP

The Azharī scholars' proposition that they would organize an upcoming conference to resolve the dilemma of the caliphate sparked a flurry of enthusiasm among Muslims across the world, and their letters and telegrams poured in to the committee's secretariat. The Cairene committee had sent out multiple copies of the Supreme Islamic Body of Egypt's decision for distribution to Muslims in other lands, frequently in more than one language as was appropriate to their destination.[25] The initial and subsidiary recipients of these and other conference-related materials often reciprocated by expressing their indebtedness and joy over the important work being undertaken by the caliphate committee.[26] To cite the embellished words of M. A. Gamiet, who served as chairman of the South African Khilafat Committee and was prominent in Cape Town politics, "I feel that the Muslims of Egypt, in organizing the World Muslim Conference, have earned the undying gratitude of the world of Islam. It is appropriate that the mother of the world [Egypt] should call the children of Islam to deliberate, on this world-wide question."[27] And others, such as one Haḍramī correspondent from Singapore, recognized that the committee's prestigious affiliation with al-Azhar University endowed its members with the persuasive authority necessary to educate and convince other Muslims of the caliphate's vital significance and the proper means that should be employed to resurrect it (*qabūl al-ḥaqq minkum aqrabu min qabūlihi min ghayrikum*).[28]

In their eagerness regarding the caliphate committee's undertakings, many offered suggestions aimed at guaranteeing the conference's success, alongside their devout supplications. The pan-Islamist Druze notable al-Amīr Shakīb Arslān (1869–1946), for instance, wanted to ensure the fullest possible representation of Muslim nations and urged the committee to send representatives to the more remote regions of the Muslim world. In particular, Java, Russia, China, the Philippines, Siam (Thailand), "Central" Africa (for which he lists at least eighteen locations by name),[29] Albania, Bosnia, Romania, and Cyprus drew his attention. By contrast, Arslān felt that regular correspondence with prominent scholars and leaders of "the well-known lands of Syria-Palestine,

Iraq, India, Yemen, Hijaz, Afghanistan, al-Maghrib, and the like" would constitute sufficient encouragement for them to organize delegations for the conference.[30] It was his hopes that such a diverse gathering would allow Muslims across the world to become better acquainted with one another and begin to cooperate more fully towards a global Islamic renaissance. He desired that no group of Muslims be left out, whether it was Morocco with their local caliph, predominantly Shi'i Iran, which he estimated was one-third Sunni, or Zaydī-ruled Yemen, which he estimated was two-thirds Sunnis of the Shāfiʿī school, so that the conference could be truly global in scope.[31] In Singapore, the modernizing Ḥaḍramī sayyid ʿAbdullāh bin Muḥammad Ṣadaqah Daḥlān al-Makkī also urged that the caliphate committee send out their publications in even more languages to reach the global span of Muslims; all possible languages would have been ideal in his view, but at the very least "the famous Islamic languages like Arabic, Persian, Hindi or Urdu, Javanese, Malay, Chinese, and Turkish" would do.[32]

And writing from Bosnia and Algeria respectively, ʿUmar Luṭfī Ibrāhīm al-Buṣnawī and the modernist reformer ʿAbd al-Ḥamīd Bin Bādīs (1889–1940) made inquiries regarding the appointment of conference delegates to represent the various Muslim lands. Eager to attend the conference himself, Ibn Bādīs acknowledged that convening regional committees to elect representatives would be impossible in the Algerian case, while the designation of delegates by the central caliphate committee in Cairo, according to "the person's fame among his people," would be plausible.[33] al-Buṣnawī, on the other hand, sought to institutionalize the selection of delegates according to earlier conference models where this had been the subject of extensive discussion.[34] Later on, al-Buṣnawī further offered to bring documents regarding papal election procedures to the caliphate conference to facilitate and prompt discussion of the future caliph's election, despite the differences he openly acknowledged between Muslim and Catholic institutional models of leadership.[35]

Even so, the subtle comparisons contemporaries made between the papacy and the caliphate in the early twentieth century remind us of the striking ways in which Muslim and Catholic efforts to recalibrate and revitalize centuries-old religious institutions with broad transregional appeal were shaped and challenged by the dynamics of a newly emerging world system of nation-states. The papacy had lost its territorial and political sovereignty when the Kingdom of Italy invaded and took over the Papal States in 1861 followed by the symbolic loss of Rome itself in 1870. Pope Pius IX (1792–1878) declared himself a prisoner inside the Vatican and refused to set foot outside its walls until the Papal States were restored, an insistence religiously adhered to by his successors. And Catholics loyal to the Vatican annually mourned the September 20th anniversary of Rome's loss by holding special mass for nearly six decades. Yet the painful ignominy also helped spur the widening reach of the papacy in consolidating its authority, ecclesiastical power, and social influence. The year 1870 had also seen the promulgating of the dogma of papal infallibility, which was gradually accompanied by increasing the appointments of Roman-educated bishops, centralizing the ecclesiastical decision-making process, utilizing papal encyclicals and apostolic letters to address social issues and state-church relations, and mobilizing popular support through the modern means of social organizations, political parties, and the press.[36]

In the aftermath of World War I, the Vatican saw itself as essential in restoring a disoriented world to proper order. Recalling the past prominence of the Catholic Church, Pius XI (1857–1939) lamented in his first encyclical in 1922:

> No merely human institution of today can be as successful in devising a set of international laws which will be in harmony with world conditions as the Middle Ages were in the possession of that true League of Nations, Christianity.... There exists an institution able to safeguard the sanctity of the law of nations. This institution is a part of every nation; at the same time it is above all nations. She enjoys, too, the highest authority, the fullness of the teaching power of the Apostles. Such an institution is the Church of Christ. She alone is adapted to do this great work, for she is not only divinely commissioned to lead mankind, but moreover, because of her very make-up and the constitution which she possesses, by reason of her age-old traditions and her great prestige, which has not been lessened but has been greatly increased since the close of the War, cannot but succeed in such a venture where others assuredly will fail.

Over the course of the 1920s, it was increasingly through the tools of international law and diplomacy that the Holy See sought to regain its primacy in Europe. The Vatican established diplomatic relations with over two-dozen countries and contracted eleven concordats in the 1920s that redefined the relationship between church and state in a bid to "reassert its traditional influence over education, public offices, and European foreign affairs." Ironically, as José Casanova has argued, it was the loss of territorial sovereignty that allowed the papacy to "be reconstituted as the core of a transnational religious regime." And arguably, the discourse-based foundation of Islam as a world system—one that was not restricted to a specific empire or economy—had enabled it also to flourish for over a thousand years and coincide with alternative ways of configuring the world, as John Voll has elucidated.[37] In the early twentieth century, Muslims around the world actively imagined ways to retain and reconfigure the caliphate that had so potently symbolized that interconnected discursive community or *ummah*.

A SPIRITUAL BODY

Especially in preparation for the international Cairo conference, Muslim intellectuals and activists began recording their ideas for the resurrection of a modern caliphate. One such figure, Mohammad Barakatullah (ca. 1857–1927),[38] had led a colorful life arguing against British imperialism for the sake of India's political independence. Born in Bhopal, India, to a Bhopal state servant, Barakatullah was in the words of the British criminal intelligence officer James Campbell Ker (1878–1961) "a very clever youth" who left home around 1883 to work as a tutor and continue his studies in Khandwa and Bombay, and eventually England.[39] By 1903, he was in New York propagating against the British rule of India and began consorting and cooperating with Irish nationalists, even hosting joint Irish-Indian meetings twice a week in 1908 at his New York home.[40] In February 1909, he departed for Japan to assume an appointment as a professor of Hindustani at the University of Tokyo, where he also published a pan-Islamic periodical entitled *Islamic Fraternity*. The British government's perception of the journal's increasingly anti-British tone in its nationalist and pan-Islamic arguments led to the journal's suppression in 1912 by the Japanese government, and in 1914 even Barakatullah's teaching contract at the University of Tokyo was not renewed.[41] Barakatullah had toured Istanbul, Cairo, and St. Petersburg in 1911, but now he returned to the United States to join the Ghadar Party based in California in May 1914 and then some months later traveled to Berlin to help the Indian committee there agitate for his country's independence.[42] In collaboration with the Germans, he joined their wartime mission to Afghanistan in 1915, building on his ties with the Afghani ruling elite from his earlier days in England, in the hope of paving the way for India's liberation.[43] On December 1, 1915, the Indian members of this German mission even declared a provisional government of India (*Hukumat-e Muvaqata-e Hind*) in Kabul, with Barakatullah proclaimed as the government-in-exile's prime minister.[44] Barakatullah remained in Kabul after the departure of the German military leader and diplomatic representative in 1916 at least through the end of 1917, when he was contacted by an Indian committee based in Stockholm.[45] By 1924, Barakatullah was a well-known international figure, whom one translator of the Qur'an into English, Abdullah Yusuf Ali, inordinately described as "a scholar of Islamic religion, history, and literature" with extensive experience abroad in England, the United States, Japan, Central Asia, and Central Europe.[46]

Following the Turkish abolition of the Ottoman Caliphate, Barakatullah published a treatise in 1924 entitled *The Khilafet*, which differs strikingly from his lengthy career agitating for India's temporal sovereignty in its concern to place the caliphate on an elevated spiritual plane, devoid of politics.[47] Putting aside the question of whether the Grand National Assembly of Ankara was endowed with the requisite authority to abolish the caliphate on its own or not, Barakatullah rather acknowledged the new reality created by this painful *fait accompli*. And convinced that the "religious and spiritual institutions in Egypt," which had announced a conference in Cairo for the following March 1925 would exert their utmost to resolve the dilemma of the caliphate, Barakatullah sought to contribute his own deliberations conceived with contemporary circumstances in mind.[48] In short, Barakatullah urged:

> When the representatives of the Moslem countries will meet in Cairo in March 1925, by the invitation of the religious institutions of Egypt for the election of the new Khalif, it is earnestly hoped, that the holy and spiritual Assembly will be gracious enough to pay proper attention to the statements and reasons sincerely presented in these pages. If they be convinced of the genuineness and honesty of the proposal it is hoped and trusted that they will elect for the post of Khalif a man who will be only the spiritual head of Islam, will have nothing to do with politics, whom all Islamic communities—whether independent or subject to non-Moslem governments—should recognise as the focus of the spiritual brotherhood, and whose orders will be directed to the sacerdotal, moral, educational, religious and spiritual welfare of the Islamic Fraternity throughout the world.[49]

The novelty and thrust of Barakatullah's proposal was that the new caliph be a solely spiritual figure, who would shun all political affairs. In his words, "The changes of time have rendered the union of the scattered tribes of Islam over the face of the earth under one temporal head practically well-nigh impossible, so the spiritual head of the Islamic world must religiously eschew every and any kind of interference in political affairs of the Faithful the world over."[50] In keeping with this new role that Barakatullah envisioned for the caliph, he found it inadvisable for any of the current Muslim rulers to assume the position. For him, the termination of the Ottoman Caliphate offered a fresh opportunity for a return to the righteous model of the first four caliphs, with an emphasis on the idealized purity and sublimity of its spiritual authority and power. Temporal rulers, Barakatullah argued, would recreate the worldly mistakes initiated by Muʿāwiyah, who founded the Umayyad dynasty, become a focal point for European intrigue, retard the development of their individual nations, and earn the mistrust and suspicion of the civilized world.[51]

In advocating this position, Barakatullah explicitly conceptualized his restructured model of the caliphate as an imitation of the modern papacy. Curiously viewing the loss of Constantinople, the "Second Rome," as the impetus for the Renaissance, Barakatullah ascribed "the separation of the temporal from the spiritual government" a central role in the revival of true spirit. It was Constantine's adoption of Christianity as a state religion and Muʿāwiyah's transformation of the caliphate into an absolute monarchy that had held their followers back from the expression of religious enthusiasm and progress, by subjecting them to the yoke of despotism. At the same time as Pope Pius XI bewailed the beleaguered state of missions in the aftermath of the Great War, Barakatullah admired their comparative success. "The Christian missions" revived by the Pope and perpetuated by the Protestants, he duly noted, "are models of religious zeal and stability. They have left no spot on the face of the earth where they have not gone and delivered the message of the Gospel." Muslims, he postulated, would not need the protection of empires and kingdoms, because, unlike Christian missionaries, they would "never interfere in political affairs of any country at all." In promoting a depoliticized caliphate, Barakatullah therefore imagined a parallel with the history of Christianity that was key to restoring the vivacity of Islam. He argued, "There will be no harm in establishing the Khilafet on the model of the Papacy, because Islam has no infallibility of the Khalif, no ecclesiastical hierarchy and no absolute submission to the decree of the Church." In Barakatullah's mind, the loss of empire previously associated with the caliphs would translate into the dawn of a new era of learning and revival among Muslims.[52]

Therefore, Barakatullah advocated for the inauguration of a predominantly spiritual leader as caliph, who would foster and maintain the ties of a global Islamic brotherhood, minus the political union, in arenas such as the training of imams, the organization of the annual pilgrimage, relief efforts to regions struck by natural disasters, and the propagation of the Islamic faith throughout the world.[53] To assist the caliph in the management and execution of his sacred duties, Barakatullah proposed the election of an administrative council, whose members would have backgrounds in the fields of religion, philosophy, science, and history, and from whom future caliphs could be elected. These deputies would supervise the Ministry of Religion (to organize mosques, schools, and religious foundations), the Ministry of Finance (*Bayt al-Māl* or the Public Treasury with revenues coming from incumbent and voluntary charity (*zakāt* and *ṣadaqah*)), the Ministry of Education and Research (that would conduct teaching, the writing of histories and textbooks, and propagate modern sciences), and the Ministry of Propaganda or Missionary Organization (that would spread the message of Islam).[54] For the seat of this centralized spiritual authority, Barakatullah evaluated a few possibilities: Istanbul would be an ideal metropolis as a sacred center under both Christianity and Islam, Medina would be suitable as the Prophet Muḥammad's city were it not for the region's political instability and foreign dependence, and Cairo would be an illustrious and favorable choice given its association with multiple civilizations, empires, and past caliphates. Making reference to the sixteenth-century transfer of the caliphate from the Cairene Abbasids to the Ottomans, Barakatullah concludes, "The Khilafet had really come from Cairo to Constantinople. If it goes from Constantinople to Cairo, it is going back home." And connecting Cairo's venerable history as a caliphal capital with its hosting the upcoming caliphate conference, Barakatullah declares his ultimate aspiration, "If the representatives of the Moslem communities assemble at Cairo next year, elect the Khalif and become responsible for the maintenance of the sacred institution, it will mark a new era of life and activity for Islam, almost like the new era after the Hegira."[55]

Ironically, it was only upon reading Barakatullah's treatise in late August 1924 that the deposed Ottoman caliph Abdülmecid learned of the preparations for the caliphate conference in Cairo. As late as May 21, 1924, Abdülmecid continued to express his hopes that the international Islamic conference he had

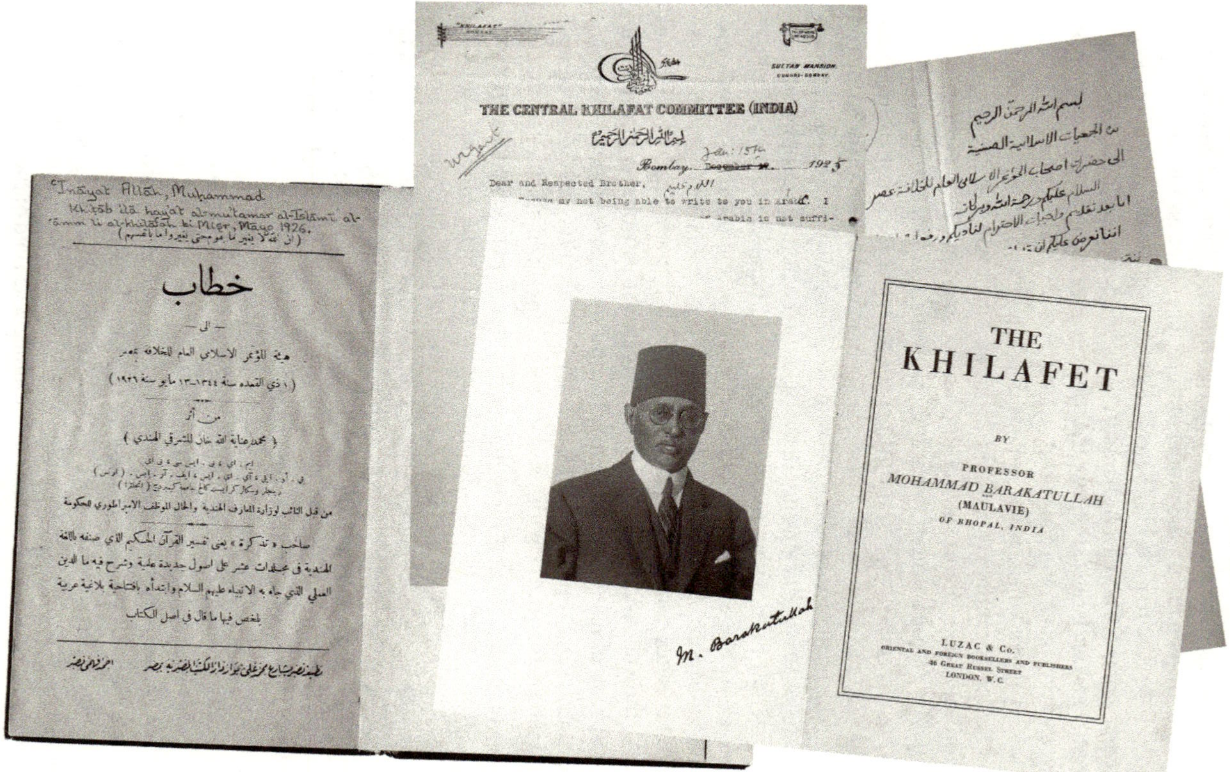

FIGURE 18. Indian and Chinese appeals to the Cairene Caliphate Congress.

Images from Mohammad Barakatullah, *The Khilafet* (London 1924); ʿInāyatullāh Khān al-Mashriqī, *Khiṭāb* (Cairo 1926), and A. L., 7780 Tārīkh 76421, file no. 112, August 18, 1925 and A. L., 7780 Tārīkh 76421, file no. 117, January 15, 1925, courtesy of al-Azhar Library.

called for shortly after his deposition would eventually materialize, although the moderation of his tone, as recorded by his personal secretary, indicates he was starting to have some doubts on the matter. At least, he felt, by that point he had tried his best to preserve the caliphal institution. But three months later, on August 29, 1924, news finally arrived of the Cairo caliphate conference, through Barakatullah's work *The Khilafet*, and Abdülmecid had clearly not been consulted or even informed. He was no doubt dismayed, but recalled that the odd silence that had followed the initial telegrams sent to him in exile had given him an inkling. With great generosity of spirit, Abdülmecid prayed that his enterprising brothers in faith who were organizing the international conference would achieve an auspicious resolution to the dilemma of the caliphate and hoped that his complete lack of involvement would allow for free discussion of the issue and increase the conference's chance of success. Yet Abdülmecid also had his doubts given the current conditions of the Islamic world. Barakatullah's propositions, for instance, he considered to be a valuable contribution, intriguing and compatible with Islam, at least in theory, but, on the whole, entirely impractical. Nothing more was left in Abdülmecid's hands, however, so, as his former secretary observed, he resigned himself to following the flow of events from a distance and praying for the eventual success of the Islamic conference to resolve the dilemma of the caliphate.[56]

A CALIPHAL COUNCIL

While Barakatullah urged the prospective conference organizers and attendees to elect a solely spiritual leader as caliph, other thinkers like ʿInāyatullāh Khān al-Mashriqī (1888–1963) moved even further away from the notion of a single traditional figurehead for the Muslim community. Born in 1888 in Amristar, India, al-Mashriqī was first educated at home by his literary father, who worked as a petition writer, but also composed poetry and books.[57] Some of these poems, his *Qaṣāʾid*, were written in praise of the Ottoman sultan-caliph Mehmed V Vahideddin, whom he eulogizes, no doubt due to the great distance from the actual happenings of Istanbul, "for introducing constitutional reforms and emancipating the country."[58] From an early age, al-Mashriqī commenced his education at missionary and government schools and colleges in Amristsar, and then Lahore, where he received a master's degree in mathematics within one year, before departing to study at Cambridge University on a scholarship in October 1907. There, he received honors in Mathematics (1909), Oriental Languages (1911), Natural Sciences (1911), and Mechanical Sciences (1912), before returning back to India in December 1912. He chose to enter the field of education and served variously as the vice principal of the Islamia College in Peshawar (beginning in March 1913), the junior assistant secretary in the Government of India's Education Department (starting in October 1917), and the headmaster of the government high school in Peshawar—a post that he would hold for ten years from October 1919 through 1929.[59] Ideologically, during this time period, al-Mashriqī composed a work entitled *al-Tadhkirah*, where he seems to have advocated a militarist interpretation of Islam, which was censured as early as July 1924 by the Muslim scholar Syed Suleman Nadvi and heavily criticized by other Indian Muslim scholars in the 1930s, after al-Mashriqī's founding of the Khaskar Movement in 1931.[60] And perhaps it was through his friendship with some Khilafat Movement leaders, like Maulana Muhammad Ali Jauhar and Hakim Ajmal Khan,[61] that al-Mashriqī was acquainted with and managed to procure an invitation to the Cairerene Caliphate Conference in 1926.

In anticipation of making a speech to his fellow conference delegates gathered in Cairo, the Indian educator al-Mashriqī penned his thoughts in Arabic under the appropriate title *Khiṭāb* ("Speech").[62] al-Mashriqī's vision for the post-Ottoman caliphal era involved a five-point program, the keystone of which was to do away with the idea of a single person functioning as caliph. No one was endowed with the essential qualities of complete freedom, palpable power, awe-inspiring magnitude, strength, and aptitude, in his view, and he considered it far more important to establish secure foundations for the institution of the caliphate rather than merely to elect and appoint a nominal head. Until such a time when electing an individual as caliph would become both feasible and desirable again, al-Mashriqī suggested instead that the international Islamic conference organization itself function as caliph.[63]

In support of the caliphate conference assuming leadership of the Muslim community, al-Mashriqī envisioned that the conference organization would remain an independent and continuous institution, based at al-Azhar University under the guidance of the Shaykh al-Azhar. The location of its annual meetings, however, would vary from one year to the next and be chosen by means of an election. al-Mashriqī, in contradistinction to Barakatullah, felt that the separation of *dīn* and *dunyā*, or of the spiritual and temporal realms, was one of the main problems besetting the Muslim community of his day, and therefore, the caliph, and by extension his novel caliphate organization, could not be relegated only to spiritual concerns. As a result, al-Mashriqī called for this new institution to establish a comprehensive system of representation and leadership on religious, legal, and social issues throughout Muslim lands, from the minute local level of villages and provinces up to the national and ultimately international scene. To execute the decisions and duties of this caliphate conference, a central bank or *Bayt al-Māl* would first collect people's alms and charity through local branches and then distribute the funds. According to al-Mashriqī, the absolute impartiality of the caliphate conference's members was critical to achieving its global credibility and success, and he, therefore, recorded in his *Khiṭāb* a naive plea for his fellow delegates at Cairo to disassociate themselves from any political parties, legal schools of thought, Sufi orders,

FIGURE 19. Members of Sarekat Islam in Java, including Tjokroaminoto (seated second from right). Image courtesy "Leden van de Sarekat Islam," Universiteit Leiden, Special Collections, KITLV, Image Code 8092, photograph from the collection of Godard Arend Johannes Hazeu (1870–1929) H 1083 (34).

and basic sectarian distinctions (such as Sunni and Shi'i) and instead solely identify themselves as Muslims.[64]

In the Indonesian archipelago, a coalition of Sarekat Islam,[65] Muhammadiyah,[66] and Al-Irshad[67] convened a special meeting in Surabaya of their local and national leaders as well as locally influential scholars on October 4 and 5, 1924, to discuss whether or not to send a delegation to the upcoming conference in Cairo. Setting the meeting's tone, Sarekat Islam leader Raden Oemar Said Tjokroaminoto (1882–1934) gave a soaring emotional speech about all Muslims' need for a caliph as their temporal and spiritual leader. And the Muhamadiyah leader Haji Fakhruddin (1890–1929) further proposed that rather than taking instantaneous decisions, a caliphate committee should be established to deliberate carefully and pave the way for the necessary delegation to Cairo. The committee that was established as a result of these suggestions, the Central Comité Chilafat, was comprised of both traditionalist and reformist representatives and prepared an extraordinary Indies All Islam Congress (*Kongres al-Islam Hindia*) held on December 24–26, 1924, also in Surabaya.[68] As recorded in the Javanese press as well as British consular and official Dutch reports, it was resolved that the cornerstone of the delegates' mandate was to advocate that the powers and functions traditionally associated with the caliph be transferred to an elected permanent council (*majlis khilāfah*) with binding religious authority over Muslims worldwide. This caliphate council would include representatives of all Muslim countries and elect from among its members the president, called the caliph, who would supervise the execution and enforcement of the council's decisions, with the assistance of other appointed officials as necessary. In the reporting of one Dutch official, another proposal entailed that "the costs of the caliphate council will be jointly borne by all Muslims, and will be divided among the various countries in accordance with their capacity." Although the Javanese Muslims who gathered to discuss these views preferred that the council be located in the holy city of Mecca, which was politically independent, they left the final decision, as well as the finer details of financing, open to the views of other Muslims who were also expected to convene in Cairo.[69]

A TRADITIONAL CALIPH

Unable to send representatives to Cairo, the Islamic Associations of China (*al-Jamʿiyyāt al-Islāmiyyah al-Ṣīniyyah*) prepared a letter on August 18, 1925, to the conference's organizers to convey their views on the caliphate for consideration. The authors reported that these Chinese Muslim associations were of one opinion regarding the issue, namely that one of the most knowledgeable, virtuous, and upright (*aʿlamuhum wa-aḥsanuhum khuluqan wa-arshaduhum diyānatan*) descendants of the Prophet Muḥammad should be elected as caliph. As for his duties as caliph, they felt it should be limited to establishing those matters connected to the Sacred Law (*al-Sharīʿah*) without any involvment in political affairs (*al-siyāsah*). If no one from the progeny of the Prophet Muḥammad was deserving of this position, however, they felt it should be filled by one of the outstanding religious scholars of the time, without regard to genealogy.[70] Thus, the model they were suggesting for further consideration entailed a traditional view of the caliph as an individual, with a rather interesting twist on the question of genealogy. Their preference for a direct descendant of the Prophet Muḥammad constricted the question of genealogy far more narrowly than customary among the Sunni community, but they were also willing to dispense with the genealogical considerations altogether, thrusting aside the lineage necessary for imams among the Shi'i community, in the greater interests of scholarship, upright character, and religiosity.

By contrast, Shakīb Arslān based his own assessment of how to restore and preserve the caliphate upon intentionally practical considerations regarding the widespread recognition of Abdülmecid's rights to this position among his contemporaries. Under ideal circumstances, Arslān rejected the notion of a strictly spiritual caliphate, as the Turks had recently contrived in 1922 with the election of Abdülmecid as a caliph stripped of temporal power. But he was certain that if the rest of the Muslim world deprived Abdülmecid of the caliphate, following his expulsion by the new Turkish Republic, there would be a caliph in every country, or in other words, the unity of the Muslim world would be deeply fractured. In his estimate, during the summer of 1924, ninety to ninety-five percent of the Muslim world agreed on the caliphate of Abdülmecid and to negate it would merely open Pandora's box. Abdülmecid's pervasive recognition as caliph supplanted and fulfilled the intent of the traditional requirement for a caliph's Qurashī lineage, according to Arslān, and therefore, what remained as problematic, in terms of his qualifications for caliphal office, was his lack of temporal power—a shortcoming that could be tolerated in the short term given the condition of the Muslim world.[71]

Yet where would the Caliph Abdülmecid reside and preside? Colonized Muslim countries were not suitable in Arslān's view, leaving only Afghanistan, Iran, Hijaz, Yemen, Najd, and Egypt as options. Neither the Amīr of Afghanistan nor the King of Egypt would tolerate a caliph in their midst, nor would the Iranians acknowledge the caliphate per se. The King of Hijaz al-Ḥusayn had proclaimed himself as caliph, and the Sulṭān of Najd Ibn Saʿūd was unlikely to want a caliph in or near his diminutive territory. All of which, according to Arslān, left Yemen as the only viable option. In its spacious lands, Abdülmecid could be acknowledged as the caliph of the Muslim world and Imam Yaḥyā as his governing sultan, following the juristic and historical model of the caliphate and sultanate under the Buyids, Seljuqs, and Mamluks and simultaneously preserving all of Imām Yaḥyā's rights as the leader of the Zaydīs in Yemen. Especially encouraging, from Arslān's perspective, was that Imam Yaḥyā had already chivarously offered refuge to Abdülmecid and the entire Ottoman family.[72]

Yet, for Arslān, this division of the caliphate and sultanate was only a temporary solution. More preferable in the long run was either for Imam Yaḥyā to demonstrate that he was capable of running an organized state and therefore be more seriously considered for the caliphate himself or for Egypt to gain its complete independence and develop an army commeasurate with the size of its population (as the key indicator of its full independence) and become the most appropriate location for the caliphate. In contrast to William Cleveland's assessment that Arslān definitively considered Egypt to be the most suitable throne of all for the caliphate, Arslān was far more circumspect, aknowledging its lack of independence and questioning when the Egyptians might actually gain it. Certainly, were they to achieve complete independence, Egypt would become an ideal seat for the Islamic caliphate. But that happening any time soon was far from certain. Therefore, a better option in Arslān's estimation was reinstating Abdülmecid as caliph under Imam Yaḥyā's protection in Yemen for the short term.[73] This evaluation, however, was one to which Rashīd Riḍā strenuously objected in his cordial private correspondence with Arslān as well as in the pages of *al-Manār*, where he laid out both of their personal perspectives, without giving away Arslān's identity—hoping that the friendly debate between the two of them would help elicit further discussion and reflection upon these critical issues.[74]

A GLOBAL ELECTORATE

Purporting to have studied the issue of the caliphate from all possible angles, whether legal, historical, or political, the famed Syrian intellectual Rashīd Riḍā also composed a letter of his own to the Cairo conference delegates. To give strength to his arguments, Riḍā enumerated his own qualifications on the subject: he had written a book and articles regarding the caliphate[75] as well as helped with the organization of the conference through cooperation with the central committee and membership in one of its branches.[76] In October 1924, Riḍā had published his views on the current situation of the Muslim community and what could be done to restore the caliphate. For Riḍā, the despotism of Abdülhamid and then the Unionists, followed by the extremism of the Kemalists, had marred the history of the Ottoman Caliphate. He considered the divestment of the caliphate's temporal power in 1922 to be unacceptable and was dismayed by his contemporaries' seeming complacency toward this calamity. The final blow, in 1924, only removed the empty shell of the caliphate that had already been deprived of its substance two years prior. Riḍā expressed his satisfaction that as the shock of his contemporaries subsided they too had begun to reflect intelligently upon the situation and called for Muslims of all vocations to gather together and resolve the dilemma of caliphal absence in consultation with one another. The absolutist and then hollow Ottoman Caliphate had been an obstacle to restoring an ideal caliphate for their times, given the intensity of people's devotion to it, and upon its removal, Riḍā articulated his vision for the future. The caliphate conference called by the *Hay'at Kibār al-'Ulamā'* in Egypt should establish a viable system for the imamate, comprising of civil laws that would manifest the sublimity of Islamic legislation and an educational system that would combine religious guidance and temporal benefits and increase the solidarity and cooperation among Muslims. Secondly, the conference should elect a caliph who would actually implement these civil laws in the lands under his rule and supervise the implementation of the revitalized educational system. And in this manner, the religious and political powers of the caliph would be rejoined.[77]

Privately, however, Riḍā's correspondence with Shakīb Arslān following the abolition of the Ottoman Caliphate reveals his recurring frustration with the way his colleagues were organizing the international conference that he had called for and deemed to be so essential.[78] Nevertheless, he was eager that his views on the caliphate be heard by those in actual attendance at the conference in Cairo so that they would receive due consideration. For Riḍā, the difficulty of actually appointing an ideal caliph under current circumstances had become fully apparent by 1926.[79] And as he had articulated to Arslān in private, his greatest hope was not that the conference attendees would agree to elect an imam who would somehow be agreeable to all Muslims, but that the conference delegates establish a system that would eventually lead to such an election.[80]

In this vein, Riḍā therefore articulated a number of key steps in his open letter to the conference delegates that would facilitate this lofty goal in the interim period. First was the search for appropriate electors (*ahl al-ḥall wa'l-'aqd*) among all Muslim peoples, and, where there were none to be found, concentrated efforts to create room for their emergence over time. His second recommendation was the establishment of a system that would foster sustained cooperation and interaction among these international representatives, along modern lines, whether that be in the form of an official party, society of some sort, or union. This global network of electors, in Riḍā's view, was necessary for securing a caliph's universal acclaim and for inaugurating a caliphal system that would correspond to the requirements of their age. Essential components of this system, for Riḍā, were the absence of any potential for authoritarianism and tyranny, the caliph's complete, and not partial, qualification for his position, and a thoroughly sound Islamic legal foundation. Based on definitive scriptural sources, the modern caliphal system would also exemplify Islamic legal principles advocating justice, mercy, true equality, independent legal reasoning (*ijtihād*) on speculative issues, public good, ease, the alleviation of hardship, and the permissibility of necessities that would otherwise be considered interdicted matters, among other Islamic legal principles of enduring benefit. As for those Muslim peoples who lacked full independence, Riḍā envisioned a strong spiritual and religious connection with the caliphal domain since they would be deprived from fully submitting to the Islamic caliphate's sovereignty and governance. In expectation of another international conference, Riḍā also offered to elaborate upon these themes and recommendations in greater detail in a treatise or book that would pave the way for a revived modern caliphate.[81]

DAMPENING HOPES

By the time the conference had convened in Cairo, however, internal Egyptian affairs had significantly dampened people's spirited support for the enterprise, both within the country and internationally. Officially, King Fu'ād displayed his complete disinterest in the position of caliph, even when Sa'd Zaghlūl had inquired if he would be interested in assuming the post in March 1924. Yet as the Azhar-affiliated caliphate conference committees proliferated throughout the country, it became clear that Ḥasan Nash'at Pasha, with close ties to the palace, was actively supporting their formation. Although King Fu'ād denied any knowledge of these committees and their activities to an inquisitive Zaghlūl, the suspicions of Egypt's political parties were not allayed. It was a particularly worrisome development that the king might be attempting to strengthen his own hand against domestic political opposition by means of the caliphate, especially since Nashʾat had established the royalist Ittiḥād party on January 10, 1925, to counter the parliamentary power of the Wafd. And with the eruption of controversy over the Liberal Constitutionalist scion ʿAlī ʿAbd al-Rāziq's book *al-Islām wa-Uṣūl al-Ḥukm* in 1925, even the fragile alliance between the Ittiḥādists and the Liberal Constitutionalists, who had initially supported Egypt's sponsoring the conference as well as procuring the caliphate for Egypt, was broken.[82] As Lord Lloyd later assessed these developments for the British Foreign Office:

> The influence exercised by Hassan Nashat Pasha over leading dignitaries of Al Azhar, and the alleged dependence of the ulama upon palace favour, have led to a belief that King Fuad is working through the Azhar Committee to secure his own election to the Caliphate.... In the present state of Egyptian politics, such a candidature could not but arouse keen opposition, even though it existed in the malice of imagination only.[83]

The dismal reality was that all of the major political parties (al-Wafd, the Liberal Constitutionalists, and al-Ḥizb al-Waṭanī) united against the royalist Ittiḥādists and the prospect of King Fuʾād amassing even more adversarial clout as caliph.[84] Determined to thwart any such plans, Egypt's political organizations, through their major newspapers, turned their pens against the caliphate conference as a mere vehicle to further King Fuʾād's ambitions.[85]

In response to this domestic political crisis, the central caliphate committee attempted to salvage the conference by deferring it for one full year to May 1926 and then, on February 3, 1926, truncated its original agenda by omitting any mention of the specific selection of a caliph,[86] but the publicity damage had already been done. Prospective participants from abroad had become increasingly wary about the conference's true aims, and some of them wrote to the secretariat for clarification. Corresponding from Tunisia on November 1, 1924, for instance, the nationalist leader Aḥmad Tawfīq al-Madanī (1899–1983), who headed the Tunisian Committee of the Caliphate, sought to learn if internal Egyptian differences over the goals of the conference had been resolved at last, and, if not, how the conference organizers could anticipate a successful outcome amid divisive domestic opposition.[87] Presuming a hidden agenda, King Fayṣal of Mesopotamia also asked the Cairo-based secretariat about their real intentions for the conference (*al-ghāyah al-ḥaqīqiyyah*).[88] Imam Yaḥyā announced that he agreed in principle on the basic tenets of the caliphate conference, but the fact that he prevented the distribution of its materials in Yemen betrays a deep-seated suspicion, on his part, regarding the organizers' motives.[89]

As a result of these widespread suspicions about the actual goals of the Cairo caliphate conference, international representation and attendance in May 1926 greatly suffered. Most noticeably absent was any official delegation from India and its Central Khilafat Committee. In the two years that elapsed after the Cairene caliphate committee's auspicious announcement, the initial support of the Indian Central Khilafat Committee dissolved into hesitation and then ultimately rejection of the conference's objectives.[90] In August and September 1925, the Russian Muslim Mufti Rızaeddin bin Fahreddin (1859–1936) expressly sought to join his Indian brothers in Islam in protesting the convening of the caliphate conference in Cairo and issued an official declaration from the Oremburg Spiritual Assembly based in Ufa. He decried British imperialist power and influence over Egypt as its protectorate, arguing that it would hinder Muslims gathered for a conference in Cairo from achieving their goals. Rather, he deemed the sacred city of Mecca to be a more desirable location, provided that an absence of imperialist interference could be guaranteed.[91] In all likelihood, given these views and his position as a Russian religious official, it was Mufti Rızaeddin, whom British officials erroneously impugned as a "Bolshevik agent," who had telegraphed Ibn Saʿūd in 1926 to suggest Mecca as an alternative venue for the caliphate conference, free from the pernicious British influence adversely affecting Cairo.[92]

During a stopover in Mecca, on the way to the caliphate conference in Cairo, half of the dispatched Indonesian delegation also fell under the sway of these concerns circulating the Muslim world and never completed their journey. After the postponement of the Cairene conference in January 1925 for at least one year, the Indonesian coalition between reformists and traditionalists had disintegrated, with each group seeking to send its own representatives to Cairo. The traditionalist association Nahdatul Ulama was born in January 1926 as a result of these activities to resolve the caliphal dilemma, but logistical problems prevented the dispatch of their two elected delegates, Kiai Asnawi of Kudus and Kiai Bisri Sjansuri of Jombang. Two reformists from West Sumatra, Abdul Karim Amrullah and Abdullah Ahmad, were able to proceed to Cairo. But the reformist delegates elected anew in February 1926 for the Indies All Islam Congress (*Kongres al-Islam Hindia*) never made it past Mecca.[93] In justifying their decision to a rather incensed audience back home, these elected delegates, the Javanese Sarekat Islam leader Tjokroaminoto and the Javanese adviser to Muhammadiyah in Surabaya Kiai Hadji Mas Mansur, cited the opinions of Ibn Saʿūd, Arabian religious teachers, Russian Muslims visiting Mecca,[94] and, equally damningly, a group of Indonesian students studying at al-Azhar,[95] organized under the name "Perhimpoenan Pendjaga Indonesia." Their cosmopolitan consensus predicted that the caliphate conference would bear no fruit because of the vocal internal opposition against the stance of the Azharī scholars within Egypt, a point that Tjokroaminoto underscored with the subversive revelation that "the rector of the high school of Al Azhar, who was the President of the Centraal Chilafaat Comite at Cairo and who sent the invitation to the Moslems in Indonesia, was under the influence of the King of Egypt and

British gold." As Tjokroaminoto came to believe in Mecca and successfully convinced the rest of the Indies All Islam Congress, the ultimate goal of the Cairo conference was "conferring the dignity of the Caliphate upon King Fuad of Egypt," through the exertion of British influence.[96] This proposition was one that the Javanese activists Tjokroaminoto and Hadji Mansoer, like so many of their international Muslim cohorts, preemptively declined to entertain.

Further, some of those invited to attend the conference were in fact barred from entering Cairo at the last minute out of consideration for the interests of European colonial powers. One Russian Muslim intellectual, Musa Carullah (Bigiyef) (1875–1949),[97] who had been delegated to attend the conference on behalf of Moscow's Muslims, was denied a visa in Istanbul, on account of the bad press given to the conference by the Russian Mufti Rızaeddin and fear of his attempting to spread Bolshevism and anti-British sentiments in Cairo. Faced with this unexpected rebuff, Musa Carullah wrote a lengthy and scathing letter to the caliphate conference committee complaining of the unjustifiable treatment he had received, especially as they had sent a personal invitation to him to attend only a few months prior. Ironically, following Musa Carullah's being denied entry into Egypt that May, Acting British Consul S. R. Jordan reported from Jeddah in mid-July that the Kemalist representative at the Mecca conference, Edib Servet (Tör) Bey (1881–1960), "recommended [Musa Carullah] for my good offices if at any time he required a visa, and assured me of his harmlessness from a political point of view." The initial fear that he might harbor anti-imperial Bolshevik tendencies, however, prevented his taking part in the discussions over the Islamic caliphate in Cairo.[98]

A different set of colonial considerations interfered with the participation of the renowned leader of the Moroccan resistance to the Spanish in the north, Muḥammad bin ʿAbd al-Karīm al-Khaṭṭābī. A letter of invitation had been sent to him on Muḥarram 12, 1344 AH (August 2, 1925), by one of the leading caliphate conference organizers, Shaykh Muḥammad Farrāj al-Minyāwī. In October, ʿAbd al-Karīm affirmed his interest in sending a delegation to the caliphate conference, should circumstances on the Riffian front permit, and the information was much celebrated in the Egyptian press, given the resistance leader's popularity. The local acclaim surrounding this news, however, caused the Spanish authorities much consternation, and they applied to both the Egyptian and British governments in the spring of 1926 to hinder ʿAbd al-Karīm's participation in the international Islamic conference and the "indirect recognition of sovereignty and therefore of belligerency" they felt such a gesture would signify. While the British authorities debated the issue internally, not wanting to do anything "unpleasant or tiresome for ourselves just to please Spain" in the words of one bureaucrat, they dreaded the implications for themselves of ʿAbd al-Karīm's stance against a fellow colonial power. Ultimately, though, High Commissioner Lord Lloyd advised against interfering in so sensitive an issue in the local political climate, therefore leaving the Spanish authorities to pursue the case with the Egyptian government. Fortunately for the Spanish, the Egyptian government would prove to be far more accommodating. In its desire to maintain good relations with Spain, the Egyptian Foreign Ministry decided to deny ʿAbd al-Karīm and any of his representatives entry into the country, labeling them with the illegitimacy of rebels: "pour témoigner de son désir de maintenir meilleures relations avec [le] gouvernement espagnol il est disposé [de] refuser entrée [aux] délègués dit rebel en territoire égyptien." And no Riffian delegation would attend the Cairene Caliphate Conference.[99]

In total, in response to the 610 invitations reissued to institutions and individuals in February and March 1926, only twenty-nine foreign delegates, in addition to Egypt's own fifteen, actually attended the caliphate conference in Cairo in May 1926. Invitations had been sent to Syria, Palestine, Jordan, Iraq, the Hijaz, Bahrain, Kuwait, Yemen, India (a staggering 139 letters and eleven telegrams), Libya, Algeria, Tunisia, Morocco, Iran, Afghanistan, Java, Sumatra, China, Singapore, Malacca, Ethiopia, South Africa, Harar, Zanzibar, Bosnia and Herzegovina, Romania, Albania, Bulgaria, Poland, the United States, Argentina, Russia, Turkistan, the Caucasus, and Turkey. Yet only Egypt (fifteen delegates), Palestine (eight delegates), Libya (four delegates), Iraq (three delegates), Hijaz (two delegates), South Africa (two delegates), Sumatra (two delegates), Yemen (two delegates), India (one delegate), Morocco (one delegate), the Malay Sultanate of Johor (one delegate), Poland (one delegate), Syria (one delegate), and Tunisia (one delegate) were represented,[100] and not all of them by official delegations. ʿInāyatullāh Khān al-Mashriqī, for instance, attended the conference from India in a purely personal capacity, as he chose to state explicitly in his prepared speech.[101] Distance itself was sometimes a factor in limiting this participation of other Muslims in the conference proceedings, as in the case of China and Argentina; the former sent in their sincere suggestions by post and the latter requested representation by a knowledgeable Egyptian scholar in their stead.[102] For others, however, distance was no object compared to the grave importance of the conference's topic, as was the case with the Muslims of Poland and South Africa, who were represented in an official capacity by the Grand Mufti Yacoub Chenkowitz of Poland, by the Imam of Cape Town, Abou Bakr Kassiem Djemaleddine of the Muslim Association of South Africa, and by a prominent shaykh in Cape Town, Ahmed Behareddine of the South African Khilafat Committee.[103] Given the conference organizers' initial ambitions, though, the low attendance and spotty representation of the world's Muslim population was both embarrassing and disappointing.

Additionally unfortunate for the conference organizers was that many of those delegates who actually attended the forum in Cairo to discuss the caliphate brought their defensiveness along with them. Well aware of the malevolent intentions attributed to the conference's central executive committee, many of the attendees seemed to have had every intention of thwarting them. Despite the Azharī organizers' emphatic reassurances in the opening session that the

FIGURE 20. The caliphate congress in Cairo, 1926.

Image © Roger-Viollet, "Le congrès du Califat au Caire," Roger-Viollet Collections, no. 1824–25.

caliphate conference was a fully independent enterprise, the recorded proceedings from May 13 to May 19, 1926, are rife with tension. Delegates quarreled bitterly with their Egyptian hosts over procedural minutiae, minor technical definitions, basic juridical interpretations, committee undertakings—anything that could potentially lead to the election of King Fuʾād as caliph.[104]

At the climax of this conflict, the second committee formed by the conference body on Sunday, May 15, 1926, to investigate if it was possible to realize a caliphate at present, according to the specifications identified by the conference's first committee, presented its findings. In short, they felt it was impossible. As they reported back to the full body of the conference, the caliphate had been a source of awesome greatness and glory while the Muslims were a united people, but they were now divided between different governments, administrations, political interests, and even nationalist sentiments—a dismal scenario even before considering their overwhelming lack of independence and their subordination to foreign rule. How then could a true caliphate be erected under these conditions, they asked.[105] Not wanting to leave Muslims without a leader to manage their affairs, the only solution the committee could grasp was to call for consecutive conferences that would bring Muslim peoples closer to one another until they were fully able to establish a caliphate. Were this to prove unfeasible, they suggested that a council of Muslim leaders be formed and meet annually to discuss the affairs of the Muslims worldwide and thereby avert leaving the community bereft of a center. The question of what the current conference should do to elect a caliph, however, was moot.[106]

At this critical juncture, Shaykh Muḥammad al-Aḥmadī al-Ẓawāhirī intervened to save Egypt's reputation. In his personal recollections of the conference, al-Ẓawāhirī recalled how the Shaykh of al-Azhar at the time and chair of the conference, Abū'l-Faḍl al-Jīzāwī, as well as King Fuʾād himself had insisted that he attend to help clear the air (after he had been antagonistically excluded at the beginning by the conference secretary al-Shaykh Ḥusayn Wālī). Yet finding the atmosphere of the conference beyond repair, al-Ẓawāhirī sought to dissolve it as rapidly as possible to avert any disasters and thereby preserve the unity of Muslims along with the future of the caliphate. The second committee's presentation offered such an opening, but also an unsatisfactory conclusion to the conference, so al-Ẓawāhirī stood up and made an eloquent plea for its revision. He agreed wholeheartedly with the committee's findings, and thanked them for their efforts, but objected to their emphasis on the impossibility of establishing the caliphate, which he argued would thrust Muslims into depression and cut them off from all hope. Instead, he requested that the committee's report be revised to state that it *was* possible to achieve the caliphate in their age, but that the *means* for doing so had not yet been established. Say it is possible, he asserted, and encourage Muslims to work for it day and night.[107]

Surprisingly, al-Ẓawāhirī's impassioned speech was a major turning point in the conference proceedings, and the power of his rhetoric evoked enthusiasm among the conference attendees, who even broke out into spontaneous applause in the middle of his oration. The committee chair Shaykh ʿAṭāʾullāh al-Khaṭīb, Director of Charitable Endowments in Baghdad, expressed his gratitude to al-Ẓawāhirī and stressed that the difference between the Egyptian shaykh's suggestions and the committee's findings was one of wording alone, whereupon the president of the Sharīʿah courts in Palestine, Ismāʿīl al-Khaṭīb, suggested dropping the offending phrase from the original report to the acclaim of all the other conference delegates. At this point, the Egyptian director of the religious establishment in Zaqāzīq, Ibrāhīm al-Jibālī, rejoiced that the conference attendees were at last sharing and expressing a spirit of brotherhood in their efforts to elevate the nation (*waṭan*) of Islam and that the conference had accomplished its goal in diagnosing the problem regarding the caliphate as well as its cure.[108]

After a recess in the proceedings, al-Ẓawāhirī took this triumph one step further and suggested the phrasing for a formal decision to be issued by the conference, which he composed in conjunction with six other Egyptian and Palestinian delegates,[109] encapsulating the unanimity of their earlier discussion. The most vociferous thorn in the side of the conference organizers up until this point, the Tunisian ʿAbd al-Azīz al-Thaʿālabī, who had participated in the early post-abolition caliphate deliberations with Abū'l-ʿAzāʾim, was so ecstatic at this juncture that he insisted repeatedly, over al-Ẓawāhirī's objections, that Cairo be the venue for the next conference. al-Thaʿālabī effused over the freedom of opinion (*ḥurriyat al-raʾy*), open-mindedness (*saʿat al-ṣadr*), and purity of intent (*nazāhat al-maqṣid*) in Egypt, as well as its geographic centrality and outstanding scholarship, which combined to make it an ideal location, and the other foreign delegates heartily concurred. This striking transformation in the perceptions and attitudes of the conference attendees was sparked by the stunning realization that their Egyptian cohorts would not attempt to foist King Fuʾād, or indeed any other figure, upon them as caliph. At the same moment that they perceived the potential value of Cairo as a neutral setting for international discussions over the caliphate, their Egyptian hosts eagerly sought to distance themselves from the endeavor that had brought so much trouble and were merely grateful for the graceful conclusion. As al-Ẓawāhirī would later mention in his memoirs, King Fuʾād personally thanked him after the conference for his successful intervention. Upon the intense insistence of the foreign delegates at the conference, though, Cairo was listed in the final published decision as the venue for a follow-up conference with greater international representation to determine the fate of the caliphate, but no such conference was ever held.[110]

UNEXPECTED CONTINUITIES

Conventional wisdom holds that the Cairo conference of 1926 was a complete failure, certainly an understandable perspective given how little was accomplished after such great internationalist hopes. British High Commissioner Lord

FIGURE 21. Some twentieth-century portraits. Left to right, top to bottom: Shakīb Arslān, Rashīd Riḍā, ʿAbd al-Razzāq al-Sanhūrī; Aḥmad Shawqī, ʿAbd al-ʿAzīz al-Thaʿālabī; Muḥammad al-Khiḍr Ḥusayn, Mustafa Sabri, Said Nursi.

Images courtesy Mohamed Ali Eltaher Collection (eltaher.org); Hasnāʾ Dāwūd and al-Khizānah al-Dāwūdiyyah in Tetouan, Morocco and the European Council Research Project on Muslims in Interwar Europe at Utrecht University; *ʿAbd al-Razzāq al-Sanhūrī min khilāl Awrāqihi al-Shakhṣiyyah*; *Aḥmad Shawqī*; Hasnāʾ Dāwūd and al-Khizānah al-Dāwūdiyyah in Tetouan, Morocco and the European Council Research Project on Muslims in Interwar Europe at Utrecht University.

Lloyd was the first to lament that adverse conditions had created "a fiasco of what in other circumstances might have been an event of world importance," and this impression that the gathering constituted a "fiasco" was later reiterated by Elie Kedourie as well as by Israel Gershoni and James Jankowski, who noted that the conference's proceedings were "singularly unproductive," "nor was it followed by anything positive."[111] Depicting a similarly dismal image of the conference, Arnold Toynbee and Martin Kramer disregard the closing zeal of its participants by reading al-Ẓawāhirī's intervention and the selection of Cairo as the venue for another conference as another imposition by domineering Egyptians upon an unwilling and unenthusiastic audience.[112] For Kramer, "the great disappointment" of this and subsequent Muslim congresses was:

> that they failed to merge in a single organization. The establishment of a permanent organization was the professed aim of every initiative. Each one made some provision for a permanent secretariat entrusted with the convening of periodic congresses. Yet none of their congresses succeeded in perpetuating itself very long beyond adjournment.[113]

In short, a general consensus has emerged that the Cairo Caliphate Conference was a disastrous affair bereft of positive outcome.

Yet the ideas raised by the caliphate conference in Cairo managed to live beyond the travails of 1926 through the work of the Egyptian jurist Dr. ʿAbd al-Razzāq al-Sanhūrī (1895–1971). Born in Alexandria close to the turn of the century, al-Sanhūrī graduated as valedictorian from Cairo's Khedival School of Law in 1917. After working for a while in the provincial judicial system as well as teaching law, al-Sanhūrī traveled to France in 1921 to pursue his doctoral studies in both law and political science.[114] The momentous changes affecting the Ottoman Caliphate during this time period that he was abroad eventually led to his second PhD thesis at the University of Lyon, completed and published in 1926, under the title, *Le Califat: son évolution vers une société des nations orientale.*[115] Towards the middle of this project, al-Sanhūrī seems to have exuded a youthful optimism that within a matter of only a few years, another caliph would be elected to replace the deposed Ottoman caliph Abdülmecid. By the end of the project, however, al-Sanhūrī had altered his views and aspired for a more institutional solution, along the lines of an Oriental League of Nations. In this transformation, al-Sanhūrī was specifically affected by the Cairene Caliphate of 1926 as well as the general trajectory of events regarding the caliphate and its fate.[116]

The idea of an international representative council assuming the position and duties of the Islamic caliphate had been circulating among Muslims leading up to the Cairo conference of 1926, as we have seen variously articulated by the Indian activist ʿInāyatullāh Khān al-Mashriqī in his *Khiṭāb* and the proceedings of Indies All Islam Congress (*Kongres al-Islam Hindia*) in Java. The Indian Khilafat Committee was also advocating the appointment of a council to perform the duties of the caliphate.[117] And after being denied a visa to Cairo, the Russian Muslim Musa Carullah likewise informed the Egyptian correspondent of *al-Liwāʾ al-Miṣrī* in Istanbul that an elected body from among the Muslims of the world should take the place of an individual caliph who would necessarily lack full qualifications for the position.[118] In May 1926, the caliphate conference itself reaffirmed this notion of a centralized council of Muslim leaders through the official report of the second committee, on which, it is worth noting, al-Mashriqī served, along with delegates from Egypt, Iraq, South Africa, Tunisia, Morocco, Poland, Hijaz, Yemen, Palestine, Sumatra, and Libya.[119] These ideas were then recirculated by journalists reporting on the conference proceedings in the Arab press—Rashīd Riḍā's *al-Manār* being an excellent case in point.[120] And even though al-Sanhūrī was studying in France at the time, it was through such Arabic periodicals that he was able to remain abreast of these developments, as he expressly acknowledges in *Le Califat*,[121] stimulating him to contemplate deeply and elaborate further upon the compelling notion of a caliphal council, which he details in the third section of his treatise entitled, "Lʾ Avenir."

This future that al-Sanhūrī envisioned entails a gradual reestablishment of the Islamic caliphate as a modern form of governance. Since al-Sanhūrī acknowledged that it was impossible to reestablish a conventional model of the caliphate at the time he wrote *Le Califat*, he sought out a temporary solution of incomplete Islamic governance that would maintain a sense of spiritual unity among Muslims while recognizing the nationalist sentiments of his age and their desire for self-governance. al-Sanhūrī's solution also sought to create a balance of powers, separating the political and religious functions associated with a complete Islamic caliphate from one another into two distinct branches of government that would one day ideally submit to the executive power of a single president, or caliph. In order to build up to this integrated model, al-Sanhūrī felt it was vital to begin by establishing a religious organization as the crux (*al-muḥarrik al-asāsī*) of this caliphate. Structurally, this organization of Islamic religious affairs (al-Sanhūrī's initial caliphate) would be headed by an elected president, or caliph, who would preside over a supreme council and a general assembly, both of which would include full representation of all Muslim peoples. The Supreme Council, consisting of one member per Muslim country or group, would function as a consultative body advising the caliph, communicate the views and desires of their local constituents, and undertake work in five committees addressing matters of Islamic worship, finance, the annual pilgrimage, education, and foreign relations. The even larger General Assembly would meet only once a year to discuss the Supreme Council's annual report and give voice to the wishes of their peoples. Moreover, al-Sanhūrī visualized a diplomatic and international presence for this representative caliphate in order for it to protect the religious interests of Muslims, including those living under the rule of non-Muslim powers.[122]

As for the corollary political organization that al-Sanhūrī imagined, it was to function as an Eastern League of Nations, adopting the broadest civilizational notion of an Islamicate inclusive of Muslims and non-Muslims alike, and not a narrow exclusionary definition, as its parameters. The mission of this organization was to achieve internal stability and external security for its member states and their citizens, in addition to aspiring to international peace and cooperation. To lay the ground for the success of this Eastern League, al-Sanhūrī aspired to a complete renaissance of the East in all realms of knowledge and culture, in which individuals and groups alike could participate. This intellectual and cultural renaissance would then pave the way for necessary political preparations, which would begin with the formation of political parties dedicated to the concept of an Eastern League, lead to unofficial international conferences on the subject, and culminate in official parliamentary conferences that would explore areas of economic rapprochement followed by discussions of political unification. Once this Eastern League was thus fully established, and the Organization of Religious Affairs was able to implement a well-researched progressive and contemporary understanding of Islamic law, then only one step remained for the full realization of al-Sanhūrī's caliphate. Namely, the president of the Organization of Religious Affairs would assume leadership of the Eastern League, although both institutions would continue to function independently of one another. With the joint subordination of these two religious and political branches to a single elected president, al-Sanhūrī felt that he had delineated a modern model for a complete Islamic caliphate.[123]

In a fascinating example of how the collaborative articulation of ideas may lead to the formation of new realities, some have considered al-Sanhūrī to be the intellectual progenitor of the Organization of Islamic Cooperation (OIC), established in the late 1960s and 1970s as the Organization of the Islamic Conference. While undertaking the translation and publication of his father-in-law's work on the caliphate into Arabic, Tawfīq al-Shāwī details a substantial intellectual history for al-Sanhuri's *Le Califat* among key figures who contributed the formation of the OIC. al-Shāwī's own discussions beginning in 1946 with the first secretary general of the Arab League, ʿAbd al-Raḥmān ʿAzzām (1893–1976), figure prominently in this personal narrative, as do his conversations with the Palestinian mufti al-Ḥājj Amīn al-Ḥusaynī. Both of them had actively participated in the international Islamic gathering that followed the 1926 Cairene Caliphate Conference, with al-Ḥusaynī himself organizing this subsequent General Islamic Congress of 1931 in Jerusalem. The idea of the international Muslim conference had not died out, nor had its associations with the lasting dilemma of the caliphate. Accordingly these concerns were not new to either of these prominent and well-connected figures by the time al-Shāwī met with them in Paris in 1946 and began discussing al-Sanhūrī's writings on the caliphate. Through al-Shāwī's recurrent discussions with both of these individuals, he asserts that al-Ḥusaynī and ʿAzzām played a prominent role in convincing the Saudi king Fayṣal b. ʿAbd al-ʿAzīz (1906–1975) to issue the Islamic call for unity during the pilgrimage season (following al-Ḥusaynī's conference in Mogadishu) in 1965—a pivotal marker on the path to the OIC's formation.[124]

Yet al-Shāwī is not alone in his views of al-Sanhūrī's intellectual influence, and perhaps the most significant assessment comes from the Nigerien secretary general of the OIC from 1989 to 1996, Ḥāmid al-Ghābid (b. 1941). For the occasion of the OIC's twentieth anniversary in 1992, al-Ghābid commissioned the reprinting of al-Sanhūrī's *Le Califat* in the original French. In doing so, he sought to demonstrate to the French-reading public how the organization had emerged in response to the pressing need of Muslims for a contemporary institution to preserve their solidarity and cooperation with one another following the disappearance of the Ottoman Caliphate. The sudden vacuum created by the collapse of the Ottoman Caliphate was the agonizing catalyst, according to al-Ghābid, as it had represented the unity and solidarity of the Muslim community. Surely, immediate political circumstances that have been well documented, such as the Israeli occupations of the West Bank and East Jerusalem, the Golan Heights, the Gaza Strip, and the Sinai Peninsula in 1967, followed by the 1969 arson attack on the Aqṣā Mosque in Jerusalem—a sacred sanctuary for Muslims—were critical in fomenting broad support for the organization's establishment. Yet al-Ghābid's perspective speaks to a longer, more intangible trajectory of cultural resonances and intellectual foment. For al-Ghābid, it was al-Sanhūrī's genius that enabled him to imagine and delineate a contemporary structure for an international organization to take the place of the traditional caliphate and still preserve the unity of the Islamic community across the world. "And thus," he concludes, "the solidarity of Muslims in all parts of the world is now represented by an Islamic organization on an international scale that contributes internationally towards peaceful cooperation and the solidarity of humanity." Nearly two decades later, another secretary general of the OIC, the Turkish Ekmeleddin Ihsanoğlu (b. 1943), would affirm and recapitulate my own reading of al-Sanhūrī's legacy in a retrospective on the institution's first forty years.[125] Far from dissipating without leaving behind any intellectual or institutional trace, the ferment of ideas and organizational activity following the collapse of the Ottoman Caliphate in the 1920s leads us to the intriguing question of whether or not we can consider the OIC to be an alternative international model of the caliphate in the modern era.

CHAPTER 6

DEBATING A MODERN CALIPHATE

ALI ŞÜKRÜ'S BRUTALLY mutilated corpse lay half-buried in a vineyard, not far from the presidential villa Çankaya, nestled in the bucolic hills a few miles south from what was then central Ankara. It was finally discovered on April 2, 1924, after days of searching. A deputy for Trabzon in Turkey's first Grand National Assembly, Ali Şükrü was last seen dining with Mustafa Kemal's personal bodyguard Osman Ağa on March 26 before his mysterious disappearance, and cries of agony had been heard emanating from Osman Ağa's house that very evening. Marks of strangulation were clearly visible on Ali Şükrü's neck, and rumors abounded that Mustafa Kemal had personally ordered the murder the day after he had returned to Ankara from a tour of the country. Ali Şükrü had been a particularly vocal opponent of Mustafa Kemal's government as one of the nationalist Second Group members of the first assembly. The Second Group had recently established a newspaper *Tan* with Ali Şükrü as its editor; his unremitting railing, as Finefrock notes, "had become more than aggravation" for Mustafa Kemal at this crucial political juncture as he strategically planned for new elections. The Second Group had also established a publishing house under Ali Şükrü's ownership to stir public discussion of their views, and one of their first publications expounded on the future relationship between the Islamic caliphate and the Grand National Assembly. This treatise was circulated among all the other deputies on January 15, 1923. As Finefrock has encapsulated this era in Turkey, "An argument had developed in favor of the Caliph playing an important role in whatever political system was ultimately established. This view was increasingly voiced in the Assembly by both liberals and conservatives alike, with the latter beginning by early January to make it a public issue."[1] Within a matter of months, however, twenty-nine-year-old Ali Şükrü (1894–1923) had paid for the dissemination of these views with his life. Indeed, as this chapter demonstrates, the separation of the caliphate from the Ottoman Sultanate followed by the Ottoman Caliphate's abolition initiated passionate and potentially lethal debates over the caliphate's role in uncharted configurations of the modern state.

İSMAIL ŞÜKRÜ (1876–1950)

The treatise distributed by Ali Şükrü's publication house, entitled *Hilafet-i İslamiye ve Türkiye Büyük Millet Meclisi*, was written by the first assembly deputy from Karahisar (now Afyonkarahisar), İsmail Şükrü (Çelikalay) Hoca (1876–

1950), who was a religious scholar and hero of the Turkish nationalist War of Independence. Eşref Edib (Fergan) (1882–1971), the Islamic modernist founder of the Ottoman periodicals *Sirat-ı Müstakim* and *Sebilürreşad*, would later confide to the Turkish historian Kadir Mısıroğlu (b. 1933) that he had written the controversial treatise and published it under İsmail Şükrü's name, so that the acknowledged author would be covered by legislative immunity. İsmail Kara finds this possibility to be plausible, pointing to a passage from the introduction that mentions how the author collaborated with some of his scholarly friends to educate the general public at a time of great confusion. Nevertheless, Kara continues to attribute the book to İsmail Şükrü, who after all lent his name and ideas to the project at the very least. [2] One of the few individuals to receive a Medal of Independence with both green and red ribbons, İsmail Şükrü played a crucial role in organizing the early resistance movement, gathering volunteer troops and munitions, and successfully stalling enemy advances for nine months to secure Ankara for the nationalist government. In a later interview, İsmail Şükrü recalled how he had also reassured the original populace of Ankara at Mustafa Kemal's request that the resistance movement's goals were to save the homeland, religion, and Islamic law (*maksadımız memleketi, din ve şeriatı kurtarmak*), and he thereby earned their critical trust and support.[3]

Given these promises made on behalf of the war waged for Turkish independence, İsmail Şükrü felt obliged to clear up what he rather euphemistically referred to as confusion over the role of the caliphate. He affirmed that the Grand National Assembly was in unison with the Caliph Abdülmecid, whom they had elected and to whom they had declared their allegiance. And he described the caliph's lack of power as a temporary situation arising from abnormal and dire circumstances that would soon be remedied. Indeed, İsmail Şükrü insisted that the caliphate's primary duty was to administer temporal affairs, and thus the caliph should be restored to political power with a status above the assembly itself, even if he delegated some of his responsibilities to the representative body as a subordinate institution. To reduce the caliphate to a solely spiritual institution would be to replicate the weakest moments of Islamic history, like those of the late Abbasids, which had led to their destruction. Yet to invest the caliphate with political power could inaugurate another era similar to the strongest points of Ottoman history that had united these two forces. Aspirations to political strength aside, though, İsmail Şükrü also argued that this vision of the caliph as a leading political figure fulfilled the requirements of Islam. As he pointed out, Ḥanafī legal methodology, which was overwhelmingly embraced by the Turks, required the ruler's permission to substantiate the validity of the congregational prayers performed on Fridays and the two major holidays as well as to authorize the legitimate operation of the state's legal system through judicial appointments. Hence, İsmail Şükrü especially emphasized the public authority of the caliph, who should be dedicated to public service as head of state, in his vision for rectifying contemporary affairs and his contemporaries' mistaken impression of the caliphate as a solely spiritual institution.[4]

The president of the Istanbul Bar Association Lütfi Fikri Bey (1872–1934), who would eventually be tried for treason, had expressed even earlier concerns about political arrangements in the aftermath of the caliphate's political estrangement by focusing on the resulting lack of a separation of powers,[5] yet it was İsmail Şükrü's passionate and eloquent Islamic entreaty that visibly unsettled Mustafa Kemal since it had the power to capture the imagination of the nation. The heroic leader immediately called for a press conference and gave speeches in January 1923 to refute İsmail Şükrü's ideas and malign their supporters.[6] In this malleable era, it was indeed possible to restore the caliph to power and to make him the head of a constitutional monarchy instead of a president. And İsmail Şükrü had phrased this proposal as a religious obligation and duty. Mustafa Kemal wanted to avoid that path at all costs and unleashed an all-out assault in what some historians have called the battle of the pamphlets. Although political battles are rarely won through words alone, İsmail Şükrü's treatise evoked a deluge of critical responses. In this war being waged on the intellectual front, a massive 240-page compendium of articles published by the research committee of Mustafa Kemal's political partisans sought to squelch the matter, and three scholars who were members of the Grand National Assembly, Halil Hulki (Aydın) (1869–1940), İlyas Sami (Muş) (1881–1936), Mehmed Rasih (Kaplan) (1883–1952), also serialized their rejection of İsmail Şükrü's ideas, published a joint rejoinder, and promoted their own understanding of national sovereignty.[7]

MEHMED SEYYID ÇELEBIZADE (1873–1925)

Another one of the early responses to İsmail Şükrü's treatise was written at Mustafa Kemal's behest by Mehmed Seyyid Çelebizade (1873–1925) in 1923 and published anonymously.[8] Commonly known as Seyyid Bey, he was born in the cosmopolitan city of Izmir to a family that originally hailed from Central Asia. After receiving his seminary education in Izmir, Seyyid went on to study in Istanbul at the Royal Academy of Law (*Mekteb-i Hukuk-ı Şahane*), an institution shaped by secular European education models. After graduating, he worked as a lawyer, became a faculty member at his alma mater that was incorporated into the Darülfünun university system in 1908, and came to be increasingly involved in late Ottoman politics. He was especially active in the CUP, rising to become its vice president by 1910 and its president by 1911. Seyyid was elected to represent Izmir in the Ottoman Parliament in 1908, 1912, and 1914, and he was appointed to the Ottoman Senate in 1916. He was also involved in multiple legal reforms of the late Ottoman system, including the attempt to complete codification of supple Ḥanafī legal methodology into the *Mecelle* for the state in 1916. Yet his political fortunes waxed and waned along with other prominent

Unionists of the era, and the invading British forces eventually exiled Seyyid to Malta in April 1920. Roughly eighteen months later, he returned to the country in October 1921, visited Ankara, and resumed teaching Islamic legal theory at Darülfünun in Istanbul. During this period, he was also in communication with Mustafa Kemal who sought his legal advice and input. Among these concerns, the irksome treatise that İsmail Şükrü put forth needed to be countered effectively.[9]

In 1923, Seyyid based his anonymous and semi-official Turkish response *Hilafet ve Hakimiyet-i Milliye* on the premise that the caliphate was not really a religious matter. Beginning with a point of broad scholarly agreement, Seyyid explained that the caliphate was an issue that belonged among the branches of Islamic jurisprudence (*mesail-i feriye ve fıkhiyedendir*), even if it had been discussed extensively in books of theology. Therefore, Seyyid suggested, it was not a question of faith. Going even further than the classical tradition, Seyyid argued that the caliphate was therefore more of a worldly and political concern than a religious one (*hatta hilafet meselesi dini bir mesele olmaktan ziyade dünyevi ve siyasi bir meseledir*). The caliphate was a peripheral issue in Seyyid's estimation, and for evidence he pointed to a preponderance of general principles over specific delineations in Islamic scriptural texts. Seyyid therefore argued that the Muslim community held direct control over its affairs to administer as they saw fit. Any other tack was pegged as incorrect and needlessly recalcitrant (*pek yanlış fikirlere ve lüzumsuz taassuba tesadüf edilmekte*), and Seyyid expressed his hope that his composition would enlighten the minds of his contemporaries.[10]

In elevating this defining role of the Muslim community, Seyyid interprets the election of a caliph as a contract between him and the nation. Creatively utilizing Islamic contractual law to delimit the caliph's parameters, Seyyid argues that a caliph receives "power of attorney" (*akd-i vekalet*) through the electoral process on behalf of the Muslim community. In theory, every individual would participate in this election, but Seyyid explains that due to the vastness of Muslim domains the task has devolved onto the electors (*ehl-i hal ve akd*) present at the seat of the caliphate. In other words, not only was the caliph successor to the Prophet Muḥammad (*hilafet-i nübüvvet ki Hazreti Peygamberden niyabet*), he was also the deputy of the Muslim community or nation (*hilafet-i ümmet ki millet-i İslamiye tarafından niyabet*), and as such it had the right to depose him.[11] As Sami Erdem and Nurullah Ardıç have alluded, these arguments were a development of Seyyid's earlier legal justifications for removing the Ottoman sultan Abdülhamid II from office.[12] Continuing in this vein to weaken the traditional power of the Ottoman Caliphate, Seyyid sought to bolster the concept of national sovereignty as the true locus of political power in Islam. And the public duties (*vilayet-i amme*) that İsmail Şükrü had held up as evidence of the caliph's rightful role as head of state were nothing but powers that the electors delegated go the caliph on behalf of the sovereign community, which Seyyid elides into the notion of a nation.[13]

Elections were critical to validating Seyyid's notion of national sovereignty (*hakimiyet-i milliye*), and he uses them to differentiate between what he designates as genuine and fictitious caliphates. A complete caliphate or *hilafet-i kamile* was one that fulfilled all of the institution's traits and necessary preconditions, including particularly election (*intihab*) and recognition (*biat*) by the community. On the other hand, a caliphate only in name or *hilafet-i suriye* was one that did not satisfy these complete criteria, especially if it was assumed by force (*tegallüb ve istila*) and not through an electoral process. By emphasizing the necessity of election, not only was Seyyid validating the Turkish Grand National Assembly's election of Abdülmecid in 1922, he was also undercutting the sanctity and legitimacy of the Umayyad, Abbasid, and Ottoman Caliphates. Seyyid maintained that a true caliphate could not be hereditary, and he disavowed earlier jurists' attempts to recognize the assumption of a caliphate by the powerful (*ghalabah* as discussed in chapter 3) as legitimate. In reality, Seyyid wrote, all of these historical caliphates that emerged after the first thirty years of the Rightly Guided Caliphs were merely oppressive kingdoms and sultanates.[14]

Seyyid's pointed inclusion of the Ottoman sultans in this last category of oppressive rulers who did not even merit the title "caliph" certainly paved the way for their demotion and removal from power. Even in his rhetoric, Seyyid explicitly justified the necessity of placing further restrictions on them. The Rightly Guided Caliphs were of course exempted because, as representatives of the complete caliphate, they followed the Prophet and were therefore pure, hallowed, just, and compassionate. They also implemented the Qur'anic and prophetic principle of consultation (*meşveret*). By contrast, the rest of the kings and sultans among the Umayyads, Abbasids, and Ottomans indulged in various forms of oppression and tyranny and were therefore not true caliphs or successors of the Prophet. From these interpretations, Seyyid concluded that there could be no hesitation about standing up to this historical form of oppression, and any measures enacted against the traditional Ottoman sultan-caliphs would only restrict their inherently oppressive nature and ward off the harm they would inflict. It was not enough to depose and replace an oppressive sultan, since experience and history had taught Seyyid that a successor would only be worse than the one he had supplanted. Rather, Seyyid argued, "The best and soundest approach is to put the caliph in a situation where he cannot cause harm" (*en iyi ve eslem tarik halifeyi ika-yı zarar edemeyecek bir hale koymakdır*).[15]

With the context of Turkey's Grand National Assembly in mind, Seyyid's solution was for the caliph to transfer all of his rights and responsibilities to other(s), whether an individual, group, cabinet, or parliament. To defend this position, Seyyid drew specifically upon the history of the Abbasid caliphs in Mamluk Egypt that was discussed extensively in chapter 2 as an important precedent. In Seyyid's reading of the earlier works of Islamic history, Sultan Baybars decided to recognize the potentially dubious Abū'l-Qāsim Aḥmad as caliph because it corresponded with his own political goals. Even more importantly in Seyyid's view, the newly inaugurated caliph al-Mustanṣir transferred all caliphal rights and affairs of state over to Baybars without any prospect of interference. Seyyid noted that these arrangements were made publicly and legitimated by Egypt's religious scholars. Thus, Seyyid concludes, the caliphate was separated from the sultanate or political power for hundreds of years in Egypt, whereas some of Seyyid's contemporaries in Turkey, including İsmail Şükrü, hesitated or outright declined to legitimate similar restrictions on the caliphate of their day and therefore suffered in his estimation. Seyyid attempted to persuade his readers that their position was a mistake; the scholars of Egypt—including the famed ʿIzz al-Dīn b. ʿAbd al-Salām—had already permitted the separation of the caliphate from the sultanate over six hundred years ago. Seyyid argued that all possible forms of restrictions and limitations should be placed on the naked power of the Ottoman Sultanate to preserve order and attain public benefit and justice, and he pegged his intellectual and political opponents as shallow and rigid reactionaries who did not consider the realities of Islamic law.[16]

In his conclusion, Seyyid affirmed that the issue of the caliphate in his day was only a matter of custom and politics (*zamanımızda hilafet meselesi artık anane ve siyaset meselesinden başka bir şey değildir*). Given its regard for this affair, Seyyid continued, the Grand National Assembly did not abolish the caliphate (*hilafeti ilga etmemiştir*) but rather restored the institution to its earlier configuration in Mamluk Egypt so that it could no longer harm the nation (*millet*) and homeland (*memleket*) with authoritarianism. Seyyid contended that these new arrangements in Turkey put political power, or the sultanate, back in the hands of the nation, who were its rightful possessors (*saltanatında sahib-i hakikisi olan milletin yedinde ika eylemiştir*).[17] He maintained that the caliph had only received "power of attorney" from the nation, and it was the nation's right to represent itself rather than delegate its affairs. This creative twist was couched in the language of Islamic legal principles with the reinterpretation of the caliphate presented as an issue of contractual law. After all, individuals and groups had the Islamic legal right to represent themselves in transactions if they so desired, and if the caliph was merely the people's delegate, then in the same way the nation as a larger scale group (*en büyük cemaat demek olan millet*) could assume full control of its affairs without him. Yet Seyyid added the qualification that a nation so great in numbers could not actually represent itself, so rather than delegating to one individual, the caliph, could not the many members of the nation delegate their power to an elected representative assembly (*müntehab ve muntazam bir heyet-i mümessileye tefvid edemez mi*)?[18] In this manner, Seyyid articulated an Islamic modernist rationale for the Grand National Assembly's assumption of political power in Ankara.

In his speech in the assembly roughly one year later, however, Seyyid revised and rephrased these conclusions. As an elected assembly member and the minister of justice, Seyyid held the floor for seven hours, persuading his fellow delegates that it was necessary to abolish the caliphate altogether. Seyyid recapitulated the arguments of his earlier treatise to the assembly's vocal approbation and encouragement, but, as Erdem acknowledges, he took these ideas one step further. No longer was the nation limited to absolute or partial delegation of its authority. The nation did not have to transfer its authority to anyone. Instead, it could take control of its own affairs as a Republic. From his reading of Islamic law and history, there could be no objection to abolishing the Ottoman Caliphate, except that people had become accustomed to living under oppression.[19] Under the persuasion of Seyyid's influential words, the vetted second assembly members present in Ankara overwhelmingly passed the motions on March 3, 1924, to abolish the caliphate and expel the Ottoman dynasty outside of the new Turkish Republic.

A mere three days later, on March 6, 1924, Seyyid was removed from his post as minister of justice in İsmet's cabinet. Perhaps his influence had grown too great, and in any case, it was no longer necessary. As an articulate modernist Muslim jurist and an experienced Unionist politician, Seyyid posed too much of a threat and nuisance to the emerging Kemalist regime. Another estranged nationalist, Rıza Nur, who eventually had to leave Turkey to live in exile, mercilessly teased Seyyid that he had been all too quickly sidelined after Mustafa Kemal and his allies had no more use for him. Now that the caliphate was abolished, Mustafa Kemal did not want to offer substance to the notion of a Republic grounded in Islamic principles and legal foundations. Instead of incorporating Ottoman legal reforms from the codified *Mecelle* and adapting from European legal systems only what aligned with Turkish customs as Seyyid had advocated, the nascent Turkish Republic adopted the Swiss Civil Code and the Italian Criminal Code wholesale in 1926. But Seyyid did not live long enough to see it. The twenty-third article of the Teşkilat-ı Esasiye Kanunu was passed on April 20, 1924, as part of a shrewd Kemalist move to curtail unwanted influences on the still-malleable shape of governance. Accordingly, Seyyid was faced with the choice of either keeping his profession or retaining his deputyship, and he opted to return to his position as a professor at the Darülfünun in Istanbul. He died there on March 8, 1925, only one year after the caliphate's abolition. In arguing back in 1923 that political successors were necessarily worse than the oppressive rulers they supplanted (*tebeddül-i saltanat vukuunda halef, selefinden daha iyi hayırlı çıkmıyor*), it is somewhat ironic that Seyyid never seems to have contemplated the possibility that the Kemalist regime he helped establish might become more authoritarian and oppressive than the empire it had replaced.[20]

ʿALĪ ʿABD AL-RĀZIQ (1888–1966)

The reverberations of Seyyid Bey's ideas extended beyond Republican Turkey, however, and helped shape the secular nationalist arguments of ʿAlī ʿAbd al-Rāziq against Islamic governance in Egypt. ʿAbd al-Rāziq was born into a prominent Egyptian landowning family in the province of Minyā in 1888, and their family home in the city functioned as a salon for leading intellectuals at the turn of the century, including the famous Islamic modernists and liberals Muḥammad ʿAbduh (1849–1905), Qāsim Amīn (1863–1908), and Aḥmad Luṭfī al-Sayyid (1872–1963). In 1907, ʿAbd al-Rāziq's father, Ḥasan Pasha, helped establish *Ḥizb al-Ummah* or the Party of the Nation—taking the longstanding Islamic concept of community (the *ummah*) and reconceptualizing it in strictly territorial nationalist terms. As a political party of wealthy, landed proprietors of the Greater Nile Valley, the *Ḥizb al-Ummah* aimed at achieving Egyptian independence through cooperation with the British. For his own education, ʿAbd al-Rāziq was first sent to al-Azhar where he eventually completed his religious studies and then the new Egyptian University (now Cairo University) established in 1908 where he acquired secular European training under professors including the Italian Orientalist Carlo Alfonso Nallino (1872–1938). In 1912, he traveled to England intending to study economics at Oxford University, but the outbreak of World War I in 1914 prompted his return to Egypt where he was appointed as an Islamic court judge in 1915.

Following the critical historical methodology impressed upon him and others of his generation as a service to their nation by a rousing Nallino, ʿAbd al-Rāziq began considering the history of the Islamic judiciary and by extension that of Islamic governance and the caliphate from which it derived its legitimacy. This intellectual side project occupied him off and on over the years that he served as a judge, and in late October 1922 his family helped found and support the Liberal Constitutionalist party (*Ḥizb al-Aḥrār al-Dustūriyyīn*) as a political successor to the Party of the Nation (*Ḥizb al-Ummah*). ʿAbd al-Rāziq's brothers were leading members and financial backers of the new secular nationalist party and its newspaper *al-Siyāsah*, and ʿAbd al-Rāziq himself made an unsuccessful bid for the Egyptian Parliament as a Liberal Constitutionalist in the 1923 and 1924 two-stage elections following the promulgation of Egypt's new constitution in 1923. The more popular nationalist Wafd Party swept to power through the elections, leading King Fuʾād to ask Saʿd Zaghlūl to become the country's first prime minister of the constitutional era and form a Wafd government in January 1924. Less than two months later, the Grand National Assembly abolished the Ottoman Caliphate in Turkey and the prospect of King Fuʾād becoming caliph in its wake seemed to threaten the hard-earned constitutional restrictions on his power.[21]

Rising to confront this potential political challenge to the new Egyptian constitution, ʿAbd al-Rāziq returned to his musings on governance and intentionally waded into the thick of contentious political waters. On Wednesday, April 1, 1925, ʿAbd al-Rāziq completed his reflections on the foundations of political power for publication as *al-Islām wa-Uṣūl al-Ḥukm*. In his opening phrase of the book praising God, ʿAbd al-Rāziq boldly declared that he did not fear anyone except for God (*wa-lā akhshā aḥadan siwāh*)—knowing that he was about to promulgate widely unpopular and unconventional views in the public sphere that also countered the political interests of his monarch. In the first third of his book, ʿAbd al-Rāziq seeks to dismantle the traditional understanding of a caliphate by discrediting the centuries-long religious discourse on it. First, he casts the caliphate as an inherently absolutist institution. Then, he discounts the exegetical tradition providing religious sanction for the caliphate through particular Qur'anic verses, denies the received meanings of prophetic traditions on Islamic leadership as merely generic descriptors, and negates the broad scholarly consensus on the caliphate's theoretical necessity by reinterpreting the legal concept of "consensus" or *ijmāʿ* as blanket universal approbation of specific historical manifestations and policies, thereby enabling him to assert that it never occurred. Next, he additionally critiques the idea that religious rites and public welfare depend upon the caliphate. ʿAbd al-Rāziq conceded that if Muslim jurists meant by the imamate and caliphate merely government in any shape or form, whether "absolute or limited, monarchical or republican, despotic or constitutional, democratic or socialist or Bolshevik," then he concurred. But if they meant a specific form of government, he emphatically demurred. Linguistically, ʿAbd al-Rāziq adopts a curiously oppositional stance for an Azharite throughout this first third of his exposition by referring to the intellectual output and debates of Muslim scholars on the caliphate from an outsider's perspective; he continuously uses terms like *ʿindahum* ("according to them"), *zaʿamū* ("they claim"), and *baqiya lahum* ("they still hold") that convey a disdainful distance. In drawing clear lines between himself as the author and "them," ʿAbd al-Rāziq positions himself as a European-inspired enlightened intellectual above and beyond the discursive tradition of Muslim jurists.[22]

By contrast, ʿAbd al-Rāziq expresses his affinity for the new Republican articulations of political theory set out by Seyyid Bey in his semi-official and anonymous Turkish treatise *Hilafet ve Hakimiyet-i Milliye* that was translated into Arabic by ʿAbd al-Ghanī Sanī as *al-Khilāfah wa-Sulṭat al-Ummah* and published in Egypt by al-Hilāl Press in 1924. ʿAbd al-Rāziq wholly concurs with Seyyid's argument that the contemporary caliphate was not a religious affair, but he goes even further by entirely negating divine as well as prophetic intent for the institution, which he lambasts as a catastrophe for Muslims. Moreover, ʿAbd al-Rāziq argues that the Prophet Muḥammad himself was only a messenger sent by God and not a political ruler. Starting with the question of the judiciary, ʿAbd al-Rāziq wonders at the scarcity of information on how the Prophet and the few followers he appointed during his lifetime adjudicated affairs and forms the hypothesis that the Prophet was never actually a religious head of state. The lack of a royal administrative apparatus, including a formalized judiciary, treasury, and bureaucracy, in the time of the Prophet convinces ʿAbd al-Rāziq that this is the case, as does his commitment to establishing a binary opposition between the spirituality of religion and the materiality of politics. ʿAbd al-Rāziq explicitly likens Muḥammad to his brethren in prophecy Jesus and Joseph who acknowledged the political authority of others—and noted that those prophets who combined divine mission and political rule, presumably Moses, David, and Solomon, were few. As ʿAbd al-Rāziq explains, states depend upon physical coercion, but the Qur'an and the Prophet espouse the inadmissibility of compulsion ("There is no compulsion in religion," Qur'an 2:256) and the importance of preaching with true wisdom and beauty (Qur'an 16:125) to achieve full conviction. Therefore, ʿAbd al-Rāziq holds that the Prophet Muḥammad's authority was solely spiritual because it was founded on moving people's hearts—and not like the political authority of an ordinary ruler who governed over people's bodies. Islam, ʿAbd al-Rāziq concludes, is a purely religious call to God and path of social reform—but not a political state. This intentional abstinence from governance, in ʿAbd al-Rāziq's view, explains the dearth of public officials, judges, and administrative registers during the prophetic era, which had initially sparked his interest.[23]

Following these conclusions, ʿAbd al-Rāziq seeks to undermine the foundational validity of an Islamic caliphate by considering how the Prophet never appointed a successor or caliph to follow him. ʿAbd al-Rāziq explains that God chose the Prophet Muḥammad as the best of creation to convey the divine message to all people, among every one in the "East and West, Arabs and non-Arabs, men and women, rich and poor, learned and ignorant." Then he argues that the Prophet's leadership over the Arabs during his lifetime was simply religious. By the time he passed away, God had declared the blessing of Islam to be complete, and the Prophet had not declared a successor to follow him, although Shi'is would disagree with that assessment. As a result, ʿAbd al-Rāziq contends that not only revelatory but also religious leadership of the Muslim community ended with the death of the Prophet. And the caliphate that emerged in the wake of the Prophet's death, he argues, was a new form of political, not religious, leadership. Thus, even the leadership of Abū Bakr, traditionally deemed to be the first of the few Rightly Guided Caliphs who tried to rule following prophetic guidance, was only political and not part of an informed vision of Islam. ʿAbd al-Rāziq tries to reinterpret Abū Bakr's approval for his designation as "Successor (i.e., Caliph) to the Messenger of God" (*Khalīfat Rasūlillāh*) along these lines and concludes that the religion of Islam, if not Islamic history, is free from the notion of a caliphate—and, for that matter, from the judiciary too. In his bold summation, aimed at reconfiguring contemporary Egyptian politics by thwarting King Fuʾād's caliphal ambitions, ʿAbd al-Rāziq declares that there is no religious justification to hold Muslims back from demolishing "that antiquated system" and from building their government according to "the most modern and advanced models shaped by human intellect and the strongest of what the experience of nations has shown to be the best foundations of political rule."[24] ʿAbd al-Rāziq had thrown down the gauntlet, expecting to provoke a response from religious scholars as well as from royalists, but he may not have realized the full extent of what would unfold.

Among the first to refute ʿAbd al-Rāziq's slim volume was Rashīd Riḍā. In the pages of Egyptian nationalist newspapers and his Islamic modernist periodical *al-Manār*, Riḍā decried *al-Islām wa-Uṣūl al-Ḥukm* as the latest assault on Islam since the erasure of the Ottoman Sultanate, the Turks' devastating abolition of the caliphate, and their creation of a secular republic with no reference to Islamic principles. This contemporary political and intellectual incursion was more pernicious than the Crusades, Riḍā argued, because it turned Muslims against one another. And what ʿAbd al-Rāziq had argued in his book to the effect that there was no foundation for the caliphate, imamate, government, or political or judicial legislation in Islam was such a reprehensible innovation that it had never crossed the minds of any Sunni, Shi'i, Kharijite, Jahmite, Mu'tazilite, or even those deviants who had claimed an esoteric understanding of Islam. It contradicted innumerable clear, definitive texts. And Riḍā was horrified how ʿAbd al-Rāziq could suggest that Muslim interpretations of the seminal history of Abū Bakr as caliph from his day until the present were invalid and misguided; it was an assault on communal memory and devotion. Even more so for Riḍā, it was an attack on the sanctity, legitimacy, and perpetuation of Islamic law in all its many forms. How could ʿAbd al-Rāziq seek to destroy Islamic legislation in favor of nations' recent experimentations, including the Bolshevik revolution? How strange, he wondered, that the propagator of this atrocious proposal to make the Egyptian government as atheistic as Ankara was an Azhar graduate and Islamic court judge from an honorable family. Given the author's association with the Azhar system, Riḍā called upon the *Mashyakhat al-Azhar* to repudiate the contents of his book *al-Islām wa-Uṣūl al-Ḥukm* and not remain silent lest their silence be misinterpreted as consent.[25]

In the middle and end of June 1925, religious scholars sent at least three formal complaints to the head of the Azhar system, Shaykh al-Azhar Muḥammad Abū'l-Faḍl al-Jīzāwī (1874–1927). On June 23, for instance, sixty-three religious scholars wrote an open letter requesting that the Shaykh al-Azhar rise to the challenge of defending Islam in an age of encroaching atheism. Their concerns over ʿAbd al-Rāziq's aberrant publication are framed by an anxiety to affirm the positive role of religious scholars in contemporary Egypt. Therefore, they recapitulate that state law declares that Islam is the official religion of Egypt and that the mission of the Azhar is to preserve religion and graduate capable religious functionaries. Based on their understanding of the Sacred Law, the purpose of the religious sciences, its scholars, and the institution of al-Azhar itself is:

> to protect religion and convey beneficial knowledge, to support and defend that beneficial knowledge within all possible legal means, to spread sacred, clement guidance among Muslims, to encourage public benefit and discourage general harm, to oppose heterodoxy, clarify misconceptions, and counter poor morals and behavior.

In an age when religious scholars benefited from greater numbers, financial security, and access to printed texts, they wondered what excuse could possibly hold their professional cohort back from countering the growing ignorance of Sacred Law and the vocal antagonism toward it among Europeanized elites? Religious scholars' restrained silence in recent years regarding these uninformed assaults against Islamic norms and rulings, they argued, had been interpreted as a sign of weakness. And today's "star" in these hostile efforts had thrust his book *al-Islām wa-Uṣūl al-Ḥukm* on an unsuspecting public without soliciting feedback and input from his scholarly peers. Although he claimed the authority of an Azharite scholar and Islamic legal court judge, the author's book was filled with immense religious doubt and uncertainty and negated the obvious and well-known components of Islam (*al-ma ʿlūm min al-dīn bi'l-ḍarūrah*). He denied the caliphate and went to great lengths to reproach the entire Muslim community that has believed in it from the time of Abū Bakr to the present—without any regard for the Prophet's Companions or the Rightly Guided Caliphs among them. Moreover, they noted, the author denied the Islamic validity of the judiciary and all other forms of governance, and he went so far as to insinuate that the prophetic model ended with his death and Muslims should not continue to follow it as an embodied source of religious guidance. The scholars worried that the author advocated in its stead that Muslims should arrange all of their affairs according to the latest ideas of European and American Christian men and opponents of religion. Troubled by this prescription, the open-letter writers implored the Shaykh al-Azhar to defend and support religion with clear evidence-based proofs within all of the legal means available to him and to help the great institution of al-Azhar participate in public discourse. In an era of rapidly shifting political and intellectual transformations, these religious scholars sought to preserve a meaningful and authoritative role for Islamic conceptions of law and ethics as well as its proficient interpreters.[26]

By July, the head of al-Azhar decided to intervene in the growing controversy and initiated official proceedings to censure ʿAbd al-Rāziq as a former graduate and present religious functionary. Based on article 101 of a law passed in 1911 regarding al-Azhar University and religious institutes, the Shaykh al-Azhar convened the Council of Leading Scholars (*Hay ʾat Kibār al-ʿUlamā ʾ*) to consider whether the contents of ʿAbd al-Rāziq's book befitted an official religious scholar. The consequences of a potential negative ruling were exacting; according to Article 101, a former graduate could be erased from the registers of al-Azhar University for behavior unbecoming of a religious scholar, and his employment in any public office requiring these nullified religious qualifications would be terminated. On July 29, 1925, ʿAbd al-Rāziq was informed of the impending proceedings as well as the seven charges laid against him and asked to prepare his defense before the twenty-five-member council. The initial review date was pushed back one week from August 5 to August 12 to allow ʿAbd al-Rāziq additional time to prepare his case, although he protested the shortness of this duration and the very undertaking against him. In person, on August 12, ʿAbd al-Rāziq prefaced his remarks in defense of his work by denying the standing of the Council of Leading Scholars to reprimand him. And in an intriguing argument for the validity of his views, ʿAbd al-Rāziq likened himself to the minor Najadāt sect, discussed in chapter 3, which broke off from the other Kharijites and did not believe in the obligatory nature of Islamic leadership. For the senior religious scholars gathered to evaluate his case, however, ʿAbd al-Rāziq's voluntary comparison of his opinions to those of a deviant, anarchist offshoot of a maligned, militant sectarian group only confirmed their negative assessment of his work. In the end, the Shaykh al-Azhar and Council of Leading Scholars unanimously affirmed all seven charges against ʿAbd al-Rāziq, determined that they did not befit a religious scholar and official, and published a thirty-one-page summary of their evaluation. Not content with a mere executive summary, two members of the council, the former Egyptian grand mufti Muḥammad Bakhīt al-Muṭīʿī (1854–1935) and the Mālikī scholar Yūsuf al-Dijwī (1840–1946), would soon publish over six hundred more pages of detailed critiques refuting ʿAbd al-Rāziq's work.[27]

The task of discharging ʿAbd al-Rāziq from his position as an Islamic court judge in consequence of this ruling, however, was quickly embroiled in multiple sets of political machinations in anticipation of impending elections in Egypt. The order dismissing ʿAbd al-Rāziq from his post needed to be authorized by the minister of justice, ʿAbd al-ʿAzīz Fahmī Pasha (1870–1951), who was also the chairperson of the Liberal Constitutionalist Party to which ʿAbd al-Rāziq and his eminent family belonged. Early on, the minister of justice privately expressed to Acting British High Commissioner Neville Henderson that he would rather resign from the Egyptian cabinet than sign the papers for ʿAbd al-Rāziq's dismissal, but nevertheless he would feel obliged to execute the order if the request came from his fellow cabinet members—out of loyalty to his colleagues. But first the minister of justice attempted to find a way out of the dilemma by forwarding the order for ʿAbd al-Rāziq's dismissal to the government's legal council for advice—in essence, he queried, did Article 101 regarding the unworthy conduct of religious scholars actually apply to the current situation? The acting prime minister and chairperson of the royalist Unionist Party, Yaḥyā Ibrāhīm Pasha (1861–1936), was enraged by these obfuscating tactics, as well as the presumption that non-Muslim lawyers in the legal department should advise on an exclusively Muslim religious affair, and demanded that the papers be returned to the cabinet for execution. Bad blood between the two men, who also led opposing political parties, certainly did not help matters—nor did the king and his advisors' desire to be rid of the Liberal Constitutionalists and their allies. A heated argument ensued between the two ministers, and the acting prime minister consulted the British Residency and Egyptian Palace (in that order) and resolved to have the minister of justice resign. Meanwhile, the acting British high commissioner had arranged for the quiet return of the papers regarding ʿAbd al-Rāziq without comment from the Egyptian government's legal advisors, and the remaining members of the cabinet had convinced the minister of justice to comply.[28]

The acting British high commissioner's overriding concern—as he reminded all the concerned parties repeatedly—was to preserve the fragile coalition between royalist Unionists and Liberal Constitutionalists in the cabinet to prevent Saʿd Zaghlūl and his Wafd Party from returning to power in the upcoming elections. Indeed, as Henderson reported back to the British Foreign Office in September 1925:

> As [the acting Egyptian prime minister] was well aware, I had always done whatever it was possible for me to do to preserve the unity of front among the opponents of the Saadists, and I was still convinced that the best course would be to preserve that unity until Saad, as the result of the elections, had been definitely crushed.... My object was a stable Government, which could not be achieved until the elections had resulted in the downfall and final discrediting of Saad Zaghlul.

And more to the point, Henderson reflected, "The dispute between the two parties is no immediate concern to His Majesty's Government, except in so far as it increases or diminishes the prospect of Saad's defeat at the elections." The Egyptian Palace, however, was keen to push the rigorous interior minister Ismāʿīl Ṣidqī Pasha (1875–1950) out of the cabinet "in order to gain unrestricted liberty of action and propaganda in this all-important Ministry" to use it to the advantage of royalists in advance of the elections. Therefore, the interior minister's tacit alliance with the Liberal Constitutionalists presented a politically convenient opportunity to force his resignation. Some Liberal Constitutionalists feared dismal results at the polls vis-à-vis the Wafd without the enveloping prestige to be gained by cooperating with the king and remaining on the cabinet. Yet rather than "continue to regard the downfall of Saad Zaghlul as their primary object" as the British advised, other Liberal Constitutionalists began to view the threat of a young and vigorous royalist like Nashʾat Pasha with even more dread than an aging Saʿd Zaghlūl who did not seem to have much longer to live. And with the resignation from the Liberal Constitutionalist Party of the former Egyptian grand mufti Bakhīt who had served on the council that censured ʿAbd al-Rāziq, the party itself began to shift away from a broad coalition of different perspectives to adopt a narrower and more strident secularist tack.[29]

In the end, it was the perfect storm. The acting prime minister and chairperson of the royalist Unionist Party insisted on the resignation and then outright dismissal of the minister of justice and chairperson of the Liberal Constitutionalist Party despite the latter's renewed sense of cooperation over the case of ʿAbd al-Rāziq. The Liberal Constitutionalists were duly outraged, and the party overwhelmingly voted that the remaining two Liberal Constitutionalist ministers, one of agriculture and the other of charitable endowments, should resign—despite the eager efforts of the other Unionist ministers to apologize and amend matters. The independent interior minister tendered his resignation in solidarity—it was accepted by the palace with indecent alacrity. And in good faith, the Liberal Constitutionalist ministers of agriculture and charitable endowments could no longer withdraw their resignations. Ultimately, the king reconstituted a cabinet composed entirely of loyal Unionists. ʿAbd al-Rāziq had become a footnote in these elaborate political maneuverings, but nonetheless the Ministry of Justice finally dismissed him from his post on September 17, and the order was dated retroactively to match the date of the Council of Leading Scholars's decision to discipline him on August 12, 1925, along with explicit affirmation of their religious and legal authority.[30]

Putting politics aside in a private moment, the Egyptian nationalist Saʿd Zaghlūl, who formed the focal point in much of these electoral calculations, shared his personal qualms over ʿAbd al-Rāziq's book with an aide. One evening, on August 20, about a week after the Council of Leading Scholar's decision and some weeks before the ensuing cabinet crisis, their conversation veered to the question of the caliphate and ʿAbd al-Rāziq's publication. Zaghlūl had read *al-Islām wa-Uṣūl al-Ḥukm* with great interest in order to evaluate the extent to which the campaign against ʿAbd al-Rāziq was justified or not, and his first impression of the book was to wonder how a religious scholar could use such language on the topic of the caliphate. Zaghlūl noted that he had read a lot of works by Orientalists, yet none of them had attacked Islam with such sharpness and vehemence as ʿAbd al-Rāziq. Zaghlūl found ʿAbd al-Rāziq to be ignorant of the foundations of his religion and simplistic in some of his ideas, especially in negating the civil legal dimension of Islam and its guidance on matters of governance. He also considered the council's disciplinary action against ʿAbd al-Rāziq to be fully justified according to the law as well as basic reason and intellect; of course, the religious officials would discharge someone from their midst who had sought to undermine their institutions. Regardless of the potential interference of the palace in instigating these charges out of desire for the caliphate, Zaghlūl held fast to the notion that what the scholars did was their unassailable duty and right (*mahmā kāna al-bāʿith fa-inna al-ʿulamāʾ faʿalū mā huwa wājib wa-ḥaqq wa-lā tuwajjah ilayhim adnā malāmah fīh*). What truly pained Zaghlūl was rather that some impressionable youths would be deluded by the ideas Abd al-Rāziq put forward without proper investigation or study and not realize that his book sought to demolish the firmly established foundations of Islam.[31]

MUḤAMMAD AL-KHIḌR ḤUSAYN (1876–1958)

A family friend of the ʿAbd al-Rāziq brothers, Muḥammad al-Khiḍr Ḥusayn was surprised at the poor quality of scholarship in ʿAlī ʿAbd al-Rāziq's treatise. Of notable Algerian descent from the Sharifian Idrisid dynasty on his father's side, al-Khiḍr was born in 1876 in the Tunisian countryside among his mother's family who were famous for their religious scholarship and piety. At the age of twelve, he moved to the capital Tunis and two years later in 1889 began his religious studies at the famed university of Zaytūna, which had graduated Ibn Khaldūn several centuries before. By 1903, al-Khiḍr had earned the highest *ʿālimiyyah* degree certifying his erudition, and he began working as a judge within two years, only to resign in 1906 after giving a speech about "Freedom in Islam" while chafing at the prolonged French occupation. Thereafter, al-Khiḍr was active in opposing the French and Italian colonization of North Africa and traveled between Istanbul, Damascus, Cairo, and Tunis. He even cooperated with Enver Paşa during his wartime stint in the Ottoman cabinet, whereas the punitive Ottoman governor of Syria Cemal Paşa (1872–1922) had al-Khiḍr imprisoned for several months until Enver Paşa interceded on his behalf. He returned from Istanbul to Damascus under the short-lived independent Arab kingdom of Fayṣal. But following the French invasion there too, al-Khiḍr settled in Egypt in 1921. In Cairo, he took and passed al-Azhar Universiy's *ʿālimiyyah* examination in 1922, earning him the distinction of joining the official ranks of Azharites as well, and al-Khiḍr continued to be actively involved in the political and intellectual issues of his day.

During this period, he frequented the ʿAbd al-Rāziq family home and participated in the engaging discussions held there, enjoying the prominent clan's respect and warm regard. In anticipation of the publication of *al-Islām wa-Uṣūl al-Ḥukm*, the family asked al-Khiḍr for the mailing addresses of a number of Muslim leaders and intellectuals in order to send them copies of the forthcoming book, which he dutifully supplied. After al-Khiḍr received his own complimentary copy, he sat down to read it with anticipation. Despite approaching the book and its author with an open heart and mind, he was shocked to find that a work purportedly written over a ten-year period could be so shoddy. He was also concerned that ʿAbd al-Rāziq's status as an Azharite would cloak his secularist assertions in legitimacy. al-Khiḍr began to write a response, subjecting ʿAbd al-Rāziq's claims to further investigation; the lengthy book that resulted, *Naqḍ Kitāb al-Islām wa-Uṣūl al-Ḥukm*, was published within a year and sold out within a month of its release.[32]

From al-Khiḍr's perspective, ʿAbd al-Rāziq had portrayed the caliphate as a dark and grotesque caricature of itself—expediently distorting religious texts and their lofty ideals in order to be able to reject them out of hand. In the first chapter, for example, ʿAbd al-Rāziq grossly exaggerated the religious obedience due to a caliph. Unmoored from the discursive Islamic tradition, ʿAbd al-Rāziq twisted scholars' words to imply that the caliph was elevated to a semi-divine status and deserved blind and absolute obedience from his subjects. al-Khiḍr retorted that Muslim scholars maintained one should only follow a caliph in what was recognizably good (*maʿrūf*)—not in any evil that he might perpetrate. al-Khiḍr also clarified how the caliph's authority was limited, the caliph was accountable for his actions, and one should discuss, critique, and even reject a caliph's policies as needed. He regarded a caliph's power as being no greater than that of the head of a constitutional government. And he wondered at ʿAbd al-Rāziq's dubious methodology in using literary anecdotes of uncertain authenticity from *al-ʿIqd al-Farīd* over clear, veracious texts from *Ṣaḥīḥ al-Bukhārī* and *Ṣaḥīḥ Muslim*, dropping from quotations key words that clarified their meaning, twisting other words beyond linguistic recognition, and taking phrases out of context to convey an impression that contradicted both the original passage and its classical commentators. al-Khiḍr also found it odd that ʿAbd al-Rāziq sought to box Islamic political traditions into European political philosophical categories where they did not fit. And al-Khiḍr even found it necessary to correct ʿAbd al-Rāziq's understanding of Thomas Hobbes (1588–1679).[33]

Even more outrageous in al-Khiḍr's eyes was ʿAbd al-Rāziq's dismissal of scriptural texts, analytical legal tools, and the rich history of Muslim engagement with political theory. While ʿAbd al-Rāziq claimed a dearth of Qur'anic verses and prophetic accounts validating the caliphate, al-Khiḍr cited a wealth of them. And in tracing the legislative weight of early scholarly consensus, al-Khiḍr argued that Islam had opened the horizons for intellectual investigation so that people could reach certainty based on clear proof and evidence. He invoked the verse "Do not follow blindly what you do not know to be true" (Qur'an 17:36) and lauded the early generations of Muslims' intellectual independence and freedom of thought—which made their areas of agreement all the more striking. As for the later divergence of al-Aṣamm, al-Khiḍr was bemused by ʿAbd al-Rāziq's misidentification of him as the Sufi mystic Ḥātim al-Aṣamm (d. 237/852) instead of the radical rationalist Abū Bakr ʿAbd al-Raḥmān b. Kaysān al-Aṣamm—which only underscored the contemporary Egyptian author's scholastic ineptitude. And on the question of political theory, al-Khiḍr cited the myriad contributions of dozens of Muslim authors over the centuries, be they early interpreters of Plato and Aristotle under the Abbasid Caliphate or later Muslim philosophers, jurists, and statesmen. al-Khiḍr further noted how Muslim rulers historically supported intellectual inquiry and the flourishing of arts and sciences. And in his own rebuttals of ʿAbd al-Rāziq's views, al-Khiḍr cites repeatedly from al-Juwaynī's seminal treatise that figured prominently in chapter 3, *Ghiyāth al-Umam*, revealing the vivacious endurance of the juristic tradition of Islamic political thought well into the twentieth century and several decades before the work's publication in 1980 from the original manuscripts. al-Khiḍr also cites on occasion from the writings of Aristotle and Montesquieu (1689–1755), among other European political theorists, revealing the breadth of his sources and interests. On the question of contemporary Islamic governance, al-Khiḍr was baffled by ʿAbd al-Rāziq's suggestions that a caliphate could theoretically take any political form including absolute, despotic, or Bolshevik ones, because, as al-Khiḍr argued, it was impossible for a caliphate to be absolute since it should be constrained by the law, or despotic since God and His prophet stressed the importance of consultation, or Bolshevik since Islamic law protected the property rights of individuals.[34]

In al-Khiḍr's frank estimation, the caliphate was in essence like a constitutional monarchy. The Islamic legal tradition required that the head of state be just, brave, erudite, wise, and experienced and that his government depend upon the indispensible principle and path of consultation. Such a caliphate, al-Khiḍr argued, was a sacred truth that Muslims needed so long as they continued to aspire to dignity and independence. And al-Khiḍr invoked stirring memories of the illustrious past of Muslims under earlier caliphates that promoted free public education and literacy while Europe—outside of Muslim Spain—scarcely had schools or colleges and restricted learning to the select few. al-Khiḍr acknowledged that the mere terms "caliph" and "caliphate" were not incantations; one could not simply label a ruler or government by them and expect it to heal every ill or to restore dignity and social justice all at once. Dignity and justice, al-Khiḍr contended, had to be earned through diligence, determination, and political wisdom. As he fondly remembered the Islamic caliphate, it had let people taste the sweetness of broad social justice and enabled them to experience the serenity of refined character and manners.[35]

As for the Prophet Muḥammad, al-Khiḍr affirmed his spiritual authority in the hearts of his community who believed in the truth and wisdom of the message he conveyed from God. But he also affirmed the necessity of social regulation—faith was not enough to deter people from socially harmful actions when overwhelmed by waves of passions, anger, or short-sighted interests. In order to preserve people's lives, property, and dignity, spiritual authority was not sufficient; it also required executive authority to institute civil and criminal law. Accordingly, al-Khiḍr explains, the authority of God's Messenger touched people's hearts, as a metaphor for belief and spirituality, and extended to their bodies, as a metaphor for social interaction and accountability. He was responsible for guiding and directing his followers to what was beneficial—as a wellspring of life—and his leadership was simultaneously religious and political. As al-Khiḍr elaborates, God conferred both of these dimensions of religious and political leadership, specifically in the Prophet's case, as guidance for humanity.

The Prophet's immediate successors, or caliphs, attempted to emulate his exemplary model, albeit without the benefit of direct access to continuing divine revelation. And al-Khiḍr marvels at ʿAbd al-Rāziq's audacity in claiming that the leadership of the Prophet's successors had no religious foundation or coloring. The caliphate of the Prophet's closest friend Abū Bakr, al-Khiḍr affirms, was an Islamic government striving to rule in accordance with divine guidance. As al-Khiḍr maintains, Abū Bakr and the other Rightly Guided Caliphs sought to lead the Muslim community according to its foundational principles and to fulfill the aims of the Sacred Law (*Sharīʿah*) to protect people's lives, religion, families, intellects, and property. al-Khiḍr argued that rather than offering an "antiquated system," Islam presented profound insights to help advance the social and political sciences, fruitful principles to help devise superior laws, and key foundations to help elevate human dignity.[36] In later years, the former Ottoman şeyhülislam Mustafa Sabri would commend both al-Khiḍr's and Bakhīt's detailed critiques "from head to toe" of *al-Islām wa-Uṣūl al-Ḥukm* with an estimation that he did not easily bestow upon the works of other scholars: "perfect" (*mükemmel*).[37]

MUSTAFA SABRİ (1869–1954)

In November 1922, the Ottoman scholar who had served at the pinnacle of the empire's religious hierarchy, the former şeyhülislam Mustafa Sabri, fled Istanbul for his life,[38] but facing the harsh consequences—even enduring exile—because of his outspoken political and intellectual views was not a new experience for this leading traditionalist scholar. Mustafa Sabri was born in the town of Tokat in the central Black Sea region of Anatolia on June 21, 1869, and completed memorizing the Qur'an before he was ten. He began his early education in Tokat before persuading his mother to intercede for his father's permission to continue his religious studies in Kayseri. From there, he went on to pursue more advanced studies in Istanbul, where he met and studied with Gümülcineli Ahmet Asım (1836–1911), the Şeyhülislam Office's Commissioner of Seminary Education (*Ders Vekili*). Mustafa Sabri's powerful intellect and depth of knowledge so impressed the distinguished scholar and administrator that he awarded Mustafa Sabri a diploma (*icazet*) within two years, encouraged him to take the advanced *Rüus* examinations as early as 1890, and married his stellar pupil to his own daughter in 1892. Mustafa Sabri's professional career included appointments teaching in seminaries, discoursing in the prestigious imperial lecture series, and working as private librarian for the Ottoman sultan Abdülhamid II. Politically, Mustafa Sabri bristled at the restrictions on free speech in the Hamidian era, and after the 1908 Young Turk Revolution, Mustafa Sabri actively strove to realize a constitutional democracy. He was elected as a Unionist candidate to the restored Ottoman Parliament in 1908 but became disillusioned with the CUP the following year when they blocked his popular legislative efforts to expand the codification and application of Islamic law in the *Mecelle* as the state's legal system.

Thereafter, Mustafa Sabri ranked among the prominent members of opposition to the Unionists and was repeatedly targeted for retaliation over the years. In 1913, after the CUP had to stage a coup to regain power, the party lost all semblance of tolerance with the vicissitudes of multi-party politics and openly arrested and deported hundreds of opposition members. Mustafa Sabri hastily fled abroad, leaving his property behind to be confiscated by the Unionist regime, which eventually managed to arrest him in Romania in 1917 and internally exile him to Bilecik in Anatolia. There he remained until Sultan Vahideddin issued amnesty to political prisoners in October 1918. [39] It was in this massive upheaval following World War I that Mustafa Sabri was first appointed as şeyhülislam in March 1919—a position from which he would resign and be reappointed four times over the next year and half. In total, Mustafa Sabri served a little over eight months as şeyhülislam in multiple cabinets of Damat Ferid Paşa during this tumultuous era.[40] And the disintegration of the Ottoman Empire soon found Mustafa Sabri a much-maligned refugee in Egypt because of his staunch opposition to the maneuverings of Mustafa Kemal whom many Egyptians revered as a new hero of Islam.[41]

Following the hostile reception in Egypt of his criticisms of the budding Kemalist revolution, Mustafa Sabri departed for Lebanon in January 1924.[42] Over the next month, he completed a book decrying what he called the blatant rejection of the blessings of religion, the caliphate, and the universal Muslim community, or *al-Nakīr ʿalā Munkirī al-Niʿmah min al-Dīn wa'l-Khilāfah wa'l-Ummah.* The appearance of Seyyid Bey's then-anonymous Turkish treatise *Hilafet ve Hakimiyet-i Milliye* along with Rashīd Riḍā's book *al-Khilāfah* in 1923 helped stir Mustafa Sabri to compose his own work. Riḍā's book was generally good and beneficial, he acknowledged, but even that critic of Westernization at the expense of Islam had not accurately diagnosed the perilous malady at the core. The rest of Egypt's religious scholars and intellectuals, as Mustafa Sabri deemed it, fared even worse in their assessments. Therefore, Mustafa Sabri sought to clarify that the new Turkish regime's separation of the caliphate from political power was actually intended to uproot Islamic law and religious practice over the long term. The noticeable change in the treatment of the Caliph Abdülmecid for no apparent reason over this short span of time told Mustafa Sabri that the ruling faction aimed to abolish the caliphate gradually, transfer power to Mustafa Kemal, and strip the state of its religious nature. Indeed, Mustafa Sabri's very definition of a caliphate implied as much: it was religious governance continuing to represent the Prophet Muḥammad in his community to the best of its ability. Therefore the Turkish Grand National Assembly had already taken the first step to strip the religious element from government by separating out the caliphate in November 1922. The caliphate, he explained, was a form of government, and just as one could not conceive of constitutional government or absolutist government without an actual government, so too was the caliphate devoid of meaning if it did not attempt to represent prophetically inspired governance and implement Islamic law.[43]

In response to those who would justify the Turkish nationalist distinction between a caliphate and a sultanate by harkening back to earlier moments in Islamic history, as analyzed in chapter 2, Mustafa Sabri wondered as an aside why they would pick the low points of the institution's past to emulate, but nevertheless he rejected any comparison between the two sets of arrangements. Past rulers required a formal investiture from caliphs to substantiate their legitimacy—but it was rather the reverse situation in contemporary Turkey with the Caliph Abdülmecid appearing to be the government's appointee. Moreover, such delegation in the past stipulated the ruler's execution of Islamic law, which was a far cry from the Kemalists' efforts to distance government from the caliphate to avoid being bound by religiosity. What happened in the past, Mustafa Sabri continued to argue, was run-of-the-mill assumptions of power (*al-taghallub al-ʿādī*) without any attempt to erode religious authority and influence or to separate it from worldly affairs. What was happening in the present, however, consisted more of a rebellion against Islam than against the individual person of the caliph. Epistemologically, Kemalists were not imitating historical models of the Islamic caliphate, Mustafa Sabri explained, they were instead drawing inspiration from French revolutionary principles separating church and state. In the past, delegated Muslim rulers (*mulūk*) conjoined their power with Islamic governance, so in actuality the caliphate transferred to these people who were entrusted with upholding Islamic legal rulings.[44] Mustafa Sabri's argument that the caliphate could not be distinguished from its actual implementation (*idh lā tanfakk al-khilāfah ʿan al-fiʿl*) continued the lengthy Islamic legal discourse discussed in chapter 3 that recognized the state's actual executive as its legal head (*al-imām al-aʿẓam*) or caliph. If Mustafa Kemal had wanted, Mustafa Sabri pointed out, he could have had himself recognized as caliph, following this tradition, and Muslims around the world would have happily acquiesced. He was after all widely hailed as the hero of Islam and the restorer of its glory, and Muslims no longer felt compelled to limit a caliph's lineage to Quraysh alone as they had with the Abbasid caliphs in Baghdad and Cairo. That Mustafa Kemal did not choose this path was proof of his clique's aversion to the state's religious character: Mustafa Kemal and his collaborators took what they wanted, political power, and tossed aside what they despised, the Islamic caliphate.[45]

In Mustafa Sabri's estimation, an Islamic caliphate was necessarily comprised of two essential components: government (*ḥukūmah*) and faithful representation of the Prophet (*niyābah*). Neither element without the other could be designated a caliphate. Yet in *al-Nakīr*, Mustafa Sabri also opened the door of caliphal designation more widely: any Islamic government that fulfilled these two conditions might be considered a caliphate. In other words, even though it was customary to recognize only one caliphate at a time, Mustafa Sabri embraced the prospect of multiplicity. Indeed, he argued that if it was permissible, even necessary, for there to be multiple governments to conduct the affairs of Muslims in distant lands, then there was no obstacle to recognizing multiple caliphates since it meant those governments would be Islamically inspired. He conceded that it would be preferable for there to be one caliph for all Muslims, as Riḍā had wished, but Mustafa Sabri could not help but doubt whether that was at all possible given contemporary circumstances. Ever the jurist, Mustafa Sabri was keenly focused on the application of Islamic law in realistic terms, not abstract ideals. His resolution of allowing for multiple Islamically inspired governments therefore stemmed from Islamic legal guidelines on the caliphate that recognized and perpetuated its essential elements of religious governance in a new landscape of emerging nation-states. Nevertheless, Mustafa Sabri still hoped that there might be a chance for the restoration of the Ottoman Caliphate to power—perhaps the Grand National Assembly might be persuaded by the Islamic world's displeasure with their experiment separating the caliphate and sultanate to try to dissemble their true colors and rescind the separation.[46] Yet it was not to be.

Less than one month after Mustafa Sabri completed his book on February 7, 1924, the Turkish Grand National Assembly confirmed his initial grim assessment and abolished the Ottoman Caliphate once and for all. Mustafa Sabri inserted a strident addendum to his Arabic book *al-Nakīr* on March 20 noting that the regime's actions affirmed all that he had written in the book. In writing the manuscript, he said, he had aimed to establish two overarching facts: first, that the Kemalists, who were Unionists by another name, were enemies of religion, and second, that they were despotic tyrants and enemies of freedom too. In the aftermath of the caliphate's abolition, though, Mustafa Sabri also sought to respond to some of the specific claims circulating in Republican Turkish newspapers. Without mentioning Seyyid Bey by name, Mustafa Sabri refuted his argument that the Muslim community no longer needed a caliph who was only their delegate anyway and dispensable now that they had decided to take matters into their own hands. The caliph was not a delegate, Mustafa Sabri asserted, but rather the Prophet's successor. And the Muslim community's assuming direct control of its affairs would mean abolishing all forms of government (not just the caliphate) and inaugurating a state of anarchy instead. If the Muslim community had truly wanted to rid itself of delegated representatives, that would necessarily include the Grand National Assembly in Ankara too.

Yet Mustafa Sabri also refuted the newspapers' assertions that these dramatic changes, including the abolition of the caliphate and the Islamic legal courts, were an expression of popular will. If that were the case, he countered, what was the need to establish Independence Tribunals all over Turkey to threaten people with the death penalty for voicing support for the caliphate, the legal courts, and religiosity? And what was the need to pass the High Treason Law branding expression of these views as a treasonable crime? Rather Mustafa Sabri described the unfortunate Turkish nation as deeply devout. And he placed culpability for this dastardly turn of events squarely at the feet of its commanding leader, Mustafa Kemal, who had carefully cultivated the laic revolutionary climate. Muslims elsewhere, like those in Egypt, had unwittingly poured immense sums of money into supporting this effort all the while thinking that they were supporting the caliphate. Would they now support the preservation of Islam among Turks, Mustafa Sabri wondered? With the rise of an assertively secular and atheistic regime built on the demolition of the Ottoman Empire that had done so much to sustain Islamic values and institutions, the religious scholar was deeply concerned about the future of Turks, Turkey, and Muslims everywhere.[47]

Mustafa Sabri later published an Ottoman Turkish article recapitulating the pith of a caliphate in light of these developments. Muslims deserved a government that would try to follow the path of the Prophet Muḥammad as closely as possible, he argued, and an individual worthy of succeeding him should be head of state. It was no excuse to claim disingenuously that there was no one worthy of this task in order to abolish the caliphal institution, since it was rare for any one to represent the magnificent and magnanimous Prophet adequately. For that reason, Mustafa Sabri explained, Islamic works of jurisprudence utilized the phrase *imamet-i kübra* to refer to state leadership rather than the term *hilafet*, or caliphate, which implied succession to the Prophet's rule. Yet there could be no hesitation in trying so long as an Islamic state with a leader acting more or less consistently with the Prophet's great work was deemed necessary. Mustafa Kemal, Mustafa Sabri explicated, did not abolish the caliphate due to a dearth of people worthy of the Prophet's caliphate or due to the impossibility of uniting Muslims in the present. Instead, Mustafa Sabri interpreted Kemal's actions as a reflection of the value that the leader placed on religious guidance:

> Perhaps he abolished [the caliphate] because he did not consider the Prophet worthy of being followed [*istihlafa şayan*] and because he was convinced that the implementation of Islamic laws based on Qur'anic verses and prophetic traditions was worthless in this civilized century—which is absolutely no different from saying that Islam could not have any value in this civilized century. All of the Ankara government's actions in the name of the Turkish revolution as well as the following statements of this government's most authoritative dignitaries attest loudly to these facts.

For proof, Mustafa Sabri quoted the Turkish minister of justice Mahmut Esat (Bozkurt) (1892–1943) that it was nonsensical to tie the Turkish nation to medieval rules in a time of modern civilization. This attitude, Mustafa Sabri felt, was an injustice to the many merits of Islamic history and to the inherent value that Islam had to offer people in every day and age.[48]

To add insult to injury, Egypt's Supreme Council decision to no longer recognize the caliphate of the exiled Abdülmecid highlighted a painful paradox. Mustafa Sabri was outraged that the country's religious scholars had not come to his defense when he had publicly argued only a matter of months before[49] that the caliphate could not be separated from political power (*sulṭah* in Arabic and *saltanat* in Turkish). Now Egyptian scholars themselves deployed this argument to delegitimize the defenseless caliphate of Abdülmecid—but where were they, he asked, when Egypt's journalists were attacking Mustafa Sabri in the press left and right for those same views? In Mustafa Sabri's acrimonious reading, they had known it was the truth all along but only raised their voices to follow in the trails of the Kemalist regime. Why had they remained silent from November 1922 to March 1924 and hence complicit to the caliphate's assassination, Mustafa Sabri wondered? Then afterwards why hadn't they initiated the caliphate's resuscitation on a new and surer footing by first denouncing Ankara's destruction of the sacred institution?[50]

Mustafa Sabri tried to assume this vast undertaking himself. After roughly eight more months in Lebanon from the time of the caliphate's abolition, Mustafa Sabri moved again to Romania, then relocated in 1927 to Gümülcine, or Komotini, in Western Thrace, which had become part of modern Greece. From these former lands of the Ottoman Empire, Mustafa Sabri kept abreast of and continued to censure developments in the new and nearby Turkish Republic. During these years of exile in neighboring Europe, Mustafa Sabri penned a series of articles on Islamic governance or "İslam'da İmamet-i Kübra" that were published in his Ottoman Turkish-language journal *Yarın* and later collected as a single volume. In part, Mustafa Sabri highlighted the contradictions of the Ankara government's past claims: in 1922, it was acceptable to separate the caliphate from the government as a unique entity, but in 1924, Ankara explained that the caliphate meant government in order to abolish it entirely. And he continued to underscore the new regime's underlying irreligious bent.[51]

Moreover, the publication of ʿAlī ʿAbd al-Rāziq's book *al-Islām wa-Uṣūl al-Ḥukm* and its swift translation into Turkish as *İslamiyet ve Hükümet*[52] gravely concerned Mustafa Sabri. For all of Seyyid Bey's pernicious arguments, Mustafa Sabri was astounded to discover that ʿAbd al-Rāziq went even further to negate the place of a caliphate in Islam. The Ankara clique had improperly utilized a prophetic ḥadīth to dismiss the legal validity of post-Rāshidūn caliphs and rationalize the institution's abolition, but, inconceivably, ʿAbd al-Rāziq negated the Islamic foundations for the reign of the first few caliphs altogether. Mustafa Sabri found this position absurd, but the enthusiasm with which it was received in Ankara only confirmed his misgivings that the true purpose of abolishing the caliphate was to secularize governance. ʿAbd al-Rāziq's article in the Egyptian newspaper *al-Siyāsah* openly supported the Ankara government and underscored their shared interests. Yet Mustafa Sabri also noticed that Ömer Rıza's Turkish translations distorted the original Arabic text in some places to create the illusion of a more definitive rejection of Islamic governance than the author originally conveyed. Perplexed by the resulting textual and religious inconsistencies, Mustafa Sabri wondered how something that God had focused so much on in His Book could have nothing to do with Islam. Or, he inquired, were some parts of the Qur'an religious and others not? As for ʿAbd al-Rāziq's contention that the caliphs later in Islamic history had been reduced to mere symbols without political power, Mustafa Sabri demurred, arguing that numerous Islamic governments had legitimately substituted for the caliphate by establishing Islamic principles and regulations. He reiterated that he accepted a regular ruler as a caliph if he protected people's religious and worldly affairs and attempted to follow in the Prophet's footsteps, and he affirmed his view that Islamic government was necessarily constitutional. In light of these proffered arguments and contemporary political developments in Turkey, Mustafa Sabri worried that antireligious governments in the wake of the caliphate's abolition would inescapably affect the nature of Islamic principles and sovereignty.[53]

In 1928, the Republic of Turkey finally removed the mention of Islam as the state's religion from its constitution. In response, Mustafa Sabri declared that the Kemalists had finally dropped their masks to reveal their true identities. Mustafa Sabri noted that Mustafa Kemal had divulged the deception involved in the revolution's early years during his marathon speech of October 1927, and had confessed that he included the provision stating Islam as the official religion of the country merely to assuage some deputies who could not leave the beliefs of the past behind in order to abolish the caliphate—all the while planning to abolish this provision as soon as possible.[54] Mustafa Sabri acknowledged the genius behind Mustafa Kemal's strategy to lead people step by step to irreligiosity through one compromise after another, yet he could hardly condone it. On the contrary, he condemned the deceit that had kept unwary people complacent through the presence of this lifeless phrase in the Turkish constitution. And now he rebuffed the new tactics that depicted its removal as harmless. Implementation of Islamic law previously belonged to the caliphate, and when it was abolished in 1924 that responsibility was, at least theoretically, transferred to the Grand National Assembly. Yet these new modifications removed even that. Proponents of this amendment asked rhetorically how a state could have a religion; could it pray or fast? Mustafa Sabri mocked their selective reification: How could a state have a language but not a religion? Was it not commonly said that the state made war or made peace? Trying to clear the haze, Mustafa Sabri explained that the rhetorical notion of a state consists in reality of a people (*millet*), a homeland (*memleket*), and a government (*hükümet*). Therefore, "to abrogate the religion of a state is to abrogate the religion of the nation," he argued, for how could a nation stay religious (*dinli*) when the government is explicitly irreligious (*dinsiz*), utilizing the contrasting Turkish terms to be *with* or *without* religion. A government is necessary to enjoin the good in society and to dissuade the harmful (*marufu emir ve münkeri nehy* or *al-amr bi'l-ma'rūf wa'l-nahy 'an al-munkar*), and Mustafa Sabri observed that even Christian nations that separate religion from worldly affairs do not entirely renounce religion's interest in and relevance to politics. Moreover, Mustafa Sabri explicated, Islam does not allow its followers to think only of themselves; it encourages them to think about general public interest and concerns.[55]

Ironically, the secularist policies of Turkey continued to persecute Mustafa Sabri in neighboring Greece and ultimately dislodged the eminent scholar from his nettling perch. Seeking rapprochement between the two countries, the Greek prime minister Eleftherios Venizelos (1864–1936) promised the Kemalist regime to defuse the irksome activities of Mustafa Sabri and other religious scholars who were agitating for change. Accordingly, the Greek government halted publication of *Yarın* in 1930 and exiled the scholarly refugee to far-off Patras, the regional capital of the Peloponnesian peninsula in western Greece. Mustafa Sabri was displaced from a city with a sizeable Turkish Muslim population bordering contemporary Turkey to an overwhelmingly Greek Orthodox Christian center in the far west that had been one of the starting points of the 1821 Greek Revolution. Welcomed by the local Christian clergy but feeling sorely isolated, Mustafa Sabri sought asylum elsewhere and ultimately received permission to settle in Egypt with his family.[56]

Arriving in Cairo on January 20, 1932, (during the holy month of Ramaḍān), Mustafa Sabri received a warmer welcome this time around and would stay in Egypt for the last twenty-two years of his life with renewed purpose. Developments in Turkey had borne out his predictions of authoritarian secularization, and the classically trained Ottoman scholar was highly respected and integrated into Egypt's intellectual circles. He actively participated in the country's profound discussions and heated debates. In 1942, one of Mustafa Mustafa Sabri's publications, *al-Qawl al-Faṣl bayn Alladhīna Yu'minūna bi'l-Ghayb wa'lladhīna Lā Yu'minūn*, came to the attention of Egypt's heir to the throne Prince Muḥammad 'Alī Tawfīq (1875–1955), and he invited the aging scholar to his Manyal Palace. There, he apologized for not being the one to visit Mustafa Sabri in person and for not having known of his presence in Cairo earlier. Upon the Egyptian prince's insistence, Mustafa Sabri thereafter received a royal honorary stipend in addition to the one bestowed by Egypt's Ministry of Charitable Endowments.[57]

With the definitive establishment of an assertively secular Republic of Turkey built on the ashes of the Ottoman Caliphate and the increasing exclusion of religion from Egypt's political sphere, Mustafa Sabri retrained his focus on the epistemological and ontological struggles of contemporary Muslims. As Mehmet Kadri Karabela argues:

> Sabri emphasized that the epistemic structure of Islamic thought had collapsed. As a result, the Muslim intellect would have to learn how to conceptualize and to formulate systematically *its own positions* on what "being" (ontology) is and what "knowledge" (epistemology) is *in terms intelligible to others,* as this would enable them to present the Muslim faith as a living and comprehensible phenomenon in their own age.[58]

Three years after the end of the Second World War, Mustafa Sabri began to crystalize these critical thoughts into his four-volume magnum opus *Mawqif al-ʿAql wa'l-ʿIlm wa'l-ʿĀlam min Rabb al-ʿĀlamīn wa-ʿIbādihi al-Mursalīn,* which he hoped would help educated Muslims grasp contemporary intellectual and philosophical issues from a solid foundation and thereby maintain their theological integrity. Sound knowledge, he held, was the critical link between religion and the world and would ultimately help them achieve success in their everyday lives and their hereafter. In elucidating this path forward, Mustafa Sabri further hoped that he would at long last fulfill his father's wishes by exhibiting scholarly devotion and thus achieve divine pleasure.[59]

After strenuously trying to hold on to conceptions of the caliphate rooted in Islamic law, Mustafa Sabri acknowledged that securing its actual implementation had slipped out of his grasp. He had argued that maintaining the religious character of governance was at the heart of an Islamic caliphate and that it was possible—even necessary—for there to be many such constitutional governments emulating prophetic guidance to the best of their ability. Yet faced with the surge of secular governance and modern European philosophies, Mustafa Sabri shifted to an even more basic struggle for the rest of his life: preserving the cognitive frameworks of Islam for a new generation of Muslims.

SAİD NURSİ (1876–1960)

In the aftermath of World War I, the devastating defeat of the Ottoman Empire weighed heavily upon another religious scholar, the Kurdish Said Nursi, who hailed from the village of Nurs in the Eastern provinces. Gifted with a prodigious memory, Nursi rapidly absorbed scores of religious texts to the extent that one of his *medrese* teachers first named him, Bediuzzaman or "The Wonder of the Age." In 1892, Nursi was politically awakened by the vision of Ottomanism and freedom eloquently articulated by Namık Kemal (1840–88) in his famous *Rüya* or *Dream.* And he was also inspired by reports of Jamāl al-Dīn al-Afghānī's (1839–97) pan-Islamism and the efforts of the Sanūsiyyah spiritual order to defend North Africa from colonial incursion. Arriving in Istanbul in late 1907, Nursi developed close ties to the CUP and avidly advocated an Islamic vision of constitutionalism in his speeches and writing over the next decade. Upon the declaration of war in 1914, Nursi immediately volunteered, serving first as a regimental chaplain (*müftü*) of the Thirty-Third Division in Van and later as a regimental commander of the militia that in local and imperial memory valiantly defended his home province of Bitlis against Russian invasion. After holding off the Russian forces, Nursi and his surviving troop of volunteers became prisoners of war in March 1916. Over two long years later, Nursi was able to escape amid the confusion of the Bolshevik Revolution and eventually made his way back to Istanbul, arriving in June 1918. The leading Unionist newspaper *Tanin* commemorated his arrival.[60]

Nursi was especially close to the prominent Unionist Enver Paşa during this early period. Enver offered to publish the scholar's Arabic treatise on the miraculousness of the Qur'an, *Ishārat al-I'jāz*, written on the Eastern front, but Nursi suggested that Enver procure the valuable paper instead. Still in his post as Ottoman war minister, Enver also wrote to Şeyhülislam Musa Kazım on August 10, 1918, requesting that Nursi, commensurate with his learning and service, be appointed as one of the founding members of the official Islamic Academy, *Dar'ül-Hikmet'il-İslamiye*. While serving on this council, Nursi used his salary to publish many of his early epistles, and from his official perch, he assailed the British who had occupied the Ottoman capital. There, Nursi overlapped with Mustafa Sabri; both were involved in the Association of Seminary Teachers (*Cemiyet-i Müderrisin*) established in 1919 and were affiliated with the Offices of the Şeyhülislam.[61] Yet their political views differed starkly.

In occupied Istanbul, Nursi vigorously defended the Turkish War of Independence then being waged in Anatolia. When the Şeyhülislam's Office issued a fatwa in April 1920 condemning the national resistance movement, Nursi retorted in print:

> A fatwa issued by a government and Şeyhülislam's Office in a country under enemy occupation and under the command and constraint of the British is defective and should not be heeded. Those operating against the enemy invasion are not rebels. The fatwa must be rescinded.

And in his *Hutuvat-ı Sitte*, Nursi tried to counter British manipulation of such differences between political and ideological contingents and to muster support for the national resistance movement with religious argumentation. On the strength of this service to the nationalist cause, Mustafa Kemal and other Unionist leaders of the resistance movement repeatedly invited Nursi to join them in Ankara. Nursi declined, citing his preference to stay in the heat of existential battle in Istanbul, but he continued to offer advice to the nascent Grand Nationalist Assembly that he deemed as the new center of the Islamic World (*alem-i İslam'ın mütemerkiz noktası*).[62]

By late 1922, Nursi acquiesced and arrived in Ankara, only to become disillusioned with the increasingly irreligious tone and dismal direction he saw its leadership adopting. By that point, the Bolsheviks had killed Enver in Central Asia, and his rival Mustafa Kemal had consolidated his dominance of the nationalist movement following the momentous victory in Sakarya. The Turkish assembly had separated the Ottoman Caliphate from the sultanate, arrogating the powers of the latter for itself. A little over a week later, a formal motion in the assembly recognized Nursi's presence there on November 9, 1922. And after everyone greeted the well-known scholar with applause, the speaker welcomed him to the podium, where he offered encouraging words and prayers. On November 23, 1922, Nursi wrote a personal letter to Mustafa Kemal, whom he respectfully addressed as "The Hero of the Islamic World" (*Alem-i İslam kahramanı Paşa Hazretlerine*)—beneath an elegantly penned heading of the Qur'anic verse enjoining believers to pray (4:103). Nursi's ten points of advice were subsequently circulated among the assembly deputies roughly three months later as a separate letter addressed to them, urging that they perform their Islamic duties, and especially the five daily prayers. Nursi stressed that not only did the assembly now represent the sultanate, but it also had to represent the caliphate adequately in order to ward off dissension, corruption, and disunity. Through their acts of piety, the deputies could constitute a collective spirit that would soar in the modern age, and the person of caliph could only undertake his duties by relying upon such a collectivity. The deputies must not let that special community be ruined by abandoning the lofty standards of Islam. Nursi even recalled scolding an offended Mustafa Kemal, who was reportedly displeased with the resulting swelling of religious sentiment and practice in his midst, and the Kurdish scholar emphasized that Qur'anic guidance should inspire any future changes. In turn, Mustafa Kemal offered Nursi a lucrative and prestigious preaching post out in the Eastern Provinces, which had recently belonged to Shaykh al-Sanūsī, as well as status as a deputy and official scholar, all of which Nursi declined. While Mustafa Sabri had recognized the writing on the wall and fled the country in 1922, Nursi chose another path the following year in Ankara and declared his intention to abandon political engagement all together and plunge into spiritual retreat.[63]

After the dust of the Unionist and Kemalist revolutions had settled, Nursi would decide that the Ottoman Caliphate had already died in 1326 of the Rumi calendar, corresponding to the aftermath of the CUP's decision to depose Sultan Abdülhamid II in 1909.[64] Even though Nursi had criticized the despotic tendencies of the Hamidian era, he later recognized that sultan's reign as the last one to combine a potent caliphate and sultanate in one unified government, executed by the bureaucracies of the şeyhülislam and the grand vizier respectively. But while in the throes of an idealistic future, Nursi had envisioned the caliphate first as an Ottoman constitutional and consultative institution in the 1910s and then as a nationalist collective and representative one in the 1920s. By the 1930s though, Nursi had concluded that the caliphate had simply reached its age limit, and he had washed his hands of any political aspirations on its behalf. In 1925, as the unrest led by the Naqshbandi Shaykh Said spread through Southeast Anatolia, Nursi scathingly criticized the very idea of rebellion as contravening Islamic law and morality (*Sharī'ah*) and dissuaded some

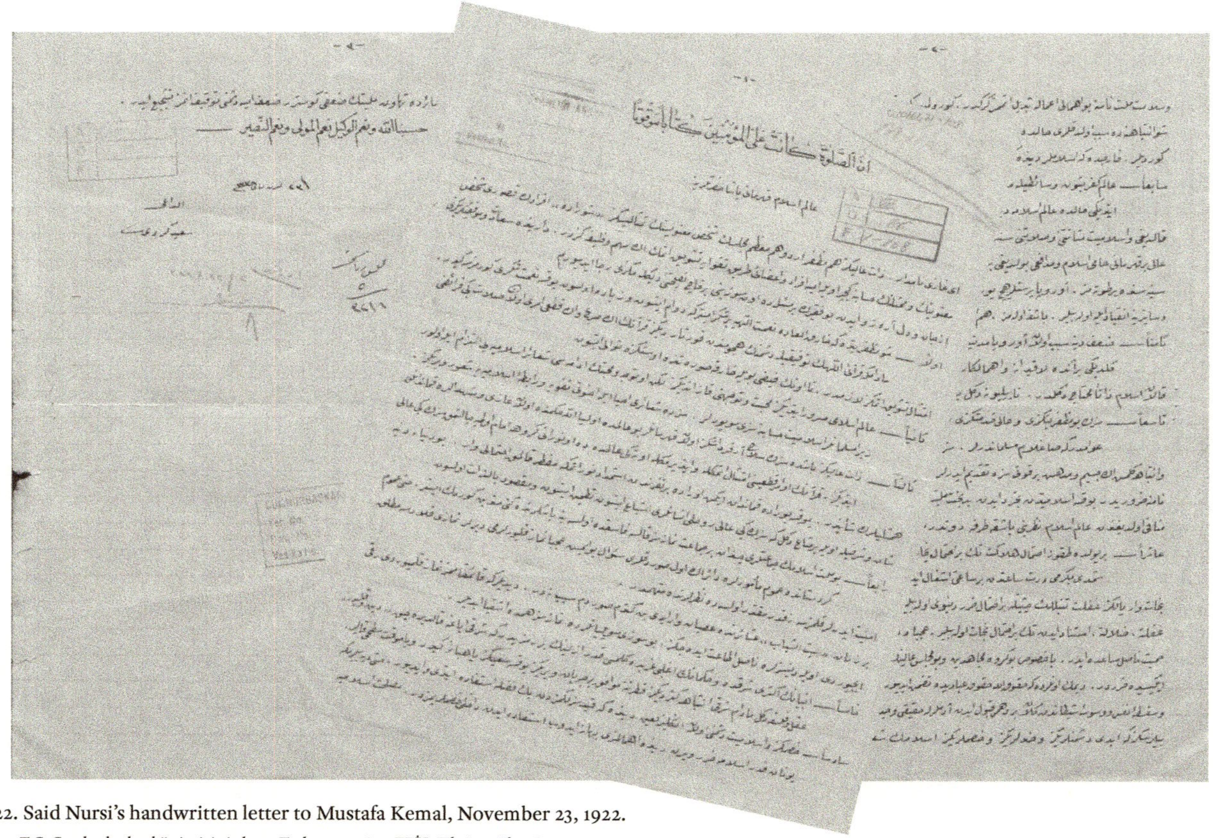

FIGURE 22. Said Nursi's handwritten letter to Mustafa Kemal, November 23, 1922.

Image courtesy T.C. Cumhurbaşkanlığı Arşivi, Ankara, Turkey, 01016471 EBİS, Fihrist 1, Ek-108.

tribes from any involvement. Instead of politics, Nursi was preoccupied with what he perceived to be a greater mission, preserving people's faith in an age of materialist philosophy and atheism.

Yet the Kemalist regime had not yet finished with him, and among the major fault lines were some eschatological predictions that Nursi had made in occupied Istanbul, while working at the official Islamic Academy. In particular, Nursi's early interpretations of the Antichrist (*deccal* in Turkish and *dajjāl* in Arabic) came to be read as subversive. An indictment drawn up in 1948 objected to one passage in Nursi's essay, known as the Fifth Ray (*Beşinci Şua*),[65] that had interpreted a prophetic tradition in modern terms, envisioning one possible antichrist among several who bore an unnerving resemblance to Mustafa Kemal in light of his policies and demeanor many years later. In his defense, Nursi explained:

> Forty years ago and the year before Freedom, I came to Istanbul. At the time, the Japanese Commander-in-Chief had asked the Muslim scholars some questions of religious content. The Istanbul *hocas* asked me about them, and taking this opportunity, they also asked me about many other things. In short, they asked me about a prophetic report (*ḥadīth*) that says: "At the end of time a fearsome person will get up in the morning and 'This is a disbeliever' will be found written on his forehead." I explained, "An astonishing person will come to lead this nation. He will get up in the morning, put a hat on his head, and make others wear it." After this answer, they asked: "Won't those who wear it become disbelievers?" I said, "The hat will be worn on the head, and it will say: 'Do not go into prostration [in prayer].' But the faith in the head will make the hat prostrate and, God willing, become Muslim." Then they said: "The same person will drink a [kind of] water, a hole will open in his hand, and through this behavior it will become known that he is Süfyan?" I replied to answer: "There is a saying that someone who is very wasteful has a hole in his hand. That is, possessions do not remain in his hand; they flow away and are lost. Thus, that fearsome person will be addicted to *rakı* [a Turkish alcoholic beverage], which is a sort of water; he will become ill through it, and he will become infinitely wasteful and make others accustomed to being wasteful too." Then one of them asked: "When he dies, Satan will shout out to the world from the obelisk in Istanbul: 'So-and-so has died!'" At that time I said, "The news will be announced by telegraph." But some time later I heard that the radio had been invented, and I understood that my earlier response was not complete. So eight years later, while in the Darü'l-Hikmet, I said, "It will be broadcast throughout the world by radio, like Satan." Then they asked me questions about the barrier of Zülkarneyn [*Dhū'l-Qarnayn*], Gog and Magog, the Dabbetü'l-Arz [*Dābbat al-Arḍ*], the Antichrist, and the second coming of Jesus (God's peace be upon him). I also answered them. Some of these answers are even partly written in my old treatises.[66]

Decades after these predictions, the Turkish Republican state establishment was disconcerted by the possible perception of the nation's fearless leader, Mustafa Kemal Atatürk, as an antichrist. He was after all known for adopting and forcing others to wear European-style hats on penalty of death, indulging in lavish extravagances, and ultimately succumbing to his alcoholism. But when faced with the objections of official religious functionaries, Nursi affirmed the validity of his interpretation within the scope of ḥadīth sciences. And he pointed to another ḥadīth of the Prophet Muḥammad as evidence that it was conceivable for such predictions to miraculously come true, namely the prophetic statement that the caliphate will continue with the sons of my uncle al-ʿAbbās until it passes into the destructive hands of the antichrist. In multiple places, Nursi clearly identifies the Mongol commander Hülegü as the antichrist fulfilling this particular prophecy.[67] And although Nursi does not explicitly draw out these conclusions for the court, the resulting parallel between Hülegü as an antichrist who ended the Abbasid Caliphate and Mustafa Kemal as a modern antichrist who abolished the Ottoman Caliphate is striking. In response to the state's security concerns though, Nursi insisted that his prior commentary in the *Fifth Ray* "dispels doubts on questions of belief, does not disturb public order, is not confrontational, and only gives information, does not specify any individuals, and sets out a scholarly truth in general form." Furthermore, it had been kept confidential and withheld from circulation to avoid causing dissension, that is, until the courts themselves had made it public.[68]

Although Nursi's allegorical insights had been expressed long before the declaration of the Turkish Republic and its revolutionary Kemalist policies, justice in the Republican court system could be prosecuted retroactively. In articulating his defense in Afyon in 1948, Nursi was weary of nearly two decades of persecution. By that point, he had been repeatedly exiled to remote regions, interrogated, imprisoned, put in solitary confinement, poisoned, tried, and acquitted for nonexistent crimes against the state. Mustafa Kemal had effectively eliminated his Unionist competition by 1926, but an apolitical religious revival inspired by the charismatic Nursi posed a more lasting perceived threat. The never-ending accusations and charges against him, Nursi exclaimed, were all various guises to confront the same issue, whether it was called composing his collected writings, the "*Risale-i Nur*," "organizing a political society," "founding a Sufi order," or "the possibility of breaching security and disturbing public order."[69] Since the courts had found only a small smattering of words to be objectionable based on a superficial reading, Nursi saw no reason why the authorities could not simply excise the passages in question and permit the free circulation of his compositions that people had otherwise painstakingly copied out by hand. His work as a whole, Nursi countered, was proven to preserve Islamic beliefs that were vital for the nation's success as well as securing public order and stability.[70]

In deflecting the charge of engaging in potentially seditious political activity, Nursi tried to convey to the courts that he believed in something more precious than politics. Article 163 of the Turkish Criminal Code that was established in 1926 as part of the early Republic's secularization efforts made it a crime to exploit religion for political reasons and thereby endanger the state. Yet Nursi insisted that political involvement was beneath the *Risale-i Nur* and his aspiration to serve the Qur'an through it. He had no interest in using the *Risale-i Nur* as a political tool lest impressionable people confuse "the diamond-like truths of the Qur'an" it exposed with the glass shards of politics that were inherently divisive and devoid of compassion. To the contrary, Nursi believed that the *Risale-i Nur* advanced compassion as an essential building block of public order and encouraged obedience to the law. Dabbling in the tumults of politics could only endanger one's sincerity and independence, and Nursi had entirely abandoned political activity for over two decades—evincing no lingering appetite or desire for it and not even reading or listening to newspapers over the past eight years. Why would he deign, Nursi proffered, to sacrifice all his endeavors to attain an eternal, heavenly life through serving Islamic belief and the Qur'an for the sake of a mere few years of debased worldly life?[71]

Indeed, Nursi's understanding of the superiority of the spiritual domain over the base world of politics permeated his interpretation of seminal moments in Islamic history. He addressed questions about ʿAlī and the immediate family of the Prophet's agonizing lack of political success by explaining that it was through such travails that God had prepared them for something greater: spiritual dominion. Nursi read the Qur'anic verse (48:29) as referring to the Rightly Guided Caliphs of the Sunni tradition: Abū Bakr was among *those who are in his company* as Muḥammad the Messenger of God's closest friend, ʿUmar was *firm against the disbelievers,* ʿUthmān was among those who were *tender among themselves,* and ʿAlī was later seen *kneeling and prostrating, seeking God's pleasure and bounty* as the fourth caliph. In other words, Nursi's reading of this verse affirmed the Sunni sequencing of the Muslim community's virtuous leaders following the Prophet Muḥammad's death and underscored ʿAlī's upright stance during his caliphate. Yet despite his extraordinary merits, intelligence, and abilities, ʿAlī, as some might wonder, was less successful at the helm of state than his predecessors. This discrepancy, Nursi argued, was because God was preparing the Prophet's blessed son-in-law to become the king of saints (*şah-ı velayet*) through defending religious principles in the face of Muʿāwiyah's political expediency. Likewise, the Prophet's beloved grandsons al-Ḥasan and al-Ḥusayn were destined to become the fount of spiritual guides who would inherit the prophetic mission and teach people how to balance and perfect their character. They witnessed the ugly side of worldly politics at the hands of the Umayyads so that they would not feel any attachment to it in their hearts. They lost a transient, superficial rule only to gain a permanent, resplendent one and thus became the authorities of the world's spiritual poles instead of commonplace governors. al-Ḥasan and al-Ḥusayn and their pious descendants held in check the tyranny of the Umayyads who had placed the bonds of nationalism before those of Islam. Surely, Nursi read contemporary events through the prism of this paradigmatic past. The tyrannical nationalism with which he wrestled in the early Republican era was Turkish rather than Arab, but he was devoted to forwarding the cause of a merciful Islam over chauvinistic arrogations of power and corruption.[72]

Even in the face of Turkish Republican restrictions on religious institutions, Nursi continued to espouse deep reverence for the Sufi path and its pious saints. In one of his letters, Nursi sought to clarify that Sufism was "a lovely, light-giving, spiritual, sacred truth" (*hakikat-i kudsiye*) and lamented how some superficial scholars and heedless politicians aimed to destroy the spiritual path and "dry up this pure source of the water of life." Spiritually, people seeking success in the hereafter could attain immense benefit from following a Sufi path, or *ṭarīqah*, in keeping with the prophetic way, and Sufis had managed to safeguard belief at the most critical junctures. Hence, Nursi maintained, it was precisely these networks of Sufis that had preserved the Ottoman Caliphate for so long. These spiritual orders, he explained, had been the most eminent and effective means of spreading and strengthening the sacred bonds of brotherhood among Muslims and protecting their domains. "What preserved Istanbul, the center of the Caliphate for five hundred and fifty years," Nursi elaborated:

> was the lights of monotheism that poured out from five hundred locations in Istanbul. And an important support for believers in that center of Islam was the powerful faith of the devout invoking God in the dervish lodges behind those grand mosques, crying out "Allah! Allah!," and going into rapture with the spiritual pleasure derived from gnosis of God.[73]

These spiritual devotees had preserved Islamic belief in the Ottoman capital, and the lights of this pure monotheism had in turn protected the seat of the caliphate for centuries.

In fact, the demise of the Ottoman Caliphate in Nursi's eyes stemmed from its politicians' loss of religious direction in the same way that the governing elite of the late Abbasids had deviated and perished. For Nursi, this was another allegorical interpretation of a prophetic tradition. Nursi recalled that the Prophet Muḥammad was reported to have said that if his community continued to be upright, it would have one day. And if it did not continue to be upright, it would have half a day. Utilizing a Qur'anic verse (32:5) to measure a metaphysical day in terms of a thousand years, Nursi creatively argued that the ḥadīth did not refer to the end of time but rather to the duration of the Muslim community's rule and sovereignty under an Islamic caliphate. In his analysis, the Abbasid Caliphate lasted for half a day or roughly five hundred years since its politicians lost their way, and because the Muslim community as a whole had not deviated from the Straight Path, the Ottoman Caliphate came to its assistance for another five hundred years or so. For Nursi, the demise of the Ottoman Caliphate, calamitous as it was, affirmed a miraculous prediction of the Prophet Muḥammad centuries ago.[74]

Yet if the maelstrom of the Ottoman Caliphate's abolition constituted a major calamity—as had the loss of the Abbasid Caliphate before,[75] Nursi's insight that turbulence ultimately gives life to greater benefit meant that he still retained immense hope for the future and anticipated the good that would come out of all this turmoil. For Nursi, the future promised even stronger bonds of brotherhood that would be rooted in Islamic principles of compassion.[76] In naming his collection of essays *Risale-i Nur*, or *The Epistles of Light*, he may have hoped that his readers—or students as he called them—would become luminous beacons of guidance in the way of the saints of the Islamic tradition before. In this understanding, saints and students alike called for public order and stability in the outward domain and filled the inner world of the soul with light and serenity.

EPILOGUE

THE SWIRL OF RELIGIOUS HOPES AND ASPIRATIONS

The [Muslim] Brothers believe that the caliphate is the symbol of Islamic unity and the manifestation of the bond between Muslim communities and that it is an Islamic rite about which Muslims must think and pay attention to its affair. And the caliph is essential to many laws in God's religion.... Therefore, the Muslim Brothers place the idea of the caliphate and working to restore it at the head of their programs, and they believe that this needs much indispensable preparatory work.

—ḤASAN AL-BANNĀ, FOUNDER OF THE SOCIETY OF MUSLIM BROTHERS, 1938[1]

"I seek refuge in God from Satan and politics!"

—SAİD NURSİ, AUTHOR OF *RİSALE-İ NUR*, 1928[2]

IN THE MID-1920S, a young Egyptian was profoundly disturbed by the contemporary ills of his society, so much so that it kept him awake at night, unable to sleep and find rest as he searched for a possible solution. The Turks, he lamented, had recently abolished the caliphate in 1924, thereby leaving the global Muslim community bereft of its traditional source of political and religious leadership—even if the venerable institution's reach had dwindled to the level of potent symbolism. And a wave of moral dissolution was overwhelming the intellectual trends, social venues, and institutions of Cairo, where he was studying. Something, he felt, clearly had to be done.[3] The epiphany of this young man, Ḥasan al-Bannā (1906–49), would spark the formation of the region's first Islamic mass movement in 1928 and the grandfather of contemporary Islamist movements around the globe. As al-Bannā himself acknowledged, the burning issue of the recently lost Islamic caliphate was central in principle to the socio-political movement that he established, the Society of Muslim Brothers. And in various forms it has remained essential to the agenda of several contemporary Islamist movements of widely divergent strains.

Among Islamists, the ways in which the underlying significance of the caliphate's abolition in the 1920s has been interpreted and harnessed in service of a particular agenda varies greatly from one group to another. Over the years, the Society of Muslim Brothers has articulated a modernist, accommodationist, and gradualist solution to the dilemma of caliphal absence by placing an emphasis on comprehensive social, educational, cultural, economic, and political reform as well as international cooperation among Muslim-majority countries. On the other hand, the ideologically purist, radical, revolutionary, and paradoxically non-violent "Liberation Party" or Ḥizb al-Taḥrīr frames democracy, capitalism, and nationalism as obstacles to their vision of the Islamic caliphate as an utopian panacea for the ills of the twentieth and twenty-first centuries. Conversely, the avowed non-violence of Ḥizb al-Taḥrīr in their call for the caliphate has constituted a major source of irritation for Salafi jihadists, as readily evident in the treatises of Ḥāmid ibn ʿAbdillāh al-ʿAlī (b. 1960) based in Kuwait and the Syrian expatriate ʿAbd al-Munʿim Muṣṭafā Ḥalīmah (also known as Abū Baṣīr al-Tarṭūṣī) based in London, who depict the caliphate as a fallen fortress that used to protect all Muslims, and they assume militant aspirations to rectify the travesties of the post-colonial world.[4]

The appearance of the most recent extremist group in this third Salafi jihadist vein, the self-proclaimed Islamic State in Iraq and Syria, also known by its pejorative Arabic acronym Daesh,[5] has shocked even the hardened militants of al-Qāʿidah with its viciousness. The product of a shattered and traumatized Iraq, Daesh continues the politics of fear, distrust, torture, and brutality that have been perpetuated by the country's ruling regimes since the late 1960s. Multiple analysts have discussed how the religious veneer of Daesh conceals a secular Baathist core leadership spurred on by the purges of Paul Bremer (b. 1941) in 2003 and Nūrī al-Mālikī (b. 1950) in 2011 that stripped hundreds of thousands of armed men of their jobs, salaries, and pensions. While unemployed former Iraqi army officers contribute extensive military expertise, infrastructure, and intelligence networks to the insurgency, the emotive rhetoric of a caliphate lures in foreign fighters who are sent off to the front lines of much-older confrontations. Not unlike past political appropriations of a caliphate, this most recent attempt seeks to capitalize on the concept's broader popular appeal even as it twists and warps the romantic religious emblem in new and unprecedented ways.[6]

Meanwhile, the overwhelming majority of Muslims abhor and reject religious extremism as aberrant, and classically trained scholars of the Islamic tradition have explicitly decried radical Muslims' unprincipled turn to violence as contravening prophetic practice and Islamic law. Prominent religious leaders like Hamza Yusuf Hanson (b. 1960), the co-founder of Zaytuna College in Berkeley, California, have elucidated that radical Muslim fringe elements do not faithfully represent the magnanimous tradition of Islam even as they utilize and distort some of its scriptural texts for unseemly ends that contradict the religion's core values. In a sermon clarifying that God gave the Prophet Muḥammad and his Companions permission to fight in order to alleviate religious persecution—so that houses of worship, specifically "monasteries, churches, synagogues, and mosques, where God's name is much invoked," would not be destroyed (Qur'an 22:39–41), Hanson bemoaned how "stupid young boys" (*ughaylamah sufaḥā'*) have shoved aside and dismissed the Islamic scholarly tradition that requires years of thoughtful training for the speedy superficiality and compounded errors of Internet searches.[7] Others, including 126 distinguished international Muslim figures who signed a lengthy open letter to the leader of the self-declared Islamic State, have also emphasized that the central Islamic principle of mercy has been perverted in the words and actions of militant groups like Daesh,[8] since mercy is considered by religious scholars to be the hallmark of Islam.[9] The open letter further ridiculed the circular logic and self-aggrandizement of Daesh in declaring all other Muslims to be non-Muslim unless they recognize the leader of Daesh as the caliph of Muslims, noting, "In this case, a caliph is nothing more than the leader of a certain group that declares more than 99% of Muslims non-Muslim."[10] And in *Refuting ISIS*, the Syrian religious scholar Muḥammad al-Ya'qūbī (b. 1963) observes how even the Salafi jihadist teacher of Daesh's supposed caliph Abū Bakr al-Baghdādī (b. 1971) censured his former pupil's ignorance of Islam saying, "He did not master one single book in theology or jurisprudence."[11] In 2014, the prominent Muslim scholar 'Abdullāh bin Bayyah (b. 1935) issued a fatwa clarifying "This is Not the Path to Paradise" in response to Daesh and established the Forum for Promoting Peace in Muslim Societies instead. This international forum later laid out the legal framework for protecting the rights of religious minorities in predominantly Muslim-majority societies.[12] In an interesting twist of history, the great-grandson of both the last Ottoman sultan-caliph Vahideddin and the last Ottoman caliph Abdülmecid II on his maternal side, Osman Rifat Ibrahim (b. 1951) who resides in Lisbon, has also denounced al-Baghdādī as an imposter not worthy of supplanting "the Caliphs of old, those men of wisdom and learning who presided over the glorious days of Islamic civilization."[13]

Despite the headline-grabbing actions of Muslim movements seeking power and control, most Muslims are not Islamists and do not share their political aspirations. According to the Gallup World Poll's extensive multi-year study of Muslim opinions in over thirty-five countries, the vast majority of Muslims aspire for better economies. Other significant hopes include greater public safety and improved educational systems. "In general," John Esposito and Dalia Mogahed observe, "Muslims see no contradiction between democratic values and religious principles."[14] The thwarted efforts of the early twentieth century to restore a caliphate have primarily dissolved into warm associations and memories of an institution that once represented Muslim piety, cosmopolitanism, and prestige. By 1926, even Aḥmad Shawqī had expressed poetically that the only caliphate left was in the literary imagination of *One Thousand and One Nights*.[15] Contemporary mainstream Muslim scholars follow in the path laid out by premodern jurists in embracing new and evolving political configurations of power by transferring the duties of the caliph to the current head of state, circumscribed by national boundaries, and signaled by such phrases as "the *imām*, i.e., the president" in contemporary texts of Islamic political jurisprudence. Spiritual sages, like Ḥabīb ʿUmar bin Ḥafīẓ (b. 1963), stress the inner metaphysical dimension of *khilāfah* as custodianship of the sublime prophetic mission over and above the polluted outer forms of political power that should be generally eschewed. He therefore advises his students to strive for purity of heart that will illuminate their lives and benefit their family, friends, and neighbors. As he explicitly counsels, "Be someone who possesses *taqwā* [God-consciousness] and do not concern yourself with the outward *khilāfah* [of political power]."[16] And many contemporary Muslims find inspiration in classical Islamic interpretations of Qur'anic verses regarding the caliphate (such as 2:30 and 6:165) that describe all people as God's trustees on earth who are responsible for its welfare.[17]

Even so, Islamist thinkers and activists who do aspire to a new political future through peaceable and sometimes violent means are not alone in their nostalgic pursuit of the past; serious Christian intellectuals like Stanley Hauerwas (b. 1940), once named "America's Best Theologian" by *Time* magazine, and his long-time friend, colleague, and collaborator David Burrell (b. 1933), also yearn for a return to Christendom. The decades-long collaboration between these two theologians, one a Protestant of the Methodist tradition and the other a Catholic priest in the Congregation of the Holy Cross, point not only to the wide range of ecclesial influences on Hauerwas but also to his aspirations for shaping the broader Christian church. In 1999, Hauerwas affirmed a Mennonite reading of his book *After Christendom?* as urging Anabaptists to be more Catholic in aspiring to "the vision of Christendom as a society in which all of life is integrated under the Lordship of Christ," Catholics to be more Anabaptist in rejecting "the sinful effort to grasp at its fullness through violence, before its eschatological time," and Protestants to be both. Or in other words, "Hauerwas is quite consistent once you see that he does want to create a Christian society (polis, societas)—a community and way of life shaped fully by Christian convictions." And one decade later, Hauerwas and Burrell openly avowed their aspirations for the return of Christendom. These inspired notions of Christendom, described by admirers as "postliberal" and by critics as "antiliberal," have been received with wide acclaim among popular and theological audiences. Indeed, in Jeffrey Stout's 2004 assessment, "Stanley Hauerwas is surely the most prolific and influential theologian now working in the United States. He has also done more than anyone else to spread the new traditionalism among Christians in the English-speaking world.... No theologian has done more to inflame Christian resentment of secular political culture."[18]

Or one could point to the twentieth-century successes of Christian Democrats in Europe who anchored their political goals in fond memories of medieval Christendom. As Jan-Werner Müller boldly states in a recent article pondering an uncertain future, "The Europe of today is a creation of Christian Democrats." With intellectual roots in the aftermath of the French Revolution, some

Catholic thinkers initially sought "to make democracy safe for religion by properly Christianizing the masses," and in the late nineteenth and early twentieth centuries the Vatican itself fostered Christian Democratic parties to promote and protect church interests without embracing the legitimacy of representative political systems. Over time, Christian Democrats grew in their independence and acceptance of democratic politics. And after World War II, Christian Democratic parties "took a leading role in constructing the postwar European order" as advocates of Atlanticism, anticommunism, and European integration. Religion, they argued, was necessary to keep governments and markets in check.

Intellectuals like the foremost European Catholic philosopher of the mid-twentieth century Jacques Maritain (1882–1973) articulated the vision of a federal Europe as a restoration of the Christian commonwealth of Christendom. The Holy Roman Empire, he argued, "was a concrete historical ideal or historic myth . . . that still impregnates our imaginations." As internationalists, Christian Democrats were the architects of the European Union and remain some of its most prominent politicians. In spite of its divisions and many challenges, Christian democracy remains "the continent's strongest political force," and its continental coalition of political parties, the European People's Party (EPP), swept the European parliamentary elections in May 2014. Political scientists, like Müller, however, question if there is enough Christian Democratic idealism left to solve the structural problems of the Eurozone as an emblem of European integration, harkening back to the days of medieval Christian empire.[19]

Likewise, a significant minority of Jews long for the rebuilding of the Temple. In the early twentieth century, Rabbi Avraham Yitzhack Hacohen Kook (1865–1935) perceived Jews' distance from the Temple Mount as deepening "the power of the memory of [its] honor and the awe of [its] sanctity," and following the Israeli military conquest of East Jerusalem in 1967, the Israeli chief rabbinate affirmed the halakhic ban against Jews entering or praying on the Temple Mount. Since then, however, the number of movements insisting on restoring a Third Temple, "as part of an idea of establishing a theocracy over the secular state" in Motti Inbari's estimation, and contravening the Orthodox halakhic ban have proliferated and greatly expanded their influence. One of the oldest of these groups, Gershon Salomon's Temple Mount Faithful began advocating for the destruction of the seventh-century monuments that comprise one of Islam's holiest sites to make way for a Third Temple in the late 1960s. As an evocative symbol of Jewish collective memory, the notion of Solomon's Temple stirs visions of religious and national redemption and a utopian future. As the ultra-Orthodox Rabbi Yosef Elboim (b. 1953), who broke away from Salomon's group in 1987 to create a more religious-based Movement for the Establishment of the Temple, expressed his hopes in 2012:

> [The Temple] will be the most precious and most joyous thing. Every good thing is attached to the Temple. At present all is desolate, and when it returns all

will be rebuilt, from the foundation. All these things shall be repaired. The Jewish culture. We will have a unified nation, a happy nation.

And discussing strategy in the same meeting with Elboim, Hillel Weiss (b. 1945), an outspoken professor of literature at Bar-Ilan University who chairs the Friends of the Temple and also seeks to restore an ancient Jewish high court of law, declared, "I want to take the movements to a place that is more sensible: a Temple-based state, where the state's entire content revolves around the Temple."[20]

For several decades now, Religious Zionists have prepared and agitated for the Temple's restoration in various ways: organizing public demonstrations, engaging in political activism, attempting to "cleanse" the Temple Mount by burning or bombing the existing mosques, drawing up architectural plans for the Third Temple, teaching the neglected religious practices of the Temple, and recreating its ritual vessels so that they are at the ready. The Temple Institute, which primarily engages in the latter two activities, receives official state recognition and funding from the Israeli Ministry of Education and on occasion from the chief rabbinate, the Jerusalem municipality, and the Ministry of Religious Affairs. Overall, seventeen percent of religious and secular Israeli Jews want to see a Third Temple built in place of Islam's Noble Sanctuary, according to a survey conducted several years ago by the joint directorate of the Temple movements in a bid to gauge their base of support and ways to increase it. These figures exclude Jewish and Christian Zionists elsewhere, particularly in the United States, who have lent substantial support in pursuit of the dream of a Third Temple. As academic scholars, like Shalom Goldman have noted, supporters of the Temple's reconstruction have been increasing dramatically in both Israel and the United States.[21]

Yet, clearly, no one would equate Ḥasan al-Bannā with Tāj al-Dīn al-Subkī, Stanley Hauerwas with Pope Innocent III, or Gershon Salomon with Judah Mosconi. As personally devout as these individuals may or may not be, they do not inhabit the same conceptual spaces across the gulf of time. The distance between the thirteenth and twentieth centuries is not only numeric; we must contemplate what time has wrought in that meaningful interval. Not only have their religious communities evolved over the passage of time, but such thinkers operate in dramatically different contexts. They interact and contend with distinctive hosts of social, intellectual, and political forces. Nor would it be conceivable to expect these figures to represent all the diverse and competing strains of their traditions. They are individuals who continue to wrestle and engage with ideas from their religious heritage.

And from my perspective, it is that very process of evocative engagement that is intriguing. By examining Muslim reactions to the disappearance of the Abbasid Caliphate in 1258 and the Ottoman Caliphate in 1924, I do not argue for their sameness. To the contrary, I have sought to convey the richness of these unique contexts and to illustrate the particularities of how Muslims grappled with these dramatic events. Yet why is it that some individuals in the twentieth and twenty-first centuries continue to think at all of the caliphate, or Christendom, or the Temple? Why does the sense of loss remain so poignant for some or the desire for restoration become so tangible? By juxtaposing the ideas and politics of the thirteenth and twentieth centuries, I have sought to trace cultural resonances across time and to witness their transformation. As Elizabeth Castelli notes in her eloquent analysis of martyrdom as "a critical building block of Christian culture," examples from the twentieth century can aptly illustrate the continuing dynamics of collective memory that were generated in the distant past.[22] In acknowledging this ongoing interpretative dynamic as a cultural grammar, we can recognize how it shapes the articulation of meanings across varying contexts, without hampering the vivacity or uniqueness of their expression. The enduring engagement is at once recognizable and distinct.

For premodern Muslims, the destruction of the Abbasid Caliphate overwhelmingly signified a rupture in the globally conceived Sunni Muslim community's connection with the Prophet Muḥammad. The Abbasid caliphs had constituted a living link to this heritage, as both descendants of the Prophet Muḥammad's uncle al-ʿAbbās and successors to the Prophet's custodianship of the Muslim community. Their loss and that of their gloriously cosmopolitan capital, Baghdad, was inconceivable. These traumatic events, wrought at the hands of the ferocious Mongols, were widely interpreted as a sign of the impending end of time and spurred much moral reflection and repentance to God. In the fluid arena of local and transregional politics, political and military elites repeatedly sought to envelop themselves in the legitimacy, prestige, and sanctity of a restored Abbasid Caliphate in Egypt and Syria. And religious scholars continued to conceptualize the Islamic caliphate as an integral component of state and society throughout the centuries of Mamluk rule, in a powerful testament to the vitality and endurance of communal memories. Yet alternative modes of connectivity to the prophetic heritage also grew in strength and prominence during this era, including the chains of transmission that bound one generation to the next through classical Islamic scholarship and spiritual training.

In the modern context, however, the surging currents of nationalism, colonialism, materialism, and internationalism were especially influential in shaping the overall tenor of intellectual and social responses to the symbolic communal loss of the Ottoman Caliphate in 1924. Nationalist politics seeking to thwart European colonial incursions and to either embrace or reject the narrowing Turkification and centralization of the Ottoman Empire helped form the reactions of Muslims in Turkey, Egypt, Syria, Palestine, India, the Indonesian Archipelago, and elsewhere. Yet the ideas generated by other traditionally trained Islamic scholars, in Turkey and Egypt in particular, more closely paralleled patterns from the past, by forging jurisprudential accommodations of new political realities and by encouraging others to focus on the everlasting Divine. Certainly the impulse of military figures and ruling elites to aggrandize their own power through harnessing the social and political capital of the caliphate had not abated by the early twentieth century; in addition to prominent displays of support for the Ottoman Caliphate from Unionists and Kemalists as they sought to consolidate their grasp on power, many rulers elsewhere longed to assume the title of caliph for themselves following the institution's abolition.

Faced with the disappearance of a traditional Islamic caliphate as represented by the Ottomans, a Pandora's box of possibilities had opened up by the 1920s. Several figures whom we have discussed illustrate some of these myriad paths forward. Islamic modernists like Seyyid Bey and ʿAlī ʿAbd al-Rāziq argued in favor of secular governance. Lay activists like Ḥasan al-Bannā organized Islamist alternatives and opposition. Jurists like Mustafa Sabri continued to accommodate changing political structures, by embracing identifiably Muslim nation-states as potential, multiple caliphates. Intellectuals like ʿAbd al-Razzāq al-Sanhūrī articulated visions of international councils along the lines of the League of Nations. And religious scholars like Said Nursi focused instead on enduring metaphysical realities and cultivating people's personal faith and character. All of these possible trajectories have persisted until the present in continually evolving, changing permutations.

NOTES

INTRODUCTION

1. Miriam Cooke and Bruce Lawrence, eds., *Muslim Networks from Hajj to Hip Hop* (Chapel Hill: University of North Carolina Press, 2005), 6.
2. Alon Confino, "History and Memory," in *The Oxford History of Historical Writing*, vol. 5 (Oxford: Oxford University Press, 2011), 44.
3. T.N.A., F. O. 371/10217/E1904, February 27, 1924, and received in the Foreign Office on March 3, 1924.
4. Ibid. Osbourne inserted his handwritten note directly after the line reporting on the abolition of the Ottoman Caliphate and the expulsion of its dynasty.
5. A. Sanhoury, *Le califat: son évolution vers une société des nations orientale* (Paris: Librairie Orientaliste Paul Geuthner, 1926), xi.
6. Bernard Lewis, *The Arabs in History* (Oxford: Oxford University Press, 1993), 168.
7. Patricia Crone, *God's Rule: Government and Islam* (NY: Columbia University Press, 2004), 250.
8. ʿAbd al-Raḥmān Ḥusayn Muḥammad, *Rithāʾ al-Mudun wa'l-Mamālik al-Zāʾilah fī'l-Shiʿr al-ʿArabī hattā Suqūṭ Gharnāṭah* (Cairo: Maṭbaʿat al-Jabalāwī, 1983), 54; Michael Cooperson, "Baghdad in Rhetoric and Narrative," *Muqarnas: An Annual on the Visual Culture of the Islamic World* 13 (1996): 99–100, 105–6.
9. Muḥammad, *Rithāʾ al-Mudun*, 93.
10. Alexander Meyrick Broadley, *How We Defended Arabi and His Friends: A Story of Egypt and the Egyptians* (London: Chapman and Hall, 1884), 231–32; Mounah Khouri, *Poetry and the Making of Modern Egypt (1882–1922)* (Leiden, Neth.: E. J. Brill, 1971), 25–26, 35–36.
11. Abū'l-Fidāʾ Ibn Kathīr, *al-Bidāyah wa'l-Nihāyah*, ed. Aḥmad Abū Mulḥim, et al. (Beirut: Dār al-Kutub al-ʿIlmiyyah, 1987), 13:268; Jalāl al-Dīn ʿAbd al-Raḥmān al-Suyūṭī, *Ḥusn al-Muḥāḍarah fī Akhbār Miṣr wa'l-Qāhirah*, ed. ʿAlī Muḥammad ʿUmar (Cairo: Maktabat al-Khānjī, 2007), 2:45–46; Burhān al-Dīn Ibrāhīm al-Bayjūrī, *Ḥāshiyat al-Imām al-Bayjūrī ʿalā Jawharat al-Tawḥīd al-Musammā Tuḥfat al-Murīd ʿalā Jawharat al-Tawḥīd*, ed. ʿAlī Jumuʿah (Cairo: Dār al-Salām, 2002), 180.
12. Egyptian newspapers, for example, published pieces with titles like "Hülegü Returns" for a letter to the editor submitted by an Iraqi woman living in Cairo describing "the second Mongol invasion in the new guise of America and its allies" or the multi-tiered title for an article, "History Repeats Itself. Baghdad Only Fell through Treachery—The American Hülegü Will Slaughter Everyone—The Mongols Invaded the Region after Muslims and Arabs Relied on Them to Settle Scores (with Each Other)." Suhaylah al-Ḥusaynī, "Hūlāgū Yaʿūd," *al-Aḥrām*, March 26, 2003, and Muḥammad ʿAbdallāh, "al-Tārīkh Yuʿīdu Nafsahu. Baghdād Lam Tusqaṭ illā bi'l-Khiyānah: Hūlāgū al-Amrīkī sa-Yadhbaḥ al-Jamīʿ: al-Mughūl Jāʾū ilā Minṭiqah baʿd an Istaʿāna bihim al-Muslimūn wa'l-ʿArab li-Taṣfiyat al-Ḥisābāt," *al-Usbūʿ*, April 14, 2003.

13. https://twitter.com/AdilAlFahim/statuses/337824359521607680; http://twitter-counter.com/AdilAlFahim. This anecdote and its stanzas were also deployed as instructive parables elsewhere online on March 15, 2012, at http://islamstory.com/ar/وعبر-احداث-التتر - محنة-
14. H.A.R. Gibb, "Constitutional Organization," in *Law in the Middle East*, ed. Majid Khadduri and Herbert Liebensy, vol. 1, *The Origin and Development of Islamic Law* (Washington, DC: Middle East Institute, 1955), 32.
15. Yuen-Gen Liang, et al., "Unity and Disunity across the Strait of Gibraltar," *Medieval Encounters* 19 (2013): 8–9; Alexander Elinson, *Looking Back at al-Andalus: The Poetics of Loss and Nostalgia in Medieval Arabic and Hebrew Literature* (Leiden, Neth,: E. J. Brill, 2009); William Granara, "Nostalgia, Arab Nationalism, and the Andalusian Chronotope in the Evolution of the Modern Arab Novel," *Journal of Arabic Literature* 36, no. 1 (2005): 57–73; Stacy Beckwith, ed., *Charting Memory: Recalling Medieval Spain* (NY: Garland Publishing, 2000).
16. Hugh Kennedy, *The Prophet and the Ages of the Caliphates* (Harlow, UK: Longman, 2004), 50–69; Fred Donner, *The Early Islamic Conquests* (Princeton, NJ: Princeton University Press, 1981), 82–90.
17. Abū ʿĪsā Muḥammad ibn ʿĪsā al-Tirmidhī, *al-Jāmiʿ al-Kabīr*, ed. Bashshār ʿAwwād Maʿrūf (Stuttgart, Ger.: Thesaurus Islamicus Foundation, 2000), 2:681 (#2891); Abū ʿAbdullāh Muḥammad ibn Yazīd Ibn Mājah al-Qazwīni, *Sunan Ibn Mājah* (Stuttgart, Ger.: Thesaurus Islamicus Foundation, 2000), 8–9 (#44–45); Abū ʻAbdillāh Aḥmad Ibn Ḥanbal, *Musnad al-Imām Aḥmad b. Ḥanbal*, ed. Shuʿayb al-Arnāʾūt (Beirut: Muʾassassat al-Risālah, 1993), 28:367, 373, 375 (#17142, #17144, 17145).
18. See, for example, the ḥadīth in the chapter on the caliphs in Abū Dāwūd Sulaymān b. al-Ashʿath al-Sijistānī, *Sunan Abī Dāwūd* (Stuttgart, Ger.: Thesaurus Islamicus Foundation, 2000) where Abū Bakr, then ʿUmar, then ʿUthmān, and then ʿAlī variously attempt to fill a bucket in a dream publicly reported to the Prophet.
19. Abū Dāwūd, *Sunan Abī Dāwūd*, 2:781 (#4648–49); al-Tirmidhī, *al-Jāmiʿ al-Kabīr*, 2:573 (#2390); Aḥmad b. Hanbal, *Musnad al-Imām Aḥmad*, 36:248, 252, 256 (#21919, #21923, #21928).
20. Abū ʿAbdillāh Muḥammad ibn Ismāʿīl al-Bukhārī, *Ṣaḥīḥ al-Bukhārī* (Stuttgart, Ger.: Thesaurus Islamicus Foundation, 2000), 1:515–16, (# 2744) 2:714, 739 (#3672, #3791) 3:1436 (#7194); Abū Dāwūd, *Sunan Abī Dāwūd*, 2:784 (#4664); al-Tirmidhī, *al-Jāmiʿ al-Kabīr*, 2:960 (#4143); Abū ʿAbd al-Raḥmān Aḥmad b. Shuʿayb al-Nasāʾī, *Sunan al-Nasāʾī* (Stuttgart, Ger.: Thesaurus Islamicus Foundation, 2000), 1:232 (#1421); Abū ʿAbd al-Raḥmān Aḥmad ibn Shuʻayb al-Nasāʾī, *Sunan al-Nasāʾī bi-Sharh al-Imamayn al-Suyūṭī wa'l-Sindī*, ed. al-Sayyid Muḥammad Sayyid, ʿAlī Muḥammad ʿAlī, and Sayyid ʿUmrān (Cairo: Dār al-Ḥadīth, 1999), 2:218–19 (#1409); Aḥmad b. Hanbal, *Musnad al-Imām Aḥmad*, 34:33–34, 98–99, 120, 138, 148 (#20392, #20448, #20473, #20499, #20516).
21. Wilferd Madelung, *Succession to Muhammad: A Study of the Early Caliphate* (NY: Cambridge University Press, 1997), 322–23. Madelung cites Aḥmad ibn Yaḥyā al-Balādhūrī's *Ansāb al-Ashrāf*, ed. Muḥammad Ḥamīd Allāh (Cairo: Maʿhad al-Makhṭūṭāt bi-Jāmiʿat al-Duwal al-ʿArabiyyah bi'l-Ishtirāk maʿ Dār al-Maʿārif bi-Miṣr, 1959), 3:40–42 and Abū Muḥammad Aḥmad ibn Aʿtham al-Kūfī's *Kitāb al-Futūḥ* (Hyderabad, India: Dāʾirat al-Maʿārif al-ʿUthmānīyah, 1968–75), 4:159–60.
22. To adapt Marshall Hodgson's reference to the "piety-minded opposition" to Marwanid Umayyad rule in *The Venture of Islam: Conscience and History in a World Civilization*, 1:241–79.

23. For studies of the Umayyads, see G. R. Hawting, *The First Dynasty of Islam: The Umayyad Caliphate AD 661–750*, 2nd ed. (London: Routledge, 2000) and in particular his bibliographical survey on pages 120–37; Patricia Crone and Martin Hinds, *God's Caliph: Religious Authority in the First Centuries of Islam* (Cambridge: Cambridge University Press, 1986); Kennedy, *The Prophet and the Ages of the Caliphates*, 82–122; Patricia Crone, *Slaves on Horses: The Evolution of the Islamic Polity* (Cambridge: Cambridge University Press, 1980), 29–57. On the question of dynastic succession, see Crone, *Government and Islam*, 33–47. And on Mu'āwiyah and 'Abd al-Malik, in particular, see the biographies, R. Stephen Humphreys, *Mu'awiya ibn Abi Sufyan: From Arabia to Empire* (Oxford: Oneworld, 2006) and Chase Robinson, *'Abd al-Malik* (Oxford: Oneworld, 2005).
24. See Jacob Lassner, *Islamic Revolution and Historical Memory: An Inquiry into the Art of 'Abbāsid Apologetics* (New Haven, CT: American Oriental Society, 1986), Roberto Marín-Guzmán, *Popular Dimensions of the 'Abbasid Revolution: A Case Study of Medieval Islamic Social History* (Cambridge, MA: Fulbright-LASPAU, 1990), Moshe Sharon, *Black Banners from the East: The Establishment of the 'Abbāsid State-Incubation of a Revolt* (Jerusalem: Magnes Press, 1983), Moshe Sharon, *Revolt: The Social and Military Aspects of the 'Abbāsid Revolution* (Jerusalem: Hebrew University, 1990), and R. Stephen Humphreys's historiographic discussion of the Abbasid revolution in his *Islamic History: A Framework for Inquiry*, rev. ed. (Princeton, NJ: Princeton University Press, 1991), 104–27; Hugh Kennedy, *Early Abbasid Caliphate: A Political History* (London: Croom and Helm, 1981), 35–45; Crone, *Slaves on Horses*.
25. Émile Tyan, *Institutions du droit public musulman: Le califat* (Paris: Ricueil Sirey, 1954), 531–41; Ira Lapidus, *A History of Islamic Societies* (Cambridge: Cambridge University Press, 2002), 126–36; Dominique Sourdel, "The 'Abbasid Caliphate," in *The Cambridge History of Islam* (Cambridge: Cambridge University Press, 1970), 104–39; Kennedy, *The Early Abbasid Caliphate*, 135–213; Kennedy, *The Prophet and the Ages of the Caliphates*, 147–345; Bertold Spuler, "The Disintegration of the Caliphate in the East," in *The Cambridge History of Islam* (Cambridge: Cambridge University Press, 1970), 143–74; John Donohue, *The Buwayhid Dynasty in Iraq 334 H. / 945 to 403 H. / 1012: Shaping Institutions for the Future* (Leiden, Neth.: E. J. Brill, 2003); Ann Lambton, *Continuity and Change in Medieval Persia: Aspects of Administrative, Economic, and Social History, 11th–14th Century* (London : I. B. Tauris, 1988); A. H. Siddiqui, "Caliphate and Kingship in Medieval Persia," in *Islamic Culture* 9 (1935): 560–70, vol. 10 (1936): 97–126, 260–80, vol. 11 (1937): 37–59; Eric Hanne, *Putting the Caliph in His Place* (Madison, NJ: Farleigh Dickinson University Press, 2007).
26. Shams al-Dīn Muḥammad b. Aḥmad b. 'Uthmān al-Dhahabī, *Siyar 'Alām al-Nubalā'* (Beirut: Dār al-Fikr, 1997), 16:181–214, 228–30, 419–27; Angelika Hartmann, "al-Nāṣir li-Dīn Allāh, Abū'l-'Abbās Aḥmad," in the *Encyclopaedia of Islam*, 2nd ed.
27. Abū'l-Faraj Jamāl al-Dīn Grīgūriyūs Ibn al-'Ibrī, *Tārīkh al-Zamān*, ed. Isḥāq Armaleh (Beirut: Dār al-Mashriq, 1986), 288–89; Abū'l-Faraj Jamāl al-Dīn Grīgūriyūs Ibn al-'Ibrī, *Tārīkh Mukhtaṣar al-Duwal* (Beirut: al-Maṭba'ah al-Kāthūlikiyyah, 1958), 254–55; Jamāl al-Dīn Muḥammad ibn Sālim Ibn Wāṣil, *Mufarrij al-Kurūb fī Ākhbār Banī Ayyūb*, ed. Jamāl al-Dīn al-Shayyāl and Ḥasanayn Muḥammad Rabī' (Cairo: Maṭba'at Jāmi'at Fu'ād al-Awwal, 1953), 5:321–32, 318; Ẓahīr al-Dīn 'Alī b. Muḥammad b. Maḥmūd b. Abī'l-'Izz b. Aḥmad b. Isḥāq b. Ibrāhīm al-Kāzarūnī al-Baghdādī al-Shāfi'ī, *Mukhtaṣar al-Tārīkh*, ed. Muṣṭafā Jawwād (Baghdad: Wizārat al-I'lām, Mudīriyyat al-Thaqāfah al-'Āmmah, 1970), 268; Quṭb al-Dīn Mūsā b. Muḥammad al-Yūnīnī al-Ba'labakkī al-Ḥanbalī, *Dhayl Mir'āt al-Zamān* (Hyderabad, India: Dā'irat al-Ma'ārif al-'Uthmāniyyah, 1954), 1:254–56; Muḥammad b. 'Alī b. Ṭabāṭabā Ibn al-Ṭiqṭaqā, *Tārīkh*

al-Duwal al-Islāmiyyah: wa-huwa Kitāb al-Fakhrī fī'l- Ādāb al-Sulṭaniyyah wa'l-Duwal al-Islāmiyyah (Beirut: Dār Ṣādir, 1960), 333; Shihāb al-Dīn Aḥmad b. ʿAbd al-Wahhāb al-Nuwayrī, *Nihāyat al-Arab fī Funūn al-Adab*, vol. 23, ed. Aḥmad Kamāl Zakī and Muḥammad Muṣṭafā Ziyādah (Cairo: al-Hayʾah al-Miṣriyyah al-ʿĀmmah li'l-Kitāb, 1980), 323; al-Malik al-Muʾayyad ʿImād al-Dīn Ismāʿīl b. ʿAlī Abū'l-Fidā, *al-Mukhtaṣar fī Akhbār al-Bashar*, ed. Muḥammad Zaynhum ʿAzab (Cairo: Dār al-Maʿārif, 1999), 3:234; Shams al-Dīn Muḥammad b. Aḥmad b. ʿUthmān al-Dhahabī, *Tārīkh al-Islām wa-Wafayāt al-Mashāhīr wa'l-Aʿlām*, ed. ʿUmar ʿAbd al-Salām Tadmurī (Beirut: Dār al-Kitāb al-ʿArabī, 1999), 258–60; al-Dhahabī, *Siyar ʿAlām al-Nubalāʾ*, 16:431; Zayn al-Dīn ʿUmar b. al-Muẓaffar Ibn al-Wardī, *Tatimmat al-Mukhtaṣar fī Akhbār al-Bashar*, ed. Aḥmad Rifʿat al-Badrāwī (Beirut: Dār al-Maʿrifah, 1970), 2:284; Mughulṭāy b. Qilīj b. ʿAbdillāh, *al-Ishārah ilā Sīrat al-Muṣṭafā wa-Tārīkh Man baʿdahu min al-Khulafāʾ*, ed. Muḥammad Niẓām al-Dīn al-Futayyiḥ (Damascus: Dār al-Qalam and Beirut: Dār al-Shāmiyyah, 1996), 559; Muḥammad Ibn Shākir al-Kutubī, *Fawāt al-Wafayāt wa'l-Dhayl ʿalayhā*, ed. Iḥsān ʿAbbās (Beirut: Dār Ṣādir, 1973), 2:231; Muḥammad Ibn Shākir al-Kutubī, *ʿUyūn al-Tawārīkh*, vol. 20, ed. Fayṣal al-Sāmir and Nabīlah ʿAbd al-Munʿim Dāwūd (Baghdad: Dār al-Rashīd, 1980), 20:133; Ṣalāḥ al-Dīn Khalīl b. Aybak al-Ṣafadī, *al-Wāfī bi'l-Wafayāt*, vol. 17, ed. Dorthea Krawulsky (Beirut: Franz Steiner Stuttgart, 1991), 641–42; Abū Muḥammad 'Abd Allāh ibn As'ad ibn 'Alī ibn Sulaymān al-Yāfi'ī al-Yamanī al-Makkī, *Mirʾāt al-Jinān wa-ʿIbrat al-Yaqẓān fī Maʿrifat mā Yuʿtabar min Ḥawādith al-Zamān*, (Beirut: Muʾassasat al-Aʿlamī li'l-Maṭbū'āt, 1970), 4:139; Tāj al-Dīn Abū'l-Naṣr ʿAbd al-Wahhāb b. ʿAlī b. ʿAbd al-Kāfī al-Subkī, *Ṭabaqāt al-Shāfiʿiyyah al-Kubrā*, ed. Maḥmūd Muḥammad al-Ṭanāḥī and ʿAbd al-Fattāḥ Muḥammad al-Ḥulw (Cairo: Maṭbaʿat ʿĪsā al-Bābī al-Ḥalabī, [1964–1976]), 8:262, 269, 272; Ibn Kathīr, *al-Bidāyah wa'l-Nihāyah* (1994), 13:171; Badr al-Dīn al-Ḥasan ibn ʿUmar Ibn Ḥabīb al-Ḥalabī, "Durrat al-Aslāk fī Dawlat al-Atrāk," Arabe Collection, Manuscript 4680, folio 25v, Bibliothèque nationale de France, Paris, France; al-Malik al-Ashraf al-Rasūlī al-Ghassānī Ismāʿīl, *al-ʿAsjad al-Masbūk wa'l-Jawhar al-Maḥkūk fī Ṭabaqāt al-Khulafāʾ wa'l-Mulūk*, ed. Shākir ʿAbd al-Munʿim (Beirut: Dār al-Turāth al-Islāmī and Baghdad: Dār al-Bayān, 1975), 632; Jalāl al-Dīn ʿAbd al-Raḥmān b. Abī Bakr al-Suyūṭī, *Tārīkh al-Khulafāʾ* (Beirut: Dār al-Jīl, 1994), 530–31.

28. Abū'l-ʿAbbās Aḥmad b. ʿAlī al-Qalqashandī, *Ṣubḥ al-Aʿshā fī Ṣināʿat al-Inshā* (Cairo: al-Muʾassasah al-Miṣriyyah al-ʿĀmmah li'l-Ṭibāʿah wa'l-Nashr, 1964), 4:19, 5:562.
29. Identified as the military commander Sharaf al-Dīn Iqbāl al-Sharābī by al-Kāzarūnī, the seventh-century historian of Baghdad Ibn al-Buzūrī, al-Dhahabī, and the unconfirmed author of *al-Ḥawādith al-Jāmiʿah*, ascribed to Ibn al-Fuwaṭī. al-Kāzarūnī, *Mukhtaṣar al-Tārīkh*, 266; *Kitāb al-Ḥawādith wa-Huwa al-Kitāb al-Musammā Wahman bi'l-Ḥawādith al-Jāmiʿah wa'l-Tajārib al-Nāfiʿah wa'l-Manṣūb li'l-Fuwaṭī*, ed. Bashshār ʿAwwād Maʿrūf and ʿImād ʿAbd al-Salām Raʾūf (Beirut: Dār al-Gharb al-Islāmī, 1997), 188; al-Dhahabī, *Tārīkh al-Islām*, 64:455. For a definition of the post, see al-Qalqashandī, *Ṣubḥ al-Aʿshā*, 4:10, 5:469.
30. This is most likely al-Amīr Abū Hāshim Yūsuf b. al-Ẓāhir Muḥammad b. al-Nāṣir Aḥmad, whom al-Ṣafadī mentions was revered by his brothers and cousins and was nominated for the caliphate. Aside from al-Mustanṣir and a brother who died in 631/1233, the eponyms of his other brothers, except for one, are as follows: Abū'l-Faḍl or Abū'l-Fatḥ Sulaymān known as al-Ḥājj, Abū'l-Qāsim ʿAlī known as al-Sabtī, Abū'l-Muẓaffar or Abū Manṣūr al-Ḥasan known as al-Turkī. The last brother is Abū'l-Futūḥ Ḥabīb, whose eponym is not listed but is less likely to be al-Khafājī given al-Ṣafadī's biography of Abū Hāshim Yūsuf. Ṣalāḥ al-Dīn Khalīl b. Aybak al-Ṣafadī, *al-Wāfī bi'l-Wafayāt*, vol. 29, ed.

Maher Jarrar (Beirut: al-Kitāb al-ʿArabī Berlin, 1997), 333–34; al-Kāzarūnī, *Mukhtaṣar al-Tārīkh*, 257; *al-Ḥawādith al-Jāmiʿah*, 189; al-Malik al-Ashraf, *al-ʿAsjad*, 632-33.

31. Ibn Wāṣil, *Mufarrij al-Kurūb*, 5:318; al-Yūnīnī, *Dhayl Mirʾāt al-Zamān*, 1:255; al-Dhahabī, *Siyar*, 16:426, 431; al-Dhahabī, *Tārīkh al-Islām*, 64:454, 66:259; al-Subkī, *Ṭabaqāt al-Shāfiʿiyyah*, 8:262.

32. Abū'l-Futūḥ Ḥabīb b. al-Ẓāhir who had gone to pledge his allegiance thinking erroneously that his brethren had preceded him. ʿAbd al-Raḥmān Sunbuṭ Qanītū al-Irbilī, *Khulāṣat al-Dhahab al-Masbūk Mukhtaṣar min Siyar al-Mulūk* (Baghdad: Maktabat al-Muthannā, [1964]), 290 and *al-Ḥawādith al-Jāmiʿah*, 189.

33. *Khulāṣat al-Dhahab al-Masbūk*, 290–91; al-Malik al-Ashraf, *al-ʿAsjad*, 510–11.

34. As noted by the editors of *al-Ḥawādith al-Jāmiʿah*, Bashshār ʿAwwād Maʿrūf and ʿImād ʿAbd al-Salām Raʾūf, in their footnote on page 189. Reports of the secrecy surrounding al-Muṣtaʿṣim's ascension pervades the seventh/thirteenth- and eighth/fourteenth-century sources, including al-Dhahabī, *Tārīkh al-Islām*, 64:454–46 who cites Ibn al-Buzūrī.

35. al-Makīn Jirjis Ibn al-ʿAmīd, *Akhbār al-Ayyūbiyyīn*, ed. Claude Cahen (Cairo: Maktabat al-Thaqāfah al-Dīniyyah, 1989), 45; Rukn al-Dīn Baybars al-Manṣūrī, *Zubdat al-Fikrah fī Tārikh al-Hijrah*, ed. Donald Richards (Beirut: Das Arabische Buch, 1998), 38–39; al-Nuwayrī, *Nihāyat al-Arab*, 23:324; Ṣārim al-Dīn Ibrāhīm b. Muḥammad b. Aydamūr al-ʿAlāʾī Ibn Duqmāq, *Nuzhat al-Anām fī Tārīkh al-Islām (628/1230–659/1261)*, ed. Samīr Ṭabbārah (Beirut: al-Maktabah al-ʿAṣriyyah li'l-Ṭibāʿah wa'l-Nashr, 1999), 240.

36. He is frequently identified as Abū Bakr, although Ibn al-Ṭiqṭaqā calls this a mistake since the sons' names were Abū'l-ʿAbbās Aḥmad, Abū'l-Faḍāʾil Abd al-Raḥmān, and Abū'l-Manāqib Mubārak. Ibn al-Ṭiqṭaqā, *al-Fakhrī*, 333.

37. Jamāl al-Dīn Muḥammad b. Sālim Ibn Wāṣil, *Die Chronik des ibn Wāsil (646/1248–659/1261)*, ed. Mohamed Rahim (Wiesbaden, Ger.: Harrassowitz Verlag, 2010), 154; al-Yūnīnī, *Dhayl Mirʾāt al-Zamān*, 1:86; Abū'l-Fidā, *al-Mukhtaṣar*, 3:233; al-Dhahabī, *Tārīkh al-Islām*, 66:34; Ibn al-Wardī, *Tatimmat al-Mukhtaṣar*, 2:282; Ibn Shākir al-Kutubī, *ʿUyūn al-Tawārīkh*, 20:131; al-Subkī, *Ṭabaqāt al-Shāfiʿiyyah*, 8:263. The Yemeni ruler and historian, al-Malik al-Ashraf, echoes this Syrian historiography in *al-ʿAsjad*, 625.

38. Ibn al-ʿAmīd, *Akhbār al-Ayyūbiyyīn*, 45; Ibn Wāṣil, *Die Chronik*, 154; al-Yūnīnī, *Dhayl Mirʾāt al-Zamān*, 1:86; Abū'l-Fidā, *al-Mukhtaṣar*, 3:233; al-Dhahabī, *Tārīkh al-Islām*, 66:34; Ibn al-Wardī, *Tatimmat al-Mukhtaṣar*, 2:282; Ibn Shākir al-Kutubī, *ʿUyūn al-Tawārīkh*, 20:131; al-Subkī, *Ṭabaqāt al-Shāfiʿiyyah*, 8:263; al-Malik al-Ashraf, *al-ʿAsjad*, 625.

39. Muʾayyad al-Dīn Muḥammad b. Aḥmad b. ʿAlī b. Muḥammad al-ʿAlqamī was appointed as al-Mustaʿṣim's vizier in 642/1244, and he died shortly after the Mongol conquest of Baghdad in either Jumādā al-Ūlā or Jumādā al-Ākhirah 656 / May or June 1258.

40. ʿAbd al-Raḥmān ibn Ismāʿīl Abū Shāmah, *Tarājim Rijāl al-Qarnayn al-Sādis wa'l-Sābiʿ*, 2nd ed., ed. Muḥammad Zāhid b. al-Ḥusayn al-Kawtharī (Beirut: Dār al-Jīl, 1974), 198–99; Ibn al-ʿAmīd, *Akhbār al-Ayyūbiyyīn*, 45; Ibn Wāṣil, *Die Chronik*, 154; Baybars al-Manṣūrī, *Zubdat al-Fikrah*, 38–39; al-Yūnīnī, *Dhayl Mirʾāt al-Zamān*, 1:86; al-Nuwayrī, *Nihāyat al-Arab*, 23:324; al-Dhahabī, *Tārīkh al-Islām*, 66:34; Ibn al-Wardī, *Tatimmat al-Mukhtaṣar*, 2:282; Ibn Shākir al-Kutubī, *ʿUyūn al-Tawārīkh*, 20:131–32; al-Yāfiʿī, *Mirʾāt al-Jinān*, 4:137, 147; al-Subkī, *Ṭabaqāt al-Shāfiʿiyyah*, 8:263; Ibn Kathīr, *al-Bidāyah wa'l-Nihāyah*, 13:168; Ibn Ḥabīb al-Ḥalabī, "Durrat al-Aslāk fī Dawlat al-Atrāk," Arabe Collection, Manuscript 4680, folio 26r, Bibliothèque nationale de France, Paris, France; Abū'l-Fidā, *al-Mukhtaṣar*, 3:233; al-Malik al-Ashraf, *al-ʿAsjad*, 625–26; Ibn Duqmāq, *Nuzhat al-Anām*, 240. Ibn al-ʿAlqamī is reported to have shared his intentions with the

caliph's Shi'I deputy over Irbil, Tāj al-Dīn Abū'l-Makārim Muḥammad b. Naṣr b. Yaḥyā Ibn al-Ṣalāyā (d. 656/1258), who is said, by some, to have tried warning the caliph to no avail; see, for example, *al-Ḥawādith al-Jāmi'ah*, 337; Baybars al-Manṣūrī, *Zubdat al-Fikrah*, 38–39; al-Yūnīnī, *Dhayl Mir'āt al-Zamān*, 1:87; Ibn al-Wardī, *Tatimmat al-Mukhtaṣar*, 2:282–83; Ibn Shākir al-Kutubī, *'Uyūn al-Tawārīkh*, 20:132; al-Subkī, *Ṭabaqāt al-Shāfi'iyyah*, 8:263–66.

41. Abū Shāmah, *Tarājim*, 198–99; Ibn al-'Amīd, *Akhbār al-Ayyūbiyyīn*, 45; Ibn Wāṣil, *Die Chronik*, 154; Baybars al-Manṣūrī, *Zubdat al-Fikrah*, 39; al-Yūnīnī, *Dhayl Mir'āt al-Zamān*, 1:87; Abū'l-Fidā, *al-Mukhtaṣar*, 3:233; al-Nuwayrī, *Nihāyat al-Arab*, 23:324; Abū Bakr b. 'Abdillāh b. Aybak Ibn al-Dawādārī, *Kanz al-Durar wa-Jāmi' al-Ghurar*, ed. Ulrich Haarmann (Cairo: Schwarz Freiburg, Maṭba'at 'Īsā al-Bābī al-Ḥalabī, 1971), 8:34; al-Dhahabī, *Tārīkh al-Islām*, 66:34; Ibn al-Wardī, *Tatimmat al-Mukhtaṣar*, 2:282; Mughulṭāy b. Qilīj b. 'Abdillāh, *al-Ishārah*, 559; Ibn Shākir al-Kutubī, *'Uyūn al-Tawārīkh*, 20:131–32; al-Subkī, *Ṭabaqāt al-Shāfi'iyyah*, 8:263; al-Yāfi'ī, *Mir'āt al-Jinān*, 4:137, 138; al-Malik al-Ashraf, *al-'Asjad*, 625–26; Ibrāhīm b. Muḥammad b. Aydamūr al-'Alā'ī Ibn Duqmāq, *al-Jawhar al-Thamīn fī Siyar al-Khulafā' wa'l-Mulūk wa'l-Salāṭīn*, ed. Sa'īd 'Abd al-Fattāḥ 'Āshūr ([Mecca]: al-Mamlakah al-'Arabiyyah al-Sa'ūdiyyah, Jāmi'at Umm al-Qurā, Markaz al-Baḥth al-'Ilmī wa-Iḥyā' al-Turāth al-Islāmī, Kulliyāt al-Sharī'ah wa'l-Dirāsāt al-Islāmiyyah, [1982]), 175–76; Ibn Duqmāq, *Nuzhat al-Anām*, 240. Ibn al-'Amīd reports that the vizier's treachery is famous.

42. Ibn Wāṣil, *Die Chronik*, 154; al-Yūnīnī, *Dhayl Mir'āt al-Zamān*, 1:86–87, 255; Abū'l-Fidā, *al-Mukhtaṣar*, 3:233; al-Nuwayrī, *Nihāyat al-Arab*, 23:324; al-Dhahabī, *Siyar*, 16:431; al-Dhahabī, *Tārīkh al-Islām*, 64:453–54, 66:34, 259; Ibn al-Wardī, *Tatimmat al-Mukhtaṣar*, 2:283–84; Ibn Shākir al-Kutubī, *'Uyūn al-Tawārīkh*, 20:132; al-Ṣafadī, *al-Wāfī bi'l-Wafayāt*, 17:357–58, 360; al-Subkī, *Ṭabaqāt al-Shāfi'iyyah*, 8:262; Ibn Kathīr, *al-Bidāyah wa'l-Nihāyah*, 13:168, 169; Ibn Ḥabīb al-Ḥalabī, "Durrat al-Aslāk fī Dawlat al-Atrāk," Arabe Collection, Manuscript 4680, folio 26r, Bibliothèque nationale de France, Paris, France; Ibn Duqmāq, *al-Jawhar al-Thamīn*, 176–77. In the obituary of al-Mustanṣir, Ibn Wāṣil places the blame for the subsequent reduction of the caliphal army upon al-Musta'ṣim's companions, although the recently published critical edition of the last section of his manuscript specifies Ibn al-'Alqamī by name. Ibn Wāṣil, *Mufarrij al-Kurūb*, 5:317, 321–22 and Ibn Wāṣil, *Die Chronik*, 154.

43. Ibn al-'Amīd, *Akhbār al-Ayyūbiyyīn*, 44; al-Kāzarūnī, *Mukhtaṣar al-Tārīkh*, 270–72; Ibn Wāṣil, *Die Chronik*, 155; *al-Ḥawādith al-Jāmi'ah*, 354–55; Baybars al-Manṣūrī, *Zubdat al-Fikrah*, 36–37; al-Yūnīnī, *Dhayl Mir'āt al-Zamān*, 1:87–88; Abū'l-Fidā, *al-Mukhtaṣar*, 3:233; Ibn al-Dawādārī, *Kanz al-Durar*, 8:34; al-Dhahabī, *Tārīkh al-Islām*, 66:35; Ibn al-Wardī, *Tatimmat al-Mukhtaṣar*, 2:283; Ibn Shākir al-Kutubī, *'Uyūn al-Tawārīkh*, 20:132–33; al-Subkī, *Ṭabaqāt al-Shāfi'iyyah*, 8:270; al-Malik al-Ashraf, *al-'Asjad*, 626–27; Ibn Duqmāq, *al-Jawhar al-Thamīn*, 177–78. The irony that the caliph's army was routed on the day of 'Āshūrā', the tenth of Muḥarram, when al-Ḥusayn was betrayed and massacred, seems to go unnoticed, except perhaps by al-Dhahabī who notes the day in passing.

44. Ibn Wāṣil, *Die Chronik*, 155-56; al-Yūnīnī, *Dhayl Mir'āt al-Zamān*, 1:88; Abū'l-Fidā, *al-Mukhtaṣar*, 3:233; al-Dhahabī, *Siyar*, 16:436; al-Dhahabī, *Tārīkh al-Islām*, 66:32; Ibn al-Wardī, *Tatimmat al-Mukhtaṣar*, 2:283; Ibn Shākir al-Kutubī, *'Uyūn al-Tawārīkh*, 20:133; al-Subkī, *Ṭabaqāt al-Shāfi'iyyah*, 8:270; Ibn Kathīr, *al-Bidāyah wa'l-Nihāyah*, 13:168; al-Yāfi'ī, *Mir'āt al-Jinān*, 4:138; al-Malik al-Ashraf, *al-'Asjad*, 630–31.

45. al-Kāzarūnī, *Mukhtaṣar al-Tārīkh*, 272; *al-Ḥawādith al-Jāmi'ah*, 356; Ibn Shākir al-Kutubī, *'Uyūn al-Tawārīkh*, 20:133.

46. Ibn Wāṣil, *Die Chronik*, 155-56; al-Yūnīnī, *Dhayl Mir'āt al-Zamān*, 1:88–89; Abū'l-Fidā, *al-Mukhtaṣar*, 3:233; al-Dhahabī, *Siyar*, 16:436; al-Dhahabī, *Tārīkh al-Islām*, 66:35–36; Ibn al-Wardī, *Tatimmat al-Mukhtaṣar*, 2:283; Ibn Shākir al-Kutubī, *'Uyūn al-Tawārīkh*, 20:133; al-Subkī, *Ṭabaqāt al-Shāfi'iyyah*, 8:270; al-Yāfi'ī, *Mir'āt al-Jinān*, 4:138; al-Malik al-Ashraf, *al-'Asjad*, 630–31. al-Kāzarūnī explains that the caliph went out to the Mongols after his safety was assured, *Mukhtaṣar al-Tārīkh*, 272–73.
47. Ibn al-Ṭiqṭaqā, *al-Fakhrī*, 338.
48. al-Dhahabī, *al-Mukhtār min Tārīkh al-Jazarī*, Manuscript 1147, folio 80, Köprülü Collection, Süleymaniye Library, Istanbul, Turkey; al-Dhahabī, *Siyar*, 16:437; al-Dhahabī, *Tārīkh al-Islām*, 66:260–61; al-Ṣafadī, *al-Wāfī bi'l-Wafayāt*, 17:642–43; Ibn al-Dawādārī, *Kanz al-Durar*, 8:36. Ibn al-Dawādārī records, from Ibn Wāṣil (604–97/1208–98), Jamāl al-Dīn Ibn Raṭlayn's statement in 698/1298. And al-Dhahabī copied this information out of the earlier history of al-Jazarī (658–739/1260–1338) to use as material for his own works.
49. According to the author of *al-Ḥawādith al-Jāmi'ah*, the only people who were spared were Baghdādī merchants with fermans of protection from the Mongols and people who took refuge with them, the Vizier Ibn al-'Alqamī, *Ṣāḥib al-Dīwān* al-Dāmaghānī, or *Ḥājib al-Bāb* al-Dawāmī (who had gone out with the vizier to meet the Mongols), *al-Ḥawādith al-Jāmi'ah*, 359. Ibn al-'Ibrī also mentions that the Christian community was also spared in the initial Mongol onslaught in his *Tārīkh al-Zamān*, 308, 313.
50. For relevant studies of the Mongols, see David Morgan, *The Mongols* (Oxford: Blackwell Publishing, 2007) and his bibliographic survey of works since 1985 on pages 181–206 of this second edition; Peter Jackson, *The Mongols and the West, 1221–1410* (Harlow, UK: Pearson Longman, 2005); Thomas Allsen, *Culture and Conquest in Mongol Eurasia* (Cambridge: Cambridge University Press, 2001); Reuven Amitai-Preiss and David Morgan, eds., *The Mongol Empire and Its Legacy* (Leiden, Neth.: E. J. Brill, 1999); Peter Golden, *Nomads and Sedentary Societies in Medieval Eurasia* (Washington, DC: American Historical Association, 1998), 40–44; Thomas Allsen, "The Rise of the Mongolian Empire and Mongolian Rule in North China," in *The Cambridge History of China, Volume 6, Alien Regimes and Border States, 907–1368*, ed. Herbert Franke and Denis Twitchett (Cambridge: Cambridge University Press, 1994), 321–413; Robert Marshall, *Storm from the East: From Ghengis Khan to Khubilai Khan* (Berkeley: University of California Press, 1993); Lambton, *Continuity and Change in Medieval Persia*, 15–20, 173–84; David Morgan, *Medieval Persia, 1040–1797* (London: Longman, 1988), 79–82; Thomas Allsen, *Mongol Imperialism: The Policies of the Grand Qan Möngke in China, Russia, and the Islamic Lands, 1251–1259* (Berkeley: University of California Press, 1987); John Andrew Boyle, *The Mongol World Empire: 1206–1370* (London: Variourum Reprints, 1977); Hodgson, *The Venture of Islam*, 2:286–92; J. J. Saunders, *The History of the Mongol Conquests* (London: Routledge and K. Paul, 1972), 44–70; John Andrew Boyle, ed., *The Cambridge History of Iran*, vol. 5, *The Saljuq and Mongol Periods* (Cambridge: Cambridge University Press, 1968).
51. I explore the intermeshed complexities and implications of the Ottoman conquest of Cairo discussed in this section further in an independent article.
52. Wolfgang Drechsler, *De Saracenis et Turcis Chronicon: item de origine et progressu et fine Machometi* (Argentorati: Iucundus, 1550), 37; Wolfgang Drechsler, *Chronicon Saracenicum et Turcicum*, ed. Georgius Fabricius and Johannes Rosinus (Lipsiae: J. C. Wohlfart, 1689), 139, 153–55; M. de M---- d'Ohsson, *Tableau général de l'empire: divisé en deux parties, I l'une comprend la législation mahométane; l'autre, l'histoire de l'empire othoman*

(Paris: De l'imprimerie de monsieur Firmin Didot, 1788), 1:232; M. de M--- d'Ohsson, *Oriental Antiquities, and General View of the Othoman Customs, Laws, and Ceremonies* (Philadelphia: Select Committee and Grand Lodge of Enquiry, 1788), 161.

53. Notably, Vasiliĭ Vladimirovich Bartold, "Khalif i Sultan," in *Mir Islama* 1 (1912): 345–400; Carlo Alfonso Nallino, *Notes on the Nature of the "Caliphate" in General and on the Alleged "Ottoman Caliphate"* [English Translation of *Appunti sulla natura del "califfato" in genere e sul presunto "califfato ottoman"*] (Rome: Press of the Foreign Office, 1919); Thomas W. Arnold, *The Caliphate* (Oxford: Clarendon Press, 1924).

54. N. Ahmet Asrar, "The Myth about the Transfer of the Caliphate to the Ottomans," *Journal of the Regional Cultural Institute* 5, no. 2 and 3 (Spring and Summer 1972): 115–16; Naimur Rahman Farooqi, *Mughal-Ottoman Relations: A Study of Political and Diplomatic Relations between Mughal India and the Ottoman Empire, 1556–1748* (Delhi: IdIrah-i AdaIiyat-i Delli, 1989), 181–86; Azmi Özcan, *Pan-Islamism: Indian Muslims, the Ottomans and Britain (1877–1924)*, (Leiden, Neth.: E. J. Brill, 1997), 2–3; Azmi Özcan, "Hilafet: Osmanlı Dönemi," in *İslam Ansiklopedesi* (Istanbul: *Türkiye Diyanet Vakfı*, 1998), 17:546–48; M. Naeem Qureshi, *Pan-Islam in British Indian Politics: A Study of the Khilafat Movement, 1918–1924* (Leiden, Neth.: E. J. Brill, 1999), 13; Azmi Özcan, "The Ottomans and the Caliphate," in *The Great Ottoman-Turkish Civilization*, ed. Kemal Çiçek (Ankara: Yeni Türkiye, 2000), 181–86.

55. Lütfi Paşa, *Makhṭūṭ Khalāṣ al-Ummah fī Ma'rifat al-A'immah li-Ṣadr al-'Aẓam Luṭfī Pāşā*, ed. Mājidah Makhlūf (Zaqāzīq, Egypt: Markaz Buḥūth Āsiyā, 2001); Hulusi Yavuz, *Siyaset ve Kültür Tarihi Açısından Osmanli Devleti ve İslamiyet* (Istanbul: İz Yayıncılık, 1991), 73–110; Hamilton A. R. Gibb, "Luṭfī Paşa on the Ottoman Caliphate," *Oriens* 15 (1962): 287–95; Ahmet Çelebi Vakfiyesi, Konya, 923/1517, B.O.A., Ev.Vkf 3/14; İskender Paşa Vakfiyesi, Diyarbakr, 973/1565, B.O.A., Ev.Vkf 1/8; Özcan, "Hilafet: Osmanlı Dönemi," 546; Feridun Bey, *Mecmua-yi Münşeat-i Selâtin* (Istanbul: 1274–75 [1857–58]), 1:437–44, 500–501; B.O.A., MD V 70; Tayyib Gökbilgin, "Kanunî Sultan Süleyman Devri Müesseseler ve Teşkilâtına Işık Tutan Bursa Şer'iyye Sicillerinden Örnekler," in *İsmail Hakkı Uzunçarşılı'ya Armğan* (Ankara: Türk Tarih Kurumu Yayınları, 1976), 96–99.

56. J. W. Redhouse, *A Vindication of the Ottoman Sultan's Title of "Caliph;" Shewing Its Antiquity, Validity, and Universal Acceptance* (London: Effingham Wilson Royal Exchange, 1877).

57. Mümtaz'er Türköne, *Siyasi İdeoloji olarak İslamcılığın Doğuşu* (Istanbul: İletişim Yayınları, 1991); Cezmi Eraslan, *II. Abdülhamid ve İslam Birliği: Osmanlı Devleti'nin İslam Siyaseti: 1856–1908* (Istanbul: Ötüken Neşriyat, 1992); Selim Deringil, *The Well-Protected Domains: Ideology and the Legitimation of Power in the Ottoman Empire 1876 – 1909* (London: I. B. Tauris, 1999); Azmi Özcan, *Pan-Islamism*, 40–63; Kemal Karpat, *The Politicization of Islam: Reconstructing Identity, State, Faith, and Community in the Late Ottoman State* (Oxford: Oxford University Press, 2001), 225–33, 240; Erik Jan Zürcher, *Turkey: A Modern History* (London: I. B. Tauris, 2004), 79; M. Şükrü Hanioğlu, *A Brief History of the Late Ottoman Empire* (Princeton, NJ: Princeton University Press, 2008), 129–30, 142.

58. Türköne, *Siyasi İdeoloji*; Eraslan, *II. Abdülhamid ve İslam Birliği*; Özcan, *Pan-Islamism*, 40–63; Karpat, *The Politicization of Islam*, 176–78, 233–34, 235–40; Zürcher, *Turkey*, 81; Hanioğlu, *Late Ottoman Empire*, 130.

59. Israel Gershoni and James Jankowski, *Egypt, Islam, and the Arabs: The Search for Egyptian Nationhood, 1900–1930* (NY: Oxford University Press, 1986), 5.

60. Gershoni and Jankowski, *Egypt, Islam, and the Arabs*, 10; Özcan, *Pan-Islamism*, 137–45, 146–62; Özcan, "Hilafet: Osmanlı Dönemi," 17:548–49; Özcan, "The Ottomans and the Caliphate," 186; T.N.A., F. O. 684/2/File 111, pp. 4–7, March 10, 1924 (Syria); T.N.A., F. O. 174/303/77, March 15, 1924 (Morocco); Cemil Aydin, *The Politics of Anti-Westernism in Asia: Visions of World Order in Pan-Islamic and Pan-Asian Thought* (NY: Columbia University Press, 2007), 96–97, 230. For pro-Ottomanism sentiments and activities during World War I in Egypt, India, and Iraq, see Gershoni and Jankowski, *Egypt, Islam, and the Arabs*, 23–28, Özcan, *Pan-Islamism*, 168–87, Ismāʿīl Nurī Ḥamīdī, "Mawqif Ahālī Baghdād tijāh Quwwāt al-ʿUthmāniyyah khilāl al-Ḥarb al-ʿĀlamiyyah al-Ūlā" (unpublished paper, August 2008), and Mustafa Sabri, *al-Nakīr ʿalā Munkirī al-Niʿmah min al-Dīn wa'l-Khilāfah wa'l-Ummah* (Beirut: al-Maṭbaʿah al-ʿAbbāsiyyah, 1342 [1924], 215–16.

61. For a poignant and succinct description of the demographic and economic impact of World War I, see Zürcher, *Turkey*, 163–65.

62. The Ottoman *şeyhülislam* Yasincizade Abdülvahhab Efendi wrote a treatise, *Khulāṣat al-Burhan fī Iṭāʿat al-Sultan* (Istanbul, 1247/1831), summarizing Muslim obedience due to the contemporary caliph Mahmud II, which is mentioned in Seyfettin Ersahin, "The Ottoman ʿUlemāʾ and the Reforms of Mahmud II" (Master's thesis, University of Manchester, 1990), 36–55.

63. For the striking continuities linking the thought of the Young Turks in opposition to Abdülhamid II during 1889 to 1908 and in the Second Constitutional Period (1908–18) to later Kemalist ideology, see M. Şükrü Hanioğlu, *The Young Turks in Opposition* (Oxford: Oxford University, 1995), 3–32, 200–216; M. Şükrü Hanioğlu, *Preparation for a Revolution: The Young Turks, 1902–1908* (Oxford: Oxford University Press, 2001), 3–7, 289–318; M. Şükrü Hanioğlu, "Garbcılar: Their Attitudes toward Religion and Their Impact on the Official Ideology of the Turkish Republic," *Studia Islamica* 86, no. 2 (1997): 133–58; M. Şükrü Hanioğlu, "Blueprints for a Future Society: Late Ottoman Materialists on Science, Religion, and Art," in *Late Ottoman Society: The Intellectual Legacy*, ed. Elisabeth Özdalga (London: Routledge, 2005), 28–116; Erik Jan Zürcher, "Ottoman Sources of Kemalist Thought," in *Late Ottoman Society: The Intellectual Legacy*, ed. Elisabeth Özdalga (London: Routledge, 2005), 14–27. Particularly striking is Mustafa Kemal's statement to Abdullah Cevdet "Doctor, until now you have written about many things. Now we may bring them to realization" (cited in Hanioğlu, "Garbcılar," 147). For discussions of education in the late Ottoman Empire, see Benjamin Fortna, *Imperial Classroom: Islam, the State, and Education in the Late Ottoman Empire* (Oxford: Oxford University Press, 2003); Selçuk Akşin Somel, *The Modernization of Public Education in the Ottoman Empire, 1839–1908* (Leiden, Neth.: E. J. Brill, 2001); Mehmet Alkan, "Modernization from Empire to Republic and Education in the Process of Nationalism," in *Ottoman Past and Today's Turkey*, ed. Kemal Karpat (Leiden, Neth.: E. J. Brill, 2000), 47–132; Elizabeth Frierson, "Unimagined Communities: State, Press, and Gender in the Hamidian Era" (PhD diss., Princeton University, 1996); Elizabeth Frierson, "Unimagined Communities: Women and Education in the Late Ottoman Empire, 1876–1909" *Critical Matrix* 9, no. 2 (Fall 1995): 55–90; Hasan Ali Koçer', *Türkiye'de Modern Eğitimin Doğuşu ve Gelişimi, 1773–1923* (Ankara: Milli Eğitim Bakanlığı, 1991); Bayram Kodaman, *Abdülhamid Devri Eğitim Sistemi* (Ankara: Türk Tarih Kurumu Basımevi, 1988); Osman Nuri Ergin, *Türkiye Maarif Tarihi* (Istanbul: Eser Neşriyat, 1977). On the reforms under Mahmud II and during the Tanzimat, also see Halil Inalcık, "Application of the Tanzimat and Its Social Effects," *Archivum Ottomanicum* 5

(1973): 91–128, Roderic Davison, *Reform in the Ottoman Empire 1851–1876* (NY: Gordian Press, 1973), Carter Findley, *Bureaucratic Reform in the Ottoman Empire: The Sublime Porte, 1789–1922* (Princeton, NJ: Princeton University Press, 1980), and Carter Findley, *Ottoman Civil Officialdom* (Princeton, NJ: Princeton University Press, 1989).

64. See Şükrü Hanioğlu's excellent summation in *A Brief History of the Late Ottoman Empire*, 111–21. For further details on the Young Ottomans in particular, see Şerif Mardin, *The Genesis of Young Ottoman Thought: A Study in the Modernization of Turkish Political Ideas* (Syracuse, NY: Syracuse University Press, 2000).
65. Hanioğlu, *Late Ottoman Empire*, 201.
66. Erik Jan Zürcher, *The Unionist Factor: The Role of the Committee of Union and Progress in the Turkish National Movement, 1905–1926* (Leiden, Neth.: E. J. Brill, 1984), 68–105; Erik Jan Zürcher, *Political Opposition in the Early Turkish Republic: The Progressive Republican Party, 1924–1925* (Leiden, Neth.: E. J. Brill, 1991), 11–15; Zürcher, *Turkey*, 135–36, 141–43, 147–51.
67. Zürcher, "Ottoman Sources of Kemalist Thought," 21; Erik Jan Zürcher, "The Vocabulary of Muslim Nationalism," *International Journal of the Sociology of Language* 137 (1999): 81–92; Erik Jan Zürcher, "Young Turks, Ottoman Muslims and Turkish Nationalists: Identity Politics," in *Ottoman Past and Today's Turkey*, ed. Kemal Karpat (Leiden, Neth.: E. J. Brill, 2000), 150–79.
68. Zürcher, *The Unionist Factor*, 45–67, 106–41; Zürcher, *Political Opposition in the Early Turkish Republic*, 15–23; Zürcher, *Turkey*, 156–59; Masayuki Yamuchi, *The Green Crescent under the Red Star: Enver Pasha in Soviet Russia, 1919–1922* (Tokyo: Institute for the Study of Languages and Cultures of Asia and Africa, 1991), 37–63.
69. The most detailed account of this process is found in Michael Martin Finefrock, "From Sultanate to Republic: Mustafa Kemal Ataturk and the Structure of Turkish Politics, 1922–1924," (PhD diss., Princeton University, 1976).
70. Özcan, *Pan-Islamism*, 187; Finefrock, "From Sultanate to Republic," 13. See, for instance, the underlying premise of the National Pact, *Misak-ı Milli*, (adopted by the Sivas Congress in September 1919 and the Ottoman Parliament in January 1920) to fight for "the continued existence of a stable Ottoman Sultanate and society," which includes the necessity of ensuring "the security of the city of Istanbul, which is the seat of the Caliphate of Islam, the capital of the Sultanate, and the headquarters of the Ottoman Government... from every threat," included in Mustafa Budak, *İdealden Gerçeğe: Misak-ı Millî'den Lozan'a Dış Politika* (Istanbul: Küre Yayınları, 2002), 155–59, 515–18 and Cengiz Sunay, *Son Karar: Misak-ı Milli, Son Osmanlı Meclisi'nin Yakın Tarihine Yön Veren Kararı* (Istanbul: Doğan Kitap, 2007), 82–86 and translated in J. C. Hurewitz, *Diplomacy in the Near and Middle East: A Documentary Record* (Princeton, NJ: D. Van Nostrand, 1956), 2:74–75. Also note Mustafa Kemal's proclamations circulated among the Turkish populace on April 21, 1920, that the Grand National Assembly would open in two days time and undertake "such vital duties of the utmost importance as saving the independence of the country and the exalted post of the Caliphate and the Sultanate" and on April 25, 1920, which included the supplication for God's mercy on and success for whomever worked to save the caliph, the sultan, the nation, and the country; both proclamations are cited in Ali Satan, *Halifeliğin Kaldırılması* (Istanbul: Gökkubbe, 2008), 115–16. For a rich discussion of the caliphate during the National Struggle, see Satan, *Halifeliğin Kaldırılması*, 105–37.
71. Zürcher, *Turkey*, 139, 151.
72. *T.B.M.M. Zabıt Ceridesi*, Devre I, Cilt 24, Içtima Senesi 3 (October 30, 1338 [1922]), 279–312 (Ottoman script), 269–98 (Latin script) and (November 1, 1338 [1922]), 316–29

(Ottoman script), 304–15 (Latin script); Rıza Nur, *Hayat ve Hatıratım* (Istanbul: Altındağ Yayınevi, 1968), 3:967–72; Finefrock, "From Sultanate to Republic," 57–90.

73. Finefrock, "From Sultanate to Republic," 106, 16, 22–36, 86–90.
74. Ali Şükrü was the owner of a publishing house that published Karahisar deputy İsmail Şükrü (Çelikalay)'s treatise *Iilafet-i İslamiyye ve Türkiye Büyük Millet Meclisi*, which argued that since the caliphate was a temporal and spiritual position of leadership, the caliph could be elevated to a chief of state and thereby avoid the potential disintegration of the Grand National Assembly over whom to elect as President. Ali Şükrü was also the owner of the newly established, vociferous opposition newspaper, *Tan*. For further details, see the beginning of chapter 6.
75. Finefrock, "From Sultanate to Republic," 191–209; Zürcher, *Political Opposition in the Early Turkish Republic*, 25–27, 124–25; Zürcher, *Turkey*, 159.
76. Finefrock, "From Sultanate to Republic," 102–5, 108, 165–68, 170–73, 177–90, 205–6; Zürcher, *Political Opposition in the Early Turkish Republic*, 25–31.
77. It is worth noting that one-fourth of the army was under the command of the conservative general and Turkish independence war hero Kazım (Karabekir) Paşa, who was purposefully not informed of Mustafa Kemal's plans to abolish the caliphate.
78. Finefrock, "From Sultanate to Republic," 279–96, 110–32, 260–63, 266–73.
79. *T.B.M.M. Zabıt Ceridesi*, Devre II, Cilt 6, Içtima Senesi 1 (February 27, 1340 [1924]), 405, 429–31 (Latin script); *T.B.M.M. Zabıt Ceridesi*, Devre II, Cilt 7, Içtima Senesi 1 (March 3, 1340 [1924]), 29–78 (Ottoman script), 28–69 (Latin script); Kemaleddin Nomer, *Şeriat, Hilafet, Cumhuriyet, Laiklik: Dini ve Tarihi Gerçeklerin Belgeleri* (Istanbul: Boğaziçi Yayınları, 1996), 297–409; Hasan Hüseyin Ceylan, *Büyük* Oyun, vol. 3, *Hilafetin Kaldırılması* (Ankara: Rehber Yayıncılık, 1995).
80. Marshall Hodgson, "The Unity of Later Islamic History," in *Rethinking World History: Essays on Europe, Islam, and World History*, ed. Edmund Burke III (Cambridge: Cambridge University Press, 1993), 189. For "a small but distinctive strain" of Persianate Sufi stories interpreting the Mongol conquests, see Devin Deweese, "'Stuck in the Throat of Chingīz Khan:' Envisioning the Mongol Conquests in Some Sufī Accounts from the 14th to 17th Centuries," in *History and Historiography of Post-Mongol Central Asia and the Middle East: Studies in Honor of John E. Woods*, ed. Judith Pfeiffer and Sholeh Quinn (Wiesbaden, Ger.: Harrassowitz Verlag, 2006), 23–60.
81. Maurice Halbwachs, *The Collective Memory*, trans. Francis Ditter Jr. and Vida Yazdi Ditter (NY: Harper Colophon Books, 1980); Maurice Halbwachs, *On Collective Memory*, ed. Lewis Cosner (Chicago: University of Chicago Press), 1992; Elizabeth Castelli, *Martyrdom and Memory: Early Christian Culture Making* (NY: Columbia University Press, 2004), 13; Patrick Hutton, *History as an Art of Memory* (Hanover, NH: University Press of New England, 1993), 79. Castelli offers an exceptional overview of the development of collective memory as a theoretical concept and its significance for interdisciplinary discussions of the past, 10–24. Other valuable contributions include Danièle Hervieu-Léger, "Religion as Memory," in *Religion: Beyond a Concept*, ed. Hent de Vries (NY: Fordham University Press, 2008), 245–58, 879–80, Jeffrey Olick and Joyce Robbins, "Social Memory Studies: From 'Collective Memory' to the Historical Sociology of Mnemonic Practices," *Annual Review of Sociology* 24 (1999): 105–40, and Alon Confino, "Collective Memory and Cultural History: Problems of Method," *American Historical Review* 102, no. 5 (1997): 1386–1403.

CHAPTER 1. VISIONS OF A LOST CALIPHAL CAPITAL: BAGHDAD, 1258 CE

1. Natalie Zemon Davis and Randolph Starn, "Introduction to Special Issue on Memory and Counter-Memory," *Representations* 26 (Spring 1989): 4.
2. Jalāl al-Dīn al-Rūmī (1207–73 CE), *The Essential Rumi*, trans. Coleman Barks with John Moyne (NY: HarperCollins, 2004), 17.
3. Ẓahīr al-Dīn ʿAlī b. Muḥammad b. Maḥmūd b. Abī'l-ʿIzz b. Aḥmad b. Isḥāq b. Ibrāhīm al-Kāzarūnī al-Baghdādī al-Shāfiʿī, *Maqāmah fī Qawāʿid Baghdād fī'l-Dawlah al-ʿAbbāsiyyah*, ed. Kūrkīs ʿAwwād and Mīkhāʾīl ʿAwwād (Baghdad: Maṭbaʿat al-Irshād, 1962), 7–10; Ibn al-Kāzarūnī, *Mukhtaṣar al-Tārīkh*, 6–22; *al-Ḥawādith al-Jāmiʿah*, 536–37; Shams al-Dīn Muḥammad b. Aḥmad b. ʿUthmān al-Dhahabī, *al-Muʿjam al-Mukhtaṣṣ*, ed. Muḥammad al-Ḥabīb al-Hīlah (Taif, Saudi Arabia: Maktabah al-Ṣiddīq, 1998), 172–73; Ṣalāḥ al-Dīn Khalīl b. Aybak al-Ṣafadī, *al-Wāfī bi'l-Wafayāt*, vol. 22, ed. Ramzī Baʿalbakī (Wiesbaden, Ger.: Franz Steiner Verlag, 1983), 140–41; al-Subkī, *Ṭabaqāt al-Shāfiʿiyyah al-Kubrā*, 10:367–68; Abū'l-Faḍl Shihāb al-Dīn Aḥmad b. ʿAlī b. Muḥammad Ibn Ḥajar al-ʿAsqalānī, *al-Durar al-Kāminah fī Aʿyān al-Miʾah al-Thāminah*, (Beirut: Dār al-Jīl, 1978), 3:119; Taqiyy al-Dīn Abū Bakr b. Aḥmad b. Muḥammad Ibn Qāḍī Shuhbah, *Ṭabaqāt al-Shāfiʿiyyah* (Hyderabad, India: Maṭbaʿat Majlis Dāʾirat al-Maʿārif al-ʿUthmānīyah, 1978–80), 2:239–40; Jamāḷ al-Dīn Abū'l-Maḥāsin Yūsuf Ibn Taghribirdī, *al-Manhal al-Ṣāfī wa'l-Mustawfā baʿd al-Wāfī* (Cairo: Maṭbaʿat Dār al-Kutub al-Miṣriyyah, 1999), 8:171.
4. Ibn al-Kāzarūnī, *Maqāmah fī Qawāʿid Baghdād*, 14–15.
5. Ibid., 16–29.
6. *al-Ḥawādith al-Jāmiʿah*, 363; Ibn Shākir al-Kutubī, *ʿUyūn al-Tawārīkh*, 20:129; al-Dhahabī, *Tārīkh al-Islām*, 66:37; Ibn Kathīr, *al-Bidāyah wa'l-Nihāyah*, 13:196; al-Suyūṭī, *Tārīkh al-Khulafāʾ*, 538.
7. Muḥammad al-Hāshimī, "Saʿdī al-Shīrāzī," *al-Yaqīn* 1, no. 17 (February 17, 1923): 500.
8. Joseph De Somogyi, "A Qasida on the Destruction of Baghdad by the Mongols," *Bulletin of the School of Oriental and African Studies* (1933): 48.
9. For a concise summary of these political developments, see Fred Donner, "Muhammad and the Caliphate: Political History of the Islamic Empire up to the Mongol Conquest," in *Oxford History of Islam*, ed. John Esposito (Oxford: Oxford University Press, 1999), 29–58.
10. John Voll, "Islam as a Special World System," *Journal of World History* 5, no. 2 (Fall 1994): 220. Indeed, as Marshall Hodgson first suggested in 1960: "Despite its unexampled dispersion throughout the Eastern Hemisphere—in Europe, Africa, India, China, Central Eurasia, and the Far South East—Islam [especially from 1000 to 1800 CE] maintained not only religious but even some measure of social bonds among its scattered communities. In this way it came closer than any other medieval society to establishing a common world order of social and even cultural standards, such as it was in fact accomplished in some respects after the advent of European world hegemony in the nineteenth century." Hodgson, "The Unity of Later Islamic History," 176.
11. Ira Lapidus, "Sultanates and Gunpowder Empires," in *Oxford History of Islam*, ed. John Esposito (Oxford: Oxford University Press, 1999), 356–68.
12. Donner, "Muhammad and the Caliphate," 32, 60.
13. Shams al-Dīn Abū ʿAbdillāh Muḥammad b. Aḥmad b. Abī Bakr al-Qurṭubī, *al-Tadhkirah fī Aḥwāl al-Mawtā wa-Umūr al-Ākhirah*, ed. Yūsuf ʿAlī Badawī (Dār Ibn Kathīr, 1999), 3:191–93.

14. *al-Ḥawādith al-Jāmiʿah*, 363–64; Ibn Shākir al-Kutubī, *Fawāt al-Wafayāt*, 2:233–35; Ibn Shākir al-Kutubī, *ʿUyūn al-Tawārīkh*, 20:137–40. For an excellent discussion of *waʿẓ* as hortatory preaching, see Linda Jones, *The Power of Oratory in the Medieval Muslim World* (Cambridge: Cambridge University Press, 2012), 158-92.
15. Tāj al-Dīn ʿAbd al-Wahhāb al-Subkī, *Muʿīd al-Niʿam wa-Mubīd al-Niqam*, 3rd ed. Muḥammad ʿAlī al-Najjār, Abū Zayd Shalabī, and Muḥammad Abū'l-ʿUyūn (Cairo: Maktabat al-Khānjī, 1996), 112–13. On the utilization of mosque space for *waʿẓ*, see Hatim Mahamid, "Mosques as Higher Educational Institutions in Mamluk Syria," *Journal of Islamic Studies* 20, no. 2 (2009): 208–11.
16. Abū Shāmah, *Tarājim*, 213; al-Dhahabī, *Tārīkh al-Islām*, 66:75; ʿAlī b. Abī'l-Faraj b. al-Ḥusayn al-Baṣrī, "al-Manāqib al-ʿAbbāsiyyah wa'l-Mafākhir al-Mustanṣiriyyah," Arabe Collection, Manuscript 6144, folio 3v, Bibliothèque nationale de France, Paris, France.
17. Peter Brown, *Through the Eye of a Needle: Wealth, the Fall of Rome, and the Making of Christianity in the West, 350–550 AD* (Princeton, NJ: Princeton University Press, 2012), xxiii–xxiv.
18. The final compendium of his teachers, compiled by al-Ḥāfiẓ Ibn Saʿd al-Ḥanbalī (703–59 AH), would ultimately encompass the biographies of some 188 scholars. al-Ḥāfiẓ Shams al-Dīn Abī Abdillāh Ibn Saʿd al-Ṣāliḥī al-Ḥanbalī, *Muʿjam al-Shuyūkh li-Tāj al-Dīn ʿAbd al-Wahhāb b. ʿAlī al-Subkī*, ed. Bashshār Maʿrūf, Rāʾid al-ʿAnbakī, and Muṣṭafā al-Aʿẓamī (Beirut: Dār al-Gharb al-Islāmī, 2004). Jonathan Berkey enumerates twenty female scholars among those who taught al-Subkī in "al-Subkī and His Women," *Mamlūk Studies Review* 14 (2010): 1–17.
19. al-Subkī, *Ṭabaqāt al-Shāfiʿiyyah al-Kubrā*, 1:3–11, 10:398–99; al-Dhahabī, *al-Muʿjam al-Mukhtaṣṣ*, 152; Ṣalāḥ al-Dīn Khalīl b. Aybak al-Ṣafadī, *al-Wāfī bi'l-Wafayāt*, vol. 19, ed. Riḍwān al-Sayyid (Wiesbaden, Ger.: Franz Steiner Verlag, 1993), 315–16; Waliyy al-Dīn Abū Zurʿah Aḥmad b. ʿAbd al-Raḥīm b. al-Ḥusayn Ibn al-ʿIrāqī, *al-Dhayl ʿalā ʿIbar fī Khabar Man ʿAbar*, ed. Ṣāliḥ Mahdī ʿAbbās (Beirut: Muʾassasat al-Risālah, 1989) 2:303–5; Taqiyy al-Dīn Abū Bakr b. Aḥmad b. Muḥammad Ibn Qāḍī Shuhbah al-Dimashqī, *Tārīkh Ibn Qāḍī Shuhbah*, ed. Adnan Darwich (Damascus: Institut Français de Damas, 1994), 3:372–75; Taqiyy al-Dīn Abū Bakr b. Aḥmad b. Muḥammad Ibn Qāḍī Shuhbah al-Dimashqī, *Ṭabaqāt al-Shāfiʿiyyah*, 3:140–43; Ibn Ḥajar al-ʿAsqalānī, *al-Durar al-Kāminah*, 2:425–28; Jamāl al-Dīn Abū'l-Maḥāsin Yūsuf Ibn Taghribirdī, *al-Nujūm al-Zāhirah fī Mulūk Miṣr wa'l-Qāhirah* (Cairo: Wizārat al-Thaqāfah wa'l-Irshād al- Qawmī [Ṭabʿah Musawwarah ʿan Ṭabʿat Dār al-Kutub]), 11:108–9; Shams al-Dīn Ibn Ṭulūn, *Quḍāt Dimashq*, ed. Ṣalāḥ al-Dīn al-Munajjid (Damascus: Maṭbuʿāt al-Majmaʿ al-ʿIlmī al-ʿArabī, 1956), 105–6; Shihāb al-Dīn ʿAbd al-Ḥayy b. Aḥmad b. Muḥammad Ibn al- ʿImād, *Shadharāt al-Dhahab fī Akhbār man Dhahab*, ed. ʿAbd al-Qādir al-Arnāʾūt and Muḥammad al-Arnāʾūt (Damascus: Dār Ibn Kathīr, 1991), 8:378–80; ʿAbd al-Ḥayy b. ʿAbd al-Kabīr al-Kattānī, *Fihris al-Fahāris wa'l-Ithbāt wa-Muʿjam al-Maʿājim wa'l-Mashyakhāt wa'l-Musalsalāt*, ed. Iḥsān ʿAbbās (Dār al-Gharb al-Islāmī, 1982), 2:1037–38.
20. Tāj al-Dīn al-Subkī, *Ṭabaqāt al-Shāfiʿiyyah al-Kubrā*, 1:23, 206–9, 9:101, 10:398–99; al-Dhahabī, *al-Muʿjam al-Mukhtaṣṣ*, 152; Ibn al-ʿIrāqī, *al-Dhayl ʿalā ʿIbar*, 2:305; Ibn Qāḍī Shuhbah, *Tārīkh*, 3:374; al-Kattānī, *Fihris al-Fahāris*, 3:1038.
21. Tāj al-Dīn al-Subkī, *Ṭabaqāt al-Shāfiʿiyyah al-Kubrā*, 1:23–30, 207; Muḥammad al-Ṣādiq Ḥusayn, *al-Bayt al-Subkī* (Cairo: Dār al-Kātib al-Miṣrī, 1948), 20–21; al-Ṣafadī, *al-Wāfī bi'l-Wafayāt*, 19:316, Ibn al-ʿIrāqī, *al-Dhayl ʿalā ʿIbar*, 2:304; Ibn Qāḍī Shuhbah, *Ṭabaqāt al-Shāfiʿiyyah*, 3:143; Ibn Ḥajar al-ʿAsqalānī, *al-Durar al-Kāminah*, 2:426; Ibn al- ʿImād, *Shadharāt al-Dhahab*, 8:380. For a solid refutation of George Makdisi's

influential interpretation of al-Subkī's *Ṭabaqāt al-Shāfiʿiyyah al-Kubra* regarding the establishment of Ashʿarī theology, see Khaled El-Rouayheb's "From Ibn Ḥajar al-Haytamī (d. 1566) to Khayr al-Dīn al-Alūsī (d. 1899): Changing Views of Ibn Taymiyya among Non-Hanbalī Sunni Scholars," in *Ibn Taymiyya and His Times*, ed. Yossef Rapoport and Shahab Ahmed (Oxford: Oxford University Press, 2010), especially pages 295–97.

22. al-Ṣafadī, *al-Wāfī bi'l-Wafayāt*, 19:316; al-Subkī, *Ṭabaqāt al-Shāfiʿiyyah al-Kubrā*, 1:30; Ibn Qāḍī Shuhbah, *Tārīkh*, 3:374–75; Ibn Qāḍī Shuhbah, *Ṭabaqāt al-Shāfiʿiyyah*, 3:142; Ibn Ḥajar al-ʿAsqalānī, *al-Durar al-Kāminah*, 2:426; Hajjī Khalīfah Kātip Çelebi Muṣṭafā b. ʿAbdillāh al-Qusṭanṭinī, *Kashf al-Ẓunūn ʿan Asāmī al-Kutub wa'l-Funūn* (Beirut: Dār al-Fikr, 1982), 3:1101; Ibn al-ʿImād, *Shadharāt al-Dhahab*, 8:379.
23. Patrick Hutton, "Collective Memory and Collective Mentalities: The Halbwachs-Ariès Connection," *Historical Reflections* 15, no 2 (1988), 313.
24. al-Subkī, *Ṭabaqāt al-Shāfiʿiyyah al-Kubrā*, 8:259, 261, 272.
25. Halbwachs, *The Collective Memory*, 22–87; see pages 63–71 about the living bonds between generations.
26. Yosef Hayim Yerushalmi, *Zakhor: Jewish History and Jewish Memory* (Seattle: University of Washington Press, 1982), 5, 11, 31–34. Yerushalmi's work has inspired a rich debate over the relationship between Jewish collective memory and history writing, including Amos Funkenstein's response arguing for a traditional Jewish historical consciousness in "Collective Memory and Historical Consciousness," *History and Memory* 1, no. 1 (1989): 5–26, David Myers's critique of Funkenstein in " 'Zakhor': A Super-Commentary," *History and Memory* 4, no. 2 (1992): 129–48, Robert Chazan's discussion of historical narrative in "The Timebound and the Timeless: Medieval Jewish Narration of Events," *History and Memory* 6, no. 1 (1994): 5–34, and Gabrielle Spiegel's elaboration of the "fundamentally liturgical nature of Jewish historical memory" in "Memory and History: Liturgical Time and Historical Time," *History and Theory* 41, no. 2 (2002): 149–62.
27. For a more expansive treatment of the place of prophetic traditions in Islamic civilization, see Jonathan Brown's introduction, *Hadith: Muhammad's Legacy in the Medieval and Modern World* (Oxford: Oneworld, 2009).
28. For a path-breaking analysis of Islamic legal reasoning, focused on "Medinese Praxis" or *ʿamal*, see Umar F. Abd-Allah Wymann-Landgraf, *Malik and Medina: Islamic Legal Reasoning in the Formative Period* (Leiden, Neth.: E. J. Brill, 2013).
29. Paul Connerton, *How Societies Remember* (Cambridge: Cambridge University Press, 1989), 44–48, 61.
30. al-Bukhārī, *Ṣaḥīḥ al-Bukhārī*, 1:123 (#634), 3:1230, 1465 (#6076, #7333); Abū'l-Ḥasan Muslim b. al-Ḥajjāj al-Qushayrī al-Naysābūrī, *Ṣaḥīḥ Muslim* (Stuttgart, Ger.: Thesaurus Islamicus Foundation, 2000), 1:530 (#3197); *Sunan Abī Dāwūd* 1:335 (#1972), *Sunan al-Nasāʾī*, 2:495 (#3075); Aḥmad b. Hanbal, *Musnad al-Imām Aḥmad*, 22:312, 418–19, 460–61 (#14419, 14553, 14618), 23:286 (#15041).
31. Ibn Shākir al-Kutubī, *ʿUyūn al-Tawārīkh*, 20:140. It seems possible that this poet is the same figure as one Abū'l-Ḥusayn Muḥammad b. al-Ḥusayn b. Abī Bakr b. al-Ḥasan b. Aḥmad al-Shurūbī al-Mawṣilī who was born in 579 AH and discussed by Ibn al-Shaʿʿār al-Mawṣilī in his *Qalāʾid al-Jumān*, 6:149.
32. Ibn Shākir al-Kutubī, *Fawāt al-Wafayāt*, 2:232.
33. al-Yūnīnī, *Dhayl Mirʾāt al-Zamān*, 1:85.
34. Ibn Wāṣil, *Die Chronik*, 153; al-Yūnīnī, *Dhayl Mirʾāt al-Zamān*, 1:85; Ibn Shākir al-Kutubī, *ʿUyūn al-Tawārīkh*, 20:130. Their writings reflect the reiteration of this sentiment in the Syrian historiographic tradition. al-Yūnīnī's usage of *afḍaʿ* (horrendous,

tragic) instead of Ibn Wāṣil's *aqṭa'* (piercing, sharp, decisive) may reflect authorial discretion or scribal alteration.

35. Ibn al-Dawādārī, *Kanz al-Durar*, 8:29, 34.
36. al-Dhahabī, *Tārīkh al-Islām*, 66:37.
37. Ibn Wāṣil, *Die Chronik*, 157.
38. al-Dhahabī, "al-Mukhtār min Tārīkh al-Jazarī," Köprülü Collection, Manuscript 1147, folio 80, Köprülü Manuscript Library, Istanbul, Turkey; al-Dhahabī, *Siyar*, 16:437; al-Dhahabī, *Tārīkh al-Islām*, 66:260–61; al-Ṣafadī, *al-Wāfī bi'l-Wafayāt*, 17:642–43; Ibn al-Dawādārī, *Kanz al-Durar*, 8:36; Ibn Kathīr, *al-Bidāyah wa'l-Nihāyah*, 13:168–69.
39. Minhāj al-Dīn al-Juzjānī, *Ṭabaqāt-i Nāṣirī: A General History of the Muhammadan Dynasties of Asia from A.H. 194 (810 A.D.) to A.H. 658 (1260 A.D.)*, trans. H. G. Raverty (New Delhi: Oriental Books Reprint Corporation, 1970), 2:1252–53.
40. Ibid.; Ibn al-'Ibrī, *Tārīkh al-Zamān*, 308; al-Subkī, *Ṭabaqāt al-Shāfi'iyyah*, 8:271.
41. Ḥusām al-Dīn was tried and executed on Muḥarram 6, 661 / November 22, 1262, with his written pledge advising against attacking the caliphate and Baghdad serving as proof of his guilt. Rashiduddin Fazlullah, *The Compendium of Chronicles (Classical Writings of the Medieval Islamic World: Persian Histories of the Mongol Dynasties, vol. 3)*, trans. Wheeler Thackston (London: I. B. Tauris, 2012), 350, 363.
42. Ibid., 350; Naṣīr al-Dīn al-Ṭusī, "Chigūnagī-i Rūydād-i Baghdād," in 'Alā al-Dīn 'Aṭā Malik ibn Muḥammad al-Juvaynī, *Taḥrīr-i Navīn: Tārīkh-i Jahāngushāy* (Tehran: Amīr Kabīr, 1983), 396–97. al-Ṭusī's epistle is translated by John Andrew Boyle in his "The Death of the Last 'Abbasid Caliph: A Contemporary Muslim Account," *Journal of Semitic Studies* 6, no. 1 (1961): 145–61 and further discussed by Georgii Michaelis Wickens in his "Nasir ad-Din Tusi on the Fall of Baghdad: A Further Study," *Journal of Semitic Studies* 7, no. 1 (1962): 23–35. Abdulhadi Hairi also grapples with the implications of Rashīd al-Dīn's passage in "Naṣīr al-Dīn al-Ṭusī: His Alleged Role in the Fall of Baghdad," in *Ve Congres International d'Arabisants et d'Islamisants, Bruxelles, 31 Août–6 Septembre 1970* (Brussels: Centre pour l'Étude des Problèmes du Monde Musulman Contemporain, 1971), 255–66.
43. David Morgan, John Andrew Boyle, H. G. Raverty, Shihāb al-Dīn al-Nuwayrī, and Ibn Ḥabīb al-Ḥalabī discuss this point and, in the case of the modern historians, provide parallel examples of such honorable treatment accorded to other Mongols put to death; see Morgan, *The Mongols*, 133; John Andrew Boyle, "The Death of the Last 'Abbasid Caliph," 152; al-Juzjānī, *Ṭabaqāt-i Nāṣirī*, trans. H. G. Raverty, 2:1185, 1253–54; al-Nuwayrī, *Nihāyat al-Arab*, 23:324; Ibn Ḥabīb al-Ḥalabī, "Durrat al-Aslāk fī Dawlat al-Atrāk," Arabe Collection, Manuscript 4680, folio 24v, Bibliothèque nationale de France, Paris, France.
44. Abū Shāmah, *Tarājim*, 199; al-Juzjānī, *Ṭabaqāt-i Nāṣirī*, 2:1253–54; Ibn al-'Ibrī, *Tārīkh al-Zamān*, 308; Ibn al-Kāzarūnī, *Mukhtaṣar al-Tārīkh*, 273–74; Ibn Wāṣil, *Die Chronik*, 156; Qanītū al-Irbilī, *Khulāṣat al-Dhahab al-Masbūk*, 291; *al-Ḥawādith al-Jāmi'ah*, 357; Baybars al-Manṣūrī, *Zubdat al-Fikrah*, 37; al-Yūnīnī, *Dhayl Mir'āt al-Zamān*, 1:85, 89; Ibn al-Ṭiqṭaqā, *al-Fakhrī*, 336; al-Nuwayrī, *Nihāyat al-Arab*, 23:324; Abū'l-Fidā, *al-Mukhtaṣar*, 233; al-Dhahabī, *Siyar*, 16:436–37; al-Dhahabī, *Tārīkh al-Islām*, 66:261; Ibn al-Wardī, *Tatimmat al-Mukhtaṣar*, 2:282, 284; Mughulṭāy b. Qilīj b. 'Abdillāh, *al-Ishārah*, 559; Ibn Shākir al-Kutubī, *Fawāt al-Wafayāt*, 2:231; Ibn Shākir al-Kutubī, *'Uyūn al-Tawārīkh*, 20:130, 134; al-Yāfi'ī, *Mir'āt al-Jinān*, 4:138, 139; al-Subkī, *Ṭabaqāt al-Shāfi'iyyah*, 8:270–71; Ibn Kathīr, *al-Bidāyah wa'l-Nihāyah*, 13:169, 171; Ibn Ḥabīb al-Ḥalabī, "Durrat al-Aslāk fī Dawlat al-Atrāk," Arabe Collection, Manuscript 4680,

folio 24v, Bibliothèque nationale de France, Paris, France; al-Malik al-Ashraf, *al-ʿAsjad*, 631; Ibn Duqmāq, *Nuzhat al-Anām*, 239; Ibn Duqmāq, *al-Jawhar al-Thamīn*, 178.

45. Ibn Shākir al-Kutubī, *ʿUyūn al-Tawārīkh*, 20:142.
46. Ibid., 20:139.
47. Ibn Shākir al-Kutubī, *Fawāt al-Wafayāt*, 2:234.
48. *al-Ḥawādith al-Jāmiʿah*, 363–64; Ibn Shākir al-Kutubī, *ʿUyūn al-Tawārīkh*, 20:137.
49. al-Hāshimī, "al-Shīrāzī," 498.
50. *al-Ḥawādith al-Jāmiʿah*, 364. For an historical reconstruction of the destroyed mausolea of the Abbasid caliphs, see Terry Allen, "Tombs of the ʿAbbāsid Caliphs in Baghdād," *Bulletin of the School of Oriental and African Studies* 47, no. 3 (1983): 421–31.
51. Ibn Shākir al-Kutubī, *ʿUyūn al-Tawārīkh*, 20:142.
52. al-Malik al-Ashraf, *al-ʿAsjad al-Masbūk*, 632.
53. Rashīd al-Dīn, *Jāmiʿ al-Tawārīkh*, vol. 2, pt. 1, 294: "*Aṣbaḥnā lanā dārun ka-jannātin wa-firdaws / wa-amsaynā bi lā dārin kaʾan lam taghna biʾl-ams.*" In Wheeler Thackston's English translation: "We woke up in the morning in a palace like paradise, but we went to bed without a palace with which we could not dispense yesterday," Rashiduddin Fazlullah, *The Compendium of Chronicles*, 3:354.
54. Lisan al-Din Ibn al-Khatib, *Raqm al-Ḥulal fī Naẓm al-Duwal*, ed. ʿAdnān Darwīsh (Damascus: Manshūrāt Wizārat al-Thaqāfah, 1990), 122. Other contemporary examples with similar exclamations include al-Yūnīnī, *Dhayl Mirʾāt al-Zamān*, 1:256 and Ibn al-Kāzarūnī, *Mukhtaṣar al-Tārīkh*, 280, along with nearly all of the historical works I examined.
55. al-Subkī, *Ṭabaqāt al-Shāfiʿiyyah*, 8:273.
56. ʿIbn Kathīr, *al-Bidāyah waʾl-Nihāyah*, 13:268; al-Suyūṭī, *Ḥusn al-Muḥāḍarah*, 2:45–46; al-Bayjūrī, *Ḥāshiyat al-Imām al-Bayjūrī ʿalā Jawharat al-Tawḥīd*, 180.
57. Ibn Wāṣil, *Die Chronik*, 156; al-Yūnīnī, *Dhayl Mirʾāt al-Zamān*, 1:89; *al-Ḥawādith al-Jāmiʿah*, 359; al-Dhahabī, *Tārīkh al-Islām*, 66:36; al-Dhahabī, *al-ʿIbar*, 5:226; Abū Muḥammad ʿAbdullāh b. Asʿad b. ʿAlī b. Sulaymān ʿAfīf al-Dīn al-Yāfiʿī al-Yamanī al-Makkī, *Mirʾāt al-Jinān wa-ʿIbrat al-Yaqẓān* (Hyderabad, India: Maṭbaʿat Dāʾirat al-Maʿārif al-Niẓāmiyyah, 1920), 4:137; al-Subkī, *Ṭabaqāt al-Shāfiʿiyyah*, 8:271; Ibn Kathīr, *al-Bidāyah waʾl-Nihāyah*, 13:170; Ibn Ḥabīb al-Ḥalabī, "Durrat al-Aslāk fī Dawlat al-Atrāk," Arabe Collection, Manuscript 4680, folio 24v, Bibliothèque nationale de France, Paris, France; al-Malik al-Ashraf, *al-ʿAsjad al-Masbūk*, 631.
58. *al-Ḥawādith al-Jāmiʿah*, 359; Baybars al-Manṣūrī, *Zubdat al-Fikrah*, 37; al-Dhahabī, *Tārīkh al-Islām*, 66:39; Ibn Ḥabīb al-Ḥalabī, "Durrat al-Aslāk fī Dawlat al-Atrāk," Arabe Collection, Manuscript 4680, folio 24v, Bibliothèque nationale de France, Paris, France; Ibn Duqmāq, *Nuzhat al-Anām*, 238; Ibn Duqmāq, *al-Jawhar al-Thamīn*, 178.
59. Ibn Kathīr, *al-Bidāyah waʾl-Nihāyah*, 13:169.
60. *al-Ḥawādith al-Jāmiʿah*, 363; Ibn Shākir al-Kutubī, *ʿUyūn al-Tawārīkh*, 20:137.
61. Ibn Shākir al-Kutubī, *ʿUyūn al-Tawārīkh*, 20:141.
62. al-Yūnīnī, *Dhayl Mirʾāt al-Zamān*, 1:89; *al-Ḥawādith al-Jāmiʿah*, 360; Baybars al-Manṣūrī, *Zubdat al-Fikrah*, 37; al-Dhahabī, *Tārīkh al-Islām*, 66:36; al-Dhahabī, *Siyar*, 16:436; al-Dhahabī, *al-ʿIbar*, 5:226; Ibn Shākir al-Kutubī, *ʿUyūn al-Tawārīkh*, 20:135; al-Yāfiʿī, *Mirʾāt al-Jinān*, 4:137; al-Subkī, *Ṭabaqāt al-Shāfiʿiyyah*, 8:271; Ibn Kathīr, *al-Bidāyah waʾl-Nihāyah*, 13:169; Ibn Ḥabīb al-Ḥalabī, "Durrat al-Aslāk fī Dawlat al-Atrāk," Arabe Collection, Manuscript 4680, folio 24v, Bibliothèque nationale de France, Paris, France; ʿAbd al-Raḥmān Ibn Khaldūn al-Maghribī, *Kitāb al-ʿIbar wa-Diwān al-Mubtadaʾ waʾl-Khabar fī Ayyām al-ʿArab waʾl-ʿAjam waʾl-Barbar wa-Man ʿĀṣarahum min Dhawiʾl-Sulṭān al-Akbar* (Beirut: Dār al-Kitāb al-Lubnānī, 1958), 3:1106, 5:1150; al-

Malik al-Ashraf, *al-ʿAsjad al-Masbūk*, 631; Ibn Duqmāq, *al-Jawhar al-Thamīn*, 178; Ibn Duqmāq, *Nuzhat al-Anām*, 239; Paul Meyvaert, "An Unknown Letter of Hulagu, Il-Khan of Persia, to King Louis IX of France," *Viator: Medieval and Renaissance Studies* 11 (1980): 256.

63. *al-Ḥawādith al-Jāmiʿah*, 359; Ibn Kathīr, *al-Bidāyah wa'l-Nihāyah*, 13:170.

64. Ibn al-Ṭiqṭaqā, *al-Fakhrī*, 336.

65. Abū Shāmah, *Tarājim*, 198–99; Ibn al-ʿAmīd, *Akhbār al-Ayyūbiyyīn*, 45; Rashīd al-Dīn, *Jāmiʿ al-Tawārīkh*, vol. 2, pt. 1, 292; Ibn Kathīr, *al-Bidāyah wa'l-Nihāyah*, 13:169; Ibn Ḥabīb al-Ḥalabī, "Durrat al-Aslāk fī Dawlat al-Atrāk," Arabe Collection, Manuscript 4680, folio 24v, Bibliothèque nationale de France, Paris, France; *al-Ḥawādith al-Jāmiʿah*, 359; Baybars al-Manṣūrī, *Zubdat al-Fikrah*, 37; al-Dhahabī, *Tārīkh al-Islām*, 66:39; Ibn Shākir al-Kutubī, *ʿUyūn al-Tawārīkh*, 20:130; Ibn Duqmāq, *Nuzhat al-Anām*, 238.

66. *al-Ḥawādith al-Jāmiʿah*, 357-8; Ibn al-Kāzarūnī, *Mukhtaṣar al-Tārīkh*, 274–77; Baybars al-Manṣūrī, *Zubdat al-Fikrah*, 37; Ibn al-Ṭiqṭaqā, *al-Fakhrī*, 336; al-Nuwayrī, *Nihāyat al-Arab*, 23:324; al-Dhahabī, *Siyar*, 16:437; al-Dhahabī, *Tārīkh al-Islām*, 66:262; Ibn Shākir al-Kutubī, *ʿUyūn al-Tawārīkh*, 20:134; Ibn Kathīr, *al-Bidāyah wa'l-Nihāyah*, 13:169, 171.

67. al-Hāshimī, "al-Shīrāzī," 497–98.

68. Taqiyy al-Dīn Abū Muḥammad Ismaʿīl b. Ibrahīm Ibn Abī Yusr Shākir b. ʿAbdillāh b. Muḥammad b. ʿAbdillāh al-Tanūkhī al-Dimashqī's family originally hailed from Maʿarrah, although he was born and lived in Damascus. He excelled in many areas of the literary arts, was known as *Musnid al-Shām*, and worked in the chancery of the Ayyubid sultan al-Nāṣir Dāwūd. al-Dhahabī, *Tārīkh al-Islām*, 68:88–90; al-Dhahabī, *al-ʿIbar*, 5:299; Ibn Shākir al-Kutubī, *Fawāt al-Wafayāt*, 1:170–72; Ṣalāḥ al-Dīn Khalīl b. Aybak al-Ṣafadī, *al-Wāfī bi'l-Wafayāt*, vol. 9, ed. Josef Van Ess (Wiesbaden, Ger.: Franz Steiner Verlag, 1974), 71–74; Ibn Taghribirdī, *al-Manhal al-Ṣāfī*, 2:383–86; Ibn al-ʿImād, *Shadharāt al-Dhahab*, 7:590.

69. al-Dhahabī, *Tārīkh al-Islām*, 66:38.

70. al-Subkī, *Ṭabaqāt al-Shāfʿiyyah*, 8:272–73.

71. al-Malik al-Ashraf, *al-ʿAsjad al-Masbūk*, 627.

72. Ibn al-Kāzarūnī, *Maqāmah fī Qawāʿid Baghdād*, 12–13; ʿAbbās ʿAzzāwī, *al-Taʿrīf bi'l-Muʾarrikhīn* (Baghdād: Sharikat al-Tijārah wa'l-Ṭibāʿah, 1957), 128–29.

73. Ibn al-Kāzarūnī, *Mukhtaṣar al-Tārīkh*, 274–77.

74. Ibid., 12, 274–77; Kamāl al-Dīn Abū'l-Faḍl ʿAbd al-Razzāq b. Aḥmad Ibn al-Fuwaṭī, *Majmaʿ al-Ādāb fī Muʿjam al-Alqāb*, ed. Muḥammad al-Kāẓim (Tehran: Mu'assasat al-Ṭibāʿah wa-al-Nashr, Wizārat al-Thaqāfah wa-al-Irshād al-Islāmī, 1995), 5:112–14.

75. The palace received its name from the Amīr Muẓaffar al-Dīn Abū'l-Fatḥ Sūsiyān, who was known as Abu Shumlah al-Turkumānī al-Khūzistānī, and died in 596/1200. The author of *al-Ḥawādith al-Jāmiʿah* indicates that his palace was located on the Canal of ʿĪsā (named after the Abbasid prince who redug it), which flows from the Euphrates roughly eastward in a semi-circle into the Tigris, specifically near the Thorn Bridge (*Qanṭarat al-Shawq*) and the street of Ibn Rizq Allāh. See the maps and details offered by Guy Le Strange. *al-Ḥawādith al-Jāmiʿah*, 288–89; Ibn al-Kāzarūnī, *Mukhtaṣar al-Tārīkh*, 274–75; Ibn al-Fuwaṭī, *Majmaʿ al-Ādāb*, 5:275; George Le Strange, *Baghdad during the Abbasid Caliphate from Contemporary Arabic and Persian Sources* (Westport, CT: Greenwood Press, 1983), 49–56, 71–76, 81–94, 151–53, 156–57.

76. One of her sisters had also been buried there a few years earlier in 647/1249. *al-Ḥawādith al-Jāmiʿah*, 288–89, 317.

77. Ibn al-Kāzarūnī, *Mukhtaṣar al-Tārīkh*, 274–77; Ibn al-Fuwaṭī, *Majma' al-Ādāb*, 1:388–89, 5:112–14, 310. Devin Deweese suggests that Ibn al-Fuwaṭī's *Majma' al-Ādāb* "appears in part to reflect the broader project of the late Ilkhanid period, aimed at integrating the Mongols into the Islamic world." Devin Deweese, "Cultural Transmission and Exchange in the Mongol Empire: Notes from the Biographical Dictionary of Ibn al-Fuwaṭī," in *Beyond the Legacy of Genghis Khan*, ed. Lind Komaroff (Leiden, Neth.: E. J. Brill, 2006), 13.
78. Meir Ydit, "Av, the Ninth of," in *Encyclopaedia Judaica*, 2nd ed. (NY: Thomson Gald, 2007), 2:714–16; *The Jewish Study Bible*, ed. Adele Berlin and Marc Zvi Brettler (Oxford: Oxford University Press, 2004), 1587–1602; Alan Mintz, *Ḥurban: Responses to Catastrophe in Hebrew Literature* (NY: Columbia University Press, 1984), 23; Adele Berlin, *Lamentations: A Commentary* (Louisville, KY: Westminister John Knox Press, 2002), 10–12, 41–61; Yerushalmi, *Zakhor*, 35. Christl Maier also argues that the female personification of Jerusalem "can be traced back to an ancient tradition of personified cities and to an anthropomorphic image of God, both of which create a relationship between the deity and the people as a female collective" as well as for the recital of Lamentations in a public mourning setting inclusive of all survivors of the catastrophe in exilic times. Christl Maier, *Daughter Zion, Mother Zion* (Minneapolis, MN: Fortress Press, 2008), 28–29, 60–93, 144–45.
79. al-Hāshimī, "al-Shīrāzī," 496.
80. Baybars al-Manṣūrī, *Zubdat al-Fikrah*, 38; Ibn Duqmāq, *Nuzhat al-Anām*, 239; Ibn Duqmāq, *al-Jawhar al-Thamīn*, 179; Ibn Taghribirdī, *al-Nujūm al-Zāhirah*, 7:53.
81. Ibn Kathīr, *al-Bidāyah wa'l-Nihāyah*, 13:170.
82. al-Subkī, *Ṭabaqāt al-Shāfi'iyyah*, 8:271–72.
83. al-Dhahabī, *Tārīkh al-Islām*, 66:38, 4680; Ibn Ḥabīb al-Ḥalabī, "Durrat al-Aslāk fī Dawlat al-Atrāk," Arabe Collection, Manuscript 4680, folio 25r, Bibliothèque nationale de France, Paris, France; Badr al-Dīn al-Ḥasan ibn 'Umar Ibn Ḥabīb al-Ḥalabī, "Durrat al-Aslāk fī Dawlat al-Atrāk," Tārīkh Collection, Manuscript 235/1, folio 12v, The Institute of Arab Manuscripts, Cairo, Egypt.
84. Shams al-Dīn al-Qurṭubī, *al-Tadhkirah*, 3:193; Muḥammad Shams al-Ḥaqq 'Aẓīmābādī, *'Awn al-Ma'būd: Sharḥ Sunan Abī Dāwūd ma' Sharḥ Ibn Qayyim al-Jawziyyah*, ed. 'Abd al-Raḥmān Muḥammad 'Uthmān (Medina: Muḥammad 'Abd al-Muḥsin, 1968), 11:416.
85. al-Subkī, *Ṭabaqāt al-Shāfi'iyyah*, 8:271–72.
86. Baybars al-Manṣūrī, *Zubdat al-Fikrah*, 37; Ibn Kathīr, *al-Bidāyah wa'l-Nihāyah*, 13:169. On Islamic notions of domestic privacy articulated by jurists from seventh to the thirteenth centuries, see Eli Alshech, "'Do Not Enter Homes Other than Your Own': The Evolution of the Notion of a Private Domestic Sphere in Early Sunnī Islamic Thought," *Islamic Law and Society* 11, no. 3 (2004): 291–332. For the prophetic distinction between private and public domains, see Wymann-Landgraf, *Malik and Medina*, 242–46.
87. al-Hāshimī, "al-Shīrāzī," 495.
88. Ibn Khaldūn, *Kitāb al-'Ibar*, 3:1106, 5:1150.
89. Rashīd al-Dīn, *Jāmi' al-Tawārīkh*, vol. 2, pt. 1, 291–93; *al-Ḥawādith al-Jāmi'ah*, 359; Ṣafiyy al-Dīn 'Abd al-Mu'min b. al-Khaṭīb 'Abd al-Ḥaqq b. 'Abdillāh b. 'Alī b. Mas'ūd al-Baghdādī al-Ḥanbalī, *Marāṣid al-Iṭṭilā' 'alā Asmā' al-Amkinah wa'l-Biqā'* (Dār Iḥyā' al-Kutub al-'Arabiyyah, n.d.), 1:209; al-Dhahabī, *Tārīkh al-Islām*, 66:39; Ibn Ḥabīb al-Ḥalabī, "Durrat al-Aslāk fī Dawlat al-Atrāk," Arabe Collection, Manuscript 4680, folio 24v, Bibliothèque nationale de France, Paris, France.

90. Rashīd al-Dīn, *Jāmi' al-Tawārīkh*, vol. 2, pt. 1, 291–93. In Wheeler Thackston's English translation: "Most of the holy places like the caliph's mosque, the Musa-Jawad shrine, and the tombs in Rusafa were burned," Rashiduddin Fazlullah, *The Compendium of Chronicles*, 3:354.
91. Abū Shāmah, *Tarājim*, 199.
92. al-Yūnīnī, *Dhayl Mir'āt al-Zamān*, 1:89; Rashīd al-Dīn, *Jāmi' al-Tawārīkh*, vol. 2, pt. 1, 289; *al-Ḥawādith al-Jāmi'ah*, 359–60; al-Dhahabī, *Tārīkh al-Islām*, 66:36, 39; Ibn Shākir al-Kutubī, *'Uyūn al-Tawārīkh*, 20:135; al-Subkī, *Ṭabaqāt al-Shāfi'iyyah*, 8:271; Ibn Kathīr, *al-Bidāyah wa'l-Nihāyah*, 13:170; Veteran *National Geographic* photographer and journalist Tom Abercrombie (1931–2006) once commented about the aftermath of an earthquake in Lar, Iran, "'I don't know if you've ever smelled 10,000 dead bodies,'... taking a deep draw on his pipe. 'But it's something you'll never forget'" (Patricia Sullivan, "Thomas J. Abercrombie; Photographer for National Geographic Magazine," *Washington Post*, Friday, April 7, 2006.
93. *al-Ḥawādith al-Jāmi'ah*, 360.
94. Ibn al-'Ibrī, *Tārīkh al-Zamān*, 309; al-Yūnīnī, *Dhayl Mir'āt al-Zamān*, 1:89; *al-Ḥawādith al-Jāmi'ah*, 359–60; Ibn Shākir al-Kutubī, *'Uyūn al-Tawārīkh*, 20:135; al-Malik al-Ashraf, *al-'Asjad al-Masbūk*, 645; Ibn Kathīr, *al-Bidāyah wa'l-Nihāyah*, 13:170.
95. His full name was al-'Adl al-Amīr Jamāl al-Dīn Abū'l-Manṣūr Sulaymān b. al-'Adl Fakhr al-Dīn Abī'l-Qāsim 'Abdillāh b. al-'Adl Amīn al-Dīn Abī'l-Ḥasan 'Alī Ibn Raṭlayn al-Ḥanbalī al-Baghdādī.
96. *Ataynā naṭlubu manāzilanā wa-ahlanā fa wajadnāhā kharāb balāqi' bi-ghayr anīs wa-lā mukhbir.*
97. al-Dhahabī, "al-Mukhtār min Tārīkh al-Jazarī," Köprülü Collection, Manuscript 1147, folios 79–81, Köprülü Manuscript Library, Istanbul, Turkey; al-Dhahabī, *Siyar*, 16:436–37; al-Dhahabī, *Tārīkh al-Islām*, 66:260–61; Ibn al-Dawādārī, *Kanz al-Durar*, 8:34–36.
98. For additional musical scores of *maqām mukhālif*, see Rob Simms, *The Repertoire of Iraqi Maqam* (Oxford: Scarecrow Press, 2004), 180–86.
99. Ḥammūdī al-Wardī, *al-Maqām al-Mukhālif* (Baghdad: Maṭba'at As'ad, 1969), 5; 'Abbās al-'Azzāwī, *al-Mūsiqā al-'Irāqiyyah fī 'Ahd al-Muhgūl wa'l-Turkumānī min Sanat 656/1258 ilā Sanat 941/1534* (Baghdad: Shirkat al-Tijārah wa'l-Ṭibā'ah al-Maḥdūdah, 1951), 103, 108–9.
100. Amnon Shiloah, *Music in the World of Islam: A Socio-Cultural Study* (Detroit: Wayne University Press, 1995), 119–20.
101. Rahim AlHaj, "When the Soul Is Settled: Music of Iraq" (Washington, DC: Smithsonian Folkways Recordings, 2006).
102. Amir Elsaffar, personal correspondence, February 16, 2007.
103. *al-Ḥawādith al-Jāmi'ah*, 541–42; Abū'l-Ma'ālī Muḥammad Ibn Rāfi' al-Sallāmī, *Tārīkh 'Ulamā' Baghdād al-musammā Muntakhab al-Mukhtār* (Baghdad: Maṭba'at al-Ahālī, 1938), 233; al-Dhahabī, *Siyar*, 17:156; al-Dhahabī, *Tārīkh al-Islām*, 70:373–74; Ibn Shākir al-Kutubī, *Fawāt al-Wafayāt*, 4:263–64; 38–39; Ṣalāḥ al-Dīn al-Munajjid, *Yāqūt al-Musta'ṣimī* (Beirut: Dār al-Kitāb al-Jadīd, 1985), 10–32, 38–39; Sheila Blair, "Yāqūt and His Followers," in *Manuscripta Orientalia: International Journal for Oriental Manuscript Research* 9, no. 3 (2003): 39–47.
104. Ibn Shākir al-Kutubī, *'Uyūn al-Tawārīkh*, 20:141.
105. Ibid., Halbwachs, *The Collective Memory*, 22–49; Hutton, *History as an Art of Memory*, 79; Sa'dī, *Kolliyat-i Sa'di*, ed. Muhammad 'Ali Foroughi (Tehran: Sazman-e Chap o Intisharat-e Javidan, n.d.), 503–4. I would like to thank Carl Ernst for his elegant

translation of Sa'dī's elegy "On the Fall of the Abbasid Caliphate" from the Persian. A brief biography of Atābak Abū Bakr (d. 658/1260) is included in Henry George Keene, *An Oriental Biographical Dictionary Founded on Materials Collected by the Late Thomas William Beale* (London: W. H. Allen and Company, 1894), 393.

106. Ibn Shākir al-Kutubī, *'Uyūn al-Tawārīkh*, 20:141–42.
107. Ibid., 20:138.
108. *wā lahfatī, wā waḥdatī, wā ḥayratī / wā waḥshatī, wā harra qalbī al-'ānī.* al-Kutubī, *Fawāt al-Wafayāt*, 2:234.
109. al-Baghdādī, *Marāṣid al-Iṭṭilā'*, 1:209.
110. Ibn Kathīr, *al-Bidāyah wa'l-Nihāyah*, 13:169.
111. Baybars al-Manṣūrī, *Zubdat al-Fikrah*, 37–38.
112. Abū Ja'far Aḥmad b. Ibrāhīm Ibn al-Zubayr al-Thaqafī, *al-Zamān wa'l-Makān*, ed. Muḥammad b. Sharīfah (Casablanca: Maṭba'at al-Najāḥ al-Jadīdah, 1993), 103.
113. Zakariyyā b. Muḥammad b. Maḥmūd al-Qazwīnī, *Āthār al-Bilād wa-Akhbār al-'Ibād* (Beirut: Dār Ṣadir, 1960), 317.
114. Mughulṭāy, *al-Ishārah*, 559–60.
115. Ibn Ḥabīb al-Ḥalabī, "Durrat al-Aslāk fī Dawlat al-Atrāk," Arabe Collection, Manuscript 4680, folio 24v, Bibliothèque nationale de France, Paris, France.
116. Brett Whalen, *Dominion of God: Christendom and Apocalypse in the Middle Ages* (Cambridge: Harvard University Press, 2009), 3, 132.
117. Ibid., 58, 151, 168, 177–203; John Tolan, *Saracens: Islam in the Medieval European Imagination* (NY: Coulmbia University Press, 2002), 201, 194–213; Roger Bacon, *Opus Majus of Roger Bacon*, trans. Robert Belle Burke (Philadelphia: University of Pennsylvania Press, 1928), 1:287, 351.
118. Abū Shāmah, *Tarājim*, 190–3; al-Qurṭubī, *al-Tadhkirah*, 3:247, 251; Ibn Wāṣil, *Die Chronik*, 151; Ibn al-Zubayr, *al-Zamān wa'l-Makān*, 102–3; Ibn Kathīr, *al-Bidāyah wa'l-Nihāyah*, 13:161–62; Ibn Ḥabīb al-Ḥalabī, "Durrat al-Aslāk fī Dawlat al-Atrāk," Arabe Collection, Manuscript 4680, folios 18r–18v, Bibliothèque nationale de France, Paris, France; al-Malik al-Ashraf, *al-'Asjad al-Masbūk*, 620; Victor E. Camp and M. John Roobol, "The Arabian Continental Alkali Basalt Province: Part I. Evolution of Harrat Rahat, Kingdom of Saudi Arabia," *Geological Society of America Bulletin* 101, Issue 1 (January 1989): 71–95. The basalt lava flow resulting from this historical eruption in 654 AH / 1256 CE has also been analyzed in detail by geologists V. E. Camp, P. R. Hooper, M. J. Roobol, and D. L. White in their article "The Madinah Eruption, Saudi Arabia: Magma Mixing and Simultaneous Extrusion of Three Basaltic Chemical Types," *Bulletin of Volcanology* 49 (1987): 489–508.
119. Abū Shāmah, *Tarājim*, 190–93; Ibn al-Zubayr, *al-Zamān wa'l-Makān*, 102; *al-Ḥawādith al-Jāmi'ah*, 332; al-Dhahabī, *Siyar*, 16:434–35; al-Dhahabī, *al-'Ibar*, 5:215–16; Ibn Kathīr, *al-Bidāyah wa'l-Nihāyah*, 13:162.
120. Abū Shāmah, *Tarājim*, 190–92; al-Qurṭubī, *al-Tadhkirah*, 3:251; Ibn al-Zubayr, *al-Zamān wa'l-Makān*, 102; Ibn Kathīr, *al-Bidāyah wa'l-Nihāyah*, 13:161; al-Malik al-Ashraf, *al-'Asjad al-Masbūk*, 620.
121. Abū Shāmah, *Tarājim*, 190–93.
122. Ibid., 191–92; *al-Ḥawādith al-Jāmi'ah*, 332.
123. al-Bukhārī, *Ṣaḥīḥ al-Bukhārī*, 3:1438 (#7203); Muslim, *Ṣaḥīḥ Muslim*, 2:1222 (#7473); Muḥyī'l-Dīn Abū Zakariyyā Yaḥyā b. Sharaf al-Nawawī, *Ṣaḥīḥ Muslim bi-Sharḥ al-Nawawī* (Beirut: Dār al-Fikr, 1981), 18:30; Abū'l-Faḍl Shihāb al-Dīn Aḥmad b. 'Alī b. Muḥammad Ibn Ḥajar al-'Asqalānī, Ibn Ḥajar al-'Asqalānī, *Fatḥ al-Bārī bi-Sharḥ Ṣaḥīḥ al-Bukhārī*, (Cairo: Dār Iḥyā' al-Turāth al-'Arabī, 1929), 13:66–68; Badr al-Dīn Abū

Muḥammad Maḥmūd b. Aḥmad al-ʿAynī, *ʿUmdat al-Qārī bi-Sharḥ Ṣaḥīh al-Bukhārī* (Beirut: Muḥammad Amīn Damj, [1970]), 24:212–14.

124. Abū Shāmah, *Tarājim*, 191 (*hādhihi dalāʾil al-qiyāmah*); al-Qurṭubī, *al-Tadhkirah*, 3:247, 251; Ibn Wāṣil, *Die Chronik*, 151; Ibn al-Zubayr, *al-Zamān wa'l-Makān*, 102–3; Ibn Kathīr, *al-Bidāyah wa'l-Nihāyah*, 13:162.

125. al-Qurṭubī, *al-Tadhkirah*, 3:251; al-Subkī, *Ṭabaqāt al-Shāfiʿiyyah*, 8:267; al-Dhahabī, *Siyar*, 16:434–35; al-Dhahabī, *al-ʿIbar*, 5:215–16.

126. Abū Shāmah, *Tarājim*, 190, 193; Ibn al-Zubayr, *al-Zamān wa'l-Makān*, 103; al-Dhahabī, *al-ʿIbar*, 5:215–16; Ibn al-Wardī, *Tatimmat al-Mukhtaṣar*, 2:281; Ibn Kathīr, *al-Bidāyah wa'l-Nihāyah*, 13:162; Ibn Ḥabīb al-Ḥalabī, "Durrat al-Aslāk fī Dawlat al-Atrāk," Arabe Collection, Manuscript 4680, folio 18v, Bibliothèque nationale de France, Paris, France; Ibn Ḥajar, *Fatḥ al-Bārī*, "ʿAlāmāt al-Nubuwwah."

127. Ibn al-Wardī, *Tatimmat al-Mukhtaṣar*, 2:281.

128. Abū Shāmah, *Tarājim*, 193; Ibn Ḥabīb al-Ḥalabī, "Durrat al-Aslāk fī Dawlat al-Atrāk," Arabe Collection, Manuscript 4680, folio 18v, Bibliothèque nationale de France, Paris, France.

129. Jalāl al-Dīn al-Suyūṭī, *Kifāyat al-Ṭālib al-Labīb fī Khaṣāʾiṣ al-Ḥabīb* (Hyderabad, India: Dāʾirat al-Maʿārif al-Niẓāmiyyah, 1902), 150.

130. Ibn Kathīr, *al-Bidāyah wa'l-Nihāyah*, 13:162.

131. Abū Shāmah, *Tarājim*, 189–94; al-Qurṭubī, *al-Tadhkirah*, 3:251; Ibn Wāṣil, *Die Chronik*, 151; al-Yūnīnī, *Dhayl Mirʾāt al-Zamān*, 1:4–11; *al-Ḥawādith al-Jāmiʿah*, 332–35; Abū'l-Fidā, *al-Mukhtaṣar fī Akhbār al-Bashar*, 3:232; Shihāb al-Dīn Aḥmad b. ʿAbd al-Wahhāb al-Nuwayrī, *Nihāyat al-Arab fī Funūn al-Adab*, vol. 29, ed. Muḥammad Ḍiyāʾ al-Dīn al-Rayyis (Cairo: al-Hayʾah al-Miṣriyyah li'l-Kitāb, 1992), 449–55. al-Dhahabī, "al-Mukhtār min Tārīkh al-Jazarī," Köprülü Collection, Manuscript 1147, folio 77, Köprülü Manuscript Library, Istanbul, Turkey; al-Dhahabī, *Siyar*, 16:434–35; al-Dhahabī, *Tārīkh al-Islām*, 66:18–24; al-Dhahabī, *al-ʿIbar*, 5:215–16; Ibn al-Wardī, *Tatimmat al-Mukhtaṣar*, 2:281; Ibn Shākir al-Kutubī, *ʿUyūn al-Tawārīkh*, 20:86–92; al-Subkī, *Ṭabaqāt al-Shāfiʿiyyah*, 8:267; Ibn Kathīr, *al-Bidāyah wa'l-Nihāyah*, 13:161–62; Ibn Ḥabīb al-Ḥalabī, "Durrat al-Aslāk fī Dawlat al-Atrāk," Arabe Collection, Manuscript 4680, folios 19r–19v, Bibliothèque nationale de France, Paris, France; al-Malik al-Ashraf, *al-ʿAsjad al-Masbūk*, 614–16, 619–21.

132. The printed version of this stanza is incorrect, and the textual corruption *lam yafna* ("did not perish") neither fits the poetic meter (*khafīf*) nor the historical context (in implying that the people of Baghdad "did not perish" as the Mongols gathered against them). The phrase as written in two copies of the manuscript held in the Bibliothèque nationale de France and the Köprülü Manuscript Library appears to read *lam yaghna* ("did not prosper"). Taking into account the poetic meter as well as the shape and dotting of the letters in the manuscripts, I suggest another phrase along the lines of *lam yafuz* ("did not escape") may have been originally intended.

133. ʿAbd al-Raḥmān ibn Ismāʿīl Abū Shāmah, "Kitāb al-Dhayl ʿalā al-Rawḍatayn," Arabe Collection, Manuscript 5852, folio 213 verso, Bibliothèque nationale de France, Paris, France; ʿAbd al-Raḥmān ibn Ismāʿīl Abū Shāmah,"Kitāb al-Dhayl ʿalā al-Rawḍatayn," Fazıl Ahmed Paşa Collection, Manuscript 1080, folio 107b, Köprülü Manuscript Library, Istanbul, Turkey; Abū Shāmah, *Tarājim*, 194.

134. al-Subkī, *Ṭabaqāt al-Shāfiʿiyyah*, 8:266–67.

135. al-Qurṭubī, *al-Tadhkirah*, 3:251.

136. Ibn Wāṣil, *Die Chronik*, 151. Ibn Wāṣil also discusses the predictions of ʿAlī b. ʿAbdillāh b. al-ʿAbbās that his progeny (the Abbasids) would asume the caliphate and retain it

until the uncouth from Khurasan (*al-ʿilj min Khurāsān*) would wrest it away from them (157).

137. al-Bukhārī, *Ṣaḥīḥ al-Bukhārī*, 2:567–68, 706–7 (#2964–66, 3629, 3632–34); Muslim, *Ṣaḥīḥ Muslim*, 2:1225 (#7494–98); Abū Dāwūd, *Sunan Abī Dāwūd*, 2:717 (#4305–6); al-Tirmidhī, *al-Jāmiʿ al-Kabīr*, 2:570, 575 (#2376, 2403); al-Nasāʾī, *Sunan al-Nasāʾī*, 2:517 (#3190); Ibn Mājah, *Sunan Ibn Mājah*, 592, 601–2 (#4210, 4235–38,); al-Nawawī, *Ṣaḥīḥ Muslim bi-Sharḥ al-Nawawī*, 18:36–37; Badr al-Dīn al-ʿAynī, *ʿUmdat al-Qārī*, 14:301; *Sharḥ Sunan Abī Dāwūd*, 11:410–12; Shams al-Dīn Muḥammad b. ʿAbd al-Raḥmān al-Sakhāwī, *al-Qanāʿah fī mā Yaḥsun al-Iḥāṭah min Ashrāṭ al-Sāʿah*, ed. Muḥammad b. ʿAbd al-Wahhāb al-ʿUqayl (Riyadh, Saudi Arabia: Maktabat Aḍwāʾ al-Salaf, 2002), 121.
138. al-Qurṭubī, *al-Tadhkirah*, 3:191–93; Ibn al-Zubayr, *al-Zamān wa'l-Makān*, 103–4; al-Sakhāwī, *Ashrāṭ al-Sāʿah*, 121–25; al-Nawawī, *Sharḥ Ṣaḥīḥ Muslim*, 18:248–49; *Sharḥ Sunan Abī Dāwūd*, 11:412–16.
139. al-Nawawī, *Sharḥ Ṣaḥīḥ Muslim*, 18:248–49.
140. al-Qurṭubī, *al-Tadhkirah*, 3:191.
141. Ibid.
142. Ibn Ḥajar al-ʿAsqalānī, *Fatḥ al-Bārī*, 12:63; Badr al-Dīn al-ʿAynī, *ʿUmdat al-Qārī*, 14:200; Abu'l-ʿUlā Muḥammad ʿAbd al-Raḥmān b. ʿAbd al-Raḥīm al-Mubārakfūrī, *Tuḥfat al-Aḥwadhī bi-Sharḥ Jāmiʿ al-Tirmidhī*, ed. ʿIṣām al-Ṣabābaṭī (Cairo: Dār al-Ḥadīth, 2001), 6:74–75.
143. al-Dhahabī, *Tārīkh al-Islām*, 66:38–39.
144. al-Hāshimī, "al-Shīrāzī," 497.
145. Ibn Khaldūn, *Kitāb al-ʿIbar*, 5:791.
146. Th. Emil Homerin, "Reflections on Poetry in the Mamluk Age," *Mamlūk Studies Review* 1 (1997): 66, 78–79.
147. Or alternatively: "market" (*sūq*) in Joseph de Somogyi's reading in "A Qasida," 44, 46.
148. al-Dhahabī, *Tārīkh al-Islām*, 66:38.
149. William Graham eloquently discusses the centrality of the *isnād* in connecting members of the Muslim community with their heritage in his article "Traditionalism in Islam: An Essay in Interpretation," *Journal of Interdisciplinary History* 23, no. 3, Religion and History (Winter 1993): 495–522.

CHAPTER 2. RECAPTURING LOST GLORY AND LEGITIMACY

1. Hodgson, "The Unity of Later Islamic History," 187.
2. Abū Ḥāmid al-Ghazalī, *Iḥyāʾ ʿUlūm al-Dīn* (Amman, Jord.: Dār al-Kutub al-ʿIlmiyyah, 1992), 2:154.
3. Ibn Wāṣil celebrates how Ṣalāḥ al-Dīn al-Ayyūbī had established public recognition of the Abbasids in Egypt in his history dedicated to the Ayyubid prince al-Malik al-Ṣāliḥ Najm al-Dīn, appropriately called "al-Tārīkh al-Ṣāliḥī." Süleymaniye Manuscript Library, Fatih 4224, folio 196, Istanbul, Turkey.
4. al-Malik al-Nāṣir Ṣalāḥ al-Dīn Yūsuf b. al-Malik al-ʿAzīz Muḥammad b. al-Malik al-Ẓāhir Ghāzī, who died in Shawwāl 658 / September 1260. Ibn Wāṣil, *Die Chronik*, 138-9; al-Yūnīnī, *Dhayl Mirʾāt al-Zamān*, 1:484–85; Ibn al-Dawādārī, *Kanz al-Durar*, 8:86–87; al-Dhahabī, *Siyar*, 17:155; al-Ṣafadī, *al-Wāfī*, 6:317–18; al-Ṣafadī, *ʿAyān* 1:208–9; Mufaḍḍal Ibn Abī'l-Faḍāʾil, *Kitāb al-Nahj al-Sadīd wa'l-Durr al-Farīd fīmā baʿd Tārīkh Ibn al-ʿAmīd*, vol.1, ed. E. Blochet (Turnhout, Belg.: Editions Brepols, 1982), 1:435. For an overview of his reign, see R. Stephen Humphreys, *From Saladin to the Mongols: The*

Ayyubids of Damascus, 1193–1260 (Albany: State University of New York Press, 1977), 309–63.

5. For details of his flight, the treacherous role played by al-Zayn al-Ḥāfiẓī, and al-Malik al-Nāṣir's ultimate death in Mongol captivity, see Abū Shāmah, *Tarājim*, 206, 211, 212; Abū'l-ʿAbbās Shams al-Dīn Aḥmad b. Muḥammad Ibn Khallikān, *Wafayāt al-Aʿyān wa Anbāʾ Abnāʾ al-Zamān*, ed. Iḥsān ʿAbbās (Beirut: Dār al-Thaqāfah, 1968), 4:10; Ibn al-ʿIbrī, *Tārīkh al-Zamān*, 314–18; Ibn al-ʿIbrī, *Tārīkh Mukhtaṣar al-Duwal*, 278–81; Ibn Wāṣil, *Die Chronik*, 198; Faḍl Allāh b. Abī'l-Fahkr al-Ṣuqāʿī al-Naṣrānī al-Kātib, *Tālī Kitāb Wafayāt al-Aʿyān*, ed. Jacqueline Sublet (Damascus: al-Maʿhad al-Fransī bi-Dimashq, 1974), 78–79, 85, 166–69; al-Yūnīnī, *Dhayl Mirʾāt al-Zamān*, 1:358–59, 461–69, 2:126–27, 134–50; Ibn al-ʿAmīd, *Akhbār al-Ayyūbiyyīn*, 45–50; Baybars al-Manṣūrī, *Kitāb al-Tuḥfah al-Mulūkiyyah fi'l-Dawlah al-Turkiyyah*, ed. ʿAbd al-Ḥamīd Ṣāliḥ Ḥamādān (Cairo: al-Dār al-Miṣriyyah al-Lubnāniyyah, 1987), 41–45; Baybars al-Manṣūrī, *Zubdat al-Fikrah*, 48–50, 52–53; Abū'l-Fidā, *al-Mukhtaṣar fī Akhbār al-Bashar*, 3:239–44, 252–53; Ibn al-Wardī, *Tatimmat al-Mukhtaṣar*, 2:291–96, 304–5; al-Dhahabī, *Tārīkh al-Islām*, 66:402–4; al-Dhahabī, *Siyar*, 16:450–51; al-Dhahabī, *al-ʿIbar*, 5:241–42, 256–57; Ibn Shākir al-Kutubī, *ʿUyūn al-Tawārīkh*, 20:222–23, 226, 257–63; Ibn Shākir al-Kutubī, *Fawāt al-Wafāyat*, 3:77–78, 4:363–66; al-Ṣafadī, *al-Wāfī bi'l-Wafayāt*, 29:311–14; Shihāb al-Dīn Aḥmad b. ʿAbd al-Wahhāb al-Nuwayrī, *Nihāyat al-Arab fī Funūn al-Adab*, vol. 27, ed. Saʿīd ʿĀshūr (Cairo: al-Hayʾah al-Miṣriyyah li'l-Kitāb, 1985), 386–90; al-Nuwayrī, *Nihāyat al-Arab*, 29:381–92; Ibn al-Dawādārī, *Kanz al-Durar*, 8:45–47, 57–59.
6. Abū Shāmah, *Tarājim*, 207–9; Ibn Khallikān, *Wafayāt al-Aʿyān*, 4:155; Ibn al-ʿIbrī, *Tārīkh al-Zamān*, 317–19; Ibn al-ʿIbrī, *Tārīkh Mukhtaṣar al-Duwal*, 280–82; Ibn Wāṣil, *Die Chronik*, 213–17; al-Ṣuqāʿī al-Naṣrānī, *Tālī Kitāb Wafayāt al-Aʿyān*, 128–29, 181; al-Yūnīnī, *Dhayl Mirʾāt al-Zamān*, 1:360–70, 2:28–29, 35–36; Ibn al-ʿAmīd, *Akhbār al-Ayyūbiyyīn*, 53–54; Muḥyī'l-Dīn Ibn ʿAbd al-Ẓāhir, *al-Rawḍ al-Zāhir fī Sīrat al-Malik al-Ẓāhir*, ed. ʿAbd al-Azīz b. ʿAbdallāh al-Khuwayṭir (Riyadh, Saudi Arabia: n.p., 1976), 63–67; Baybars al-Manṣūrī, *Zubdat al-Fikrah*, 50–52; Baybars al-Manṣūrī, *Tuḥfah*, 43–44; Baybars al-Manṣūrī, *Mukhtār al-Akhbār: Tārīkh al-Dawlah al-Ayyūbiyyah wa Dawlat al-Mamālīk al-Baḥriyyah*, ed. ʿAbd al-Ḥamīd Ṣāliḥ Ḥamdān (Cairo: al-Dār al-Miṣriyyah al-Lubnāniyyah, 1993), 11; Abū'l-Fidā, *al-Mukhtaṣar fī Akhbār al-Bashar*, 3:238, 245–47; Ibn al-Wardī, *Tatimmat al-Mukhtaṣar*, 2:297–300; al-Dhahabī, *Tārīkh al-Islām*, 66:352–56; al-Dhahabī, *Siyar*, 16:447; al-Dhahabī, *al-ʿIbar*, 5:242–43, 247; Shams al-Dīn Muḥammad b. Aḥmad b. ʿUthmān al-Dhahabī, *Duwal al-Islām* (Hyderabad, India: Maṭbaʿat Dāʾirat al-Maʿārif al-Niẓāmiyyah, 1337 AH), 2:125; Ibn Shākir al-Kutubī, *ʿUyūn al-Tawārīkh*, 20:226–28, 241–44; Ibn Shākir al-Kutubī, *Fawāt al-Wafayāt*, 3:202–3; Ṣalāḥ al-Dīn Khalīl b. Aybak al-Ṣafadī, *al-Wāfī bi'l-Wafayāt*, vol. 24, ed. Muḥammad ʿAdnān al-Bakhīt and Muṣṭafā al-Ḥiyārī (Wiesbaden, Ger.: Franz Steiner Verlag, 1993), 252–53; al-Nuwayrī, 29:470–77; Ibn al-Dawādārī, *Kanz al-Durar*, 8:46–53, 59–60; Ibn Abī'l-Faḍāʾil, *al-Nahj al-Sadīd*, 1:435. For an overview of the events leading up to and including the battle of ʿAyn Jālūt, see Reuven Amitai-Preiss, *Mongols and Mamluks: The Mamluk-Īlkhānid War, 1260–1281* (Cambridge: Cambridge University Press, 1995), 26–45. For a detailed military history of the battle itself, also see John Masson Smith Jr., "Ayn Jalut: Mamluk Success or Mongol Failure?," *Harvard Journal of Asiatic Studies* 44, no. 2 (1984): 307–45.
7. Abū Shāmah, *Tarājim*, 210; Ibn Khallikān, *Wafayāt al-Aʿyān*, 4:155; Ibn al-ʿIbrī, *Tārīkh al-Zamān*, 319; Ibn al-ʿIbrī, *Tārīkh Mukhtaṣar al-Duwal*, 282; Ibn Wāṣil, *Die Chronik*, 218–19; al-Ṣuqāʿī al-Naṣrānī, *Tālī Kitāb Wafayāt al-Aʿyān*, 50, 129; al-Yūnīnī, *Dhayl*

Mir'āt al-Zamān, 1:370–72, 2:1–2, 29–30; Ibn al-ʿAmīd, *Akhbār al-Ayyūbiyyīn*, 54–55; Ibn ʿAbd al-Ẓāhir, *al-Rawḍ al-Zāhir*, 67–68; Baybars al-Manṣūrī, *Zubdat al-Fikrah*, 53–55; Baybars al-Manṣūrī, *Tuḥfah*, 45; Baybars al-Manṣūrī, *Mukhtār*, 11–13; Abū'l-Fidā, *al-Mukhtaṣar fī Akhbār al-Bashar*, 247–48; Ibn al-Wardī, *Tatimmat al-Mukhtaṣar*, 2:300–301; al-Dhahabī, *Tārīkh al-Islām*, 66:352–53, 355; al-Dhahabī, *Siyar*, 17:305; al-Dhahabī, *al-ʿIbar*, 5:243; al-Dhahabī, *Duwal al-Islām*, 2:125–26; Ibn Shākir al-Kutubī, *ʿUyūn al-Tawārīkh*, 20:228–29, 241; Ibn Shākir al-Kutubī, *Fawāt al-Wafayāt*, 1:237–38; 3:202–3; Ṣalāḥ al-Dīn Khalīl b. Aybak al-Ṣafadī, *al-Wāfī bi'l-Wafayāt*, vol. 10, ed. Ali Amara and Jacqueline Sublet (Wiesbaden, Ger.: Franz Steiner Verlag, 1980), 332–33; al-Ṣafadī, *al-Wāfī*, 24:253; al-Nuwayrī, 29:477–78; Shihāb al-Dīn Aḥmad b. ʿAbd al-Wahhāb al-Nuwayrī, *Nihāyat al-Arab fī Funūn al-Adab*, vol. 30, ed. Muḥammad ʿAbd al-Hādī Shaʿīrah (Cairo: al-Hay'ah al-Miṣriyyah li'l-Kitāb, 1990), 13–14; Ibn al-Dawādārī, *Kanz al-Durar*, 8:60–62, 87; Ibn Abī'l-Faḍā'il, *al-Nahj al-Sadīd*, 1:407–8, 410, 435–36.

8. Ibn Shākir al-Kutubī, *Fawāt al-Wafayāt*, 2:352; Baybars al-Manṣūrī, *Mukhtār al-Akhbār*, 12–13. For further discussion of the interactions between ʿAlā' al-Dīn Aydekin Bunduqdār and Sultan al-Malik al-Ṣāliḥ Najm al-Dīn Ayyūb b. al-Malik al-Kāmil Muḥammad, see their biographies in al-Ṣafadī, *al-Wāfī bi'l-Wafayāt*, 9:491–92 and Ṣalāḥ al-Dīn Khalīl b. Aybak al-Ṣafadī, *al-Wāfī bi'l-Wafayāt*, vol. 10, 55–58.
9. Richard Bulliet, "Religion and the State in Islam: From Medieval Caliphate to the Muslim Brotherhood," University of Denver Center for Middle East Studies Occasional Paper Series, Paper No. 2, (2013), 3.
10. Julia Smith, *Europe after Rome: A New Cultural History, 500–1000* (Oxford: Oxford University Press, 2007), 15, 253–97; Raymond Van Dam, *Rome and Constantinople: Rewriting Roman History during Late Antiquity* (Waco, TX: Baylor University Press, 2010), 66; Lucy Grig and Gavin Kelly, "Introduction: From Rome to Constantinople," in *Two Romes: Rome and Constantinople in Late Antiquity*, ed. Lucy Grig and Gavin Kelly (Oxford: Oxford University Press, 2012), 11–12; Margaret Alexiou, *The Ritual Lament in Greek Tradition* (Cambridge: Cambridge University Press, 1974); Walter Emil Kaegi, *Byzantium and the Decline of Rome* (Princeton, NJ: Princeton University Press, 1968).
11. Abū'l-ʿAbbās Aḥmad (631–56/1233–58) and Abū'l-Faḍā'il ʿAbd al-Raḥmān (633–66/1235–58).
12. Abū'l-Faḍl or Abū'l-Fatḥ Sulaymān al-Ḥājj, Abū'l-Qāsim ʿAlī al-Sabtī, Abū'l-Muẓaffar (and it is also said Abu Manṣūr) al-Turkī and al-Ḥasan, Abū Hāshim Yūsuf, and Abū'l-Futūḥ Ḥabīb. al-Kāzarūnī, *Muktaṣar al-Tārīkh*, 257; *al-Ḥawādith al-Jāmiʿah*, 189, 358; al-Ṣafadī, *al-Wāfī*, 29:333–34; al-Malik al-Ashraf, *al-ʿAsjad*, 632.
13. al-Muʾayyad Abū ʿAbdillāh al-Ḥusayn and al-Muwaffaq Abū ʿAlī Yaḥyā the sons of al-Malik al-Muʿazzam Abū'l-Ḥasan ʿAlī, who had been the younger of the Caliph al-Nāṣir's own two sons and nominated to succeed his father to the caliphate instead of his older brother al-Ẓāhir. Instead, he died on Friday, 20 Dhū'l-Qaʿdah 612 / March 11, 1216. al-Kāzarūnī, *Muktaṣar al-Tārīkh*, 248; *al-Ḥawādith al-Jāmiʿah*, 189, 358; al-Malik al-Ashraf, *al-ʿAsjad*, 633.
14. Cf. my discussion of this point in the introduction.
15. While the majority of sources contemporary to these events state that Abū'l-ʿAbbās remained hidden in Baghdad until the beginning of 657/1259, another young contemporary, Shāfiʿ b. ʿAlī b. ʿAbbās al-Kātib (649–730/1252–1330) provides a colorful addition to the story of Abū'l-ʿAbbās's escape. He states that the Mongols had intended to build a structure over him (to bury him alive as it were) but that the builder whom they employed, likely Ibn al-Bannā' himself, had mercy on him and took Abū'l-ʿAbbās out to the Bedouins instead. Shāfiʿ b. ʿAlī b. ʿAbbās al-Kātib, *Kitāb Ḥusn al-Manāqib*

al-Sirriyyah al-Muntazi'ah min al-Sīrah al-Ẓāhiriyyah, ed. 'Abd al-Azīz b. 'Abdallāh al-Khuwayṭir (Saudi Arabia: Maṭābi' al-Quwwāt al-Musallaḥah, 1976), 54–55.

16. al-Yūnīnī, *Dhayl Mir'āt al-Zamān*, 1:483–84; Ibn Aybak al-Dawādārī, *Kanz al-Durar*, 8:86; al-Dhahabī, *Siyar 'Alām al-Nubalā'*, 17:155; al-Ṣafadī, *al-Wāfī bi'l-Wafayāt*, 6:217; Ṣalāḥ al-Dīn Khalīl b. Aybek al-Ṣafadī, *A'yān al-'Aṣr wa-A'wān al-Naṣr*, ed. 'Alī Abū Zayd, et al. (Beirut: Dār al-Fikr al-Mu'āṣir, 1998), 1:208; Ibn Abī'l-Faḍā'il, *al-Nahj al-Sadīd*, 434–35. Ibn al-Bannā' reported to contemporaries that the planet Venus (*Kawkab al-Ṣubḥ*) had disappeared from sight upon the death of al-Musta'ṣim and did not reappear until the emergence of Abū'l-'Abbās—a cosmological coincidence that inspired much commotion and admiration among the Bedouin.
17. As the Bedouin of 'Ubādah used to reside in the region between Baghdad and Mosul, with some of them also congregating around the Damascene pasture, the added presence of one of their elders suggests a reasonable set of arrangements for the journey further west. The Banū 'Ubādah are the offspring of 'Ubādah b. 'Uqayl b. Ka'b b. Rabī'ah b. 'Āmir and therefore related to the Banū Khafājah through their common forefather 'Uqayl. Shihāb al-Dīn Abī'l-'Abbās Aḥmad b. Yaḥyā Ibn Faḍl Allāh al-'Umarī, *Masālik al-Abṣār wa-Mamālik al-Amṣār*, ed. Dorothea Krawulsky (Beirut: al-Markaz al-Islāmī li'l-Buḥūth, 1985), 112, 148; al-Nuwayrī, *Nihāyat al-Arab*, 2:340–41; Abū'l-'Abbās Aḥmad al-Qalqashandī, *Qalā'id al-Jumān fī'l-Ta'rīf bi Qabā'il al-Zamān*, ed. Ibrāhīm al-Abyārī (Cairo and Beirut: Dār al-Kutub al-Islāmiyyah, Dār al-Kitāb al-Miṣrī, Dār al-Kitāb al-Lubnānī, 1982), 119, 122–23; Abū'l-'Abbās Aḥmad al-Qalqashandī, *Nihāyat al-Arab fī Ma'rifat Ansāb al-'Arab*, ed. Ibrāhīm al-Abyārī (Cairo and Beirut: Dār al-Kutub al-Islāmiyyah, Dār al-Kitāb al-Miṣrī, Dār al-Kitāb al-Lubnānī, 1980), 335; al-Qalqashandī, *Ṣubḥ al-A'shā*, 1:341–43.
18. Ibn Shaddād, *Tārīkh al-Malik al-Ẓāhir*, 39.
19. These highly influential descendents of the family of Rabī'ah used to reside in geographical Syria, Iraq, and the Hijaz. Ibn Faḍl Allāh al-'Umarī, *Masālik*, ed. Krawulsky, 112–16; al-Qalqashandī, *Qalā'id*, 76–79; al-Qalqashandī, *Nihāyah*, 110; al-Qalqashandī, *Ṣubḥ al-A'shā*, 1:324–25.
20. Abū Muḥannā Sharaf al-Dīn 'Īsā b. Muḥannā. Al-Yūnīnī, *Dhayl Mir'āt al-Zamān*, 4:231–32; al-Ṣuqā'ī al-Naṣrānī, *Tālī Kitāb Wafayāt al-A'yān*, 110; al-Dhahabī, *Tārīkh al-Islām*, 69:155–56; al-Dhahabī, *Siyar*, 17:337–38.
21. These highly influential descendents of the family of Rabī'ah used to reside in geographical Syria, Iraq, and the Hijaz. Ibn Faḍl Allāh al-'Umarī, *Masālik*, ed. Krawulsky, 112–16; al-Qalqashandī, *Qalā'id*, 76–79; al-Qalqashandī, *Nihāyah*, 110; al-Qalqashandī, *Ṣubḥ al-A'shā*, 1:324–25.
22. al-Yūnīnī, *Dhayl Mir'āt al-Zamān*, 1:484–85; Ibn al-Dawādārī, *Kanz al-Durar*, 8:86–87; al-Dhahabī, *Siyar*, 17:155; al-Ṣafadī, *al-Wāfī*, 6:317–18; al-Ṣafadī, *A'yān al-'Aṣr*, 1:208–9; Mufaḍḍal Ibn Abī'l-Faḍā'il, *Kitāb al-Nahj al-Sadīd wa'l-Durr al-Farīd fīmā ba'd Tārīkh Ibn al-'Amīd*, vol.1, ed. E. Blochet (Turnhout, Belg.: Editions Brepols, 1982), 1:435.
23. Abū Shāmah, *Tarājim*, 207–9; Ibn Khallikān, *Wafayāt al-A'yān*, 4:155; Ibn al-'Ibrī, *Tārīkh al-Zamān*, 317–19; Ibn al-'Ibrī, *Tārīkh Mukhtaṣar al-Duwal*, 280–82; al-Ṣuqā'ī al-Naṣrānī, *Tālī Kitāb Wafayāt al-A'yān*, 128–29, 181; al-Yūnīnī, *Dhayl Mir'āt al-Zamān*, 1:360–70, 2:28–29, 35–36; Ibn al-'Amīd, *Akhbār al-Ayyūbiyyīn*, 53–54; Ibn 'Abd al-Ẓāhir, *al-Rawḍ al-Zāhir*, 63–67; Baybars al-Manṣūrī, *Zubdat al-Fikrah*, 50–52; Baybars al-Manṣūrī, *Kitāb al-Tuḥfah al-Mulūkiyyah fī'l-Dawlah al-Turkiyyah*, 43–44; Baybars al-Manṣūrī, *Mukhtār al-Akhbār*, 11; Abū'l-Fidā, *al-Mukhtaṣar fī Akhbār al-Bashar*, 3:238, 245–47; Ibn al-Wardī, *Tatimmat al-Mukhtaṣar*, 2:297–300; al-Dhahabī, *Tārīkh al-Islām*, 66:352–56; al-Dhahabī, *Siyar*, 16:447; al-Dhahabī, *al-'Ibar*, 5:242–43, 247;

Shams al-Dīn Muḥammad b. Aḥmad b. ʿUthmān al-Dhahabī, *Duwal al-Islām* (Hyderabad, India: Maṭbaʿat Dāʾirat al-Maʿārif al-Niẓāmiyyah, 1337 AH), 2:125; Ibn Shākir al-Kutubī, *ʿUyūn al-Tawārīkh*, 20:226–28, 241–44; Ibn Shākir al-Kutubī, *Fawāt al-Wafayāt*, 3:202–3; Ṣalāḥ al-Dīn Khalīl b. Aybak al-Ṣafadī, *al-Wāfī bi'l-Wafayāt*, vol. 24, ed. Muḥammad ʿAdnān al-Bakhīt and Muṣṭafā al-Ḥiyārī (Wiesbaden, Ger.: Franz Steiner Verlag, 1993), 252–53; al-Nuwayrī, 29:470–77; Ibn al-Dawādārī, *Kanz al-Durar*, 8:46–53, 59–60; Ibn Abī'l-Faḍāʾil, *al-Nahj al-Sadīd*, 1:435. For an overview of the events leading up to and including the battle of ʿAyn Jālūt, see Reuven Amitai-Preiss, *Mongols and Mamluks: The Mamluk-Īlkhānid War, 1260–1281* (Cambridge: Cambridge University Press, 1995), 26–45. For a detailed military history of the battle itself, also see John Masson Smith Jr., "Ayn Jalut: Mamluk Success or Mongol Failure?," 307–45.

24. Al-Yūnīnī, *Dhayl Mirʾāt al-Zamān*, 1:485; al-Dhahabī, *Siyar*, 17:155; al-Ṣafadī, *al-Wāfī*, 6:318; al-Ṣafadī, *Aʿyān*, 1:208, 209; Ibn Abī'l-Faḍāʾil, *al-Nahj al-Sadīd*, 1:435. For a careful study of al-Yūnīnī's work, see Li Guo, *Early Syrian Historiography: al-Yūnīnī's Dhayl Mirʾāt al-Zamān* (Leiden, Neth.: E. J. Brill, 1998).
25. Ibn al-Dawādārī, *Kanz al-Durar*, 8:87 and Ibn Abī'l-Faḍāʾil, *al-Nahj al-Sadīd*, 1:435–36.
26. al-Yūnīnī, *Dhayl Mirʾāt al-Zamān*, 1:485–86; al-Dhahabī, *Siyar*, 17:155; al-Ṣafadī, *al-Wāfī*, 6:318; al-Ṣafadī, *Aʿyān*, 1:209; Ibn Abī'l-Faḍāʾil, *al-Nahj al-Sadīd*, 1:435. Abū'l-ʿAbbās, the Amīr Sayf al-Dīn Qilij al-Baghdādī, the Amīr Sharaf al-Dīn ʿĪsā b. Muhannā, the Amīr Sayf al-Dīn ʿAlī b. Ṣaqr b. Makhlūl, ʿUmar b. Makhlūl, and all of the populous Āl Faḍl (except for the sons of Ḥudhayfah) went on to retake the towns of ʿĀnah, al-Ḥadīthah, Hīt, and al-Anbār. At the end of Dhū'l-Ḥijjah 658 / late November or early December 1260, this aggregated force also defeated a group of Mongols in battle at al-Fallūjah, killing over one thousand horsemen, along with Ankūrk and eighty other commanders. But when the Muslim forces heard that the Mongol commander Qarabughā had arrived with a larger army, they decided to return to Ḥimyah and were followed on the way back by the Mongols, who eventually desisted from this pursuit.
27. Abū Shāmah, *Tarājim*, 210; Ibn Khallikān, *Wafayāt al-Aʿyān*, 4:155; Ibn al-ʿIbrī, *Tārīkh al-Zamān*, 319; Ibn al-ʿIbrī, *Tārīkh Mukhtaṣar al-Duwal*, 282; Ibn Wāṣil, *Die Chronik*, 204–12, 230–31, 218–19; al-Ṣuqāʿī al-Naṣrānī, *Tālī Kitāb Wafayāt al-Aʿyān*, 50, 129; al-Yūnīnī, *Dhayl Mirʾāt al-Zamān*, 1:370–72, 2:1–2, 29–30; Ibn al-ʿAmīd, *Akhbār al-Ayyūbiyyīn*, 54–55; Ibn ʿAbd al-Ẓāhir, *al-Rawḍ al-Zāhir*, 67–68; Baybars al-Manṣūrī, *Zubdat al-Fikrah*, 53–55; Baybars al-Manṣūrī, *Tuḥfah*, 45; Baybars al-Manṣūrī, *Mukhtār*, 11–13; Abū'l-Fidā, *al-Mukhtaṣar fī Akhbār al-Bashar*, 247–48; Ibn al-Wardī, *Tatimmat al-Mukhtaṣar*, 2:300–301; al-Dhahabī, *Tārīkh al-Islām*, 66:352–53, 355; al-Dhahabī, *Siyar*, 17:305; al-Dhahabī, *al-ʿIbar*, 5:243; al-Dhahabī, *Duwal al-Islām*, 2:125–26; Ibn Shākir al-Kutubī, *ʿUyūn al-Tawārīkh*, 20:228–29, 241; Ibn Shākir al-Kutubī, *Fawāt al-Wafayāt*, 1:237–38; 3:202–3; Ṣalāḥ al-Dīn Khalīl b. Aybak al-Ṣafadī, *al-Wāfī bi'l-Wafayāt*, vol. 10, ed. Ali Amara and Jacqueline Sublet (Wiesbaden, Ger.: Franz Steiner Verlag, 1980), 332–33; al-Ṣafadī, *al-Wāfī*, 24:253; al-Nuwayrī, 29:477–78; Shihāb al-Dīn Aḥmad b. ʿAbd al-Wahhāb al-Nuwayrī, *Nihāyat al-Arab fī Funūn al-Adab*, vol. 30, ed. Muḥammad ʿAbd al-Hādī Shaʿīrah (Cairo: al-Hayʾah al-Miṣriyyah li'l-Kitāb, 1990), 13–14; Ibn al-Dawādārī, *Kanz al-Durar*, 8:60–62, 87; Ibn Abī'l-Faḍāʾil, *al-Nahj al-Sadīd*, 1:407–8, 410, 435–36.
28. al-Yūnīnī, *Dhayl Mirʾāt al-Zamān*, 1:485–86; al-Dhahabī, *Siyar*, 17:155; al-Ṣafadī, *al-Wāfī*, 6:318; al-Ṣafadī, *Aʿyān*, 1:209; Ibn Abī'l-Faḍāʾil, *al-Nahj al-Sadīd*, 1:435. For the time being, Abū'l-ʿAbbās returned to the safety of ʿĪsā b. Muhannā's domain.
29. al-Yūnīnī, *Dhayl Mirʾāt al-Zamān*, 1:486; al-Dhahabī, *Siyar*, 17:155; al-Ṣafadī, *al-Wāfī*, 6:318; al-Ṣafadī, *Aʿyān*, 1:209.

30. al-Yūnīnī, *Dhayl Mir'āt al-Zamān,* 1:486; al-Dhahabī, *Siyar,* 17:155; al-Ṣafadī, *al-Wāfī,* 6:318; al-Ṣafadī, *A'yān,* 1:209.
31. al-Ṣuqā'ī al-Naṣrānī, *Tālī Kitāb Wafayāt al-A'yān,* 2; al-Yūnīnī, *Dhayl Mir'āt al-Zamān,* 1:486; Ibn al-Dawādārī, *Kanz al-Durar,* 8:72; al-Dhahabī, *Siyar,* 16:427; al-Dhahabī, *Tārīkh al-Islām,* 66:407; Ibn Shākir al-Kutubī, *'Uyūn al-Tawārīkh,* 20:251; al-Ṣafadī, *al-Wāfī,* 7:384; Ibn Abī'l-Faḍā'il, *al-Nahj al-Sadīd,* 1:423. In the seventh/thirteenth and eighth/fourteenth centuries, the Khafājah Bedouins used to reside in the area of Iraq circumscribed by Hīt and al-Anbār, Bi'r Mallāḥā, al-Kūfah, Qā'im 'Anqā', and al-Tharthār, as far as al-Muthannā but not al-Baṣrah. Ibn Faḍl Allāh al-'Umarī, *Masālik al-Abṣār,* ed. Krawulsky, 148. The Banū Khafājah are the progeny of Khafājah b. 'Amr b. 'Uqayl b. Ka'b b. Rabī'ah b. 'Āmir. See Shihāb al-Dīn Aḥmad b. 'Abd al-Wahhāb al-Nuwayrī, *Nihāyat al-Arab fī Funūn al-Adab,* vol. 2 (Cairo: Maṭba'at Dār al-Kutub al-Miṣriyyah, 1924), 340; al-Qalqashandī, *Qalā'id,* 122-3; al-Qalqashandī, *Nihāyat,* 246–47; al-Qalqashandī, *Ṣubḥ al-A'shā,* 1:243.
32. Ibn 'Abd al-Ẓāhir, *al-Rawḍ al-Zāhir,* 99; Ibn Shaddād, *Tārīkh al-Malik al-Ẓāhir,* 330; al-Yūnīnī, *Dhayl Mir'āt al-Zamān,* 1:441, 2:94–95, 123; Ibn Shākir al-Kutubī, *'Uyūn al-Tawārīkh,* 20:251; al-Nuwayrī, *Nihāyat al-Arab,* 30:28–29; Ibn al-Dawādārī, *Kanz al-Durar,* 8:72; Ibn Abī'l-Faḍā'il, *al-Nahj al-Sadīd,* 1:423–24. al-Yūnīnī describes these ten leaders as belonging to the Banī Mahārish, which is a subset of Khafājah, as is observable through the way al-Yūnīnī cites some of the same individuals as Ibn Shaddād (613–84/1217–85) and through al-Qalqashandī's (756–821/1355–1418) citation of the common progenitor Mahārish in the lineage of a prominent member of Khafājah, Khiḍr b. Badrān b. Muqlid b. Sulaymān b. Mahārish, mentioned in relation to Abū'l-Qāsim's later exploits (*Qalā'id,* 123). The appellation Banū Mahārish is also utilized by Ibn al-Dawādārī (alive at least until 736/1335), al-Dhahabī (673–748/1274–1348), and al-Ṣafadī (696–764/1297–1363).
33. Ibn 'Abd al-Ẓāhir, *al-Rawḍ al-Zāhir,* 99; al-Nuwayrī, *Nihāyat al-Arab,* 30:29.
34. Ibn 'Abd al-Ẓāhir, *al-Rawḍ al-Zāhir,* 99; Shāfi', *Ḥusn al-Manāqib,* 37; al-Yūnīnī, *Dhayl Mir'āt al-Zamān,* 1:441–42, 2:95–96, 123; 'Izz al-Dīn Muḥammad ibn 'Alī Ibn Shaddād, *Tārīkh al-Malik al-Ẓāhir [al-Rawḍ al-Zāhir Sīrat al-Malik al-Ẓāhir],* ed. Aḥmad Ḥuṭayṭ (Beirut: Franz Steiner, 1983), 330; al-Ṣuqā'ī al-Naṣrānī, *Tālī Kitāb Wafayāt al-A'yān,* 2; Baybars al-Manṣūrī, *Zubdat al-Fikrah,* 60; Baybars al-Manṣūrī, *Tuḥfah,* 47; Baybars al-Manṣūrī, *Mukhtār,* 15; al-Dhahabī, *Siyar,* 16:427; Ibn Shākir al-Kutubī, *'Uyūn al-Tawārīkh,* 20:251; al-Ṣafadī, *al-Wāfī,* 7:384; al-Nuwayrī, *Nihāyat al-Arab,* 23:327, 30:29; Ibn al-Dawādārī, *Kanz al-Durar,* 8:72–73; Ibn Abī'l-Faḍā'il, *al-Nahj al-Sadīd,* 1:424. al-Yūnīnī gives the date of his arrival as the ninth of Rajab. al-Nuwayrī mistakenly conflates the day of Abū'l-Qāsim's arrival with the ceremonious day on which he was given *bay'ah,* and Ibn al-Dawādārī similarly conflates the day of his *bay'ah* with that of the later *taqlīd* ceremony; hence his observation that some people report it as occurring on Thursday while others say it was Monday. On the architectural history of this processional route, see Nasser Rabbat, *Staging the City: Or How Mamluk Architecture Coopted the Streets of Cairo* (Berlin: EB-Verlag, 2014) and Dina Ghaly, "The Shāri' al-A'ẓam in Cairo: Its Topography and Architecture in the Mamluk Period," (PhD diss., University of Toronto, 2004).
35. P. M. Holt, "Some Observations on the 'Abbasid Caliphate of Cairo," *Bulletin of the School of Oriental and African Studies* 47, no. 3 (1984), 501–3 and Stefan Heidemann, *Das Aleppiner Kalifat (A.D. 1261): Vom Ende Kalifates in Baghdad über Aleppo zu den Restaurationen in Kairo* (Leiden, Neth.: E. J. Brill, 1994); see the review article by Reuven Amitai-Preiss, "The Fall and Rise of the 'Abbāsid Caliphate," *Journal of the American Oriental Society* 113, no. 3 (July–September 1996): 487–94.

36. On Baybars' subsequent projection of legitimacy through epigraphic inscriptions connecting him with this restored caliphate, see Denise Aigle, "Les inscriptions de Baybars dans le Bilād al-Šām: Une expression de la légitimité du pouvoir," *Studia Islamica* 97 (2003): 57–85 and Denise Aigle, "Legitimizing a Low-Born, Regicide Monarch: The Case of the Mamluk Sultan Baybars and the Ilkhans in the Thirteenth Century," in *Representing Power in Ancient Inner Asia: Legitimacy, Transmission and the Sacred*, ed. Isabelle Carleux, et al. ([Bellingham, WA]: Center for East Asian Studies, Western Washington University, 2010), 61–94.
37. *al-Ṭawāshī* appears to refer to Mukhtār al-Baghdādī's being a eunuch and not to the military rank, since most of the primary sources cited below refer alternatively to a "servant from Baghdad" (*khādim min al-Baghādidah*). David Ayalon demonstrates the military sense of the term among authors from the early Mamluk period, including Ibn Shaddād (613–84/1217–85), Baybars al-Manṣūrī (645–725/1247–1325), and Ibn Faḍl Allāh al-ʿUmarī (700–749/1301–49) in his "Studies on the Structure of the Mamluk Army—II," *Bulletin of the School of Oriental and African Studies* 15, no. 3 (1953): 464–67. For later usages of the term by Ibn Khaldūn (732–84/1332–1406), al-Qalqashandī (756–821/1355–1418), and al-Maqrīzī (766–845/1364–1442) as synonomous with "eunuch," see Ayalon's other works, his "The Eunuchs in the Mamluk Sultanate," in *Studies in Memory of Gaston Wiet*, ed. Myriam Rosen-Ayalon (Jerusalem: Institute of Asian and African Studies, 1977), 267–69, his "On the Eunuchs in Islam," in *Jerusalem Studies in Arabic and Islam* (Jerusalem: Magnes Press, 1979), 79, and his *Eunuchs, Caliphs and Sultans* (Jerusalem: Magnes Press, 1999), 262, 265–66 as well as Shaun Marmon, *Eunuchs and Sacred Boundaries in Islamic Society* (Oxford: Oxford University Press, 1995), 41–42 and M. Plessner, "Ṭawāshī," in *The Encyclopaedia of Islam*, 1st ed.
38. This group consisted of al-Qāḍī Jamāl al-Dīn Yaḥyā (*Nāʾib al-Ḥukm al-ʿAzīz bi-Miṣr al-Maḥrūsah*), al-Faqīh ʿAlam al-Dīn Ibn Rashīq (*al-Muftī*), al-Qaḍī Ṣadr al-Dīn Mawhūb al-Jazarī, Najīb al-Dīn al-Ḥarrānī, and Sadīd al-Dīn al-Tirmidhī (*Nāʾib al-Ḥukm biʾl-Qāḥirah*). Ibn ʿAbd al-Ẓāhir, *al-Rawḍ al-Zāhir*, 100; Shāfiʿ, *Ḥusn al-Manāqib*, 37; al-Nuwayrī, *Nihāyat al-Arab*, 23:327.
39. Tāj al-Dīn Abū Muḥammad ʿAbd al-Wahhāb b. Khalaf b. Badr al-Alāmī Ibn Bint al-Aʿazz. al-Subkī, *Ṭabaqāt*, 8:318–23.
40. Ibn Wāṣil, *Die Chronik*, 231; al-Yūnīnī, *Dhayl Mirʾāt al-Zamān*, 2:187; Ibn ʿAbd al-Ẓāhir, *al-Rawḍ al-Zāhir*, 99; Shāfiʿ, *Ḥusn al-Manāqib*, 37; Baybars al-Manṣūrī, *Zubdat al-Fikrah*, 61; al-Nuwayrī, *Nihāyat al-Arab*, 23:328, 30:29.
41. Ibn ʿAbd al-Ẓāhir, *al-Rawḍ al-Zāhir*, 99–101; Shāfiʿ, *Ḥusn al-Manāqib*, 37–38; al-Yūnīnī, *Dhayl Mirʾāt al-Zamān*, 1:442–43, 451–52, 2:95–96, 97–98, 123; Ibn Shaddād, *Tārīkh al-Malik al-Ẓāhir*, 330; Baybars al-Manṣūrī, *Zubdat al-Fikrah*, 60–61; Baybars al-Manṣūrī, *Tuḥfah*, 47; Baybars al-Manṣūrī, *Mukhtār*, 15–16; al-Ṣuqāʿī al-Naṣrānī, 2; Abū Shāmah, *Tarājim*, 213; Abūʾl-Fidā, *al-Mukhtaṣar fī Akhbār al-Bashar*, 3:253; Ibn al-Wardī, *Tatimmat al-Mukhtaṣar*, 2:305; al-Dhahabī, *Tārīkh al-Islām*, 66:406–8; al-Dhahabī, *Siyar*, 16:427–28; al-Dhahabī, *al-ʿIbar*, 5:252, 258; al-Dhahabī, *Duwal al-Islām*, 2:127; Ibn Shākir al-Kutubī, *ʿUyūn al-Tawārīkh*, 20:251–52; al-Ṣafadī, *al-Wāfī*, 7:384–85; al-Nuwayrī, *Nihāyat al-Arab*, 23:327–28; 30:29–30; Ibn al-Dawādārī, 8:73; Ibn Abīʾl-Faḍāʾil, 1:424; Ibn Ḥabīb al-Ḥalabī, "Durrat al-Aslāk fī Dawlat al-Atrāk," Arabe Collection, Manuscript 4680, folios 43r–43v, Bibliothèque nationale de France, Paris, France.
42. Abū Shāmah, *Tarājim*, 213; al-Yūnīnī, *Dhayl Mirʾāt al-Zamān*, 1:452.
43. Ibn ʿAbd al-Ẓāhir, *al-Rawḍ al-Zāhir*, 100; Shāfiʿ, *Ḥusn al-Manāqib*, 37; Baybars al-Manṣūrī, *Zubdat al-Fikrah*, 61; Baybars al-Manṣūrī, *Mukhtār*, 15–16.

44. I.e., both the Mamluk and non-Mamluk contingents, the former possessing a more elevated status than the more populous latter group, which also included some religious officials, see al-Qalqashandī, *Ṣubḥ al-Aʿshā,* 1:15–16. For a fuller exposition, cf. David Ayalon, "Studies on the Structure of the Mamluk Army—I," *Bulletin of the School of Oriental and African Studies* 15, no. 2 (1953): 203–28 and Ayalon, "Studies on the Structure of the Mamluk Army—II," 448–76.
45. Abū Shāmah, *Tarājim,* 213; al-Yūnīnī, *Dhayl Mirʾāt al-Zamān,* 1:452.
46. Abū Shāmah, *Tarājim,* 213; al-Yūnīnī, *Dhayl Mirʾāt al-Zamān,* 1:451–52; Ibn ʿAbd al-Ẓāhir, *al-Rawḍ al-Zāhir,* 100–101; Shāfiʿ, *Ḥusn al-Manāqib,* 36–37; Baybars al-Manṣūrī, *Zubdat al-Fikrah,* 61; Baybars al-Manṣūrī, *Mukhtār,* 16; Baybars al-Manṣūrī, *Tuḥfah,* 47; Ibn Shākir al-Kutubī, *ʿUyūn al-Tawārīkh,* 20:287; al-Ṣafadī, *al-Wāfī,* 7:384; al-Nuwayrī, *Nihāyat al-Arab,* 23:328. Heidemann has thoroughly studied the extant coinage from this era in his *Das Aleppiner Kalifat (A.D. 1261),* 205–371; see Amitai-Preiss' review article, "The Fall and Rise of the ʿAbbāsid Caliphate," 492–93.
47. al-Ṣuqāʿī al-Naṣrānī, *Tālī Kitāb Wafayāt al-Aʿyān,* 143; al-Dhahabī, *Siyar,* 17:329.
48. The prestigious Shāfiʿī legal college inside of Damascus, begun by Nūr al-Dīn Zanjī (r. 541–65/1174–46), continued by al-Malik al-ʿĀdil Sayf al-Dīn Abū Bakr b. Ayyūb (r. 592–615/1196–1218), and completed by al-Malik al-Muʿaẓẓim (r. 615–24/1218–27), where the chief justices of geographical Syria frequently taught (the first being Jamāl al-Dīn al-Miṣrī who died in Rabīʿ al-Awwal 623 / March 1226). ʿIzz al-Dīn Abū ʿAbdillāh Muḥammad b. ʿAlī b. Ibrāhīm Ibn Shaddād, *al-Aʿlāq al-Khaṭīrah fī Dhikr Umarāʾ al-Shām wa'l-Jazīrah,* ed. Sāmī al-Dahhān (Damascus: al-Maʿhad al-Faransī li'l-Dirāsāt al-ʿArabiyyah, 1956), 240; al-Subkī, *Ṭabaqāt,* 8:366; al-Dhahabī, *Tārīkh al-Islām,* 63: 178–79.
49. Abū Shāmah, *Tarājim,* 213; al-Yūnīnī, *Dhayl Mirʾāt al-Zamān,* 1:452; al-Dhahabī, *Siyar,* 16:428.
50. Abū Shāmah, *Tarājim,* 213.
51. Ibn Shaddād, *Tārīkh al-Malik al-Ẓāhir,* 278.
52. See al-Yūnīnī, *Dhayl Mirʾāt al-Zamān,* 1:443–49, 2:98–103; Ibn ʿAbd al-Ẓāhir, *al-Rawḍ al-Zāhir,* 102–10; Shāfiʿ, *Ḥusn al-Manāqib,* 38–44; Baybars al-Manṣūrī, *Zubdat al-Fikrah,* 61–65; al-Nuwayrī, *Nihāyat al-Arab,* 30:30–35; Ibn al-Dawādārī, *Kanz al-Durar,* 8:73–79, 94; Ibn Kathīr, *al-Bidāyah wa'l-Nihāyah,* 13:357. In addition to his role in crafting the official foundations for the Mamluk regime as a legitimate sultanate, Fakhr al-Dīn Abū Isḥāq Ibrāhīm b. Luqmān b. Aḥmad b. Muḥammad later rose to greater prominence as its vizier. His house in al-Manṣūrah was also where King Louis IX of France was imprisoned after being defeated in battle in Egypt on the Seventh Crusade in 647/1250.
53. Ibn ʿAbd al-Ẓāhir, *al-Rawḍ al-Zāhir,* 101, 110; Shāfiʿ, *Ḥusn al-Manāqib,* 38, 44; al-Yūnīnī, *Dhayl Mirʾāt al-Zamān,* 1:443, 2:98, 123–24; Baybars al-Manṣūrī, *Zubdat al-Fikrah,* 61, 65; Baybars al-Manṣūrī, *Mukhtār,* 16–17; al-Ṣuqāʿī al-Naṣrānī, *Tālī Kitāb Wafayāt al-Aʿyān,* 2; al-Dhahabī, *Tārīkh al-Islām,* 66:407; al-Dhahabī, *Siyar,* 16:428; al-Dhahabī, *al-ʿIbar,* 5:252, 258–59; Ibn Shākir al-Kutubī, *ʿUyūn al-Tawārīkh,* 20:253; al-Ṣafadī, *al-Wāfī,* 7:384–85; al-Nuwayrī, *Nihāyat al-Arab,* 23:328, 30:30; Ibn al-Dawādārī, *Kanz al-Durar,* 8:73; Ibn Abī'l-Faḍāʾil, *al-Nahj al-Sadīd,* 1:424–25; Ibn Ḥabīb al-Ḥalabī, "Durrat al-Aslāk fī Dawlat al-Atrāk," Arabe Collection, Manuscript 4680, folios 43r–34v, Bibliothèque nationale de France, Paris, France. For other discussions of al-Mustanṣir's ascension in Cairo, and later that of al-Ḥākim, see Syedah Fatima Sadeque, *Baybars I of Egypt* (Pak.: Oxford University Press, 1956), 43–46; David Ayalon, "Studies on the Transfer of the ʿAbbāsid Caliphate from Bağdād to Cairo," *Arabica* 7, no. 1 (1960): 41–59;

Abdul-Aziz Khowaiter, *Baibars the First: His Endeavours and Achievements* (London: Green Mountain Press, 1978), 34–36; P. M. Holt, "Some Observations," 501–7; P. M. Holt, *The Age of the Crusades* (London: Longman, 1986), 92–94; Peter Thorau, *The Lion of Egypt: Sultan Baybars I and the Near East in the Thirteenth Century* (London: Longman, 1987), 110–19; Amitai-Preiss, *Mongols and Mamluks*, 56–57.

54. al-Yūnīnī, *Dhayl Mir'āt al-Zamān*, 1:450–51, 2:104; Ibn 'Abd al-Ẓāhir, *al-Rawḍ al-Zāhir*, 111; Shāfi', *Ḥusn al-Manāqib*, 45; Ibn al-Dawādārī, *Kanz al-Durar*, 8:80–81; Ibn Abī'l-Faḍā'il, *al-Nahj al-Sadīd*, 1:426–28; Hodgson, *The Venture of Islam*, 2:279–85; Robert Irwin, "'Futuwwa': Chivalry and Gangsterism in Medieval Cairo," *Muqarnas* 21 (2004): 161–70; Erik Ohlander, *Sufism in an Age of Transition: 'Umar al-Suhrawardī and the Rise of the Islamic Mystical Brotherhoods* (Leiden, Neth.: E. J. Brill, 2008), 23–27, 271–72; Herbert Mason, *Two Statesmen of Medieval Islam: Vizir Ibn Hubayra (499–560 AH / 1105–1165 AD) and Caliph an-Nāṣir Li-Dīn Allāh (553–622 AH / 1158–1225 AD)*, 119–32; Angelika Hartmann, *an-Nāṣir li-Dīn Allāh (1180–1225)* (Berlin: Walter de Gruyter, 1975), 92–108; Qamar ul-Hoda, "The Prince of Diplomacy: Shaykh 'Umar al-Suhrawardi's Revolution for Sufism, Futuwwa Groups, and Politics under Caliph al-Nāsir," *History of Sufism* 3 (2001): 257–78; Angelika Hartmann, "al-Nāṣir Li-Dīn Allāh;" Franz Taeschner, "Futuwwa," in *The Encyclopaedia of Islam*, 2nd ed.; Muṣṭafā Jawād, "al-Futuwwah mundhu al-Qarn al-Awwal li'l-Hijrah ilā al-Qarn al-Thālith 'Ashar minhā," in Abū 'Abdillāh Muḥammad b. Abī'l-Makārim Ibn al-Mi'mār al-Baghdādī, *Kitāb al-Futuwwah*, ed. Muṣṭafā Jawād, et al. (Baghdad: Maktabat al-Muthannā, 1958), 3–99.

55. Abū Shāmah, *Tarājim*, 213; Ibn Wāṣil, *Die Chronik*, 232; al-Dhahabī, *Tārīkh al-Islām*, 66:75; al-Yūnīnī, *Dhayl Mir'āt al-Zamān*, 1:453, 2:107.

56. al-Yūnīnī, *Dhayl Mir'āt al-Zamān*, 1:453, 2:107–8; Ibn Shākir al-Kutubī, *'Uyūn al-Tawārīkh*, 20:288–89; Ibn Abī'l-Faḍā'il, *al-Nahj al-Sadīd*, 1:450–52.

57. al-Yūnīnī, *Dhayl Mir'āt al-Zamān*, 1:486; al-Dhahabī, *Siyar*, 17:155; al-Ṣafadī, *al-Wāfī*, 6:318; al-Ṣafadī, *A'yān*, 1:209.

58. al-Yūnīnī, *Dhayl Mir'āt al-Zamān*, 1:455; Ibn al-Dawādārī, *Kanz al-Durar*, 8:80–81; Ibn Abī'l-Faḍā'il, *al-Nahj al-Sadīd*, 1:429.

59. Ibn Wāṣil, *Die Chronik*, 226–28; al-Yūnīnī, *Dhayl Mir'āt al-Zamān*, 1:440, 2:93, 119–20; Ibn 'Abd al-Ẓāhir, *al-Rawḍ al-Zāhir*, 97; Baybars al-Manṣūrī, *Zubdat al-Fikrah*, 69–70; Abū'l-Fidā, *al-Mukhtaṣar fī Akhbār al-Bashar*, 3:251; Ibn al-Wardī, *Tatimmat al-Mukhtaṣar*, 2:303; Ibn Shākir al-Kutubī, *'Uyūn al-Tawārīkh*, 20:250; al-Nuwayrī, *Nihāyat al-Arab*, 30:44; Ibn al-Dawādārī, *Kanz al-Durar*, 8:70, 72; Ibn Abī'l-Faḍā'il, *al-Nahj al-Sadīd*, 1:421, 423. The Egyptian contemporaries Ibn 'Abd al-Ẓāhir (620–92/1223–92) and Baybars al-Manṣūrī also include the Ashrafiyyah among those Mamluks who left Damascus with al-Barlī. al-Barlī is an Arabic rendering for the Ölberli clan of the Qipchaq nomadic confederation; see Peter Golden, "Cumanica II: The Ölberli (Ölperli): The Fortunes and Misfortunes of an Inner Asian Nomadic Clan," *Archivum Eurasiae Medii Aevi* 6 (1986): 13–14.

60. Ibn Shaddād, *Tārīkh al-Malik al-Ẓāhir*, 38–39, 241, 285, 287, 334; Ibn Wāṣil, *Die Chronik*, 227–31; al-Ṣuqā'ī al-Naṣrānī, *Tālī Kitāb Wafayāt al-A'yān*, 18; al-Yūnīnī, *Dhayl Mir'āt al-Zamān*, 1:439–40, 2:93–94, 104–5,120–22; Ibn 'Abd al-Ẓāhir, *al-Rawḍ al-Zāhir*, 75, 97–98, 122; Baybars al-Manṣūrī, *Zubdat al-Fikrah*, 60, 69–70; Shāfi', *Ḥusn al-Manāqib*, 46; Abū'l-Fidā, *al-Mukhtaṣar fī Akhbār al-Bashar*, 3:251–52; Ibn al-Wardī, *Tatimmat al-Mukhtaṣar*, 2:303–4; al-Nuwayrī, *Nihāyat al-Arab*, 30:43–44; Ibn al-Dawādārī, *Kanz al-Durar*, 8:72; Ibn Abī'l-Faḍā'il, *al-Nahj al-Sadīd*, 1:422–23.

61. al-Yūnīnī, *Dhayl Mir'āt al-Zamān*, 1:486; al-Dhahabī, *Siyar*, 17:155; al-Ṣafadī, *al-Wāfī*, 6:318; al-Ṣafadī, *A'yān*.

62. al-Yūnīnī, *Dhayl Mir'āt al-Zamān,* 2:105–6; Ibn ʿAbd al-Ẓāhir, *al-Rawḍ al-Zāhir,* 75, 97–99, 113; Ibn Shaddād, *Tārīkh al-Malik al-Ẓāhir,* 241, 285; al-Ṣuqāʿī al-Naṣrānī, *Tālī Kitāb Wafayāt al-Aʿyān,* 18; al-Nuwayrī, *Nihāyat al-Arab,* 30:44. The representatives of al-Barlī who entered Aleppo on his behalf were ʿAlam al-Dīn Tuqṣubā al-Nāṣirī and Sayf al-Dīn Kikildī. In the unlikely event that al-Barlī arrived on the first or second of Ramaḍān, those dates would coincide with the last two days of July.

63. Even the father of the famous Ibn Taymiyyah, Shihāb al-Dīn ʿAbd al-Ḥalīm, pledged his allegiance to al-Ḥākim as caliph. Abū Shāmah, *Tarājim,* 215; al-Yūnīnī, *Dhayl Mir'āt al-Zamān,* 1:486; al-Dhahabī, *Siyar,* 17:155; al-Dhahabī, *al-ʿIbar,* 5:252–53; al-Dhahabī, *Duwal al-Islām,* 2:127; al-Ṣafadī, *al-Wāfī,* 6:318; al-Ṣafadī, *Aʿyān,* 1:209. The missing folio of the Ibn Abī'l-Faḍā'il manuscript (1:427–28) must contain information on al-Ḥākim, and possibly also on al-Barlī, as is discernible from the continuation of a sentence on the following page (1:429). The first to point out that al-Barlī paid allegiance to al-Ḥākim was P. M. Holt in his "Some Observations on the ʿAbbāsid Caliphate of Cairo," 501, although within the same sentence acknowledging this *bayʿah,* al-Ḥākim is summarily dispatched by al-Barlī to Mesopotamia. Passing reference is also made in Amitai-Preiss, *Mongols and Mamluks,* 62. The significance of this Aleppan caliphate receives fuller treatment in Heidemann, *Das Aleppiner Kalifat (A.D. 1261)*; see the review article by Reuven Amitai-Preiss, "The Fall and Rise of the ʿAbbāsid Caliphate," 487–94.

64. Abū Shāmah, *Tarājim,* 213–14; al-Ṣuqāʿī al-Naṣrānī, *Tālī Kitāb Wafayāt al-Aʿyān,* 2, 50; al-Yūnīnī, *Dhayl Mir'āt al-Zamān,* 1:450–51, 453, 2:104, 106–8, 124; Ibn ʿAbd al-Ẓāhir, *al-Rawḍ al-Zāhir,* 111–12; Shāfiʿ, *Ḥusn al-Manāqib,* 45; Baybars al-Manṣūrī, *Zubdat al-Fikrah,* 66; Baybars al-Manṣūrī, *Mukhtār,* 18; Abū'l-Fidā, *al-Mukhtaṣar fī Akhbār al-Bashar,* 3:253–54; Ibn al-Wardī, *Tatimmat al-Mukhtaṣar,* 2:305–6; al-Dhahabī, *Tārīkh al-Islām,* 66:408–9; al-Dhahabī, *Siyar,* 16:429; al-Dhahabī, *al-ʿIbar,* 5:252, 259; al-Dhahabī, *Duwal al-Islām,* 2:127; Ibn Shākir al-Kutubī, *ʿUyūn al-Tawārīkh,* 20:254; al-Ṣafadī, *al-Wāfī,* 7:385–86; al-Nuwayrī, *Nihāyat al-Arab,* 30:36–37; Ibn al-Dawādārī, *Kanz al-Durar,* 8:80–81; Ibn Abī'l-Faḍā'il, *al-Nahj al-Sadīd,* 1:426–27. Also note how al-Yūnīnī reports, "When the news arrived of al-Barlī's taking of al-Bīrah and his return to Aleppo, and the departure of al-Ḥalabī therefrom, the Sultan set out with his army to Birkat al-Jubb with the Caliph and the sons of the [deceased] ruler of Mosul on the nineteenth of the month of Ramaḍān" (2:106–7) and the centrality that Ibn ʿAbd al-Ẓāhir assigns to this matter by placing resolution of the al-Barlī affair before all else (113–14).

65. Abū Shāmah, *Tarājim,* 215; al-Ṣuqāʿī al-Naṣrānī, *Tālī Kitāb Wafayāt al-Aʿyān,* 3; al-Yūnīnī, *Dhayl Mir'āt al-Zamān,* 1:454–55, 486, 2:108–10, 122, 152; Ibn ʿAbd al-Ẓāhir, *al-Rawḍ al-Zāhir,* 112–13; Baybars al-Manṣūrī, *Tuḥfah,* 47–48; Baybars al-Manṣūrī, *Mukhtār,* 18–19; Baybars al-Manṣūrī, *Tuḥfah,* 47–48; Abū'l-Fidā, *al-Mukhtaṣar fī Akhbār al-Bashar,* 3:255; Ibn al-Wardī, *Tatimmat al-Mukhtaṣar,* 2:307; al-Dhahabī, *Tārīkh al-Islām,* 66:409; al-Dhahabī, *Siyar,* 16:429, 17:155; al-Dhahabī, *al-ʿIbar,* 5:252–53; al-Dhahabī, *Duwal al-Islām,* 2:127; al-Ṣafadī, *al-Wāfī,* 6:318, 7:386; al-Nuwayrī, *Nihāyat al-Arab,* 23:330, 30:37, 44; Ibn al-Dawādārī, *Kanz al-Durar,* 8:82; Ibn Abī'l-Faḍā'il, *al-Nahj al-Sadīd,* 1:428–29.

66. Abū Shāmah, *Tarājim,* 215–16; Ibn al-ʿIbrī, *Tārīkh al-Zamān,* 322; al-Ṣuqāʿī al-Naṣrānī, *Tālī Kitāb Wafayāt al-Aʿyān,* 2–3; al-Yūnīnī, *Dhayl Mir'āt al-Zamān,* 1:454–57, 500, 2:108–12, 164, 187; Ibn ʿAbd al-Ẓāhir, *al-Rawḍ al-Zāhir,* 111–12; Shāfiʿ, *Ḥusn al-Manāqib,* 33, 44–46; Baybars al-Manṣūrī, *Zubdat al-Fikrah,* 66–68; Baybars al-Manṣūrī, *Tuḥfah,* 47–48; Abū'l-Fidā, *al-Mukhtaṣar fī Akhbār al-Bashar,* 3:254; Ibn al-Wardī, *Tatimmat al-Mukhtaṣar,* 2:305–6; al-Dhahabī, *Tārīkh al-Islām,* 66:409; al-Dhahabī, *Siyar,* 16:429,

17:155; al-Dhahabī, *al-'Ibar,* 5:252–53, 259; al-Dhahabī, *Duwal al-Islām,* 2:127; Ibn Shākir al-Kutubī, *'Uyūn al-Tawārīkh,* 20:253–56; al-Ṣafadī, *al-Wāfī,* 6:318, 7:385–86; al-Ṣafadī, *A'yān,* 1:209; al-Nuwayrī, *Nihāyat al-Arab,* 23:328–31, 30:36–37; Ibn al-Dawādārī, *Kanz al-Durar,* 8:79–80, 82–84; Ibn Abī'l-Faḍā'il, *al-Nahj al-Sadīd,* 1:425–26, 429–32; Ibn Ḥabīb al-Ḥalabī, "Durrat al-Aslāk fī Dawlat al-Atrāk," Arabe Collection, Manuscript 4680, folios 47v–47r, Bibliothèque nationale de France, Paris, France.

67. Abū Shāmah, *Tarājim,* 215; al-Ṣuqā'ī al-Naṣrānī, *Tālī Kitāb Wafayāt al-A'yān,* 3; al-Yūnīnī, *Dhayl Mir'āt al-Zamān,* 1:454–55, 486, 2:108–10, 122, 152; Ibn 'Abd al-Ẓāhir, *al-Rawḍ al-Zāhir,* 112–13; Shāfi', *Ḥusn al-Manāqib,* 45–46; Baybars al-Manṣūrī, *Zubdat al-Fikrah,* 68; Baybars al-Manṣūrī, *Tuḥfah,* 47–48; Baybars al-Manṣūrī, *Mukhtār,* 18–19; Baybars al-Manṣūrī, *Tuḥfah,* 47–48; Abū'l-Fidā, *al-Mukhtaṣar fī Akhbār al-Bashar,* 3:254–55; Ibn al-Wardī, *Tatimmat al-Mukhtaṣar,* 2:306–7; al-Dhahabī, *Tārīkh al-Islām,* 66:409; al-Dhahabī, *Siyar,* 16:429, 17:155; al-Dhahabī, *al-'Ibar,* 5:252–53; al-Dhahabī, *Duwal al-Islām,* 2:127; al-Ṣafadī, *al-Wāfī,* 6:318, 7:386; al-Nuwayrī, *Nihāyat al-Arab,* 23:330, 30:37, 44; Ibn al-Dawādārī, *Kanz al-Durar,* 8:82; Ibn Abī'l-Faḍā'il, *al-Nahj al-Sadīd,* 1:428–29.

68. Abū Shāmah, *Tarājim,* 216; Ibn Shaddād, *Tārīkh al-Malik al-Ẓāhir,* 330; al-Yūnīnī, *Dhayl Mir'āt al-Zamān,* 1:483–84, 486–87, 2:153; Ibn 'Abd al-Ẓāhir, *al-Rawḍ al-Zāhir,* 141; Abū'l-Fidā, *al-Mukhtaṣar fī Akhbār al-Bashar,* 3:255; Ibn al-Wardī, *Tatimmat al-Mukhtaṣar,* 2:307; al-Dhahabī, *Siyar,* 17:155; Ibn Shākir al-Kutubī, *'Uyūn al-Tawārīkh,* 20:266; Ibn Shākir al-Kutubī, *Fawāt al-Wafayāt,* 1:68; al-Ṣafadī, *al-Wāfī,* 6:318; al-Ṣafadī, *A'yān,* 1:209; al-Nuwayrī, *Nihāyat al-Arab,* 23:331, 30:79; Ibn al-Dawādārī, *Kanz al-Durar,* 8:86; Ibn Abī'l-Faḍā'il, *al-Nahj al-Sadīd,* 1:434.

69. Details of this incident are relayed by Ibn al-'Amīd, *Akhbār al-Ayyūbiyyīn,* 46–47, Baybars al-Manṣūrī, *Zubdat al-Fikrah,* 33–34, Baybars al-Manṣūrī, *Tuḥfah,* 40–41, and al-Nuwayrī, *Nihāyat al-Arab,* 29:378, 433–38. For Baybars's defeat of the Shahrazūriyyah, see Ibn 'Abd al-Ẓāhir, *al-Rawḍ al-Zāhir,* 62–63. For related discussions of the Baḥriyyah's role, see also al-Ṣuqā'ī al-Naṣrānī, *Tālī Kitāb Wafayāt al-A'yān,* 166–67; al-Yūnīnī, *Dhayl Mir'āt al-Zamān,* 1:342; Abū'l-Fidā, *al-Mukhtaṣar fī Akhbār al-Bashar,* 3:232, 234, 237, 238, 244; Ibn al-Wardī, *Tatimmat al-Mukhtaṣar,* 2:280, 285–86, 289, 290, 293; Ibn Shākir al-Kutubī, *'Uyūn al-Tawārīkh,* 20:135–36, 212–13; al-Nuwayrī, *Nihāyat al-Arab,* 29:471. Also see Stephen Humphreys, *From Saladin to the Mongols: The Ayyubids of Damascus, 1193–1260* (Albany: State University of New York Press, 1977), 341–44.

70. al-Khiḍr's lust for power was said to date from the days of his proximity to al-Malik al-Mu'izz during that Mamluk ruler's reign. He was later imprisoned for attempting to ingratiate himself with the ruling officials at the expense of other wealthy persons, whose names he wrote on a piece of paper and placed beneath the jewel-stone of a ring that he presented as belonging to the Vizier Sharaf al-Dīn Hibat Allāh b. Ṣā'id al-As'ad al-Fā'izī (d. 655 or 656 AH); see al-Ṣuqā'ī al-Naṣrānī, *Tālī Kitāb Wafayāt al-A'yān,* 162–64; al-Yūnīnī, *Dhayl Mir'āt al-Zamān,* 1:80–83; al-Dhahabī, *Tārīkh al-Islām,* 66:220–21; Ṣalāḥ al-Dīn Khalīl b. Aybak al-Ṣafadī, *al-Wāfī bi'l-Wafayāt,* vol. 27, ed. Otfried Weintritt (Wiesbaden, Ger.: Franz Steiner Verlag, 1997), 276–77. The individuals named were said to have had valuable deposits entrusted to them by the deceased vizier, for whom the ring was supposed to have served as a reminder. After some turmoil, the forgery was uncovered, and a few lines of satirical poetry were even composed on the occasion to ridicule al-Khiḍr's ignoble acts; see the following note for references. This scenario might correspond to the accusations brought against al-Rashīd Jamāl al-Dīn al-Ḥusayn b. Baṣāṣah and others during the reign of al-Malik al-Ẓāhir, which were cleared upon

investigation, as mentioned in Ibn ʿAbd al-Ẓāhir, *al-Rawḍ al-Zāhir*, 78 and Baybars al-Manṣūrī, *Mukhtār*, 14.

71. News of this matter's decisive resolution reached Damascus one month later in Rajab. Abū Shāmah, *Tarājim*, 217–18; al-Yūnīnī, *Dhayl Mirʾāt al-Zamān*, 2:170–72; al-Dhahabī, *Tārīkh al-Islām*, 66:413–14; Ibn Shākir al-Kutubī, *ʿUyūn al-Tawārīkh*, 20:272–73; Ṣalāḥ al-Dīn Khalīl b. Aybak al-Ṣafadī, *al-Wāfī bi'l-Wafayāt*, vol. 13, ed. Muḥammad al-Ḥujayrī (Wiesbaden, Ger.: Franz Steiner Verlag, 1984), 331–32.
72. Holt, "Some Observations," 502–3.
73. Ibn Shaddād, *Tārīkh al-Malik al-Ẓāhir*, 291, 333–34; Ibn Faḍl Allāh al-ʿUmarī, *Masālik*, ed. Krawulsky, 116–18; al-Ṣafadī, *Aʿyān*, 5:462–63; Ibn ʿAbd al-Ẓāhir, *al-Rawḍ al-Zāhir*, 98; Baybars al-Manṣūrī, *Zubdat al-Fikrah*, 70; al-Qalqashandī, *Qalāʾid*, 79; al-Yūnīnī, *Dhayl Mirʾāt al-Zamān*, 4:231–32; Shāfiʿ, *Ḥusn al-Manāqib*, 77; al-Dhahabī, *Tārīkh al-Islām*, 69:155; al-Dhahabī, *Siyar*, 17:337–38; al-Dhahabī, *al-ʿIbar*, 5:344; al-Dhahabī, *Duwal al-Islām*, 2:143; al-Ṣuqāʿī al-Naṣrānī, *Tālī Kitāb Wafayāt al-Aʿyān*, 110; Ibn al-Wardī, 2:332; Ibn Shākir al-Kutubī, *ʿUyūn al-Tawārīkh*, 20:344; al-Nuwayrī, *Nihāyat al-Arab*, 30:37; Shihāb al-Dīn Aḥmad b. ʿAbd al-Wahhāb al-Nuwayrī, *Nihāyat al-Arab fī Funūn al-Adab*, vol. 31, ed. al-Bāz al-ʿAzīzī (Cairo: al-Hayʾah al-Miṣriyyah li'l-Kitāb, 1990), 120–21.
74. Ibn Shaddād, *Tārīkh al-Malik al-Ẓāhir*, 39–40, 334; al-Yūnīnī, *Dhayl Mirʾāt al-Zamān*, 1:440, 2:94; Shāfiʿ, *Ḥusn al-Manāqib*, 97–98; al-Ṣafadī, *Aʿyān*, 5:462–63; Ibn al-Dawādārī, *Kanz al-Durar*, 8:72; Ibn Abī'l-Faḍāʾil, *al-Nahj al-Sadīd*, 1:423; Ibn Faḍl Allāh al-ʿUmarī, *Masālik*, ed. Krawulsky, 117–18. For more on the rivalry between these two families for the position of *amīr*, see M. A. Hiyari, "The Origins and Development of the Amīrate of the Arabs during the Seventh/Thirteenth and Eighth/Fourteenth Centuries," *Bulletin of the School of Oriental and African Studies* 3 (1975): 509–24.
75. Abū Shāmah, *Tarājim*, 218; Ibn Shaddād, *Tārīkh al-Malik al-Ẓāhir*, 38–39; al-Ṣuqāʿī al-Naṣrānī, *Tālī Kitāb Wafayāt al-Aʿyān*, 4; al-Yūnīnī, *Dhayl Mirʾāt al-Zamān*, 1:492–93, 2:157–58; Ibn ʿAbd al-Ẓāhir, *al-Rawḍ al-Zāhir*, 114; Shāfiʿ, *Ḥusn al-Manāqib*, 46; Baybars al-Manṣūrī, *Zubdat al-Fikrah*, 70; al-Nuwayrī, *Nihāyat al-Arab*, 30:45; Ibn al-Dawādārī, *Kanz al-Durar*, 8:88; Ibn Abī'l-Faḍāʾil, *al-Nahj al-Sadīd*, 1:436–38.
76. Ibn Shaddād, *Tārīkh al-Malik al-Ẓāhir*, 287; al-Yūnīnī, *Dhayl Mirʾāt al-Zamān*, 1:493–94, 2:158; Ibn ʿAbd al-Ẓāhir, *al-Rawḍ al-Zāhir*, 128–29, 133–35; Shāfiʿ, *Ḥusn al-Manāqib*, 51; Baybars al-Manṣūrī, *Zubdat al-Fikrah*, 70, 77–78; Abū'l-Fidā, *al-Mukhtaṣar fī Akhbār al-Bashar*, 3:255; Ibn al-Wardī, *Tatimmat al-Mukhtaṣar*, 2:307; al-Nuwayrī, *Nihāyat al-Arab*, 30:59–60; Ibn al-Dawādārī, *Kanz al-Durar*, 8:88; Ibn Abī'l-Faḍāʾil, *al-Nahj al-Sadīd*, 1:438–39. At this point, following al-Barlī's arrival, al-Malik al-Ẓāhir wrote *ilā jamīʿ nuwwāb al-Shām an yukhallū al-bilād wa-yanḍammū ilā Dimashq* (al-Yūnīnī, Dhayl Mirʾāt al-Zamān, 2:158). This rapprochement between al-Barlī and al-Malik al-Ẓāhir was short-lived as the Mamluk sultan issued orders for al-Barlī's arrest and imprisonment on Monday, Rajab 28, 661 / June 7, 1263 and he died in captivity; Ibn Shaddād, *Tārīkh al-Malik al-Ẓāhir*, 334; al-Yūnīnī, *Dhayl Mirʾāt al-Zamān*, 1:533, 2:194; Ibn ʿAbd al-Ẓāhir, *al-Rawḍ al-Zāhir*, 166–70; Shāfiʿ, *Ḥusn al-Manāqib*, 51; Baybars al-Manṣūrī, *Zubdat al-Fikrah*, 84; Abū'l-Fidā, *al-Mukhtaṣar fī Akhbār al-Bashar*, 3:255; Ibn al-Wardī, *Tatimmat al-Mukhtaṣar*, 2:307; Ibn Shākir al-Kutubī, *ʿUyūn al-Tawārīkh*, 20:289–90; al-Nuwayrī, *Nihāyat al-Arab*, 30:84–87; al-Dawādārī, *Kanz al-Durar*, 8:96.
77. According to Abū Shāmah, who was present for their initial appearance on Saturday, Dhū'l-Qaʿdah 27, 660 / October 13, 1262 in Damascus, the roughly two hundred or so Mongols had been members of Hülegü's army that were defeated and dispersed by his

Mongol adversary, Berke. Abū Shāmah's Egyptian counterpart Ibn ʿAbd al-Ẓāhir, however, recounts that al-Malik al-Ẓāhir's Damascene representative, al-Amīr ʿAlāʾ al-Dīn Aydakīn al-Ḥājj al-Ruknī, reported that they were actually companions of Berke who had been sent to support Hülegü militarily until the two Mongol leaders had come into disagreement with one another and therefore Berke had ordered them to return to him, and if they could not, to make their way to the Mamluk sultan of Egypt. For further discussion of the phenomenon of military immigration to the Mamluks and their integration, see David Ayalon, "The Wafidiya in the Mamluk Kingdom," *Islamic Culture* 25 (1951): 89–104, Nakamachi Nobutaka, "The Rank and Status of Military Refugees in the Mamluk Army: A Reconsideration of the *Wāfidīyah*," *Mamlūk Studies Review* 10 (2006): 55–81, and Reuven Amitai, "Mamluks of Mongol Origin and Their Role in Early Mamluk Political Life," *Mamlūk Studies Review* 12 (2008): 119–37.

78. Abū Shāmah, *Tarājim*, 220–21; Ibn Shaddād, *Tārīkh al-Malik al-Ẓāhir*, 330; al-Yūnīnī, *Dhayl Mirʾāt al-Zamān*, 1:496–98, 530, 2:156, 161–62, 186–90; Ibn ʿAbd al-Ẓāhir, *al-Rawḍ al-Zāhir*, 135–38, 141–45; Shāfiʿ, *Ḥusn al-Manāqib*, 51–53; Baybars al-Manṣūrī, *Zubdat al-Fikrah*, 78–80; Baybars al-Manṣūrī, *Mukhtār*, 24; Baybars al-Manṣūrī, *Tuḥfah*, 51; Abū'l-Fidā, *al-Mukhtaṣar fī Akhbār al-Bashar*, 3:255–56; Ibn al-Wardī, *Tatimmat al-Mukhtaṣar*, 2:307–8; al-Dhahabī, *Siyar*, 17:155; al-Dhahabī, *al-ʿIbar*, 5:258, 263–64; al-Dhahabī, *Duwal al-Islām*, 2:128–29; Ibn Shākir al-Kutubī, *ʿUyūn al-Tawārīkh*, 20:287; Ibn Shākir al-Kutubī, *Fawāt al-Wafayāt*, 1:68–69; al-Ṣafadī, *al-Wāfī*, 6:318; al-Ṣafadī, *Aʿyān*, 1:209–10; al-Nuwayrī, *Nihāyat al-Arab*, 23:331–32, 30:62–64, 79; Ibn al-Dawādārī, *Kanz al-Durar*, 8:87, 90–94; Ibn Abī'l-Faḍāʾil, *al-Nahj al-Sadīd*, 1:436, 442–48; Ibn Ḥabīb al-Ḥalabī, "Durrat al-Aslāk fī Dawlat al-Atrāk," Arabe Collection, Manuscript 4680, folios 49v–50r, Bibliothèque nationale de France, Paris, France. Yaacov Lev bases his discussion in "Symbiotic Relations: Ulama and the Mamluk Sultans," *Mamlūk Studies Review* 13 (2009), 13–14 on the 2004 Tadmūrī edition of the last section of Ibn Wāṣil's *Mufarrij al-Kurūb* which erroneously presents later additions to the text by another author as authentic and original to it. As Mohamed Rahim includes in his 2010 edition, Ibn Wāṣil dictated *Mufarrij al-Kurūb* up to the year 659 AH and did not narrate all the events of that year or the tumultuous changes thereafter; see his *Die Chronik*, ix–xii, 154–55.

79. al-Yūnīnī, *Dhayl Mirʾāt al-Zamān*, 2:161–62, 186–91; Ibn ʿAbd al-Ẓāhir, *al-Rawḍ al-Zāhir*, 139–47, 173; Shāfiʿ, *Ḥusn al-Manāqib*, 51–55; Baybars al-Manṣūrī, *Zubdat al-Fikrah*, 80, 82–85; al-Dhahabī, *al-ʿIbar*, 5:258; al-Nuwayrī, *Nihāyat al-Arab*, 23:331, 30:62–65, 79; Ibn al-Dawādārī, *Kanz al-Durar*, 8:87, 90–94; Ibn Abī'l-Faḍāʾil, *al-Nahj al-Sadīd*, 1:436, 442–48; Holt, "Some Observations," 503; Holt, *The Age of the Crusades*, 93–94; Amitai-Preiss, "The Fall and Rise," 491–92; Heidemann, *Das Aleppiner Kalifat (A.D. 1261)*, 160–73; Amitai-Preiss, *Mongols and Mamluks*, 62–63. Anne Broadbridge further analyzes these early relations between the Mamluks and the Golden Horde in her book *Kingship and Ideology in the Islamic and Mongol Worlds* (Cambridge: Cambridge University Press, 2008), 50–58.

80. Ibn ʿAbd al-Ẓāhir, *al-Rawḍ al-Zāhir*, 245, 247.

81. Ibid., al-Kāzarūnī, *Mukhtaṣar al-Tārīkh*, 274; *al-Ḥawādith al-Jāmiʿah*, 357–58; Baybars al-Manṣūrī, *Zubdat al-Fikrah*, 38; al-Ṭiqṭaqā, *al-Fakhrī*, 333; al-Dhahabī, *Tārīkh al-Islām*, 66:262; al-Dhahabī, *Siyar*, 16:437; Ibn Shākir al-Kutubī, *Fawāt al-Wafayāt*, 2:134; al-Ṣafadī, *al-Wāfī*, 17:642; Ibn Kathīr, *al-Bidāyah wa'l-Nihāyah*, 13:169; al-Yāfiʿī, *Mirʾāt al-Jinān*, 4:139; al-Malik al-Ashraf, *al-ʿAsjad*, 632.

82. al-Ṣuqāʿī al-Naṣrānī, *Tālī Kitāb Wafayāt al-Aʿyān*, 11–12; al-Dhahabī, *Siyar*, 17:310; al-Ṣafadī, *al-Wāfī*, 9:323–24.

83. Ibn ʿAbd al-Ẓāhir, *al-Rawḍ al-Zāhir*, 100; Shāfiʿ, *Ḥusn al-Manāqib*, 37–38; Baybars al-Manṣūrī, *Zubdat al-Fikrah*, 61; al-Nuwayrī, *Nihāyat al-Arab*, 23:327–28.
84. Ibn ʿAbd al-Ẓāhir, *al-Rawḍ al-Zāhir*, 245, 247.
85. Ibn al-Kāzarūnī, *Mukhtaṣar al-Tārīkh*, 274–76; Ibn al-Fuwaṭī, *Majmaʿ al-Ādāb*, 1:388–89, 2:69, 4:116, 138, 5:314; *al-Ḥawādith al-Jāmiʿah*, 288–89, 317; Carole Hillenbrand, "Mustarshid," in *The Encyclopaedia of Islam*, 2nd ed. Ibn al-Kāzarūnī also mentions that al-Mubārak had four children: three sons, Abū Naṣr Muḥammad, Abū Aḥmad ʿAbdullāh, and Abū Hāshim Yūsuf, and a daughter al-Mubārakah. Ibn al-Fuwaṭī also notes that Abū Naṣr Muḥammad narrated prophetic transmissions from his grandfather al-Mustaʿṣim that he had heard from his father.
86. Ibn ʿAbd al-Ẓāhir, *al-Rawḍ al-Zāhir*, 248.
87. Abū'l-Fidā, *al-Mukhtaṣar fī Akhbār al-Bashar*, 3:253; Ibn al-Wardī, *Tatimmat al-Mukhtaṣar*, 2:305.
88. al-Dhahabī, *Duwal al-Islām*, 2:127.
89. Ibn ʿAbd al-Ẓāhir, *al-Rawḍ al-Zāhir*, 248.
90. Baybars al-Manṣūrī, *Zubdat al-Fikrah*, 362–63; Baybars al-Manṣūrī, *Tuḥfah*, 162; Abū'l-Fidā, *al-Mukhtaṣar fī Akhbār al-Bashar*, 4:59; Shams al-Dīn Muḥammad b. Aḥmad b. ʿUthmān al-Dhahabī, *Dhayl al-ʿIbar fī Khabar Man Ghabar (701–764 A.H.)*, ed. Abū Hājir Muḥammad al-Saʿīd b. Basyūnī Zaghlūl (Beirut: Dār al-Kutub al-ʿIlmiyyah, 1985), 4:4; Shams al-Dīn Muḥammad b. Aḥmad b. ʿUthmān al-Dhahabī, *Duwal al-Islām*, ed. Ḥasan Ismāʿīl Marwah (Beirut: Dār Ṣādir, 1999), 2:232; Ibn al-Wardī, *Tatimmat al-Mukhtaṣar*, 2:356; Ibn Shākir al-Kutubī, *Fawāt al-Wafayāt*, 1:68–69; al-Ṣafadī, *al-Wāfī*, 6:317; al-Ṣafadī, *Aʿyān*, 1:210; al-Nuwayrī, *Nihāyat al-Arab*, 23:332; Ibn Ḥabīb al-Ḥalabī, "Durrat al-Aslāk fī Dawlat al-Atrāk," Arabe Collection, Manuscript 4680, folios 243v–244r, Bibliothèque nationale de France, Paris, France; Dorothea Russell, "A Note on the Cemetery of the Abbasid Caliphs of Cairo and the Shrine of Saiyida Nafīsa," *Ars Islamica* 6, no. 2 (1939): 168–74; Doris Behrens-Abouseif, *Cairo of the Mamluks: A History of the Architecture and Its Culture* (London: I. B. Tauris, 2007), 126–27.
91. al-Yūnīnī, *Dhayl Mirʾāt al-Zamān*, 1:505–6, 2:174–75; Ibn Shākir al-Kutubī, *Fawāt*, 2:351; al-Subkī, *Ṭabaqāt al-Shāfiʿiyyah al-Kubrā*, 8:215. Or consider the statement of al-Malik al-Ẓāhir regarding Ibn ʿAbd al-Salām: "The one who testified is worth more than a thousand witnesses."
92. al-Yūnīnī, *Dhayl Mirʾāt al-Zamān*, 2:96; Ibn ʿAbd al-Ẓāhir, *al-Rawḍ al-Zāhir*, 100; Shāfiʿ, *Ḥusn al-Manāqib*, 37; Abū'l-Fidā, *al-Mukhtaṣar fī Akhbār al-Bashar*, 3:253; Ibn al-Wardī, *Tatimmat al-Mukhtaṣar*, 2:305; Ibn Shākir al-Kutubī, *ʿUyūn al-Tawārīkh*, 20:252; al-Ṣafaḍī, *al-Wāfī*, 7:385; al-Subkī, *Ṭabaqāt al-Shāfiʿiyyah al-Kubrā*, 8:215.
93. al-Dhahabī, *Siyar*, 16:427 and al-Dhahabī, *Tārīkh al-Islām*, 66:409. The minor linguisitic variations of the version in al-Dhahabi's *Tārīkh al-Islām* include "*fa-lammā faraghnā al-bayʿah*," "*maṣṭabah fākhirah*," "*iḍribū hādhihi*" rather than "*fa-lammā ʿaqadnā al-bayʿah*," "*maṣṭabah nāfirah*," "*akhribū hādhihi*."
94. al-Yūnīnī, *Dhayl Mirʾāt al-Zamān*, 1:442–43, 2:97–98; Ibn ʿAbd al-Ẓāhir, *al-Rawḍ al-Zāhir*, 142–45; Baybars al-Manṣūrī, *Zubdat al-Fikrah*, 78–80; Shāfiʿ, *Ḥusn al-Manāqib*, 51–53. See my discussion of the Qur'anic verse 4:59 in the following chapter.
95. Abū Shāmah, *Tarājim*, 213; al-Yūnīnī, *Dhayl Mirʾāt al-Zamān*, 1:442, 2:95, 187; Ibn ʿAbd al-Ẓāhir, *al-Rawḍ al-Zāhir*, 99–100, 141–42; Shāfiʿ, *Ḥusn al-Manāqib*, 37, 51–52; Baybars al-Manṣūrī, *Zubdat al-Fikrah*, 60–61, 78; Baybars al-Manṣūrī, *Tuḥfah*, 47, 51; Baybars al-Manṣūrī, *Mukhtār*, 15–16; al-Dhahabī, *Tārīkh al-Islām*, 66:406–7; al-Dhahabī, *Duwal al-Islām*, 2:128–29; al-Ṣafadī, *al-Wāfī*, 7:384; al-Nuwayrī, *Nihāyat al-Arab*, 30:29.

As Mounira Chapoutot-Remadi observes, "Aussi le khalife était-il moins un chef réel et actif des ʿulamā qu'un symbole. Le symbole de l'orthodoxie sunnite triomphante à l'intérieur comme à l'extérieur." Mounira Chapoutot-Remadi, "Une institution mal connue: le khalifat abbaside du Caire," *Les cahiers de Tunisie* 20, no. 77–78 (1972): 23.

96. Abū Shāmah, *Tarājim*, 213, 221; Ibn Shaddād, *Tārīkh al-Malik al-Ẓāhir*, 248; al-Yūnīnī, *Dhayl Mirʾāt al-Zamān*, 1:434, 530, 2:87–89, 186; Baybars al-Manṣūrī, *Zubdat al-Fikrah*, 60, 78; Ibn al-Wardī, 2:284; al-Dhahabī, *Tārīkh al-Islām*, 66:406; al-Dhahabī, *Siyar*, 16:427; al-Dhahabī, *al-ʿIbar*, 5:231; Ibn Shākir al-Kutubī, *ʿUyūn al-Tawārīkh*, 20:212, 222, 247, 251, 287; al-Ṣafadī, *al-Wāfī*, 7:384; al-Nuwayrī, *Nihāyat al-Arab*, 23:326, 330–31; Ibn al-Dawādārī, *Kanz al-Durar*, 8:38, 45, 67, 73.

97. al-Dhahabī, *Siyar*, 16:427.

98. al-Yūnīnī, *Dhayl Mirʾāt al-Zamān*, 1:434, 530, 2:87, 186.

99. Ibid., 1:550, 2:87–88. Relating to this point, David Ayalon is correct in refuting Richard Hartmann's theory of the early Mamluk recognition of the Hafsid Caliphate, even though, contrary to Ayalon's initial presumption, al-Yūnīnī does in fact indicate that al-Mustanṣir billāh Muḥammad b. Yaḥyā b. ʿAbd al-Wahhāb was prayed for as caliph within his domains. Ayalon, "Studies on the Transfer," 54.

100. Ibn Shākir al-Kutubī, *ʿUyūn al-Tawārīkh*, 20:212, 222, 247; Ibn al-Dawādārī, *Kanz al-Durar*, 8:38, 45, 67.

101. Ibn al-Dawādārī, *Kanz al-Durar*, 8:86.

102. Ibn Abī'l-Faḍāʾil, *al-Nahj al-Sadīd*, 1:416.

103. Ibn Shākir al-Kutubī, *ʿUyūn al-Tawārīkh*, 20:266, 287.

104. al-Suyūṭī, *Tārīkh al-Khulafāʾ*, 540, 541, 542.

105. Ibn Duqmāq, *al-Jawhar al-Thamin*, 179–80.

106. ʿAlī b. Abī'l-Faraj al-Baṣrī, "al-Manāqib al-ʿAbbāsiyyah wa'l-Mafākhir al-Mustanṣiriyyah," Arabe Collection, Manuscript 6144, folios 2r, 3v, 4r, 148v–149r, Bibliothèque nationale de France, Paris, France, which I analyze further in a separate article.

107. Baybars al-Manṣūrī, *Tuḥfah*, 51.

108. Ibn Ḥabīb al-Ḥalabī, "Durrat al-Aslāk fī Dawlat al-Atrāk," Arabe Collection, Manuscript 4680, folio 43v, Bibliothèque nationale de France, Paris, France. Here, he plays on the linguistic affinity between gardens (*jinān*) and the emotions or soul (*janān*) and their metaphorical fruits.

109. However, Abū'l-Fidā's (682–732/1273–1331) universal history, along with its continuation by Ibn al-Wardī (689–749/1290–1349), conveys skepticism towards one of the candidates, al-Mustanṣir, through use of the verb *zaʿama* for "to claim," with its connotations of falsehood. In fact, Abū'l-Fidā, and by extension Ibn al-Wardī, directs more attention to al-Mustanṣir's dark coloring and popular nickname al-Zarabīnī; see Abū'l-Fidā, *al-Mukhtaṣar fī Akhbār al-Bashar*, 3:253; Ibn al-Wardī, *Tatimmat al-Mukhtaṣar*, 2:305. Amitai-Preiss also notes that Heidemann analyzes al-Ḥakim's lineage in his *Das Aleppiner Kalifat (A.D. 1261)*, 72–75, 373–78. And Ibn Ḥabīb al-Ḥalabī eloquently praises al-Ḥakim's lineage in his "Durrat al-Aslāk fī Dawlat al-Atrāk," Arabe Collection, Manuscript 4680, folio 243v, Bibliothèque nationale de France, Paris, France.

110. Baybars al-Manṣūrī, *Tuḥfah*, 47. al-Ḥākim's noble heritage is also duly praised on page 51.

111. al-Yūnīnī, *Dhayl Mirʾāt al-Zamān*, 2:96, 123; Ibn ʿAbd al-Ẓāhir, *al-Rawḍ al-Zāhir*, 100; ʿAlī b. Abī'l-Faraj al-Baṣrī, "al-Manāqib al-ʿAbbāsiyyah wa'l-Mafākhir al-Mustanṣiriyyah," Arabe Collection, Manuscript 6144, folio 4v, 148v, Bibliothèque nationale de France, Paris, France; Baybars al-Manṣūrī, *Zubdat al-Fikrah*, 61; al-Dhahabī, *al-ʿIbar*, 5:258; Ibn Shākir al-Kutubī, *ʿUyūn al-Tawārīkh*, 20:252; al-Ṣafadī, *al-Wāfī*, 7:384–85; al-Nuwayrī, *Nihāyat al-Arab*, 23:328.

112. al-Yūnīnī, *Dhayl Mir'āt al-Zamān,* 2:96–97, 187; al-Dhahabī, *Tārīkh al-Islām,* 66:407–8; Ibn Shākir al-Kutubī, *'Uyūn al-Tawārīkh,* 20:252–53; al-Ṣafaḍī, *al-Wāfī,* 7:385; Ibn 'Abd al-Ẓāhir, *al-Rawḍ al-Zāhir,* 138.
113. al-Yūnīnī, *Dhayl Mir'āt al-Zamān,* 2:95, 186; al-Dhahabī, *Siyar,* 16:428; al-Dhahabī, *al-'Ibar,* 5:259; Ibn Shākir al-Kutubī, *'Uyūn al-Tawārīkh,* 20:251–52; al-Ṣafaḍī, *al-Wāfī,* 7:385.
114. Abū Shāmah, *Tarājim,* 214–16, 221; Ibn Shaddād, *Tārīkh al-Malik al-Ẓāhir,* 330; al-Ṣuqā'ī al-Naṣrānī, *Tālī Kitāb Wafayāt al-A'yān,* 2–3; al-Yūnīnī, *Dhayl Mir'āt al-Zamān,* 1:434, 530, 2:95, 163, 186; Ibn 'Abd al-Ẓāhir, *al-Rawḍ al-Zāhir,* 99, 141; Shāfi', *Ḥusn al-Manāqib,* 37, 51; Baybars al-Manṣūrī, *Zubdat al-Fikrah,* 60, 78; Baybars al-Manṣūrī, *Tuḥfah,* 47, 51; Baybars al-Manṣūrī, *Mukhtār,* 15; al-Dhahabī, *Siyar,* 16:427, 17:154; al-Dhahabī, *Tārīkh al-Islām,* 66:406; al-Dhahabī, *Duwal al-Islām,* 2:127, 128; Ibn Shākir al-Kutubī, *Fawāt al-Wafayāt,* 1:68; al-Ṣafadī, *al-Wāfī,* 6:317, 7:384; al-Ṣafadī, *A'yān,* 1:208; al-Nuwayrī, *Nihāyat al-Arab,* 30:79; Ibn al-Dawādārī, *Kanz al-Durar,* 8:81–82.
115. Baybars al-Manṣūrī, *Zubdat al-Fikrah,* 60.
116. al-Dhahabī, *Dhayl,* 373, 375–76; Ibn al-Wardī, *Tatimmat al-Mukhtaṣar,* 356, 364–451, 465–66, 468–73; Ibn Faḍl Allāh, *Masālik al-Abṣār fī Mamālik al-Amṣār,* ed. Kāmil Salmān al-Jabūrī (Beirut: Dār al-Kutub al-'Ilmiyyah, 2010), 27:324, 358–60; al-Ṣafadī, *al-Wāfī,* 15:349–50; al-Ṣafadī, *A'yān,* 2:419–21, 2:220–21; Ibn Kathīr, *al-Bidāyah wa'l-Nihāyah,* 14:21, 49–51, 53–58, 184, 187, 188, 190, 198–99, 202–3; Ibn Khaldūn, *Kitāb al-'Ibar,* 3:1111–12, 5:947–48; Ibrāhīm b. Muḥammad Ibn Duqmāq, *al-Jawhar al-Thamīn fī Sayr al-Khulafā' wa'l-Mulūk wa'l-Salāṭīn,* ed. Sa'īd 'Abd al-Fattāḥ 'Āshūr (Mecca: Jāmi'at Umm al-Qurā, 1982), 188–90, 329–68; Ibrāhīm b. Muḥammad Ibn Duqmāq, *al-Nafḥah al-Miskiyyah fī'l-Dawlah al-Turkiyyah,* ed. 'Umar 'Abd al-Salām Tadmurī (Beirut: al-Maktabah al-'Aṣriyyah, 1999), 111–16, 136, 138–41; Aḥmad al-Qalqashandī, *Ma'āthir al-Ināfah fī Ma'ālim al-Khilāfah,* ed. 'Abd al-Sattār Aḥmad Farrāj (Kuwait: Wizārat al-Irshād wa'l-Inbā', 1964), 2:132–33, 145–46, 148–50; Taqiyy al-Dīn Aḥmad b. 'Alī al-Maqrīzī, *al-Mawā'iẓ wa'l-I'tibār fī Dhikr al-Khiṭaṭ wa'l-Āthār,* ed. Ayman Fu'ād Sayyid (London: al-Furqān Islamic Heritage Foundation, 2002), 3:775, 784–85; Ibn Qāḍī Shuhbah, *Tārīkh Ibn Qāḍī Shuhbah,* ed. 'Adnān Darwīsh (Damascus: Institut Français de Damas, 1994), 1:135–36, 201; Ibn Ḥajar, *al-Durar al-Kāminah,* 1:137, 2:141–44; Ibn Taghribirdī, *Mawrid al-Laṭāfah,* 1:242–46, 2:2:56–70; Ibn Taghribirdī, *al-Manhal al-Ṣāfī,* 1:308–9; Ibn Taghribirdī, *al-Nujūm al-Zāhirah,* 9:3–115, 10:290–91; al-Suyūṭī, *Tārīkh al-Khulafā',* 552–69; al-Suyūṭī, *Ḥusn al-Muḥāḍarah,* 2:55–70; Ibn al-'Imād, *Shadharāt al-Dhahab,* 8:222, 296; Muḥammad b. Aḥmad Ibn Iyās, *Badā'i al-Zuhūr fī Waqā'i' al-Duhūr,* ed. Muḥammad Muṣṭafā (Wiesbaden, Ger.: Franz Steiner, 1975), 1:410, 487. al-Qalqashandī also includes copies of al-Ḥakim II's subsequent designation of Mamluk sultans, the description of one such ceremony, and an official letter composed on his behalf by the Egyptian chancery, 2:242–43, 3:39–60, 3:324–31.
117. Muḥammad b. 'Alī Ibn Ḥamzah al-Ḥusaynī, *Min Dhuyūl al-'Ibar,* ed. Muḥammad Rashād 'Abd al-Muṭṭalib (Kuwait: Maṭba'at Ḥukūmat al-Kuwayt, n.d.), 350–51; Ibn Khaldūn, *Kitāb al-'Ibar,* 3:1112, 5:948; Ibn Duqmāq, *al-Jawhar al-Thamīn,* 8–10, 193–94, 441; Ibn Duqmāq, *al-Nafḥah al-Miskiyyah,* 7–10, 223; al-Qalqashandī, *Ma'āthir al-Ināfah,* 2:167, 174–75, 181; Ibn al-'Irāqī, *al-Dhayl 'ala al-'Ibar fī Khabar Man Ghabar,* ed. Ṣāliḥ Mahdī 'Abbās (Beirut: Mu'assasat al-Risālah, 1989), 1:97–98, 2:429–31, 461–63; Taqiyy al-Dīn Aḥmad b. 'Alī al-Maqrīzī, *Durar al-'Uqūd al-Farīdah fī Tarājim al-A'yān al-Mufīdah,* ed. Maḥmūd al-Jalīlī (Beirut: Dār al-Gharb al-Islāmī, 2002), 2:209–10; al-Maqrīzī, *al-Mawā'iẓ,* 3:778, 785–86; Ibn Qāḍī Shuhbah, *Tārīkh,* 2:543; Ibn Ḥajar, *Dhayl al-Durar,* 118–19; Shihāb al-Dīn Abu'l-Faḍl Aḥmad b. 'Alī Ibn Ḥajar, *Inbā' al-Ghumr*

bi-Abnā' al-'Umr, ed. Muḥammad 'Abd al-Mu'īd Khān (Beirut: Dār al-Kutub al-'Ilmiyyah, 1986), 1:4, 230–35; Ibn Taghribirdī, *Mawrid al-Laṭāfah*, 1:248–51, 2:103–5; Ibn Taghribirdī, *al-Nujūm al-Zāhirah*, 11:148–55; al-Sakhāwī, *al-Ḍaw' al-Lāmi' li-Ahl al-Qarn al-Tāsi'* (Beirut: Manshūrāt Dār Maktabat al-Ḥayāh, 1934), 7:168; al-Suyūṭī, *Tārīkh al-Khulafā'*, 570–72; al-Suyūṭī, *Ḥusn al-Muḥāḍarah*, 2:70–72; Ibn al-'Imād, *Shadharāt al-Dhahab*, 9:1166; Ibn Iyās, *Badā'i al-Zuhūr*, 1:188, 205–10.

118. The later accounts of Ibn Qāḍī Shuhbah, who was a child of around five at the time, and Ibn Taghribirdī, who was born eighteen years later, also detail the content of the accused's statements, though their remarks give the air of common rumblings of disgruntlement reserviced and magnified for the occasion (and possibly later complaints written into the historical record). In their words, the caliph was accused of aspiring to regain the throne for himself as the more legitimate Islamic leader, having only designated Barqūq as a sultan unwillingly, while the Mamluk proved to be an oppressive ruler who usurped people's wealth.

119. Ibn Khaldūn, *Kitāb al-'Ibar*, 3:1112, 5:1015–18; Ibn Duqmāq, *al-Jawhar al-Thamīn*, 458, 461; Ibn Duqmāq, *al-Nafḥah al-Miskiyyah*, 240; al-Qalqashandī, *Ma'āthir al-Ināfah*, 2:184–85, 187–202; Ibn al-'Irāqī, *al-Dhayl 'ala al-'Ibar*, 2:544; al-Maqrīzī, *Durar al-'Uqūd*, 1:297–303, 2:210–11; al-Maqrīzī, *al-Mawā'iẓ*, 3:779–81, 786; Ibn Qāḍī Shuhbah, *Tārīkh*, 3:109–10, 186–89, 269; Ibn Ḥajar, *Dhayl al-Durar*, 118–19; Ibn Ḥajar, *Inbā' al-Ghumr*, 1:4, 2:128–31, 217, 221, 239–40, 4:59; Ibn Taghribirdī, *al-Manhal al-Ṣāfī*, 2:87–89; Ibn Taghribirdī, *Mawrid al-Laṭāfah*, 1:251–54, 2:109–13; Ibn Taghribirdī, *al-Nujūm al-Zāhirah*, 11:234–37, 245; al-Sakhāwī, *al-Ḍaw' al-Lāmi'*, 2:96–98, 7:168; al-Suyūṭī, *Tārīkh al-Khulafā'*, 573–75; al-Suyūṭī, *Ḥusn al-Muḥāḍarah*, 2:72–73; Ibn al-'Imād, *Shadharāt al-Dhahab*, 9:116; Ibn Iyās, *Badā'i al-Zuhūr*, 1:332–34, 377; Lutz Wiederhold, "Legal-Religious Elite, Temporal Authority, and the Caliphate in Mamluk Society: Conclusions Drawn from the Examination of a 'Zahiri Revolt' in Damascus in 1386," in *International Journal of Middle East Studies* 31, no 2 (April 1999): 203–35; Nasser Rabbat, "Who Was al-Maqrīzī? A Biographical Sketch," *Mamlūk Studies Review* 7, no. 2 (2003), 12–15.

120. Ibn Khaldūn, *Kitāb al-'Ibar*, 3:1112–13, 5:1018–75; Ibn Duqmāq, *al-Jawhar al-Thamīn*, 463–70; Ibn Duqmāq, *al-Nafḥah al-Miskiyyah*, 250–53; al-Qalqashandī, *Ma'āthir al-Ināfah*, 2:184–85, 187–202; Ibn al-'Irāqī, *al-Dhayl 'alā al-'Ibar*, 2:545; al-Maqrīzī, *Durar al-'Uqūd*, 2:211; al-Maqrīzī, *al-Mawā'iẓ*, 3:781, 786; Ibn Qāḍī Shuhbah, *Tārīkh*, 3:262–78; Ibn Ḥajar, *Dhayl al-Durar*, 119; Ibn Ḥajar, *Inbā' al-Ghumr*, 2:311–56, 3:1–8; Ibn Taghribirdī, *Mawrid al-Laṭāfah*, 1:253–54, 2:110–13; Ibn Taghribirdī, *al-Nujūm al-Zāhirah*, 11:260–62, 268–70; al-Sakhāwī, *al-Ḍaw' al-Lāmi'*, 7:168; al-Suyūṭī, *Tārīkh al-Khulafā'*, 573; al-Suyūṭī, *Ḥusn al-Muḥāḍarah*, 2:73–74; Ibn al-'Imād, *Shadharāt al-Dhahab*, 9:116; Ibn Iyās, *Badā'i al-Zuhūr*, 1:398–99; Walter Fischel, *Ibn Khaldūn in Egypt: His Public Functions and His Historical Research (1382–1406)*, Berkeley: University of California Press, 1967), 35–39, 75–76.

121. Ibn Khaldūn, *Kitāb al-'Ibar*, 3:1113.

122. al-Maqrīzī, Ibn Ḥajar, and Ibn Taghribirdī offer the most detailed accounts of al-Musta'īn's reign, whereas al-Qalqashandī analyzes al-Musta'īn's official documents at greater length. al-Qalqashandī, *Ma'āthir al-Ināfah*, 2:202–9, 3:193, 264–65; al-Maqrīzī, *Durar al-'Uqūd*, 2:206–7, 211–15; al-Maqrīzī, *al-Mawā'iẓ*, 3:786–87; Ibn Ḥajar, *Inbā' al-Ghumr*, 7:52–74, 115–16, 8:213–14; Ibn Taghribirdī, *Mawrid al-Laṭāfah*, 1:255–57, 2:133–35; Ibn Taghribirdī, *al-Nujūm al-Zāhirah*, 12:1–33, 13:51, 146–47, 189–208, 14:2–3, 16; al-Sakhāwī, *al-Ḍaw' al-Lāmi'*, 4:19–20; al-Suyūṭī, *Tārīkh al-Khulafā'*, 575–78; al-

Suyūṭī, *Ḥusn al-Muḥāḍarah*, 2:74–77; Ibn Iyās, *Badāʿi al-Zuhūr*, 1:747, 823–28; Ibn al-ʿImād, *Shadharāt al-Dhahab*, 9:295–96.

123. Jalāl al-Dīn al-Suyūṭī, who lived and died near the end of the Mamluk Sultanate, and Ibn Iyās, who lived through its conquest by the Ottomans, refer in their works to the fame of Ibn Ḥajar's poem. al-Suyūṭī, *Tārīkh al-Khulafāʾ*, 575–77; al-Suyūṭī, *Ḥusn al-Muḥāḍarah*, 2:75–76; Ibn Iyās, *Badāʿi al-Zuhūr*, 1:747, 823–28.

124. Heidemann, *Das Aleppiner Kalifat (A.D. 1261)*, 68; Amitai-Preiss, "The Fall and Rise of the ʿAbbāsid Caliphate," 488.

125. Ibn Qāḍī Shuhbah, *Tārīkh*, 1:364; Ibn Khaldūn, *Kitāb al-ʿIbar*, 3:1113; Muḥibb al-Dīn Abū'l-Walīd Muḥammad Ibn al-Shiḥnah, *Rawḍat al-Manāẓir fī Akhbār al-Awāʾil wa'l-Awākhir* (Beirut: Dār al-Kutub al-ʿIlmiyyah, 1997), 296; al-Maqrīzī, *Durar al-ʿUqūd*, 1:427–30; Ibn Ḥajar, *Inbāʾ al-Ghumr*, 7:27, 33–34; al-Sakhāwī, *al-Ḍawʾ al-Lāmiʿ*, 2:313; al-Suyūṭī, *Ḥusn al-Muḥāḍarah*, 2:73; al-Suyūṭī, *Tārīkh al-Khulafāʾ*, 578; Carl Ernst, *Eternal Garden: Mysticism, History, and Politics at a South Asian Sufi Center* (Albany: State University of New York Press, 1992), 55–59; H. Nelson Wright, *The Coinage and Metrology of the Sultāns of Delhī* (New Delhi: Oriental Books Reprint, 1974); Richard Eaton, *The Rise of Islam and the Bengal Frontier, 1204–1760* (Berkeley: University of California Press, 1993), 23–32, 38–40, 47, 324; Paul Wittek, *Rise of the Ottoman Empire: Studies in the History of Turkey, Thirteenth–Fifteenth Centuries*, ed. Colin Heywood (NY: Routledge, 2012), 89–90, 141; Tanvir Anjum, *Chishtī Sufis in the Sultanate of Delhi, 1190–1400: From Restrained Indifference to Calculated Defiance* (Oxford: Oxford University Press, 2011), 247–49; Blain Auer, *Symbols of Authority in Medieval Islam: History, Religion, and Muslim Legitimacy in the Delhi Sultanate* (London: I. B. Tauris, 2012), 104–34; Mohammad Habib and Khaliq Ahmad Nizami, eds., *A Comprehensive History of India* (Delhi: People's Publishing House, 1970), 5:537–38; Muḥammad ʿAbd al-ʿĀl Aḥmad, "Aḍwāʾ Jadīdah ʿalā Iḥyāʾ al-Khilāfah al-ʿAbbāsiyyah," (unpublished paper, 1987), 46–70.

CHAPTER 3. CONCEPTUALIZING THE CALIPHATE, 632–1517 CE

1. See, for example, Muḥammad Saʿīd Ramaḍān al-Būṭī, *Fiqh al-Sīrah al-Nabawiyyah* (Damascus: Dār al-Fikr, 1991), 490–507, its English translation, M. Saʿīd Ramaḍān al-Būṭī, *The Jurisprudence of the Prophetic Biography and a Brief History of Rightly Guided Caliphs*, trans. Nancy Roberts (Damascus: Dār al-Fikr, 2010), 582–603, and Meraj Mohiuddin, *Revelation: The Story of Muhammad* (Scottsdale, AZ: Whiteboard Press, 2015), 340–41.

2. Abū'l-Maʿālī ʿAbd al-Malik b. Abdillah al-Juwaynī, *Ghiyāth al-Umam fī Iltiyāth al-Ẓulam*, ed. ʿAbd al-ʿAẓīm al-Dīb, 2nd ed. (Cairo: Maṭbaʿat Nahḍat Miṣr, 1401 AH), 22–26; ʿAbdullāh b. ʿUmar b. Sulaymān al-Damījī, *al-Imāmāh al-Uẓmā ʿinda Ahl al-Sunnah wa'l-Jamāʿah* (Riyadh, Saudi Arabia: Dār Ṭaybah, 1987), 54–64; ʿAbdullah Muḥammad Muḥammad al-Qāḍī, *al-Siyāsah al-Sharʿiyyah: Maṣdar li'l-Taqnīn bayna al-Naẓariyyah wa'l-Taṭbīq*, (Ṭanṭā, Egypt: Maṭbaʿat Dār al-Kutub al-Jāmiʿiyyah al-Ḥadīthah, 1989), 406–12; Ṣalāḥ al-Ṣāwī, *al-Wajīz fī Fiqh al-Khilāfah* (Cairo: Dar al-Iʿlām al-Dawlī, 1994), 21–24.

3. Ibn Khaldūn, *Kitāb al-ʿIbar*, 1:339.

4. Ibid., 1:339, 401–2; al-Juwaynī, *Ghiyāth al-Umam*, 22–26; Qalqashandī, *Ma'āthir al-Ināfah*, 1:8–28; al-Damījī, *al-Imāmāh al-Uẓmā*, 25–42; al-Qāḍī, *al-Siyāsah al-Shar'iyyah*, 398–406; al-Ṣāwī, *al-Wajīz*, 5–14.
5. Abū Ja'far Muḥammad b. Jarīr al-Ṭabarī, *Jāmi' al-Bayān fī Tafsīr al-Qur'ān* (Bulaq, Egypt: al-Maṭba'ah al-Kubrā al-Amīriyyah, 1905), 5:93–95.
6. Abū 'Abdillāh Muḥammad b. Aḥmad al-Anṣārī al-Qurṭubī, *al-Jāmi' li-Aḥkām al-Qur'ān*, ed. Aḥmad 'Abd al-'Alīm al-Bardūnī, 3rd ed. (Cairo: Dār al-Qalam and Dār al-Kitāb al-'Arabī, 1966), 5:258–61.
7. Wadād al-Qāḍī, "The Term 'Khalīfah' in Early Exegetical Literature," *Die Welt des Islams* 28 (1988): 394–97, 408–10.
8. Abū Muḥammad 'Alī b. Aḥmad Ibn Ḥazm al-Ẓahirī, *al-Fiṣal fī'l-Milal wa'l-Ahwā' wa'l-Niḥal*, ed. Muḥammad Ibrāhīm Naṣr and 'Abd al-Raḥmān 'Umayrah (Beirut: Dār al-Jīl, 1995), 4:149–50.
9. Such as the explication of al-Nawawī in his *Sharḥ Saḥīḥ Muslim*; al-Damījī, *al-Imāmāh al-Uẓmā*, 49–54; al-Ṣāwī, *al-Wajīz*, 19–21.
10. Abū Bakr 'Abd al-Raḥmān b. Kaysān b. al-Aṣamm (d. 200/816 or 201/817) was among the sixth ṭabaqah of the Mu'tazilites; among the contemporaries of Abu'l Hudhayl Muḥammad ibn al-Hudhayl al-'Allāf who died 227 or 235 AH. Ibn Ḥajar al-'Asqalānī, *Lisān al-Mizān* (Beirut: Dār Iḥyā' al-Turāth al-'Arabī, 1996), 4:288; Aḥmad ibn Yaḥyā Ibn al-Murtaḍā, *Kitāb Ṭabaqāt al-Mu'tazilah*, ed. Susanna Diwlad-Wilzer (Beirut: al-Maṭba'ah al-Kāthūlīkiyyah in kommission bei Franz Steiner Verlag GMBH, 1961), 56; Abū'l-Qāsim al-Balkhī, al-Qāḍī 'Abd al-Jabbār, and al-Ḥākim al-Jushamī, *Faḍl al-I'tizāl wā-Ṭabaqāt al-Mu 'tazilah*, ed. Fu'ad al-Sayyid (Tunis: al-Dār al-Tawfiqiyyah), 267; al-Qāḍī Abd al-Jabbār al-Hamadhānī and Aḥmad ibn Yaḥyā Ibn al-Murtaḍā, *Firaq wa-Ṭabaqāt al-Mu'tazilah [al-Munyah wa'l-Amal fī Sharḥ Kitāb al-Milal wa'l-Niḥal]*, ed. 'Alī Sāmī al-Nashshār and 'Iṣām al-Dīn Muḥammad 'Alī (Alexandria, Egypt: Dār al-Maṭbū'āt al-Jāmi'iyyah, 1972), 65.
11. Hishām b. 'Amr al-Fūṭī (also known as al-Fuwaṭī) al-Shaybānī, who died 215/830, was among the sixth ṭabaqah of the Mu'tazilīs; among the contemporaries of Abu'l Hudhayl Muḥammad ibn al-Hudhayl al-'Allāf who died 227 or 235 AH. The editor of al-Baghdādī's *al-Farq bayn al-Firaq* notes a difference of opinion regarding the pronunciation of this *nisbah*, with some people saying al-Fūṭī (in reference to the singular *fūṭah*) and others saying al-Fuwaṭī (in reference to the plural *fuwat*). Indeed, in his entry on Hishām b. 'Amr in *Lisān al-Mizān*, Ibn Ḥajar al-'Asqalānī clearly writes out the vocalization of al-Fūṭī with words "*al-Fūṭī bi damm al-fā' wa iskān al-waw*." Ibn Ḥajar, *Lisān al-Mizān*, 7:268–69; al-Dhahabī, *Siyar 'Alām al-Nubalā*, ed. Shu'ayb al-Arna'ūt and Muḥammad Na'īm (Beirut: Mu'assasat al-Risālah, 1986), 546–47; 'Abd al-Qāhir ibn Ṭāhir ibn Muḥammad al-Baghdādī al-Isfarā'īnī al-Tamīmī al-Baghdādī, *al-Farq bayn al-Firaq*, ed. Muḥammad Muḥyī'l-Dīn 'Abd al-Ḥamīd (Cairo: Maktabat Muḥammad 'Alī Ṣabīḥ, n.d.), 159–64; Abū'l-Fatḥ Muḥammad ibn 'Abd al-Karīm ibn Abī Bakr Aḥmad al-Shahrastānī, *al-Milal wa'l-Niḥal*, ed. 'Abd al-Amīr 'Alī Muhannā and 'Alī Ḥasan Fā'ūr (Beirut: Dār al-Ma'rifah, 1990), 1:85–87; Ibn al-Murtaḍā, *Ṭabaqāt al-Mu'tazilah*, 61; *Faḍl al-I'tizāl*, 271; *Firaq wa-Ṭabaqāt al-Mu'tazilah*, 69.
12. The Najadāt are the followers of Najdah b. 'Āmir al-Nakh'ī al-Ḥanafī al-Ḥarūrī, who died 69 or 70 AH. Ibn Ḥajar, *Lisān al-Mizān*, 7:168–69; al-Dhahabī, *al-'Ibar*, 4:74, 77; al-Baghdādī, *al-Farq bayn al-Firaq*, 87–90; al-Shahrastānī, *al-Milal wa'l-Niḥal*, 1:141–44; R. Rubinacci, "Nadjadat," in *The Encyclopaedia of Islam*, 2nd ed.
13. For a detailed analysis of these views of the Najadāt and the Mu'tazilites al-Aṣamm and al-Fuwaṭī, see Patricia Crone, "A Statement by the Najdiyya Khārijites on the Dispensi-

bility of the Imamate," *Studia Islamica* 88 (1998): 55–76 and Patricia Crone, "Ninth-Century Muslim Anarchists," *Past and Present* 167 (May 2000): 3–28. Crone, *Government and Islam*, 54–69; al-Damījī, *al-Imāmah al-Uẓmā*, 45–46; al-Qādī, *al-Siyāsah al-Shar'iyyah*, 412–14; al-Ṣāwī, *al-Wajīz*, 16–17.

14. Ibn Ḥazm, *al-Fiṣal fi'l-Milal wa'l-Ahwā' wa'l-Niḥal*, 4:148.
15. al-Qurṭubī, *al-Jāmi' li-Aḥkām al-Qur'ān*, 1:264.
16. al-Juwaynī, *Ghiyāth al-Umam*, 22–23.
17. Ibid., 180–239; Abū'l-Ḥasan 'Alī b. Muḥammad al-Māwardī, *al-Aḥkām al-Sulṭāniyyah wa'l-Wilāyāt al-Dīniyyah*, ed. Aḥmad Mubārak al-Baghdādī (al-Manṣūrah: Dār al-Wafā' 1989), 22–24; Abū Ya'lā Muḥammad b. al-Ḥusayn Ibn al-Farrā', *al-Aḥkām al-Sulṭāniyyah* (Cairo: Muṣṭafā al-Bābī al-Ḥalabī, 1966), 27–28; al-Qalqashandī, *Ma'āthir al-Ināfah*, 1:74–80; al-Damījī, *al-Imāmah al-Uẓmā*, 331–464; 'Alī Jumu'ah, *al-Ḥukm al-Shar'ī 'inda al-Uṣūliyyīn* (Cairo: Dār al-Salām, 2002), 171; al-Qāḍī, *al-Siyāsah al-Shar'iyyah*, 472–531; al-Ṣāwī, *al-Wajīz*, 47–51; Crone, *Government and Islam*, 286–314; Tyan, *Institutions du droit public musulman*; Ann K. S. Lambton, *State and Government in Medieval Islam: An Introduction to the Study of Islamic Political Theory* (Oxford: Oxford University Press, 1981), 18–19, 58, 73, 91–92; Ann K. S. Lambton, "Khalīfa: In Political Theory," in *The Encyclopedia of Islam*, 2nd ed.; Wilferd Madelung, "Imāma," in *The Encyclopaedia of Islam*, 2nd ed.
18. Ibn al-Farrā', *al-Aḥkām al-Sulṭāniyyah*, 28; al-Māwardī, *al-Aḥkām al-Sulṭāniyyah*, 24; al-Damījī, *al-Imāmah al-Uẓmā*, 375–420; Jumu'ah, *al-Ḥukm al-Shar'ī*, 171; al-Qāḍī, *al-Siyāsah al-Shar'iyyah*, 532–63; al-Ṣāwī, *al-Wajīz*, 52–57.
19. al-Nawawī, *Sharh Saḥīḥ Muslim*, 1:398.
20. Abū Ḥāmid Muḥammad b. Muḥammad al-Ghazālī, *al-Iqtiṣād fī'l-'Itiqād*, ed. Hüseyin Atay (Ankara: Nur Matbaası, 1962), 240.
21. Wael Hallaq, "Was the Gate of Ijtihad Closed?," *International Journal of Middle East Studies* 16, no. 1 (March 1984), 13–16; Wael Hallaq, "Caliphs, Jurists and the Saljūqs in the Political Thought of Juwaynī," *Muslim World* 74, no. 1 (January 1984): 32–38; Crone, *Government and Islam*, 219–49, 286–314.
22. al-Ḥasan b. 'Alī b. Isḥāq b. al-'Abbās al-Ṭūsī. al-Subkī, *Ṭabaqāt al-Shāfi'iyyah*, 4:322–27.
23. As his previous work on the foundations of Islam, which included a section on theology, *al-Risālah al- Niẓāmiyyah fī'l-Arkān al-Islāmiyyah* had come to be known as *al-Niẓāmī*. al-Juwaynī also recommends an abbreviated title of *al-Ghiyāthī* for his *Ghiyāth al-Umam fī Iltiyāth al-Ẓulam*. Both abbreviations contain allusions to their illustrious benefactor, Niẓām al-Mulk. See al-Juwaynī, *Ghiyāth al-Umam*, 7–14, 18. Also worth mentioning is al-Juwaynī's lavish praise of the person to whom *al-Ghiyāthī* was presented in the entry for Niẓām al-Mulk compiled by the Shāfi'ī biographer Tāj al-Dīn 'Abd al-Wahhāb al-Subkī in his *Ṭabaqāt al-Shāfi'iyyah*, 4:314–15.
24. al-Juwaynī, *Ghiyāth al-Umam*, 19–305. These initial foundations are relayed in further detail by Wael Hallaq in his "Caliphs, Jurists and the Saljūqs."
25. Ibid., 307.
26. The appearance of another more qualified non-Qurashī, however, would not necessitate the former's deposition as a rule, since the *mafḍūl* (surpassed acceptable person) is not deposed upon the emergence of the *fāḍil* (superior one). Ibid., 308–10, 313–14.
27. Ibid., 310–11.
28. Ibid., 311.
29. Ibid., 312–13.
30. Here, the combination of lineage and scholarship is evaluated against political ability and independence.

31. Ibid., 313–15.
32. Ibid., 316–18. By this point, al-Juwaynī had already recorded his preference in the first foundational segment of the book for the opinion of Abū'l-Ḥasan al-Ash'arī (260–324/ 873 -935) that the minimum number of electors necessary to contract an imamate is only one, see al-Juwaynī, *Ghiyāth al-Umam,* 69–72.
33. An elector who whimsically refuses to validate the single candidate would necessarily be disqualified from the position due to his insistence on opposing the interests of the community.
34. al-Juwaynī, *Ghiyāth al-Umam,* 318–20.
35. Ibid., 320–24.
36. Ibid., 324–26.
37. Ibid., 326–28.
38. Ibid., 328–54.
39. Ibid., 354–84.
40. In Arabic: *intiqāl al-maḥall 'inda dhahāb maḥall al-ḥukm.* Jumu'ah, *al-Ḥukm al-Shar'ī,* 171–72. In this section of *al-Ḥukm al-Shar'ī,* the former grand mufti of Egypt Alī Jumu'ah al-Shāfi'ī discusses al-Juwaynī's third scenario of the total absence of the imamate, which more clearly illustrates his point of how Islamic laws may be perpetuated despite the disappearance of the original ruling's locus. al-Juwaynī's second scenario, discussed above, while also illustrative of this juristic process, is a bit more intricate given the actual presence of a caliph although it is *as if* he is in fact absent. I discuss this legal interpretation as well as al-Juwaynī's third imagined scenario of total anarchy in greater detail in another article.
41. al-Juwaynī uses this phrase in *al-Ghiyāthī* as an ironic play on the name of the contemporary Abbasid caliph, *al-Qā'im bi-Amrillāh.* See, for example, al-Juwaynī, *Ghiyāth al-Umam,* 355.
42. See, for instance, Ibn Kathīr, *al-Bidāyah wa'l-Nihāyah,* 14:46–48.
43. Gibb, "Constitutional Organization," 22–23; Sir Hamilton Gibb and Harold Bowen, *Islamic Society and the West: A Study of the Impact of Western Civilization on Moslem Culture in the Near East* (London: Oxford University Press, 1950), vol. 1, pt. 1, 32–33; Lambton, *State and Government,* 139–43.
44. Gibb, "Constitutional Organization," 23–24; Lambton, *State and Government,* 143–51. To cite Gibb's dramatic words, Ibn Taymiyyah "in his effort to cleanse Islam of its accretions of heresy, deviations, and abuses, and to preach to a return to the purity of early doctrine and practice, inevitably attacked the web of juristic argument regarding the caliphate."
45. Also referred to as *shawkah.*
46. Lambton, *State and Government,* 139.
47. Malcolm Kerr, *Islamic Reform: The Political and Legal Theories of Muḥammad 'Abduh and Rashīd Riḍa* (Berkeley: University of California Press, 1966), 50.
48. Gibb, "Constitutional Organization," 22–23. See also Sir Hamilton Gibb and Harold Bowen, *Islamic Society and the West,* vol. 1, pt. 1, 32–33.
49. Gibb, "Constitutional Organization," 23.
50. Madelung, "Imāma;" Crone, *Government and Islam,* 136–37.
51. Badr al-Dīn Muḥammad b. Ibrāhīm Ibn Jamā'ah, *Taḥrīr al-Aḥkām fī Tadbīr Ahl al-Islām,* ed. Fu'ād 'Abd al-Mun'im Aḥmad, 3rd ed. (Qatar: Dār al-Thaqāfah and Ri'āsat al-Maḥākim al-Shar'iyyah wa'l-Shu'ūn al-Dīniyyah, 1988).
52. Cf. my earlier discussion of al-Juwaynī's views in detail on this point.
53. al-Juwaynī, *Ghiyāth al-Umam,* 326.

54. Lambton, *State and Government*, 141–42.
55. Kerr, *Islamic Reform*, 50.
56. Ibn Jamā'ah, *Taḥrīr al-Aḥkām*, 45–46.
57. Ibid., 58–60.
58. al-Suyūṭī, *Ḥusn al-Muḥāḍarah*, 2:83–101.
59. al-Maqrīzī, *al-Mawā'iz*, 3:784.
60. Ibn Jamā'ah, *Taḥrīr al-Aḥkām*, 45.
61. Ibid., 61.
62. Ibid., 61–73. Ibn Jamā'ah also notes the secondary opinion that *ulū'l-amr* refers to religious scholars (*wa-ulu'l-amr hum al-imām wa-nuwwābuhu 'inda al-aktharīn wa-qīla hum al-'ulamā'*).
63. Ibid., 51.
64. Henri Laoust, *Essai sur les doctrines sociales et politiques de Taḳī-d-dīn Aḥmad b. Taimīya* (Cairo: Imprimerie de l'institut français d'archéologie orientale, 1939). For further details on Laoust's fundamental misreading of Ibn Taymiyyah's views on the caliphate, see my article Mona Hassan, "Modern Interpretations and Misinterpretations of a Medieval Scholar: Apprehending the Political Thought of Ibn Taymiyya," in *Ibn Taymiyya and His Times*, ed. Shahab Ahmed and Yossef Rapoport (Oxford: Oxford University Press, 2010), 338–66. The rest of this section is adapted from part of that article, which offers a fuller discussion of Ibn Taymiyyah's scholarship on the caliphate as well as later academic and Islamist representations of them.
65. Ibn Taymiyyah, *Majmū' Fatāwā Shaykh al-Islām Aḥmad b. Taymiyyah*, ed. 'Abd al-Raḥmān b. Muḥammad Ibn Qāsim (Cairo: Dār al-Raḥmah, n.d.), 35:18–32.
66. Ibid. A recent book commends these detailed arguments on Ibn Taymiyyah's legal responsa for demonstrating "the fatal flaw" of previous scholarship that presumed Ibn Taymiyyah demolished classical Islamic theories of the caliphate. But the author also mischaracterizes my analysis as a static "'nothing-new' position" rather than acknowledging how I locate Ibn Taymiyyah's creative corpus as part of a dynamic discursive tradition. This oversimplification stems in part from his contention that Muslim scholars wrote on the caliphate *as theologians* and not jurists. Yet it is evident that works such as al-Juwaynī's *al-Ghiyāthī*, written within the theoretical tradition of legal methodology or *uṣūl al-fiqh*, do not allow for such simple dichotomies. Similarly intertwined juridical and theological conceptualizations were in fact pivotal for most subsequent scholars, such as al-Ghazālī, Ibn Jamā'ah, and Ibn Taymiyyah, among others. Rather than artificially bifurcating jurists and theologians, who often excelled in the domains of both law and theology, we must recognize how multiple modes of inquiry were integral to shaping ongoing Muslim discussions of the caliphate over time. Cf. Ovamir Anjum, *Politics, Law, and Community in Islamic Thought: The Taymiyyan Moment* (Cambridge: Cambridge University Press, 2012), 28–29, 252–54.
67. Ironically enough, this is precisely the prophetic ḥadīth that Laoust identifies as the inspiration for Ibn Taymiyyah's rejection of the caliphate. For the ḥadīth, see al-Nawawī, *Sharḥ Ṣaḥīḥ Muslim*, 12:473–74; Ibn Ḥajar al-'Asqalānī, *Fatḥ al-Bārī*, 13:258–59; Ibn Mājah, *Sunan Ibn Mājah*, 3:400.
68. Ibn Taymiyyah, *Majmū' Fatāwā*, 35:20.
69. Ibn Taymiyyah, *Minhāj al-Sunnah fī Naqḍ Kalām al-Shī'ah wa'l-Qadariyyah* (Bulaq, Egypt: al-Maṭba'ah al-Kubrā al-Amīriyyah, 1903), 1:27.
70. Ibid., 1:8.
71. Ibid., 3:131.
72. Ibn Taymiyyah, *Majmū' Fatāwā*, 35:24–32.

73. Ibn Taymiyyah, *Minhāj al-Sunnah,* 3:131.
74. Ibn Taymiyyah, *Majmūʿ Fatāwā,* 35:20.
75. Ibid., 35:5–9, 20.
76. Ibn Taymiyyah, *al-Siyāsah al-Sharʿiyyah fī Iṣlāḥ al-Rāʿī wa'l-Raʿiyyah* (Beirut: Dār al-Kutub al-ʿIlmiyyah, n.d.). This work was translated by Omar Farrukh under the slightly misleading title *Ibn Taimiyya on Public and Private Law in Islam, or Public Policy in Islamic Jurisprudence* (Beirut: Khayats, 1966). I elaborate on understanding this work as a piece of advice literature in Hassan, "Modern Interpretations and Misinterpretations of a Medieval Scholar," 346–49. In response to my recognition of Ibn Taymiyyah's avowed intentions to offer beneficial advice to his contemporaries, Ovamir Anjum relies upon calcified classifications of what constitutes advice literature to assert that jurists, like Ibn Taymiyyah, did not write them. His ahistorical assertion, however, obscures more than it reveals by supposing an irreconcilable rift in neatly characterizing the influences on an author and his writings as either "Persian" (advice literature) or "Islamic" (scripture, law, and theology)—but not conceivably both. In discounting the possibility of convergence, Anjum even goes so far as to disparage the rich, human complexity of the prominent scholar al-Māwardī who writes in both genres as evincing "a multiple-personality disorder" for varying his style and approach when writing in different contexts. If anything, Anjum's move to pathologize multiplicity underscores the soundness of my emphasis on the premodern significance of genre in shaping Ibn Taymiyyah's innovative work. Anjum, *Politics, Law, and Community in Islamic Thought,* 28–29, 252–54.
77. Ibn Taymiyyah, *al-Siyāsah al-Sharʿiyyah,* 7–9.
78. Ibn Taymiyyah, *Minhāj al-Sunnah,* 1:28 (*al-aʾimmah hum al-umarāʾ wulāt al-umūr*), 3:131 (*al-nās yusammūna wulāt umūr al-Muslimīn al-khulafāʾ*).
79. Ibn Taymiyyah, *al-Siyāsah al-Sharʿiyyah,* 21–22.
80. Ibid., 13–28.
81. Ibid., 137–43.
82. Stefan Winter, "Shams al-Dīn Muḥammad ibn Makkī 'al-Shahīd al-Awwal' (d. 1384) and the Shiʿah of Syria," *Mamlūk Studies Review* 3 (1999): 149–82.
83. Tariq al-Jamil, "Ibn Taymiyya and Ibn Muṭahhar al-Ḥillī: Shi'i Polemics and the Struggle for Authority in Medieval Islam," in *Ibn Taymiyya and His Times,* ed. Shahab Ahmed and Yossef Rapoport (Oxford: Oxford University Press, 2009), 229–46 and Hassan, "Modern Interpretations and Misinterpretations of a Medieval Scholar," 338–43.
84. Shams al-Dīn Muḥammad al-Dhahabī, "al-Muqaddimah al-Zahrā fī Īḍāḥ al-Imāmah al-Kubrā," ʿAqāʾid Taymūr Collection, Manuscript, 59, folios 1–17, Egyptian National Library, Cairo, Egypt; Shams al-Dīn Muḥammad al-Dhahabī, "Risālah fī'l-Imāmah al-ʿUẓmā," Reisülküttap Collection, Manuscript 1185/2, folios 126–133; Süleymaniye Manuscript Library, Istanbul, Turkey; Shams al-Dīn Muḥammad al-Dhahabī, "Laṭīfah Tataʿallaqu bi'l-Imāmah al-ʿUẓmā," Nuruosmaniye Collection, Manuscript 34 Nk 4976/3, folios 20–23, Nuruosmaniye Manuscript Library, Istanbul, Turkey.
85. See note 84.
86. al-Dhahabī, "al-Muqaddimah al-Zahrāʾ fī Īḍāḥ al-Imāmah al-Kubrā," ʿAqāʾid Taymūr Collection, Manuscript 59, folio 6, Egyptian National Library, Cairo, Egypt; al-Dhahabī, "Risālah fī'l-Imāmah al-ʿUẓmā," Reisülküttap Collection, Manuscript 1185/2, folio 128, Süleymaniye Manuscript Library, Istanbul, Turkey; al-Dhahabī, "Laṭīfah Tataʿallaqu bi'l-Imāmah al-ʿUẓmā," Nuruosmaniye Collection, Manuscript 34 Nk 4976/3, folio 21, Nuruosmaniye Manuscript Library, Istanbul, Turkey.

87. Hassan, "Modern Interpretations and Misinterpretations of a Medieval Scholar," 356–59; Ibn Taymiyyah, *Majmūʿ Fatāwā*, 28:531–34, 552; al-Dhahabī, *Dhayl al-Tārīkh*, 257, 259–63; al-Dhahabī, *Siyar*, 17:503–4; al-Subkī, *Ṭabaqāt al-Shāfiʿiyyah al-Kubrā*, 9:103.
88. Reuven Amitai-Preiss, "Mongol Imperial Ideology and the Ilkhanid War against the Mamluks," in *The Mongol Empire and Its Legacy*, ed. Reuven Amitai-Preiss and David O. Morgan (Leiden, Neth.: E. J. Brill, 1999), 61–62.
89. al-Dhahabī, *Siyar*, 17:155; Shams al-Dīn Muḥammad b. Aḥmad al-Dhahabī, *Muʿjam al-Shuyūkh: al-Muʿjam al-Kabīr* (Taif, Saudi Arabia: Maktabat al-Ṣiddīq, 1988), 1:34–35; al-Dhahabī, *al-Muʿjam al-Mukhtaṣṣ*, 12–14; al-Subkī, *Ṭabaqāt al-Shāfiʿiyyah al-Kubrā*, 8:15; Ibn Kathīr, "Ṭabaqāt al-Shāfiʿiyyah," Garrett Collection, Yahuda section, Manuscript 4993, folios 276a and 276b, Princeton University Library, Princeton, NJ; Ibn Kathīr, *al-Bidāyah wa'l-Nihāyah* (1994), 13:361–62; al-Yāfiʿī, *Mirʾāt al-Jinān*, 4:225; Ibn Qāḍī Shuhbah, *Ṭabaqāt al-Shāfiʿiyyah*, 2:204–6; Ibn Taghribirdī, *al-Manhal al-Ṣāfī*, 1:229–31; Sherman Jackson, "The Primacy of Domestic Politics: Ibn Bint al-Aʿazz and the Establishment of Four Chief Judgeships in Mamlūk Egypt," *Journal of the American Oriental Society* 115, no. 1 (1995): 60.
90. al-Dhahabī, "al-Muqaddimah al-Zahrāʾ fī Īḍāḥ al-Imāmah al-Kubrā," ʿAqāʾid Taymūr Collection, Manuscript 59, folios 1–17, Egyptian National Library, Cairo, Egypt; al-Dhahabī, "Risālah fi'l-Imāmah al-ʿUẓmā," Reisülküttap Collection, Manuscript 1185/2, folios 126–133; Süleymaniye Manuscript Library, Istanbul, Turkey; al-Dhahabī, "Laṭīfah Tataʿallaqu bi'l-Imāmah al-ʿUẓmā," Nuruosmaniye Collection, Manuscript 34 Nk 4976/3, folios 20–23; Nuruosmaniye Manuscript Library, Istanbul, Turkey; al-Dhahabī, *Tārīkh al-Islām*, 66:75–76, 80–81, 86, 406–9; al-Dhahabī, *Dhayl al-Tārīkh*, 16, 373, 375–76; al-Dhahabī, *Siyar*, 16:426–29, 17:154–55, 549; al-Dhahabī, *al-ʿIbar*, 5:252–53, 258–59, 263; al-Dhahabī, *Dhayl al-ʿIbar*, 17, 214; al-Dhahabī, *Duwal al-Islām*, 2:157, 186; al-Subkī, *Ṭabaqāt al-Shāfiʿiyyah al-Kubrā*, 9:100–123, 10:398–99.
91. For a recent study on how Syrian congregational mosques were utilized for educational purposes in the Mamluk era, see Mahamid, "Mosques as Higher Educational Institutions in Mamluk Syria," 188–212.
92. al-Subkī, *Ṭabaqāt al-Shāfiʿiyyah al-Kubrā*, 10:139–338; al-Dhahabī, *al-Muʿjam al-Mukhtaṣṣ*, 152, 166–67.
93. al-Subkī, *Muʿīd al-Niʿam*, 1–13; al-Subkī, *Ṭabaqāt al-Shāfiʿiyyah al-Kubrā*, 1:208–9.
94. al-Subkī, *Muʿīd al-Niʿam*, 13–16.
95. Ibid., 16–21.
96. al-Subkī, *Ṭabaqāt al-Shāfiʿiyyah al-Kubrā*, 1:208.
97. Ibid., 9:103.
98. El-Rouayheb, "From Ibn Ḥajar al-Haytamī (d. 1566) to Khayr al-Dīn al-Alūsī (d. 1899)," 295–97; Wilfred Madelung, "The Spread of Maturidism and the Turks," in *Religious Schools and Sects in Medieval Islam* (London: Variorum Reprints, 1985), 110.
99. Yossef Rapoport, "Legal Diversity in the Age of *Taqlīd*: The Four Chief *Qāḍīs* under the Mamluks," *Islamic Law and Society* 10, no. 2 (2003): 201–28; Jackson, "The Primacy of Domestic Politics," 52–65.
100. Najm al-Dīn Ibrāhīm b. ʿAlī al-Ṭarsūsī, *Tuḥfat al-Turk fī mā Yajibu an Yuʿmala fi'l-Mulk*, ed. Riḍwān al-Sayyid (Beirut: Dār al-Ṭalīʿah li'l-Ṭibāʿah wa'l-Nashr, 1992), 18–21.
101. Ibid., 60–65, 71.
102. Ibid., 65.

103. Ibid., 65–71. Baki Tezcan also discusses these points of comparison between the two schools as evidence that the Turks' political successes were not due to their Hanafi affiliation in "Hanafism and the Turks in al-Ṭarsūsī's *Gift for the Turks*," *Mamlūk Studies Review* 17 (2011), 72–76, 85–86.

104. al-Maqrīzī, *Durar al-ʿUqūd*, 2:383–410; al-Sakhāwī, *al-Ḍawʾ al-Lāmiʿ*, 4:146–49; Fischel, *Ibn Khaldūn in Egypt*, 1–6, 15–25, 30–41, 167–69; Syed Farid Alatas, "Ibn Khaldūn," in *The Wiley-Blackwell Companion of Major Social Theorists* (West Sussex, UK: Wiley-Blackwell, 2011), 12.

105. Ibn Khaldūn, *Kitāb al-ʿIbar*, 3:337–38, 341, 359–60, 386–87.

106. Ibid., 3:358–70.

107. Ibid., 3:1113.

108. Ibn Taghribirdī, *al-Manhal al-Ṣāfī*, 4:103–38.

109. Ibn Khaldūn does not specify which member of the Cairene Abbasid dynasty approached Timur, but it could not have been the second caliph who substituted for al-Mutawakkil and was deposed in 791/1389, because he had already died in 801/1399.

110. Ibn Taghribirdī, *al-Manhal al-Ṣāfī*, 7:143–44.

111. Ibn Khaldūn, *Kitāb al-ʿIbar*, 7:1211–14; Ibn Khaldūn, "Riḥlat Ibn Khaldūn," Aya Sofya Collection, Manuscript 3200, folio 81, Süleymaniye Manuscript Library, Istanbul, Turkey; Walter Fischel, *Ibn Khaldūn and Tamerlane: Their Historic Meeting in Damascus, 1401 A.D. (803 A.H.)* (Berkeley and Los Angeles: University of California Press, 1952), 39–41.

112. al-Qalqashandī, *Qalāʾid*; al-Qalqashandī, *Nihāyah*; al-Qalqashandī, *Ṣubḥ*; al-Maqrīzī, *Durar al-ʿUqūd*, 1:312–13; Ibn Taghribirdī, *al-Manhal al-Ṣāfī*, 1:351–52; al-Sakhāwī, *al-Ḍawʾ al-Lāmiʿ*, 2:8; Ibn al-ʿImād, *Shadharāt al-Dhahab*, 9:218–19; C. E. Bosworth, "A 'Maqāma' on Secretaryship: al-Qalqashandī's 'al-Kawākib al-Durriyya fī'l-Manāqib al-Badriyya,'" in *Bulletin of the School of Oriental and African Studies* 27, no. 2 (1964): 291–98; C. E. Bosworth, "al-Ḳalḳashandī," in *The Encyclopaedia of Islam*, 2nd ed.

113. In the middle of the work, al-Qalqashandī notes that he was writing as of 819 AH, which correspondes to 1416 CE. al-Qalqashandī, *Maʾāthir al-Ināfah*, 1:1–5, 2:209–10, 218, 221–23, 3:375–81; Ibn Ḥajar, *al-Durar al-Kāminah*, 7:115–16, 9:173; Ibn Taghribirdī, *Mawrid al-Laṭāfah*, 1:258–59; Ibn Taghribirdī, *al-Nujūm al-Zāhirah*, 15:489–90; Ibn Taghribirdī, *al-Manhal al-Ṣāfī*, 5:301–5; al-Sakhāwī, *al-Ḍawʾ al-Lāmiʿ*, 3:215; al-Suyūṭī, *Tārīkh al-Khulafāʾ*, 578–81; al-Suyūṭī, *Ḥusn al-Muḥāḍarah*, 2:78–79; Ibn Iyās, *Badāʾiʿ al-Zuhūr*, 2b:12.

114. al-Qalqashandī, *Maʾāthir al-Ināfah*, 1:2, 8, 13-14; al-Qalqashandī, *Ṣubḥ al-Aʿshā*, 5:444–47. In his article analyzing the Molla Çelebi collection manuscript of *Maʾāthir al-Ināfah* written in 905/1499, İbrahim Kafesoğlu notes further locations where al-Qalqashandī reproduced material from *Ṣubḥ al-Aʿshā*: "Kalkaşandi'nin Bilinmeyen Bir Esseri Meâsirülʾ-İnâfe," *Tarih Dergisi* 8, no. 11–12 (1956): 99–104.

115. al-Qalqashandī, *Maʾāthir al-Ināfah*, 1:29–31.

116. Ibid., 1:37–39, 2:256–59; Rabbat, "Who Was al-Maqrīzī?," 7–8.

117. al-Qalqashandī, *Maʾāthir al-Ināfah*, 1:46–47, 2:255–56.

118. Ibid., 1:70–72, 74–80, 2:232.

119. Ibid., 2:274–317, 337–53.

120. Ibid., 3:39–76, 100–121, 121–37, 194–98.

121. Ibid., 2:224–32, 237–44, 3:322–31.

122. ʿAlī b. Aḥmad b. Muḥammad b. Abī Bakr b. Muḥammad al-Shīrāzī, "Tuḥfat al-Mulūk wa'l-Salāṭīn," Ijtimāʿ Taymūr Collection, Manuscript 72, folios 3–10, 653, Egyptian Na-

tional Library, Cairo, Egypt; al-Sakhāwī, *al-Ḍaw' al-Lāmi'*, 5:189; Kātip Çelebi, *Kashf al-Ẓunūn 'an Asāmī al-Kutub wa'l-Funūn*, 1:375; 'Umar Riḍā Kaḥḥālah, *Mu'jam al-Mu'allifīn: Tarājim Muṣannifī al-Kutub al-'Arabiyyah* (Beirut: Mu'assassat al-Risālah, 1993), 2:399–400; Ibn Taghribirdī, *Mawrid al-Laṭāfah*, 2:158–63.

123. 'Alī b. Aḥmad al-Shīrāzī, "Tuḥfat al-Mulūk wa'l-Salāṭīn," Ijtimā' Taymūr Collection, Manuscript 72, folios 69–78, Egyptian National Library, Cairo, Egypt.
124. Ibid., 78–79.
125. Ibid., 79–82, 88, 91–92. On folios 88 and 91, al-Shīrāzī also comments how the selection of the caliph by the eminent electors of Egypt suffices the rest of the Muslim community and relieves them of the collective obligation to elect a caliph.
126. Ibid., 82–88.
127. Ibid., 69–110.
128. Ibid., 83, 85, 87–89, 99–100, 105–10.
129. Ibid., 69–110.
130. Shams al-Dīn Muḥammad b. 'Abd al-Raḥmān al-Sakhāwī, "Tārīkh Khulafā' wa-Salāṭīn Miṣr," Aya Sofya Collection, Manuscript 3266, folios 29–30, 119, Süleymaniye Manuscript Library, Istanbul, Turkey; Ibn Ḥajar, *al-Durar al-Kāminah*, 9:173; Ibn Taghribirdī, *al-Manhal al-Ṣāfī*, 4:275–312, 5:301–5, 183–84, 6:51–53; Ibn Taghribirdī, *Mawrid al-Laṭāfah*, 1:258–65, 2:158–63; Ibn Taghribirdī, *al-Nujūm al-Zāhirah*, 15:465–559, 16:1–30; al-Sakhāwī, *al-Ḍaw' al-Lāmi'*, 3:166–67, 215, 269; al-Suyūṭī, *Tārīkh al-Khulafā'*, 578–83; al-Suyūṭī, *Ḥusn al-Muḥāḍarah*, 2:78–79, 106; Ibn Iyās, *Badā'i al-Zuhūr*, 2b:12, 230, 288; Dimitris Kastritsis, "Conquest and Political Legitimation in the Early Ottoman Empire," in *Byzantines, Latins, and Turks in the Eastern Mediterranean World after 1150*, ed. Jonathan Harris, Catherine Holmes, and Eugenia Russell (Oxford: Oxford University Press, 2012), 221–45.
131. Marlis Saleh, "Al-Suyūṭī and His Works: Their Place in Islamic Scholarship from Mamluk Times to the Present," *Mamlūk Studies Review* 5 (2001), 74; 'Abd al-Qādir al-'Aydarūsī, *al-Nūr al-Sāfir 'an Akhbār al-Qarn al-'Āshir*, ed. Aḥmad Ḥālū, Muḥammad al-Arnā'ūṭ, and al-Karam al-Būshī (Beirut: Dār Ṣādir, 2001), 90.
132. al-Suyūṭī, *Tārīkh al-Khulafā'*, 581–82; al-Suyūṭī, *Ḥusn al-Muḥāḍarah*, 2:78–79; al-Sakhāwī, *al-Ḍaw' al-Lāmi'*, 3:269, 11:72–73; al-'Aydarūsī, *al-Nūr al-Sāfir*, 91; Najm al-Dīn Muḥammad al-Ghazzī, *al-Kawākib al-Sā'irah bi-A'yān al-Mi'ah al-'Āshirah*, ed. Khalīl al-Manṣūr (Beirut: Dār *al-Kutub* al-'Ilmīyah, 1997), 227. al-Sakhāwī notes the date of al-Mustakfī III's death as the second day of 855/1451 and the elder al-Suyūṭī's death in the following month. al-'Aydarūsī specifies it was on the fifth, and al-Ghazzī comments that Jalāl al-Dīn al-Suyūṭī was five years and seven months old at the time of his father's death.
133. al-Suyūṭī, *Tārīkh al-Khulafā'*, 579.
134. Ibid., 584; al-Suyūṭī, *Ḥusn al-Muḥāḍarah*, 2:80.
135. My unpublished research on "Social Conflict in the Administration of Mamluk Charitable Endowments: Jalāl al-Dīn al-Suyūṭī's Legal Opinions and Management of the Baybarsiyyah," which originally inspired the topic of this book, analyzed al-Ṣuyūṭī's fatwa "al-Inṣāf fī Tamyīz al-Awqāf" from *al-Ḥāwī li'l-Fatāwī* in connection with his experiences managing Baybars al-Jāshankīr's foundation. Similar work and a translation of this fatwa was later independently published by Rebecca Skreslet Hernandez in "Sultan, Scholar, and Sufi: Authority and Power Relations in al-Suyūṭī's Fatwā on Waqf," *Islamic Law and Society* 20, no. 4 (2013): 333–70. Also see Leonor Fernandes, "The Foundation of Baybars al-Jashnakir: Its Waqf, History, and Architecture," *Muqarnas* 4

(1987): 21–42 and Albert Arazi, "Al-Risāla al-Baybarsiyya d'al-Suyūṭī: Un document sur les problèmes d'un *waqf* sultanien sous les derniers Mamlūks," *Israel Oriental Studies* 9 (1979): 329–53.

136. Jean-Claude Garcin, "Histoire, opposition, politique et piétisme traditionaliste dans le Ḥusn al Muḥādarat de Suyûti," *Annales Islamologiques* 7 (1967), 36–37; Saleh, "Al-Suyūṭī," 76–79; Hallaq, "Was the Gate of Ijtihad Closed?," 27–28; Elizabeth Sartain, *Jalāl al-Dīn al-Suyūṭī: Biography and Background* (Cambridge: Cambridge University Press, 1975), 1:61–72, 2:205–14; al-Sakhāwī, *al-Ḍaw' al-Lāmi'*, 4:67–69; Ibn Iyās, *Badā'i' al-Zuhūr fī Waqā'i al-Duhūr*, ed. Muḥammad Muṣṭafā (Cairo: Dār Iḥyā' al-Kutub al-'Arabiyyah, 1963), 3:339.

137. Jalāl al-Dīn al-Suyūṭī, *al-Radd 'alā Man Akhlada ilā al-Arḍ wa-Jahila anna al-Ijtihād fī Kull 'Aṣr Farḍ*, ed. Khalīl al-Mays (Beirut: Dār al-Kutub al-'Ilmiyyah, 1983), 82. al-Suyūṭī's framing of al-Juwaynī's discussion of *ijtihād* indicates his familiarity with the author's other treatment of the topic. And al-Suyūṭī explicitly uses al-Juwaynī's *Ghiyāth al-Umam* (also known as *al-Ghiyāthī*) as a precedent for the naming of his treatise on non-Arabic origin words in the Qur'an; see *The Mutawakkili of As-Suyuti*, ed. William Bell (Cairo: Nile Mission Press, 1926), 15–16, 33.

138. Jalāl al-Dīn al-Suyūṭī, "Kitāb al-Ināfah fī Rutbat al-Khilāfah," Reisülküttap Collection, Manuscript 1185, folios 141a–146a, Süleymaniye Manuscript Library, Istanbul, Turkey.

139. Jalāl al-Dīn al-Suyūṭī, "al-Asās fī Manāqib Banī'l-Abbās," Reisülküttap Collection, Manuscript 1185, folios 134a–140b, Süleymaniye Manuscript Library, Istanbul, Turkey; Jalāl al-Dīn al-Suyūṭī, "al-Asās fī Manāqib Banī'l-Abbās," Manisa Akhisar Zeynelzade Collection, Manuscript 45 Ak Ze 419/12, folios 192b–197a, Manisa İl Halk Library, Manisa, Turkey. In *al-Ḍaw' al-Lāmi'*, al-Sakhāwī accuses al-Suyūṭī of plagiarizing much of this treatise from Ibn Ḥajar al-'Asqalānī (4:68), although al-Suyūṭī refuted the charge in his manuscript "al-Kāwī fī Tārīkh al-Sakhāwī." Sartain offers further defense in her biography *Jalāl al-Dīn al-Suyūṭī*, 1:74–77. Nevertheless, the accusation indicates a wider circulation of similar notions and compositions among an earlier generation of scholars.

140. al-Suyūṭī, "al-Asās fī Manāqib Banī'l-Abbās," Reisülküttap Collection, Manuscript 1185, folios 136a–136b, Süleymaniye Manuscript Library, Istanbul, Turkey; Muslim, *Ṣaḥīḥ Muslim*, 2:1032 (#6378), *Ṣaḥīḥ Muslim bi-Sharḥ al-Nawawī* (Beirut: Dār al-Fikr, 1981), 15:179–80.

141. al-Suyūṭī, "al-Asās fī Manāqib Banī'l-Abbās," Reisülküttap Collection, Manuscript 1185, folios 136a, 140a, Süleymaniye Manuscript Library, Istanbul, Turkey; al-Bukhārī, *Ṣaḥīḥ al-Bukhārī*, 1:190 (#1018), 2:734, 740 (#3757, #3796); Ibn Ḥajar al-'Asqalānī, *Fatḥ al-Bārī bi-Sharḥ Ṣaḥīḥ al-Bukhārī*, 2:398–99, 7:77.

142. al-Suyūṭī, "al-Asās fī Manāqib Banī'l-Abbās," Reisülküttap Collection, Manuscript 1185, folios 136b–140a, Süleymaniye Manuscript Library, Istanbul, Turkey.

143. Jonathan Brown, "Did the Prophet Say It or Not? The Literal, Historical, and Effective Truth of Ḥadīths in Early Sunnism," *Journal of the American Oriental Society* 129, no. 2 (2009): 279–85 and "Even If It's Not True It's True: Using Unreliable Ḥadīths in Sunni Islam," *Islamic Law and Society* 18 (2011): 1–52.

144. al-Tirmidhī rates this particular ḥadīth as *ḥasan gharīb*, a fair transmission having limited corroboration, and comments "innamā na'rifuhu min hādhā al-wajh." al-Ḥākim rates it as *ṣaḥīḥ* or sound. al-Tirmidhī, *al-Jāmi' al-Kabīr*, 2:963 (#4158).

145. Lassner, *Islamic Revolution and Historical Memory*, 25–30, 39–40; Sharon, *Black Banners from the East*, 75–99.

146. al-Suyūṭī, "Kitāb al-Ināfah fī Rutbat al-Khilāfah," Reisülküttap Collection, Manuscript 1185, folio 145a, Süleymaniye Manuscript Library, Istanbul, Turkey; al-Suyūṭī, "al-Asās

fī Manāqib Banī'l-Abbās," Reisülküttap Collection, Manuscript 1185, folios 139a–139b, Süleymaniye Manuscript Library, Istanbul, Turkey; Jonathan Brown, "Did the Prophet Say It or Not?," 281–82; Sharon, *Black Banners from the East*, 94.

147. al-Suyūṭī, *Tārīkh al-Khulafā'*, 6–9.

CHAPTER 4. MANIFOLD MEANINGS OF LOSS: OTTOMAN DEFEAT, EARLY 1920S

1. Mohammad Barakatullah, *The Khilafet* (London: Luzac and Company Oriental and Foreign Booksellers and Publishers, 1924), 1.
2. Aḥmad Shawqī, "Dam'ah wa'btisāmah," *al-Ahrām*, October 24, 1923; Aḥmad Shawqī, *al-Shawqiyyāt*, ed. 'Alī 'Abd al-Mun'im 'Abd al-Ḥamīd (Cairo: al-Shirkah al- Miṣriyyah al-'Ālamiyyah li'l-Nashr and Longman, 2000), 1107.
3. Mustafa Sabri, "Khiṭāb Maftūḥ li-Amīr al-Shu'arā' Shawqī Bey," *al-Muqaṭṭam*, October 27, 1923; Mustafa Sabri, *Mawqif al-'Aql wa'l-'Ilm wa'l-'Ālam min Rabb al-'Ālamīn* ([Cairo]: Dār Iḥyā' al-Kutub al-'Arabiyyah, 'Īsā al-Bābī al-Ḥalabī wa-Shurakā'uh, 1950), 1:363.
4. Mustafa Sabri, *al-Nakīr 'alā Munkirī al-Ni'mah min al-Dīn wa'l-Khilāfah wa'l-Ummah* (Beirut: al-Maṭba'ah al-'Abbāsiyyah, 1342 [1924]), 39–41.
5. Aḥmad Shawqī, "Taklīl Anqarah wa-'Azl al-Astānah," *al-Ahrām,* November 28, 1923; Shawqī, *al-Shawqiyyāt*, 277.
6. Aḥmad Shawqī, "Khilāfat al-Islām," *al-Akhbār*, April 15, 1924; Shawqī, *al-Shawqiyyāt*, 250.
7. "Min Jalālat al-Khalīfah ilā Amīr al-Shu'arā'," *al-Akhbār*, May 21, 1924.
8. Mustafa Sabri, *Mawqif*, 1:464–65; Mustafa Sabri, *al-Nakīr*, 217–18.
9. Shawqī, "Khilāfat al-Islām," *al-Akhbār*, April 15, 1924; Shawqī, *al-Shawqiyyāt*, 251–52. Shawqī, however, continues on to clarify his position by affirming that truth above all merits the devotion of his pen. Truth itself, he decides, is more sacred and more deserving of his allegiance than Mustafa Kemal, and yet, Shawqī still cannot fully break away from the glorious image of his earlier compositions. Hesitant, or perhaps incapable of shattering all of the hopes he had placed in Mustafa Kemal, Shawqī concludes that the president of the nascent Turkish Republic has been deluded by the ardent adulation of the masses and pleads that this potentially noble leader receive sincere advice so that he might be set aright.
10. Mustafa Sabri, *Mawqif*, 1:464–65.
11. Ibid., 1:22–23, 99–101.
12. See, for example, Ahmet Çelebi Vakfiyesi, Konya, 923/1517, B.O.A., Ev.Vkf 3/14; İskender Paşa Vakfiyesi, Diyarbakr, 973/1565, B.O.A., Ev.Vkf 1/8; Özcan, "Hilafet: Osmanlı Dönemi," 546; Feridun Bey, *Mecmua-yi Münşeat-i Selâtin*, 1:437–44, 500–501; Gökbilgin, "Kanunî Sultan Süleyman," 96–99; *Makhṭūṭ Khalāṣ al-Ummah fī Ma'rifat al-A'immah*; Gibb, "Luṭfī Paşa," 295; Yavuz, *Osmanli Devleti ve İslamiyet*, 73–110.
13. S. Tufan Buzpinar, "The Question of Caliphate under the Last Ottoman Sultans," in *Ottoman Reform and Muslim Regeneration*, ed. Itzchak Weismann and Fruma Zachs (London: I. B. Tauris, 2005), 17–36; Brian Glyn Williams, *The Crimean Tatars: The Diaspora Experience and the Forging of a Nation* (Leiden, Neth.: E. J. Brill, 2001); B.O.A., Name-i Hümayun Defteri IX/1, 25; Cevdet Paşa, *Tarih-i Cevdet* (Istanbul: Matbaa-yi Osmaniye, 1893), 1:359.
14. Marshall Poe, "Moscow, the Third Rome: The Origins and Transformations of a 'Pivotal Moment,'" *Jahrbücher für Geschichte Osteuropas, Neu Folge* 49 (2001): 412–29; John

Meyendorff, "Was There Ever a 'Third Rome?' Remarks on the Byzantine Legacy in Russia," in *The Byzantine Tradition after the Fall of Constantinople*, ed. John Yiannias (Charlottesville: University of Virginia Press, 1991), 45–60; Daniel Rowland, "The Third Rome or the New Israel?," *Russian Review* 55, no. 4 (1996): 591–614; Colin Wells, *Sailing from Byzantium: How a Lost Empire Shaped the World* (NY: Random House, 2007), 275–77.

15. Stephen Baehr, "From History to National Myth: *Translatio Imperii* in Eighteenth-Century Russia," *Russian Review* 37, no. 1 (1978): 1–13; Stephen Baehr, *The Paradise Myth in Eighteenth-Century Russia: Utopian Patterns in Early Secular Russian Literature and Culture* (Stanford, CA: Stanford University Press, 1991), 18–21, 49–55. On the eighteenth-century Russian fascination with imperial Rome, also see Andrew Kahn, "Readings of Imperial Rome from Lomonosov to Pushkin," *Slavic Review* 52, no. 4 (1993): 745–68 and Jurij Lotman and Boris Uspenkij, "Echoes of the Notion 'Moscow as the Third Rome' in Peter the Great's Ideology," trans. N.F.C. Owen, in *The Semiotics of Russian Culture*, ed. Ann Shukman (Ann Arbor: Michigan Slavic Contributions, 1984), 53–67.
16. Poe, "Moscow, the Third Rome," 412–29; Judith Kalb, *Russia's Rome: Imperial Visions, Messianic Dreams, 1890–1940* (Madison: University of Wisconsin Press, 2008); Anna Frajlich, *The Legacy of Ancient Rome in the Russian Silver Age* (Amsterdam: Rodopi, 2007); Peter Duncan, *Russian Messianism: Third Rome, Holy Revolution, Communism and After* (London: Routledge, 2000).
17. Türköne, *Siyasi İdeoloji*; Eraslan, *II. Abdülhamid ve İslam Birliği*; Deringil, *The Well-Protected Domains*; Özcan, *Pan-Islamism*, 40–63; Karpat, *The Politicization of Islam*, 176–78, 233–34, 235–40; Zürcher, *Turkey*, 79, 81; Hanioğlu, *Late Ottoman Empire*, 129–30, 142.
18. van Bruinessen, "Muslims of the Dutch East Indies and the Caliphate Question," 264.
19. See Qureshi, *Pan-Islam in British Indian Politics*; Özcan, *Pan-Islamism*, 189–204; Mim Kemal Öke, *Hilafet Hareketi: Güney Asya Müslümanları'nın İstiklal Davası ve Türk Milli Mücadelesi 1919–1924* (Ankara: Kültür ve Turizm Bakanlığı, 1988); Gail Minault, *The Khilafat Movement: Religious Symbolism and Political Mobilization in India* (NY: Columbia University Press, 1982); A. C. Niemeijer, *The Khilafat Movement in India 1919–1924* (The Hague: Martinus Nijhoff, 1972).
20. Shawqī, *al-Shawqiyyāt*, 252. On Ethem the Ciracassian, see Bülent Bilmez, "A Nationalist Discourse of Heroism and Treason: The Construction of an 'Official' Image of Çerkes Ethem (1886–1948) in Turkish Historiography, and Recent Challenges," in *Untold Histories of the Middle East: Recovering Voices from the 19th and 20th Centuries*, ed. Amy Singer, Christoph Neumann, and Selçuk Akşin Somel (London: Routledge, 2011), 106–23, as well as Emrah Cilasun, *Bâki İlk Selam: Çerkes Ethem* (Istanbul: Belge Yayınları, 2004).
21. van Bruinessen, "Muslims of the Dutch East Indies and the Caliphate Question," 261, 266–67; Hasan Arifin Melayu, "Islam and Politics in the Thought of Tjokroaminoto (1882–1934)," (Master's thesis, McGill University, 2000), 73–80. For a fuller study of Southeast Asian constructions of Islamic nationhood, see Michael Francis Laffan's *Islamic Nationhood and Colonial Indonesia: The Umma below the Winds* (NY: Routledge, 2003).
22. Gail Minault, "Indian Muslims' Reactions to the Abolition of the Caliphate in 1924: The Collapse of a Nationalist Political Alliance," *Les Annales de l'autre Islam*, no. 2 (1994): 246, 250.

23. Shawqī, *al-Shawqiyyāt*, 438; Khouri, *Poetry and the Making of Modern Egypt*, 111.
24. Gershoni and Jankowski, *Egypt, Islam, and the Arabs*, 73–74.
25. Shawqī, *al-Shawqiyyāt*, 251.
26. Article published in *Amān-i Afghān* on March 18, 1924, T.N.A., F. O. 371/10218/E4392, May 19, 1924.
27. T.N.A., F. O. 371/10218/E2823, March 31, 1924.
28. Muḥammad ʿAbd al-Muṭṭalib, *Dīwān ʿAbd al-Muṭṭalib*, ed. Ibrahīm al-Abyārī and ʿAbd al-Ḥāfiẓ Shalabī, 1st ed.(Cairo: Maṭbaʿat al-Iʿtimād, n.d.), 253.
29. T.N.A., F. O. 371/10217/E2593, March 11, 1924. For a general picture of Bosnian reactions to the Ottoman Caliphate's abolition, see Jasna Samic, "Le Califat en Bosnie et les réactions à son abolition," *Les Annales de l'autre Islam*, no. 2 (1994): 325–27.
30. "al-Khalīfah al-ʿArabī," *Alif Bāʾ*, March 8, 1924, T.N.A., F. O. 684/2/File 111, pp. 4–7, March 10, 1924. Yūsuf al-ʿĪsā established *Alif Bāʾ* in Damascus on September 1, 1920; Philippe de Ṭarrāzī, *Tārīkh al-Ṣiḥāfah al-ʿArabiyyah: Yaḥtawī ʿalā Akhbār Kull Jarīdah wa-Majallah ʿArabiyyah* (Beirut: al-Maṭbaʿah al-Amrīkiyyah, 1933), 4:48–49.
31. T.N.A., F. O. 174/303/77, March 15, 1924.
32. T.N.A., F. O. 406/53/no. 22, March 29, 1924; According to the *Foreign Office List* for 1947, pp. 156–57, Sir Reader William Bullard (born December 5, 1885, and retired on March 20, 1946) was appointed H. M. agent and consul at Jeddah on June 16, 1923—a post that he held until December 30, 1930, *Foreign Office List and Diplomatic and Consular Year Book*, 59 vols. (London: Harrison and Sons, 1907–65). He died on May 24, 1976, Ann Lambton, "Obituary: Sir Reader William Bullard," *Bulletin of the School of Oriental and African Studies* 40, no. 1 (1977): 130–34.
33. Open letter published in the *Corriere di Tripoli* on April 5, 1924, T.N.A., F. O. 371/10218/E3833, April 22, 1924, and also published in the Egyptian newspaper *al-Ahrām* on May 8, 1924, Ḥilmī Aḥmad ʿAbd al-ʿĀl Shalabī, "Intihāʾ al-Khilāfah al-ʿUthmāniyyah 1924" (Master's thesis, ʿAyn Shams University, Cairo, 1977), 269–70.
34. "Masʾalat al-Khilāfah: Raʾy Faḍīlat Shaykh Jāmiʿ al-Azhar," *al-Akhbār*, March 15, 1924; Zakariyyā Sulaymān Bayyūmī, *Mawqif Miṣr min al-Mutaghayyirāt fī Turkiyā bayn al-Ḥarbayn al-ʿĀlamiyyatayn 1918–1938* (Cairo: Dār al-Kitāb al-Jāmiʿī, n.d.), 86; Shalabī, "Intihāʾ al-Khilāfah al-ʿUthmāniyyah 1924," 250; T.N.A., F. O. 371/10217/E2322, March 17, 1924; T.N.A., F. O. 371/10110/E3657, April 30, 1924.
35. I.e., the Ankara Government, T.N.A., F. O. 371/10110/E3657, April 30, 1924.
36. Article from the Albanian *Shpresa Kombëtare* on March 19, 1924, T.N.A., F. O. 371/10218/E2823, March 31, 1924.
37. T.N.A., F. O. 371/10218/E3791, May 1, 1924, see, for example, the reports from Madras, March 16, 1924, and Assam, March 22, 1924; T.N.A., F. O. 371/10110/E3657, April 30, 1924, also underlines that news of the caliph's deposition and the caliphate's abolition "caused consternation in India" and that the "News of expulsion of Caliph caused revulsion of popular sentiment." It also contains a statement jointly issued by the Central Khilafat Committee and the Jamiat-ul-Ulama and published in the *Times of India Weekly* on March 22, 1924, "The news received from Turkey regarding the deposition of the Khalifa and the abolition of the institution of the Khilafat has naturally caused great consternation among the Mussalmans and surprised and disturbed other communities in India."
38. And who said, as late as November 1922, that matters relating to the caliphate were of concern to the entire Muslim world and not alone for Turkey to decide; Finefrock, "From Sultanate to Republic," 82–83. For promises made during the national resistance

movement, also see Mustafa Kemal's proclamations in support of the caliphate to the Turkish populace in the introduction's notes as well as the discussions later in this chapter and chapter 6.

39. Aḥmad Shawqī, "Khilāfat al-Islām," *al-Akhbār*, April 15, 1924; Shawqī, *al-Shawqiyyāt*, 250.
40. T.N.A., F. O. 371/10217/E2593, March 11, 1924.
41. T.N.A., F. O. 371/10218/E3098, March 29, 1924; Viscount Edmund Henry Hyman Allenby (born April 23, 1861) was appointed high commissioner of Egypt on October 14, 1919, and resigned on August 23, 1925, *Foreign Office List* (1926), 153–54.
42. T.N.A., F. O. 371/10218/E5885, June 2, 1924.
43. Ibid. and T.N.A., F. O. 371/10218/E3791, May 1, 1924, see, for example, the report from Calcutta, March 17, 1924.
44. T.N.A., F. O. 371/10218/E3791, May 1, 1924, see, for example, the report from Delhi, March 27, 1924; T.N.A., F. O. 371/10110/E3657, April 30, 1924; T.N.A., F. O. 371/10110/E4212, May 14, 1924; Minault, "Indian Muslims' Reactions," 255.
45. These eight persons included Dr. Mukhtar Ahmed Ansari of Delhi; Hakim Mohamed Ajmal Khan Sahib of Delhi; Maulvi Mufti Kifayetullah Sahib, President of the Jamiat-ulema-i-hind; Mr. Mohamed Marmaduke Pickthall, editor of the "Bombay Chronicle"; Maulana Sulaiman Nadvi of the Shibli Academy in Azamgarh; Mr. Tassaduq Ahmed Khan Sherwani of Aligarh; Chaudhri Khuliquzzaman, Chairman of the Municipal Board, Lucknow; and Haji Abdullah Haroon; T.N.A., F. O. 424/261/no. 21–22.
46. T.N.A., F. O. 371/10110/E3657, April 30, 1924.
47. T.N.A., AIR 23/406/F2019, October 7, 1924; T.N.A., AIR 23/406/F2121, October 14, 1924; T.N.A., AIR 23/406/F2143, February 3, 1925; T.N.A., F. O. 371/10110/E3657, April 30, 1924, also reports of the caliphate committee's suggesting to the Turkish Red Crescent Mission upon its arrival in India on March 31, 1924, that Mustafa Kemal assume the position of caliph—a suggestion that is said to have been received favorably at the time.
48. Aḥmad Muḥarram, *Dīwān Muḥarram: al-Siyāsiyyāt min ʿĀm 1922 ḥattā ʿĀm 1945*, ed. Maḥmūd Aḥmad Muḥarram (Kuwait: Maktabat al-Falāḥ, n.d.), vol. 1, pt. 2:627.
49. Ibid.
50. T.N.A., F. O. 424/260/no. 60 (E2358/1752/44), March 12, 1924, and T.N.A., F. O. 424/260/no. 73 (E2591/1752/44), March 19, 1924; Sir Ronald Charles Lindsay (born May 3, 1877, and retired on October 17, 1939) was appointed H.M. representative at Constantinople on February 2, 1924, and promoted to be ambassador extraordinary and plenipotentiary there on March 1, 1925, where he served until October 12, 1926, *Foreign Office List* (1940), 327.
51. T.N.A., H. W. 12/56/no. 016165, March 20, 1924.
52. T.N.A., F. O. 424/260/no. 73 (E2591/1752/44), March 19, 1924.
53. Ibid.
54. Finefrock, "From Sultanate to Republic," 191–202; Zürcher, *Political Opposition in the Early Turkish Republic*, 26.
55. T.N.A., F. O. 424/260/no. 60 (E2358/1752/44), March 12, 1924, and T.N.A., F. O. 424/260/no. 73 (E2591/1752/44), March 19, 1924.
56. T.N.A., F. O. 424/260/no. 73 (E2591/1752/44), March 19, 1924.
57. Article published in *Amān-i Afghān*, March 18, 1924, T.N.A., F. O. 371/10218/E4392.
58. T.N.A., F. O. 424/260/No. 52 (E2126/1752/44), March 5, 1924; Sir Nevile Meyrick Henderson (born June 10, 1882, and retired March 1940) served as *chargé d'affaires* in Constantinople from October 14, 1920, until he became acting counsellor on December 16, 1921. On May 1, 1922, he was promoted to be counsellor of the embassy at Constantinople

and served as the acting British high commissioner there during the periods July 1–30, 1922, November 16, 1922–February 12, 1924, and June 5–September 18, 1924, *Foreign Office List* (1941), 274–75. He would later be the British ambassador to the Third Reich.

59. T.N.A., F. O. 424/260/no. 73 (E2591/1752/44), March 19, 2004.
60. T.N.A., F. O. 424/261/no. 20 (E6454/32/44), July 23, 1924.
61. Seçil Akgün, *Halifeliğin Kaldırılması ve Laiklik, 1924–1928* (Ankara: Turhan Kitabevi, 1985), 223; Çetin Özek, *100 Soruda: Türkiyede Gerici Akımlar* (Istanbul: Gerçek Yayınevi, 1968), 80.
62. Ali Fuat Cebesoy, *Siyasi Hatiralar* (Istanbul: Vatan Neşriyatı, 1957), 1:316–17.
63. T.N.A., F. O. 424/261/no. 102 (E11553/32/44), December 17, 1924.
64. Erik-Jan Zürcher, "Review," *International Journal of Middle East Studies* 45, no. 2 (2013), 398.
65. T.N.A., F. O. 424/261/no. 20 (E6454/32/44), July 23, 1924.
66. T.N.A., F. O. 424/261/no. 102 (E11553/32/44), December 17, 1924.
67. T.N.A., AIR 23/406/F2092, December 16, 1924.
68. Ibid.
69. Also see, for example, Lindsay's assessment of the progressive opposition in paragraph five of T.N.A., F. O. 424/261/no. 93 (E10614/32/44), November 24, 1924.
70. Zürcher, Political Opposition in the Early Turkish Republic, 32–52; "Rauf Bey'in Riyasetinde Yeni Bir 'Cumhuriyet' Fırkası," *Tanin,* November 10, 1924; "Terakkiperver Cumhuriyet Fırkası Resmen Teşekkül Etti," *Tanin,* November 18, 1924.
71. *TBMM Zabıt Ceridesi,* Devre II, Cilt 7, Içtima Senesi 1 (March 3, 1340 [1924]), 38–40 (Ottoman script), 35–36 (Latin script); "Maqam-ı Hilafetin İlgası," *Tevhid-i Efkar,* March 4, 1924.
72. Mohammad Iqbal, "The Principle of Movement in the Structure of Islam," in *Six Lectures on the Reconstruction of Religious Thought in Islam* (Lahore, Pak.: Kapur Art Printing Works, 1930), 220; Muhammad Qasim Zaman, "South Asian Islam and the Idea of the Caliphate," in *Demystifying the Caliphate,* ed. Madawi Al-Rasheed, Carool Kersten, and Marat Shterin (NY: Columbia University Press, 2013), 60. In the exact words of Iqbal's wishful reading of the Grand National Assembly's decision, "Turkey's Ijtihad is that according to the spirit of Islam the Caliphate or Imamate can be vested in a body of persons, or an elected Assembly."
73. *TBMM Zabıt Ceridesi,* Devre II, Cilt 7, Içtima Senesi 1 (March 3, 1340 [1924]); "Meclis, Tarihimizde Yeni Bir Fasıl Açan Dört Kanunu da Aynen Kabul Etti," *İkdam,* March 4, 1924.
74. This wording from the nine-point electoral platform is cited in Mete Tunçay, *T. C.'nde Tek-Parti Yönetimi'nin Kurulması, 1923–1931* (Istanbul: Cem Yayınevi, 1992), 355. In the assembly, the minutes record Halit stating, "'Türkiye Büyük Millet Meclisi makam-ı hilafetin istinatgahıdır ve makam-ı hilafet beynel'islam bir makam-ı mualladır,' dedik."
75. Including Mustafa Bey, deputy of Tokat; Çayıroğlu Hilmi Bey, deputy of Ankara; and Ragıp Bey, deputy of Zonguldak.
76. Halit also reiterated his disappointment in the transgression of the People's Party against their avowed principles in an interview given to a local newspaper, *Acıkgöz Gazetesi,* on July 26, 1924. *TBMM Zabıt Ceridesi,* Devre II, Cilt 7, Içtima Senesi 1 (March 3, 1340 [1924]), 38–40 (Ottoman script), 35–36 (Latin script); "Maqam-ı Hilafetin İlgası," *Tevhid-i Efkar,* March 4, 1924; Ziya Göğem, *Kurmay Albay Daday'lı Halit Beğ Akmansu (1884–1953)* (Istanbul: Halk Basımevi, 1954–56), 1:271–72, 2:306; Kadir Mısıroğlu, *Üç Hilâfetçi Şahsiyet* (Istanbul: Sebil Yayınevi, 1995), 294–306; Nomer, *Şeriat, Hilâfet, Cumhuriyet, Laiklik,* 333–34.

77. After his resignation from the People's Party, its members personally stonewalled Halit and refused to even greet him. Göğem, *Kurmay Albay Daday'lı Halit Beğ*, 1:272–73.
78. Kadirbeyoğlu, *Kadirbeyoğlu Zeki Bey'in Hâtıraları*, ed. Ömer Faruk Lermioğlu (Istanbul: Sebil Yayınevi, 2007), 54, 174–97; Uğur Üçüncü, *İkinci Dönem TBMM'de Bir Muhalifin Portresi: Kadirbeyzade Zeki Bey* (Konya, Turk.: Çizgi Kitabevi, 2011), 41–56, 109; Mısıroğlu, *Üç Hilâfetçi Şahsiyet*, 17–144; Alexander Balistreri, "Turkey's Forgotten Political Opposition: The Demise of Kadirbeyoğlu Zeki Bey, 1919–1927," *Die Welt des Islams* 55 (2015): 141–85.
79. *Efendiler biz saltanata düşman değiliz, eşhasa düşmanız. Zira bugünkü günde gördüğüm vaziyet şudur: Cumhuriyet, devam ettiği halde saltanata doğru yürüyor.*
80. *TBMM Zabıt Ceridesi*, Devre II, Cilt 7, Içtima Senesi 1 (March 3, 1340 [1924]), 33–37, 41–44 (Ottoman script), 31–34, 37–40 (Latin script); "Maqam-ı Hilafetin İlgası," *Tevhid-i Efkar*, March 4, 1924; Kadirbeyoğlu, *Kadirbeyoğlu Zeki Bey'in Hâtıraları*, 198–211; Üçüncü, *İkinci Dönem TBMM'de Bir Muhalifin Portresi*, 184–99; Mısıroğlu, *Üç Hilâfetçi Şahsiyet*, 17–144; Nomer, *Şeriat, Hilâfet, Cumhuriyet, Laiklik*, 321–26.
81. Kadirbeyoğlu, *Kadirbeyoğlu Zeki Bey'in Hâtıraları*, 200–262; Üçüncü, *İkinci Dönem TBMM'de Bir Muhalifin Portresi*, 158–67; Mısıroğlu, *Üç Hilâfetçi Şahsiyet*, 17–144.
82. Kemal Öztürk, *İlk Meclis: Belgesel* (Istanbul: Inkılab Yayınları, 1999), 171–72; Finefrock, "From Sultanate to Republic," 327.
83. Rıza Nur, *Hayat ve Hatıratım*, 3:968–72; 4:1282–86.
84. T.N.A., F. O. 424/261/no. 93 (E10614/32/44), November 24, 1924.
85. Finefrock, "From Sultanate to Republic," 205–9.
86. Akgün, *Halifeliğin Kaldırılması*, 225–26; Özek, *100 Soruda*, 80; *Tanin*; T.N.A., F. O. 424/261/no. 20 (E6454/32/44), July 23, 1924. As Gavin Brockett noted in his article "Collective Action and the Turkish Revolution: Towards a Framework for the Social History of the Atatürk Era, 1923–38," *Middle Eastern Studies* 34, no. 4 (1998): 44–66: "British consular reports constitute a particularly revealing source all too often discounted on the grounds that they were written by observers unfamiliar with and unsympathetic to the society they described. Nevertheless, given the paucity of other written records, these documents cannot be ignored; indeed, written by officials stationed in major Anatolian cities and responsible for traveling throughout the country, they present astute observations of Anatolian society in this important period, and frequently provide details and perspectives concerning collective action found nowhere else."
87. Özek, *100 Soruda*, 80; Akgün, *Halifeliğin Kaldırılması*, 225.
88. *al-Akhbār*, May 27, 1924; Fatḥī Aḥmad Shalabī, *al-Azhar wa'l-Khilāfah al-Islāmiyyah fī'l-ʿAsr al-Ḥadīth* (Cairo: n.p., 2003), 244.
89. T.N.A., F. O. 371/10218/E3177, March 27, 1924 (Aleppo, Syria).
90. The revolt broke out in February 1925 and lasted for a few months until it was suppressed.
91. Martin van Bruinessen, "Popular Islam, Kurdish Nationalism and Rural Revolt: The Rebellion of Shaikh Said in Turkey (1925)," in *Mullas, Sufis and Heretics: The Role of Religion in Kurdish Society: Collected Articles* (Istanbul: Isis Press, 2000), 144, 146, 148; Martin van Bruinessen, *Agha, Shaikh and State: The Social and Political Structures of Kurdistan* (London: Zed Books Limited, 1992), 265, 280, 281–82; Robert Olson, *The Emergence of Kurdish Nationalism and the Sheikh Said Rebellion, 1880–1925* (Austin: University of Texas Press, 1989), 41.
92. van Bruinessen, "Popular Islam, Kurdish Nationalism and Rural Revolt," 144.
93. Ibid., 154.

94. Ibid., 148–49; van Bruinessen, *Agha, Shaikh and State*, 282–84, 298; Olson, *The Emergence of Kurdish Nationalism*, 42–47; T.N.A., F. O. 371 (1924): E11093/11093/95; T.N.A., AIR 5/556.
95. van Bruinessen, *Agha, Shaikh and State*, 268–69. Zürcher points out that "Propaganda leaflets and letters found on the rebels made clear both the Kurdish-nationalist aspect (with demands for a Kurdish national government) and the Islamic character (with demands for the restoration of the Caliphate) [of the 1925 rebellion]," *Political Opposition in the Early Turkish Republic*, 81.
96. Robert Olson and William Tucker, "The Shaikh Sait Rebellion in Turkey (1925): A Study in the Consolidation of a Developed Uninstitutionalized Nationalism and the Rise of Incipient (Kurdish) Nationalism," *Die Welt des Islams* 18, no. 3–4 (1978): 200–201. Ergün Aybars also remarks, "Asiler dağıttıkları bildirilerde 'Hilafetsiz müsülmanlık olmaz' diyor," in his *İstiklal Mahkemeleri, 1920–1927* (İzmir, Turk.: Doküz Eylul Üniversitesi Yayınları, 1988), 272.
97. T.N.A., F. O. 424/262/no. 180 (E3541/1091/44), June 9, 1925.
98. Olson, *The Emergence of Kurdish Nationalism*, 108–27; van Bruinessen, *Agha, Shaikh and State*, 289–91; van Bruinessen, "Popular Islam, Kurdish Nationalism and Rural Revolt," 143, 152; Olson and Tucker, "The Shaikh Sait Rebellion in Turkey (1925)," 204–5; Tunçay, *T. C.'nde Tek-Parti Yönetimi'nin Kurulması*, 128, 136; Aybars, *İstiklal Mahkemeleri*, 282–85.
99. Zürcher, *Political Opposition in the Early Turkish Republic*, 80–81; Olson, *The Emergence of Kurdish Nationalism*, 123–24; van Bruinessen, *Agha, Shaikh and State*, 290; Olson and Tucker, "The Shaikh Sait Rebellion in Turkey (1925)," 203; Tunçay, *T. C.'nde Tek-Parti i Yönetimi'nin Kurulması*, 135; Aybars, *İstiklal Mahkemeleri*, 271–73.
100. Olson, *The Emergence of Kurdish Nationalism*, 108–27; van Bruinessen, *Agha, Shaikh and State*, 289–91; van Bruinessen, "Popular Islam, Kurdish Nationalism and Rural Revolt," 143, 152; Olson and Tucker, "The Shaikh Sait Rebellion in Turkey (1925)," 204–5; Aybars, *İstiklal Mahkemeleri*, 282–327.
101. Olson, *The Emergence of Kurdish Nationalism*, 126.
102. Zürcher, *Political Opposition in the Early Turkish Republic*, 81–86; Olson, *The Emergence of Kurdish Nationalism*, 124; Zürcher, *The Unionist Factor*, 140; van Bruinessen, "Popular Islam, Kurdish Nationalism and Rural Revolt," 143; Olson and Tucker, "The Shaikh Sait Rebellion in Turkey (1925)," 203–4; Tunçay, *T. C.'nde Tek-Parti Yönetimi'nin Kurulması*, 137–42; Mete Tunçay, *Türkiye'de Sol Akımlar, 1908–1925* (Ankara: Ankara Üniversitesi—Siyasal Bilgiler Fakültesi Yayınları, 1967), 187–88; Aybars, *İstiklal Mahkemeleri*, 273–80.
103. Zürcher, *Political Opposition in the Early Turkish Republic*, 86–87, 88; Zürcher, *The Unionist Factor*, 140–41; Tunçay, *T. C.'nde Tek-Parti Yönetimi'nin Kurulması*, 142–46; Tunçay, *Türkiye'de Sol Akımlar*, 188; Aybars, *İstiklal Mahkemeleri*, 280, 331–37, 366–76; Olson and Tucker, "The Shaikh Sait Rebellion in Turkey (1925)," 204.
104. Tunçay, *Türkiye'de Sol Akımlar*, 189–90; Zürcher, *Political Opposition in the Early Turkish Republic*, 87; Aybars, *İstiklal Mahkemeleri*, 385–91.
105. Zürcher, *Political Opposition in the Early Turkish Republic*, 90–91; Olson and Tucker, "The Shaikh Sait Rebellion in Turkey (1925)," 206–9; Tunçay, *T. C.'nde Tek-Parti Yönetimi'nin Kurulması*, 146–49; Aybars, *İstiklal Mahkemeleri*, 301–4, 358–66; T.N.A., F. O. 371/262/no. 180 (E3541/1091/44), June 9, 1925.
106. T.N.A., F. O. 424/262/no. 138 (E2076/194/44), March 31, 1925.
107. Zürcher, *Political Opposition in the Early Turkish Republic*, 91–94; Zürcher, *The Unionist Factor*, 141–62; Zürcher, *Turkey*, 174, Aybars, *İstiklal Mahkemeleri*, 423–70.

108. See Hasan Kayali, *Arabs and Young Turks: Ottomanism, Arabism, and Islamism in the Ottoman Empire, 1908–1918* (Berkeley: University of California Press), 1997.
109. "al-Yawm al-Tārīkhī al-Mashhūd fī'l-ʿĀṣimah: Inʿiqād al-Bayʿah li-Ṣāḥib al-Jalālah al-Hāshimiyyah," *al-Qiblah,* March 6, 1924; Niḍāl Dāwūd al-Muʾminī, *al-Sharīf al-Ḥusayn ibn ʿAlī wa'l-Khilāfah* (Amman, Jord.: Manshūrāt Lajnat Tārīkh al-Urdun, 1996), 185–96, 209–22, 234–49; T.N.A., F. O. 686/71/no. 8, p. 112, March 5, 1924; T.N.A., F. O. 371/10217/E2308, March 5, 1924.
110. Joshua Teitelbaum, "Sharif Husayn ibn Ali and the Hashemite Vision of the Post-Ottoman Order: From Chieftaincy to Suzerainty," *Middle Eastern Studies* 34, no. 1 (January 1998): 103–22; Timothy Paris, *Britain, the Hashemites and Arab Rule, 1920–1925* (London: Frank Cass, 2003), 321–24, 342–46. For Sharīf Ḥusayn's interactions with the French from 1914 to 1917, also see Dan Eldar, "French Policy towards Husayn, Sharif of Mecca," *Middle Eastern Studies* 26, no. 3, (1990): 329–50.
111. Interview with Sharīf Hussein in the camp at Shūnah in Transjordan, published in the *Manchester Guardian* on March 13, 1924, T.N.A., F. O. 371/10217/E2286.
112. "al-Yawm al-Tārīkhī al-Mashhūd fī'l-ʿĀṣimah," *al-Qiblah,* March 6, 1924.
113. T.N.A., F. O. 371/10217/E2157, March 8, 1924; T.N.A., F. O. 371/10217/E2285, March 11, 1924.
114. In striking contrast with *al-Qiblah*'s assertion, the British director of criminal intelligence in Singapore noted on July 11, 1924, that "the feeling here and in Penang [from where the students originated] and Malacca is against King Hussein and we know of certain people recently returned from the pilgrimage who have been spreading anti-Hussein propaganda." T.N.A., F. O. 686/71/no. 37, pp. 92–95, April 16, 1924; T.N.A., F. O. 371/10218/E3934, April 16, 1924; T.N.A., F. O. 686/71/no. 39, pp. 52–55, April 22, 1924; T.N.A., F. O. 371/10218/E4375, April 22, 1924; T.N.A., F. O. 686/71/no. 129, pp. 19–22, 24–25, April 30–July 16, 1924; T.N.A., F. O. 686/71/F3145, pp. 8–10, June 30, 1924.
115. van Bruinessen, "Muslims of the Dutch East Indies and the Caliphate Question," 270; Deliar Noer, *The Modernist Muslim Movement in Indonesia, 1900–1942* (Oxford: Oxford University Press, 1973), 299; William Clarence-Smith, "The Hadrami *Sada* and the Evolution of an Islamic Religious International, c. 1750s to 1930s," in *Religious Internationals in the Modern World: Globalization and Faith Communities since 1750*, ed. Abigail Green and Vincent Viaene (NY: Palgrave Macmillan, 2012), 244–45.
116. Minault, *The Khilafat Movement,* 206–7; Qureshi, *Pan-Islam in British Indian Politics,* 380–81.
117. See Suleiman Mousa, "A Matter of Principle: King Hussein of the Hijaz and the Arabs of Palestine," *International Journal of Middle East Studies* 9, no. 2 (April 1978): 183–94.
118. Muhammad Muslih, "The Rise of Local Nationalism in the Arab East," in *The Origins of Arab Nationalism,* ed. Rashid Khalidi, et al. (NY: Columbia University Press, 1991), 171; Mary C. Wilson, "The Hashemites, the Arab Revolt, and Arab Nationalism," in *The Origins of Arab Nationalism,* ed. Rashid Khalidi, et al. (NY: Columbia University Press, 1991), 214–15, 217.
119. Wilson, "The Hashemites," 218–19.
120. Finbarr Barry Flood, *The Great Mosque of Damascus: Studies on the Making of an Umayyad Visual Culture* (Leiden, Neth.: E. J. Brill, 2001).
121. "al-Mubāyaʿah bi'l-Khilāfah," *Filasṭīn,* March 14, 1924; "Inʿiqād al-Bayʿah al-ʿĀmmah bi'l-Imāmah al-Kubrā li-Ṣāḥib al-Jalālah al-Hāshimiyyah Amīr al-Muʾminīn," *al-Qiblah,* March 13, 1924; "Mubāyaʿat Kāffat al-Aqṭār al-Sūriyyah bi'l-Khilāfah," *al-Qiblah,* March 17, 1924; "al-Khalīfah al-ʿArabī," *Alif Bāʾ*, March 8, 1924, T.N.A., F. O. 684/2/File 111,

pp. 4–7, March 10, 1924; T.N.A., F. O. 684/2/File 111, p. 3, March 7, 1924; T.N.A., F. O. 371/10217/E2106, March 7, 1924; T.N.A., F. O. 371/10217/E2663, March 10, 1924; al-Mu'minī, *al-Sharīf al-Ḥusayn*, 249–52.

122. *Fatā al-'Arab*, March 14, 1924, T.N.A., F. O. 684/2/File 111, p. 13–16, March 15, 1924. Ma'rūf al-Arna'ūt established *Fatā al-'Arab* in Damascus on February 18, 1920; Ṭarrāzī, *Tārīkh al-Ṣiḥāfah al-'Arabiyyah*, 4:46–47. I regret that I was unable to consult the periodical collections of al-Assad National Library and other local repositories following the outbreak of hostilities in Syria.

123. "al-Mubāya'ah bi'l-Khilāfah," *Filasṭīn*, March 14, 1924; "Mubāya'at Kāffat al-Aqṭār al-Sūriyyah bi'l-Khilāfah," *al-Qiblah*, March 17, 1924.

124. Yasser Tabbaa, "Survivals and Archaisms in the Architecture of Northern Syria, ca. 1080–ca. 1150," *Muqarnas* 10 (1993): 29–41.

125. "Mubāya'at Kāffat al-Aqṭār al-Sūriyyah bi'l-Khilāfah," *al-Qiblah*, March 17, 1924; T.N.A., F. O. 371/10217/E2213, March 11, 1924; T.N.A., F. O. 371/10217/E2660, March 11, 1924.

126. "al-Mubāya'ah bi'l-Khilāfah," *Filasṭīn*, March 14, 1924; "al-Amīr Sa'īd al-Jazā'irī, 1883–1966," *Sūriyyatunā* 1, no. 46 (2012): 16–17; T.N.A., F. O. 371/10217/E2131, March 9, 1924; T.N.A., F. O. 371/10217/E2655, March 13, 1924. Sa'īd al-Jazā'irī later decried these pledges of allegianc to Sharīf Ḥusayn as caliph and formed an association called *Jam'iyyat al-Khilāfah al-Islāmiyyah* in Damascus, with branches in Aleppo and Beirut, to coordinate the proper restoration of an Islamic caliphate, in communication with Muslims in Egypt and India; "Jam'iyyat al-Khilāfah al-Sūriyyah," *al-Balāgh*, April 2, 1924, and "Ḥawl Mas'alat al-Khilāfah," *al-Balāgh*, April 8, 1924.

127. *al-Zahrah* 3, no. 17–18 (March 1924): 399–402; "al-Mubāya'ah bi'l-Khilāfah," *Filasṭīn*, March 14, 1924; "In'iqād al-Bay'ah al-'Āmmah," *al-Qiblah*, March 13, 1924; al-Mu'minī, *al-Sharīf al-Ḥusayn*, 224–26; T.N.A., F. O. 371/10217/E2217, March 10, 1924; T.N.A., F. O. 371/10217/E2276, March 13, 1924; T.N.A., F. O. 371/10217/E2310, March 13, 1924; T.N.A., F. O. 684/2/File 111, p. 9, March 10, 1924; T.N.A., F. O. 684/2/File 111, p. 10, March 13, 1924; T.N.A., F. O. 684/2/File 111, p. 25, March 14, 1924. On March 15, 1924, a delegation from Nablus set off to Shūnah to recognize Sharīf Ḥusayn's caliphate along with the rest of Palestine, see T.N.A., F. O. 684/2/File 111, p. 26. *Filasṭīn* also reproduces the telegraph pledge of allegiance sent by Palestinian students of law at the Syrian University in Damascus on the second page of its March 21, 1924 issue.

128. Ḥannā al-Baḥrī, "Li-takun Fardiyyah: al-Jināyah al-Faẓī'ah allatī Tammat bi'stishhād al-Maghfūr lahu al-Marḥūm al-Ustādh Jamīl al-Baḥrī, Aḥad Ṣāhibay al-Maktabah al-Waṭanaiyyah wa-Jarīdat al-Zuhūr wa-Majallat wa-Maṭba'at al-Zahrah," *al-Zuhūr*, September 22, 1930. On the fallout from al-Baḥrī's unfortunate murder, see Noah Haiduc-Dale, *Arab Christians in British Mandate Palestine: Communalism and Nationalism, 1917–1948* (Edinburgh: Edinburgh University Press, 2012), 103–9. On al-Baḥrī's literary stature and contributions, see Salma Khadra Jayyusi, ed., *Anthology of Modern Palestinian Literature* (NY: Columbia University Press, 1992), 12, 74.

129. *al-Zahrah* 3, nos. 17–18 (March 1924): front matter–406. al-Baḥrī established *al-Zahrah* in Haifa on May 1, 1922; Ṭarrāzī, *Tārīkh al-Ṣiḥāfah al-'Arabiyyah*, 4:140–41.

130. Rashid Khalidi, *The Iron Cage: The Story of the Palestinian Struggle for Statehood* (Boston: Beacon Press, 2006), 90–104; Salim Tamari, "Issa al Issa's Unorthodox Orthodoxy: Banned in Jerusalem, Permitted in Jaffa," *Jerusalem Quarterly* 59 (2014): 16–36; Ṭarrāzī, *Tārīkh al-Ṣiḥāfah al-'Arabiyyah*, 4:70–71; Muḥammad Sulaymān, *Tārīkh al-Ṣiḥāfah al-Filisṭīniyyah 1876–1976* (Athens: Bisan Press, 1987), 1:83–87. al-'Īsā founded *Filasṭīn* in Jaffa on January 14, 1911, with his cousin Yūsuf al-'Īsā (d. 1948), who in 1918 moved to Damascus where he established another prominent newspaper, *Alif Bā'*, in 1920.

131. Ruba Kana'an, "Waqf, Architecture, and Political Self-Fashioning: The Construction of the Great Mosque of Jaffa by Muhammad Aga Abu Nabbut," *Muqarnas* 18 (2001): 120–40.
132. "Akhbār Maḥalliyyah," *Filasṭīn,* March 11, 1924.
133. "Ilghā' al-Khilāfah fī Turkiyyā wa-Ta'thīruh," *Filasṭīn,* March 7, 1924; "Akhbār Maḥalliyyah," *Filasṭīn,* March 11, 1924.
134. "Wafd Jalālat al-Malik fī'l-Majdal," *Filistīn,* April 1, 1924.
135. T.N.A., F. O. 371/10217/E2655, March 13, 1924; Ṭarrāzī, *Tārīkh al-Ṣiḥāfah al-'Arabiyyah,* 4:10–11. Aḥmad 'Abbās al-Azharī established *al-Ḥaqīqah* in Beirut on February 6, 1909, and the British consul notes that "a perquisition was actually made at the house of [the newspaper owner] Abbas Kemal, who is an Egyptian subject."
136. T.N.A., F. O. 371/10217/E2738, March 15, 1924; T.N.A., F. O. 684/2/File 111, pp. 11–15, March 15, 1924; T.N.A., F. O. 371/10218/E2994, March 22, 1924; T.N.A., F. O. 684/2/File 111, pp. 20–22, March 22, 1924; T.N.A., F. O. 371/10218/E3174, March 15, 1924; T.N.A., F. O. 371/10218/E3422, March 31, 1924; T.N.A., F. O. 371/10218/E4030, April, 22, 1924; T.N.A., F. O. 684/2/File 111, pp. 31–32, April 22, 1924.
137. T.N.A., F. O. 371/10218/E3174, March 15, 1924.
138. T.N.A., F. O. 371/10218/E3185, March 27, 1924; T.N.A., F. O. 371/10218/E3647, April 12, 1924.
139. T.N.A., F. O. 371/10217/E2738, March 15, 1924; T.N.A., F. O. 684/2/File 111, pp. 11–15, March 15, 1924.
140. T.N.A., F. O. 371/10218/E2994, March 22, 1924; T.N.A., F. O. 684/2/File 111, pp. 20–22, March 22, 1924.
141. "Ḥaqqī al-'Aẓm wa'l-Khilāfah," *Filasṭīn,* March 21, 1924; 'Abd al-Qadīr's speech was published in a description of "The Silent Protest" in the Damascene newspaper *'Umrān* on March 22, 1924, and translated in T.N.A., F. O. 684/2/File 111, pp. 20–22, March 22, 1924; T.N.A., F. O. 371/10217/E2738, March 15, 1924; T.N.A., F. O. 684/2/File 111, pp. 11–15, March 15, 1924; T.N.A., F. O. 371/10218/E2994, March 22, 1924; al-Mu'minī, *al-Sharīf al-Ḥusayn,* 256–58. Ilyās Kūzmā and Qiblān al-Riyāshī established *'Umrān* in Damascus on October 20, 1920; Ṭarrāzī, *Tārīkh al-Ṣiḥāfah al-'Arabiyyah,* 4:48–49.
142. Ibid.; T.N.A., F. O. 371/10218/E4030, April, 22, 1924; T.N.A., F. O. 684/2/File 111, pp. 31–32, April 22, 1924.
143. T.N.A., F. O. 371/10218/E2994, March 22, 1924; T.N.A., F. O. 684/2/File 111, pp. 20–22, March 22, 1924.
144. Ibid.; T.N.A., F. O. 371/10218/E3185, March 27, 1924; al-Mu'minī, *al-Sharīf al-Ḥusayn,* 258.
145. T.N.A., F. O. 424/260/no. 55, March 12, 1924; T.N.A., F. O. 371/10217/E2298, March 12, 1924.
146. T.N.A., F. O. 371/10217/E2157 March 8, 1924; T.N.A., F. O. 371/10217/E2188, March 11, 1924.
147. T.N.A., F. O. 371/10217/E2205, March 11, 1924.
148. T.N.A., F. O. 371/10217/E2275, March 13, 1924.
149. T.N.A., F. O. 371/10217/E2488, March 20, 1924; T.N.A., F. O. 371/10218/E3038, April 1, 1924; T.N.A., F. O. 371/10218/E3629, March 17, 1924.
150. T.N.A., F. O. 371/10217/E2308, March 13, 1924; T.N.A., F. O. 371/10217/E2382, March 17, 1924; T.N.A., F. O. 371/10217/E2722, March 22, 1924.
151. T.N.A., F. O. E2097/2097/91, March 13, 1924; T.N.A., F. O. 371/10217/E2395, March 19, 1924; T.N.A., F. O. 371/10217/E2722, March 22, 1924; "Obituary: Dr. Naji al-Aṣil," *Iraq* 25, no. 2 (1963): ii–vi.

152. T.N.A., F. O. 371/10218/E2760, March 17, 1924; T.N.A., F. O. 371/10218/E3020, March 22, 1924; T.N.A., F. O. 371/10218/E3175, March 15, 1924; T.N.A., F. O. 371/10218/E3180, March 27, 1924; T.N.A., F. O. 371/10217/E2736, March 27, 1924.
153. T.N.A., F. O. 371/10218/E2760, March 17, 1924; *al-Taqaddum* was established by Shukrī Kanaydir in Aleppo on October 15, 1908, then again on May 21, 1909, by the Kanaydir brothers; Ṭarrāzī, *Tārīkh al-Ṣiḥāfah al-ʿArabiyyah,* 4:54–55.
154. T.N.A., F. O. 371/10218/E3020, March 22, 1924.
155. T.N.A., F. O. 371/10218/E3175, March 15, 1924.
156. T.N.A., F. O. 371/10218/E3422, March 31, 1924.
157. T.N.A., F. O. 371/10217/E2213, March 11, 1924; T.N.A., F. O. 371/10110/E4212, May 13, 1924; T.N.A., F. O. 371/11475/E3123, May 20, 1926; T.N.A., F. O. 371/11475/E3586, June 9, 1926.
158. *al-Muqtabas,* May 22, 1924, T.N.A., F. O. 684/2/File 111, pp. 37–38, May 23, 1924; T.N.A., F. O. 371/10218/E2898, March 17, 1924; T.N.A., F. O. 371/10218/E4913, May 23, 1924; T.N.A., AIR 23/406/2400, March 20, 1925.
159. *al-Muqaṭṭam,* May 10, 1924, T.N.A., F. O. 684/2/File 111, pp. 35–36, May 17, 1924.
160. T.N.A., F. O. 686/71, p. 2, October 27, 1924; T.N.A., F. O. 686/71, p. 11, October 21, 1924; T.N.A., F. O. 686/71, p. 12, October 23, 1924; T.N.A., F. O. 686/71, pp. 235–37, December 18, 1924; T.N.A., F. O. 684/2/File 111, pp. 2–3, March 7, 1924; T.N.A., F. O. 684/2/File 111, pp. 2–3, March 10, 1924.
161. T.N.A., F. O. 371/10186/E2511, March 21, 1924. For reactions in the French press to the Ottoman Caliphate's abolition see Jean-Louis Bacqué-Grammont, "Regards des autorités françaises et de l'opinion parisienne sur le califat d'Abdülmecid Efendi," *Les Annales de L'Autre Islam,* no. 2 (1994): 325–27 and Jean-Louis Bacqué-Grammont, "L'Abolition du califat vue par la presse quotidienne de Paris en Mars 1924," *Revue des études islamiques* 50 (1982): 208–48. For a longer trajectory of French ruminations over the caliphate, see Wajīh al-Kawtharānī, "Masʾalat al-Khilāfah fī'l-Siyāsāt al-Dawliyyah wa'l-Afkār al-Maḥalliyyah," in *al-ʿAlāqāt al-Dawliyyah bayn al-Uṣūl al-Islāmiyyah wa-bayn Khibrat al-Tārīkh al-Islāmī,* ed. Nādiyah Maḥmūd Muṣṭafā and Sayf al-Dīn ʿAbd al-Fattāḥ (Cairo: Jāmiʿat al-Qāhirah, Kulliyyat al-Iqtiṣād wa'l-ʿUlūm al-Siyāsiyyah, Markaz al-Buḥūth wa'l-Dirāsāt al-Siyāsiyyah, 2000), 2:897–918 and Henry Laurens, "France et le califat," *Turcica* 31 (1999): 149–83.
162. D.W.Q., *Maḥāfiẓ ʿĀbidīn* #357, telegraphs dated March 4 and March 8, 1924, letter dated March 7, 1924; Fatḥī Aḥmad Shalabī, *al-Azhar wa'l-Khilāfah al-Islāmiyyah fī'l-ʿAṣr al-Ḥadīth,* 72–73, 192; T.N.A., F. O. 371/10217/E2038, March 6, 1924; T.N.A., F. O. 371/10218/E4392, April 21, 1924; T.N.A., F. O. 371/10110/E4212, May 13, 1924; T.N.A., F. O. 371/11475/E3123, May 20, 1926; T.N.A., F. O. 371/11475/E3586, June 9, 1926.
163. D.W.Q., *Maḥāfiẓ ʿĀbidīn* #357, letter dated March 7, 1924; Shalabī, *al-Azhar wa'l-Khilāfah,* 72; T.N.A., F. O. 371/10217/E2038, March 6, 1924; T.N.A., F. O. 371/10218/E3192, March 12, 1924; T.N.A., F. O. 371/10218/E4392, April 21, 1924; T.N.A., F. O. 371/11475/E3123, May 20, 1926; T.N.A., F. O. 371/11475/E3586, June 9, 1926.
164. Shalabī, *al-Azhar wa'l-Khilāfah,* 79; T.N.A., F. O. 371/10217/E2038, March 6, 1924; T.N.A., F. O. 371/10218/E4392, April 21, 1924; T.N.A., F. O. 371/11475/E3123, May 20, 1926; T.N.A., F. O. 371/11475/E3586, June 9, 1926.
165. Shalabī, *al-Azhar wa'l-Khilāfah,* 147; T.N.A., F. O. 686/71, p. 2, October 27, 1924; T.N.A., F. O. 686/71, p. 11; T.N.A., F. O. 686/71, October 21, p. 12, October 21, 1924; T.N.A., F. O. 686/71, p. 11, October 23, 1924; T.N.A., F. O. 686/71, pp. 235–37, December 18, 1924; T.N.A., F. O. 684/2/no. 22, pp. 2–4, November 27, 1924; T.N.A., F. O. 371/11475/E3123,

May 20, 1926; T.N.A., F. O. 371/11475/E3586, June 9, 1926; T.N.A., F. O. 371/11433/E2219, March 26, 1926; T.N.A., F. O. 371/11476/E3179, May 25, 1926.

166. Shalabī, *al-Azhar wa'l-Khilāfah*, 72; T.N.A., F. O. 371/10217/E2038, March 6, 1924; T.N.A., F. O. 371/11920/W8257, August 26, 1926.

167. Qureshi, *Pan-Islam in British Indian Politics*, 382.

168. Shalabī, *al-Azhar wa'l-Khilāfah*, 149; Finefrock, "From Sultanate to Republic"; Claudia Gazzini, "Jihad in Exile: Ahmad al-Sharif al-Sanusi 1918–1933" (Master's thesis, Princeton University, 2004), 78–89; T.N.A., F. O. 371/10217/E2038, March 6, 1924; T.N.A., F. O. 371/10218/E4392, April 21, 1924; T.N.A., F. O. 371/11433/E2219, March 26, 1926.

169. T.N.A., F. O. 371/10218/E4392, April 21, 1924.

170. Özcan, *Pan-Islamism*, 204; Qureshi, *Pan-Islam in British Indian Politics*, 383; Öke, *Hilafet Hareketi*, 122; T.N.A., AIR 23/406/F2019, October 7, 1924; T.N.A., AIR 23/406/F2121, October 14, 1924; T.N.A., AIR 23/406/F2143, February 3, 1925; T.N.A., F. O. 371/10110/E3657, April 30, 1924.

171. T.N.A., F. O. 371/10218/E3791, March 27, 1924.

172. T.N.A., F. O. 174/303/77, Box 303, March 15, 1924.

CHAPTER 5. IN INTERNATIONAL PURSUIT OF A CALIPHATE

1. D.W.Q., *Maḥāfiẓ ʿĀbidīn* #357, "The Conspiracy of the Kemalists against Islam."

2. Salih Keramet Nigar, *Halife İkinci Abdülmecid: yurdundan nasıl sürüldü, sonra nerelerde yaşadı, ne zaman ve nerede öldü, ne zaman ve nerede gömüldü?* (Istanbul: İnkılap ve Aka Kitabevleri, 1964), 10–19; O. Gazi Aşiroğlu, *Son Halife Abdülmecid* (Istanbul: Burak Yayınevi, 1992), 91–95; Murat Bardakçı, "Hanedan Yayınları ve Halife Abdülmecid'in 'Yeşil Kitab'ı," *Müteferrika*, no. 3 (Summer 1994): 55–57; T.N.A., F. O. 371/10217/E2265, March 13, 1924; T.N.A., F. O. 371/10218/E5236, June 14, 1924; *al-Ahrām*, March 10, 1924; "Nidāʾ Jalālat al-Khalīfah ʿAbdulmajīd Khān ilā al-ʿĀlam al-Islāmī," *al-Siyāsah*, March 13, 1924; "Manshūr al-Khalīfah li'l-ʿĀlam al-Islāmī," *al-Akhbār*, March 17, 1924.

3. Murat Bardakçı, "Hanedan Yayınları," 57; T.N.A., F. O. 371/10217/E2265, March 13, 1924.

4. Sebastian Conrad and Dominic Sachsenmaier, eds., *Competing Visions of World Order: Global Moments and Movements, 1880s–1930s* (Basingstoke, UK: Palgrave Macmillan, 2007), 3–16; Akira Iriye, *Global Community: The Role of International Organizations in the Making of the Contemporary World* (Berkeley: University of California Press, 2002), 11, 16–17, 22, 27–28; Akira Iriye, *Cultural Internationalism and World Order* (Baltimore: John Hopkins University Press, 1997), 54–89; James Gelvin and Nile Green, eds., *Global Muslims in the Age of Steam and Print* (Berkeley: University of California Press, 2014), 1–22; Lisa Moses Leff, *Sacred Bonds of Solidarity: The Rise of Jewish Internationalism in Nineteenth-Century France* (Stanford, CA: Stanford University Press, 2006), 236; Malachi Hacohen, *Jacob and Esau: Jewish European History between Empire and Nation* (Cambridge: Cambridge University Press, forthcoming); Guiliana Chamedes, "The Vatican and the Reshaping of the European International Order after World War I," *Historical Journal* (December 2013): 957, 964; Cemil Aydin, *The Politics of Anti-Westernism in Asia: Visions of World Order in Pan-Islamic and Pan-Asian Thought* (NY: Columbia University, 2007), 11–12, 127–60.

5. The Indian Khilafat Committee was also reputed to have communicated with Syrian nationalists regarding their hasty allegiance to King Ḥusayn as caliph. This correspondence, in combination with the instigation of French and Turkish agents against King Ḥusayn and in favor of an Islamic congress instead, was supposed to have inspired a

growing movement in Syria and Palestine in favor of an Islamic congress to settle the question. King Ḥusayn's candidacy for the caliphate was also undermined by his inability to achieve Palestinian independence. T.N.A., F. O. 371/10110/E3657, April 30, 1924; T.N.A., F. O. 371/11475/E3123, May 20, 1926; T.N.A., F. O. 371/11475/E3586, June 9, 1926.

6. *Amān-i Afghān*, March 18, 1924, in T.N.A., F. O. 371/10218/E4392, May 19, 1924.
7. Shalabī, *al-Azhar wa'l-Khilāfah*, 144; *al-Niẓām*, March 9, 1924.
8. Ṭāriq al-Bishrī, *al-Muslimūna wa'l-Aqbāṭ fī Iṭār al-Jamā'ah al-Waṭaniyyah* (Cairo: Dār al-Shurūq, 1988), 303; Shalabī, *al-Azhar wa'l-Khilāfah*, 145–46, 155–56; *al-Akhbār*, March 16, 1924, March 22, 1924; *al-Ahrām*, March 17, 1924. A descendant of Mehmed 'Alī on both sides of his family, Prince 'Umar Ṭūṣūn published in French as Omar Toussoun.
9. T.N.A., F. O. 424/57/no. 297, May 15, 1926; al-Bishrī, *al-Muslimūna wa'l-Aqbāṭ*, 303–4; Shalabī, *al-Azhar wa'l-Khilāfah*, 143–44, 147–48, 158–59, 171–72; "Mas'alat al-Khilāfah," *al-Balāgh*, April 14, 1924 .
10. Shalabī, *al-Azhar wa'l-Khilāfah*, 77–78; *al-Akhbār*, March 13, 1924.
11. Shalabī, *al-Azhar wa'l-Khilāfah*, 78; *al-Akhbār*, March 16, 1924.
12. al-Bishrī, *al-Muslimūna wa'l-Aqbāṭ*, 282; Shalabī, *al-Azhar wa'l-Khilāfah*, 80–81; *al-Siyāsah*, March 21, 1924; *al-Ahrām*, March 21, 1924; *al-Akhbār*, March 23, 1924.
13. "Qarār al-Hay'ah al-'Ilmiyyah al-Dīniyyah al-Islāmiyyah al-Kubrā bi'l-Diyār al-Miṣriyyah fī Sha'n al-Khilāfah," *Majallat al-Mu'tamar al-Islāmī al-'Āmm li'l-Khilāfah bi-Miṣr* 1 (October 1924): 20; al-Bishrī, *al-Muslimūna wa'l-Aqbāṭ*, 282–83; Shalabī, *al-Azhar wa'l-Khilāfah*, 82–83.
14. "Qarār al-Hay'ah al-'Ilmiyyah al-Dīniyyah al-Islāmiyyah al-Kubrā," *Majallat al-Mu'tamar al-Islāmī*, 21–23; "al-Khilāfah wa'l-Mu'tamar al-Islamī: Qarār Kibār al-'Ulamā' al-Rasmiyyīn fi'l-Qāhirah," *al-Manar* 25, no. 5 (Dhu'l-Qa'dah 29, 1342 / July 2, 1924): 367–70.
15. D.W.Q., The New Secret Archives from 1918–1939, *Maḥfaẓah* 1524, *Milaff* 1/2/24. In addition, when Abdülmecid's aide de camp Salih Keramet (Nigar) beseeched the Egyptian government to save his master from the dire fate of penury while in exile, financial aid was not forthcoming. See "Taqrīr 'an Ḥālat al-Khalīfah al-Sābiq 'Abd al-Majīd," D.W.Q., *Maḥāfiẓ 'Ābidīn* #357, *Tābi' Awrāq al-Khilāfah al-Islāmiyyah*, Memoranda from the Légation Royale d'Egypte à Paris, March–May, 1924.
16. Here, 'Izzat Pasha seems to overlook the British occupation of Istanbul from 1918 to 1923.
17. D.W.Q., *Maḥāfiẓ 'Ābidīn* #357, *al-Malik wa'l-Khilāfah: Dūsiyat al-'Arā'iḍ al-Marfū'ah bi-Mubāya'at Ḥaḍrat Ṣāḥib al-Jalālah al-Malik bi'l-Khilāfah al-Islāmiyyah, Māris 1924*, Letter from the Légation Royale d'Egypte à Londres, March 7, 1924.
18. Ibid.
19. Secret British documents also indicate that, immediately after the caliphate's abolition, "a Cabinet meeting was held on 4th March and it was decided that Egypt should summon a Muslim congress—King Fuad's claims to the Caliphate were favourably discussed." T.N.A., F. O. 371/10110/E3657, April 30, 1924.
20. al-Bishrī, *al-Muslimūna wa'l-Aqbāṭ*, 303, 304; Shalabī, *al-Azhar wa'l-Khilāfah*, 143, 146–47; *al-Niẓām*, March 28, 1924; T.N.A., F. O. 424/57/no. 296, May 15, 1926; T.N.A., F. O. 424/57/no. 297, May 15, 1926; T.N.A., F. O. 371/11476/E3178, May 25, 1926; T.N.A., F. O. 371/11476/E3179, May 25, 1926.
21. al-Bishrī, *al-Muslimūna wa'l-Aqbāṭ*, 304; Shalabī, *al-Azhar wa'l-Khilāfah*, 155, 165; *al-Akhbār*, April 14, 1924, May 19, 1924, May 21, 1924; T.N.A., F. O. 424/57/no. 296, May 15, 1926; T.N.A., F. O. 424/57/no. 297, May 15, 1926; T.N.A., F. O. 371/11476/E3178, May

25, 1926; T.N.A., F. O. 371/11476/E3179, May 25, 1926; "Mas'alat al-Khilāfah," *al-Balāgh*, April 14, 1924; "Mas'alat al-Khilāfah: Shubuhāt," *al-Balāgh*, April 16, 1924; "Ḥawl Mas'alat al-Khilāfah," *al-Balāgh*, April 25, 1924; "Mas'alat al-Khilāfah wa-Sumuww al-Amīr 'Umar Ṭūsūn," *al-Balāgh*, May 10, 1924.

22. al-Bishrī, *al-Muslimūna wa'l-Aqbāṭ*, 304; Shalabī, *al-Azhar wa'l-Khilāfah*, 155.
23. T.N.A., F. O. 424/57/no. 296, May 15, 1926; T.N.A., F. O. 371/11476/E3178, May 25, 1926.
24. For instance, the response of the Indian delegation mentioned in Shalabī, *al-Azhar wa'l-Khilāfah*, 150–51; al-Bishrī, *al-Muslimūna wa'l-Aqbāṭ*, 304.
25. A. L., 7780 *Tārīkh* 76421, file no. 33, January 27, 1924; A. L., 7780 *Tārīkh* 76421, file no. 37, October 4, 1924; A. L., 7780 *Tārīkh* 76421, file no. 41, October 11, 1924; A. L., 7780 *Tārīkh* 76421, file no. 43, n.d.; A. L., 7780 *Tārīkh* 76421, file no. 48, November 1, 1924; A. L., 7780 *Tārīkh* 76421, file no. 68, November 23, 1924; A. L., 7780 *Tārīkh* 76421, file no. 88, January 25, 1925; A. L., 7780 *Tārīkh* 76421, file no. 99, April 21, 1925.
26. A. L., 7780 *Tārīkh* 76421, file no. 34, September 27, 1924; A. L., 7780 *Tārīkh* 76421, file no. 37, October 4, 1924; A. L., 7780 *Tārīkh* 76421, file no. 41, October 11, 1924; A. L., 7780 *Tārīkh* 76421, file no. 43, n.d.; A. L., 7780 *Tārīkh* 76421, file no. 48, November 1, 1924; A. L., 7780 *Tārīkh* 76421, file no. 68, November 23, 1924; A. L., 7780 *Tārīkh* 76421, file no. 88, January 25, 1925; A. L., 7780 *Tārīkh* 76421, file no. 99, April 21, 1925.
27. A. L., 7780 *Tārīkh* 76421, file no. 99, April 21, 1925. Muhammad Arshad Gamiet's earlier work with the South African Malay Association, which he established in 1909, "with the aim of furthering educational and social advancement of the Muslims of Cape Town" is discussed in Ebrahim Mahomed Mahida, *History of Muslims in South Africa: A Chronology* (Durban-Westvilieday: South African History Online, 1993) at http://www.sahistory.org.za/pages/library-resources/online-books.htm, page "1900–'20s." Gamiet was also president of the Cape Malay Association established in June 1925; see Éric Germain, "L'Afrique du Sud dans la politique «panislamique» de l'empire ottoman," *Turcica* 31 (1999): 135.
28. A. L., 7780 *Tārīkh* 76421, file no. 43, n.d. This is 'Abdullāh bin Ṣadaqah Daḥlān al-Makkī who is discussed further in the following paragraph.
29. Senegal, Senegambia, Niger, Liberia, Sierra Leone, Sokoto, Bornu, Adamawa, Cameroon, Kanem, Wadai, Zanzibar, the Comoros Islands, Madagascar, Harar, Somalia, Ethopia, and the Galla.
30. A. L., 7780 *Tārīkh* 76421, file no. 71, November 29, 1924. For Arslan's transnational networks, see Raja Adal, "Constructing Transnational Islam: The East-West Network of Shakib Arslan," in *Intellectuals in the Modern Islamic World: Transmission, Transformation, Communication*, ed. Stéphane A. Dudoignon, Komatsu Hisao, and Kosugi Yasushi (London: Routledge, 2006), 176–210. For further discussion of his pan-Islamic ideals, see William Cleveland, *Islam against the West: Shakib Arslan and the Campaign for Islamic Nationalism* (Austin: University of Texas, 1985) and Mahmoud Haddad, "The Ideas of Amir Shakib Arslan: Before and after the Collapse of the Ottoman Empire," in *Views from the Edge: Essays in Honor of Richard W. Bulliet*, ed. Neguin Yavari, Lawrence G. Potter, and Jean-Marc Ran Oppenheim (NY: Columbia University Press, for The Middle East Institute, Columbia University, 2004), 101–15. For his reflections on the Ottomans and Mustafa Kemal Atatürk, also see al-Amīr Shakīb Arslān, *Tārīkh al-Dawlah al-'Uthmānīyah*, ed. Ḥasan al-Samāḥī Suwaydān (Damascus: Dār Ibn Kathīr, 2001), Najīb al-Bu'aynī, *Dhikrayāt al-Amīr Shakīb Arslān: 'an al-Ḥarb al-Kawniyyah al-Ūlā wa-'an al-Majā'ah fī Sūrīyā wa-Lubnān* (Beirut: Nawfal, 2001), and William Cleveland, "Atatürk Viewed by His Arab Contemporaries: The Opinion of Sati' al-Husri and Shakib Arslan," *International Journal of Turkish Studies* 2, no. 2 (1982): 15–23.

31. As he clarifies in his letter to Rashīd Riḍā dated May 12, 1924, and reproduced in Aḥmad al-Sharabāṣī, *Amīr al-Bayān Shakīb Arslān* (Cairo: Dār al-Kitāb al-ʿArabī, 1963), 2:655–57; 668. This letter to Riḍā that precedes his letter to the conference secretariat offers a more detailed delineation of this idea. He envisioned at least five delegations in total, which would be financed by the Egyptian government: one to India, Afghanistan, Siam, all the various parts of Java, the Philippines, and China; one to Bukhara, *jnwh* (possibly a misprinting of Khiva), Ufa, Caucauses, Romania, Bulgaria, Bosnia, and Albania; one to Sudan, Ethopia, Somalia, Zanzibar, and Uganda; one to Darfur, Wadai, *al-Bājirmī*, Bornu, Sokoto, the lands of Niger, Senegal, Senegambia, Ghana Liberia; one to Iran and Kurdistan; and possibly additional delegations to Morocco, Algeria, Tunisia, Libya, Turkey, Kurdistan, Iraq, Syria, Palestine, Yemen, Najd, Hijaz, Amman, Kuwait, and Bahrain, although letters to their leaders and prominent scholars could suffice.
32. A. L., 7780 *Tārīkh* 76421, file no. 43, n.d.; Natalie Mobini-Kesheh, *The Hadrami Awakening: Community and Identity in the Netherlands East Indies, 1900–1942* (Ithaca, NY: Southeast Asia Program Publications, Cornell University, 1999), 36, 96. At one point, Daḥlān was also head of the modern educational foundation *al-Jamʿiyyah al-Khayriyyah* (or *Djamiat Chair*) established in 1905 in Batavia and led by Haḍramī sayyids. Further details on *Djamiat Chair* can be found in Noer, *The Modernist Movement in Indonesia*, 58–63, in his longer section on the origins and growth "The Arab Community" of Indonesia. For more on the mobile Haḍramī elite of Southeast Asia, also see Engseng Ho, *The Graves of Tarim: Genealogy and Mobility across the Indian Ocean* (Berkeley: University of California Press, 2006), Ulrike Freitag, *Indian Ocean Migrants and State Formation in Hadhramaut: Reforming the Homeland* (Leiden, Neth.: E. J. Brill, 2003), and Ulrike Freitag and William Clarence-Smith, eds., *Hadhrami Traders, Scholars and Statesmen in the Indian Ocean, 1750s–1960s* (Leiden, Neth.: E. J. Brill 1997).
33. A. L., 7780 *Tārīkh* 76421, file no. 37, October 4, 1924. Well over a decade later, in May 1938, Ibn Bādīs published a piece in *al-Shihāb* on the caliphate entitled "al-Khilāfah am Jamāʿat al-Muslimīn," *al-Shihāb* 14, no. 2 (May 1938): 61–63, which is republished in *Ibn Bādīs: Ḥayātuhu wa-Āthāruh,* ed. ʿAmmār al-Ṭālibī (Beirut: Dār al-Gharb al-Islāmī, 1983), 3:410–12 and Maḥmūd Qāṣim, *al-Imām ʿAbd al-Ḥamīd bin Bādīs: al-Zaʿīm al-Rūḥī li-Ḥarb al-Taḥrīr al-Jazāʾiriyyah* (Cairo: Dār al-Maʿārif, n.d.), 136–37. For other studies of Ibn Badīs, see James McDougall, *History and the Culture of Nationalism in Algeria* (Cambridge: Cambridge University Press, 2006), 12–17, 60–71, 122–29; Gabriel Pirický, "Modernist Interpretation of Islam and the Legacy of Muslim Reformism: Sayyid Ahmad Khan and Abdulhamid Ben Badis," in *Slovak Contributions to the 19th International Congress of Historical Sciences,* ed. Dušan Kováč (Bratislava, Slovakia: VEDA, 2000), 27–36; Ali Merad, *Ibn Badis: commentateur du coran* (Paris: Librarie orientaliste Paul Geuthner, 1971); Turkī Rābiḥ, *al-Shaykh ʿAbd al-Ḥamīd bin Bādīs: Falsafatuhu wa-Juhūduhu fī'l-Tarbiyyah wa'l-Taʿlīm* (Algeria: al-Shirkah al-Waṭaniyyah li'l-Nashr wa'l-Tawzīʿ, n.d.); Turkī Rābiḥ, *al-Shaykh ʿAbd al-Ḥamīd bin Bādīs: Bāʿith al-Nahḍah al-Islāmiyyah al-ʿArabiyyah fi'l-Jazāʾir al-Ḥadīthah* (Riyadh, Saudi Arabia: Dār al-ʿUlūm, 1983); Muḥammad Bahī al-Dīn Sālim. *Ibn Bādīs: Fāris al-Iṣlāḥ wa'l-Tanwīr* (Cairo: Dār al-Shurūq, 1999); Māzin Ṣalāḥ Muṭabbaqānī, *ʿAbd al-Ḥamīd bin Bādīs: al-ʿĀlim al-Rabbānī wa'l-Zaʿīm al-Siyāsī* (Damascus: Dār al-Qalam, 1989); Muḥammad Fatḥī ʿUthmān, *ʿAbd al-Ḥamīd bin Bādīs: Rāʾid al-Ḥarakah al-Islāmiyyah fī'l-Jazāʾir al-Muʿāṣirah* (Kuwait: Dār al-Qalam, 1987); Sabri Hizmetli, *Cezayir Bağımsızlık Mücadelesi Önderi Bin Badis* (Ankara: Türkiye Diyanet Vakfı, 1994).
34. A. L., 7780 *Tārīkh* 76421, file no. 41, October 11, 1924.
35. A. L., 7780 *Tārīkh* 76421, file no. 68, November 23, 1924.

36. José Casanova, "Globalizing Catholicism and the Return to a 'Universal Church,'" in *Religion in the Process of Globalization*, ed. Peter Beyer (Ger.: Ergon Verlag, 2001), 201–26; José Casanova, "Public Religions Revisited," in *Religion: A Concept*, ed. Hent de Vries (NY: Fordham University Press, 2008), 101–19; David Kertzer, *The Pope and Mussolini: The Secret History of Pius XI and the Rise of Fascism in Europe* (NY: Random House, 2014); Frank Coppa, "Italy: The Church and the *Risorgimento*," in *The Cambridge History of Christianity*: *World Christianities c. 1815–1914*, vol. 7(Cambridge: Cambridge University Press, 2006), 8:233–49; John Pollard, "The Papacy," in *The Cambridge History of Christianity*: *World Christianities c. 1914–2000*, vol. 9 (Cambridge: Cambridge University Press, 2006), 9:29–49; Chamedes, "The Vatican," 955–76.
37. Pius XI, *Ubi Arcano Dei Consilio* (December 23, 1922), *Encyclicals—Pius XI—The Holy See—The Holy Father*, http://www.vatican.va/holy_father/pius_xi/encyclicals/documents/hf_p-xi_enc_23121922_ubi-arcano-dei-consilio_en.html; Kertzer, *The Pope and Mussolini*, 49; Chamedes, "The Vatican," 956; Casanova, "Globalizing Catholicism," 201; Casanova, "Public Religions Revisited," 113–19; Voll, "Islam as a Special World System," 213–26. Given all the discussion about "an international organization which shall bring peace and order to the people of the world," the historian of the First Crusade August C. Krey (1887–1961) also sought to "sketch again the outlines of one of the most successful of those attempts" spearheaded by the papacy from Gregory VII to Boniface VIII in his article, "The International State of the Middle Ages," *American Historical Review* 28, no. 1 (October 1922): 1–12.
38. Harish Puri, *Ghadar Movement: Ideology Organisation and Strategy* (Amritsar, India: Guru Nanak Dev University, 1993), 252–53. Barakatullah died on September 20, 1927, in San Francisco, California. His headstone in Sacramento's Old City Cemetery reads "Maulavi Muhammad Barakatullah. Born Bhopal India. Died Sept 20 1927 San Francisco. Aged 60 years. World famous scholar and patriot, great leader of Indian nationalism, and reformer of modern Islam. May his soul rest in peace." According to Puri, a biography of Barakatullah was written in Urdu by a devoted follower, M. Irfan, *Barakatullah Bhopali* (Bhopal: Irfan Publications, 1969). And aspects of Barakatullah's early activism are discussed in Prithwindra Mukherjee's 1985 PhD dissertation, "Les origines intellectuelles du mouvement d'indépendance de l'Inde (1893–1918)." In 1926, Barakatullah was visited by Jawaharlal Nehru in Switzerland to communicate the unintentionally negative impact of the Comintern in India's propaganda, and shortly before Barakatullah's death the following year, arrangements, that may likely have not been implemented, were made for him and Nehru to visit Comintern together to improve coordination of the anti-British struggle. See the details in Sobhanlal Datta Gupta, "The Comintern and the Indian Revolutionaries in Russia in 1920s," *Calcutta Historical Journal* 18, no. 2 (July–December 1996): 160–61. As Qureshi notes, however, "Barakatullah once explained to *Izveshsia*, the Indians were neither socialists nor communists. They wanted to expel the British from the East and that had made them seek Bolshevik help," *Pan-Islam in British Indian Politics*, 255. Barakatullah's participation in the Ghadar Movement based in California receives further treatment in Maia Ramnath, *Haj to Utopia* (Berkeley: University of California Press, 2011), 222–32.
39. James Campbell Ker, *Political Trouble in India, 1907–1917* (Calcutta: Superintendent Government Printing, 1917), 132; Thomas Hughes, "German Mission to Afghanistan, 1915–1916," *German Studies Review* 25, no. 2 (October 2002): 458.
40. Hughes, "German Mission to Afghanistan," 452, 458; Ker, *Political Trouble in India, 1907–1917*, 225.

41. Aydin, *The Politics of Anti-Westernism in Asia*, 113–14, 230, 235; Ker, *Political Trouble in India, 1907–1917*, 132–35.
42. Hughes, "German Mission to Afghanistan," 452, 458; Ker, *Political Trouble in India, 1907–1917*, 135, 239; Puri, *Ghadar Movement*, 102; Hans-Ulrich Seidt, "From Palestine to the Caucasus—Oskar Niedermayer and Germany's Middle Eastern Strategy in 1918," *German Studies Review* 24, no. 1 (February 2001): 3. For the organizational and ideological history of the Ghadar party, see Harish Puri, "Revolutionary Organization: A Study of the Ghadar Movement," *Social Scientist* 9, no. 2/3 (September–October 1980): 53–66 and the second edition of his book, *Ghadar Movement*, which examines the period from party's inception in 1913 up until 1947.
43. Hughes, "German Mission to Afghanistan," 452; Puri, *Ghadar Movement*, 112; Seidt, "From Palestine to the Caucasus," 3; Ker, *Political Trouble in India, 1907–1917*, 132–35; Qureshi, *Pan-Islam in British Indian Politics*, 81.
44. Hughes, "German Mission to Afghanistan," 469–70; Puri, *Ghadar Movement*, 112–13; Qureshi, *Pan-Islam in British Indian Politics*, 79.
45. Seidt, "From Palestine to the Caucasus," 3.
46. Barakatullah, *The Khilafet*, foreword by Abdullah Yusuf Ali.
47. Barakatullah, *The Khilafet*. Qureshi briefly discusses Barakatullah's treatise as articulating his vision for a caliphate with solely spiritual powers in contrast to the views of some Indian Khilafatists who preferred to see Mustafa Kemal as caliph; see Qureshi, *Pan-Islam in British Indian Politics*, 383.
48. Barakatullah, *The Khilafet*, 2, 53–55.
49. Ibid., 62–63.
50. Ibid., 61.
51. Ibid., 55–58.
52. Ibid., 23, 48–51, 81–83; Pius XI, *Ubi Arcano Dei Consilio* (December 23, 1922). In his 1922 encyclical, the pope grieved, "The evil results of the Great War, as they affect the spiritual life, have been felt all over the world, even in out-of-the-way and lonely sections of far-off continents. Missionaries have been forced to abandon the field of their apostolic labors, and many have been unable to return to their work, thus causing interruptions to and even abandonment of those glorious conquests of the Faith which have done so much to raise the level of civilization, moral, material, and religious."
53. Barakatullah, *The Khilafet*, 61–63.
54. Ibid., 63–80.
55. Ibid., 96–97.
56. Nigar, *Halife İkinci Abdülmecid*, 29–34.
57. Muhammad Aslam Malik, *Allama Inayatullah Mashraqi: A Political Biography* (Oxford: Oxford University Press, 2000), 1–2; Hira Lal Seth, *The Khaksar Movement (and Its Leader Allama Mashraqi)* (Delhi: Discovery, 1985), 14. For other works on al-Mashriqī and the Khaksar Movement he would later establish in 1931, see Nasim Yousaf, *Pakistan's Freedom and Allama Mashriqi: Statements, Letters, Chronology of Khaksar Tehrik (Movement) Period: Mashriqi's Birth to 1947* (NY: AMZ Publications, 2004); Iftikhar Malik, "Regionalism or Personality Cult? Allama Mashriqi and the Tehreek-i-Khaksar in Pre-1947 Punjab," in *Region and Partition: Bengal, Punjab and the Partition of the Subcontinent*, ed. Ian Talbot and Gurharpal Singh (Oxford: Oxford University Press, 1999): 42–94; Nasim Yousaf, *Hidden Facts behind British India's Freedom: A Scholarly Look into Allama Mashraqi and Quaid-e-Azam's Political Conflict* (Liverpool, NY: AMZ Publications, 2007); Shan Muhammad, *Khaksar Movement in India* (Meerut, India:

Meenakshi Prakashan [1972]); Y. B. Mathur, "The Khāksār Movement," *Studies in Islam: Quarterly Journal of the Indian Institute of Islamic Studies* 6, no. 1 (1969): 27–62; Hira Lal Seth, *The Khaksar Movement under Searchlight, and the Life Story of Its Leader Allama Mashraqi*, (Lahore, Pak.: Hero Publications, 1943).

58. Malik, *Allama Inayatullah Mashraqi*, 2.
59. Ibid., 2–5; Seth, *The Khaksar Movement*, 14–15.
60. Syed Suleman Nadvi, "Tazkirah ka Muhakmah," *al-Maarif* (July 1924): 85–91, cited by Malik, *Allama Inayatullah Mashraqi*, 40–51; Seth, *The Khaksar Movement*, 16–21.
61. Malik, *Allama Inayatullah Mashraqi*, 6.
62. ʿInāyatullāh Khān al-Mashriqī, *Khiṭāb, 13 May 1926, Muʾtamar-i Khilāfat, Qāhirah, Miṣr* (Rawalpindi, Pak.: Furūgh-i Islām Foundation, n.d.). *Khiṭāb* is not the conference proceedings "in Urdu translation" as noted by Martin Kramer on page 87 of his *Islam Assembled: The Advent of the Muslim Congresses* (NY: Columbia University Press, 1986), but rather the Arabic speech that al-Mashriqī prepared for the conference. My gratitude to Professor İsmail Kara of Marmara Üniversitesi for sharing his copy of this text with me.
63. al-Mashriqī, *Khiṭāb*, 25–26. He advocated *qiyām hādhā al-muʾtamar maqām al-amīr* [i.e., *amīr al-muʾminīn*] *fīnā*.
64. Ibid., 9–24.
65. Noer discusses the origin and growth of Sarekat Islam as a political movement from 1911–42 in *The Modernist Muslim Movement in Indonesia*, 101–53.
66. Noer discusses the origin and growth of *Muhammadijah* as an educational and social movement in *The Modernist Muslim Movement in Indonesia*, 73–83.
67. al-Irshād (or *Al-Irsjad*) splintered off from *Djamiat Chair*, see Noer, *The Modernist Muslim Movement in Indonesia*, 63–69.
68. van Bruinessen, "Muslims of the Dutch East Indies and the Caliphate Question," 271–73. For a detailed discussion of Tjokroaminoto's pan-Islamic views, see Melayu's Master's thesis, "Islam and Politics in the Thought of Tjokroaminoto (1882–1934)," 81–88.
69. van Bruinessen, "Muslims of the Dutch East Indies and the Caliphate Question," 273–74; T.N.A., F. O. 371/11084/W1038, January 3, 1925; T.N.A., F. O. 371/11084/W5354, May 4, 1925; T.N.A., F. O. 371/11084/W8727, August, 10, 1925; T.N.A., F. O. 371/11924/W252, January 11, 1926; T.N.A., F. O. 371/11476/E2360, March 11, 1926, including excerpts from the newspapers *Nieuwe Soerabaisasche Courant* and *Java Bode* of March 9, 1926; T.N.A., F. O. 371/11476/E2970, April 17, 1926; T.N.A., F. O. 371/11476/E2971, April 20, 1926; T.N.A., F. O. 371/11475/E3123, May 20, 1926; T.N.A., F. O. 371/11475/E3586, June 9, 1926.
70. A. L., 7780 *Tārīkh* 76421, file no. 112, August 18, 1925. For discussion of the intellectual exchange between Egypt and China in the early twentieth century, see Zvi Ben-Dor Benite, "Taking ʿAbduh to China: Chinese-Egyptian Intellectual Contact in the Early Twentieth Century," in *Global Muslims in the Age of Steam and Print*, ed. James Gelvin and Nile Green (Berkeley: University of California Press, 2014), 249–67.
71. al-Sharabāṣī, *Amīr al-Bayān Shakīb Arslān*, 2:647–60, 664–70. These letters of Arslān's are dated May 12, 1924, and July 3, 1924.
72. Ibid.
73. Ibid.; Cleveland, "Atatürk Viewed by His Arab Contemporaries," 20–21.
74. al-Amīr Shakīb Arslān, *al-Sayyid Rashīd Riḍā aw-Ikhā Arbaʿīn Sanah* (Damascus: Maṭbaʿat Ibn Zaydūn, 1937), 330–35, 356–58; Riḍā states that he also published these views in the sixth article in al-Manār issued on Muḥarram 19, 1343 / August 20, 1924. Riḍā's letters to Arslān are dated Dhu'l Qaʿdah 8, 1342 / [June 11, 1924] and Muḥarram 19, 1343 / August 20, [1924]). Although Arslān's reproduction of the June 1924 letter in

1937 intentionally omits most of the details of Riḍā's initial objections, Arslān's own response dated July 3, 1924, is an attempt to clarify and justify his position further.

75. For the best overview of Rashīd Riḍā's changing views on the caliphate up until 1923, articulated in his aforementioned articles and book as well as his private communications, see Mahmoud Haddad's article, "Arab Religious Nationalism in the Colonial Era: Rereading Rashīd Riḍā's Ideas on the Caliphate," *Journal of the American Oriental Society* 117, no. 2 (April–June, 1997): 253–77, which is based on his unpublished doctoral dissertation: Mahmoud Osman Haddad, "Rashīd Riḍā and the Theory of the Caliphate: Medieval Themes and Modern Concerns" (PhD diss., Columbia University, 1989). Also see Albert Hourani's analysis in *Arabic Thought in the Liberal Age, 1798–1939* (Cambridge: Cambridge University Press, 1983), 239–44. Earlier discussions by Henri Laoust, Malcom Kerr, and Hamid Enayet focus primarily on aspects of Riḍā's 1922 treatise on the caliphate, *al-Khilāfah aw al-Imāmah al-ʿUẓmā* (Cairo: Maṭbaʿat al-Manār, 1922). See Henri Laoust, *Le califat dans la doctrine de Rašīd Riḍā* (Beirut: l'Institut français de Damas, 1938); Kerr, *Islamic Reform*, 153–86, 220–21; Hamid Enayet, *Modern Islamic Political Thought* (Austin: University of Texas Press, 1982), 69–83.

76. Muḥammad Rashīd Riḍā, "Mudhakkirah muqaddimah ilā muʾtamar al-khilāfah al-ʿāmm fī Miṣr al-Qāhirah," *al-Manār* 27, no. 2 (May 13, 1926): 138. In a letter to Arslān dated Jumādā al-ʿŪlā 14, 1343 / Kanūn Awwal 11 [or December 11, 1924], Riḍā mentioned that he had been included on the Califate Conference committee that determined whom to invite to the conference and kept record of who had accepted; see Arslān, *al-Sayyid Rashīd Riḍā*, 373.

77. Rashīd Riḍā,"{*waʾtamirū baynakum bi-maʿruf*}," *Majallat al-Muʾtamar al-Islāmī al-ʿĀmm li'l-Khilāfah bi-Miṣr* 1 (Rabīʿ al-Awwal 1343 / October 1924): 3–14; Rashīd Riḍā, "Muʾtamar al-Khilāfah: {*waʾtamirū baynakum bi-maʿruf*}," *al-Manār* 25, no. 7 (Rabīʿ al-Awwal 29, 1343 / October 28, 1924): 525–34.

78. Arslān, *al-Sayyid Rashīd Riḍā*, 352, 366–68. The first letter is dated Jumādā al-Ākhirah 6, 1343 / January 1, [1925], and the other letter written during 1924–25 is missing its dated first page. The internal references of this second letter, in relation to the other letters of Riḍā and Arslān's correspondence, seem to place it in the late spring or summer of 1924.

79. Riḍā, "Mudhakkirah muqaddimah ilā muʾtamar al-khilāfah al-ʿāmm fī Miṣr al-Qāhirah," 138.

80. Arslān, *al-Sayyid Rashīd Riḍā*, 335. This letter from Riḍā to Arslān is dated Dhū'l-Qaʿdah 8, 1342 / [June 11, 1924].

81. Riḍā, "Mudhakkirah muqaddimah ilā muʾtamar al-khilāfah al-ʿāmm fī Miṣr al-Qāhirah," 138–43.

82. al-Bishrī, *al-Muslimūna wa'l-Aqbāṭ*, 281–90; Shalabī, *al-Azhar wa'l-Khilāfah*, 167–72, 175–89, 193–94.

83. T.N.A., F. O. 371/11439/3178, May 25, 1926; T.N.A., F. O. 406/57/no. 296, May 25, 1926. See chapter 6 for further details.

84. al-Bishrī, *al-Muslimūna wa'l-Aqbāṭ*, 299–300; Shalabī, *al-Azhar wa'l-Khilāfah*, 187–92.

85. As evinced by the pages of *al-Balāgh*, *Kawkab al-Sharq*, *al-Siyāsah*, and *al-Liwāʾ al-Miṣrī*.

86. Ḥusayn Wālī, "Taʾjīl ʿaqd al-muʾtamar al-islāmī al-ʿāmm li'l-khilāfah bi-Miṣr ilā sanah li-asbāb muhimmah," *Majallat al-Muʾtamar al-Islāmī al-ʿĀmm li'l-Khilāfah bi-Miṣr* 4 (January 1925): 81–99; Muḥammad Farrāj al-Minyāwī, "Ḥawl taʾjīl al-muʾtamar," *Majallat al-Muʾtamar al-Islāmī al-ʿĀmm li'l-Khilāfah bi-Miṣr* 4 (January 1925): 110–14; Shalabī, *al-Azhar wa'l-Khilāfah*, 96–100.

87. A. L., 7780 *Tārīkh* 76421, file no. 48, Rabīʿ al-Thānī 3, 1343 / November 1, 1924; Aḥmad Tawfīq al-Madanī, *Ḥayāt Kifāḥ: Mudhakkirāt* (Algeria: al-Sharikah al-Waṭaniyyah li'l-Nashr wa'l-Tawzīʿ, 1976), 1:324–28; McDougall, *History and the Culture of Nationalism in Algeria*; Julia Clancy-Smith, *Rebel and Saint: Muslim Notables, Populist Protest, Colonial Encounters (Algeria and Tunisia, 1800–1904)* (Berkeley: University of California Press, 1994), 251.
88. A. L., 7780 *Tārīkh* 76421, file dated February 17, 1926.
89. A. L., 7780 *Tārīkh* 76421, file no. 59, November 18, 1924, A. L., 7780 *Tārīkh* 76421, file no. 89, January 29, 1925, A. L., 7780 *Tārīkh* 76421, file no. 114, May 20, 1925; *al-Muqattam*, May 20, 1926. For a political history of Imam Yaḥyā and Yemen from around 1900 to 1948, see Paul Dresch, *A History of Modern Yemen* (Cambridge: Cambridge University Press, 2000), 1–57.
90. A. L., 7780 *Tārīkh* 76421, file no. 3, n.d.; A. L., 7780 *Tārīkh* 76421, file no. 116, April 1925; A. L., 7780 *Tārīkh* 76421, file no. 117, January 15, 1925; A. L., 7780 *Tārīkh* 76421, file no. 120, July 14, 1925; A. L., 7780 *Tārīkh* 76421, file no. 122, August 6, 1925; Shalabī, *al-Azhar wa'l-Khilāfah*, 207; Fakhr al-Dīn al-Aḥmadī al-Ẓawāhirī, *al-Siyāsah wa'l-Azhar min Mudhakkirāt Shaykh al-Islām al-Ẓawāhirī* (Cairo: Maṭbaʿat al-ʿItimād, 1945), 213–14.
91. İsmail Türkoğlu, *Rusya Türkleri Arasındaki Yenileşme Hareketinin Öncülerinden Rızaeddin Fahreddin* (İstanbul: Ötüken Neşriyat, 2000), 269–76; T.N.A., F. O. 371/11446/E4319, July 3, 1926.
92. T.N.A., F. O. 371/11476/E2146, March 31, 1926.
93. Noer, *The Modernist Muslim Movement in Indonesia*, 136, 222–34; van Bruinessen, "Muslims of the Dutch East Indies and the Caliphate Question," 274–77; Melayu, "Islam and Politics in the Thought of Tjokroaminoto (1882–1934)," 84–86.
94. In addition to Mufti Rızaeddin bin Fahreddin and Musa Carullah (Bigiyef), the "Russian and Turkestan delegation" to Mecca in 1926 included Abdurrahman Ömeri (delegated to represent the Muslims of Astrakhan), Tahir İlyasi (delegated to represent the Muslims of Kazan), Abdülvahid Kari (delegated by the Tashkent Muftiate to represent the Muslims of Turkestan), Mehdi Makuli (delegated to represent the Kazakhs), Muslihiddin Halil (delegated by the Crimean Muftiate), and either Ziaeddin-bin-Qawameddin or Keşşaf Tercümani (contemporary British and Russian sources differ over the identity of this sixth delegate). British Vice-Consul S. R. Jordan in Jeddah reported with grave concern that the Java representatives "Mohammed Said Tjokorominato, Haji Mansur, and Jeran Taib" were constant visitors to the residence of the six "Soviet delegates" last named above in Mecca. T.N.A., F. O. 371/11446/E4319, July 3, 1926; T.N.A., F. O. 371/11433/E4186, June 23, 1926; Türkoğlu, *Rızaeddin Fahreddin*, 271; *Islâm Mecellesi* no. 8 (20) December 1926: 795.
95. For studies of Indonesian students at al-Azhar, see William Roff, "Indonesian and Malay Students in Cairo in the 1920s," *Indonesia* (Cornell University) 9 (1970), 73–87; Mona Abaza, *Changing Images of Three Generations of Azharites in Indonesia* (Singapore: Institute of Southeast Asian Studies, 1993); Mona Abaza, *Islamic Education, Perceptions and Exchanges: Indonesian Students in Cairo* (Paris: Association Archipel, 1994).
96. T.N.A., F. O. 371/11476/E2092, March 2, 1926; T.N.A., F. O. 371/11476/E2623, March 25, 1926; T.N.A., F. O. 371/11476/E6347, October 8, 1926; T.N.A., F. O. 371/11433/E6480, October 23, 1926; T.N.A., F. O. 371/11924/pp. 53–54 (W3728).
97. The best available biography of Musa Carullah (Bigiyef) is Ahmet Kanlıdere, *Kadimle Cedit arasında Musa Carullah: Hayatı, Eserleri, Fikirleri* (Istanbul: Dergâh Yayınları, 2005).

98. al-Ẓawāhirī, *Mudhakkirāt Shaykh al-Islām al-Ẓawāhirī*, 214; Türkoğlu, *Rızaeddin Fahreddin*, 271; A. L., 7780 *Tārīkh* 76421, file no. 2, p. 23, n.d.; T.N.A., F. O. 371/11433/ 4677, July 15, 1926. The invitation was sent to Musa Carullah in Kazan, Russia, on February 20, 1926. And Mehmet Görmez mentions that he was delegated to represent the Kashghar Muslims at the caliphate conference, although Türkoğlu's source of information regarding his representation of Moscow's Muslims is more reliable, see Mehmet Görmez, *Musa Carullah Bigiyef* (Ankara: Türkiye Diyanet Vakfı, 1994), 38–39.

99. *Nashrat al-Azhar*, November 27, 1925; A. L., 7780 *Tārīkh* 76421, file no. 127, October 8, 1925; T.N.A., F. O. 371/11920/W2249, March 17, 1926; T.N.A., F. O. 371/11920/W3227, April 10, 1926; D.W.Q., The New Secret Archives from 1918–39, *Maḥfaẓah* 1524, *Milaff* 1/2/24, Telegram dated March 13, 1926, and Response dated March 25, 1926; T.N.A., F. O. 407/202/no. 20, April 30, 1926; T.N.A., F. O. 371/11582/J1144, April 30, 1926. The British high commissioner Lord Lloyd further reported that "the exclusion of Riffi delegates by the Egyptian Government, at the request of the Spanish Government, has, however, aroused some outcry in the Opposition papers."

100. A. L., 7780 *Tārīkh* 76421, file no. 2., n.d.; D.W.Q., *Maḥāfiẓ ʿĀbidīn* #357, file 35-8-1 Conference et Congrès: Congrès Islamique du Khalifat, 1926, Procès verbaux des séances du Congrès Général Islamique du Khalifat du Caire du 13 au 19 Mai 1926.

101. al-Mashriqī, *Khiṭāb*, 26. al-Mashriqī clarifies, "I am not at all a delegate from India in that sense nor a representative of any of its people" (*Mā anā bi-mandūb min al-Hind fī hādhā al-maʿnā aw mumaththil ayy shaʿb minhum*).

102. A. L., 7780 *Tārīkh* 76421, file no. 112, August, 18, 1925; *al-Muqaṭṭam*, May 29, 1926; Shalabī, *al-Azhar wa'l-Khilāfah*, 246.

103. A. L., 7780 *Tārīkh* 76421, file no. 104, April 24, 1925; A. L., 7780 *Tārīkh* 76421, file no. 99, April 21, 1925; A. L., 7780 *Tārīkh* 76421, file no. 107, July 1, 1925; A. L., 7780 *Tārīkh* 76421, file no. 118, July 17, 1925; D.W.Q., *Maḥāfiẓ ʿĀbidīn* #357, file 35-8-1, Congrès Islamique du Khalifat, 1926, May 13–19, 1926; Germain, "L'Afrique du Sud," 135. Germain notes that the names of these two South African representatives are also spelled as Abubaker Gamieldien or Abubakar Jamal al-Din and Achmat Behardien, Ahmed Behaeddine, or Ahmad Bahadur Yan.

104. D.W.Q., *Maḥāfiẓ ʿĀbidīn* #357, file 35-8-1, Congrès Islamique du Khalifat, 1926, May 13–19, 1926; Riḍā, "Mudhakkirāt Muʾtamar al-Khilāfah al-Islāmiyyah," *al-Manār* 27, no. 3 (June 11, 1926): 208–32; vol. 27, no. 4 (July 10, 1926): 280–94; vol. 27, no. 5 (August 18, 1926): 370–77; vol. 27, no. 6 (September 7, 1926): 449–58.

105. The committee singled out for mention: *al-difāʿ ʿan ḥawzat al-dīn fī jamīʿ bilād al-muslimīn wa-tanfīdh aḥkām al-sharīʿah al-gharrāʾ fīhā*.

106. D.W.Q., *Maḥāfiẓ ʿĀbidīn* #357, file 35-8-1, Congrès Islamique du Khalifat, 1926, May 13–19, 1926; Riḍā, "Mudhakkirāt Muʾtamar al-Khilāfah al-Islāmiyyah," 27:370–77.

107. al-Ẓawāhirī, *Mudhakkirāt Shaykh al-Islām al-Ẓawāhirī*, 215–17; D.W.Q., *Maḥāfiẓ ʿĀbidīn* #357, file 35-8-1, Congrès Islamique du Khalifat, 1926, May 13–19, 1926; Riḍā, "Mudhakkirāt Muʾtamar al-Khilāfah al-Islāmiyyah," 27:449–52.

108. D.W.Q., *Maḥāfiẓ ʿĀbidīn* #357, file 35-8-1, Congrès Islamique du Khalifat, 1926, May 13–19, 1926; Riḍā, "Mudhakkirāt Muʾtamar al-Khilāfah al-Islāmiyyah," 27:452–54.

109. Shaykh Aḥmad Hārūn, al-Sayyid Muḥammad al-Biblāwī, al-Shaykh Ḥasan Abū Saʿūd, al-Shaykh Muḥammad ʿAbd al-Laṭīf al-Faḥḥām, al-Shaykh Khalīl Khālidī, and al-Shaykh Ibrāhīm al-Jibālī.

110. D.W.Q., *Maḥāfiẓ ʿĀbidīn* #357, file 35-8-1, Congrès Islamique du Khalifat, 1926, May 13–19, 1926; Riḍā, "Mudhakkirāt Muʾtamar al-Khilāfah al-Islāmiyyah," 27:454–58; al-Ẓawāhirī, *Mudhakkirāt Shaykh al-Islām al-Ẓawāhirī*, 216–17.

111. T.N.A., F. O. 371/11476/E3304, May 22, 1926; Elie Kedourie, "Egypt and the Caliphate, 1915–52," in *The Chatham House Version and Other Middle-Eastern Studies*, new ed. (London: Brandeis University Press, 1984), 195; Gershoni and Jankowski, *Egypt, Islam, and the Arabs*, 65–66.
112. Arnold Toynbee, *Survey of International Affairs 1925: The Islamic World since the Peace Settlement* (London: Oxford University Press, 1927), 88–90; Kramer, *Islam Assembled*, 100–101.
113. Kramer, *Islam Assembled*, 166.
114. Ḍiyā' Shīt Khaṭṭāb, *al-Maghfūr lahu al-'Allāmah 'Abd al-Razzāq Aḥmad al-Sanhūrī, 1895–1971* (Baghdad: Maṭba'at al-'Ānī, 1971), 3–4; *'Abd al-Razzāq al-Sanhūrī min khilāl Awrāqihi al-Shakhṣiyyah*, ed. Nādiyah al-Sanhūrī and Tawfīq al-Shāwī (Cairo: al-Zahrā' li'l-I'lām al-'Arabī, 1988), 31–35, 49–224; Enid Hill, *Al-Sanhuri and Islamic Law: The Place and Significance of Islamic Law in the Life and Work of 'Abd al-Razzaq Ahmad al-Sanhuri Egyptian Jurist and Scholar 1895–1971*, Cairo Papers in Social Science, no. 10 (Cairo: American University Press, 1987), 1–2.
115. Sanhoury, *Le califat*. He titled his first doctoral dissertation, which he completed in 1925 also at the University of Lyon, *Les restrictions contractuelles à la liberté individuelle de travail dans la jurisprudence anglaise* (Paris: Marcel Biard, 1925).
116. Sanhoury, *Le califat*, 314, 605–7; 'Abd al-Razzāq al-Sanhūrī, *Fiqh al-Khilāfah wa-Taṭawwuruhā li-Tuṣbiḥa 'Uṣbat Umam Sharqiyyah* (Beirut: Mu'assasat al-Risālah, 2001), 370–71.
117. T.N.A., F. O. 371/11475/E3123, May 20, 1926; T.N.A., F. O. 371/11475/E3586, June 9, 1926.
118. *al-Liwā' al-Miṣrī*, May 25, 1926; Shalabī, *al-Azhar wa'l-Khilāfah*, 245–46.
119. D.W.Q., *Maḥāfiẓ 'Ābidīn* #357, file 35-8-1, Congrès Islamique du Khalifat, 1926, May 13–19, 1926. The respective names of these other committee members were Shaykh Muḥammad Muṣṭafā al-Marāghī, Shaykh 'Aṭā'ullāh al-Khaṭīb Effendi, Abū Bakr Jamāl al-Dīn Effendi, Shaykh Muḥammad al-Ṣāliḥī al-Tūnisī, Sayyid Muḥammad al-Ṣiddīq, Yacoub Chenkovitch Effendi, Sharīf Yaḥyā 'Adnān Pasha, Sayyid al-Mīrghanī al-Idrīsī, Muḥammad Murād Effendi, Doctor Hājj Abdullāh Aḥmad, and His Excellency Sayyid al-Idrīsī al-Sanūsī.
120. Riḍā, "Mudhakkirāt Mu'tamar al-Khilāfah al-Islāmiyyah," 27:208–32, 280–94, 370–77, 449–58. Several articles in Stéphane A. Dudoignon, Komatsu Hisao, and Kosugi Yasushi, ed., *Intellectuals in the Modern Islamic World: Transmission, Transformation, Communication* (London: Routledge, 2006) discuss the transregional impact of *al-Manār*.
121. Sanhoury, *Le Califat*, 577–79.
122. Ibid., 569–77; al-Sanhūrī, *Fiqh al-Khilāfah*, 339–44.
123. Sanhoury, *Le Califat*, 573, 578–607; al-Sanhūrī, *Fiqh al-Khilāfah*, 341, 345–66.
124. Tawfīq al-Shāwī, "Sharḥ wa-Taqyīm li-Mashrū' I'ādat al-Khilāfah 'inda al-Sanhūrī," in 'Abd al-Razzāq al-Sanhūrī, *Fiqh al-Khilāfah wa-Taṭawwuruhā li-Tuṣbiḥa 'Uṣbat Umam Sharqiyyah* (Beirut: Mu'assasat al-Risālah, 2001), 384–87; Kramer, *Islam Assembled*, 123–41. Other institutional milestones included the gatherings held: on September 25, 1969, in Rabat after the arson of the Aqṣā Mosque in Jerusalem one month prior; on March 1970, in Jeddah when the first Islamic Conference of Foreign Ministers established a permanent General Secretariat; on February 29–March 4, 1972, in Jeddah when the OIC charter was ratified by Muslim foreign ministers; and on January 25–28, 1981, in Mecca when the OIC goals of supporting Muslim solidarity and avoiding division were further articulated.

125. Sanhoury, *Le califat*; al-Sanhūrī, *Fiqh al-Khilāfah*, 19–24; Ekmeleddin Ihsanoğlu, *The Islamic World in the New Century: The Organization of the Islamic Conference, 1969–2009* (London: Hurst and Company, 2010), 16. Ekmeleddin Ihsanoğlu, who incorporates my analysis of al-Sanhūrī's *Le califat* into the historical background of the OIC, served as its secretary general from 2005 to 2014. In addition to this intellectual legacy, analysts of the OIC have pointed back to a series of distinct Muslim conferences on a range of topics from the 1920s to the 1960s as institutional precedents for international gatherings of Muslim solidarity. See Noor Ahmad Baba, *Organization of the Islamic Conference: Theory and Practice of Pan-Islamic Cooperation* (Karachi, Pak.: Oxford University Press, 1994), 25–55 and Saad Khan, *Reasserting International Islam: A Focus on the Organization of the Islamic Conference and Other Islamic Institutions* (Oxford: Oxford University Press, 2001), 1–21.

CHAPTER 6. DEBATING A MODERN CALIPHATE

1. Finefrock, "From Sultanate to Republic," 106–7, 113–18, 169–77; Ahmet Kekeç, *Ali Şükrü Cinayeti: Birinci Meclise Yapılan Darbe ve Faili Meşhur Bir Vak'a* (Istanbul: İşaret Yayınları, 1994); Zürcher, *Turkey*, 159; "Ali Şükrü Bey'in Guyubeti Dolayısıyla Dün Büyük Millet Meclis'inde Cereyan Eden Müzakerat ve Hükümet Reisinin Bu Husustaki Beyanatı," *Hakimiyet-i Milliye*, March 30, 1923; "Büyük Millet Meclis'inde Ali Şükrü Bey Hadisesi Hakkında Adliye Vekili İzahatta Bulunmuş ve Bazı Kanunlar Müzakere ve Kabul Olunmuştur," *Hakimiyet-i Milliye*, April 1, 1923.
2. İsmail Kara, *Hilafet Risâleleri* (Istanbul: Klasik, 2014), 6:13–15; Kadir Mısıroğlu, *Osmanoğulları'nın Dramı: Elli Gurbet Yılı, 1924–1974* (Istanbul: Sebil Yayınevi, 1974), 110.
3. İsmail Şükrü, *Hilafet-i İslamiye ve Türkiye Büyük Millet Meclisi* (Ankara: Ali Şükrü Matbaası, 1339 [1923]); İsmail Şükrü (Çelikalay), *Hilafet-i İslamiye ve Türkiye Büyük Millet Meclisi* (Istanbul: Bedir Yayınevi, 1993), 18–26.
4. İsmail Şükrü, *Hilafet-i İslamiye ve Türkiye Büyük Millet Meclisi*; Sami Erdem, "Cumhuriyet'e geçis sürecinde hilafet teorisine alternatif yaklaşımlar: Seyyid Bey Örneği," *Divan* 2 (1996): 119–46; Nurullah Ardıç, *Islam and the Politics of Secularism: The Caliphate and Middle Eastern Modernization in the Early 20th Century* (London: Routledge, 2012), 275–76.
5. Lütfi Fikri, *Hükümdarlık Karşısında Milliyet, Mesuliyet ve Tefrik-i Kuva Mesa'ili* (Istanbul: Akşam Matbaası, 1338 [1922]); Lütfi Fikri, *Meşrutiyet ve Cumhuriyet* (Istanbul: Ahmet İhsan ve Şürekası Matbaası, 1339 [1923]); Mehmet Çulcu, *Hilafetin Kaldırılması sürecinde Cumhuriyetin İlanı ve Lütfi Fikri Davası* (Istanbul: Kastaş Yayınları, 1991).
6. Arı İnan, *Gazi Mustafa Kemal Atatürk'ün 1923 Eskişehir-İzmit Konuşmaları* (Ankara: Türk Tarih Kurumu, 1982).
7. *Hilafet ve Milli Hakimiyet* (Ankara: Matbuat ve İstihbarat Matbaası, 1339 [1923]); İlyas Sami, "İslam'da Hilafet," *Hakimiyet-i Milliye*, January 19, 1923 and January 24, 1923; Rasih, "İslam'da Hilafet ve Tesis-i Hükümet," *Hakimiyet-i Milliye*, January 17, 1923, January 19, 1923, January 22, 1923, January 23, 1923, January 24, 1923, and January 26, 1923; Hoca Halil Hulki, Hoca İlyas Sami, ve Hoca Rasih, *Hakimiyet-i Milliye ve Hilafet-i İslamiye* (Ankara: Yeni Gün Matbaası, 1341 [1924]); Tunçay, *T. C.'nde Tek-Parti*, 64–67; Ardıç, *Islam and the Politics of Secularism*, 274–82; Finefrock, "From Sultanate to Republic," 107, 109–19.
8. Sami Erdem, "Seyyid Bey: Hayatı ve Eserleri," in *Türk Hukuk ve Siyaset Adamı Seyyit Bey Sempozyumu*, ed. Osman Karadeniz, A. Bülent Baloğlu, and A. Bülent Ünal (İzmir,

Turk.: İzmir İlahiyat Fakültesi Vakfı Yayınları, 1999), 27; Ardıç, *Islam and the Politics of Secularism*, 283, 349.

9. Erdem, "Seyyid Bey: Hayatı ve Eserleri," 11–16; Michelangelo Guida, "Seyyid Bey and the Abolition of the Caliphate," *Middle Eastern Studies* 44, no. 2 (2008): 275–76.
10. [Mehmed Seyyid], *Hilafet ve Hakimiyet-i Milliye* (Ankara: n.p., 1339 [1923]), 1–5.
11. Ibid., 25–31.
12. Erdem, "Seyyid Bey," 27; Ardıç, *Islam and the Politics of Secularism*, 284; Seyyid, *Usul-i Fıkıh* (Istanbul: Matbaa-yı Amire, 1917), 1:100–162.
13. [Seyyid], *Hilafet ve Hakimiyet-i Milliye*, 36, 38–40.
14. Ibid., 13–17, 25–31. Seyyid recognized election (*intihab*) and appointment (*istihlaf*) as the only two legitimate means of caliphal accession.
15. Ibid., 41–57.
16. Ibid., 57–67.
17. Ibid., 72–73.
18. Ibid., 41–42.
19. *T.B.M.M. Zabıt Ceridesi*, Devre II, Cilt 7, Içtima Senesi 1 (March 3, 1340 [1924]), 44–70 (Ottoman script), 40–61 (Latin script); Seyyid Bey, *Hilafetin Mahiyet-i Şeriyesi* (Ankara: Türkiye Büyük Millet Meclisi Matbaası, 1340 [1924]); Erdem, "Cumhuriyet'e geçis sürecinde hilafet teorisine alternatif yaklaşımalar," 142; Erdem, "Seyyid Bey," 17–20.
20. "Yeni Kabine İsmet Paşa'nın Riyasetinde Teşekkül Etti," *Tevhid-i Efkar*, March 7, 1924; Guida, "Seyyid Bey," 277; Erdem, "Seyyid Bey," 18–24; Rıza Nur, *Hayat ve Hatıratım*, 3:967–72; [Seyyid], *Hilafet ve Hakimiyet-i Milliye*, 57.
21. Muḥammad ʿImārah, *al-Islām wa-Uṣūl al-Ḥukm li-ʿAlī ʿAbd al-Rāziq* (Beirut: al-Muʾassasah al-ʿArabiyyah li'l-Dirāsāt wa'l-Nashr, 1972); Muḥammad ʿImārah, *Maʿrakat al-Islām wa-Uṣūl al-Ḥukm* (Cairo: Dār al-Shurūq, 1997); James Broucek, "The Controversy of Shaykh 'Ali 'Abd al-Raziq" (PhD diss., Florida State University, 2012); Walid Kazziha, "The Jarīdah-Ummah Group and Egyptian Politics," *Middle Eastern Studies* 13, no. 3 (1977): 373–85; Donald Malcolm Reid, *Cairo University and the Making of Modern Egypt* (Cambridge: Cambridge University Press, 1990); Afaf Lutfi al-Sayyid Marsot, *Egypt's Liberal Experiment: 1922–1936* (Berkeley: University of California Press, 1977); T.N.A, J2461/2350/16, August 13, 1925.
22. ʿAlī ʿAbd al-Rāziq, *al-Islām wa-Uṣūl al-Ḥukm: Bahth fī'l-Khilāfah wa'l-Ḥukūmah fī'l-Islām*, ed. Mamdūḥ Ḥaqqī (Beirut: Manshūrat Maktabat al-Ḥayāt, [1966]), 7–24, 37–47, 65–86.
23. Ibid., 23, 83, 93–105, 111–29, 135–56; [Seyyid Bey], *al-Khilāfah wa-Sulṭat al-Ummah*, trans. ʿAbd al-Ghanī Sanī (Cairo: Maṭba'at al-Hilāl, 1342/1924).
24. ʿAbd al-Rāziq, *al-Islām wa-Uṣūl al-Ḥukm*, 165–77, 181–86, 191–201.
25. Rashīd Riḍā, "al-Islām wa-Uṣūl al-Ḥukm," *al-Manār* 26, no. 2 (June 21, 1925): 100–104; Rashīd Riḍā, "al-Islām wa-Uṣūl al-Ḥukm [II]," *al-Manār* 26, no. 3 (July 21, 1925): 213; Rashīd Riḍā, "al-Islām wa-Uṣūl al-Ḥukm [III]," *al-Manār* 26, no. 3 (July 21, 1925): 230–32.
26. *Radd Hayʾat Kibār al-ʿUlamāʾ ʿalā Kitāb Islām wa-Uṣūl al-Ḥukm li'l-Shaykh ʿAlī ʿAbd al-Rāziq* (Cairo: al-Maṭbaʿah al-Yūsufiyyah, 1344/1925); Riḍā, "Ḥukm," 263–93.
27. *Radd Hayʾat Kibār al-ʿUlamāʾ*; Riḍā, "Ḥukm," 362–93; T.N.A., J2350/2350/16, August 13, 1925; T.N.A., J2461/2350/16, August 13, 1925; T.N.A., F. O. 371/10888/J2990; ʿImārah, *Maʿrakat al-Islām wa-Uṣūl al-Ḥukm*, 93–101; "Mudhakkirāt al-Shaykh ʿAlī ʿAbd al-Rāziq," *al-Siyāsah*, August 13, 1925; Muḥammad Bakhīt al-Muṭīʿī, *Ḥaqīqat al-Islām wa-Uṣūl al-Ḥukm* (Cairo: al-Maṭbaʿah al-Salafiyyah, 1344 [1926]); Yūsuf al-Dijwī, *Radd Ṣāḥib al-Faḍīlah al-Ustādh al-Kabīr al-Shaykh Yūsuf al-Dijwī ʿalā Kitāb al-Shaykh ʿAlī*

'Abd al-Rāziq al-Islām wa-Uṣūl al-Ḥukm (Cairo: Maṭba'at al-Samāḥ, 1927). On Bakhīt's role as mufti and continued involvement in Egyptian society, see Jakob Skovgaard-Petersen, *Defining Islam for the Egyptian State: Muftis and Fatwas of the Dār al-Iftā* (Leiden, Neth.: E. J. Brill, 1997), 133–45.

28. T.N.A., J2461/2350/16, August 13, 1925; T.N.A., J2664/29/16, September 11, 1925; T.N.A., J2746/29/16, September 12, 1925; T.N.A., J2836/29/16, September 19, 1925; Riḍā, "Ḥukm," 383–87.
29. T.N.A., J2674/29/16, September 4, 1925; T.N.A., J2591/2350/16, September 7, 1925; T.N.A., J2626/29/16, September 9, 1925; T.N.A., J2650/29/16, September 10, 1925; T.N.A., J2664/29/16, September 11, 1925; T.N.A., J2659/29/16, September 10, 1925; T.N.A., J2746/29/16, September 12, 1925; T.N.A., J2836/29/16, September 19, 1925; T.N.A., F. O. 371/10888/J3204; Riḍā, "Ḥukm," 386–87.
30. T.N.A., J2591/2350/16, September 7, 1925; T.N.A., J2626/29/16, September 9, 1925; T.N.A., J2650/29/16, September 10, 1925; T.N.A., J2664/29/16, September 11, 1925; T.N.A., J2665/29/16, September 11, 1925; T.N.A., J2666/29/16, September 12, 1925; T.N.A., J2746/29/16, September 12, 1925; T.N.A., J2919/29/16, September 26, 1925; T.N.A., F. O. 371/10888/J2919; T.N.A., F. O. 371/10888/J3142; Riḍā, "Ḥukm," 383–91.
31. Muḥammad Ibrāhīm Jazīrī, *Sa'd Zaghlūl: Dhikrayāt Tārikhiyyah Ṭarīfah* (Cairo: Dār Akhbār al-Yawm, 1954), 91–93.
32. 'Imārah, *Ma'rakat al-Islām wa-Uṣūl al-Ḥukm*, 175–85, 215–16.
33. Ibid., 218–33, 289.
34. Ibid., 235–85.
35. Ibid., 286–90.
36. Ibid., 293–423. al-Khiḍr offers a line-by-line rebuttal of 'Abd al-Rāziq's arguments and methods, which is too extensive to recount in full detail.
37. Mustafa Sabri, *Hilafet ve Kemalizm*, ed. Sadık Albayrak (Istanbul: Araştırma Yayınları, 1992), 122. *Onun kitabını Mısır'ın en büyük alimlerinden iki yüce zat, Şeyh Bahiyt ve Muhammed el-Hazar* [*sic., el-Hızır*] *Hüseyin, baştan ayağa kadar takip ve tetkik ederek mükemmel eserler yazmışlardır.*
38. Rıza Tevfik, *Biraz da Ben Konuşayım* (Istanbul: İletişim Yayıncılık, 1993), 232–75.
39. Mufarriḥ ibn Sulaymān al-Qawsī, *Muṣṭafā Ṣabrī: al-Mufakkir al-Islāmī wa'l-'Ālim al-'Ālamī wa-Shaykh al-Islām fī'l-Dawlah al-'Uthmānīyah Sābiqan, 1286–1373 H / 1869–1954 M* (Damascus: Dār al-Qalam, 2006), 77–136; Amit Bein, "'Ulama and Political Activism in the Late Ottoman Empire: The Political Career of Şeyhülislam Mustafa Sabri Efendi (1869–1954)," in *Guardians of Faith in Modern Times: 'Ulama' in the Middle East*, ed. Meir Hatina (Leiden, Neth.: E. J. Brill, 2009), 67–82; Mehmet Kadri Karabela, "One of the Last Ottoman Şeyhulislams, Mustafa Sabri Efendi (1869–1954): His Life, Works and Intellectual Contributions" (PhD diss., McGill University, 2003), 36–44.
40. al-Qawsī, *Muṣṭafā Ṣabrī*, 92–93; Karabela, "One of the Last Ottoman Şeyhulislams," 44–46; Bein, "'Ulama and Political Activism in the Late Ottoman Empire," 82–86.
41. Ḥusayn, *al-Ittijāhāt al-Waṭaniyyah*, 2:28–30.
42. al-Qawsī, *Muṣṭafā Ṣabrī*, 144; Karabela, "One of the Last Ottoman Şeyhulislams," 47.
43. Mustafa Sabri, *al-Nakīr*, 3–15, 23–30, 52–54.
44. Sabri's specific wording bears mention: *al-khilāfah intaqalat bi'l-fi'l ilā man ta'ahhada an yaf'ala fi'l al-khulafā' min iqāmat al-aḥkām al-shar'iyyah, wa mā baqiya fī'l-khulafā' fa-'ibārah 'an al-ism al-baḥt, idh lā tanfakk al-khilāfah 'an al-fi'l.*
45. Ibid., 31–34.
46. Ibid., 39–41, 197.
47. Ibid., 198–223.

48. Mustafa Sabri, *Hilafet ve Kemalizm,* 70–74.
49. Mustafa Sabri, "Shaykh al-Islām al-Sābiq yabsuṭu ārā'ahu wa-yudāfi'u 'an nafsihi wa-yaḥmilu 'alā khuṣūmih," *al-Ahrām,* December 2, 1922; Mustafa Sabri, "Khiṭāb Maftūḥ"; Mustafa Sabri, "Takrīr al-Tadhkīr," *al-Muqaṭṭam,* November 4, 1923; Mustafa Sabri, "Man al-Mahjū fī Shi'r Amīr al-Shu'arā'?," *al-Muqaṭṭam,* November 8, 1923.
50. Sabri, *Hilafet ve Kemalizm,* 76–80.
51. William Charles Brice, *An Historical Atlas of Islam* (Leiden, Neth.: E. J. Brill, 1981), 329–31; Karabela, "One of the Last Ottoman Şeyhulislams," 48; al-Qawsī, *Muṣṭafā Ṣabrī,* 256–57, 349–54, 489; Sabri, *Hilafet ve Kemalizm,* 115–16. Sabri wrote the first installation of "İslam'da İmamet-i Kübra, yani Hilafet-i Muazzama-yı İslamiye" in 1926 and published it on the front page of his twelfth issue of *Yarın* on Friday, December 16, 1927. For *Yarın*'s editorial interventions regarding the "non-exchangeable" Muslim inhabitants of Western Thrace, see Yannis Bonos, "Crossing the Borders in Reality and in Press: The Case of the Newspapers *Yeni Adım* and *Yarın* in the Late 1920s," *European Journal of Turkish Studies* 12 (2011): 2–15.
52. 'Alī 'Abd al-Rāziq, *İslamiyet ve Hükümet,* trans. Ömer Rıza (Istanbul: Kitaphane-yi Sudi, 1927).
53. Mustafa Sabri, *Hilafet ve Kemalizm,* 113–45.
54. Mustafa Kemal, *Nutuk* (Ankara: n.p., 1927); Mustafa Kemal Atatürk, *Nutuk,* ed. Bedi Yazıcı (Istanbul: n.p, 1995), 678, 694. Sabri reiterated Mustafa Kemal's admissions in the November 10, 1927 issue of *Yarın.*
55. Mustafa Sabri, *Hilafet ve Kemalizm,* 172–84, 220–22.
56. al-Qawsī, *Muṣṭafā Ṣabrī,* 145–48, 257.
57. Ibid., 148–56, 340–45. Two years earlier in 1940, two younger Egyptian princes Muḥammad 'Abd al-Mun'im (1899–1979) and Muḥammad 'Alī Ibrāhīm (1900–1977) married the last Ottoman caliph's and last Ottoman sultan's shared grandchildren Fatma Neslişah Sultan (1921–2012) and Zehra Hanzade Sultan (1923–98) respectively. These Ottoman princesses were the daughters of the deposed caliph Abdülmecid's son Şehzade Ömer Faruk (1898–1969) and the deposed sultan Vahideddin's daughter Sabiha Sultan (1894–1971), whom Mustafa Kemal had once sought to marry. Their sister Necla Heybetullah Sultan (1926–2006) married another scion of Egypt's Mehmed Ali dynasty, Prince 'Amr Ibrāhīm (1903–77), in 1943.
58. Karabela, "One of the Last Ottoman Şeyhulislams," 34. Emphasis in original.
59. Mustafa Sabri, *Mawqif,* 1–16.
60. Şükran Vahide, *Islam in Modern Turkey: An Intellectual Biography of Bediuzzaman Said Nursi,* ed. Ibrahim Abu-Rabi (Albany: State University of New York Press, 2005), 3–129; Bediüzzaman Said Nursi, *Tarihçe-i Hayat* (Istanbul, Envar Neşriyat, 1993), 30–116.
61. Vahide, *Islam in Modern Turkey,* 104–5, 112, 131–44; Nursi, *Tarihçe-i Hayat,* 259.
62. Vahide, *Islam in Modern Turkey,* 143–55; Nursi, *Tarihçe-i Hayat,* 138–42; Bediüzzaman Said Nursi, *Risale-i Nur Külliyatı* (Istanbul: Nesil, 2006), 2:2055–59.
63. *T.B.M.M. Zabıt Ceridesi,* Devre I, Cilt 24, İçtima Senesi 3 (November 9, 1338 [1922]), 457 (Ottoman script), 439 (Latin script); "Bediüzzaman'dan Mustafa Kemal'e Namaz Beyannamesi," *Derin Tarih* 36 (March 2015), 88–91; Vahide, *Islam in Modern Turkey,* 167–73; Nursi, *Tarihçe-i Hayat,* 139–42; Bediüzzaman Said Nursi, *al-Mathnawi al-Nuri: Seedbed of the Light,* trans. Huseyin Akarsu (Somerset, NJ: Light, 2007), 150–54.
64. Said Nursi, "On Sekizinci Lem'a," *Lem'alar* [Ottoman-script edition], (Istanbul: Sözler Neşriyat, 1995), 262–64. This epistle has been excised from the modern Turkish editions in Latin script.

65. Said Nursi, "Beşinci Şua," *Şualar* (Istanbul: Envar Neşriyat, 1956), 578–96; Nursi, "The Fifth Ray," *The Rays: Reflections on Islamic Belief, Thought, Worship and Action*, trans. Hüseyin Akarsu (Clifton, NJ: Tughra Books, 2010), 351–74.
66. Nursi, "On Dördüncü Şua," *Şualar*, 358–59. This section is excised from Tughra Books's 2010 English translation.
67. Ibid., 401, 506, 580. As for drinking *rakı*, Mustafa Kemal was in the habit of consuming half a liter to one liter of it per day; Zürcher, *The Unionist Factor*, 144.
68. Nursi, "On Dördüncü Şua," *Şualar*, 354.
69. Ibid., 347–48.
70. Ibid., 389; Nursi, *Tarihçe-i Hayat*, 255.
71. Nursi, "On Dördüncü Şua," *Şualar*, 347–577; Nursi, "On Üçüncü Mektub," *Mektubat* (Istanbul: Envar Neşriyat, 1993), 48–49; Nursi, "The Fourteenth Ray," *The Rays*, 327–41. Nursi's thirteenth letter is not fully translated in Hüseyin Akarsu's 2007 English translation entitled *The Letters*.
72. Nursi, "On Beşinci Mektub" and "On Dokuzuncu Mektub: Mucizat-ı Ahmediye," *Mektubat*, 53–58, 98–104; Nursi, "Dördüncü Lem'a" and "Yedinci Lem'a," *Lem'alar* (Istanbul: Envar Neşriyat, 1993), 20–26, 30–31, 35–37; Nursi, "The Fifteenth Letter" and "The Nineteenth Letter," *The Letters: Epistles on Islamic Thought, Belief, and Life*, trans. Hüseyin Akarsu (Clifton, NJ: Tughra Books, 2007), 93–96, 126–33; Nursi, "The Fourth Gleam" and "The Seventh Gleam," *The Gleams: Reflections on Qur'anic Wisdom and Spirituality*, trans. Hüseyin Akarsu (Clifton, NJ: Tughra Books, 2008), 35–44, 50, 55–57.
73. Nursi, "Yirmi Dokuzuncu Mektub," *Mektubat*, 443–46; Nursi, "The Twenty-Ninth Letter," *The Letters*, 426–29. The translations excerpted above are mine.
74. Nursi, "Beşinci Şua," *Şualar*, 589–90; Bediüzzaman Said Nursi, "Sekizinci Şua," *Sikke-i Tasdik-i Gaybi* (Istanbul: Şahdamar Yayınları, 2008), 125–26; Nursi, "On Sekizinci Lem'a," *Lem'alar* [Ottoman-script edition], 262–64; Abdülkadir Badıllı, *Risale-i Nur'un Kudsi Kaynakları* (Istanbul: Envar Neşriyat, 2011), 752–53; Nursi, "The Fifth Ray," *The Rays*, 366. The "On Sekizinci Lem'a" was excised from the Turkish versions in Latin script.
75. Nursi, "On Birinci Şua," *Şualar*, 269. This section is excised from Tughra Books's 2010 English translation entitled *The Rays*.
76. Nursi, "Hakikat Çekirdekleri," *Mektubat*, 473; Nursi, "Epigrams," *Letters*, 451.

EPILOGUE. THE SWIRL OF RELIGIOUS HOPES AND ASPIRATIONS

1. Ḥasan al-Bannā, *Risālat al-Mu'tamar al-Khāmis* (n.p.), 57–58.
2. Nursi, "On Üçüncü Mektub, Üçüncü Sual," *Mektubat*, 48–49; Nursi, "Yirimi İkinci Mektup, Birinici Mebhas, Dördüncü Vecih, Dördüncü Düstur," *Mektubat*, 267. Nursi repeats this statement in his "Thirteenth Letter" written in 1929 and his "Twenty-First Letter" written in 1928.
3. Ḥasan al-Bannā, *Mudhakkirāt al-Da'wah wa'l-Dā'iyah* (Cairo: Dār al-Kitāb al-'Arabī, n.d.), 47-50; al-Bannā, *Risālat al-Mu'tamar al-Khāmis*, 7.
4. Islamist movements have produced a vast body of materials addressing the Islamic caliphate, including political treatises, debates, memoirs, journal articles, and online contributions. Some examples include Yusuf al-Qaraḍāwī's *Qaḍāyā al-Mu'āṣirah wa'l-Khilāfah*, ed. al-Sayyid Yāsīn (Cairo: Mīrīt li'l-Nashr wa'l-Ma'lūmāt, 1999) and Zaynab

al-Ghazālī's series of articles envisioning the path to regaining the caliphate "al-Ṭarīq li-ʿAwdat al-Khilāfah" in the monthly *al-Liwāʾ al-Islāmī*, vol. 43 (June, July, and August 1988) from the Society of Muslim Brothers; the founder of Ḥizb al-Taḥrīr Taqiyy al-Dīn al-Nabhānī's book on the necessity of the caliphate, *al-Dawlah al-Islāmiyyah* (1952), and his successor ʿAbd al-Qadīm Zallūm's book *Kayfa Hudimat al-Khilāfah* (1962) dwelling on the destruction of the Ottoman Caliphate; as well as the jihadist theorists al-ʿAlī's treatise memorializing the fallen caliphate *Dhikrā Suqūṭ al-Khilāfah al-Islāmiyyah* and al-Tarṭūṣī's treatise seeking its reestablishment *al-Ṭarīq ilā Istiʾnāf Ḥayāt Islāmiyyah wa-Qiyām Khilāfah Rāshidah ʿalā Ḍawʾ al-Kitāb wa'l-Sunnah*, which were both disseminated on the jihadist website http://www.tawhed.ws/. I analyzed these sources and more in "Remembering the Lost Caliphate: Emotional Attachment and Longing among Islamists for an Idealized Past and a New Global Future," Conference on "Islamic Resurgence in the Age of Globalization: Myth, Memory, Emotion," The Norwegian University of Science and Technology, Trondheim, Norway, September 4–6, 2009, "Islamist Remembering and Longing for a Lost Caliphal Ideal: The Politics of Memory, Culture, and Emotion," Session on "Rethinking History, Reimagining Community," American Academy of Religion Annual Meeting, Atlanta, GA, October 30–November 1, 2010, and "Emotional Rhetoric among Islamists about a Caliphal Utopia," European Science Foundation Conference on "Demystifying the Caliphate: Advocates, Opponents and Implications for Europe," King's College, London, UK, November 12–13, 2010. Reza Pankhurst utilizes my research regarding the global aftermath of 1924 in his *The Inevitable Caliphate? A History of the Struggle for Global Islamic Union* (London: Hurst and Company, 2013) and builds on some of my insights regarding the Society of Muslim Brothers, Ḥizb al-Taḥrīr, and al-Qāʿidah.

5. Carl Ernst, "Why ISIS Should Be Called Daesh: Reflections on Religion and Terrorism," October 29, 2014, Lecture at the University of North Carolina—Chapel Hill, published online on November 11, 2014, at http://islamicommentary.org/2014/11/carl-ernst-why-isis-should-be-called-daesh-reflections-on-religion-terrorism/ and Zeba Khan, "Words Matter in 'ISIS' War, So Use 'Daesh,'" *Boston Globe* (October 9, 2014), https://www.bostonglobe.com/opinion/2014/10/09/words-matter-isis-war-use-daesh/V85GYEuasEEJgrUunodMUP/story.html.
6. Liz Sly, "Relics of Iraq's Past Call Shots for Islamic State," *Washington Post* (April 5, 2015), accessible online as Liz Sly, "The Hidden Hand behind the Islamic State Militants? Saddam Hussein's," *Washington Post* (April 4, 2015): http://www.washingtonpost.com/world/middle_east/the-hidden-hand-behind-the-islamic-state-militants-saddam-husseins/2015/04/04/aa97676c-cc32-11e4-8730-4f473416e759_story.html; Christoph Reuter, "Secret Files Reveal the Structure of Islamic State," *Spiegel Online* (April 18, 2015), http://www.spiegel.de/international/world/islamic-state-files-show-structure-of-islamist-terror-group-a-1029274-druck.html; Michael Weiss and Hassan Hassan, *ISIS: Inside the Army of Terror* (NY: Regan Arts, 2015); Joel Rayburn, *Iraq after America: Strongmen, Sectarians, Resistance* (Stanford, CA: Hoover Institution Press, 2014).
7. Hamza Yusuf Hanson, "The Crisis of ISIS: A Prophetic Prediction," A Friday Sermon delivered on September 12, 2014, at the San Ramon Valley Islamic Center, https://www.youtube.com/watch?v=hJo4B-yaxfk (published online September 19, 2014).
8. "Open Letter to Dr. Ibrahim Awwad al-Badri alias 'Abu Bakr al-Baghdadi' and to the Fighters and Followers of the Self-Declared 'Islamic State,'" (September 19, 2014), available online at http://www.lettertobaghdadi.com/pdf/Booklet-Combined.pdf; Lauren Markoe, "Muslim Scholars Release Open Letter to Islamic State Meticulously Blasting

Its Ideology," *Huffington Post* (September 24, 2014), http://www.huffingtonpost.com/2014/09/24/muslim-scholars-islamic-state_n_5878038.html.

9. See, for example, Umar Faruq Abd-Allah, "Mercy: The Stamp of Creation," (Chicago: Nawawi Foundation, 2004), available online at http://www.nawawi.org/wp-content/uploads/2013/01/Article1.pdf.
10. "Open Letter," 23.
11. Muhammad al-Yaqoubi, *Refuting ISIS: A Rebuttal of Its Religious and Ideological Foundations* (United States: Sacred Knowledge, 2015), 26–27. For additional details of al-Baghdādī's biography, see William McCants, "The Believer: How an Introvert Became the Leader of the Islamic State," The Brookings Essay (September 1, 2015), published online at http://www.brookings.edu/series/the-brookings-essay. For information on the former Iraqi intelligence officer who drew up the blueprints for the so-called Islamic State and selected Abū Bakr al-Baghdādī to "give the group a religious face," see Christoph Reuter's article in *Der Spiegel*, "Secret Files Reveal the Structure of Islamic State."
12. His Eminence Shaikh Abdallah bin Bayyah, "This Is Not the Path to Paradise: Response to ISIS," (Abu Dhabi, UAE: September 14, 2014), published online at http://binbayyah.net/english/2014/09/24/fatwa-response-to-isis/; Dina Temple-Raston, "Prominent Muslim Sheikh Issues Fatwa Against ISIS Violence," NPR (September 24, 2014), http://www.npr.org/2014/09/25/351277631/prominent-muslim-sheikh-issues-fatwa-against-isis-violence; Tom Gjelten, "Muslim Leaders Vow to Protect Rights of Religious Minorities," NPR (January 28, 2016), http://www.npr.org/sections/parallels/2016/01/28/464688623/muslim-leaders-vow-to-protect-rights-of-religious-minorities; Marrakesh Declaration, "The Rights of Religious Minorities in Predominantly Muslim Majority Communities: Legal Framework and a Call to Action (Marrakesh, Morocco: January 27, 2016), published online at http://www.marrakeshdeclaration.org/index.html.
13. Osman Rifat Ibrahim, "Why Abu Bakr al-Baghdadi Is an Imposter," *Al Jazeera*, July 14, 2014: http://www.aljazeera.com/indepth/opinion/2014/07/baghdadi-impostor-2014 7991513785260.html. Osman Rifat Ibrahim is a descendent of the Ottoman dynasty through his mother Princess Necla Heybetullah (1926–2006) as well as of the Mehmed Ali dynasty in Egypt through his father Prince ʿAmr Ibrāhīm (1903–77).
14. John Esposito and Dalia Mogahed, *Who Speaks for Islam? What a Billion Muslims Really Think* (NY: Gallup Press, 2007), 29–98. The Pew Research Center's subsequent multi-year survey across thirty-nine countries affirms that "Muslims around the world express broad support for democracy" and "strongly reject violence in the name of Islam" in "The World's Muslims: Religion, Politics, Society" (Washington, DC: Pew Research Center, 2013), 29–33, 59–72.
15. *Man bāta yaltamisu 'l-khilāfata fī'l-karā, lam yalqa ghayra khilāfat al-Ṣayyādi.* Aḥmad Shawqī, "al-Khilāfah," *al-Siyāsah*, June 7, 1926; *al-Shawqiyyāt al-Majhūlah*, ed. Muḥammad Ṣabrī (Cairo: Maṭbaʿat Dār al-Kutub wa'l-Wathā'iq al-Qawmiyyah, 2003), 2:200–203.
16. Ḥabīb ʿUmar bin Ḥafīẓ, "On the Concept of Khilāfah and the Reality of Political Power," Extract from a *Rawḥah* Lesson Commenting on Abū Ṭālib al-Makkī's *Qūt al-Qulūb* on July 30, 2013, translated and published online at http://muwasala.org/on-the-concept-of-khilafah-and-the-reality-of-political-power/ on September 2, 2013. On the definition of these two forms of caliphate: "There are two types of khilāfah. The first is the outward khilāfah which relates to political power, which is not noble and honourable in itself. Anyone may attain political power, whether they be pious or corrupt, whether

they be a believer or a disbeliever, whether they be a Prophet or a wretched person" and "The second type is the khilāfah of prophethood, which is a noble and lofty thing. It relates to understanding the speech of Allah, to our connection with Him, to attaining a pure heart and attaining His pleasure. It is the preserve of the Prophets and their followers, the pious people in every time and place."

17. See, for example, Ibrahim Abdul-Matin's discussion of the caliphate as good stewardship of the earth in *Green Deen: What Islam Teaches about Protecting the Planet* (San Francisco: Berrett-Koehler Publishers, 2010), 5, 7–8, 21, 32–33, 52, 57, 65, 75, 86, 95, 101, 111, 114, 118–19, 128, 135, 143, 150, 158, 180. For early illustrations of these spiritual teachings, see al-Ṭabarī, *Jāmiʿ al-Bayān*, 1:156–58, 8:84, Ibn Khaldūn, *Kitāb al-ʿIbar*, 1:339, and Ibn ʿAjībah, *al-Bahr al-Madīd fī Tafsīr al-Qur'ān al-Majīd*, ed. Aḥmad ʿAbdallāh al-Qurashī (Cairo: Ḥasan ʿAbbās Zakī, 1999), 1:93, 2:194. This section is inexplicably excised in the currently available English translations of Ibn Khaldun's much-celebrated theoretical introduction to history as are all the Qur'anic verses from which Ibn Khaldun derived his insights.

18. Jean Bethke Elshtain, "Theologian. Christian Contrarian," *Time* 158, no. 12 "America's Best" (September 17, 2001): 76–77; Stanley Hauerwas, *After Christendom? How the Church Is to Behave if Freedom, Justice, and a Christian Nation Are a Bad Idea*, 2nd ed. (Nashville, TN: Agingdon Press, 1999); David Burrell, "Christian-Muslim Theology: An Exercise in Creative Hermeneutics," Lecture, Duke Divinity School, October 20, 2009; John Wright, ed., *Postliberal Theology and the Church Catholic: Conversations with George Lindbeck, David Burrell, and Stanley Hauerwas* (Grand Rapids, MI: Baker Academic, 2012); Jeffrey Stout, *Democracy and Tradition* (Princeton, NJ: Princeton University Press, 2004), 140–79; "The Difference Christ Makes: Celebrating the Life, Work, and Friendship of Stanley Hauerwas," Conference, Duke Divinity School, November 1, 2013, https://www.youtube.com/playlist?list=PL-_N-pg4WXLKWqunITGE8f4UZdedUgMDD.

19. Jan-Werner Müller, "The End of Christian Democracy," *Foreign Affairs* (July 15, 2014): https://www.foreignaffairs.com/articles/western-europe/2014-07-15/end-christian-democracy; Mary Anne Perkins, *Christendom and European Identity: The Legacy of a Grand Narrative since 1789* (NY: Walter de Gruyter, 2004); Stathis Kalyvas, *The Rise of Christian Democracy in Europe* (Ithaca, NY: Cornell University Press, 1996); Thomas Kselman and Joseph A. Buttigieg, ed., *European Christian Democracy: Historical Legacies and Comparative Perspectives* (Notre Dame, IN: University of Notre Dame Press, 2003); ed. Jean-Dominique Durand, *Christian Democrat Internationalism: Its Action in Europe and Worldwide from Post World War II until the 1990s* (Brussels: P.I.E. Peter Lang, 2013).

20. Motti Inbari, *Jewish Fundamentalism and the Temple Mount: Who Will Build the Third Temple*, trans. Shaul Vardi (Albany: SUNY Press, 2009); Nir Hasson, "Temple Mount Faithful: From the Fringes to the Mainstream," *Haaretz*, October 4, 2012, http://www.haaretz.com/news/features/temple-mount-faithful-from-the-fringes-to-the-mainstream-1.468234; Shany Littman, "Following the Dream of a Third Temple in Jerusalem," *Haaretz*, October 4, 2012, http://www.haaretz.com/weekend/magazine/following-the-dream-of-a-third-temple-in-jerusalem-1.468221; Alan Balfour, *Solomon's Temple: Myth, Conflict, and Faith* (West Sussex, UK: Wiley-Blackwell, 2012), 285–86; Motti Inbari, "A Temple for All the Nations: Jewish-Christian Cooperation for the Construction of the Third Temple," *Studies in Contemporary Jewry* 24 (2010): 158–73; Shalom Goldman, *Zeal for Zion: Christians, Jews, and the Idea of the Promised Land* (Chapel Hill: University of North Carolina Press, 2009), 293–94.

21. See note 20.
22. Castelli, *Martyrdom and Memory,* 8, 172–96. In her sixth chapter, Castelli analyzes how narratives of martyrdom following the tragic 1999 Columbine High School shooting replicate premodern patterns of Christian culture-making centered on the memory of martyrdom.

BIBLIOGRAPHY

ARCHIVES

al-Azhar Library Archival Documents (A. L., Maktabat al-Azhar)
British Library Manuscripts
British National Archival Documents (T.N.A.)
Egyptian National Archival Documents (D.W.Q., Dār al-Wathā'iq al-Qawmiyyah)
Egyptian National Library Manuscripts (*Dār al-Kutub al-Qawmiyyah*)
India Office Records (I.O.R.)
The Institute of Arab Manuscripts (*Ma'had al-Makhṭūṭat al-'Arabiyyah*)
National Library of France Manuscripts (*Bibliothèque nationale de France*)
Ottoman Archives (B.O.A., *Osmanlı Arşivi Daire Başkanlığı*)
Princeton University Library Manuscripts
Süleymaniye, Köprülü, Manisa İl Halk, and Nuruosmaniye Library Manuscripts

ARABIC PERIODICALS

al-Ahrām (Cairo)
al-Akhbār (Cairo)
al-Balāgh (Cairo)
Filisṭīn (Jaffa)
Majallat al-Azhar (Cairo)
Majallat al-Mu'tamar al-Islāmī al-'Āmm li'l-Khilāfah bi-Miṣr (Cairo)
al-Manār (Cairo)
al-Muqaṭṭam (Cairo)
al-Qiblah (Hijaz)
al-Siyāsah (Cairo)
al-Zahrah (Haifa)

OTTOMAN TURKISH PERIODICALS

Hakimiyet-i Milliye (Ankara)
İkdam (Istanbul)
Tanin (Istanbul)
T.B.M.M. Zabıt Ceridesi (Ankara)
Tevhid-i Efkar (Istanbul)
Yarın (Komotini [Gümülcine])

BOOKS AND JOURNALS

Abaza, Mona. *Changing Images of Three Generations of Azharites in Indonesia*. Singapore: Institute of Southeast Asian Studies, 1993.

——. *Islamic Education, Perceptions and Exchanges: Indonesian Students in Cairo*. Paris: Association Archipel, 1994.

ʿAbd al-Muṭṭalib, Muḥammad. *Dīwān ʿAbd al-Muṭṭalib*. Edited by Ibrahīm al-Abyārī and ʿAbd al-Ḥāfiẓ Shalabī, 1st ed. Cairo: Maṭbaʿat al-Iʿtimād, n.d.

ʿAbd al-Rāziq, Alī. *al-Islām wa-Uṣūl al-Ḥukm: Bahth fīʾl-Khilāfah waʾl-Ḥukūmah fīʾl-Islām*. Edited by Mamdūḥ Ḥaqqī. Beirut: Manshūrat Maktabat al-Ḥayāt, [1966].

——. *İslamiyet ve Hükümet*. Translated by Ömer Riza. Istanbul: Kitaphane-i Sudi, 1927.

ʿAbd al-Razzāq al-Sanhūrī min khilāl Awrāqihi al-Shakhṣiyyah. Edited by Nādiyah al-Sanhūrī and Tawfīq al-Shāwī. Cairo: al-Zahrāʾ liʾl-Iʿlām al-ʿArabī, 1988.

ʿAbdallāh, Muḥammad. "al-Tārīkh Yuʿīdu Nafsahu. Baghdād Lam Tusqaṭ illa biʾl-Khiyānah: Hūlāgū al-Amrīkī sa-Yadhbaḥ al-Jamīʿ: al-Mughūl Jāʾū ilā Minṭiqah baʿd an Istaʿāna bihim al-Muslimūn waʾl-ʿArab li-Taṣfiyat al-Ḥisābāt." *al-Usbūʿ*, April 14, 2003.

Abdul-Matin, Ibrahim. *Green Deen: What Islam Teaches about Protecting the Planet*. San Francisco, CA: Berrett-Koehler Publishers, 2010.

Abū Dāwūd Sulaymān b. al-Ashʿath al-Sijistānī. *Sunan Abī Dāwūd*. Stuttgart, Ger.: Thesaurus Islamicus Foundation, 2000.

Abū Shāmah, ʿAbd al-Raḥmān ibn Ismāʿīl. *Tarājim Rijāl al-Qarnayn al-Sādis waʾl-Sābiʿ*. 2nd ed. Edited by Muḥammad Zāhid b. al-Ḥusayn al-Kawtharī. Beirut: Dār al-Jīl, 1974.

Abūʾl-Fidā, al-Malik al-Muʾayyad ʿImād al-Dīn Ismāʿīl b.ʿAlī. *al-Mukhtaṣar fī Akhbār al-Bashar*. Edited by Muḥammad Zaynhum ʿAzab. Cairo: Dār al-Maʿārif, 1999.

Abun-Nasr, Jamil. *Muslim Communities of Grace: The Sufi Brotherhoods in Islamic Religious Life*. New York: Columbia University Press, 2007.

Adal, Raja. "Constructing Transnational Islam: The East-West Network of Shakib Arslan." In *Intellectuals in the Modern Islamic World: Transmission, Transformation, Communication*, edited by Stéphane A. Dudoignon, Komatsu Hisao, and Kosugi Yasushi, 176–210. London: Routledge, 2006.

Aḥmad, Muḥammad ʿAbd al-ʿĀl. "Aḍwāʾ Jadīdah ʿalā Iḥyāʾ al-Khilāfah al-ʿAbbāsiyyah." Unpublished paper, 1987.

Akgün, Seçil. *Halifeliğin Kaldırılması ve Laiklik, 1924–1928*. Ankara: Turhan Kitabevi, 1985.

Aigle, Denise. "Les inscriptions de Baybars dans le Bilād al-Shām: Une expression de la légitimité du pouvoir." *Studia Islamica* 97 (2003): 57–85.

——. "Legitimizing a Low-Born, Regicide Monarch: The Case of the Mamluk Sultan Baybars and the Ilkhans in the Thirteenth Century." In *Representing Power in Ancient Inner Asia: Legitimacy, Transmission and the Sacred*, edited by Isabelle Carleux, et. al., 61–94. [Bellingham, WA]: Center for East Asian Studies, Western Washington University, 2010.

Alatas, Syed Farid. "Ibn Khaldūn." In *The Wiley-Blackwell Companion of Major Social Theorists*, edited by George Ritzer and Jeffrey Stepnisky, 12–29. West Sussex, UK: Wiley-Blackwell, 2011.

Alexiou, Margaret. *The Ritual Lament in Greek Tradition*. Cambridge: Cambridge University Press, 1974.

Alkan, Mehmet. "Modernization from Empire to Republic and Education in the Process of Nationalism." In *Ottoman Past and Today's Turkey*, edited by Kemal Karpat, 47–132. Leiden, Neth.: E. J. Brill, 2000.

Allen, Terry. "Tombs of the ʿAbbāsid Caliphs in Baghdād." *Bulletin of the School of Oriental and African Studies* 47, no. 3 (1983): 421–31.

Allsen, Thomas. *Culture and Conquest in Mongol Eurasia.* Cambridge: Cambridge University Press, 2001.

———. *Mongol Imperialism: The Policies of the Grand Qan Möngke in China, Russia, and the Islamic Lands, 1251–1259.* Berkeley: University of California Press, 1987.

———. "The Rise of the Mongolian Empire and Mongolian Rule in North China." In *The Cambridge History of China,* vol. 6, *Alien Regimes and Border States, 907–1368,* edited by Herbert Franke and Denis Twitchett, 321–413. Cambridge: Cambridge University Press, 1994.

Alshech, Eli. "'Do Not Enter Homes Other than Your Own': The Evolution of the Notion of a Private Domestic Sphere in Early Sunnī Islamic Thought." *Islamic Law and Society* 11, no. 3 (2004): 291–332.

al-Ālūsī, Jamāl al-Dīn. *Baghdād fi'l-Shi'r al-'Arabī min Tārīkhihā wa-Akhbārihā al-Ḥaḍāriyyah,* ([Baghdad]: al-Majma' al-'Ilmī al-'Irāqī, 1987).

Amitai-Preiss, Reuven. "The Fall and Rise of the 'Abbāsid Caliphate." *Journal of the American Oriental Society* 113, no. 3 (July–September 1996): 487–94.

———. "Mamluks of Mongol Origin and Their Role in Early Mamluk Political Life." *Mamlūk Studies Review* 12 (2008): 119–37.

———. "Mongol Imperial Ideology and the Ilkhanid War against the Mamluks." In *The Mongol Empire and Its Legacy,* edited by Reuven Amitai-Preiss and David O. Morgan, 57–72. Leiden, Neth: E. J. Brill, 1999.

———. *Mongols and Mamluks: The Mamluk-Īlkhānid War, 1260–1281.* Cambridge: Cambridge University Press, 1995.

Amitai-Preiss, Reuven and David Morgan, eds. *The Mongol Empire and Its Legacy.* Leiden, Neth.: E. J. Brill, 1999.

Anjum, Ovamir. *Politics, Law, and Community in Islamic Thought: The Taymiyyan Moment.* Cambridge: Cambridge University Press, 2012.

Anjum, Tanvir. *Chishtī Sufis in the Sultanate of Delhi, 1190–1400: From Restrained Indifference to Calculated Defiance.* Oxford: Oxford University Press, 2011.

Arazi, Albert. "Al-Risāla al-Baybarsiyya d'al-Suyūṭī: Un Document sur les problèmes d'un *waqf* sultanien sous les derniers Mamlūks." *Israel Oriental Studies* 9 (1979): 329–53.

Ardıç, Nurullah. *Islam and the Politics of Secularism: The Caliphate and Middle Eastern Modernization in the Early 20th Century.* London: Routledge, 2012.

Arnold, Thomas W. *The Caliphate.* Oxford: Clarendon Press, 1924.

Arslān, al-Amīr Shakīb. *al-Sayyid Rashīd Riḍā aw-Ikhā Arba'īn Sanah.* Damascus: Maṭba'at Ibn Zaydūn, 1937.

———. *Tārīkh al-Dawlah al-'Uthmānīyah.* Edited by Ḥasan al-Samāḥī Suwaydān. Damascus: Dār Ibn Kathīr, 2001.

Asad, Talal. *Formations of the Secular: Christianity, Islam, and Modernity.* Stanford, CA: Stanford University Press, 2003.

Aşiroğlu, O. Gazi. *Son Halife Abdülmecid.* Istanbul: Burak Yayınevi, 1992.

Asrar, N. Ahmet. "The Myth about the Transfer of the Caliphate to the Ottomans." *Journal of the Regional Cultural Institute* 5, no. 2 and 3 (Spring and Summer 1972): 111–20.

[Atatürk], Mustafa Kemal. *Nutuk.* Ankara: n.p., 1927. [Ottoman script.]

———. *Nutuk.* Edited by Bedi Yazıcı. Istanbul: n.p, 1995.

Auer, Blain. *Symbols of Authority in Medieval Islam: History, Religion, and Muslim Legitimacy in the Delhi Sultanate.* London: I. B. Tauris, 2012.

Ayalon, David. *Eunuchs, Caliphs and Sultans.* Jerusalem: Magnes Press, 1999.

———. "The Eunuchs in the Mamluk Sultanate." In *Studies in Memory of Gaston Wiet,* edited by Myriam Rosen-Ayalon, 267–96. Jerusalem: Institute of Asian and African Studies, 1977.

——. "On the Eunuchs in Islam." In *Jerusalem Studies in Arabic and Islam*. Jerusalem: Magnes Press, 1979.

——. "Studies on the Structure of the Mamluk Army—I." *Bulletin of the School of Oriental and African Studies* 15, no. 2 (1953): 203–28.

——. "Studies on the Structure of the Mamluk Army—II." *Bulletin of the School of Oriental and African Studies* 15, no. 3 (1953): 448–76.

——. "Studies on the Transfer of the ʿAbbāsid Caliphate from Baġdād to Cairo." *Arabica* 7, no. 1 (1960): 41–59.

——. "The Wafidiya in the Mamluk Kingdom." *Islamic Culture* 25 (1951): 89–104.

Aybars, Ergün. *İstiklal Mahkemeleri, 1920–1927*. İzmir, Turk.: Doküz Eylul Üniversitesi Yayınları, 1988.

al-ʿAydarūsī, ʿAbd al-Qādir. *al-Nūr al-Sāfir ʿan Akhbār al-Qarn al-ʿĀshir*. Edited by Aḥmad Ḥālū, Muḥammad al-Arnāʾūṭ, and al-Karam al-Būshī. Beirut: Dār Ṣādir, 2001.

Aydin, Cemil. *The Politics of Anti-Westernism in Asia: Visions of World Order in Pan-Islamic and Pan-Asian Thought*. NY: Columbia University Press, 2007.

[Aydın], Halil Hulki, İlyas Sami [Muş], and Mehmed Rasih [Kaplan]. *Hakimiyet-i Milliye ve Hilafet-i İslamiye*. Ankara: Yeni Gün Matbaʾası, 1341 [1924].

al-ʿAynī, Badr al-Dīn Abū Muḥammad Maḥmūd b. Aḥmad. *ʿUmdat al-Qārī bi-Sharḥ Ṣaḥīh al-Bukhārī*. Beirut: Muḥammad Amīn Damj, [1970].

ʿAẓīmābādī, Muḥammad Shams al-Ḥaqq. *ʿAwn al-Maʿbūd: Sharḥ Sunan Abī Dāwūd maʿ Sharḥ Ibn Qayyim al-Jawziyyah*. Edited by ʿAbd al-Raḥmān Muḥammad ʿUthmān. Medina: Muḥammad ʿAbd al-Muḥsin, 1968.

al-ʿAzzāwī, ʿAbbās. *al-Mūsiqā al-ʿIrāqiyyah fī ʿAhd al-Muhgūl wa'l-Turkumānī min Sanat 656/1258 ilā Sanat 941/1534*. Baghdad: Shirkat al-Tijārah wa'l-Ṭibāʿah al-Maḥdūdah, 1951.

Baba, Noor Ahmad. *Organization of the Islamic: Theory and Practice of Pan-Islamic Cooperation*. Karachi, Pak.: Oxford University Press, 1994.

Bacon, Roger. *Opus Majus of Roger Bacon*. Translated by Robert Belle Burke. Philadelphia: University of Pennsylvania Press, 1928.

Bacqué-Grammont, Jean-Louis. "L'Abolition du califat vue par la presse quotidienne de Paris en Mars 1924." *Revue des études islamiques* 50 (1982): 208–48.

——. "Regards des autorités françaises et de l'opinion parisienne sur le califat d'Abdülmecid Efendi." *Les Annales de L'Autre Islam*, no. 2 (1994): 325–27.

Badıllı, Abdülkadir. *Risale-i Nur'un Kudsi Kaynakları*. Istanbul: Envar Neşriyat, 2011.

Baehr, Stephen. "From History to National Myth: *Translatio Imperii* in Eighteenth-Century Russia." *Russian Review* 37, no. 1 (1978): 1–13.

——. *The Paradise Myth in Eighteenth-Century Russia: Utopian Patterns in Early Secular Russian Literature and Culture*. Stanford, CA: Stanford University Press, 1991.

al-Baghdādī al-Ḥanbalī, Ṣafiyy al-Dīn ʿAbd al-Muʾmin b. al-Khaṭīb ʿAbd al-Ḥaqq b. ʿAbdillāh b. ʿAlī b. Masʿūd. *Marāṣid al-Iṭṭilāʿ ʿalā Asmāʾ al-Amkinah wa'l-Biqāʿ*. Dār Iḥyāʾ al-Kutub al-ʿArabiyyah, n.d.

al-Baghdādī al-Isfarāʾīnī al-Tamīmī, ʻAbd al-Qāhir ibn Ṭāhir ibn Muḥammad. *al-Farq bayn al-Firaq*. Edited by Muḥammad Muḥyi'l-Dīn ʿAbd al-Ḥamīd. Cairo: Maktabat Muḥammad ʿAlī Ṣabīḥ, n.d.

Bakhīt al-Muṭīʿī, Muḥammad. *Ḥaqīqat al-Islām wa-Uṣūl al-Ḥukm*. Cairo: al-Maṭbaʿah al-Salafiyyah, 1344 [1926].

al-Balādhurī, Aḥmad ibn Yaḥyā. *Ansāb al-Ashrāf*. Edited by Muḥammad Ḥamīd Allāh. Cairo: Maʿhad al-Makhṭūṭāt bi-Jāmiʿat al-Duwal al-ʿArabiyyah bi'l-Ishtirāk maʿ Dār al-Maʻārif bi-Miṣr, 1959.

Balfour, Alan. *Solomon's Temple: Myth, Conflict, and Faith.* West Sussex, UK: Wiley-Blackwell, 2012.

Balistreri, Alexander. "Turkey's Forgotten Political Opposition: The Demise of Kadirbeyoğlu Zeki Bey, 1919–1927." *Die Welt des Islams* 55 (2015): 141–85.

al-Balkhī, Abū'l-Qāsim, al-Qāḍī 'Abd al-Jabbār, and al-Ḥākim al-Jushamī. *Faḍl al-I'tizāl wā-Ṭabaqāt al-Mu'tazilah.* Edited by Fu'ad al-Sayyid. Tunis: al-Dār al-Tawfiqiyyah.

al-Bannā, Ḥasan. *Mudhakkirāt al-Da'wah wa'l-Dā'iyah.* Cairo: Dār al-Kitāb al-'Arabī, n.d.

——. *Risālat al-Mu'tamar al-Khāmis.* n.p., n.d.

Barakatullah, Mohammad. *The Khilafet.* London: Luzac and Company Oriental and Foreign Booksellers and Publishers, 1924.

Bardakçı, Murat. "Hanedan Yayınları ve Halife Abdülmecid'in 'Yeşil Kitab'ı." *Müteferrika,* no. 3 (Summer 1994): 55–57.

Bartold, Vasiliĭ Vladimirovich. "Khalif i Sultan." In *Mir Islama* 1 (1912): 345–400.

al-Bayjūrī, Burhān al-Dīn Ibrāhīm. *Ḥāshiyat al-Imām al-Bayjūrī 'alā Jawharat al-Tawḥīd al-Musammā Tuḥfat al-Murīd 'alā Jawharat al-Tawḥīd.* Edited 'Alī Jumu'ah. Cairo: Dār al-Salām, 2002.

Bayyūmī, Zakariyyā Sulaymān. *Mawqif Miṣr min al-Mutaghayyirāt fī Turkiyā bayn al-Ḥarbayn al-'Ālamiyyatayn 1918–1938.* Cairo: Dār al-Kitāb al-Jāmi'ī, n.d.

Beckwith, Stacy, ed. *Charting Memory: Recalling Medieval Spain.* NY: Garland Publishing, 2000.

"Bediüzzaman'dan Mustafa Kemal'e Namaz Beyannamesi." *Derin Tarih* 36 (March 2015): 88–91.

Behrens-Abouseif, Doris. *Cairo of the Mamluks: A History of the Architecture and Its Culture.* London: I. B. Tauris, 2007.

Bein, Amit. *Ottoman Ulema, Turkish Republic: Agents of Change and Guardians of Tradition.* Stanford, CA: Stanford University Press, 2011.

——. "'Ulama and Political Activism in the Late Ottoman Empire: The Political Career of Şeyhülislâm Mustafa Sabri Efendi (1869–1954)." In *Guardians of Faith in Modern Times: 'Ulama' in the Middle East,* edited by Meir Hatina, 67–90. Leiden, Neth.: E. J. Brill, 2009.

Benite, Zvi Ben-Dor. "Taking 'Abduh to China: Chinese-Egyptian Intellectual Contact in the Early Twentieth Century." In *Global Muslims in the Age of Steam and Print,* edited by James Gelvin and Nile Green, 249–67. Berkeley: University of California Press, 2014.

Berkey, Jonathan. "al-Subkī and His Women." *Mamlūk Studies Review* 14 (2010): 1-17.

Berlin, Adele. *Lamentations: A Commentary.* Louisville, KY: Westminister John Knox Press, 2002.

Berlin, Adele and Marc Zvi Brettler, eds. *The Jewish Study Bible.* Oxford: Oxford University Press, 2004), 1587–1602.

Bilmez, Bülent. "A Nationalist Discourse of Heroism and Treason: The Construction of an 'Official' Image of Çerkes Ethem (1886–1948) in Turkish Historiography, and Recent Challenges." In *Untold Histories of the Middle East: Recovering Voices from the 19th and 20th Centuries,* edited by Amy Singer, Christoph Neumann, and Selçuk Akşin Somel, 106–23. London: Routledge, 2011.

Binder, Leonard. "'Alī 'Abd al-Rāziq and Islamic Liberalism." *Asian and African Studies* 16 (1982): 31–57.

——. *Islamic Liberalism: A Critique of Development Ideologies.* Chicago: University of Chicago Press, 1988.

al-Bishrī, Ṭāriq. *al-Muslimūna wa'l-Aqbāṭ fī Iṭār al-Jamā'ah al-Waṭaniyyah.* Cairo: Dār al-Shurūq, 1988.

Blair, Sheila. "Yāqūt and His Followers." In *Manuscripta Orientalia: International Journal for Oriental Manuscript Research* 9, no. 3 (2003): 39–47.

Bonos, Yannis. "Crossing the Borders in Reality and in Press: The Case of the Newspapers *Yeni Adım* and *Yarın* in the Late 1920s." *European Journal of Turkish Studies* 12 (2011): 2–15.

Bosworth, C. E. "al-Ḳalḳashandī." *The Encyclopaedia of Islam*, 2nd ed.

——. "A 'Maqāma' on Secretaryship: al-Qalqashandī's 'al-Kawākib al-Durriyya fī'l-Manāqib al-Badriyya.'" *Bulletin of the School of Oriental and African Studies* 27, no. 2 (1964): 291–98.

Boyle, John Andrew. "The Death of the Last ʿAbbasid Caliph: A Contemporary Muslim Account." *Journal of Semitic Studies* 6, no. 1 (1961): 145–61.

——. *The Mongol World Empire: 1206–1370*. London: Variourum Reprints, 1977.

Boyle, John Andrew, ed. *The Cambridge History of Iran,* vol. 5, *The Saljuq and Mongol Periods*. Cambridge: Cambridge University Press, 1968.

Brice, William Charles. *An Historical Atlas of Islam.* Leiden, Neth.: E. J. Brill, 1981.

Broadbridge, Anne. *Kingship and Ideology in the Islamic and Mongol Worlds.* Cambridge: Cambridge University Press, 2008.

Broadley, Alexander Meyrick. *How We Defended Arabi and His Friends: A Story of Egypt and the Egyptians*. London: Chapman and Hall, 1884.

Brockett, Gavin. "Collective Action and the Turkish Revolution: Towards a Framework for the Social History of the Atatürk Era, 1923–38." *Middle Eastern Studies* 34, no. 4 (1998): 44–66.

Broucek, James. "The Controversy of Shaykh 'Ali 'Abd al-Raziq." PhD diss., Florida State University, 2012.

Brown, Jonathan. "Did the Prophet Say It or Not? The Literal, Historical, and Effective Truth of Ḥadīths in Early Sunnism." *Journal of the American Oriental Society* 129, no. 2 (2009): 279–85.

——. "Even If It's Not True It's True: Using Unreliable Ḥadīths in Sunni Islam." *Islamic Law and Society* 18 (2011): 1–52.

——. *Hadith: Muhammad's Legacy in the Medieval and Modern World.* Oxford: Oneworld, 2009.

Brown, Peter. *Through the Eye of a Needle: Wealth, the Fall of Rome, and the Making of Christianity in the West, 350–550 AD.* Princeton, NJ: Princeton University Press, 2012.

al-Buʿaynī, Najīb. *Dhikrayāt al-Amīr Shakīb Arslān: ʿan al-Ḥarb al-Kawniyyah al-Ūlā wa-ʿan al-Majāʿah fī Sūrīyā wa-Lubnān.* Beirut: Nawfal, 2001.

Budak, Mustafa. *İdealden Gerçeğe: Misak-ı Milli'den Lozan' a Dış Politika.* Istanbul: Küre Yayınları, 2002.

al-Bukhārī, Abū ʿAbdillāh Muḥammad ibn Ismāʿīl. *Ṣaḥīḥ al-Bukhārī.* Stuttgart, Ger.: Thesaurus Islamicus Foundation, 2000.

Bulliet, Richard. "Religion and the State in Islam: From Medieval Caliphate to the Muslim Brotherhood." University of Denver Center for Middle East Studies Occasional Paper Series, Paper No. 2 (2013): 1–19.

Burrell, David. "Christian-Muslim Theology: An Exercise in Creative Hermeneutics." Lecture, Duke Divinity School, October 20, 2009.

al-Būṭī, Muḥammad Saʿīd Ramaḍān. *Fiqh al-Sīrah al-Nabawiyyah.* Damascus: Dār al-Fikr, 1991.

al-Būṭī, M. Saʿīd Ramaḍān. *The Jurisprudence of the Prophetic Biography and a Brief History of Rightly Guided Caliphs.* Translated by Nancy Roberts. Damascus: Dār al-Fikr, 2010.

Buzpinar, S. Tufan. "The Question of Caliphate under the Last Ottoman Sultans." In *Ottoman Reform and Muslim Regeneration*, edited by Itzchak Weismann and Fruma Zachs, 17–36. London: I. B. Tauris, 2005.

Camp, Victor E. and M. John Roobol. "The Arabian Continental Alkali Basalt Province: Part I. Evolution of Harrat Rahat, Kingdom of Saudi Arabia." *Geological Society of America Bulletin* 101, Issue 1 (January 1989): 71–95.

Camp, V. E., P. R. Hooper, M. J. Roobol, and D. L. "The Madinah Eruption, Saudi Arabia: Magma Mixing and Simultaneous Extrusion of Three Basaltic Chemical Types." *Bulletin of Volcanology* 49 (1987): 489–508.

Casanova, José. "Globalizing Catholicism and the Return to a 'Universal Church.'" In *Religion in the Process of Globalization*, edited by Peter Beyer, 201–25. Ger.: Ergon Verlag, 2001.

——. "Public Religions Revisited." In *Religion: A Concept*, edited by Hent de Vries, 101–19. NY: Fordham University Press, 2008.

Castelli, Elizabeth. *Martyrdom and Memory: Early Christian Culture Making*. NY: Columbia University Press, 2004.

Cebesoy, Ali Fuat. *Siyasi Hatiralar*. Istanbul: Vatan Neşriyatı, 1957.

[Çelikalay], İsmail Şükrü. *Hilafet-i İslamiye ve Türkiye Büyük Millet Meclisi*. Ankara: Ali Şükrü Matbaası, 1339 [1923].

——. *Hilafet-i İslamiyye ve Türkiye Büyük Millet Meclisi*. Istanbul: Bedir Yayınevi, 1993.

Ceylan, Hasan Hüseyin. *Büyük Oyun*, vol. 3, *Hilafetin Kaldırılması*. Ankara: Rehber Yayıncılık, 1995.

Chamedes, Guiliana. "The Vatican and the Reshaping of the European International Order after World War I." *Historical Journal* (December 2013): 955–76.

Chapoutot-Remadi, Mounira. "Une institution mal connue: le khalifat abbaside du Caire." *Les cahiers de Tunisie* 20, no. 77–78 (1972): 23.

Chazan, Robert. "The Timebound and the Timeless: Medieval Jewish Narration of Events." *History and Memory* 6, no. 1 (1994): 5–34.

Cilasun, Emrah. *Bâki İlk Selam: Çerkes Ethem*. Istanbul: Belge Yayınları, 2004.

Clancy-Smith, Julia. *Rebel and Saint: Muslim Notables, Populist Protest, Colonial Encounters (Algeria and Tunisia, 1800–1904)*. Berkeley: University of California Press, 1994.

Clarence-Smith, William. "The Hadrami *Sada* and the Evolution of an Islamic Religious International, c. 1750s to 1930s." In *Religious Internationals in the Modern World: Globalization and Faith Communities since 1750*, edited by Abigail Green and Vincent Viaene, 233–51. NY: Palgrave Macmillan, 2012.

Cleveland, William. "Atatürk Viewed by His Arab Contemporaries: The Opinion of Sati' al-Husri and Shakib Arslan." *International Journal of Turkish Studies* 2, no. 2 (1982): 15–23.

——. *Islam against the West: Shakib Arslan and the Campaign for Islamic Nationalism*. Austin: University of Texas, 1985.

Connerton, Paul. *How Societies Remember*. Cambridge: Cambridge University Press, 1989.

Confino, Alon. "Collective Memory and Cultural History: Problems of Method." *American Historical Review* 102, no. 5 (1997): 1386–1403.

——. "History and Memory." In *The Oxford History of Historical Writing*, vol. 5. Oxford: Oxford University Press, 2011.

Conrad, Sebastian and Dominic Sachsenmaier, eds. *Competing Visions of World Order: Global Moments and Movements, 1880s–1930s*. Basingstoke, UK: Palgrave Macmillan, 2007.

Cooke, Miriam and Bruce Lawrence, eds. *Muslim Networks from Hajj to Hip Hop*. Chapel Hill: University of North Carolina Press, 2005.

Cooperson, Michael. "Baghdad in Rhetoric and Narrative." *Muqarnas: An Annual on the Visual Culture of the Islamic World* 13 (1996): 99–100, 105–6.

Coppa, Frank. "Italy: The Church and the *Risorgimento*." In *The Cambridge History of Christianity*, vol. 7, *World Christianities c. 1815–1914*, edited by Sheridan Gilley, 233–49. Cambridge: Cambridge University Press, 2006.

Crone, Patricia. *God's Rule: Government and Islam*. NY: Columbia University Press, 2004.

——. "Ninth-Century Muslim Anarchists." *Past and Present* 167 (May 2000): 3–28.

——. *Slaves on Horses: The Evolution of the Islamic Polity*. Cambridge: Cambridge University Press, 1980.

——. "A Statement by the Najdiyya Khārijites on the Dispensibility of the Imamate." *Studia Islamica* 88 (1998): 55–76.

Crone, Patricia and Martin Hinds. *God's Caliph: Religious Authority in the First Centuries of Islam*. Cambridge: Cambridge University Press, 1986.

Çulcu, Mehmet. *Hilaftein Kaldırılması sürecinde Cumhuriyetin İlanı ve Lütfi Fikri Davası*. Istanbul: Kastaş Yaynları, 1991.

al-Damījī, ʿAbdullāh b. ʿUmar b. Sulaymān. *al-Imāmāh al-Uẓmā ʿinda Ahl al-Sunnah wa'l-Jamāʿah*. Riyadh, Saudi Arabia: Dār Ṭaybah, 1987.

Davis, Natalie Zemon and Randolph Starn, "Introduction to Special Issue on Memory and Counter-Memory." *Representations* 26 (Spring 1989): 1–6.

Davison, Roderic. *Reform in the Ottoman Empire 1851–1876*. NY: Gordian Press, 1973.

De Somogyi, Joseph. "A Qasida on the Destruction of Baghdad by the Mongols." *Bulletin of the School of Oriental and African Studies* (1933): 41–48.

Deringil, Selim. *The Well-Protected Domains: Ideology and the Legitimation of Power in the Ottoman Empire 1876 – 1909*. London: I.B. Tauris, 1999.

Deweese, Devin. "Cultural Transmission and Exchange in the Mongol Empire: Notes from the Biographical Dictionary of Ibn al-Fuwaṭī." In *Beyond the Legacy of Genghis Khan*, edited by Linda Komaroff, 11–29. Leiden, Neth.: E. J. Brill, 2006.

——. "'Stuck in the Throat of Chingīz Khan:' Envisioning the Mongol Conquests in Some Sufi Accounts from the 14th to 17th Centuries." In *History and Historiography of Post-Mongol Central Asia and the Middle East: Studies in Honor of John E. Woods*, edited by Judith Pfeiffer and Sholeh Quinn, 23–60. Wiesbaden, Ger.: Harrassowitz Verlag, 2006.

al-Dhahabī, Shams al-Dīn Muḥammad b. Aḥmad b. ʿUthmān. *Dhayl al-ʿIbar fī Khabar Man Ghabar (701–764 A.H.)*. Edited by Abū Hājir Muḥammad al-Saʿīd b. Basyūnī Zaghlūl. Beirut: Dār al-Kutub al-ʿIlmiyyah, 1985.

——. *Duwal al-Islām*. Hyderabad, India: Maṭbaʿat Dāʾirat al-Maʿārif al-Niẓāmiyyah, 1337 AH.

——. *Duwal al-Islām*. Edited by Ḥasan Ismāʿīl Marwah. Beirut: Dār Ṣādir, 1999.

——. *al-ʿIbar fī Khabar Man ʿAbar*. Edited by Salāḥ al-Dīn al-Munajjid. Kuwait: Dār al-Turāth al-ʿArabī, 1961.

——. *al-ʿIbar fī Khabar Man Ghabar*. Edited by Ṣalāḥ al-Dīn al-Munajjid. Kuwait: Maṭbaʿat Ḥukūmat al-Kuwayt, 1966.

——. *al-Muʿjam al-Mukhtaṣṣ*. Edited by Muḥammad al-Ḥabīb al-Hīlah. Taif, Saudi Arabia: Maktabah al-Ṣiddīq, 1998.

——. *Muʿjam al-Shuyūkh: al-Muʿjam al-Kabīr*. Taif, Saudi Arabia: Maktabat al-Ṣiddīq, 1988.

——. *Siyar ʿAlām al-Nubalā*. Edited by Shuʿayb al-Arnaʾūt and Muḥammad Naʿīm. Beirut: Muʾassasat al-Risālah, 1986.

——. *Siyar ʿAlām al-Nubalāʾ*. Beirut: Dār al-Fikr, 1997.

——. *Tārīkh al-Islām wa-Wafayāt al-Mashāhīr wa'l-Aʿlām*. Edited by ʿUmar ʿAbd al-Salām Tadmurī. Beirut: Dār al-Kitāb al-ʿArabī, 1999.

al-Dijwī, Yūsuf. *Radd Ṣāḥib al-Faḍīlah al-Ustādh al-Kabīr al-Shaykh Yūsuf al-Dijwī ʿalā Kitāb al-Shaykh ʿAlī ʿAbd al-Rāziq al-Islām wa-Uṣūl al-Ḥukm*. Cairo: Maṭbaʿat al-Samāḥ, 1927.

d'Ohsson, M. de M----. *Oriental Antiquities, and General View of the Othoman Customs, Laws, and Ceremonies*. Philadelphia: Select Committee and Grand Lodge of Enquiry, 1788.

——. *Tableau général de l'empire: divisé en deux parties, dont l'une comprend la législation mahométane; l'autre, l'histoire de l'empire othoman.* Paris: De l'imprimerie de monsieur Firmin Didot, 1788.

Donner, Fred. *The Early Islamic Conquests.* Princeton, NJ: Princeton University Press, 1981.

——. "Muhammad and the Caliphate: Political History of the Islamic Empire up to the Mongol Conquest." In *Oxford History of Islam*, edited by John Esposito, 29–58. Oxford: Oxford University Press, 1999.

Donohue, John. *The Buwayhid Dynasty in Iraq 334 H. / 945 to 403 H. / 1012: Shaping Institutions for the Future.* Leiden, Neth.: E. J. Brill, 2003.

Dresch, Paul. *A History of Modern Yemen.* Cambridge: Cambridge University Press, 2000.

Drechsler, Wolfgang. *Chronicon Saracenicum et Turcicum.* Edited by Georgius Fabricius and Johannes Rosinus. Lipsiae: J. C. Wohlfart, 1689.

——. *De Saracenis et Turcis Chronicon: item de origine et progressu et fine Machometi.* Argentorati: Iucundus, 1550.

Dudoignon, Stéphane A., Komatsu Hisao, and Kosugi Yasushi, eds. *Intellectuals in the Modern Islamic World: Transmission, Transformation, Communication.* London: Routledge, 2006.

Duncan, Peter. *Russian Messianism: Third Rome, Holy Revolution, Communism and After.* London: Routledge, 2000.

Durand, Jean-Dominique, ed. *Christian Democrat Internationalism: Its Action in Europe and Worldwide from Post World War II until the 1990s.* Brussels: P.I.E. Peter Lang, 2013.

Eaton, Richard. *The Rise of Islam and the Bengal Frontier, 1204–1760.* Berkeley: University of California Press, 1993.

Eldar, Dan. "French Policy towards Husayn, Sharif of Mecca." *Middle Eastern Studies* 26, no. 3, (1990): 329–50.

Elinson, Alexander. *Looking Back at al-Andalus: The Poetics of Loss and Nostalgia in Medieval Arabic and Hebrew Literature.* Leiden, Neth.: E. J. Brill, 2009.

El-Rouayheb, Khaled. "From Ibn Ḥajar al-Haytamī (d. 1566) to Khayr al-Dīn al-Alūsī (d. 1899): Changing Views of Ibn Taymiyya among Non-Hanbalī Sunni Scholars." In *Ibn Taymiyya and His Times*, edited by Yossef Rapoport and Shahab Ahmed, 269–318. Oxford: Oxford University Press, 2010.

Elsaffar, Amir. Personal correspondence, February 16, 2007.

Elshtain, Jean Bethke. "Theologian. Christian Contrarian." *Time* 158, no. 12 "America's Best." September 17, 2001: 76–77.

Enayet, Hamid. *Modern Islamic Political Thought.* Austin: University of Texas Press, 1982.

Eraslan, Cezmi. II. *Abdülhamid ve İslam Birliği: Osmanlı Devleti'nin İslam Siyaseti: 1856–1908.* Istanbul: Ötüken Neşriyat, 1992.

Erdem, Sami. "Cumhuriyet'e geçis sürecinde hilafet teorisine alternatif yaklaşımlar: Seyyid Bey Örneği." *Divan* 2 (1996): 119–46.

——. "Seyyid Bey: Hayatı ve Eserleri." In *Türk Hukuk ve Siyaset Adamı Seyyit Bey Sempozyumu*, edited by Osman Karadeniz, A. Bülent Baloğlu, and A. Bülent Ünal, 11–41. İzmir, Turk.: İzmir İlahiyat Fakültesi Vakfı Yayıları, 1999.

Ergin, Osman Nuri. *Türkiye Maarif Tarihi.* Istanbul: Eser Neşriyat, 1977.

Ernst, Carl. *Eternal Garden: Mysticism, History, and Politics at a South Asian Sufi Center.* Albany: State University of New York Press, 1992.

Ersahin, Seyfettin. "The Ottoman ʿUlemāʾ and the Reforms of Mahmud II." Master's thesis, University of Manchester, 1990.

Esposito, John and Dalia Mogahed. *Who Speaks for Islam? What a Billion Muslims Really Think.* NY: Gallup Press, 2007.

Farooqi, Naimur Rahman. *Mughal-Ottoman Relations: A Study of Political and Diplomatic Relations between Mughal India and the Ottoman Empire, 1556–1748*. Delhi: Idarah-i Adabiyat-i Delli, 1989.

Farrukh, Omar. *Ibn Taimiyya on Public and Private Law in Islam, or Public Policy in Islamic Jurisprudence*. Beirut: Khayats, 1966.

Feridun Bey. *Mecmua-yi Münşeat-i Selâtin*. Istanbul, 1274–75 [1857–58].

Fernandes, Leonor. "The Foundation of Baybars al-Jashnakir: Its Waqf, History, and Architecture." *Muqarnas* 4 (1987): 21–42.

Findley, Carter. *Bureaucratic Reform in the Ottoman Empire: The Sublime Porte, 1789–1922*. Princeton, NJ: Princeton University Press, 1980.

——. *Ottoman Civil Officialdom*. Princeton, NJ: Princeton University Press, 1989.

Finefrock, Michael Martin. "From Sultanate to Republic: Mustafa Kemal Ataturk and the Structure of Turkish Politics, 1922–1924." PhD diss., Princeton University, 1976.

Firaq wa-Ṭabaqāt al-Muʿtazilah [Based on the work of al-Qāḍī Abd al-Jabbār al-Hamadhānī and Aḥmad ibn Yaḥyā Ibn al-Murtaḍā's *al-Munyah wa'l-Amal fī Sharḥ Kitāb al-Milal wa'l-Niḥal*]. Edited by ʿAlī Sāmī al-Nashshār and ʿIṣām al-Dīn Muḥammad ʿAlī. Alexandria, Egypt: Dār al-Maṭbūʿāt al-Jāmiʿiyyah, 1972.

Fischel, Walter. *Ibn Khaldūn and Tamerlane: Their Historic Meeting in Damascus, 1401 A.D. (803 A.H.)*. Berkeley and Los Angeles: University of California Press, 1952.

——. *Ibn Khaldūn in Egypt: His Public Functions and His Historical Research (1382–1406)*. Berkeley: University of California Press, 1967.

Flood, Finbarr Barry. *The Great Mosque of Damascus: Studies on the Making of an Umayyad Visual Culture*. Leiden, Neth.: E. J. Brill, 2001.

Foreign Office List and Diplomatic and Consular Year Book, 59 vols. London: Harrison and Sons, 1907–65.

Fortna, Benjamin. *Imperial Classroom: Islam, the State, and Education in the Late Ottoman Empire*. Oxford: Oxford University Press, 2003.

Frajlich, Anna. *The Legacy of Ancient Rome in the Russian Silver Age*. Amsterdam: Rodopi, 2007.

Freitag, Ulrike. *Indian Ocean Migrants and State Formation in Hadhramaut: Reforming the Homeland*. Leiden, Neth.: E. J. Brill, 2003.

Freitag, Ulrike and William Clarence-Smith, eds. *Hadhrami Traders, Scholars and Statesmen in the Indian Ocean, 1750s–1960s*. Leiden, Neth.: E. J. Brill 1997.

Frierson, Elizabeth. "Unimagined Communities: State, Press, and Gender in the Hamidian Era." PhD diss., Princeton University, 1996.

——. "Unimagined Communities: Women and Education in the Late Ottoman Empire, 1876–1909." *Critical Matrix* 9, no. 2 (Fall 1995): 55–90.

Funkenstein, Amos. "Collective Memory and Historical Consciousness." *History and Memory* 1, no. 1 (1989): 5–26.

Garcin, Jean-Claude. "Histoire, opposition, politique et piétisme traditionaliste dans le Ḥusn al Muḥādarat de Suyûti." *Annales Islamologiques* 7 (1967), 33–90.

Gazzini, Claudia. "Jihad in Exile: Ahmad al-Sharif al-Sanusi 1918–1933." Master's thesis, Princeton University, 2004.

Gelvin, James and Nile Green, eds. *Global Muslims in the Age of Steam and Print*. Berkeley: University of California Press, 2014.

Germain, Éric. "L'Afrique du Sud dans la politique «panislamique» de l'empire ottoman." *Turcica* 31 (1999): 135.

Gershoni, Israel and James Jankowski. *Egypt, Islam, and the Arabs: The Search for Egyptian Nationhood, 1900–1930*. NY: Oxford University Press, 1986.

Ghaly, Dina. "The Shāriʿ al-Aʿẓam in Cairo: Its Topography and Architecture in the Mamluk Period." PhD diss., University of Toronto, 2004.

al-Ghazalī, Abū Ḥāmid Muḥammad b. Muḥammad. *Iḥyāʾ ʿUlūm al-Dīn*. Beirut: Dār al-Kutub al-ʿIlmiyyah, 1992.

——. *al-Iqtiṣād fīʾl-ʿItiqād*. Edited by Hüseyin Atay. Ankara: Nur Matbaası, 1962.

al-Ghazālī, Zaynab. "al-Ṭarīq li-ʿAwdat al-Khilāfah." *al-Liwāʾ al-Islāmī*, vol. 43, no. 3 (June, 1988): 54.

——. "al-Ṭarīq li-ʿAwdat al-Khilāfah (2)." *al-Liwāʾ al-Islāmī*, vol. 43, no. 4 (July 1988): 54.

——. "al-Ṭarīq li-ʿAwdat al-Khilāfah (3)." *al-Liwāʾ al-Islāmī*, vol. 43, no. 5 (August 1988): 44.

al-Ghazzī, Najm al-Dīn Muḥammad. *al-Kawākib al-Sāʾirah bi-Aʿyān al-Miʾah al-ʿĀshirah*. Edited by Khalīl al-Manṣūr. Beirut: Dār al-Kutub al-ʿIlmīyah, 1997.

Gibb, Hamilton A. R. "Luṭfī Paşa on the Ottoman Caliphate," *Oriens* 15 (1962): 287–95.

——. "Constitutional Organization." In *Law in the Middle East*, vol. 1, *The Origin and Development of Islamic Law*, edited by Majid Khadduri and Herbert Liebensy, 22–23. Washington, DC: Middle East Institute, 1955.

Gibb, Sir Hamilton and Harold Bowen. *Islamic Society and the West: A Study of the Impact of Western Civilization on Moslem Culture in the Near East*. London: Oxford University Press, 1950.

Göğem, Ziya. *Kurmay Albay Daday'lı Halit Beğ Akmansu (1884–1953)*. Istanbul: Halk Basımevi, 1954–56.

Gökbilgin, Tayyib. "Kanunî Sultan Süleyman Devri Müesseseler ve Teşkilâtına Işık Tutan Bursa Şer'iyye Sicillerinden Örnekler." In *İsmail Hakkı Uzunçarşılı'ya Armğan*. Ankara: Türk Tarih Kurumu Yayınları, 1976.

Golden, Peter. "Cumanica II: The Ölberli (Ölperli): The Fortunes and Misfortunes of an Inner Asian Nomadic Clan." *Archivum Eurasiae Medii Aevi* 6 (1986): 13–14.

——. *Nomads and Sedentary Societies in Medieval Eurasia*. Washington, DC: American Historical Association, 1998.

Goldman, Shalom. *Zeal for Zion: Christians, Jews, and the Idea of the Promised Land*. Chapel Hill: University of North Carolina Press, 2009.

Goldschmidt, Jr., Arthur. *Biographical Dictionary of Modern Egypt*. Boulder, CO: Lynne Rienner, 2000.

Görmez, Mehmet. *Musa Carullah Bigiyef*. Ankara: Türkiye Diyanet Vakfı, 1994.

Graham, William. "Traditionalism in Islam: An Essay in Interpretation." *Journal of Interdisciplinary History* 23, no. 3 (Winter 1993): 495–522.

Granara, William. "Nostalgia, Arab Nationalism, and the Andalusian Chronotope in the Evolution of the Modern Arab Novel." *Journal of Arabic Literature* 36, no. 1 (2005): 57–73.

Grig, Lucy and Gavin Kelly, eds. *Two Romes: Rome and Constantinople in Late Antiquity*. Oxford: Oxford University Press, 2012.

Guida, Michelangelo. "Seyyid Bey and the Abolition of the Caliphate." *Middle Eastern Studies* 44, no. 2 (2008): 275–89.

Guo, Li. *Early Syrian Historiography: al-Yūnīnī's Dhayl Mirʾāt al-Zamān*. Leiden, Neth.: E. J. Brill, 1998.

Gupta, Sobhanlal Datta. "The Comintern and the Indian Revolutionaries in Russia in 1920s." *Calcutta Historical Journal* 18, no. 2 (July–December 1996).

Habib, Mohammad and Khaliq Ahmad Nizami, eds. *A Comprehensive History of India*, vol. 5, *The Delhi Sultanat (A.D. 1206–1526)*. Delhi: People's Publishing House, 1970.

Hacohen, Malachi. *Jacob and Esau: Jewish European History between Empire and Nation*. Cambridge: Cambridge University Press, forthcoming.

Haddad, Mahmoud. "Arab Religious Nationalism in the Colonial Era: Rereading Rashīd Riḍā's Ideas on the Caliphate." *Journal of the American Oriental Society* 117, no. 2 (April–June, 1997): 253–77.

——. "The Ideas of Amir Shakib Arslan: Before and after the Collapse of the Ottoman Empire." In *Views from the Edge: Essays in Honor of Richard W. Bulliet,* edited by Neguin Yavari, Lawrence G. Potter, and Jean-Marc Ran Oppenheim, 101–15. NY: Columbia University Press, for the Middle East Institute, Columbia University, 2004.

——. "Rashīd Riḍā and the Theory of the Caliphate: Medieval Themes and Modern Concerns." PhD diss., Columbia University, 1989.

Haiduc-Dale, Noah. *Arab Christians in British Mandate Palestine: Communalism and Nationalism, 1917–1948.* Edinburgh: Edinburgh University Press, 2012.

Hairi, Abdulhadi. "Naṣīr al-Dīn al-Ṭusī: His Alleged Role in the Fall of Baghdad." In *Ve Congres International d'Arabisants et d'Islamisants, Bruxelles, 31 Août–6 Septembre 1970,* 255–66. Brussels: Centre pour l'Étude des Problèmes du Monde Musulman Contemporain, 1971.

AlHaj, Rahim. "When the Soul Is Settled: Music of Iraq." Washington, DC: Smithsonian Folkways Recordings, 2006.

Halbwachs, Maurice. *The Collective Memory.* Translated by Francis Ditter Jr. and Vida Yazdi Ditter. NY: Harper Colophon Books, 1980.

——. *On Collective Memory.* Edited by Lewis Cosner. Chicago: University of Chicago Press, 1992.

Hallaq, Wael. "Caliphs, Jurists and the Saljūqs in the Political Thought of Juwaynī." *Muslim World* 74, no. 1 (January 1984): 26–41.

——. "Was the Gate of Ijtihad Closed?," *International Journal of Middle East Studies* 16, no. 1 (March 1984): 3–41.

Ḥamīdī, Ismāʿīl Nurī. "Mawqif Ahālī Baghdād tijāh Quwwāt al-ʿUthmāniyyah khilāl al-Ḥarb al-ʿĀlamiyyah al-Ūlā." Unpublished paper, August 2008.

al-Ḥanbalī, al-Ḥāfiẓ Shams al-Dīn Abī Abdillāh Ibn Saʿd al-Ṣāliḥī. *Muʿjam al-Shuyūkh li-Tāj al-Dīn ʿAbd al-Wahhāb b. ʿAlī al-Subkī.* Edited by Bashshār Maʿrūf, Rāʾid al-ʿAnbakī, and Muṣṭafā al-Aʿẓamī. Beirut: Dār al-Gharb al-Islāmī, 2004.

Hanioğlu, M. Şükrü. "Blueprints for a Future Society: Late Ottoman Materialists on Science, Religion, and Art." In *Late Ottoman Society: The Intellectual Legacy,* edited by Elisabeth Özdalga, 28–116. London: Routledge, 2005.

——. *A Brief History of the Late Ottoman Empire.* Princeton, NJ: Princeton University Press, 2008.

——. "Garbcılar: Their Attitudes toward Religion and Their Impact on the Official Ideology of the Turkish Republic." *Studia Islamica* 86, no. 2 (1997): 133–58.

——. *Preparation for a Revolution: The Young Turks, 1902–1908.* Oxford: Oxford University Press, 2001.

——. *The Young Turks in Opposition.* Oxford: Oxford University, 1995.

Hanne, Eric. *Putting the Caliph in His Place: Power, Authority, and the Late Abbasid Caliphate.* Madison, NJ: Farleigh Dickinson University Press, 2007.

Hartmann, Angelika. *an-Nāṣir li-Dīn Allāh (1180–1225).* Berlin: Walter de Gruyter, 1975.

——. "al-Nāṣir li-Dīn Allāh, Abū'l-ʿAbbās Aḥmad." In *The Encyclopaedia of Islam,* 2nd ed.

al-Hāshimī, Muḥammad. "Saʿdī al-Shīrāzī." *al-Yaqīn* 1, no. 17 (February 17, 1923): 491–500.

Hassan, Mona. "Emotional Rhetoric among Islamists about a Caliphal Utopia." European Science Foundation on "Demystifying the Caliphate: Advocates, Opponents and Implications for Europe," King's College, London, UK. Unpublished Paper, November 12–13, 2010.

———. "Islamist Remembering and Longing for a Lost Caliphal Ideal: The Politics of Memory, Culture, and Emotion." Session on "Rethinking History, Reimagining Community." American Academy of Religion Annual Meeting, Atlanta, GA. Unpublished Paper, October 30–November 1, 2010.

———. "Modern Interpretations and Misinterpretations of a Medieval Scholar: Apprehending the Political Thought of Ibn Taymiyya." In *Ibn Taymiyya and His Times*, edited by Shahab Ahmed and Yossef Rapoport, 338–66. Oxford: Oxford University Press, 2010.

———. "Remembering the Lost Caliphate: Emotional Attachment and Longing among Islamists for an Idealized Past and a New Global Future." Conference on "Islamic Resurgence in the Age of Globalization: Myth, Memory, Emotion." The Norwegian University of Science and Technology, Trondheim, Norway. Unpublished Paper, September 4–6, 2009.

———. "Social Conflict in the Administration of Mamluk Charitable Endowments: Jalāl al-Dīn al-Suyūṭī's Legal Opinions and Management of the Baybarsiyyah." Unpublished Paper, 2002.

Hauerwas, Stanley. *After Christendom? How the Church Is to Behave if Freedom, Justice, and a Christian Nation Are a Bad Idea*, 2nd ed. Nashville, TN: Agingdon Press, 1999

Hawting, G. R. *The First Dynasty of Islam: The Umayyad Caliphate AD 661–750*, 2nd ed. London: Routledge, 2000.

Heidemann, Stefan. *Das Aleppiner Kalifat (A.D. 1261): Vom Ende Kalifates in Baghdad über Aleppo zu den Restaurationen in Kairo*. Leiden, Neth.: E. J. Brill, 1994.

Hernandez, Rebecca Skreslet. "Sultan, Scholar, and Sufi: Authority and Power Relations in al-Suyūṭī's Fatwā on Waqf." *Islamic Law and Society* 20, no. 4 (2013): 333–70.

Hervieu-Léger, Danièle. "Religion as Memory." In *Religion: Beyond a Concept*, edited by Hent de Vries, 245–58. NY: Fordham University Press, 2008.

Hilafet ve Milli Hakimiyet. Ankara: Matbuat ve İstihbarat Matbaası, 1339 [1923].

Hill, Enid. *Al-Sanhuri and Islamic Law: The Place and Significance of Islamic Law in the Life and Work of ʿAbd al-Razzaq Ahmad al-Sanhuri Egyptian Jurist and Scholar 1895–1971*. Cairo Papers in Social Science, no. 10. Cairo: American University Press, 1987.

Hillenbrand, Carole. "Mustarshid." In *The Encyclopaedia of Islam*, 2nd ed.

Hiyari, M. A. "The Origins and Development of the Amīrate of the Arabs during the Seventh/Thirteenth and Eighth/Fourteenth Centuries." *Bulletin of the School of Oriental and African Studies* 3 (1975): 509–24.

Hizmetli, Sabri. *Cezayir Bağımsızlık Mücadelesi Önderi Bin Badis*. Ankara: Türkiye Diyanet Vakfı, 1994.

Ho, Engseng. *The Graves of Tarim: Genealogy and Mobility across the Indian Ocean*. Berkeley: University of California Press, 2006.

Hodgson, Marshall. *Rethinking World History: Essays on Europe, Islam, and World History*. Edited by Edmund Burke III. Cambridge: Cambridge University Press, 1993.

———. *The Venture of Islam: Conscience and History in a World Civilization*. Chicago: University of Chicago Press, 1974.

Holt, P. M. *The Age of the Crusades*. London: Longman, 1986.

———. "Some Observations on the ʿAbbāsid Caliphate of Cairo." *Bulletin of the School of Oriental and African Studies, University of London* 47, no. 3 (1984): 501–7.

Homerin, Th. Emil. "Reflections on Poetry in the Mamluk Age." *Mamlūk Studies Review* 1 (1997): 63–85.

Hourani, Albert. *Arabic Thought in the Liberal Age, 1798–1939*. Cambridge: Cambridge University Press, 1983.

Hughes, Thomas. "German Mission to Afghanistan, 1915–1916." *German Studies Review* 25, no. 2 (October 2002): 447–76.

Humphreys, R. Stephen. *From Saladin to the Mongols: The Ayyubids of Damascus, 1193–1260.* Albany: State University of New York Press, 1977.

———. *Islamic History: A Framework for Inquiry*, rev. ed. Princeton, NJ: Princeton University Press, 1991.

———. *Mu'awiya ibn Abi Sufyan: From Arabia to Empire.* Oxford: Oneworld, 2006.

Hurewitz, J. C. *Diplomacy in the Near and Middle East: A Documentary Record.* Princeton, NJ: D. Van Nostrand, 1956.

Ḥusayn, Muḥammad Muḥammad. *al-Ittijihāt al-Waṭaniyyah fī'l-Adab al-Mu'āṣir.* Cairo: Dār al-Irshād, 1970.

Ḥusayn, Muḥammad al-Ṣādiq. *al-Bayt al-Subkī.* Cairo: Dār al-Kātib al-Miṣrī, 1948.

al-Ḥusaynī, Muḥammad b. 'Alī Ibn Ḥamzah. *Min Dhuyūl al-'Ibar.* Edited by Muḥammad Rashshād 'Abd al-Muṭṭalib. Kuwait: Maṭba'at Ḥukūmat al-Kuwayt, n.d.

al-Ḥusaynī, Suhaylah. "Hūlāgū Ya'ūd." *al-Aḥrām*, March 26, 2003.

Hutton, Patrick. "Collective Memory and Collective Mentalities: The Halbwachs-Ariès Connection." *Historical Reflections* 15, no 2 (1988): 311–22.

———. *History as an Art of Memory.* Hanover, NH: University Press of New England, 1993.

Ibn 'Abd al-Ẓāhir, Muḥyī'l-Dīn. *al-Rawḍ al-Zāhir fī Sīrat al-Malik al-Ẓāhir.* Edited by 'Abd al-Azīz b. 'Abdallāh al-Khuwayṭir. Riyadh, Saudi Arabia: n.p., 1976.

Ibn Abī'l-Faḍā'il, Mufaḍḍal. *Kitāb al-Nahj al-Sadīd wa'l-Durr al-Farīd fīmā ba'd Tārīkh Ibn al-'Amīd.* Edited by E. Blochet. Turnhout, Belg.: Editions Brepolis, 1982.

Ibn 'Ajībah, Abū'l-'Abbās Aḥmad b. Muḥammad. *al-Bahr al-Madīd fī Tafsīr al-Qur'ān al-Majīd.* Edited by Aḥmad 'Abdallāh al-Qurashī. Cairo: Ḥasan 'Abbās Zakī, 1999.

Ibn al-'Amīd, al-Makīn Jirjis. *Akhbār al-Ayyūbiyyīn.* Edited by Claude Cahen. Cairo: Maktabat al-Thaqāfah al-Dīniyyah, 1989.

Ibn Bādīs. "al-Khilāfah am Jamā'at al-Muslimīn." *al-Shihāb* 14, no. 2 (May 1938): 61–63.

[Ibn Bādīs.] *Ibn Bādīs: Ḥayātuhu wa-Āthāruh.* Edited by 'Ammār al-Ṭālibī. Beirut: Dār al-Gharb al-Islāmī, 1983.

Ibn al-Dawādārī, Abū Bakr b. 'Abdillāh b. Aybak. *Kanz al-Durar wa-Jāmi' al-Ghurar.* Edited by Ulrich Haarmann. Cairo: Schwarz Freiburg, Maṭba'at 'Īsā al-Bābī al-Ḥalabī, 1971.

Ibn Duqmāq, Ibrāhīm b. Muḥammad. *al-Jawhar al-Thamīn fī Sayr al-Khulafā' wa'l-Muluk wa'l-Salāṭīn.* Edited by Sa'īd 'Abd al-Fattāḥ 'Āshūr. Mecca: Jāmi'at Umm al-Qurā, 1982.

———. *al-Nafḥah al-Miskiyyah fī al-Dawlah al-Turkiyyah.* Edited by 'Umar 'Abd al-Salām Tadmūrī. Beirut: al-Maktabah al-'Aṣriyyah, 1999.

Ibn Duqmāq, Ṣārim al-Dīn Ibrāhīm b. Muḥammad b. Aydamūr al-'Alā'ī. *Nuzhat al-Anām fī Tārīkh al-Islām (628/1230–659/1261).* Edited by Samīr Ṭabbārah. Beirut: al-Maktabah al-'Aṣriyyah li'l-Ṭibā'ah wa'l-Nashr, 1999.

Ibn Faḍl Allāh al-'Umarī, Shihāb al-Dīn Abi'l-'Abbās Aḥmad b. Yaḥyā. *Masālik al-Abṣār fī Mamālik al-Amṣār.* Edited by Kāmil Salmān al-Jabūrī. Beirut: Dār al-Kutub al-'Ilmiyyah, 2010.

———. *Masālik al-Abṣār wa-Mamālik al-Amṣār.* Edited by Dorothea Krawulsky. Beirut: al-Markaz al-Islāmī li'l-Buḥūth, 1985.

Ibn al-Farrā', Abū Ya'lā Muḥammad b. al-Ḥusayn. *al-Aḥkām al-Sulṭāniyyah.* Cairo: Muṣṭafā al-Bābī al-Ḥalabī, 1966.

Ibn al-Fuwaṭī, Kamāl al-Dīn Abū'l-Faḍl 'Abd al-Razzāq b. Aḥmad. *Majma' al-Ādāb fī Mu'jam al-Alqāb.* Edited by Muḥammad al-Kāẓim. Tehran: Mu'assasat al-Ṭibā'ah wa'l-Nashr, Wizārat al-Thaqāfah wa'l-Irshād al-Islāmī, 1995.

Ibn Ḥajar al-'Asqalānī, Shihāb al-Dīn Abū'l-Faḍl Aḥmad b. 'Alī b. Muḥammad. *al-Durar al-Kāminah fī A'yān al-Mi'ah al-Thāminah.* Beirut: Dār al-Jīl, 1978.

——. *Inbā' al-Ghumr bi-Abnā' al-'Umr*. Edited by Muḥammad 'Abd al-Mu'īd Khān. Beirut: Dār al-Kutub al-'Ilmiyyah, 1986.

——. *Fatḥ al-Bārī bi-Sharḥ Ṣaḥīḥ al-Bukhārī*. Cairo: Dār Iḥyā' al-Turāth al-'Arabī, 1929.

——. *Lisān al-Mizān*. Beirut: Dār Iḥyā' al-Turāth al-'Arabī, 1996.

Ibn Ḥanbal, Abū 'Abdillāh Aḥmad. *Musnad al-Imām Aḥmad b. Ḥanbal*. Edited by Shu'ayb al-Arnā'ūt. Beirut: Mu'assassat al-Risālah, 1993.

Ibn Ḥazm al-Ẓahirī, Abū Muḥammad 'Alī b. Aḥmad. *al-Fiṣal fī'l-Milal wa'l-Ahwā' wa'l-Niḥal*. Edited by Muḥammad Ibrāhīm Naṣr and 'Abd al-Raḥmān 'Umayrah. Beirut: Dār al-Jīl, 1995.

Ibn al-'Ibrī, Abū'l-Faraj Jamāl al-Dīn Grīgūriyūs. *Tārīkh Mukhtaṣar al-Duwal*. Beirut: al-Maṭba'ah al-Kāthūlikiyyah, 1958.

——. *Tārīkh al-Zamān*. Edited by Isḥāq Armaleh. Beirut: Dār al-Mashriq, 1986.

Ibn al-'Imād, Shihāb al-Dīn 'Abd al-Ḥayy b. Aḥmad. *Shadharāt al-Dhahab fī Akhbār man Dhahab*. Edited by 'Abd al-Qādir al-Arnā'ūt and Muḥammad al-Arnā'ūt. Damascus: Dār Ibn Kathīr, 1991.

Ibn al-'Irāqī, Aḥmad b. 'Abd al-Raḥīm. *al-Dhayl 'ala al-'Ibar fī Khabar Man Ghabar*. Edited by Ṣāliḥ Mahdī 'Abbās. Beirut: Mu'assasat al-Risālah, 1989.

Ibn Iyās, Muḥammad b. Aḥmad. *Badā'i al-Zuhūr fī Waqā'i' al-Duhūr*. Edited by Muḥammad Muṣṭafā. Wiesbaden, Ger.: Franz Steiner, 1975.

Ibn Jamā'ah, Badr al-Dīn Muḥammad b. Ibrāhīm. *Taḥrīr al-Aḥkām fī Tadbīr Ahl al-Islām*. Edited by Fu'ād 'Abd al-Mun'im Aḥmad, 3rd ed. Qatar: Dār al-Thaqāfah and Ri'āsat al-Maḥākim al-Shar'iyyah wa'l-Shu'ūn al-Dīniyyah, 1988.

Ibn Kathīr, Abū'l-Fidā'. *al-Bidāyah wa'l-Nihāyah*. Edited by Aḥmad Abū Mulḥim, 'Alī Najīb 'Aṭawī, Fu'ād al-Sayyid, Mahdī Nāṣir al-Dīn, and 'Alī 'Abd al-Sattār. Beirut: Dār al-Kutub al-'Ilmiyyah, 1987.

Ibn Khaldūn, 'Abd al-Raḥmān b. Muḥammad. *Kitāb al-'Ibar wa Dīwān al-Mubtada' wa'l-Khabar fī Ayyām al-'Arab wa'l-'Ajam wa'l-Barbar wa Man 'Āṣarahum min Dhawī'l-Sulṭān al-Akbar*, 2nd ed. Beirut: Maktabat al-Madrasah and Dār al-Kitāb al-Lubnānī, 1958.

Ibn Khallikān, Abū'l-'Abbās Shams al-Dīn Aḥmad b. Muḥammad. *Wafayāt al-A'yān wa Anbā' Abnā' al-Zamān*. Edited by Iḥsān 'Abbās. Beirut: Dār al-Thaqāfah, 1968.

Ibn al-Khatib, Lisan al-Din. *Raqm al-Ḥulal fī Naẓm al-Duwal*. Edited by 'Adnān Darwīsh. Damascus: Manshūrāt Wizārat al-Thaqāfah, 1990.

Ibn Mājah al-Qazwīni, Abū 'Abdullāh Muḥammad ibn Yazīd. *Sunan Ibn Mājah*. Stuttgart, Ger.: Thesaurus Islamicus Foundation, 2000.

Ibn al-Murtaḍā, Aḥmad ibn Yaḥyā. *Kitāb Ṭabaqāt al-Mu'tazilah*. Edited by Susanna Diwlad-Wilzer. Beirut: al-Maṭba'ah al-Kāthūlīkiyyah in kommission bei Franz Steiner Verlag GMBH, 1961.

Ibn Qāḍī Shuhbah al-Dimashqī, Taqiyy al-Dīn Abū Bakr b. Aḥmad b. Muḥammad. *Ṭabaqāt al-Shāfi'iyyah*. Hyderabad, India: Maṭba'at Majlis Dā'irat al-Ma'ārif al-'Uthmānīyah, 1978–80.

——. *Tārīkh Ibn Qāḍī Shuhbah*. Edited by Adnan Darwich. Damascus: Institut Français de Damas, 1994.

Ibn Shaddād, 'Izz al-Dīn Abū 'Abdillāh Muḥammad b. 'Alī b. Ibrāhīm. *al-A'lāq al-Khaṭīrah fī Dhikr Umarā' al-Shām wa'l-Jazīrah*. Edited by Sāmī al-Dahhān. Damascus: al-Ma'had al-Faransī li'l-Dirāsāt al-'Arabiyyah, 1956.

——. *Tārīkh al-Malik al-Ẓāhir [al-Rawḍ al-Zāhir Sīrat al-Malik al-Ẓāhir]*. Edited by Aḥmad Ḥuṭayṭ. Beirut: Franz Steiner, 1983.

Ibn Shākir al-Kutubī, Muḥammad. *Fawāt al-Wafayāt wa'l-Dhayl 'alayhā*. Edited by Iḥsān 'Abbās. Beirut: Dār Ṣādir, 1973.

——. *ʿUyūn al-Tawārīkh*, vol. 20. Edited by Fayṣal al-Sāmir and Nabīlah ʿAbd al-Munʿim Dāwūd. Baghdad: Dār al-Rashīd li'l-Nashr, 1980.

Ibn al-Shiḥnah, Muḥibb al-Dīn Abū'l-Walīd Muḥammad. *Rawḍat al-Manāẓir fī Akhbār al-Awāʾil wa'l-Awākhir*. Beirut: Dār al-Kutub al-ʿIlmiyyah, 1997.

Ibn Taghribirdī, Jamāl al-Dīn Abū'l-Maḥāsin Yūsuf. *al-Manhal al-Ṣāfī wa'l-Mustawfā baʿd al-Wāfī*. Cairo: Maṭbaʿat Dār al-Kutub al-Miṣriyyah, 1999.

——. *Mawrid al-Laṭāfah fī Man Waliyah al-Salṭanah wa'l-Khilāfah*. Edited by Nabīl Muḥammad ʿAbd al-ʿAzīz. Cairo: Maṭbaʿat Dār al-Kutub al-Miṣriyyah, 1997.

——. *al-Nujūm al-Zāhirah fī Mulūk Miṣr wa'l-Qāhirah*. Cairo: Wizārat al-Thaqāfah wa'l-Irshād al- Qawmī [Ṭabʿah Musawwarah ʿan Ṭabʿat Dār al-Kutub]), 1972.

Ibn Taymiyyah. *Majmūʿ Fatāwā Shaykh al-Islām Aḥmad b. Taymiyyah*. Edited by ʿAbd al-Raḥmān b. Muḥammad Ibn Qāsim. Cairo: Dār al-Raḥmah, n.d.

——. *Minhāj al-Sunnah fī Naqḍ Kalām al-Shīʿah wa'l-Qadariyyah*. Bulaq, Egypt: al-Maṭbaʿah al-Kubrā al-Amīriyyah, 1903.

——. *al-Siyāsah al-Sharʿiyyah fī Iṣlāḥ al-Rāʿī wa'l-Raʿiyyah*. Beirut: Dār al-Kutub al-ʿIlmiyyah, n.d.

Ibn al-Ṭiqṭaqā, Muḥammad b. ʿAlī b. Ṭabāṭabā. *Tārīkh al-Duwal al-Islāmiyyah: wa-huwa Kitāb al-Fakhrī fi'l- Ādāb al-Sultaniyyah wa'l-Duwal al-Islāmiyyah*. Beirut: Dār Ṣādir, 1960.

Ibn Ṭulūn, Shams al-Dīn. *Quḍāt Dimashq*. Edited by Ṣalāḥ al-Dīn al-Munajjid. Damascus: Maṭbuʿāt al-Majmaʿ al-ʿIlmī al-ʿArabī, 1956.

Ibn al-Wardī, Zayn al-Dīn ʿUmar b. al-Muẓaffar. *Tatimmat al-Mukhtaṣar fī Akhbār al-Bashar*. Edited by Aḥmad Rifʿat al-Badrāwī. Beirut: Dār al-Maʿrifah, 1970.

Ibn Wāṣil, Jamāl al-Dīn Muḥammad ibn Sālim. *Die Chronik des ibn Wāsil (646/1248–659/1261)*, ed. Mohamed Rahim. Wiesbaden, Ger.: Harrassowitz Verlag, 2010.

——. *Mufarrij al-Kurūb fī Ākhbār Banī Ayyūb*. Edited by Jamāl al-Dīn al-Shayyāl and Ḥasanayn Muḥammad Rabīʿ. Cairo: Maṭbaʿat Jāmiʿat Fuʾād al-Awwal, 1953.

Ibn al-Zubayr al-Thaqafī, Abū Jaʿfar Aḥmad b. Ibrāhīm. *al-Zamān wa'l-Makān*. Edited by Muḥammad b. Sharīfah. Casablanca: Maṭbaʿat al-Najāḥ al-Jadīdah, 1993.

Ibrāhīm, Hāshim Muḥammad. "al- Khilāfah al-ʿAbbāsiyyah fī'l-Qāhirah." *Majallat al-Azhar* 22 (1950): 180–83.

——. "al-Khilāfah baʿd Fatḥ al-Atrāk li-Miṣr." *Majallat al-Azhar* 22 (1950): 272–76.

Ihsanoğlu, Ekmeleddin. *The Islamic World in the New Century: The Organization of the Islamic , 1969–2009*. London: Hurst and Company, 2010.

ʿImārah, Muḥammad. *al-Islām wa-Uṣūl al-Ḥukm li-ʿAlī ʿAbd al-Rāziq*. Beirut: al-Muʾassasah al-ʿArabiyyah li'l-Dirāsāt wa'l-Nashr, 1972.

——. *Maʿrakat al-Islām wa-Uṣūl al-Hukm*. Cairo: Dār al-Shurūq, 1997.

Inalcık, Halil. "Application of the Tanzimat and Its Social Effects." *Archivum Ottomanicum* 5 (1973): 91–128.

İnan, Arı. *Gazi Mustafa Kemal Atatürk'ün 1923 Eskişehir-İzmit Konuşmaları*. Ankara: Türk Tarih Kurumu, 1982.

Inbari, Motti. *Jewish Fundamentalism and the Temple Mount: Who Will Build the Third Temple*. Translated by Shaul Vardi. Albany: SUNY Press, 2009.

——. "A Temple for All the Nations: Jewish-Christian Cooperation for the Construction of the Third Temple." *Studies in Contemporary Jewry* 24 (2010): 158–73.

Iqbal, Mohammad. *Six Lectures on the Reconstruction of Religious Thought in Islam*. Lahore, Pak.: Kapur Art Printing Works, 1930.

al-Irbilī, Abd al-Raḥmān Sunbuṭ Qanītū. *Khulāṣat al-Dhahab al-Masbūk Mukhtaṣar min Siyar al-Mulūk*. Baghdad: Maktabat al-Muthannā, [1964].

Iriye, Akira. *Cultural Internationalism and World Order*. Baltimore: John Hopkins University Press, 1997.

——. *Global Community: The Role of International Organizations in the Making of the Contemporary World*. Berkeley: University of California Press, 2002.

Irwin, Robert. "'Futuwwa': Chivalry and Gangsterism in Medieval Cairo." *Muqarnas* 21 (2004): 161–70.

Jackson, Peter. *The Mongols and the West, 1221–1410*. Harlow, UK: Pearson Longman, 2005.

Jackson, Sherman. "The Primacy of Domestic Politics: Ibn Bint al-Aʿazz and the Establishment of Four Chief Judgeships in Mamlūk Egypt." *Journal of the American Oriental Society* 115, no. 1 (1995): 52–65.

al-Jamil, Tariq. "Ibn Taymiyya and Ibn Muṭahhar al-Ḥillī: Shiʿi Polemics and the Struggle for Authority in Medieval Islam." In *Ibn Taymiyya and His Times*, edited by Shahab Ahmed and Yossef Rapoport, 229–46. Oxford: Oxford University Press, 2009.

Jawād, Muṣṭafā. "al-Futuwwah mundhu al-Qarn al-Awwal li'l-Hijrah ilā al-Qarn al-Thālith ʿAshar minhā." In Abū ʿAbdillāh Muḥammad b. Abī'l-Makārim Ibn al-Miʿmār al-Baghdādī, *Kitāb al-Futuwwah*, edited by Muṣṭafā Jawād, Muḥammad Taqiyy al-Dīn al-Hilālī, ʿAbd al-Ḥalīm al-Najjār, and Aḥmad Nājī al-Qaysī. Baghdad: Maktabat al-Muthannā, 1958.

Jayyusi, Salma Khadra, ed. *Anthology of Modern Palestinian Literature*. NY: Columbia University Press, 1992.

Jazīrī, Muḥammad Ibrāhīm. *Saʿd Zaghlūl: Dhikrayāt Tārikhiyyah Ṭarīfah*. Cairo: Dār Akhbār al-Yawm, 1954.

Jones, Linda. *The Power of Oratory in the Medieval Muslim World*. Cambridge: Cambridge University Press, 2012.

Jumuʿah, ʿAlī. *al-Ḥukm al-Sharʿī ʿinda al-Uṣūliyyīn*. Cairo: Dār al-Salām, 2002.

al-Juwaynī, Abū'l-Maʿālī ʿAbd al-Malik b. Abdillah. *Ghiyāth al-Umam fi Iltiyāth al-Ẓulam*. Edited by ʿAbd al-ʿAẓīm al-Dīb, 2nd ed. Cairo: Maṭbaʿat Nahḍat Miṣr, 1401 AH [1980].

al-Juzjānī, Minhāj al-Dīn. *Ṭabaqāt-i Nāṣirī: A General History of the Muhammadan Dynasties of Asia from A.H. 194 (810 A.D.) to A.H. 658 (1260 A.D.)*. Translated by H. G. Raverty. New Delhi: Oriental Books Reprint Corporation, 1970.

Kadirbeyoğlu, Zeki. *Kadirbeyoğlu Zeki Bey'in Hatıraları*. Edited by Ömer Faruk Lermioğlu. Istanbul: Sebil Yayınevi, 2007.

Kaegi, Walter Emil. *Byzantium and the Decline of Rome*. Princeton, NJ: Princeton University Press, 1968.

Kafesoğlu, İbrahim. "Kalkaşandi'nin Bilinmeyen Bir Esseri Measirül'-İnafe." *Tarih Dergisi* 8, no. 11–12 (1956): 99–104.

Kaḥḥālah, ʿUmar Riḍā. *Muʿjam al-Muʾallifīn: Tarājim Muṣannifī al-Kutub al-ʿArabiyyah*. Beirut: Muʾassassat al-Risālah, 1993.

Kahn, Andrew. "Readings of Imperial Rome from Lomonosov to Pushkin." *Slavic Review* 52, no. 4. (1993): 745–68.

Kalb, Judith. *Russia's Rome: Imperial Visions, Messianic Dreams, 1890–1940*. Madison: University of Wisconsin Press, 2008.

Kalyvas, Stathis. *The Rise of Christian Democracy in Europe*. Ithaca, NY: Cornell University Press, 1996.

Kana'an, Ruba. "Waqf, Architecture, and Political Self-Fashioning: The Construction of the Great Mosque of Jaffa by Muhammad Aga Abu Nabbut." *Muqarnas* 18 (2001): 120–140.

Kanlıdere, Ahmet. *Kadimle Cedit arasında Musa Carullah: Hayatı, Eserleri, Fikirleri*. Istanbul: Dergâh Yayınları, 2005.

Kara, İsmail. *Hilafet Risâleleri*. Istanbul: Klasik, 2014.

Karabela, Mehmet Kadri. "One of the Last Ottoman Şeyhulislams, Mustafa Sabri Efendi (1869–1954): His Life, Works and Intellectual Contributions." PhD diss., McGill University, 2003.

Karpat, Kemal. *The Politicization of Islam: Reconstructing Identity, State, Faith, and Community in the Late Ottoman State.* Oxford: Oxford University Press, 2001.

Kastritsis, Dimitris. "Conquest and Political Legitimation in the Early Ottoman Empire." In *Byzantines, Latins, and Turks in the Eastern Mediterranean World after 1150*, edited by Jonathan Harris, Catherine Holmes, and Eugenia Russell, 221–45. Oxford: Oxford University Press, 2012.

Kātip Çelebi, Hajjī Khalīfah Muṣṭafā b. ʿAbdillāh al-Qusṭanṭinī. *Kashf al-Ẓunūn ʿan Asāmī al-Kutub wa'l-Funūn.* Beirut: Dār al-Fikr, 1982.

al-Kattānī, ʿAbd al-Ḥayy b. ʿAbd al-Kabīr. *Fihris al-Fahāris wa'l-Ithbāt wa-Muʿjam al-Maʿājim wa'l-Mashyakhāt wa'l-Musalsalāt.* Edited by Iḥsān ʿAbbās. Dār al-Gharb al-Islāmī, 1982.

al-Kawtharānī, Wajīh. "Masʾalat al-Khilāfah fī'l-Siyāsāt al-Dawliyyah wa'l-Afkār al-Maḥalliyyah." In *al-ʿAlāqāt al-Dawliyyah bayn al-Uṣūl al-Islāmiyyah wa-bayn Khibrat al-Tārīkh al-Islāmī*, edited by Nādiyah Maḥmūd Muṣṭafā and Sayf al-Dīn ʿAbd al-Fattāḥ, 2:897–918. Cairo: Jāmiʿat al-Qāhirah, Kulliyyat al-Iqtiṣād wa'l-ʿUlūm al-Siyāsiyyah, Markaz al-Buḥūth wa'l-Dirāsāt al-Siyāsiyyah, 2000.

Kayali, Hasan. *Arabs and Young Turks: Ottomanism, Arabism, and Islamism in the Ottoman Empire, 1908–1918.* Berkeley: University of California Press, 1997.

al-Kāzarūnī al-Baghdādī al-Shāfiʿī, Ẓahīr al-Dīn ʿAlī b. Muḥammad b. Maḥmūd b. Abī'l-ʿIzz b. Aḥmad b. Isḥāq b. Ibrāhīm. *Maqāmah fī Qawāʿid Baghdād fī'l-Dawlah al-ʿAbbāsiyyah.* Edited by Kūrkīs ʿAwwād and Mīkhāʾīl ʿAwwād. Baghdad: Maṭbaʿat al-Irshād, 1962.

———. *Mukhtaṣar al-Tārīkh.* Edited by Muṣṭafā Jawād. Baghdad: Wizārat al-Aʿlām, Mudīriyyat al-Thaqāfah al-ʿĀmmah, 1970.

Kazziha, Walid. "The Jarīdah-Ummah Group and Egyptian Politics." *Middle Eastern Studies* 13, no. 3 (1977): 373–85.

Kedourie, Elie. "Egypt and the Caliphate, 1915–52." In *The Chatham House Version and Other Middle-Eastern Studies*, new ed., 177–212. London: Brandeis University Press, 1984.

Keene, Henry George. *An Oriental Biographical Dictionary Founded on Materials Collected by the Late Thomas William Beale.* London: W. H. Allen and Company, 1894.

Kekeç, Ahmet. *Ali Şükrü Cinayeti: Birinci Meclise Yapılan Darbe ve Faili Meşhur Bir Vakʾa.* Istanbul: İşaret Yayınları, 1994.

Kennedy, Hugh. *Early Abbasid Caliphate: A Political History.* London: Croom and Helm, 1981.

———. *The Prophet and the Ages of the Caliphates.* Harlow, UK: Longman, 2004.

Ker, James Campbell. *Political Trouble in India, 1907–1917.* Calcutta: Superintendent Government Printing, 1917.

Kerr, Malcolm. *Islamic Reform: The Political and Legal Theories of Muḥammad ʿAbduh and Rashīd Riḍa.* Berkeley: University of California Press, 1966.

Kertzer, David. *The Pope and Mussolini: The Secret History of Pius XI and the Rise of Fascism in Europe.* NY: Random House, 2014.

Khalidi, Rashid. *The Iron Cage: The Story of the Palestinian Struggle for Statehood.* Boston: Beacon Press, 2006.

Khan, Saad. *Reasserting International Islam: A Focus on the Organization of the Islamic and Other Islamic Institutions.* Oxford: Oxford University Press, 2001.

Khaṭṭāb, Ḍiyāʾ Shīt. *al-Maghfūr lahu al-ʿAllāmah ʿAbd al-Razzāq Aḥmad al-Sanhūrī, 1895–1971.* Baghdad: Maṭbaʿat al-ʿĀnī, 1971.

Khouri, Mounah Abdallah. *Poetry and the Making of Modern Egypt (1882–1922).* Leiden, Neth.: E. J. Brill, 1971.

Khowaiter, Abdul-Aziz. *Baibars the First: His Endeavours and Achievements.* London: Green Mountain Press, 1978.

Kitāb al-Ḥawādith wa-Huwa al-Kitāb al-Musammā Wahman bi'l-Ḥawādith al-Jāmi'ah wa'l-Tajārib al-Nāfi'ah wa'l-Manṣūb li'l-Fuwaṭī. Edited by Bashshār 'Awwād Ma'rūf and 'Imād 'Abd al-Salām Ra'ūf. Beirut: Dār al-Gharb al-Islāmī, 1997.

Koçer, Hasan Ali. *Türkiye'de Modern Eğitimin Doğuşu ve Gelişimi, 1773–1923.* Ankara: Milli Eğitim Bakanlığı, 1991.

Kodaman, Bayram. *Abdülhamid Devri Eğitim Sistemi.* Ankara: Türk Tarih Kurumu Basımevi, 1988.

Kramer, Martin. *Islam Assembled: The Advent of the Muslim Congresses.* NY: Columbia University Press, 1986.

Krey, August C. "The International State of the Middle Ages." *American Historical Review* 28, no. 1 (October 1922): 1–12.

Kselman, Thomas and Joseph A. Buttigieg, eds. *European Christian Democracy: Historical Legacies and Comparative Perspectives.* Notre Dame, IN: University of Notre Dame Press, 2003.

al-Kūfī, Abū Muḥammad Aḥmad ibn A'tham. *Kitāb al-Futūḥ.* Hyderabad, India: Dā'irat al-Ma'ārif al-'Uthmānīyah, 1968–75.

Laffan, Michael Francis. *Islamic Nationhood and Colonial Indonesia: The Umma below the Winds.* NY: Routledge, 2003.

Lambton, Ann. *Continuity and Change in Medieval Persia: Aspects of Administrative, Economic, and Social History, 11th-14th Century.* London: I. B. Tauris, 1988.

———. "Obituary: Sir Reader William Bullard." *Bulletin of the School of Oriental and African Studies* 40, no. 1 (1977): 130–34.

Lambton, Ann K. S. "Khalīfa: In Political Theory." In *The Encyclopaedia of Islam*, 2nd ed.

———. *State and Government in Medieval Islam: An Introduction to the Study of Islamic Political Theory.* Oxford: Oxford University Press, 1981.

Laoust, Henri. *Le califat dans la doctrine de Rašīd Riḍā.* Beirut: L'Institut français de Damas, 1938.

———. *Essai sur les doctrines sociales et politiques de Taḳī-d-dīn Aḥmad b. Taimīya.* Cairo: Imprimerie de l'institut français d'archéologie orientale, 1939.

Lapidus, Ira. *A History of Islamic Societies.* Cambridge: Cambridge University Press, 2002.

———. "Sultanates and Gunpowder Empires: The Middle East." In *Oxford History of Islam*, edited by John L. Esposito, 347–93. Oxford: Oxford University Press, 1999.

Lassner, Jacob. *Islamic Revolution and Historical Memory: An Inquiry into the Art of 'Abbāsid Apologetics.* New Haven, CT: American Oriental Society, 1986.

Laurens, Henry. "France et le califat." *Turcica* 31 (1999): 149–83.

Le Strange, George. *Baghdad during the Abbasid Caliphate from Contemporary Arabic and Persian Sources.* Westport, CT: Greenwood Press, 1983.

Lev, Yaacov. "Symbiotic Relations: Ulama and the Mamluk Sultans." *Mamlūk Studies Review* 13 (2009): 1–26.

Leff, Lisa Moses. *Sacred Bonds of Solidarity: The Rise of Jewish Internationalism in Nineteenth-Century France.* Stanford, CA: Stanford University Press, 2006.

Lewis, Bernard. *The Arabs in History.* Oxford: Oxford University Press, 1993.

Liang, Yuen-Gen, Abigail Krasner Balbale, Andrew Devereux, and Camilo Gómez-Rivas. "Unity and Disunity across the Strait of Gibraltar." *Medieval Encounters* 19 (2013): 1–40.

Lotman, Jurij and Boris Uspenkij. "Echoes of the Notion 'Moscow as the Third Rome' in Peter the Great's Ideology." Translated by N.F.C. Owen. In *The Semiotics of Russian Culture*, edited by Ann Shukman, 53–67. Ann Arbor: Michigan Slavic Contributions, 1984.

Lütfi Fikri. *Hükümdarlık Karşısında Milliyet, Mesuliyet ve Tefrik-i Kuva Mesaili.* Istanbul: Akşam Matbaası, 1338 [1922].

——. *Meşrutiyet ve Cumhuriyet.* Istanbul: Ahmet İhsan ve Şürekası Matbaası, 1339 [1923]).

Lütfi Paşa. *Makhṭūṭ Khalāṣ al-Ummah fī Maʿrifat al-Aʾimmah li-Ṣadr al-ʿAẓam Luṭfī Pāşā.* Edited by Mājidah Makhlūf. Zaqāzīq, Egypt: Markaz Buḥūth Āsiyā, 2001.

al-Madanī, Aḥmad Tawfīq. *Ḥayāt Kifāḥ: Mudhakkirāt.* Algeria: al-Sharikah al-Waṭaniyyah li'l-Nashr wa'l-Tawzīʿ, 1976.

Madelung, Wilferd. "Imāma." In *The Encyclopaedia of Islam*, 2nd ed.

——. "The Spread of Maturidism and the Turks." In *Religious Schools and Sects in Medieval Islam*, 109–68. London: Variorum Reprints, 1985.

——. *Succession to Muhammad: A Study of the Early Caliphate.* NY: Cambridge University Press, 1997.

Mahamid, Hatim. "Mosques as Higher Educational Institutions in Mamluk Syria." *Journal of Islamic Studies* 20, no. 2 (2009): 208–11.

Maier, Christl. *Daughter Zion, Mother Zion.* Minneapolis, MN: Fortress Press, 2008.

al-Malik al-Ashraf al-Rasūlī al-Ghassānī Ismāʿīl. *al-ʿAsjad al-Masbūk wa'l-Jawhar al-Maḥkūk fī Ṭabaqāt al-Khulafāʾ wa'l-Mulūk.* Edited by Shākir ʿAbd al-Munʿim. Beirut: Dār al-Turāth al-Islāmī and Baghdad: Dār al-Bayān, 1975.

Malik, Iftikhar. "Regionalism or Personality Cult? Allama Mashriqi and the Tehreek-i-Khaksar in Pre-1947 Punjab." In *Region and Partition: Bengal, Punjab and the Partition of the Subcontinent*, edited by Ian Talbot and Gurharpal Singh, 42–94. Oxford: Oxford University Press, 1999.

Malik, Muhammad Aslam. *Allama Inayatullah Mashraqi: A Political Biography.* Oxford: Oxford University Press, 2000.

al-Manṣūrī, Baybars. *Kitāb al-Tuḥfah al-Mulūkiyyah fī'l-Dawlah al-Turkiyyah.* Edited by ʿAbd al-Ḥamīd Ṣāliḥ Ḥamādān. Cairo: al-Dār al-Miṣriyyah al-Lubnāniyyah, 1987.

——. *Mukhtār al-Akhbār: Tārīkh al-Dawlah al-Ayyūbiyyah wa-Dawlat al-Mamālīk al-Baḥriyyah.* Edited by ʿAbd al-Ḥamīd Ṣāliḥ Ḥamdān. Cairo: al-Dār al-Miṣriyyah al-Lubnāniyyah, 1993.

——. *Zubdat al-Fikrah fī Tārīkh al-Hijrah.* Edited by Donald Richards. Beirut: al-Maʿhad al-Almānī li'l-Abḥāth al-Sharqiyyah, 1998.

al-Maqrīzī, Taqiyy al-Dīn Aḥmad b. ʿAlī. *Durar al-ʿUqūd al-Farīdah fī Tarājim al-Aʿyān al-Mufīdah.* Edited by Maḥmūd al-Jalīlī. Beirut: Dār al-Gharb al-Islāmī, 2002.

——. *al-Mawāʿiẓ wa'l-Iʿtibār fī Dhikr al-Khiṭaṭ wa'l-Āthār.* Edited by Ayman Fuʾād Sayyid. London: al-Furqān Islamic Heritage Foundation, 2002.

Mardin, Şerif. *The Genesis of Young Ottoman Thought: A Study in the Modernization of Turkish Political Ideas.* Syracuse, NY: Syracuse University Press, 2000.

Marín-Guzmán, Roberto. *Popular Dimensions of the ʿAbbasid Revolution: A Case Study of Medieval Islamic Social History.* Cambridge, MA: Fulbright-LASPAU, 1990.

Marmon, Shaun. *Eunuchs and Sacred Boundaries in Islamic Society.* Oxford: Oxford University Press, 1995.

Marshall, Robert. *Storm from the East: From Ghengis Khan to Khubilai Khan.* Berkeley: University of California Press, 1993.

Marsot, Afaf Lutfi al-Sayyid. *Egypt's Liberal Experiment: 1922–1936.* Berkeley: University of California Press, 1977.

al-Mashriqī, ʿInāyatullāh Khān. *Khiṭāb, 13 May 1926, Muʾtamar-i Khilāfat, Qāhirah, Miṣr.* Rawalpindi, Pakistan: Furūgh-i Islām Foundation, n.d.

——. *Khiṭāb ilā Hayʾat al-Muʾtamar al-Islāmī al-ʿĀmm li'l-Khilāfāh fī Miṣr.* Cairo: Maṭbaʿat Naṣr, 1926.

Mason, Herbert. *Two Statesmen of Medieval Islam: Vizir Ibn Hubayra (499–560 AH / 1105–1165 AD) and Caliph an-Nāṣir Li-Dīn Allāh (553–622 AH / 1158–1225 AD)*. The Hague: Mouton and Company, 1972.

Mathur, Y. B. "The Khāksār Movement." *Studies in Islam: Quarterly Journal of the Indian Institute of Islamic Studies* 6, no. 1 (1969): 27–62.

al-Māwardī, Abū'l-Ḥasan ʿAlī b. Muḥammad. *al-Aḥkām al-Sulṭāniyyah wa'l-Wilāyāt al-Dīniyyah*. Edited by Aḥmad Mubārak al-Baghdādī. al-Manṣūrah: Dār al-Wafāʾ, 1989.

al-Mawṣilī, Kamāl al-Dīn Abū'l-Barakāt al-Mubārak Ibn al-Shaʿʿār. *Qalāʾid al-Jumān fī Farāʾid Shuʿarāʾ hādhā al-Zamān*. Beirut: Dār al-Kutub al-ʿIlmiyyah, 2005.

McDougall, James. *History and the Culture of Nationalism in Algeria*. Cambridge: Cambridge University Press, 2006.

McNeill, William. *The Rise of the West*. Chicago: University of Chicago Press, 1963.

Melayu, Hasan Arifin. "Islam and Politics in the Thought of Tjokroaminoto (1882–1934)." Master's thesis, McGill University, 2000.

Merad, Ali. *Ibn Badis: commentateur du coran*. Paris: Librarie orientaliste Paul Geuthner, 1971.

Meyendorff, John. "Was There Ever a 'Third Rome?' Remarks on the Byzantine Legacy in Russia." In *The Byzantine Tradition after the Fall of Constantinople*, edited by John Yiannias, 45–60. Charlottesville: University of Virginia Press, 1991.

Meyvaert, Paul. "An Unknown Letter of Hulagu, Il-Khan of Persia, to King Louis IX of France." *Viator: Medieval and Renaissance Studies* 11 (1980): 256.

Minault, Gail. "Indian Muslims' Reactions to the Abolition of the Caliphate in 1924: The Collapse of a Nationalist Political Alliance." *Les Annales de l'autre Islam*, no. 2 (1994): 245–60.

——. *The Khilafat Movement: Religious Symbolism and Political Mobilization in India*. NY: Columbia University Press, 1982.

Mintz, Alan. *Ḥurban: Responses to Catastrophe in Hebrew Literature*. NY: Columbia University Press, 1984.

Mısıroğlu, Kadir. *Osmanoğulları'nın Dramı: Elli Gurbet Yılı, 1924–1974*. Istanbul: Sebil Yayınevi, 1974.

——. *Üç Hilâfetçi Şahsiyet*. Istanbul: Sebil Yayınevi, 1995.

Mobini-Kesheh, Natalie. *The Hadrami Awakening: Community and Identity in the Netherlands East Indies, 1900–1942*. Ithaca, NY: Southeast Asia Program Publications, Cornell University, 1999.

Mohiuddin, Meraj. *Revelation: The Story of Muhammad*. Scottsdale, AZ: Whiteboard Press, 2015.

Morgan, David. *Medieval Persia, 1040–1797*. London: Longman, 1988.

——. *The Mongols*. Oxford: Blackwell Publishing, 2007.

Mousa, Suleiman. "A Matter of Principle: King Hussein of the Hijaz and the Arabs of Palestine." *International Journal of Middle East Studies* 9, no. 2 (April 1978): 183–94.

al-Mubārakfūrī, Abū'l-ʿUlā Muḥammad ʿAbd al-Raḥmān b. ʿAbd al-Raḥīm. *Tuḥfat al-Aḥwadhī bi-Sharḥ Jāmiʿ al-Tirmidhī*. Edited by ʿIṣām al-Ṣabābaṭī. Cairo: Dār al-Ḥadīth, 2001.

Mughulṭāy b. Qilīj b. ʿAbdillāh. *al-Ishārah ilā Sīrat al-Muṣṭafā wa-Tārīkh Man baʿdahu min al-Khulafāʾ*. Edited by Muḥammad Niẓām al-Dīn al-Futayyiḥ. Damascus: Dār al-Qalam, 1996.

Muḥammad, ʿAbd al-Raḥmān Ḥusayn. *Rithāʾ al-Mudun wa'l-Mamālik al-Zāʾilah fī'l-Shiʿr al-ʿArabī hattā Suqūṭ Gharnāṭah*. Cairo: Maṭbaʿat al-Jabalāwī, 1983.

Muhammad, Shan. *Khaksar Movement in India*. Meerut, India: Meenakshi Prakashan [1972].

Muḥarram, Aḥmad. *Dīwān Muḥarram: al-Siyāsiyyāt min ʿĀm 1922 ḥattā ʿĀm 1945*. Edited by Maḥmūd Aḥmad Muḥarram. Kuwait: Maktabat al-Falāḥ, n.d.

Mukherjee, Prithwindra. "Les origines intellectuelles du mouvement d'indépendance de l'Inde (1893–1918)." PhD diss., Université de Lille III, 1985.

al-Mu'minī, Niḍāl Dāwūd. *al-Sharīf al-Ḥusayn bin 'Alī wa'l-Khilāfah.* Amman, Jord.: Manshūrāt Lajnat Tārīkh al-Urdun, 1996.

al-Munajjid, Ṣalāḥ al-Dīn. *Yāqūt al-Musta'ṣimī.* Beirut: Dār al-Kitāb al-Jadīd, 1985.

Muslih, Muhammad. "The Rise of Local Nationalism in the Arab East." In *The Origins of Arab Nationalism,* edited by Rashid Khalidi, Lisa Anderson, Muhammad Muslih, and Reeva Simon, 167–85. NY: Columbia University Press, 1991.

Mustafa Sabri. *Hilafet ve Kemalizm.* Edited by Sadık Albayrak. Istanbul: Araştırma Yayınları, 1992.

——. *Mawqif al-'Aql wa'l-'Ilm wa'l-'Ālam min Rabb al-'Ālamīn.* [Cairo]: Dār Iḥyā' al-Kutub al-'Arabiyyah, 'Īsā al-Bābī al-Ḥalabī wa-Shurakā'uh, 1950.

——. *al-Nakīr 'alā Munkirī al-Ni'mah min al-Dīn wa'l-Khilāfah wa'l-Ummah.* Beirut: al-Maṭba'ah al-'Abbāsiyyah, 1342 [1924].

Muṭabbaqānī, Māzin Ṣalāḥ. *'Abd al-Ḥamīd bin Bādīs: al-'Ālim al-Rabbānī wa'l-Za'īm al-Siyāsī.* Damascus: Dār al-Qalam, 1989.

al-Muṭī'ī, Muḥammad Bakhīt. *Ḥaqīqat al-Islām wa-Uṣūl al-Hukm.* Cairo: al-Maṭba'ah al-Salafiyyah, 1344 [1926].

Myers, David. "'Zakhor': A Super-Commentary." *History and Memory* 4, no. 2 (1992): 129–48.

al-Nabhānī, Taqiyy al-Dīn. *al-Dawlah al-Islāmiyyah.* Jerusalem: Ḥizb al-Taḥrīr, 1952.

Nadvi, Syed Suleman. "Tazkirah ka Muhakmah." *al-Maarif* (July 1924): 85–91.

Nallino, Carlo Alfonso. *Notes on the Nature of the "Caliphate" in General and on the Alleged "Ottoman Caliphate"* [English Translation of *Appunti sulla natura del "califfato" in genere e sul presunto "califfato ottoman"*]. Rome: Press of the Foreign Office, 1919.

al-Nasā'ī, Abū 'Abd al-Raḥmān Aḥmad ibn Shu'ayb. *Sunan al-Nasā'ī.* Stuttgart, Ger.: Thesaurus Islamicus Foundation, 2000.

——. *Sunan al-Nasā'ī bi-Sharḥ al-Imamayn al-Suyūṭī wa'l-Sindī.* Edited by al-Sayyid Muḥammad Sayyid, 'Alī Muḥammad 'Alī, and Sayyid 'Umrān. Cairo: Dār al-Ḥadīth, 1999.

al-Nawawī, Muḥyī'l-Dīn Abū Zakariyyā Yaḥyā b. Sharaf. *Ṣaḥīḥ Muslim bi-Sharḥ al-Nawawī.* Beirut: Dār al-Fikr, 1981.

Niemeijer, A. C. *The Khilafat Movement in India 1919–1924.* The Hague: Martinus Nijhoff, 1972.

Nigar, Salih Keramet. *Halife İkinci Abdülmecid: yurdundan nasıl sürüldü, sonra nerelerde yaşadı, ne zaman ve nerede öldü, ne zaman ve nerede gömüldü?* Istanbul: İnkılap ve Aka Kitabevleri, 1964.

Nobutaka, Nakamachi. "The Rank and Status of Military Refugees in the Mamluk Army: A Reconsideration of the Wāfidīyah." *Mamlūk Studies Review* 10 (2006): 55–81.

Noer, Deliar. *The Modernist Muslim Movement in Indonesia, 1900–1942.* Oxford: Oxford University Press, 1973.

Nomer, Kemaleddin. *Şeriat, Hilafet, Cumhuriyet, Laiklik: Dini ve Tarihi Gerçeklerin Belgeleri.* Istanbul: Boğaziçi Yayınları, 1996.

Nur, Rıza. *Hayat ve Hatıratım.* Istanbul: Altındağ Yayınevi, 1968.

Nursi, Bediüzzaman Said. *The Gleams: Reflections on Qur'anic Wisdom and Spirituality.* Translated by Hüseyin Akarsu. Clifton, NJ: Tughra Books, 2008.

——. *Lem'alar.* Istanbul: Envar Neşriyat, 1993.

——. *Lem'alar* [Ottoman-script edition]. Istanbul: Sözler Neşriyat, 1995.

——. *The Letters: Epistles on Islamic Thought, Belief, and Life.* Translated by Hüseyin Akarsu. Clifton, NJ: Tughra Books, 2007.

——. *al-Mathnawi al-Nuri: Seedbed of the Light.* Translated by Huseyin Akarsu. Somerset, NJ: Light, 2007.
——. *Mektubat.* Istanbul: Envar Neşriyat, 1993.
——. *The Rays: Reflections on Islamic Belief, Thought, Worship and Action.* Translated by Hüseyin Akarsu. Clifton, NJ: Tughra Books, 2010.
——. *Risale-i Nur Külliyatı.* Istanbul: Nesil, 2006.
——. *Sikke-i Tasdik-i Gaybi.* Istanbul: Şahdamar Yayınları, 2008.
——. *Şualar.* Istanbul: Envar Neşriyat, 1993.
——. *Tarihçe-i Hayat.* Istanbul: Envar Neşriyat, 1993.
al-Nuwayrī, Shihāb al-Dīn Aḥmad b. ʿAbd al-Wahhāb. *Nihāyat al-Arab fī Funūn al-Adab,* vol. 2. Cairo: Maṭbaʿat Dār al-Kutub al-Miṣriyyah, 1924.
——. *Nihāyat al-Arab fī Funūn al-Adab,* vol. 23. Edited by Aḥmad Kamāl Zakī and Muḥammad Muṣṭafā Ziyādah. Cairo: al-Hayʾah al-Miṣriyyah al-ʿĀmmah li'l-Kitāb, 1980.
——. *Nihāyat al-Arab fī Funūn al-Adab,* vol. 27. Edited by Saʿīd ʿĀshūr. Cairo: al-Hayʾah al-Miṣriyyah li'l-Kitāb, 1985.
——. *Nihāyat al-Arab fī Funūn al-Adab,* vol. 29. Edited by Muḥammad Ḍiyāʾ al-Dīn al-Rayyis. Cairo: al-Hayʾah al-Miṣriyyah li'l-Kitāb, 1992.
——. *Nihāyat al-Arab fī Funūn al-Adab,* vol. 30. Edited by Muḥammad ʿAbd al-Hādī Shaʿīrah. Cairo: al-Hayʾah al-Miṣriyyah li'l-Kitāb, 1990.
——. *Nihāyat al-Arab fī Funūn al-Adab,* vol. 31. Edited by al-Bāz al-ʿAzīzī. Cairo: al-Hayʾah al-Miṣriyyah li'l-Kitāb, 1990.
"Obituary: Dr. Naji al-Aṣil." *Iraq* 25, no. 2 (1963): ii–vi.
Ohlander, Erik. *Sufism in an Age of Transition: ʿUmar al-Suhrawardī and the Rise of the Islamic Mystical Brotherhoods.* Leiden, Neth.: E. J. Brill, 2008.
Öke, Mim Kemal. *Hilafet Hareketi: Güney Asya Müslümanları'nın İstiklal Davası ve Türk Milli Mücadelesi 1919–1924.* Ankara: Kültür ve Turizm Bakanlığı, 1988.
Olick, Jeffrey and Joyce Robbins. "Social Memory Studies: From 'Collective Memory' to the Historical Sociology of Mnemonic Practices." *Annual Review of Sociology* 24 (1999): 105–40.
Olson, Robert. *The Emergence of Kurdish Nationalism and the Sheikh Said Rebellion, 1880–1925.* Austin: University of Texas Press, 1989.
Olson, Robert and William Tucker. "The Shaikh Sait Rebellion in Turkey (1925): A Study in the Consolidation of a Developed Uninstitutionalized Nationalism and the Rise of Incipient (Kurdish) Nationalism." *Die Welt des Islams* 18, no. 3–4 (1978): 195–211.
Özcan, Azmi. "Hilafet: Osmanlı Dönemi." In *İslam Ansiklopedesi,* 17: 546–48. Istanbul: Türkiye Diyanet Vakfı, 1998.
——. "The Ottomans and the Caliphate." In *The Great Ottoman-Turkish Civilization,* edited by Kemal Çiçek, 181–86. Ankara: Yeni Türkiye, 2000.
——. *Pan-Islamism: Indian Muslims, the Ottomans and Britain, 1877–1924.* Leiden, Neth.: E. J. Brill, 1997.
Özek, Çetin. *100 Soruda: Türkiyede Gerici Akımlar.* Istanbul: Gerçek Yayınevi, 1968.
Öztürk, Kemal. *İlk Meclis: Belgesel.* Istanbul: Inkılab Yayınları, 1999.
Pankhurst, Reza. *The Inevitable Caliphate? A History of the Struggle for Global Islamic Union.* London: Hurst and Company, 2013.
Paris, Timothy. *Britain, the Hashemites and Arab Rule, 1920–1925.* London: Frank Cass, 2003.
Perkins, Mary Anne. *Christendom and European Identity: The Legacy of a Grand Narrative since 1789.* NY: Walter de Gruyter, 2004.
Pew Research Center. "The World's Muslims: Religion, Politics, Society." Washington, DC: Pew Research Center, 2013.

Pirický, Gabriel. "Modernist Interpretation of Islam and the Legacy of Muslim Reformism: Sayyid Ahmad Khan and Abdulhamid Ben Badis." In *Slovak Contributions to the 19th International Congress of Historical Sciences,* edited by Dušan Kováč, 27–36. Bratislava, Slovakia: VEDA, 2000.

Plessner, M. "Ṭawāshī." In *The Encyclopaedia of Islam,* 1st ed.

Poe, Marshall. "Moscow, the Third Rome: The Origins and Transformations of a 'Pivotal Moment.'" *Jahrbücher für Geschichte Osteuropas, Neu Folge* 49 (2001): 412–29.

Pollard, John. "The Papacy." In *The Cambridge History of Christianity, Volume 9: World Christianities c. 1914–2000.* Edited by Hugh McLeod, 29–49. Cambridge: Cambridge University Press, 2006.

Puri, Harish. *Ghadar Movement: Ideology Organisation and Strategy.* Amritsar, India: Guru Nanak Dev University, 1993.

———. "Revolutionary Organization: A Study of the Ghadar Movement." *Social Scientist* 9, no. 2/3 (September–October 1980): 53–66.

al-Qāḍī, ʿAbdullah Muḥammad Muḥammad. *al-Siyāsah al-Sharʿiyyah: Maṣdar li'l-Taqnīn bayna al-Naẓariyyah wa'l-Taṭbīq.* Ṭanṭā, Egypt: Maṭbaʿat Dār al-Kutub al-Jāmiʿiyyah al-Ḥadīthah, 1989.

al-Qāḍī, Wadād. "The Term 'Khalīfah' in Early Exegetical Literature." *Die Welt des Islams* 28 (1988): 394–97, 408–10.

al-Qalqashandī, Abū'l-ʿAbbās Aḥmad. *Maʾāthir al-Ināfah fī Maʿālim al-Khilāfah.* Edited by ʿAbd al-Sattār Aḥmad Farrāj. Kuwait: Wizārat al-Irshād wa'l-Inbāʾ, 1964.

———. *Nihāyat al-Arab fī Maʿrifat Ansāb al-ʿArab.* Edited by Ibrāhīm al-Abyārī. Cairo: Dār al-Kutub al-Islāmiyyah, Dār al-Kitāb al-Miṣrī, Dār al-Kitāb al-Lubnānī, 1980.

———. *Qalāʾid al-Jumān fī'l-Taʿrīf bi Qabāʾil al-Zamān.* Edited by Ibrāhīm al-Abyārī. Cairo: Dār al-Kutub al-Islāmiyyah, Dār al-Kitāb al-Miṣrī, Dār al-Kitāb al-Lubnānī, 1982.

———. *Ṣubḥ al-Aʿshā fī Ṣināʿat al-Inshā.* Cairo: al-Muʾassasah al-Miṣriyyah al-ʿĀmmah li'l-Ṭibāʿah wa'l-Nashr, 1964.

Qamar ul-Huda. "The Prince of Diplomacy: Shaykh ʿUmar al-Suhrawardi's Revolution for Sufism, Futuwwa Groups, and Politics under Caliph al-Nāsir." *History of Sufism* 3 (2001): 257–78.

al-Qaraḍāwī, Yusuf. *Qaḍāyā al-Muʿāṣirah wa'l-Khilāfah.* Edited by al-Sayyid Yāsīn. Cairo: Mīrīt li'l-Nashr wa'l-Maʿlūmāt, 1999.

Qāṣim, Maḥmūd. *al-Imām ʿAbd al-Ḥamīd bin Bādīs: al-Zaʿīm al-Rūḥī li-Ḥarb al-Taḥrīr al-Jazāʾiriyyah.* Cairo: Dār al-Maʿārif, n.d.

al-Qawsī, Mufarriḥ ibn Sulaymān. *Muṣṭafā Ṣabrī: al-Mufakkir al-Islāmī wa'l-ʿĀlim al-ʿĀlamī wa-Shaykh al-Islām fī'l-Dawlah al-ʿUthmānīyah Sābiqan, 1286–1373 H / 1869–1954 M.* Damascus: Dār al-Qalam, 2006.

al-Qazwīnī, Zakariyyā b. Muḥammad b. Maḥmūd. *Āthār al-Bilād wa-Akhbār al-ʿIbād.* Beirut: Dār Ṣadir, 1960.

The Qur'an: English Translation with Parallel Arabic Text. Translated with an introduction and notes by M.A.S. Abdel Haleem. Oxford: Oxford University Press, 2010.

Qureshi, M. Naeem. *Pan-Islam in British Indian Politics: A Study of the Khilafat Movement, 1918–1924.* Leiden, Neth.: E. J. Brill, 1999.

al-Qurṭubī, Abū ʿAbdillāh Muḥammad b. Aḥmad al-Anṣārī. *al-Jāmiʿ li-Aḥkām al-Qurʾān.* Edited by Aḥmad ʿAbd al-ʿAlīm al-Bardūnī, 3rd ed. Cairo: Dār al-Qalam and Dār al-Kitāb al-ʿArabī, 1966.

al-Qurṭubī, Shams al-Dīn Abū ʿAbdillāh Muḥammad b. Aḥmad b. Abī Bakr. *al-Tadhkirah fī Aḥwāl al-Mawtā wa-Umūr al-Ākhirah.* Edited by Yūsuf ʿAlī Badawī. Damascus and Beirut: Dār Ibn Kathīr, 1999.

al-Qushayrī al-Naysābūrī, Abū'l-Ḥasan Muslim b. al-Ḥajjāj. *Ṣaḥīḥ Muslim.* Stuttgart, Ger.: Thesaurus Islamicus Foundation, 2000.

Rabbat, Nasser. *Staging the City: Or How Mamluk Architecture Coopted the Streets of Cairo.* Berlin: EB-Verlag, 2014.

——. "Who Was al-Maqrīzī? A Biographical Sketch." *Mamlūk Studies Review* 7, no. 2 (2003): 1–19.

Rābiḥ, Turkī. *al-Shaykh 'Abd al-Ḥamīd bin Bādīs: Bā'ith al-Nahḍah al-Islāmiyyah al-'Arabiyyah fī'l-Jazā'ir al-Ḥadīthah.* Riyadh, Saudi Arabia: Dār al-'Ulūm, 1983.

——. *al-Shaykh 'Abd al-Ḥamīd bin Bādīs: Falsafatuhu wa-Juhūduhu fī'l-Tarbiyyah wa'l-Ta'līm.* Algeria: al-Shirkah al-Waṭaniyyah li'l-Nashr wa'l-Tawzī', n.d.

Radd Hay'at Kibār al-'Ulamā' 'alā Kitāb Islām wa-Uṣūl al-Ḥukm li'l-Shaykh 'Alī 'Abd al-Rāziq. Cairo: al-Maṭba'ah al-Yūsufiyyah, 1344/1925.

Ramnath, Maia. *Haj to Utopia.* Berkeley: University of California Press, 2011.

Rapoport, Yossef. "Legal Diversity in the Age of *Taqlīd*: The Four Chief *Qāḍīs* under the Mamluks." *Islamic Law and Society* 10, no. 2 (2003): 201–28.

Rashīd al-Dīn Faḍl Allāh al-Hamadhānī. *Jāmi' al-Tawārīkh.* Cairo: Dār Iḥyā' al-Kutub al-'Arabiyyah, n.d.

Rashiduddin Fazlullah. *The Compendium of Chronicles (Classical Writings of the Medieval Islamic World: Persian Histories of the Mongol Dynasties, vol. 3).* Translated by Wheeler Thackston. London: I. B. Tauris, 2012.

Rayburn, Joel. *Iraq after America: Strongmen, Sectarians, Resistance.* Stanford, CA: Hoover Institution Press, 2014.

Redhouse, J. W. *A Vindication of the Ottoman Sultan's Title of "Caliph;" Shewing Its Antiquity, Validity, and Universal Acceptance.* London: Effingham Wilson Royal Exchange, 1877.

Reid, Donald Malcolm. *Cairo University and the Making of Modern Egypt.* Cambridge: Cambridge University Press, 1990.

Riḍā, Rashid. *al-Khilāfah aw al-Imāmah al-'Uẓmā.* Cairo: Maṭba'at al-Manār, 1922.

Robinson, Chase. *'Abd al-Malik.* Oxford: Oneworld, 2005.

Roff, William. "Indonesian and Malay Students in Cairo in the 1920s." *Indonesia* (Cornell University) 9 (1970), 73–87.

Rowland, Daniel. "The Third Rome or the New Israel?," *Russian Review* 55, no. 4. (1996): 591–614.

Rubinacci, R. "Nadjadat." In *The Encyclopaedia of Islam*, 2nd ed.

al-Rūmī, Jalāl al-Dīn. *The Essential Rumi.* Translated by Coleman Barks with John Moyne. NY: HarperCollins, 2004.

Russell, Dorothea. "A Note on the Cemetery of the Abbasid Caliphs of Cairo and the Shrine of Saiyida Nafīsa." In *Ars Islamica* 6, no. 2 (1939): 168–74.

Sadeque, Syedah Fatima. *Baybars I of Egypt.* Pak.: Oxford University Press, 1956.

Sa'dī. *Kolliyat-i Sa'di.* Edited by Muhammad 'Ali Foroughi. Tehran: Sazman-e Chap o Intisharat-e Javidan, n.d.

——. "On the Fall of the Abbasid Caliphate." Translated by Carl Ernst. Unpublished translation.

——. *Qaṣā'id-i Sa'dī.* Edited by Muḥammad 'Alī Furūghī. Tehran: Iqbāl, [1963].

al-Ṣafadī, Ṣalāḥ al-Dīn Khalīl b. Aybak. *A'yān al-'Aṣr wa-A'wān al-Naṣr.* Edited by 'Alī Abū Zayd, et al. Beirut: Dār al-Fikr al-Mu'āṣir, 1998.

——. *al-Wāfī bi'l-Wafayāt*, vol. 10. Edited by Ali Amara and Jacqueline Sublet. Wiesbaden, Ger.: Franz Steiner Verlag, 1980.

——. *al-Wāfī bi'l-Wafayāt*, vol. 13. Edited by Muḥammad al-Ḥujayrī. Wiesbaden, Ger.: Franz Steiner Verlag, 1984.

——. *al-Wāfī bi'l-Wafayāt*, vol. 17. Edited by Dorthea Krawulsky. Beirut: Franz Steiner Stuttgart, 1991.

——. *al-Wāfī bi'l-Wafayāt*, vol. 24. Edited by Muḥammad ʿAdnān al-Bakhīt and Muṣṭafā al-Ḥiyārī. Wiesbaden, Ger.: Franz Steiner Verlag, 1993.

——. *al-Wāfī bi'l-Wafayāt*, vol. 27. Edited by Otfried Weintritt. Wiesbaden, Ger.: Franz Steiner Verlag, 1997.

——. *al-Wāfī bi'l-Wafayāt*, vol. 29. Edited by Maher Jarrar. Wiesbaden, Ger.: Franz Steiner Verlag, 1997.

al-Sakhāwī, Shams al-Dīn Muḥammad b. ʿAbd al-Raḥmān. *al-Ḍaw' al-Lāmiʿ li-Ahl al-Qarn al-Tāsiʿ*. Beirut: Manshūrāt Dār Maktabat al-Ḥayāh, 1934.

——. *al-Qanāʿah fī mā Yaḥsun al-Iḥāṭah min Ashrāṭ al-Sāʿah*. Edited by Muḥammad b. ʿAbd al-Wahhāb al-ʿUqayl. Riyadh, Saudi Arabia: Maktabat Aḍwā' al-Salaf, 2002.

Saleh, Marlis. "Al-Suyūṭī and His Works: Their Place in Islamic Scholarship from Mamluk Times to the Present." *Mamlūk Studies Review* 5 (2001): 73–89.

Sālim, Muḥammad Bahī al-Dīn. *Ibn Bādīs: Fāris al-Iṣlāḥ wa'l-Tanwīr*. Cairo: Dār al-Shurūq, 1999.

al-Sallāmī, Abū'l-Maʿālī Muḥammad Ibn Rāfiʿ. *Tārīkh ʿUlamā' Baghdād al-musammā Muntakhab al-Mukhtār*. Baghdad: Maṭbaʿat al-Ahālī, 1938.

Samic, Jasna. "Le Califat en Bosnie et les réactions à son abolition." *Les Annales de l'autre Islam*, no. 2 (1994): 325–27.

Sanhoury, A. (Docteur en droit ès Sciences Juridique et ès Sciences Politiques). *Le califat: son évolution vers une société des nations orientale*. Paris: Librairie Orientaliste Paul Geuthner, 1926.

——. *Les restrictions contractuelles à la liberté individuelle de travail dans la jurisprudence anglaise*. Paris: Marcel Biard, 1925.

al-Sanhūrī, ʿAbd al-Razzāq. *Fiqh al-Khilāfah wa-Taṭawwuruhā li-Tuṣbiḥa ʿUṣbat Umam Sharqiyyah*. Beirut: Muʾassasat al-Risālah, 2001.

Sartain, Elizabeth. *Jalāl al-Dīn al-Suyūṭī: Biography and Background*. Cambridge: Cambridge University Press, 1975.

Satan, Ali. *Halifeliğin Kaldırılması*. Istanbul: Gökkubbe, 2008.

Saunders, J. J. *The History of the Mongol Conquests*. London: Routledge and K. Paul, 1972.

al-Ṣāwī, Ṣalāḥ. *al-Wajīz fī Fiqh al-Khilāfah*. Cairo: Dar al-Iʿlām al-Dawlī, 1994.

Seidt, Hans-Ulrich. "From Palestine to the Caucasus—Oskar Niedermayer and Germany's Middle Eastern Strategy in 1918." *German Studies Review* 24, no. 1 (February 2001): 1-18.

Seth, Hira Lal. *The Khaksar Movement (and Its Leader Allama Mashraqi)*. Delhi: Discovery, 1985.

——. *The Khaksar Movement under Searchlight, and the Life Story of Its Leader Allama Mashraqi*. Lahore, Pak.: Hero Publications, 1943.

[Seyyid Bey.] *Hilafet ve Hakimiyet-i Milliye*. Ankara: n.p., 1339 [1923].

——. *al-Khilāfah wa-Sulṭat al-Ummah*. Translated by ʿAbd al-Ghanī Sanī. Cairo: Maṭba'at al-Hilāl, 1342/1924.

Seyyid Bey. *Hilafetin Mahiyet-i Şeriyesi*. Ankara: Türkiye Büyük Millet Meclisi Matbaʿası, 1340 [1924].

——. *Usul-i Fıkıh*. Istanbul: Matbaʿa-yı Amire, [1917].

Shāfiʿ b. ʿAlī b. ʿAbbās al-Kātib. *Kitāb Ḥuṣn al-Manāqib al-Sirriyyah al-Muntaziʿah min al-Sīrah al-Ẓāhiriyyah*. Edited by ʿAbd al-Azīz b. ʿAbdallāh al-Khuwayṭir. Saudi Arabia: Maṭābiʿ al-Quwwāt al-Musallaḥah, 1976.

al-Shahrastānī, Abu'l-Fatḥ Muḥammad ibn 'Abd al-Karīm ibn Abī Bakr Aḥmad. *al-Milal wa'l-Niḥal*. Edited by ʿAbd al-Amīr ʿAlī Muhannā and ʿAlī Ḥasan Fā'ūr. Beirut: Dār al-Maʿrifah, 1990.

Shalabī, Fatḥī Aḥmad. *al-Azhar wa'l-Khilāfah al-Islāmiyyah fī'l-'Asr al-Ḥadīth.* Cairo: n.p., 2003.

Shalabī, Ḥilmī Aḥmad 'Abd al-'Āl. "Intihā' al-Khilāfah al-'Uthmāniyyah 1924." Master's thesis, 'Ayn Shams University, Cairo, 1977.

Shaqraf, 'Abd al-Mun'im Muḥammad. *al-Imām Muḥammad Māḍī Abū'l-'Azā'im.* Dār al-Ṭibā'ah al-Ḥadīthah, n.d.

al-Sharabāṣī, Aḥmad. *Amīr al-Bayān Shakīb Arslān.* Cairo: Dār al-Kitāb al-'Arabī, 1963.

Sharon, Moshe. *Black Banners from the East: The Establishment of the 'Abbāsid State-Incubation of a Revolt.* Jerusalem: Magnes Press, 1983.

——. *Revolt: The Social and Military Aspects of the 'Abbāsid Revolution.* Jerusalem: Hebrew University, 1990.

al-Shāwī, Tawfīq. "Sharḥ wa-Taqyīm li-Mashrū' I'ādat al-Khilāfah 'inda al-Sanhūrī." In 'Abd al-Razzāq al-Sanhūrī, *Fiqh al-Khilāfah wa-Taṭawwuruhā li-Tuṣbiḥa 'Uṣbat Umam Sharqiyyah.* Beirut: Mu'assasat al-Risālah, 2001.

Shawqī, Aḥmad. *al-Shawqiyyāt.* Edited by 'Alī 'Abd al-Mun'im 'Abd al-Ḥamīd. Cairo: al-Shirkah al-Miṣriyyah al-'Ālamiyyah li'l-Nashr and Longman, 2000.

[——.] *al-Shawqiyyat al-Majhūlah.* Edited by Muḥammad Ṣabrī. Cairo: Maṭba'at Dār al-Kutub wa'l-Wathā'iq al-Qawmiyyah, 2003.

al-Shaybānī, Kamāl al-Dīn Abu'l-Faḍl 'Abd al-Razzāq b. Aḥmad Ibn al-Fuwaṭī. *Majma' al-Ādāb fī Mu'jam al-Alqāb.* Edited by Muḥammad al-Kāẓim. Tehran: Mu'assasat al-Ṭibā'ah wa'l-Nashr, Wizārat al-Thaqāfah wa'l-Irshād al-Islāmī, 1995.

Shiloah, Amnon. *Music in the World of Islam: A Socio-Cultural Study.* Detroit: Wayne University Press, 1995.

Siddiqui, A. H. "Caliphate and Kingship in Medieval Persia." In *Islamic Culture* 9 (1935): 560–70, vol. 10 (1936): 97–126, 260–80, vol. 11 (1937): 37–59.

Simms, Rob. *The Repertoire of Iraqi Maqam.* Oxford: Scarecrow Press, 2004.

Skovgaard-Petersen, Jakob. *Defining Islam for the Egyptian State: Muftis and Fatwas of the Dār al-Iftā.* Leiden, Neth.: E. J. Brill, 1997.

Sly, Liz. "Relics of Iraq's Past Call Shots for Islamic State." *Washington Post.* Sunday, April 5, 2015.

Smith Jr., John Masson. "Ayn Jalut: Mamluk Success or Mongol Failure?" *Harvard Journal of Asiatic Studies* 44, no. 2 (1984): 307–45.

Smith, Julia. *Europe after Rome: A New Cultural History, 500–1000.* Oxford: Oxford University Press, 2007.

Somel, Selçuk Akşin. *The Modernization of Public Education in the Ottoman Empire, 1839–1908.* Leiden, Neth.: E. J. Brill, 2001.

Sourdel, Dominique. "The 'Abbasid Caliphate." In *The Cambridge History of Islam,* 104–39. Cambridge: Cambridge University Press, 1970.

Spiegel, Gabrielle. "Memory and History: Liturgical Time and Historical Time." *History and Theory* 41, no. 2 (2002): 149–62.

Spuler, Bertold. "The Disintegration of the Caliphate in the East." In *The Cambridge History of Islam* (Cambridge: Cambridge University Press, 1970), 143–74.

Stout, Jeffrey. *Democracy and Tradition.* Princeton, NJ: Princeton University Press, 2004.

al-Subkī, Tāj al-Dīn 'Abd al-Wahhāb b. 'Alī b. 'Abd al-Kāfī. *Mu'īd al-Ni'am wa-Mubīd al-Niqam,* 3rd ed. Edited by Muḥammad 'Alī al-Najjār, Abū Zayd Shalabī, and Muḥammad Abū'l-'Uyūn. Cairo: Maktabat al-Khānjī, 1996.

——. *Ṭabaqāt al-Shāfi'iyyah al-Kubrā.* Edited by Maḥmūd Muḥammad al-Ṭanāḥī and 'Abd al-Fattāḥ Muḥammad al-Ḥulw. Cairo: Maṭba'at 'Īsā al-Bābī al-Ḥalabī, [1964–76].

Sulaymān, Muḥammad. *Tārīkh al-Ṣiḥāfah al-Filisṭīniyyah, 1876–1976.* Athens: Bisan Press, 1987.

Sullivan, Patricia. "Thomas J. Abercrombie; Photographer for National Geographic Magazine." *Washington Post*, Friday, April 7, 2006.
Sunay, Cengiz. *Son Karar: Misak-ı Milli, Son Osmanlı Meclisi'nin Yakın Tarihine Yön Veren Kararı*. Istanbul: Doğan Kitap, 2007.
al-Ṣuqāʿī al-Naṣrānī al-Kātib, Faḍl Allāh b. Abi'l-Fahkr. *Tālī Kitāb Wafayāt al-Aʿyān*. Edited by Jacqueline Sublet. Damascus: al-Maʿhad al-Fransī bi-Dimashq, 1974.
al-Suyūṭī, Jalāl al-Dīn ʿAbd al-Raḥmān b. Abī Bakr. *Ḥusn al-Muḥāḍarah fī Akhbār Miṣr wa'l-Qāhirah*. Edited by ʾAlī Muḥammad ʿUmar. Cairo: Maktabat al-Khānjī, 2007.
——. *Kifāyat al-Tālib al-Labīb fī Khaṣāʾiṣ al-Ḥabīb*. Hyderabad, India: Dāʾirat al-Maʿārif al-Niẓāmiyyah, 1902.
——. *The Mutawakkili of As-Suyuti*. Edited by William Bell. Cairo: Nile Mission Press, 1926.
——. *al-Radd ʿalā Man Akhlada ilā al-Arḍ wa-Jahila anna al-Ijtihād fī Kull ʿAṣr Farḍ*. Edited by Khalīl al-Mays. Beirut: Dār al-Kutub al-ʿIlmiyyah, 1983.
——. *Tārīkh al-Khulafāʾ*. Beirut: Dār al-Jīl, 1994.
al-Ṭabarī, Abū Jaʿfar Muḥammad b. Jarīr. *Jāmiʿ al-Bayān fī Tafsīr al-Qurʾān*. Bulaq, Egypt: al-Maṭbaʿah al-Kubrā al-Amīriyyah, 1905.
Tabbaa, Yasser. "Survivals and Archaisms in the Architecture of Northern Syria, ca. 1080–ca. 1150." *Muqarnas* 10 (1993): 29–41.
Taeschner, Franz. "Futuwwa." In *The Encyclopaedia of Islam*, 2nd ed.
Tamari, Salim. "Issa al Issa's Unorthodox Orthodoxy: Banned in Jerusalem, Permitted in Jaffa." *Jerusalem Quarterly* 59 (2014): 16–36.
Ṭarrāzī, Philippe de. *Tārīkh al-Ṣiḥāfah al-ʿArabiyyah: Yaḥtawī ʿalā Akhbār Kull Jarīdah wa-Majallah ʿArabiyyah*. Beirut: al-Maṭbaʿah al-Amrīkiyyah, 1933.
al-Ṭarsūsī, Najm al-Dīn Ibrāhīm b. ʿAlī. *Tuḥfat al-Turk fī mā Yajibu an Yuʿmala fi'l-Mulk*. Edited by Riḍwān al-Sayyid. Beirut: Dār al-Ṭalīʿah li'l-Ṭibāʿah wa'l-Nashr, 1992.
Teitelbaum, Joshua. "Sharif Husayn ibn Ali and the Hashemite Vision of the Post-Ottoman Order: From Chieftaincy to Suzerainty." *Middle Eastern Studies* 34, no. 1 (January 1998): 103–22.
Tevfik, Rıza. *Biraz da Ben Konuşayım*. Istanbul: İletişim Yayıncılık, 1993.
Tezcan, Baki. "Hanafism and the Turks in al-Ṭarsūsī's *Gift for the Turks*." *Mamlūk Studies Review* 17 (2011): 67–86.
Thorau, Peter. *The Lion of Egypt: Sultan Baybars I and the Near East in the Thirteenth Century*. London: Longman, 1987.
Tibawi, A. L. "From Rashid Rida to Lloyd George." *Islamic Quarterly* 20/22, no. 1/2 (January–June 1978): 24–29.
al-Tirmidhī, Abū ʿĪsā Muḥammad ibn ʿĪsā. *al-Jāmiʿ al-Kabīr*. Edited by Bashshār ʿAwwād Maʿrūf. Stuttgart, Ger.: Thesaurus Islamicus Foundation, 2000.
Tolan, John. *Saracens: Islam in the Medieval European Imagination*. NY: Coulmbia University Press, 2002.
Toynbee, Arnold. *Survey of International Affairs 1925: The Islamic World since the Peace Settlement*. London: Oxford University Press, 1927.
Tunçay, Mete. *T. C.'nde Tek-Parti Yönetimi'nin Kurulması, 1923–1931*. Istanbul: Cem Yayınevi, 1992.
——. *Türkiye'de Sol Akımlar, 1908–1925*. Ankara: Ankara Üniversitesi—Siyasal Bilgiler Fakültesi Yayınları, 1967.
Türkoğlu, İsmail. *Rusya Türkleri Arasındaki Yenileşme Hareketinin Öncülerinden Rızaeddin Fahreddin*. İstanbul: Ötüken Neşriyat, 2000.
Türköne, Mümtaz'er. *Siyasi İdeoloji olarak İslamcılığın Doğuşu*. Istanbul: İletişim Yayınları, 1991.

al-Ṭusī, Naṣīr al-Dīn. "Chigūnagī-i Rūydād-i Baghdād." In ʻAlā al-Dīn ʻAṭā Malik ibn Muḥammad al-Juvaynī, *Taḥrīr-i Navīn: Tārīkh-i Jahāngushāy*. Tehran: Amīr Kabīr, 1983.

Tyan, Émile. *Institutions du droit public musulman: Le Califat*. Paris: Ricueil Sirey, 1954.

Üçüncü, Uğur. *İkinci Dönem TBMM'de Bir Muhalifin Portresi: Kadirbeyzade Zeki Bey*. Konya, Turk.: Çizgi Kitabevi, 2011.

ʻUthmān, Muḥammad Fatḥī. *ʻAbd al-Ḥamīd bin Bādīs: Rāʼid al-Ḥarakah al-Islāmiyyah fī'l-Jazāʼir al-Muʻāṣirah*. Kuwait: Dār al-Qalam, 1987.

Vahide, Şükran. *Islam in Modern Turkey: An Intellectual Biography of Bediuzzaman Said Nursi*. Edited by Ibrahim Abu-Rabi. Albany: State University of New York Press, 2005.

van Bruinessen, Martin. *Agha, Shaikh and State: The Social and Political Structures of Kurdistan*. London: Zed Books Limited, 1992.

———. "Muslims of the Dutch East Indies and the Caliphate Question." *Les Annales de lʼautre Islam*, no. 2 (1994): 264

———. "Popular Islam, Kurdish Nationalism and Rural Revolt: The Rebellion of Shaikh Said in Turkey (1925)." In *Mullas, Sufis and Heretics: The Role of Religion in Kurdish Society: Collected Articles*. Istanbul: Isis Press, 2000.

Van Dam, Raymond. *Rome and Constantinople: Rewriting Roman History during Late Antiquity*. Waco, TX: Baylor University Press, 2010.

Voll, John. "Islam as a Special World System." *Journal of World History* 5, no. 2 (1994): 213–26.

al-Wardī, Ḥammūdī. *al-Maqām al-Mukhālif*. Baghdad: Maṭbaʻat Asʻad, 1969.

Weiss, Michael and Hassan Hassan. *ISIS: Inside the Army of Terror*. NY: Regan Arts, 2015.

Wells, Colin. *Sailing from Byzantium: How a Lost Empire Shaped the World*. NY: Random House, 2007.

Whalen, Brett. *Dominion of God: Christendom and Apocalypse in the Middle Ages*. Cambridge: Harvard University Press, 2009.

Wickens, Georgii Michaelis. "Nasir ad-Din Tusi on the Fall of Baghdad: A Further Study." *Journal of Semitic Studies* 7, no. 1 (1962): 23–35.

Wiederhold, Lutz. "Legal-Religious Elite, Temporal Authority, and the Caliphate in Mamluk Society: Conclusions Drawn from the Examination of a 'Zahiri Revolt' in Damascus in 1386." *International Journal of Middle East Studies* 31, no 2 (April 1999): 203–35.

Williams, Brian Glyn. *The Crimean Tatars: The Diaspora Experience and the Forging of a Nation*. Leiden, Neth.: E. J. Brill, 2001.

Wilson, Mary C. "The Hashemites, the Arab Revolt, and Arab Nationalism." In *The Origins of Arab Nationalism*, edited by Rashid Khalidi, Lisa Anderson, Muhammad Muslih, and Reeva Simon, 204–21. NY: Columbia University Press, 1991.

Winter, Stefan. "Shams al-Dīn Muḥammad ibn Makkī 'al-Shahīd al-Awwal' (d. 1384) and the Shiʻah of Syria." *Mamlūk Studies Review* 3 (1999): 149–82.

Wittek, Paul. *Rise of the Ottoman Empire: Studies in the History of Turkey, Thirteenth–Fifteenth Centuries*. Edited by Colin Heywood. NY: Routledge, 2012.

Wright, H. Nelson. *The Coinage and Metrology of the Sultāns of Delhī*. New Delhi: Oriental Books Reprint, 1974.

Wright, John, ed. *Postliberal Theology and the Church Catholic: Conversations with George Lindbeck, David Burrell, and Stanley Hauerwas*. Grand Rapids, MI: Baker Academic, 2012.

Wymann-Landgraf, Umar F. Abd-Allah. *Malik and Medina: Islamic Legal Reasoning in the Formative Period*. Leiden, Neth.: E. J. Brill, 2013.

al-Yāfiʻī al-Yamanī al-Makkī, Abū Muḥammad 'Abd Allāh ibn As'ad ibn 'Alī ibn Sulaymān. *Mirʼāt al-Jinān wa-'Ibrat al-Yaqẓān fī Ma'rifat mā Yu'tabar min Ḥawādith al-Zamān*. Beirut: Muʼassasat al-A'lamī li'l-Maṭbū'āt, 1970.

al-Yāfiʿī al-Yamanī al-Makkī, Abū Muḥammad ʿAbdullāh b. Asaʿd b. ʿAlī b. Sulaymān ʿAfīf al-Dīn. *Mirʾāt al-Jinān wa-ʿIbrat al-Yaqẓān*. Hyderabad, India: Maṭbaʿat Dāʾirat al-Maʿārif al-Niẓāmiyyah, 1920.

al-Yaqoubi, Muhammad. *Refuting ISIS: A Rebuttal of Its Religious and Ideological Foundations*. United States: Sacred Knowledge, 2015.

Yārid, Nāzik Sābā. *Aḥmad Shawqī: Laḥn al-Mujtamaʿ wa'l-Waṭan*. Beirut: Bayt al-Ḥikmah, 1968.

Yavuz, Hulusi. *Siyaset ve Kültür Tarihi Açısından Osmanli Devleti ve İslamiyet*. Istanbul: İz Yayıncılık, 1991.

Yamuchi, Masayuki. *The Green Crescent under the Red Star: Enver Pasha in Soviet Russia, 1919–1922*. Tokyo: Institute for the Study of Languages and Cultures of Asia and Africa, 1991.

Ydit, Meir. "Av, the Ninth of." In *Encyclopaedia Judaica*, 2nd ed. NY: Thomas Gald, 2007.

Yerushalmi, Yosef Hayim. *Zakhor: Jewish History and Jewish Memory*. Seattle: University of Washington Press, 1982.

Yousaf, Nasim. *Hidden Facts behind British India's Freedom: A Scholarly Look into Allama Mashraqi and Quaid-e-Azam's Political Conflict*. Liverpool, NY: AMZ Publications, 2007.

———. *Pakistan's Freedom and Allama Mashriqi: Statements, Letters, Chronology of Khaksar Tehrik (Movement) Period: Mashriqi's Birth to 1947*. NY: AMZ Publications, 2004.

al-Yūnīnī al-Baʿlabakkī al-Ḥanbalī, Quṭb al-Dīn Mūsā b. Muḥammad. *Dhayl Mirʾāt al-Zamān*. Hyderabad, India: Dāʾirat al-Maʿārif al-ʿUthmāniyyah, 1954.

Zallūm, ʿAbd al-Qadīm. *Kayfa Hudimat al-Khilāfah*. Beirut: Dār al-Ummah, 1962.

Zaman, Muhammad Qasim. "South Asian Islam and the Idea of the Caliphate." In *Demystifying the Caliphate*, edited by Madawi Al-Rasheed, Carool Kersten, and Marat Shterin, 57–79. NY: Columbia University Press, 2013.

al-Ẓawāhirī, Fakhruddīn al-Aḥmadī. *al-Siyāsah wa'l-Azhar min Mudhakkirāt Shaykh al-Islām al-Ẓawāhirī*. Cairo: Maṭbaʿat al-ʿItimād, 1945.

Zürcher, Erik Jan. "Ottoman Sources of Kemalist Thought." In *Late Ottoman Society: The Intellectual Legacy*, edited by Elisabeth Özdalga, 14–27. London: Routledge, 2005.

———. *Political Opposition in the Early Turkish Republic: The Progressive Republican Party, 1924–1925*. Leiden, Neth.: E. J. Brill, 1991.

———. "Review." *International Journal of Middle East Studies* 45, no. 2 (2013): 397–99.

———. *Turkey: A Modern History*. London: I. B. Tauris, 2004.

———. *The Unionist Factor: The Role of the Committee of Union and Progress in the Turkish National Movement, 1905–1926*. Leiden, Neth.: E. J. Brill, 1984.

———. "The Vocabulary of Muslim Nationalism." *International Journal of the Sociology of Language* 137 (1999): 81–92.

———. "Young Turks, Ottoman Muslims and Turkish Nationalists: Identity Politics." In *Ottoman Past and Today's Turkey*, edited by Kemal Karpat, 150–79. Leiden, Neth.: E. J. Brill, 2000.

ONLINE SOURCES

Abd-Allah, Umar Faruq. "Mercy: The Stamp of Creation." Chicago: Nawawi Foundation, 2004. http://www.nawawi.org/wp-content/uploads/2013/01/Article1.pdf

al-ʿAlī, Ḥāmid ibn ʿAbdillāh. *Dhikrā Suqūṭ al-Khilāfah al-Islāmiyyah*. http://www.tawhed.ws/

"The Difference Christ Makes: Celebrating the Life, Work, and Friendship of Stanley Hauerwas." Duke Divinity School, November 1, 2013. https://www.youtube.com/playlist?list=PL-_N-pg4WXLKWqunITGE8f4UZdedUgMDD

Ernst, Carl. "Why ISIS Should Be Called Daesh: Reflections on Religion and Terrorism." October 29, 2014, Lecture at the University of North Carolina—Chapel Hill. Made available online on November 11, 2014. http://islamicommentary.org/2014/11/carl-ernst-why-isis-should-be-called-daesh-reflections-on-religion-terrorism/

Ḥabīb ʿUmar bin Ḥafīẓ. "On the Concept of Khilāfah and the Reality of Political Power." Extract from a *Rawḥah* Lesson Commenting on Abū Ṭālib al-Makkī's *Qūt al-Qulūb* on July 30, 2013, translated and published online on September 2, 2013. http://muwasala.org/on-the-concept-of-khilafah-and-the-reality-of-political-power/

Hanson, Hamza Yusuf. "The Crisis of ISIS: A Prophetic Prediction." September 19, 2014. https://www.youtube.com/watch?v=hJo4B-yaxfk

Hasson, Nir. "Temple Mount Faithful: From the Fringes to the Mainstream." *Haaretz*, October 4, 2012. http://www.haaretz.com/news/features/temple-mount-faithful-from-the-fringes-to-the-mainstream-1.468234

Ibrahim, Osman Rifat. "Why Abu Bakr al-Baghdadi Is an Imposter." *Al Jazeera*. July 14, 2014. http://www.aljazeera.com/indepth/opinion/2014/07/baghdadi-impostor-20147991513785260.html

Khan, Zeba. "Words Matter in 'ISIS' War, So Use 'Daesh.'" *Boston Globe*. October 9, 2014. https://www.bostonglobe.com/opinion/2014/10/09/words-matter-isis-war-use-daesh/V85GYEuasEEJgrUunodMUP/story.html

Littman, Shany. "Following the Dream of a Third Temple in Jerusalem." *Haaretz*. October 4, 2012. http://www.haaretz.com/weekend/magazine/following-the-dream-of-a-third-temple-in-jerusalem-1.468221

Markoe, Lauren. "Muslim Scholars Release Open Letter to Islamic State Meticulously Blasting Its Ideology." *Huffington Post*. September 24, 2014. http://www.huffingtonpost.com/2014/09/24/muslim-scholars-islamic-state_n_5878038.html

McCants, William. "The Believer: How an Introvert Became the Leader of the Islamic State." The Brookings Essay. September 1, 2015. http://www.brookings.edu/series/the-brookings-essay

Müller, Jan-Werner. "The End of Christian Democracy." *Foreign Affairs*. July 15, 2014. https://www.foreignaffairs.com/articles/western-europe/2014-07-15/end-christian-democracy

"Open Letter to Dr. Ibrahim Awwad al-Badri Alias 'Abu Bakr al-Baghdadi' and to the Fighters and Followers of the Self-Declared 'Islamic State.'" September 19, 2014. http://www.lettertobaghdadi.com/pdf/Booklet-Combined.pdf

Pius XI, *Ubi Arcano Dei Consilio* (December 23, 1922), *Encyclicals—Pius XI—The Holy See—The Holy Father*. http://www.vatican.va/holy_father/pius_xi/encyclicals/documents/hf_p-xi_enc_23121922_ubi-arcano-dei-consilio_en.html

Sly, Liz. "The Hidden Hand behind the Islamic State Militants? Saddam Hussein's." *Washington Post*. April 4, 2015. http://www.washingtonpost.com/world/middle_east/the-hidden-hand-behind-the-islamic-state-militants-saddam-husseins/2015/04/04/aa97676c-cc32-11e4-8730-4f473416e759_story.html

al-Ṭarṭūṣī, Abū Baṣīr. [ʿAbd al-Munʿim Muṣṭafa Ḥalīmah.] *al-Ṭarīq ilā Istiʾnāf Ḥayāt Islāmiyyah wa-Qiyām Khilāfah Rāshidah ʿalā Ḍawʾ al-Kitāb wa'l-Sunnah*. http://www.tawhed.ws/

SELECTED MANUSCRIPTS

Abū Shāmah, ʿAbd al-Raḥmān ibn Ismāʿīl. "Kitāb al-Dhayl ʿalā al-Rawḍatayn." Arabe Collection, Manuscript 5852, Bibliothèque nationale de France, Paris, France.

——. "Kitāb al-Dhayl ʿalā al-Rawḍatayn." Fazıl Ahmed Paşa Collection, Manuscript 1080, Köprülü Manuscript Library, Istanbul, Turkey.

al-Baṣrī, ʿAlī b. Abī'l-Faraj b. al-Ḥusayn. "al-Manāqib al-ʿAbbāsiyyah wa'l-Mafākhir al-Mustanṣiriyyah." Arabe Collection, Manuscript 6144, Bibliothèque nationale de France, Paris, France.

al-Dhahabī, Shams al-Dīn Muḥammad. "Laṭīfah Tataʿallaqu bi'l-Imāmah al-ʿUẓmā." Nuruosmaniye Collection, Manuscript 34 Nk 4976/3, folios 20-23, Nuruosmaniye Manuscript Library, Istanbul, Turkey.

——. "al-Mukhtār min Tārīkh al-Jazarī." Fazıl Ahmed Paşa Collection, Manuscript 1147, Köprülü Manuscript Library, Istanbul, Turkey.

——. "al-Muqaddimah al-Zahrā fī Īḍāḥ al-Imāmah al-Kubrā." ʿAqāʾid Taymūr Collection, Manuscript, 59, Egyptian National Library, Cairo, Egypt.

——. "Risālah fī'l-Imāmah al-ʿUẓmā." Reisülküttap Collection, Manuscript 1185/2, Süleymaniye Manuscript Library, Istanbul, Turkey.

Ibn Ḥabīb al-Ḥalabī, Badr al-Dīn al-Ḥasan ibn ʿUmar. "Durrat al-Aslāk fī Dawlat al-Atrāk." Arabe Collection, Manuscript 4680, Bibliothèque nationale de France, Paris, France.

——. "Durrat al-Aslāk fī Dawlat al-Atrāk." Tārīkh Collection, Manuscript 235/1, Institute of Arab Manuscripts, Cairo, Egypt.

Ibn Kathīr, Abū'l-Fidāʾ. "Ṭabaqāt al-Shāfiʿiyyah." Garrett Collection, Yahuda Section, Manuscript 4993, Princeton University Library, Princeton, NJ.

Ibn Khaldūn, ʿAbd al-Raḥmān b. Muḥammad. "Riḥlat Ibn Khaldūn." Aya Sofya Collection, Manuscript 3200, Süleymaniye Manuscript Library, Istanbul, Turkey.

Ibn Shākir al-Kutubī, Muḥammad. "ʿUyūn al-Tawārīkh." Tārīkh Taymūr ʿArabī Collection, Manuscript 1376, Egyptian National Library, Cairo, Egypt.

Rashīd al-Dīn Faḍl Allāh al-Hamadhānī. "Jāmiʿ al-Tawārīkh." Supplément Persan Collection, Manuscript 1113, Bibliothèque nationale de France, Paris, France.

al-Sakhāwī, Shams al-Dīn Muḥammad b. ʿAbd al-Raḥmān. "Tārīkh Khulafāʾ wa-Salāṭīn Miṣr." Aya Sofya Collection, Manuscript 3266, Süleymaniye Manuscript Library, Istanbul, Turkey.

al-Shīrāzī, Alī b. Aḥmad b. Muḥammad b. Abī Bakr b. Muḥammad. "Tuḥfat al-Mulūk wa'l-Salāṭīn." Ijtimāʿ Taymūr Collection, Manuscript 72, Egyptian National Library, Cairo, Egypt.

al-Suyūṭī, Jalāl al-Dīn ʿAbd al-Raḥmān b. Abī Bakr. "al-Asās fī Manāqib Banī'l-Abbās." Manisa Akhisar Zeynelzade Collection, Manuscript 45 Ak Ze 419/12, Manisa İl Halk Library, Manisa, Turkey.

——. "al-Asās fī Manāqib Banī'l-Abbās." Reisülküttap Collection, Manuscript 1185, Süleymaniye Manuscript Library, Istanbul, Turkey.

——. "Kitāb al-Ināfah fī Rutbat al-Khilāfah." Reisülküttap Collection, Manuscript 1185, Süleymaniye Manuscript Library, Istanbul, Turkey.

Tabrīzī, Aḥmad. "Shahanshāh Nāmah." Oriental Manuscripts Collection, Manuscript 2780, British Library, London, United Kingdom.

Ibn Wāṣil, Jamāl al-Dīn Muḥammad ibn Sālim. "al-Tārīkh al-Ṣāliḥī." Fatih Collection, Manuscript 4224, Süleymaniye Manuscript Library, Istanbul, Turkey.

INDEX

Note: page numbers followed by *f* indicate a figure.